A HISTORY OF THE ARABS IN THE SUDAN

A HISTORY OF THE ARABS IN THE SUDAN

AND SOME ACCOUNT OF THE PEOPLE WHO PRECEDED THEM AND OF THE TRIBES INHABITING DÁRFŪR

H. A. MACMICHAEL

VOLUME II

FRANK CASS & CO. LTD.
1967

Published by
FRANK CASS AND COMPANY LIMITED
67 Great Russell Street, London WC1
by arrangement with Cambridge University Press.

First Edition	1922
Second Impression	1967

Printed in Great Britain by
Thomas Nelson (Printers) Ltd., London and Edinburgh

CONTENTS

Part IV

THE NATIVE MANUSCRIPTS OF THE SUDAN

GENEALOGICAL TREES in addition to those printed in the Text

EXPLANATORY NOTE

1. Square brackets [ ] are used:

(*a*) to enclose words which do not occur in the Arabic text but which are added in the translation to complete the obvious meaning;

(*b*) to enclose a transliteration of an Arabic proper name or other word.

2. When a line of dots occurs thus, . . ., some words or sentences have been omitted in the translation. Such omissions are made in six cases:

(*a*) When there occur laudations of God following mention of His name.

(*b*) When there occur complimentary phrases, such as "upon him be blessings," which always follow mention of Muḥammad, the Prophets or the Companions.

(*c*) Where a passage is identical, or practically so, with a passage quoted elsewhere. In such a case the reference is always given.

(*d*) —Chiefly in AB and D3—where the subject-matter is of insufficient interest to warrant translation. In such a case a short *précis* is generally given of the passage omitted.

(*e*) When the author has added an explanation as to what are the vowel points of the preceding proper name: the result in such a case is made clear by the English transliteration.

(*f*) When a word is illegible: in this case the word "*illegible*" is added in brackets.

3. When it is said that a passage is identical with another the statement must be understood with the implied reservation that there may be slight grammatical variations not affecting the meaning.

4. The textual notes give obvious emendations for misprints that occur in the text, and conversions of dates from the Muham-

madan to the Gregorian calendar. As regards the former, it may be noted that throughout the MSS. there is a continuous confusion between ق and غ.

5. It is not enough merely to compare the genealogical trees and neglect the text, because several persons or tribes, whose names occur in the text, are not entered in the trees owing to their relationship to the main stock not being specifically defined.

6. In common parlance the forms "GA'ALIÍN," "'ARAKIÍN," etc. are used in all cases instead of the grammatically correct forms "GA'ALIYYŪN," "'ARAKIYYŪN," etc. In the MSS. sometimes one form and sometimes the other is used, independently of the grammatical construction. For the sake of consistency I have used, in translating the MSS., the form ending in -IYYŪN throughout.

7. The paragraphs have been numbered by the translator for the purpose of reference.

Note

The three trees following Chapter 1 of Part II illustrate the genealogical connections between the Arabian tribes to which reference is frequent in Part IV. Thus, when there is a reference to Wüstenfeld's *Register* in the notes, recourse may be had to these trees, which are compiled from that work, and the introductory note which precedes them in Vol. 1, p. 154.

PART IV

THE NATIVE MANUSCRIPTS OF THE SUDAN

INTRODUCTION

I The line of cleavage between the two great Arab groups of descendants of Ḳaḥṭán on the one hand and of Ismá'íl and 'Adnán on the other has not been obscured by the lapse of ages, nor by the tremendous unifying force of a common religion, nor by continuous intermarriage, nor by migration to distant lands. The distinction, still jealously preserved in Arabia[1], is, in another form, clearly traceable in the Sudan at the present day, and its persistence is due to the unquestioned authority of the Ḳurán and of certain of the Traditions.

As being a revelation from the very mouth of God the contents of the Ḳurán are familiar to the masses and unimpeachable both in doctrinal matters and as a storehouse of historical facts. The best authenticated traditions carry an almost equal weight.

No one familiar with the historical portions of the Ḳurán and the biography of the Prophet could be oblivious of the distinction between the Ḳaḥṭánite and the Ismá'ílite; and, in the second place, the careful preservation of pedigrees is enjoined by the Ḳurán and the traditions as an act of piety. The injunction is frequently quoted and to some extent obeyed.

Thus any respectable member of society, and particularly the *feki* whose concern is immediately with things of religion, must needs be prepared to produce his pedigree. Some of the links may be faulty—they invariably are so—but the ground is fairly sure in places, and by a system of comparison one obtains certain valuable indications.

II Corresponding to the old division between Ḳaḥṭánite and Ismá'ílite we find in the Sudan a definite line drawn between the two great groups of tribes claiming descent on the one hand from GUHAYNA and on the other from 'Abbás the uncle of the Prophet.

The period from the present day to that of the Aṣḥáb is generally shewn as covering about forty generations, and in the case of a typical *feki* or sheikh of good family one may generally accept the first five or six generations from the present as stated accurately, and

[1] See Zwemer, p. 259. "The animosity of these two races to each other is unaccountable but invincible. Like two chemical products which instantly explode when placed in contact, so has it always been found impossible for Yemenite and Maadite [*i.e.* 'Adnánite] to live quietly together."

the next eight or nine as less so. Then follow seven or eight successive ancestors whose names rest more firmly on the accepted authority of contemporary *nisbas* compiled during that Augustan age of the Sudan, the period of the early FUNG kingdom.

Beyond these are the weakest links in the chain, some fourteen or fifteen names probably due in part to the inventiveness of the genealogists of the FUNG period and their anxiety to connect their own generation with that of the immediate descendants of the Companions of the Prophet.

III In the early centuries of Islam so much attention was paid, by generations that scrupulously observed the behest of Muḥammad concerning pedigrees, to the exact inter-relationship of his Companions and their ancestors that the native scribe of the present is naturally content to accept without question the statement of any ancient genealogist whose work may be accessible to him.

The popular idea of the value of a long pedigree is easily estimated from the opening paragraphs of the larger *nisbas* that have been translated.

Unfortunately the Arab genealogies have always been almost purely patrilinear, and little account is taken of the wives and daughters and the collateral lines. It is noticeable, however, that whereas in the more recent generations the mother is not mentioned at all unless for some very special reason, her name is not infrequently given in the groups of ancestors who lived about the early FUNG period, but then only incidentally and with a view to showing which of the sons of some particular man were full brothers and which half-brothers. So, too, in the group of ancestors connecting the generations last mentioned with the better-known generations of those who lived in the seventh and eighth centuries A.D. one sometimes finds such names as "*so and so* el Khazragi," meaning that his mother was a Khazragía[1].

IV Now the traditions current among the Arabs of the Sudan on the subject of their racial origins and the circumstances and date of the migration of their forebears to the Sudan are almost entirely based upon statements they have found in the *nisbas* handed down to them, though in a few cases their stock of information has been supplemented by the result of inadequate uncritical and unenlightened foragings among the works of one or two mediaeval Arabic historians.

The Arabic historians if studied with greater care might well have saved the genealogists of the Sudan from a vast number of inaccuracies, but, as it is, they have been so neglected that, unless the context

[1] See BA, CXXXIII note.

forbids, one is often inclined to accept a similarity between two statements as corroborative evidence.

The *nisba*-writer relies as a rule upon the accuracy of the inherited or copied *nisba*, and it is only in dealing with the more recent generations that tradition, other than that derived from the *nisbas*, plays any important part.

V From among the mass of useless and untrustworthy material contained in the manuscripts it is not difficult to pick out certain definite and persistent traditions which are distinctly interesting. In addition to them there are made in passing numerous remarks and asides from which one may make some not unimportant deductions. It cannot be too often insisted that the proper method is to regard the tribal *nisbas* rather as parables than as statements of fact. Considered in that light they have a very definite value.

By piecing together such scraps of historical information as are available from the native manuscripts into an abbreviated and coherent whole one discovers to what extent the result coincides with or differs from or supplements the information similarly derivable from the works of non-Sudanese authors, whether they be mediaeval Arabs or modern European travellers; and from certain of the manuscripts one learns something of the sociology of the people and of their customs and beliefs.

VI But one must make some attempt to reply to the inevitable questions—"What is the general character of these native manuscripts?" "Who wrote them?" "What is their date?"

VII The word *nisba*, by which the majority is known, means literally a pedigree. Hence the true *nisba* is avowedly genealogical in purpose and items of narrative are only incidental to the main theme.

As a rule the author or copyist, after the usual confession of faith, if he desires to do more than give a bald list of his ancestors, recapitulates his reasons for writing the *nisba*: it is an act of piety enjoined by the Prophet, and the author had found that there was some danger of links in the genealogical chain being lost or confused[1]. Then follows a genealogical exposition, usually of the GUHAYNA or the 'Abbásid stock in the Sudan, or of both, including the author's or the copyist's own pedigree from father to son. In addition the *nisba* often contains towards the end a series of short stereotyped notes on the origin of the chief Arab tribes of the Sudan.

[1] Much of what is said about this bears a very strong resemblance to the contents of the first chapter of Ibn Khaldūn's second book, *i.e.* Vol. II in the Arabic edition. This second book, unlike the first and third, has not, I believe, been yet translated into either English or French.

This type of *nisba* is both the oldest and the commonest. Hundreds of examples must exist in the Sudan, but the great majority of them are not merely incomplete but hardly pretend to be more than extracts copied from a larger manuscript. Misreadings and omissions abound. Interpolations also occur fairly frequently, but happily the Sudanese Arab excels at the type of work that demands no mental effort whatever, and as a copyist he may count this as a merit. Where interpolations have been added the fact is almost always obvious and consequently not without use.

VIII The father of this type of *nisba* is undoubtedly that renowned but very elusive person, "el Samarḳandi." As a writer of parables in the form of genealogies he deserves a considerable meed of praise.

The second type of manuscript, sometimes included under the term *nisba*, takes the form of a semi-historical, semi-genealogical hotch-potch founded partly on *nisbas* proper and partly on some ill-digested Arabic history or encyclopaedia.

Thirdly, we have copies of a history[1] of the Fung kingdom and the Turkish period which followed it by an unknown author, who probably wrote between 1870 and 1880 but had access to older records.

Fourthly, we meet occasionally with a treasured copy of the well-known *Ṭabaḳát wad Ḍayfulla*[2], a series of biographies of the Arab holy men of the Sudan, containing many anecdotes and historical data.

Into a fifth category may be classed a number of present-day works dealing with the history of some particular region or with certain specified tribes. These are founded partly on tradition and partly on the manuscripts described[3].

IX A word must be said here as to the "Samarḳandi" referred to as the originator of the most typical *nisbas*. It must be confessed that nothing really definite is known about him at all. All we have to go upon may be summed up as follows: hardly had the Fung and their Arab allies overthrown the kingdom of Sóba in 1504 when they were threatened with invasion by Sultan Selím who had conquered Egypt in 1517. 'Omára Dūnḳas therefore thought it well to write to Selím and explain that the inhabitants of his kingdom were Arabs of exalted lineage. "With this letter he sent a book of the pedigrees of the Arab tribes in his kingdom compiled for him by el Imám el Samarḳandi, one of the learned men of Sennár; and when

[1] D 7. [2] D 3.

[3] Part IV consists of examples of all these types of MSS., and remarks as to authorship and reliability are given in each case in an introductory note.

this book reached the Sultan Selím its contents delighted him and he renounced the attack on Sennár[1]."

Of el Samarḳandi nothing more is known. He was probably one of the itinerant *fekis* who were attracted from Egypt by the fame of the new kingdom founded in the Gezíra and by the probability that in the vanity and credulity of its rulers some profit might be found for himself. His original work has entirely disappeared and the numerous "exact copies" of it that are periodically reported are never more than garbled extracts.

There are nine references to el Samarḳandi in the manuscripts that follow: four of them are in A 2, two in A 11, two in C 5, and one in D 6. From A 2 one gathers that el Samarḳandi's method was to give the pedigree and branches of the Ga'ali stock and so connect them with the BENI 'ABBÁS; then to tell how one Sulaymán of the BENI OMMAYYA migrated through Abyssinia to the Sudan about 750 A.D., when the 'Abbásids were supplanting the Ommayyads, and became ancestor of the FUNG; and finally, perhaps, to enumerate the Arab tribes of the Sudan and state very shortly from what Arabian ancestor each was descended and whence and when it migrated to the Sudan.

From A 11 one gets the same impression but is told that there were two persons named el Samarḳandi, Maḥmúd el Samarḳandi and 'Abdulla ibn Sa'íd el Samarḳandi. One of them was apparently called "el Samarḳandi the Great." C 5 adds nothing to our information. D 6 speaks of "Abu Maḥmúd el Samarḳandi." No direct information is vouchsafed in any of the manuscripts as to the date or life of el Samarḳandi; and D 7, which makes a point of mentioning such savants as came to the FUNG court, refers to no such person. To non-Sudanese literature so far as I am aware he is entirely unknown.

It would be unjustifiable, I think, to write him down a myth. His fame must rest on some basis or other of actuality. If one accept the gist of Na'úm Bey's account of him it is certainly allowable to remark that at the time when el Samarḳandi composed his work there must have been a fairly large fund of information still available about the circumstances of the entry of the Arabs into the Sudan and their tribal affinities. El Samarḳandi would naturally make use of this, and the Arab chieftains of the day would be only too eager to supply him with genealogical details and tradition concerning

---

[1] Translated from Na'úm Bey Shuḳayr, II, pp. 73, 74. Cp. Crowfoot in *A.-E. Sudan*, I, 319. Na'úm Bey, I believe, got his facts by hearsay at Khartoum about the time of the reoccupation of the Sudan.

themselves and their immediate forebears. Where links in the chain were missing no doubt others were supplied by the imagination, and the critical faculty was presumably brought into play as little as possible; but it appears to me that it is easy to over-estimate the part played by sheer inventiveness and to under-estimate the general amount of truth underlying statements which as regards the exact form in which they have survived are inaccurate in many details.

X Let us now summarise the information to be gleaned from the manuscripts as to historical and sociological matters.

No mention is made in any manuscript of an Arab immigration to the Sudan prior to the foundation of Islam. The reason is obviously the lack of interest felt for any ancestor who left Arabia in the pagan "Days of Ignorance." The desire of all was to display their fathers as pillars of the true faith.

One also notes that the tide of immigration is always represented as having been by way of the Red Sea ports or of the Nile valley[1], and generally the former[2]. Nothing is said of any tribe wandering southwards from Tripoli, Algiers or Morocco into the western kingdoms and thence eastwards into the Sudan.

The Ismá'ílitic tribes most commonly mentioned in the manuscripts as having sent branches to the Sudan are Ḳuraysh (including Beni 'Abbás and Beni Ommayya) and Ḳays 'Aylán, who include Ghatafán, Beni Dhubián (Fezára, etc.), Beni 'Abs, Thaḳíf and others.

Among the Ḳaḥṭánite group we most often meet with Ḥimyar, who include Ḳuḍá'a and Guhayna (a branch of Ḳuḍá'a), and with Beni Ghassán.

Extra stress is laid on Ḳuraysh for obvious reasons, and the Beni Ghassán are similarly favoured because the tribes of "Anṣár," Aus and Khazrag, the "Helpers of the Prophet," were of their number.

From the frequency with which Ḥimyarite names[3] occur in Ga'ali *nisbas* it would appear that some of the Arabs who claimed an 'Abbásid (Ismá'ílitic) origin were really of Ḳaḥṭánite stock.

XI As regards the various epochs at which Islamic immigration occurred the following data are available from the manuscripts.

Speaking of the conquest of Egypt by 'Amr ibn el 'Áṣi the author of D 4 says the armies of the Muhammadans penetrated "to the furthest limits of the land of the Nūba, to Dábat el Dólíb and the hills of the Nūba[4]," that is, roughly speaking, to Debba and el Ḥaráza.

[1] See D 2, IV.
[2] In particular see D 6.
[3] *E.g.* Dhu el Kilá'a and Masrūk. See BA, CXXXIII note.
[4] D 4, VI.

In the next paragraph he alludes to a further immigration in the following century.

Secondly, we are told of the FEZÁRA that they "have dwelt in the Sudan since the conquest of el Bahnasá," that is, since 'Abdulla ibn Sa'ad's expedition of 641–642[1].

Thirdly, the MAḤASS, who are Nūbian rather than Arab by race, claim to be

descended from the Anṣár who conquered the Sudan in 43 A.H. [663 A.D.] during the period of the rule of 'Abdulla ibn Abu Saraḥ [*i.e.* ibn Sa'ad], the Companion. After the conquest the KHAZRAG settled in this country....At the time of their coming to conquer the Sudan they numbered about 81,000[2].

Fourthly, the ḤAḌÁRMA are said to have migrated from Ḥaḍramaut "in the time of Ḥaggág ibn Yūsef" and settled at Sūákin[3], that is, between 662 and 713 A.D.

Fifthly, the ancestor of the MESALLAMÍA is recorded to have come to the Sudan from Syria "in the time of 'Omar ibn 'Abd el 'Azíz[4]," or between 679 and 718 A.D.

Sixthly, we have the entry of Sulaymán ibn 'Abd el Malik, the alleged Ommawi ancestor of the FUNG, into Abyssinia between 750 and 754 A.D., and his passage thence to the Sudan[5].

Seventhly, it is generally implied by genealogists of the Ga'ali group[6] that Kerdam or his son Serrár was the first of their ancestors to immigrate from Arabia.

Aḥmad ibn Ismá'íl el Wali, the author of AB, was born about 1830–1840 and his pedigree makes him the twenty-second in descent from Kerdam. The latter or Serrár would therefore, if one reckon the generation at about thirty years, seem to have immigrated in the latter part of the thirteenth century[7].

Another *nisba* says the first Ga'ali ancestor to immigrate was Ghánim (the fourth in descent from Serrár), and that he came in the middle of the thirteenth century A.D. after the fall of Baghdád before the Tartars[8].

A third document makes Ghánim's grandfather Ṣubuḥ the original settler[9]. A fourth represents the forefathers of the GA'ALIÍN

[1] A 11, LIV, and D 6, XIII. Cp. account in Part II, Chap. 2.

[2] ABC, IX, and see note thereto.

[3] BA, CLXXVI.

[4] BA, CLXXVIII.

[5] *E.g.* BA, CCXIII and note.

[6] *E.g.* BA, CXXXIII and AB, CLXVI.

[7] See Part III, Chap. 1 (*a*). One arrives at the same conclusion if one start with the reasonably legitimate assumption that 'Armán, who lived seven generations after Kerdam, was a contemporary of el Samarḳandi.

[8] ABC, XXII.

[9] D 5 (*c*).

as coming to Egypt about 969 A.D. and migrating to the Sudan about 1171[1].

Other passages suggest that the date of their coming was about 750 A.D. and the cause of it the overthrow of the Ommayyads by the 'Abbásids, but one naturally regards these with even more suspicion than the other stories[2].

Eighthly, we read that "according to Ibn Khaldūn the tribes of Arabs descended from GUHAYNA came after the Muhammadan conquest of the Northern Nūba in 1318 A.D....[3]," and this statement we have seen to be correct.

Ninthly, the RIKÁBÍA are descended from Rikáb the son of Ghulámulla. Ghulámulla, it is said[4], lived as a young man in Yemen and then moved with his father by way of the Red Sea to Dongola, where he found the people still "sunk in perplexity and error." He was the thirteenth in descent from Mūsa el Káẓim, who, we know, died about 800 A.D.[5]; and the Awlád Gábir (the fifth generation from Ghulámulla) were junior by a generation to Maḥmūd el 'Araki who flourished in the middle of the sixteenth century[6]. We may therefore hazard the second half of the fourteenth century as being very approximately the date of the immigration of Ghulámulla, the ancestor of the tribe which is known by the name of his son Rikáb.

Tenthly, the manuscript D 7, speaking of the foundation of the FUNG kingdom in 1504 A.D., says that it was followed by a largely increased immigration of Arabs into the Sudan[7].

Lastly, Ya'aḳūb el Mugelli is said[8] to have entered the Sudan and visited Sennár in 1592 A.D., and his father, the ancestor of the ZENÁRKHA, to have previously immigrated from the Yemen, that is perhaps about 1560 A.D.

XII Some of these traditions relate apparently to individuals only, but one gets a general impression of four tides of Arab immigration into the Sudan.

The first flowed through Egypt in the seventh and eighth centuries and was a natural sequel to the conquest of that country. It was probably of mixed composition and may have contained, among others, tribesmen of FEZÁRA and BENI OMMAYYA[9] and some Anṣár.

The second immigration took place in the eighth century across the Red Sea by way of Abyssinia as a result of the overthrow of the

[1] D 6, XXXIX. [2] See A 11, VII and D 6, X and notes thereto.
[3] ABC, L. [4] BA, CLXXIX, CCVII, CCVIII. [5] Wüstenfeld, I, 324.
[6] D 3, 157. The elder brother among the Awlád Gábir, Ibráhím el Bulád, came to the Sudan between 1554 and 1562 (see D 3, VI, and D 7, XV).
[7] D 7, XI. [8] ABC, LIV.
[9] *I.e.* the ancestors of the MESALLAMÍA.

Ommayyads by the 'Abbásids, and eventually resulted in the foundation of the Arab-Fung hegemony in the Gezíra.

The ancestors of the Ḥadárma or Ḥaḍáreb had similarly reached Sūákin by way of the Red Sea half a century earlier and settled on the coast—so at least say the *nisbas*; but colonies from Ḥaḍramaut had undoubtedly established themselves on the African shore at a much earlier date, and in any case the interior of the country was very little affected.

For several centuries after the rise of the 'Abbásids no immigration of tribes is mentioned by the *nisbas*. Then in the thirteenth and fourteenth centuries the conquests of the Mamlūk Sultans broke down the barrier which had been for so long presented by the Christian kingdom of Dongola and opened the way for a fresh inflow of Arabs into the Sudan. To this period belongs the great Guhayna movement, and, in so far as the Danágla-Ga'aliín group are Arabs, it is probably to the same period that their genesis must be traced, though, as we have seen, the Ga'aliín proper—the people living between the Shablūka and the embouchure of the Atbara—may not have come into existence as a tribe until the beginning of the sixteenth century.

The fourth great immigration followed the foundation of the Fung kingdom and the conquest of Egypt by Selím I: it does not seem to have been confined to any particular tribe.

XIII There is no reason to doubt the approximate correctness of this presentation if one have regard only to the dates at which the chief immigrations occurred, but the *nisbas* generally err in assuming that each tribe of the present day is descended from a single ancestor and deliberately ignoring the fact that each consists of a conglomeration of heterogeneous elements some of which may have reached the country at one time and some at another. Even apart from this it is dubious whether the particular tribal substrata to which certain periods of migration are reserved can be accepted as correct.

No mention is made of any extensive tribal movement into the Sudan occurring later than the first half of the sixteenth century; and, if one except the thin though constant infiltration of Arabs across the Red Sea from the Ḥegáz and the Yemen, it is probably correct to say there has not been any.

XIV Let us now briefly examine the sparse references that occur to the indigenous races with whom the Arab immigrants must have coalesced, though the *nisbas* naturally lay no great stress on the fact.

Muḥammad walad Dólíb the younger simply quotes Ibn Khaldūn when he states that "the original autochthonous people of the Sudan were the Nūba and the Abyssinians and the Zing[1]," but he goes on to classify the Hamag as Zing and the Fung as Nūba. "The original [home] of the Zing," he says, "is a mountain inhabited by blacks on the equator and south [of it]. Beyond them are no other peoples; and their country stretches from West Africa [*el Moghrab*] to the neighbourhood of Abyssinia[2]." Sennár, he adds, in old days contained "tribes of Zing and Nūba[3]."

Dáūd Kubára of Ḥalfa discussing the Nūbian race says that the capital of the kingdom of the Nūba was Gebel el Ḥaráza in Northern Kordofán: he also speaks of Abyssinians and Nūbians as living together round the first cataract[4]. The limits of Nūbia to the south in the seventh century, in his view, would seem to have been Debba on the river and el Ḥaráza inland[5]. When civil war broke out between the Beni 'Abbás and the Beni Ommayya in the next century, he says, many Arabs migrated and, following the steps of previous emigrants, settled in the Sudan "and mingled with the Nūbians, and took their women to wife, and intermarried with them, and made the land of Nūba their home...[6]." The same author speaks of Southern Kordofán, Dár Nūba that is, as inhabited by "Zing-Nūba[7]."

Referring to the origin of the Fung race the manuscripts commonly speak of Sulaymán 'Abd el Malik as passing through Abyssinia into the "mountains of the Fung" or "the country of the Hamag," meaning the northern Burūn country south of Roṣayreṣ, and there marrying the daughter of a local king,—whence the Fung aristocracy.

The Fung chronicle says that about 1504 A.D. the Fung and their Arab allies overthrew the Christian "Nūba," otherwise "the 'Anag, the kings of Sóba and el Ḳerri," and most of "the Nūba...scattered and fled to Fázoghli and Kordofán[8]." Similarly the Ṭabaḳát[9]: "Know that the Fung possessed and conquered the land of the Nūba early in the tenth century" (*sc.* of Islam).

Muḥammad walad Dólíb the elder classes as "'Anag" the Fun-ḳur, the aborigines of Borḳu, the people of Baḳirmi, the Dágū, and

[1] D I, CLXXVIII. [2] D I, CLXXXII. [3] D I, CLXXXIII.
[4] D 4, IV. [5] D 4, VI and XX.
[6] D 4, VII. [7] D 4, XXI.
[8] D 7, *q.v.* paras. I–X. The 'Anag, I have been assured, came originally from Sabá in southern Arabia, and their headquarters were at Sóba on the east bank. They had wonderful means of communication between Sabá and Sóba, it is said; but the story that when King Subr of Sóba fell ill his father came "by telegraph" from Sabá in one day has so taxed even the credulity of the Sudan that the retort to a cock-and-bull story is "Khubru Subru!" ("a Subr yarn!").
[9] D 3, *q.v.* para. IV.

the inhabitants of eastern and northern Kordofán, including the hills of el Ḥaráza, etc. Western and southern Kordofán, and Dárfūr, he speaks of as inhabited by NŪBA. He calls the autochthonous DANÁGLA 'ANAG, "and some remnants of them at the present day are called the NŪBA." The DINKA are "'ANAG from among the ZING[1]."

These quotations will suffice to shew that, as might have been expected, there is no really clear distinction traceable in the mind of the native historian between any of the pre-Arab races of the Sudan. All are vaguely and indiscriminately heaped together under the names "NŪBA" and "'ANAG." The term ZING is reserved for more southernly negroid tribes, but it too is used with such obvious vagueness that there would be little point in discussing the exact connotation of the term as used, with rather more exactitude, by mediaeval Arab authors[2]. The non-Arab element in the BEGA tribes of the east and some of the negroid tribes in the west is ignored by the simple expedient of providing them with shadowy Arabian ancestors or else by omitting mention of them altogether.

XV Now we have seen that in the first nine hundred odd years that followed the conquest of Egypt the Arabs who entered the Sudan gradually acquired a temporal hegemony in certain districts, but the manuscripts do not leave one with the impression that they concerned themselves very assiduously with the proselytizing of the earlier inhabitants. The reason may easily be seen: those who left Egypt for the west and south were either led to do so by the spirit of wandering and the hope of booty or driven forth by the exactions of an unsympathetic government.

Their ancient superstitions, it is true, had been re-clothed in the new garment of Islam, but the sword and not the book was still their first concern, and so long as a proper subservience was shewn to the name of Muhammadanism no exact compliance with its rules in daily life were universally exacted.

In proportion, however, as the sword gradually brought the country into subjection a more peaceful and pious type began to follow and explain the doctrine which the earlier immigrants had perforce neglected because of their own ignorance of its significance.

XVI It seems from the *nisbas* that until the latter part of the fourteenth century such Muhammadanism as existed among the people of Dongola was purely nominal—until, that is, the learned and pious Ghulámulla ibn 'Áíd settled there and began the work of

[1] D I, CXXIX–CLXX.
[2] See, however, the note to D I, XXII.

instruction in earnest. Dongola and the country north of it, being so near to Egypt, were probably converted by the end of that century, but apparently nearly two hundred years elapsed before any religious regeneration was effected south of the junction of the Niles.

Then Maḥmūd el 'Araki undertook the work. He was followed by a large group of other missionaries, of whom the most famous were perhaps Tág el Dín el Bahári, Bán el Naḳa, Dafa'alla el 'Araki and Ḥámid el 'Aṣa[1], and schools and mosques were built for the enlightenment of the people from the northern frontier of the Sudan to Sennár.

This work of instruction and conversion was enormously facilitated by the foundation of the FUNG kingdom, with its subject Arab dynasty of the 'ABDULLÁB, a branch of the RUFÁ'A, at Ḳerri near the Shablūka cataract.

The power of the FUNG king became a guarantee of peace and order throughout the northern Sudan, and his court the meeting-place of all who had any pretensions to learning. Numbers of these latter settled permanently in the Sudan, and their tombs and those of their sons and grandsons are still to be seen overshadowing the villages that have arisen round them.

From the early pioneers who were contemporaries of Dafa'alla el 'Araki and the Awlád Gábir and from their sons and pupils are descended most of the best-known religious families of the Sudan, 'ARAKIÍN, YA'AḲŪBÁB, 'OMARÁB, GHUBUSH and others; and the memory of many is still preserved in the names of villages called after them, Wad Medani, Wad el Turábi, Wad Ḥasūna, Wad Bán el Naḳa, Abu Delayḳ, etc., and in the nomenclature of the children born to the inhabitants in successive generations[2].

XVII The manuscript numbered D 3 is a series of biographical notices of these holy men, or patron-saints as they might almost be called, from the middle of the sixteenth to the beginning of the nineteenth century, and from it one gleans many interesting details of

[1] For all these see D 3. The renowned Awlád Gábir were their contemporaries but lived farther north and were successors of Ghulámulla rather than of Maḥmūd.

[2] There is a marked persistence of the same proper names in certain localities or among certain communities, *e.g.* "'Abd el Gelíl" among the GELÍLÁB, "Abu 'Aḳla" and "Ḥammad el Níl" among the 'ARAKIÍN, "Sughayerūn" among the RIKÁBÍA, etc. This is due to the habit of naming children after some holy man "for luck" and the fact that it is a common custom among the Sudanese Arabs to name the firstborn boy after his father's deceased father and a firstborn girl after her mother's deceased mother, with intent "to keep the name alive." (This does not apply exclusively to the case of a firstborn, but occasionally to that of a subsequent child.) Normally, if the grandparent were still alive, the child would not be called after him or her, but (*e.g.*) in the case of a boy, after a late brother of his father for choice. This is the normal custom but there is no hard and fast rule.

the life of the people and their common beliefs. Among the first points that strike one are the universal use of the technical Ṣūfi terminology, the disproportionate number of incidents and anecdotes that relate to divorce and remarriage[1], the wealth possessed by many of the holy men, and the obvious survivals that are in evidence of a matrilinear system[2].

[1] Lack of space and other considerations necessitated the omission of many of these stories from the translation.

[2] See, *e.g.*, D 3, Nos. 46, 85, 107, 124, 154 and 196.

MANUSCRIPT BA

Introduction

THREE copies of this work have been read and carefully compared by me: they are alluded to as MSS. 1, 2 and 3 respectively. In addition, portions of it have been incorporated by the author of AB in his work. Innumerable other copies, more or less complete or faulty, also exist in the Sudan. MS. 1 is in the possession of el Nūr Bey 'Anḳara, an ex-Dervish *amír*, at Omdurman, and it was from it, excepting where the contrary is specifically stated, that the following translation was actually taken[1].

Subsequently Sheikh el 'Abbás Muḥammad Bedr of Um Dubbán, an ex-Ḳáḍi of the Khalífa and a Mesallami by race, sent me a copy (MS. 2) taken from a MS. in his possession; and a year later Mr S. Hillelson of the Gordon College lent me a third copy (MS. 3) which had been given him by an old pupil.

All three MSS. are in close agreement, and in several cases the same errors occur in all three.

From internal evidence it is likely that MS. 1 (excepting paras. CCXXV–CCXXVIII) was copied from the original of MS. 2: the owner of the latter was very positive that the converse could not have taken place.

MSS. 1 and 2 are written in a clear fine script, but MS. 3 is written roughly and hastily.

In MS. 3 we have some of the errors of MSS. 1 and 2 repeated, but in quite a number of cases MS. 3 is right and MSS. 1 and 2 wrong.

On the other hand, MS. 3 is very carelessly written and contains many fresh slips and inaccuracies not occurring in the other two.

As regards the authorship of the original work, it appears from paragraph CCXXIII that this *nisba* was written or, more probably, copied by el Sheríf el Ṭáhir ibn 'Abdulla of the RIKÁBÍA in Dongola early in the sixteenth century (see note to para. CCXXIII and D 5 (*d*)).

I In the name of God....

II This is a pedigree giving the origins of the Arabs; for the

[1] A marginal reference of "reading (*x*) for (*y*)" means that *x* is either an obvious emendation or else the version given by MS. 2 or MS. 3 or AB as opposed to MS. 1 (*y*).

preservation and guarding of such is obligatory because of the [record of] blood-relationships that they contain.

III The object of preserving them is not to cause boastful comparisons of pedigrees; for, as was said by the Commander of the Faithful the Imám 'Omar ibn el Khaṭṭáb..."Ye know from your pedigrees how ye are connected."

IV Some of the learned say that 'Omar may have heard this from the Prophet..., but that which has no other claim to be obligatory than his [sole] authority is yet obligatory.

V But the knowledge of the pedigrees of persons who are unrelated to yourself is of no use, because the authoritative dictum does not apply to such; and the following saying of the Prophet...about one who was learned in pedigrees bears this out: "A knowledge [of them] is useless and ignorance harmless."

VI But if a man devote himself to the study of what does not concern him, his labour is impious:

VII that is in times of mutual love and affection; but in these present days of mutual hatred and jealousy the study of pedigrees is obligatory, for at the end of the age the use of abusive epithets will be prevalent, and the difficulty will not be resolved save by means of pedigrees.

VIII So [the keeping of] pedigrees has been ordained, and it is not dutiful to neglect them: in fact he who does so is a rebel, owing to the danger of disturbance being caused among the people, and trouble in the hearts of the various nations.

IX Thus the study of pedigrees is obligatory because the observance of blood-relationships is obligatory by the authority of the Book and the Law ["el Sunna"] and the Unanimities ["el Igmá'a"].

X As regards the Book, God Almighty said "Fear God by whom ye beseech one another and [honour] the womb that bore you."

XI As regards the Law, we have the saying of the Prophet... "He that puts his trust in God and the Last Day will honour his guest and observe the duties of relationship and speak good words or none at all."

XII As regards the "Unanimities," all alike have agreed that the observance of blood-relationships is specifically ordained; and he who neglects it is disobedient.

XIII In the "Traditions" it is said "The womb is suspended upon the throne [of God] and says 'Lord, honour him that honours me and cut off him that cuts me off.'"

XIV Some too have said that the observance of blood-relationships lengthens life.

XV People are reliable as to their pedigrees; and whosoever has received from his father or ancestor any charge of a pedigree is indeed whatever the pedigree in his charge shows him to be.

XVI Boastful comparisons of pedigrees are blameworthy, and it is not the part of an intelligent man to vaunt his fathers and ancestors and claim honour and respect because of the nobility of his pedigree: such a thing could only be done by a slave by virtue of his being pious;

XVII for the Prophet...said "I am the ancestor of every pious man and woman, even though it be an Abyssinian slave, etc."

XVIII Boastful comparisons of pedigree and competition to amass wealth and disdain of the poor are forbidden by the law.

XIX For God Almighty said "Verily the faithful are [all] brethren; therefore reconcile your brethren,"—that is both in affairs temporal and spiritual, for faith is the bond between the faithful both in the matter of their pedigrees and of their religion; and "reconcile your brethren" means [you should do so] if two of them quarrel and fight.—"And fear God, and rebel not against Him nor disobey His behest, that ye may be the recipients of His mercy."

XX "O ye that believe, let not men mock at other men, who are perchance better than themselves, nor let women laugh other women to scorn, who are perchance better than themselves. Neither defame one another nor abuse one another with injurious appellations. An ill name [it is to be charged with] wickedness, after [having embraced] the faith: and whoso repent not, they will be the unjust doers."

XXI On the authority of 'Omar...it is related that the Prophet... said "The Muslim is brother to the Muslim: he wrongs him not, nor abuses him; and whoso helps his brother Muslim, him will God help; and whoso relieves a Muslim from affliction, God will thereby relieve him of one of the afflictions of the day of resurrection."

XXII God Almighty said "O people, I have created you of male and female,"—that is Ádam and Eve ["Ḥowá"]; and the meaning is "You are all of the same descent, so do not make boastful comparisons between one another, for all of you are the children of the same man and woman." Others say the meaning to be "I have created each one of you in the same manner as the other, so you have no cause for invidious self-glorification and boastful comparison of pedigrees."

XXIII [God also said] "And I have made you races ['*shu'ūb*'] [and tribes]."

XXIV [The term] "*shu'ūb*" is the plural of "*sha'b*"... and denotes the sources of the tribes, such as RABÍ'A and MUḌR and EL AUS and EL KHAZRAG; and they were called "races" because from them were the tribes sprung, or, as it is also said, because in them were the tribes united.

XXV "*Ḳabáil*" ("tribes") is the plural of "*ḳabíla*," which is [a degree less than][1] "*shu'ūb*," and examples of "*ḳabáil*" are BUKR [derived] from RABÍ'A and TAMÍM from MUḌR.

XXVI Next below the "*ḳabáil*" are the "*'amáir*," of which the singular [is "*'amára*"][2]..., such as SHAYBÁN [derived] from BUKR, and DÁRIM from TAMÍM.

Next below the "*'amáir*" are the "*buṭūn*," of which the singular is "*baṭn*," such as BENI GHÁLIB and LŪAI [derived] from ḲURAYSH.

XXVII Next below the "*buṭūn*" are the "*afkhádh*," of which the singular is "*fakhdh*," such as BENI HÁSHIM and BENI OMMAYYA [derived] from LŪAI.

XXVIII Next below the "*afkhádh*" are the "*faṣáil*," of which the singular is "*faṣíla*"..., such as BENI EL 'ABBÁS [derived] from BENI HÁSHIM.

XXIX After the "*faṣáil*" come the "*'asháir*," of which the singular is "*'ashíra*," and after them there is nothing to mention at all.

XXX Now [the term] "*shu'ūb*" applies to the non-Arabs [*'agam*] and "*ḳabáil*" to the Arabs; and it is said that the "*shu'ūb*" are those that do not trace their origin [as a race to a common ancestor] but to [common] cities and villages, whereas the "*ḳabáil*" are the Arabs who trace their pedigrees to their ancestors.

XXXI Thus the [successive] grades into which the Arabs fall are six, viz. the "*sha'b*," the "*ḳabíla*," the "*'amára*," the "*baṭn*," the "*fakhdh*," and the "*faṣíla*"; and the "*sha'b*" contains [*lit.* "collects"] the "*ḳabáil*," the "*ḳabíla*" the "*'amáir*," the "*'amára*" the "*buṭūn*," the "*baṭn*" the "*afkhádh*," and the "*afkhádh*" the "*faṣáil*."

KHUZAYMA is a "*sha'b*," KENÁNA a "*ḳabíla*," ḲURAYSH an "*'amára*," ḲUṢAI a "*baṭn*," HÁSHIM a "*fakhdh*," and EL 'ABBÁS a "*faṣíla*," and so on.

XXXII "That ye may know one another." That is, that ye may know how closely ye are related to one another, and not make boastful comparisons of your pedigrees.

XXXIII Then he shewed by virtue of what type of character[3] one man acquires merit over another and gains honour in the sight of God Almighty, quoting "The noblest of you in God's sight is the most pious of you."

[1] inserting دون.
[2] inserting عمارة.
[3] reading الخصلة for الفصل.

XXXIV [So too] in the Tradition [it is said] "He who desires to be the noblest of men in God's sight, let him fear God."

XXXV Ibn 'Abbás...said "In this world honour is given to wealth, in the next to piety."

XXXVI On the authority of Samra ibn Gundub, the Prophet... said "It is wealth that is reckoned, but piety is [the true] nobleness."

XXXVII This saying is quoted by el Termidhi, who also quotes a beautiful tradition, corroborated by Abu Hurayra...: the latter says that the Prophet...was asked[1] "Which of the people is the noblest?" He replied "The noblest of them in God's sight is the most pious of them." They said "It is not of this that we ask you." He replied "The noblest of the people is Yūsef the Prophet of God, son of the prophet of God, son of the Friend of God." They said "It is not of this that we ask you." He replied "Is it of the original sources[2] of the Arabs that you ask me?" They said "Yes." He replied "The best of them in the days of ignorance is the best of them in the days of Islam, provided they are versed in knowledge ('*faḳukhū*' or, it is said '*faḳikhū*'), that is provided they have mastered the rules of the law."

XXXVIII It is related on the authority of 'Omar...that the Prophet ...on the day of the conquest [of Mekka] made the circuit [of the temple] on his she-camel [*náḳa*], and saluted the corners [of the sacred stone] with his staff [*maḥgan*]; and on leaving he found no place for his camel to kneel; so he dismounted [from it as it stood, helped] by the hands of the men, and then addressed them, and praised and glorified Almighty God, saying "Praise be to God who hath redeemed you from the brutishness[3] of the days of ignorance and pride. O people, I have created you in two types, the man of piety and justice [who is] noble in God's sight, and the miserable infidel [who is] of no account in God's sight." Then he repeated the word of God "O people, I have created you of male and female."

XXXIX Then he said "I tell you this and I ask the protection of God for myself and for you, etc."

XL Now the *maḥgan* was a stick with a bent handle, like a crook.

XLI By "the brutishness[4] of the days of ignorance" is meant their pride and boasting, the intention being to warn people of being boastful as [the people of] the days of ignorance were from pride and conceit of their fathers and ancestors.

XLII Ye are the sons of Ádam, and Ádam was formed from mud,

[1] reading قال قيل يا for قال قال.
[2] read معادن for معارف.
[3] read غبية for عيبه.
[4] read غبية for عيبة.

that is from the earth that is trodden underfoot, so how shall one be proud and boastful: one branch is no greater than another save by the will of God on account of piety.

XLIII Four things characterized the days of ignorance: boasting of their merits, speaking ill of [each other's] lineage, [excessive] lamentation, and prognostication of rain by the stars.

XLIV It has been said [by the poet] "By thy life! What is [a man's] pedigree if he be not a child of religion: so forsake not piety, trusting to your lineage. Verily by Islam was Selmán the Persian [slave] exalted, and [by his unbelief] did Abu Lahab forego his rich portion."

XLV God Almighty said "Justify not yourselves": that is "do not [pretend to be] free from sin nor boast of your deeds." And it is said that the meaning of the verse is "He knows you best, O ye faithful," *i.e.* knows your condition from the day of your creation till your last day; therefore "Justify not yourselves" with false humility and arrogance, nor say to one that you know not truly "I am better than thou" and "I am purer than thou." "Knowledge is of God," and this saying is an index [for men] to their duties, that they may take warning of what will befal: and verily God knows what will befal him that is pious, and God best knows who is the most pious, that is the greatest and most obedient and most efficient in his works. He who is tardy in works will not be speeded [to salvation] by his pedigree, and he that is speedy in works will not be retarded by his pedigree: works outweigh pedigrees; and if you are wanting in your works you have no profit in this world or the next.

XLVI They gained not the dominion and riches save by obedience to God Almighty, and by humility and self-abasement and gentleness.

XLVII And it is related on the authority of Ibn 'Abbás (God bless him) that he upon whom be the blessings of God said "There is no alternative to be accepted of the Arabs excepting Islam or the sword."

XLVIII According to Ibn Wahháb there are seven tribes whose enslavement is not permissible, namely:

- Ḳuraysh
- el Anṣár
- Muzayna
- Guhayna
- Ashga'a
- Aslam
- Ghafár

and it is related also that the Prophet said that no Arab should be enslaved. If you wish for the reference, see El Mishkát li 'l Ḳári ["The Reader's Illuminators"] with the commentary of 'Abd el Báḳi.

XLIX The tribes of the Arabs are seven, and whosoever is not included in them may lawfully be enslaved: these are

- KENÁNA
- MUZAYNA
- GUHAYNA
- ASHGA'A
- ḤIMYAR
- GHAFÁR
- ḲURAYSH

and the noblest of these is KENÁNA, because he upon whom be the blessing of God said "God chose KENÁNA from among the sons of Ismá'íl, and ḲURAYSH from KENÁNA, and BENI HÁSHIM from ḲURAYSH, and from BENI HÁSHIM he chose me, who am thus the noblest of the noblest"; and this is no [vain] boast: this account is the true one.

L Now ḤIMYAR and ṬAI and THA'ALEB and NIGM and HAMDÁN and MA'ÁFIR and BÍṢAR and ḤUḲNA and KELÁB EL AZD[1] and MUZAYNA and GUHAYNA all trace their descent to one ancestor: viz. el Maḥassi ibn Ḳaḥṭán el Maḥassi son of Ibráhím: God knows the truth.

LI Most of GUHAYNA are in the Nile-land and the west, and MUZAYNA are mixed[2] with [the inhabitants of] those parts, and ḤIMYAR are in the land of el Baṣra, and ASHGA'A in the land of Tūnis and Tripoli ["*Ṭerábulus*"], and GHAFÁR in the land of Andalusia ["*el Andalus*"] and Persia ["*Fáris*"] and Mesopotamia ["*el 'Irák*"], and KENÁNA are in the land of Mekka the noble and el Medína the glorious and Egypt and el Rūm.

LII Now when Noah, upon whom be the blessings of God, landed from the ark to inhabit the earth, one day it happened that his privy parts were exposed, and his son Ḥám looked at them and laughed and did not cover him up: then his son Sám saw him and turned his face aside and did not cover [his father]: then his son Yáfith saw him and turned his face aside and covered his father's privy parts. And when [Noah] awoke he learnt of this and he called his son Ḥám [saying] "may God change the seed of your loins and blacken your face: you shall beget none but blacks."

LIII And Ḥám begot EL HIND and EL SIND and the NŪBA and ḲURÁN and all the blacks; and Yáfith begot the TURKS and the CHINESE ["*el Ṣín*"] and BERBER and the SLAVONIANS ["*el Ṣaḳáliba*"] and GOG and MAGOG ["*Yágūg wa Mágūg*"] and FÁRISH and DÁRISH and KHÁLABḲÁ and GÁBIRSÁ; and Sám begot the Arabs and the Romans ["*el Rūm*"] and Persians ["*Fáris*"].

[1] reading كلاب الازد for كلام الازرد.
[2] reading ممتزجة (as AB) for ممزوجة.

LIV And when death was come to Noah, upon whom be the blessings of God, he called to his son Sám, his firstborn, and divided the earth between him and his brothers, and to Sám he allotted the centre of the earth, the holy land, and its environs as far as Ḥaḍramaut and 'Omán[1] as far as el Baḥrayn and 'Álig; and to his brothers he allotted the outlying portions of the land; and Sám's allotment was the best of the earth and the most fertile. Ends.

LV We will now take up the thread of the narrative.

LVI The pedigree of Guhayna is as follows:

Dhubián son of 'Abdulla son of Dahmán son of Ḳays son of Mufíḍ son of Guhayna son of Rayth son of Ghaṭafán[2] son of Sa'ad son of Ḳays son of 'Aylán son of Muḍr son of Mu'áwia son of el Ḥakam son of 'Affán son of Ams son of Ommayya son of 'Abd Shams son of 'Abd Menáf son of Ḳuṣai son of Keláb son of Murra son of Lūai son of Ghálib son of Fihr son of Málik son of Nuḍr son of Kenána son of Khuzayma son of Mudraka son of el Yás son of Muḍr son of Nizár[3] son of Ma'ad son of 'Adnán.

LVII Others say that Guhayna was son of 'Aṭía son of el Ḥasan son of el Zubayr son of el 'Awwám son of Khowaylid son of Asad son of 'Abd el 'Uzzá son of Ḳuṣai...etc.

LVIII Others say that Guhayna was son of 'Abdulla son of Unays el Guhani; and God knows the truth.

LIX Dhubián had ten sons, viz. Watíd and Fahíd and Shaṭír and Bashír and 'Ámir and 'Omrán and 'Abd el 'Azíz Maḥassi and Gudhám and Sufián Afzar and Ṣárid[4].

LX Watíd and Fahíd and Gudhám and 'Ámir and 'Omrán were, all five, sons of one mother; and Shaṭír and Bashír were sons of one mother; and 'Abd el 'Azíz Maḥassi and Ṣárid[5] were sons of one mother; and Sufián Afzar[6] was the only son of his mother.

LXI The descendants of Watíd are the KHAWÁLDA; the descendants of Fahíd the FAHÍDÁT in the West.

LXII Shaṭír begot Sulṭán only.

LXIII Sulṭán had seven sons, Musallam and Ga'afir and Ráshid and Ruwáḥ and Ḥamayd (or "Ḥamayl")[7] and Ma'ashir and Rikáb.

LXIV Muslim's sons were Fádin and Mashaykh and Moghrab and Dwayḥ and Dáūd.

LXV Fádin's descendants are the FÁDNIA; Mashaykh's[8] the MA-

1 reading عمان for امان.
2 reading غطفان for عطفا.
3 reading نزار for نذار.
4 reading صارد for صادر.
5 reading صارد for صادر.
6 reading افزر for فزر.
7 reading حميل for حميد.
8 reading مشيخ for مسيخ.

SHÁÍKHA; Moghrab's the MOGHÁRBA; Dwayḥ's the DWAYḤÍA; and Dáūd's the DÁŪDÍA.

LXVI Ga'afir's descendants are the GA'ÁFIRA; Ráshid's the ROWÁSHDA; Ruwáḥ's the RUWÁḤÍA; and Ḥamayl's the ḤAMAYLÍA, that is the ḤAMAYLÁT, and[1] a tribe called AWLÁD ḤAMAYL between el Hind and el Sind; and Ma'ashir's descendants are the MA'ÁSHIRA; and Rikáb's the RIKÁBÍA and the GENÁNA and the MEZANIYYŪN and the LAḤÁWIYYŪN and the ZUMAYLÁT: all these are the descendants of Sulṭán son of Shaṭír.

LXVII The descendants of his brother Bashír are the SHUKRÍA, and the BUÁDIRA and the UMBÁDIRÍA.

LXVIII 'Ámir begot Muḥammad only: this Muḥammad had eight sons and one daughter, the eldest of [his children].

LXIX The sons[3] were Ráfa'i and Nagaz and Duriáb and Ḥammad el 'Uláṭi and Hilál and Kelb and Muḥammad 'Áḳil and Dwayḥ[4], all sons of one mother, excepting Dwayḥ, who was the only son of his mother.

LXX The daughter was given in marriage by her father Muḥammad ibn 'Ámir to a man named Marhíṣ of the FŪL, whose children by her were Kál and Báz and el Ma'ádia and Fáliḳ and their various descendants.

LXXI The sons of Ráfa'i ibn Muḥammad were Zanfal and Shabáriḳ[5] and Ḳásim.

LXXII The descendants of Zanfal are the ZENÁFLA, of Shabáriḳ the SHABÁRḲA, and of Ḳásim the ḲAWÁSMA and the MAḤÁMÍD.

LXXIII The descendants of 'Abd el 'Azíz Maḥassi are the MAḤASS, of Gudhám the GUDHÁMIYYŪN, and of Ṣárid[6] the ṢOWÁRDA.

LXXIV The sons of Ḥammad el 'Uláṭi son of Muḥammad 'Ámir were Maḥmūd and Ḥasan Ma'árak[7] and Fūáḳ and 'Ón.

LXXV Maḥmūd had five sons, Raḥál and Dárish and Kūákir and 'Áíl and Fakhdh.

LXXVI The descendants of Raḥál are the ROWÁḤLA, of Dárish the DOWÁRISHA, of Kūákir the KŪÁKÍR, and of Fakhdh the FOWÁKHIDHÍA.

LXXVII The sons of Ḥasan Ma'árak son of Ḥammad el 'Uláṭi were Durrak and 'Asham and Dasham[8].

LXXVIII The sons of Durrak were Ḥamar and Ḥamrán.

LXXIX The sons of 'Asham were Nágiḥ and Náíl and Tha'alib and 'Othmán and 'Amūd and Ḥalū and 'Affan.

[1] inserting و.
[2] reading والام بادرية for واللام بادية.
[3] reading فالاولاد for فلاولاد.
[4] reading دويح for رويح.
[5] reading شبارق for بشارق.
[6] reading صارد for صادر.
[7] reading معارك for معراك.
[8] reading دشم for رشم.

LXXX The descendants of Nágiḥ are the NAWÁGIḤA, of Náíl the NAWÁÍLA, of Tha'alib the THA'ALIBA, of 'Othmán the 'OTHMÁNÍA.

LXXXI The sons of 'Amūd were Ḳerayn and Bashḳar and Zamlūṭ and 'Isayl and Ḥasan and Ḥasán and Shiblá, and Ferag by a concubine.

LXXXII The descendants of Ḳerayn are the ḲERAYNÁT, of Bashḳar the BASHÁḲIRA, of Zamlūṭ the ZAMÁLṬA, of 'Isayl the 'ISAYLÁT, of Ḥasan the ḤASANÍA, of Ḥasán the ḤASÁNÍA, of Shiblá the SHIBAYLÁT, and of Ferag the MUFÁRIGA and the FARAGÁB and the MUWÁRIGA.

LXXXIII The descendants of Ḥalū are the ḤALÁWIYYŪN, of 'Affan the 'AFFANÁB[1].

LXXXIV The sons of Dasham were Bedr and Zayd and Ḥegázi and Fáḍil and Thaḳíf and Zuhayr.

LXXXV The descendants of Bedr are the BEDRIYYŪN, of Zayd the ZŪÁÍDA, of Ḥegázi the ḤEGÁZÁB, of Fáḍil the FAḌLIYYŪN, of Thaḳíf the THAḲÍFIYYŪN, and of Zuhayr the ZUHAYRIYYŪN.

LXXXVI The descendants of Fūáḳ son of Ḥammad el 'Uláṭi are the SHUKRÁB.

LXXXVII The sons of his brother 'Ón were Thábit and Ṣábir and Sárib and Gurfán and Missír and Ma'atūḳ, and among his descendants are the THAWÁBITA[2] and the SHAḲLÁB and the SHUKRÁB and the 'ABDULLÁB and the TUNGURÁB and KUNGÁRA and, it is said, BORNŪ and BORḲŪ and AFNŪ and MADAḲA and FELLÁTA and the MESSÍRÍA and 'OḲAYL,—all of them descendants of 'Ón[3] son of Ḥammad el 'Uláṭi.

LXXXVIII Kelb son of Muḥammad 'Ámir had five sons, Ṭurfa and Aḥmar and Serḥán and Ḳalḳál and Dágir.

LXXXIX Ṭurfa had seven sons, Ḳalíma and Gáma'i and Sulaym and Belū and Maní'a and Minba'a and Sandál.

XC The descendants of Ḳalíma are the THAḲRA, some of whom are pagans and some Muḥammadans: the descendants of Gáma'i are the BENI GÁMA'I, of Sulaym the BENI SULAYM, of Maní'a the MANÁ'A and the BURNÍT and the ḲUMDAR and KHAWÁBIRA[4] and the DABAYTÍA: and I do not know any descendants of Minba'a. The descendants of Belū are the BELŪ.

XCI The descendants of Aḥmar are the ḤAMRÁN and the ḤAMAYRÍA and the KERÍMÍA and the BERÁGHÍTH in the West.

XCII The sons of Serḥán son of Kelb son of Muḥammad 'Ámir were Zamal and Mazan and Laḥū.

1 reading العفناب for العقباب.
2 reading ثوابتة for توابتة.
3 reading عون for عدن.
4 reading خوابرة for حوابرة.

XCIII The descendants of Zamal are the Zamalát, of Mazan the Mazaynía, and of Laḥū the Laḥáwiyyūn.

XCIV The descendants of Ḳalḳál are the Ḳaláḳla in the land of Tūnis; and of Dágir the Dawágira in the East, and they are the people of el Nūḳ el Bakht.

XCV The descendants of Sandál son of Ṭurfa son of Kelb son of Muḥammad 'Ámir are the Sanádalíb, and those of Hilál son of Muḥammad 'Ámir are the Beni Yezíd.

XCVI The son of 'Omrán son of Dhubián was 'Ámir, whose sons were the 'Amárna and Sabíḳ and Ḍabí'a and Akírít and Adayḳim and 'Áṭif.

XCVII The descendants of Sabíḳ are the Sabíḳiyyūn, of Ḍabí'a the Ḍabí'át, of Akírít [the] Kurtán[1], of Adayḳim the Daḳímiyyūn, and of 'Áṭif the 'Awáṭifa, and also the Gerábí'a. These are all the descendants of 'Omrán.

XCVIII The sons of Sufián Afzar were Zayád and 'Abs and Hilál.

XCIX The descendants of Zayád are the Ḥuḍūr and the Zayádía.

C The son of 'Abs was Ḥammad el Afzar, whose sons were Kabsh and Sha'ūf.

CI The sons of Kabsh were Ribayḳ and Berára and Ḳerri and 'Aṭawi.

CII Of these the son of Sha'ūf was Ṣábir only. Ṣábir's son was Ṣárim, and Ṣárim's sons were Sálim el Hamám and Abza'a and Gerár.

CIII The sons [of Gerár] were Barakát and Ḥayla and Abu Ḥagūl.

CIV The sons of Abza'a were Nūr and Nūrán[2].

CV The sons of Nūr were Dál and Mázin.

CVI Mázin's sons were 'Awál and Ma'ál and 'Abd el 'Ál and Baghdád.

CVII Baghdád's descendants are the Bagháda.

CVIII The descendants of 'Abd el 'Ál are the Shenábla, and of Ma'ál the Ma'ália.

CIX The sons of 'Awál were 'Áḳil and Gikhays and 'Abd el Báḳi and Sahal and Ḥámid and Ḥammad.

CX The descendants of 'Áḳil are the Ma'áḳla, of Gikhays the Gikhaysát, of 'Abd el Báḳi the Bawáḳi, of Sahal the Na'ímát, and of Ḥámid the Habábín and the Feráḥna and the Merámra and the Nawáḥia, and the Gilaydát[3], whose mother was Bakhíta el Ṣughayra, [Ḥámid's] freedwoman.

[1] reading كرتان for كرات. [2] reading نوران for نولان.
[3] reading جليدات for جليلات.

CXI The descendants of Ḥammad are the AWLÁD AḲOI[1] and the MEGÁNÍN: or, according to [another] account [the latter] are descendants of Ḥámid and their father was called Magnūn.

CXII The son of Hilál son of Sufián Afzar was Ḥasan el Hiláli, whose mother was a concubine; and his sons were Ferag and Nūḥ and Dóka and their mother was Lūla.

CXIII Dóka's sons were Shilluk and Dínka and Ibráhím and Dekín.

CXIV The son of Ibráhím was Aṣbíḥ, and Aṣbíḥ's sons were Ganḳ and Funḳur and Káf and Ūlū el Gháya.

CXV Dekín had five sons, Kíra and Kirán and Káranḳū and Dóka and Aywa.

CXVI And it is said that the ḲÁÍDÁB and the MAHÍDÁB and the 'AFṢA and the BÁḲÁB and the MESÁ'ÍD and the ḲARÁFÍD and the KHAGÍLÁT and the KÁSIRÁB and the SHUKRÁB and the MA'ÁÍDA and their subdivisions are all of the stock of Muḥammad ibn 'Ámir.

CXVII The BEGÁ and the KHÁS and the BÁRÍA and the ḲURA'ÁN and the MÍDÓB and ZAGHÁWA[2] are said [by some] to be originally from Makáda, and by others to be among the descendants of the Gin that deceived the prophet of God Sulaymán son of Dáūd, upon both of them be the blessings of God, when he was away from his wife, namely Hafháf son of Shamákh.

CXVIII There is a difference of opinion as to the KAWÁHLA, the sons of Káhil: some say they are among the above, and some that they are descended from el Zubayr ibn el 'Awwám: God knows the truth best.

CXIX Similarly there is a difference of opinion about the FELLÁTA: some say they are the sons of Fellát son of Uḳbá son of Yásir, [who], when he converted the people of the West, married the daughter of the Sultan of the infidels. Their language is that of their mother's people.

CXX And [men] have disputed about these tribes as to their being descended from the Gin, and said "How could the Gin have offspring by a human woman, because the Gin is not of human descent?" God knows the truth best.

CXXI Compare the story of Balḳís[3] and how it is said that her mother was a female Gin: [but] knowledge belongs to Almighty God.

CXXII If you wish for the explanation refer to [the remarks in] the Ḥáshia of el Gemal [on the passages] wherein God says "*And I made [Noah's] offspring [to be] those who survived*" and "*And I have made*

[1] reading اقوي for قوي. [2] reading زغاوة for زقاوي.
[3] reading بلقيس for بلقيسة.

you races and tribes that ye may know one another. Verily the noblest of you in God's sight is the most pious of you," and there you will find it.

CXXIII Now the tribe of GUHAYNA became [*lit.* "reached"] fifty-two tribes in the land of Sóba on the Blue Nile under the rule of the FUNG, but most [of them] are in the West, [namely in] Tūnis and Bornūḥ.

CXXIV Zubayr had two sons, 'Abdulla and Ḥasan. The descendants of 'Abdulla are the KAWÁHLA, and the son of Ḥasan was 'Aṭía; and some say that the descendants of 'Aṭía are GUHAYNA: God knows the truth best.

CXXV The BENI YŪNIS and BENI SÍRA and BENI HAMZA are all branches of the descendants of Hilál son of Muḥammad 'Ámir.

CXXVI The descendants of Muḥammad 'Áḳil are the BENI 'ÁḲIL and the BENI HUZAYL and the BENI MAṬAYR and the BENI 'UTAYBA and the BENI YAḲŪM and the BENI MUKHALLAD and BENI YŪNIS and BENI MERÍN: these [tribes] are his own proper descendants.

CXXVII The SHÁMÍA and the MA'ÁÍDA are the descendants of 'Áíd son of Khamsín.

CXXVIII The 'AWÁMRA and BENI 'OMRÁN and BENI KELB and BENI RÁFA'I and BENI 'ULÁṬI[1] and BENI 'ÁḲIL and BENI DWAYḤ and BENI DURIÁB are all GUHAYNA and very closely related. Here ends what I have learnt of the pedigree of GUHAYNA; and knowledge belongs to God Almighty.

CXXIX Now as regards GA'AL, what is to be found here is as follows:

CXXX ḲURAYSH were in the time of the Prophet (God bless him) eighty tribes, and [similarly] GUHAYNA were eighty tribes:

CXXXI and accounts differ as to the BENI MA'AMŪR and HILÁL, some saying they belong to ḲURAYSH and some to GUHAYNA.

CXXXII Now GA'AL are [descended from] BENI EL 'ABBÁS (God bless him), and they should not be called a tribe [*ḳabíla*] but rather one of the branches of BENI HÁSHIM. They are only called "GA'AL" because their forefather, whose name was Ibráhím, was known as "Ga'al" from the fact that he was a generous man, to whom in time of famine the feeble branches allied themselves, and he used to say to them "*ga'alnákum minná*" ["we have made you a part of ourselves"]: so he was surnamed "Ga'al."

CXXXIII Now the man who collected all the tribes of GA'AL together was Kerdam son of Abu el Dís son of Ḳuḍá'a son of Ḥarḳán son of Masrūḳ son of Aḥmad el Yemáni son of Ibráhím Ga'al son of Idrís son of Ḳays son of Yemen son of el Khazrag son of 'Adí son of

[1] reading علاطي for علاط.

Ḳuṣáṣ son of Kerab son of Háṭil son of Yáṭil son of Dhu el Kilá'a el Ḥimyari son of Ḥimyar son of Sa'ad son of el Faḍl son of 'Abdulla son of el 'Abbás, God bless him.

CXXXIV This is the account given by some, but the following is given by the generality of genealogists: Serrár son of Kerdam son of Abu el Dís son of Ḳuḍá'a son of Ḥarḳán son of Masrūḳ son of Aḥmad el Ḥegázi son of Muḥammad el Yemeni son of Ibráhím Ga'al son of Sa'ad son of el Faḍl son of 'Abdulla son of el 'Abbás, the uncle of the best of men, upon him be the blessing of God, son of 'Abd el Muṭṭalib son of Háshim son of 'Abd Menáf son of Ḳuṣai son of Keláb son of Murra son of Ka'ab son of Lūai son of Ghálib son of Fihr son of Málik son of el Nuḍr son of Kenána son of Khuzayma son of Mudraka son of el Yás son of Muḍr son of Nizár[1] son of Ma'ad son of 'Adnán.

CXXXV Beyond that we will not go since he upon whom be the blessings of God warned us against so doing.

CXXXVI And whosoever is not enrolled among his descendants, that is [among the descendants] of the Sultan Kerdam, is not a Ga'ali.

CXXXVII Now his father Abu el Dís had two sons: one of them was called Tergam, but I do not know of his having any descendants, and the other was el Sulṭán Ḥasan Kerdam son of Abu el Dís.

CXXXVIII He, it is said, had ten sons: seven of them returned to el Kūfa; and those that are known and whose descendants are preserved and recorded in the genealogies are three, viz. Dūla and Tamím and Serrár.

CXXXIX The descendants of Dūla are the SAḲÁRANG[2], the kings of Gebel Teḳali; the descendants of Tamím are the TOMÁM; and the sons of Serrár were Samra and Samayra and Mismár.

CXL Samra had four sons, Bedayr and 'Abd el Raḥman Abu Shayḥ and Ṭerayfi and Aḥmad Abu Rísh.

CXLI The descendants of Bedayr are the BEDAYRÍA, of 'Abd el Raḥman Abu Shayḥ the SHUWAYḤÁT, of Ṭerayfi the ṬERAYFÍA, and of Aḥmad Abu Rísh the RÍASH[3].

CXLII The descendants of Samayra are the GHODIÁT[4] and the ḲUNAN and the ḲUṢÁṢ and the BAṬAḤÍN.

CXLIII Mismár had four sons, Sa'ad el Feríd and three sons by [another] mother, Ṣubuḥ Abu Merkha and Rubáṭ and Nebíh.

CXLIV Sa'ad el Feríd had three sons, Ḳaḥṭán and Selma and Ḥammad.

[1] reading نزار for نذار.

[2] reading سقارنج for سقارج.

[3] reading رياش for دياش.

[4] reading غديات for قديات.

CXLV Ḳaḥṭán had six sons, or, it is said, seven; and the latter is the more correct: they were Ṣubuḥ and Faḍl and Manṣūr and Maḳít and Miás and Muḥammad el Ḍub and Maḳbūḍ.

CXLVI The descendants of Ṣubuḥ are the ṢUBḤÁ, of Faḍl the FAḌLIYYŪN, of Manṣūr the MANÁṢRA, of Maḳít the MAḲÁÍTA, of Miás the MIÁÍSA, of Muḥammad el Ḍub the ḌUBÁB, and of Maḳbūḍ the MEḲÁBḌA.

CXLVII The sons of Selma were Ḥákim and Gábir.

CXLVIII The descendants of Ḥákim are the ḤÁKIMÁB, the kings of Arḳó, and the descendants of Gábir are the GÁBIRÁB or GAWÁBRA or GÁBIRÍA.

CXLIX Ḥammad begot Fahíd. The sons of Fahíd were Guma'a and Gáma'i and Ḥammad, [also] called Ḥámid: they were three in number.

CL The descendants of Guma'a are the GIMA'A, of Gáma'i the GAWÁMA'A, of Ḥammad (or Ḥámid) the AḤÁMDA[1] and the ḤAMMADA; and it is said that among his descendants are also the NAWÁÍBA[2] and the SALÁMÁT and BORḲU.

CLI Rubáṭ had five sons, 'Awaḍ and Ḳuraysh and Khanfar and Muḳbal and 'Abayṭá.

CLII The descendants of 'Awaḍ are the 'AWAḌÍA, of Ḳuraysh the ḲURAYSHÁB, of Khanfar the KHANFARÍA, of Muḳbal the MUḲÁBLA, and of 'Abayṭá the 'ABṬA.

CLIII The descendants of Nebíh son of Mismár are the NEBAH.

CLIV Ṣubuḥ Abu Merkha had three sons, Ḥammad el Akrat and Ḥamayd el Nawám and Ḥamaydán.

CLV The descendants of Ḥammad[3] el Akrat are the MÁGIDÍA and the KURTÁN, and of Ḥamayd el Nawám the NAWÁMÍA and the MANṢŪRÁB and the ṢANDÍDÁB.

CLVI The sons of Ḥamaydán were Ghánim and Sháíḳ, whose mother was Ḥamáma the daughter of [Ḥamaydán's] uncle Rubáṭ ibn Mismár, and Ḥasabulla and Muṭraf (ancestor of the ḤASABÍA), whose mother was the daughter of Ḥáshi el Ḳumri el Fungáwía, and four sons of another mother, Ghaním and Ghanam, or Ghanūm, and Gamí'a and Malik el Zayn.

CLVII The descendants of Sháíḳ are the SHÁÍḲÍA.

CLVIII Ghánim had three sons, Ḍíáb and Ḍūáb and Gamū'a. The descendants of Gamū'a are the GAMŪ'ÍA: the sons of Ḍíáb were Bishára and Náṣir.

[1] reading الاحامدة for اللحمدة. [2] reading نوايبة (as AB) for نوابية.
[3] reading حمد for محمد.

CLIX The descendants of Bishára are the Mírafáb and the 'Abd el Raḥmanáb Zaydáb of Berber and the Fáḍláb and the Serayḥáb and the Ḥasanáb, who live from Berber to the land of Zóra.

CLX The descendants of Náṣir are the Náṣiráb who inhabit Gebel Berayma on the White Nile.

CLXI The sons of Ḍūáb were 'Armán and Abu Khamsín.

CLXII The sons of Abu Khamsín were Muḥammad and Ḥammad el Bahkarūb.

CLXIII Muḥammad's descendants are the Muḥammadáb of Gerayf Ḥamdulla, the Ḳaríbáb, the Belíáb and the Kitíáb.

CLXIV The descendants of Ḥammad el Bahkarūb are the Awgáb.

CLXV The sons of 'Armán were Zayd and Mukábir and Shá'a el Dín and Tumayr and Sa'íd and Naṣrulla and 'Abd el 'Ál and Musallam and Gebel and Gabr and 'Adlán.

CLXVI The descendants of Zayd are the Zaydáb, of Mukábir[1] the Mukábiráb, and of Shá'a el Dín the Sha'adínáb.

CLXVII 'Abd el 'Ál had twenty-four sons, [including] Muḥammad el Á'war and Kabūsh and 'Abd el Kabír and Ḥasabulla and Ráfa'a and Gádulla and Khiḍr and Káltūt and Kasr and Beshr and Mūsa and 'Omar and Shaddū and Ḳadabū and Tisa'a Kulli and Muḥammad el Nigayḍ.

CLXVIII The descendants of Muḥammad el Á'war are the 'Omarab, of Kabūsh the Kabūsháb and the Ḳandíláb, of 'Abd el Kabír the 'Asháníḳ, of Ḥasabulla the Ḥasabulláb, of Ráfa'a the Ráfa'áb, of Gádulla the Gódaláb, of Khiḍr the Khiḍráb, of Káltūt the Kaltíáb, but of Kasr and Beshr his brother I know of no descendants.

CLXIX The descendants of Mūsa are the Mūsíáb; the descendants of 'Omar are at the village of the Tumayráb at el Sára and are called the 'Omaráb of Sára; and the descendants of Tisa'a Kulli and the tenth of them [*sic*] Muḥammad el Nigayḍ are the Kálíáb.

CLXX The descendants of Musallam are the Musallamáb, of Gebel the Gebeláb, and of Gabr the Gábráb or "Gabáráb."

CLXXI 'Adlán[2] had thirty sons, namely the four Karákisa, whose mother was the daughter of 'Ali Karḳūs; and Shuḳl el Kamál; and the four Sitnáb, whose mother was [Sitna daughter of...and the four 'Abūdatáb whose mother was] the daughter of 'Abūda; and Náfa'a and Nafí'a[3] and 'Abd el Dáim and 'Abd el Ma'abūd, the mother of all of whom was the daughter of Ádam Ḥalayb; and Muḥammad 'Ali and Abu Selíma and Barakát, who were sons of

[1] reading اما مكابر for اماكابر. [2] reading عدلان for عدنان.
[3] reading نفيع for نبيع.

another mother; and Muḥammad Feríd; and 'Abūda and Yóiy and Tūayr and Abu Bukr and 'Awaḍ and 'Abd el Raḥman Bádiḳis and Wahhayb and Kunna and Ba'ashóm.

CLXXII The four KARÁKISA are well known: the descendants of Shuḳl el Kamál are the SHUḲÁL: the descendants of four of the Sitnáb are the SITNÁB, and of four of the 'ABŪDATÁB[1] the 'ABŪDATÁB[1], and of Náfa'a the NÁFA'ÁB, and of Nafí'a the NIFÍ'ÁB, and of 'Abd el Dáím the 'ÁLÍÁB and their subdivisions, and of 'Abd el Ma'abūd I know no descendants. The descendants of Muḥammad 'Ali are the SA'ADÁB, and I do not know of any descendants of Abu Selíma and Barakát. The descendants of the Mek Muḥammad are the MUḤAMMADÁB, of 'Abūda the 'ABŪDÁB, of Yóiy the YÓIYÁB at Ḳóz Bara, and I do not know of any descendants of Tūayr[2] and Abu Bukr and 'Awaḍ and 'Abd el Raḥman Bádiḳis.

The descendants of Wahhayb are the WAHÁHÍB near Berber, of Kunna the KUNNÁWIYYŪN, of Ba'ashóm the BA'ÁSHÍM and the people of el 'Arashḳól and the SABA'ÁNÍA and the people of Kabūshía.

CLXXIII The 'ABÁBSA are the descendants of 'Abdulla Abu Ga'afir el Saffáḥ, the first of the BENI EL 'ABBÁS to hold the power, and they live at el Ráí and el Shūra and are a mighty tribe.

CLXXIV The FÁDNÍA are the descendants of the noble Sayyid, el Sayyid Muḥammad ibn el Ḥanafiá, son of the most noble Imám 'Ali son of Abu Ṭálib, God bless him and honour him; and there is much told of them, and God knows best.

CLXXV The GA'ÁFIRA are the family of Ga'afir son of Ḳaḥṭán of the tribe of ṬAI, said to be a descendant of Ḥátim el Ṭái, and they are renowned for generosity.

CLXXVI The ḤAḌÁRMA were originally nomads in Ḥaḍramaut and migrated to the mainland in the time of el Ḥaggág ibn Yūsef of the tribe of Thaḳíf and dwelt on the well-known island of Sūákin on the shore of the Red Sea on the mainland of the Sudan.

CLXXVII The GABARTA are originally Arabs.

CLXXVIII The MESALLAMÍA (spelt with SA and double L) are the family of Musallam son of Ḥegáz son of 'Áṭif of the tribe of BENI OMMAYYA. He migrated from Syria in the time of 'Omar ibn 'Abd el 'Azíz, God bless him, and settled on the mainland of the Sudan.

CLXXIX The RIKÁBÍA are the descendants of Rikáb son of Sheikh Ghulámulla[3] son of el Sayyid 'Áíd son of el Maḳbūl son of Sheikh Aḥmad, son of Sheikh 'Omar el Zíla'í, who dwelt at el Ḥalía, a village

[1] reading عبودتاب for عبدوتاب. [2] reading تویر for نذير.

[3] reading غلام الله for قلام الله.

in Yemen, and was son of Maḥmūd son of Háshim son of Mukhṭár son of 'Ali son of Serág son of Muḥammad son of Abu el Ḳásim son of el Imám Zámil son of el Sayyid Mūsa el Káẓim son of el Sayyid Ga'afir el Ṣádiḳ son of el Sayyid Muḥammad el Bákir son of el Sayyid Zayn el 'Ábdín son of the most noble el Sayyid el Ḥusayn son of the Commander of the Faithful the Imám 'Ali son of Abu Ṭálib, God bless him and honour him.

CLXXX [Now not only] the branches and subdivisions of the RIKÁBÍA [but also] the persons who have become fused with them by intermarriage belong to them, for he upon whom be the blessings of God said "the son of a daughter of the tribe belongs to the tribe itself."

CLXXXI Now Sheikh Ghulámulla[1] had two sons, Rikáb and Rubáṭ. Rikáb had five sons and one daughter, 'Abdulla and 'Abd el Nebi and Ḥabíb and 'Agíb, all four sons by the same mother, and Zayd by another mother.

CLXXXII The sons of 'Abdulla were Ḥagág and Ḥág. The descendants of Ḥág are the DÓÁLÍB.

CLXXXIII The son of Ḥagág was Sheikh 'Ali Abu Ḳurūn, whose sons were Ak·ḥal and Farḳa, and their descendants are among the KAWÁHLA EL DUNÍÁB, and some of them are in the Teḳali hills.

CLXXXIV The sons of 'Abd el Nebi were Máshir and Shakár.

CLXXXV The descendants of Máshir are the ṢÁDIḲÁB, the stock of Sheikh 'Abd el Ṣádiḳ, and the SAMAYRÁB, the sons of Muḥammad son of Máshir, and some branches [who are] with the SHUKRÍA.

CLXXXVI The ḤADÁḤÍD and the KELBA and the GENÁNA[2] are said to be GUHAYNA by origin, but they became fused in race with Máshir by intermarriage.

CLXXXVII The son of Shakár was Ḥasan, and his descendants are in Dongola.

CLXXXVIII The descendants of Ḥabíb are at the village of el Ṣabábi on the Blue Nile.

CLXXXIX The descendants of 'Agíb are the ḤALÍMÁB, the sons of Sheikh Ḥammad Abu Ḥalíma.

CXC The sons of Zayd were 'Abd el Raḥím and 'Abd el Raḥman. The descendants of 'Abd el Raḥím are the TUMAYRÁB, and the 'Akázáb[3], the sons of his son el Ḥág Mágid.

CXCI The descendants of 'Abd el Raḥmán are the SHABWÁB[4] and the BAHGÁB.

[1] reading غلام الله for قلام الله.
[2] reading جنانة for جغانة.
[3] reading عكازاب for عكاراب.
[4] reading شبواب for شبراب.

CXCII The son of Rubáṭ was Selím, who had six sons, Ruzaym and Dahmash and 'Abd el Rázik̩ and Muṣbáḥ, [these four] being the sons of one mother, el Ganíba the daughter of his uncle Rikáb, and Muḥammad 'Ón, whose mother was 'Ónía, and Hadhlūl[1], whose mother was the daughter of Malik el Kanísa [*i.e.* "King of the Church"].

CXCIII Ruzaym had a son, Ḥammad, whose son[2] was Sheikh Muḥammad, nicknamed Ḥabíb Nesi.

CXCIV The sons of Dahmash were the *feki* 'Ali and Manófali.

CXCV The sons of the *feki* 'Ali were Manófali and Aḥmad and Muḥammad and 'Abd el Kerím and 'Abd el Ḥafíẓ and 'Abd el Raḥman: I do not know their descendants.

CXCVI The only son of Manófali son of Dahmash was 'Ísa, whose only son was the *feki* Ḥammad, whose sons were 'Abd el Fattáḥ and 'Abd el Malik and Ibráhím.

CXCVII 'Abd el Fattáḥ had a son, 'Abd el Bári, who had a son 'Abd el Básiṭ, whose sons were Muṣṭafá and 'Abd el Ṣummad: I do not know their descendants.

CXCVIII The descendants of 'Abd el Malik son of Ḥammad son of 'Ísa [son of Manófali] son of Dahmash son of Selím son of Rubáṭ are a family of *fak̩írs* at Kenár and Ṭaha (?).

CXCIX The sons of his brother Ibráhím were four, Ḥusayn and Idrís and Faḍlulla and Muḥammad.

CC The sons of Ḥusayn were Ibráhím and el Ṭayyib and Muḥammad and Manír: God knows who were the descendants of these four.

CCI The sons of Idrís son of Ibráhím son of Ḥammad son of 'Ísa son of Manófali son of Dahmash son of Selím son of Rubáṭ were Muḥammad and 'Ali and Ibráhím. God knows who were their descendants.

CCII The sons of Faḍlulla son of Ibráhím son of the said Ḥammad were Ḥasabulla and Muḥammad el Fezári. I am not sure of Ḥasabulla's descendants: the sons of Muḥammad el Fezári were Aḥmad and Idrís and Ibráhím: I do not know the descendants of any of the three.

CCIII The son of 'Abd el Rázik̩ son of Selím son of Rubáṭ was [called] Sheikh Selím after his grandfather, and his son was el Ḥág Belíla, whose son was Sheikh Ḥasan, whose sons were Málik and Belíla and K̩uraysh and 'Abaydi, the descendants of all of whom are at Kenár[3] and Gebel Abu Tubr, and also Dáūd.

[1] reading هذلول for هزلول. [2] reading ولد for اولاد.
[3] reading كنار for كنا.

CCIV The descendants of Muṣbáḥ are the AWLÁD ḤAMAYDA at el 'Aḍáḍ, and some of them are with the KABÁBÍSH.

CCV The son of Muḥammad 'Ón son of Selím was Gábir, whose sons were the four famous men, the learned Sheikh Ibráhím el Būlád and the pious recluse el Sheikh 'Abd el Raḥman and the learned Sheikh Ismá'íl el Wali and Sheikh 'Abd el Raḥím. These are the four sons of Gábir, and their stock is called the GÁBIRÁB and is well known.

CCVI The descendants of Hadhlūl[1] son of Selím son of Rubáṭ son of Sheikh Ghulámulla[2] son of el Sayyid 'Áíd, etc., are the AWLÁD MŪSÁ walad Merín at Gebel el Ḥaráza.

CCVII But the name Rikáb applies to three persons, namely, Rikáb son of Ka'ab, and Rikáb son of Sulṭán son of Shaṭír, of the seed of 'Abdulla el Guhani, and Rikáb son of Sheikh Ghulámulla[3] (son of el Sayyid 'Áíd son of el Maḳbūl son of Sheikh Aḥmad son of Sheikh 'Omar el Zíla'í), who [Ghulámulla] was brought up at el Ḥalía, a village in Yemen, on an island called Nowáwa.

CCVIII His father had proceeded from el Ḥalía and settled on one of the islands of the Red Sea called Sákia; and thence he migrated with his sons to Dongola and settled there because that place was sunk in perplexity and error owing to the absence of men who could read and were learned. So when he settled there he built up the mosques and read the Ḳurán and taught knowledge direct to his children and disciples, the sons of the Muslims.

CCIX Here ends this blessed genealogical tree that contains the pedigrees of all the Arabs.

CCX As he, upon whom be the blessing of God, said, "Him that wishes injury to Ḳuraysh may God injure"; and again "They advanced Ḳuraysh and did not surpass it"; and again "The Imáms are from Ḳuraysh"; and again "Ḳuraysh was a light between the hands of God Almighty 2000 years before he created the children of Adam, God bless him; and that light glorifies God, and the Angels take up the chorus and glorify Him also."

CCXI The Prophet, upon whom be the blessings of God, said "A succession of rulers drawn from Ḳuraysh gives security to the land: Ḳuraysh has thrice been shewn glorious: and if any tribe of the Arabs [seeks to] supplant Ḳuraysh they are partizans of Satan." This [tradition] is quoted by Abu Nu'aym in the "Ḥilya."

CCXII The following is a list of the tribes that are offshoots of Ḳuraysh: BENI SHAYBA, BENI ḤELB, BENI UNAIS, BENI YEZÍD, BENI THAḲÍF, BENI ḤALÁF, BENI MU'ÁWÍA, BENI MÁLIK, BENI KHAFÍF,

[1] reading هذلول for هزلول. [2] reading غلام الله for قلام الله.
[3] reading غلام الله for قلام الله.

Beni Náḍir, Beni Harán, Beni Muḥammad, Beni Huzayl[1], Beni Zabíb, Beni Ḳáfiḍ, Beni Khuzám, Beni Makhzūm[2], and Beni 'Adíl, all of them Ḳuraysh; and the above is on the authority of el Sheikh Muḥammad el Hindi and el Sheikh Aḥmad el Shámi who wrote on the authority of el Sheikh el Ag·hūri who again wrote on the authority of el Imám Aḥmad ibn Idrís, author of *Kitáb el Ma'áref fí Aṣūl el 'Arab* ["the Book of what is known concerning the origins of the Arabs"].

CCXIII The 'Amriyyūn (spelt with *'amr*...) are the family of Sulaymán son of 'Abd el Malik son of Marwán the Ommawi. He migrated from Syria in the time of Abu Ga'afir 'Abdulla el Saffáḥ, the first of the Beni el 'Abbás to hold the Khalífate, and settled in Abyssinia; and when Sulaymán heard that the said Abu Ga'afir had set himself to seek out the Beni Ommayya after their dispersal into different countries and had finally overtaken Muḥammad ibn el Walíd ibn Háshim in the land of Andalusia and killed him, he fled from Abyssinia to the Sudan [*berr el Sūdán*] and dwelt there and married the daughter of one of the kings of the Sudan and begot by her two sons, one named Dáūd and the other Ans. Then Sulaymán died and the names of his sons became corrupted in the local dialect, and Dáūd was called "Oudūn," and Ans "Ounsa."

CCXIV The descendants of Ounsa are the Ounsáb, and of Oudūn the Oudūnáb, and the power passed in succession from king to king until finally they became the kings of the Sudan renowned in history.

CCXV The Beni 'Ámir are the family of 'Ámir and settled in Abyssinia and were its chieftains; and they are renowned for bravery and courage, and are a mighty tribe.

CCXVI Now the date of the commencement of the dynasty of the Fūng in the kingdom of Sennár was the beginning of the year 910. The first of them was the Sultan 'Omára Dūnḳas, whom they used to call "King of the Sun and the Darkness" ["Malik el Shams wa el Ẓull"], and he reigned forty-two years. The following were his successors in turn:

'Abd el Ḳádir	reigned	twelve	years
Náil	,,	eleven	,,
'Omára abu Sakínín	,,	eight	,,
Dekín Síd el 'Áda	,,	nineteen	,,
Dūda	,,	nine	,,
Ṭanbul	,,	four	,,
'Abd el Ḳádir	,,	five	,,
Ounsa	,,	twelve	,,

[1] reading هزيل for هديل. [2] reading مخزوم for مخذوم.

'Adlán, his son[1], reigned twelve years. And it was he that fought at Karkóg. And after he had vanquished and slain the Sheikh 'Agíb the Fūng deposed him.

Bádi Síd el Ḳūm reigned nineteen years

Rubáṭ, his son, reigned twenty-seven years

Bádi, son of Abu Duḳn, reigned thirty-nine years. He was a ruler after God's own heart and was a follower of Sídi 'Abd el Ḳádir el Gayli.

Ounsa, son of Náṣir the brother of Abu Duḳn, reigned four years

Bádi el Aḥmar	reigned	twenty-nine years
Ounsa and King Nūl	,,	seven years
Bádi, son of Nūl	,,	thirty-nine years
Náṣir, son of Bádi, and Ismá'íl	,,	twelve years

CCXVII Here ends the Fūng dynasty. The power was now transferred to the Hamag. The first of these was Náṣir walad Muḥammad; and the grace of God was with him and he so extended his kingdom that it had no bounds save the [seven] climates. He reigned twelve years.

CCXVIII His successor was the Sheikh Idrís, his brother, who reigned five years and a half.

CCXIX The next kings were Muḥammad walad Ragab and Muḥammad walad Náṣir: they reigned four years and a half.

CCXX After them Muḥammad walad Ibráhím reigned for two years.

CCXXI After him succeeded Muḥammad walad 'Adlán and ruled twelve years.

CCXXII Here end the Kings of Sennár, lords of power and strength. After them the power was transferred to the Turks in the year 1230 after the Hegira of the Prophet, to whom be the highest honour and salutations.

CCXXIII Now this manuscript was copied from a manuscript that was found in the writing of el feki Muḥammad ibn el feki el Nūr el Gábirábi of the stock of the four sons of Gábir, [and] I found his son, Ibráhím ibn el feki Muḥammad, saying of it that he copied it from the manuscript of his father Gábir son of Muḥammad 'Ón son of Selím son of Rubáṭ, and that it was mentioned therein that it was in the writing of el Sheríf el Ṭáhir son of el Sheríf 'Abdulla son of el Sheríf el Ṭáhir son of el Sayyid 'Áíd: and I confide the matter to God and his Prophet, upon whom be the blessings of God, and refer [all] knowledge of the matter to God Almighty to whom glory be.

1 reading ولده عدلان for ولد عدلان.

CCXXIV Here ends the blessed genealogical tree that unites the pedigrees of the Arabs all together; and God is our help.

CCXXV This manuscript was completed by the hand of its writer, the *faḳír* of God Almighty, el 'Ebayd Muḥammad 'Abd el Raḥman; and its owner is el Nūr Bey, known as 'Anḳara, son of Muḥammad.

CCXXVI May God protect the writer and the owner and all faithful Muḥammadans, both men and women, the living and the dead.

CCXXVII The writing of it was finally completed on the forenoon of Tuesday the 24th of Rabí'a in the year 1325[1], at Omdurmán. End. Praise God.

CCXXVIII In the name of God the compassionate and merciful, he upon whom be the blessings of God said "Ye know from your pedigrees how ye are related." El Nūr el Malik [is] son of el Malik Muḥammad son of el Malik Mattí son of el Malik Ibráhím son of el Malik Ḥasan son of el Malik Muḥammad Khayr son of el Malik 'Omar son of el Malik Faḍl son of el Malik Khiḍr son of el Malik Abu Sowár son of el Malik 'Abd el Manán son of el Malik Muḥammad Fūráwi son of el Malik el Yás son of el Malik Ibráhím son of el Malik Khiḍr son of el Malik el Nuṣr son of el Malik Mattí son of el Malik Muḥammad son of el Malik Mūsa son of el Malik Sáb el Yal son of el Malik Mūsa, king of the Dufár, son of Dahmash son of Muḥammad el Bedayr son of Samra son of Serrár son of the Sultan Ḥasan Kerdam son of Abu el Dís son of Ḳuḍá'a son of Ḥarḳán son of Masrūḳ son of Aḥmad el Yemáni son of Ibráhím Ga'al son of Idrís son of Ḳays son of Yemen son of el Khazrag son of 'Adí son of Ḳuṣáṣ son of Kerab son of Háṭil son of Yáṭil son of Dhu el Kilá'a el Ḥimyari[2], who was descended on his mother's side from the tribe of Ḥimyar[3], son of Ḥimyar son of Sa'ad el Anṣári, who was descended on his mother's side from the Anṣár, son of el Faḍl son of 'Abdulla son of el 'Abbás son of 'Abd el Muṭṭalib son of Háshim son of 'Abd Menáf son of Ḳuṣai son of Keláb son of Murra son of Lūai son of Ghálib son of Fihr son of Málik son of el Nuḍr[4] son of Kenána son of Khuzayma son of Mudraka son of el Yás son of Muḍr son of Nizár[5] son of Ma'ad son of 'Adnán. End.

CCXXIX The poet says on this subject

"how many a father owes the nobility which he possesses to his son, even as 'Adnán owes his to the Prophet of God."

CCXXX Here ends [this work] with praise to God [for] the grace of his assistance.

[1] 1906 A.D. [2] reading الحميري for الحمير. [3] reading حمير for حميرة. [4] reading النضر for النصر. [5] reading نزار for نذار.

BA (NOTES)

I MSS. 1, 2 and 3 all begin and continue alike. Where differences occur, other than merely clerical errors and unimportant grammatical variations, a note will be found of the fact.

II Cp. C 5 (*a*), VII.

The phrase which I have translated "Because of the [record of] blood-relationships that they contain" is لما فيه من صلة الرحم. The literal meaning of الرحم is "the womb," and so "parentage," etc., and صلة is from the root وصل meaning to join one thing to another: hence صلة is also used for "a gift" or "a favour," and وصل رحمه comes to mean "He acted well by his relatives." In these *nisbas* the phrase and its variations are very common and apparently suggest less the good treatment of one's relatives than the preservation of one's relationships.

III Cp. BA, XXXII; AB, XLIX; A 3, II; A 4, I; A 9, II; A 11, II; B 1, III; C 3, II; C 5 (*a*), VI.

The quotation is تعلموا من انسابكم ما تصلون به ارحامكم and is very common. Ibn Khaldūn gives it in his second book (ed. ar. vol. II, p. 4).

IV Cp. AB, LI, where this saying is attributed to el Shádhali.

V Cp. AB, LII and LV for the first sentence, and AB, LV; B 1, IV, etc., for the tradition. The Arabic (in BA) is علم لا ينفع وجهل لا يضرّ, or (in AB) وجهالة لا تضرّ...

The tradition is quoted (in the second form) by Ibn Khaldūn in his second book (ed. ar. vol. II, p. 3).

VI Cp. AB, LVIII.

After "concern him" AB adds as a gloss من دينه, *i.e.* "from the point of view of religion." The words are attributed by AB to Yūsef ibn 'Omar.

VII Cp. AB, LXIV and B 1, IV.

The Arabic in MS. No. 2 is as follows:

وفي آخر الزمان يحصل فيه ملكالا نزاب ولا يتخلصون الا بالانساب

The meaning is that people will take to calling each other slaves and base-born, and the truth or falsity of the assertion will only be susceptible of proof by the means of pedigrees. For الانزاب No. 1 gives الاتراب. AB and B 1 give العرب: the word انزاب was no doubt unfamiliar.

IX Cp. AB, LXVII and C 5 (*a*), VII.

The Arabic is فواجب تعليم الانساب لان صلة الرحم واجبة. Cp. para. II.

By the "Igmá'a" here is meant "the unanimous consent" of the Companions to the genuineness or validity of a particular tradition or rule (see Sell, *Essays on Islam*, p. 259; and Huart, pp. 236–7).

For the "Sunna," aptly called "the Blackstone of Islam," see Hamilton's *Hedaya*, pp. xv *et seq*. Cp. D 3, LXVI (end).

X Cp. AB, LXVIII.

The quotation is from the 4th chapter of the Ḳurán (see Sale, p. 53).

XI Cp. AB, LXIX.

XII Cp. AB, LXX.

XIII Cp. AB, LXXIII, and C 5 (*a*), V.

The Arabic is صل من وصلني واقطع من قطعني.

The tradition is given by el Bokhári in the chapter *Kitáb Tafsír el Ḳurán* as a commentary on the Kuranic phrase وتقطعوا ارحامكم as follows:

"It is related on the authority of Abu Hurayra...concerning the Prophet...that God created the world, and when he had completed it the womb arose and seized him by the loins and said 'Stop! This is the time for me to beseech Thee that I be not cut off.' And God said 'Art thou indeed willing that I honour him that honours thee, and cut off him that cuts thee off?' The womb said 'Yea, O Lord.' Then God said 'Let it be so.'" (See el Zebaydi, vol. II, p. 117.)

"El 'arsh" is the word for the imperial throne of God (see Sale's *Koran*, p. 28 of the text). A tradition quoted by Sell (p. 30) probably gives the key to the meaning, viz. قلوب المومنين عرش الله تعالى, *i.e.* "The hearts of the faithful are the throne of God Almighty."

XIV Cp. AB, LXXIV.

XV Cp. AB, XXVI and D 5 (*c*), XVIII. MS. No. 2 gives the final words of the paragraph as فانه عليما حاز, MS. No. 1 as فانه على ما حاز.

XVI Cp. AB, CIV, CV.

XVIII Cp. AB, CX.

XIX For both quotations, down to the end of para. XX, see Ḳurán, ch. 49 (Sale, p. 382). After the words "that is" *sc.* "the faithful are brethren."

XXII Cp. AB, CXI; A 9, I; C 3, I; C 5 (*a*), III.

The quotation is a continuation of that in paras. XIX and XX.

XXIII Cp. AB, CXX; A 3, III; A 8, I; C 3, I; C 5 (*a*), III.

A continuation of the last quotation. The words "and tribes" are omitted by mistake.

XXIV *et seq*. Cp. AB, CXXI *et seq*.

These paragraphs, up to and including XXXI, are by way of parenthesis. The explanation concerning the correct designation of the various divisions and subdivisions of mankind into nations, tribes, etc., is prefaced in AB by the words "According to el Kházin" (for whom see note on AB, CIX). The subject is treated by Wüstenfeld in the introduction to his *Register* (*q.v.* pp. ix–xi). He shews that the traditional nomenclature is to be traced to Muḥammad Abu el Ḥasan ibn Muḥammad Abu Ga'afir, a *sheríf* known as "'Obaydulla," the author of the *Tahdhíb el Insáb wa Niháyat el Á'ḳáb*. "'Obaydulla" gives ten relative divisions, of each of which he gives the exact distinctive connotation, and adds definitions, quotations, and illustrative examples. His divisions are as follows:

1. *gidhm*, *e.g.* 'Adnán, the forefather of the Ismá'ílitic stocks, or Ḳaḥṭán, the forefather of the Yemenite stocks. All the Arabs traced descent to one or the other.
2. *gumhūr*, *e.g.* MA'AD.
3. *sha'b* „ NIZÁR.
4. *ḳabíla* „ MUḌR.
5. *'amára* „ descendants of EL YÁS.
6. *baṭn* „ KENÁNA.
7. *fakhdh* „ ḲURAYSH.
8. *'ashíra* „ ḲUṢAI.
9. *faṣíla* „ 'ABD MENÁF.
10. *raht* (a group of less than 10), *e.g.* BENI HÁSHIM.

Or, "another example":

FIHR	= *a sha'b.*
ḲUṢAI	= *a ḳabíla.*
HÁSHIM	= *a 'amára.*
'ALI	= *a baṭn.*
EL ḤASAN	= *a fakhdh*
	etc.

The names of the forefathers given do not form an unbroken line of pedigree in either case.

Wüstenfeld's quotation from "'Obaydulla," though short, contains two of the stock quotations found in BA and AB, viz. the one to the effect that any pedigree traced beyond 'Adnán is spurious, and the other "I have created you male and female and made you..., etc." (see paras. XXII and XXIII).

XXIV The Arabic for what I have translated "The sources of the tribes" is رؤس القبائل (*lit.* "the heads of the tribes"). "'Obaydulla" likewise employs a simile on these lines.

With him

sha'b	corresponds to the	head
ḳabíla	„ „	breast
'amára	„ „	hand
baṭn	„ „	stomach
fakhdh	„ „	liver
'ashíra	„ „	two legs
faṣíla	„ „	foot
raht	„ „	toes

Of the above terms *ḳabíla* is the only one commonly used in the Sudan. The usual terms for subdivisions of the *ḳabíla* are *ḥashimbayt* (*pl. ḥashimbuyūt*), a house-group, *fera'a* (*pl. ferū'a*), a branch, *badana* (*pl. badanát*), properly a trunk, and occasionally *rákūba* (*pl. ruwákíb*), an offshoot. In Kordofán *badana* is used (by the western tribes) to denote the main subdivisions of the tribe. The other terms are all used loosely: *ḥashimbayt* is of general use; *fera'a* is less technical, and *rákūba* is rare and literary. On this subject see Jaussen, pp. 112–114.

After رؤس القبائل BA rightly gives مثل ("such as"): AB by mistake gives من ("from").

XXV MS. No. 3 also omits the دون. AB inserts it.

XXVI "SHAYBÁN" is certainly correct. AB (the original) gives كيسان ("such as Yasán"—a non-existent tribe), instead of كشيبان. Here we have evidence that the corresponding passages in BA and AB were taken from different sources.

XXX This paragraph is in AB prefaced by "It is said that...."

XXXI The first half of this paragraph is omitted in AB.

XXXII Cp. BA, III; AB, CXX; A 3, III; A 8, II; A 7, I; C 5 (*a*), III.

The quotation continues the previous one (para. XXIII), from ch. 49 of the Ḳurán. A 3 omits the explanatory part of this paragraph.

XXXIII Cp. AB, CXV; A 3, III; C 3, I.

"He," as appears from AB, is el Kházin.

This quotation, a very common one, is again from ch. 49 of the Ḳurán. MS. 3 here correctly gives الخصلة, MSS. 1 and 2 wrongly give الفصل.

XXXVII Cp. AB, CXVI. This tradition is given by el Bokhári in the chapters entitled *Kitáb badi el Khalḳ* and *Manáḳibu Ḳurayshin* (see el Zebaydi, vol. II, pp. 38 and 46).

"Yūsef" is Joseph, and "The Friend of God" ("el Khalíl") is Abraham. One generation is omitted.

The word translated "original sources" is معادن. AB gives this correctly, but apparently none of the copyists of BA knew the word.

XXXVIII Cp. AB, CXVII.

For "she-camel" BA gives "*náḳa*" and BA "*raḥála*." The camel was called "el Ḳaṣwá" and was the famous one on which the Prophet fled from Mekka. The second half of this paragraph occurs in AB, CVI and CXVII in a different setting.

AB and MS. 3 of BA give غبية for عيبة (MSS. 1 and 2).

XLI Cp. AB, CVIII.

XLII Cp. AB, CIX and A 8, I.

XLIV Abu Lahab was the uncle of the Prophet. Ch. 111 of the Ḳurán is devoted to cursing him for his opposition to Islam.

XLV The quotation is from ch. 53 of the Ḳurán.

XLVII Cp. AB, CXXX.

XLVIII Cp. AB, CXXXI, CXXXII; A 3, IV; and D 1, LXXXIV.

The tradition occurs in el Bokhári (chapter *Manáḳibu Ḳurayshin*, see el Zebaydi, vol. II, p. 46) in the following words:

عن ابي هُريرة رضى الله عنه قال قال رسول الله صلى الله عليه وسلم
قريش والانسارُ وجُهَينةُ ومُزَيْنةُ وأسلَمُ وأشْجَعُ وغفارُ مواليّ ليس لهم مَوْلَى
دون الله ورسولِه

"'Abd el Báḳi" is 'Abd el Báḳi ibn Yūsef el Zurḳáni (for whom see Ḥagi Khalfa's *Lexicon*, vol. V, p. 447). He was born 1020 A.H. and died in 1099 A.H. (1688 A.D.).

The word مشكات means literally a niche in a wall wherein to place a lamp.

The seven great Arabian tribes mentioned will all be found in Wüstenfeld. By "el Anṣár" are meant AUS and KHAZRAG.

XLIX Cp. AB, CXXXIV, CXXXV; and A 3, V.

AB prefaces the paragraph by "In some reliable records I have found that...." Of the seven tribes given six are identical (though the order is varied) with those given in AB, but in place of ḲURAYSH AB gives KHUZAYMA (as also does D 1, LXXXV). AB again gives "Who am thus the noblest of the noblest of the noblest..." and omits from "And this is..." to "true one." MS. 3 spells GHAFÁR قفار.

L Cp. AB, CXXXVIII, CXXXIX; B 1, II; B 3, I.

For "NIGM" AB and B 1 give "LAGM": B 3 gives "NIGM." AB, B 1, and B 3 all add GUDHÁM to the list.

The tribes mentioned seem to be mostly, if not all, Ḳaḥṭánite tribes descended from 'Abd Shams. "NIGM" (or "Lagm") may be a corruption of LAKHM. "BÍṢAR" is mentioned by Mas'ūdi (chap. XXXI) as a son of Ham who migrated westwards to Egypt, and was the father of Miṣr, but he seems out of place here. B 1 reads "Bíṣ." "ḤUḲNA" (حقنة) may be a corruption of GAFNA (جفنة) (for whom see D 1, 194). "KELÁB EL AZD" should possibly be "KELÁB (or KELB) and EL AZD," both well-known tribes. MSS. 1 and 2 give "KELÁM EL AZRAD," and MS. 1 "KELÁB EL AZRAD."

"El Maḥassi" is apocryphal. After "Ḳaḥṭán" AB continues "And another version is that el Maḥassi was the son of the prophet Ibráhím... but I have not found this true." The author of BA seems to have combined the two versions. MS. 1 gives "el Maḥassi son of Ḳaḥṭán son of el Maḥassi...etc.," which more nearly agrees with B 1; but I have followed MS. 2 here.

LI Cp. AB, CXXXVI, and D 1, LXXXIV, LXXXV.

All three MSS. of BA give ممزوجة for ممتزجة (AB).

The version of AB differs from BA as follows:

(*a*) *re* GUHAYNA, the words "and the west" are omitted.
(*b*) „ ḤIMYAR, after "el Baṣra" AB adds "and Persia" ["Fáris"].
(*c*) „ ASHGA'A, after "Tūnis" AB adds "and Andalusia."
(*d*) „ GHAFÁR, AB substitutes "el Baṣra" for "Andalusia and Persia."
(*e*) „ KENÁNA, after "Egypt" AB adds "and Syria."

There is a large colony of MUZAYNA at the S.E. end of the Sinai Peninsula. They claim to be Ḥarb by origin and their chief branch is the 'Alowna, a name which occurs more than once in the Sudan as that of a tribal division. See Na'ūm Bey, *Hist. Sinai...*, p. 112, for the Muzayna.

LII This and the following three paragraphs do not occur in AB.

For the story of Noah and Ham cp. el Ṭabari, p. 107.

LIII By Ḳurán are meant the ḲURA'ÁN, a wide term generally applied in the Sudan to the negroid element among the TIBBU. They almost certainly represent the ancient GARAMANTES and are the "GORAN" of Leo Africanus (see MacMichael, *Tribes...*, pp. 235 *et seq.*).

For "EL HIND" and "EL SIND" and GOG and MAGOG see notes to D 1, LVI and LXX.

As regards "FÁRISH" and "DÁRISH" and "KHÁLABḲÁ" and "GÁBIRSÁ" (MS. 3 "GABŪSÁ") I fancy the Kurdish tribes are meant. Mas'ūdi (ch.

XLVI, p. 254) speaks of various Kurdish tribes who allege descent from 'Adnán and among them occur "the BÁRISÁN and the KHALÍA and the GÁBÁRḲÍA.

LIV "'Álig" is Raml 'Álig, a series of great sandhills famous as the scene in pre-Islamic times of the destruction of the tribe of Wabár (see Mas'ūdi, ch. XLVII, p. 288).

LVI Here is confusion: from Rayth to Muḍr is correct (see Wüstenfeld, H), but this Muḍr, father of 'Aylán, is the Muḍr mentioned five lines later as son of Nizár, and the series of names intervening between the two mentions of Muḍr, viz. Mu'áwia to el Yás, have got into the text by some error: this series is in itself too slightly inaccurate: Ka'ab is omitted between Murra and Lūai, and the relationships of Mu'áwia and el Ḥakam to 'Affán are wrongly shewn, and the father of 'Affán and son of Ommayya was Abu el 'Aṣi (see Wüstenfeld, U and V).

MS. 3 gives وهمان for دهمان and ريش for ريث.

MSS. 1, 2, 3, all give عطفا by error for غطفان.

The Dhubián intended in this passage is certainly Dhubián the son of Baghíḍ (for which Mufíḍ is probably an error), and grandson of Rayth ibn Ghaṭafán: he was brother of 'Abs and father of Fezára, both of which names occur very frequently in *nisbas* in conjunction with that of Dhubián. Cp. ABC, XXVIII.

There was a Dahmán who was descended from Rayth in the fifth degree (see Wüstenfeld, H).

Fihr is the same as Ḳuraysh.

LVII Cp. BA, CXXIV and ABC, XXVI.

From el Zubayr to Ḳuṣai is correct (see Wüstenfeld, T). The rest is apparently pure invention, though identical with B 1, XXIV. MS. 1 gives خولد by error for خويلد.

LVIII See ABC, XXVI.

'Abdulla ibn Unays is the "'Abdulla el Guhani" from whom so many Sudan Arab tribes claim descent. He sometimes appears (*e.g.* in D 1, LXXVI) as "son of Anas" or "son of Anas ibn Málik," "Anas" being in such cases a corruption of Unays and the insertion of Málik due to the fact that the famous divine Málik was son of Anas.

'Abdulla "el Guhani" belonged to the family of ḲUḌÁ'A and was not, strictly speaking, a Guhayni at all, but was so nicknamed. He was a descendant of Ḳuḍá'a through 'Imram and Taghlib, whereas Guhayna was descended from Ḳuḍá'a through Aslam (see Wüstenfeld, 2). Wüstenfeld (p. 21) gives the following details concerning him:

He lived among the family of Salíma ibn Sa'ad, a Khazragi, in Medína and was named "el Guhani" although not descended from Guhayna. After he had embraced Islam he joined Mu'ádh ibn Gebel in destroying the idols of Salíma, was one of the "Seventy" at el 'Aḳaba, and fought at Oḥod. He was also entrusted by the Prophet with the duty of getting rid of Khálid ibn Sufián, the chief of the Laḥián Arabs. Having accomplished this (in 625 A.D., see Muir's *Life*..., p. 267) he returned to Muḥammad, who presented him with his staff saying "This shall be a token between me and thee on the Day of Resurrection. Verily, few on that day shall have wherewithal to lean upon." 'Abdulla was known in consequence as "Dhu Mikhṣara" ("He of the Staff"). He lived at A'ráf near Medína and was once summoned by Muḥammad to Medína and stayed there all night in the mosque: this night was known thenceforth as "The night of el Guhani." He died in 54 A.H. and left four sons, 'Aṭía, 'Amr, Ḍamra, and 'Abdulla.

Muir also mentions (pp. 337–8) that in 627 A.D. he assassinated the Jewish chief Abu el Hukayk, and in 628 A.D. his successor also.

For the connection between him and Dhubián, the ancestor of the GUHAYNA of the Sudan, see note to D 1, LXXXVI.

LIX Cp. B 1, VI; B 3, II; D 1, LXXXIX, etc.

All the GUHAYNA group of *nisbas* say Dhubián had ten sons, and the names vary but little. "Shaṭír" is sometimes (*e.g.* AB) written Shatír: for "Gudhám" MS. 2 gives "Guzám": "Sufián Afzar" is a fake, two men being combined into one. "Afzar" is a reminiscence of Fezára the son of the Dhubián of para. LVI. The variations in the details of this and following paragraphs will be seen by reference to the trees.

LXII–LXV AB (CXLI, CXLII) speaks of "Sulṭán who was ancestor of seven tribes," and continues, "I have omitted mention of them for fear of prolixity, but whoever wishes to know them should refer to the manuscript copied from *The Noble Gift and Rare Excellence* by el Imám el Sháfa'i, from which he [*sc.* the copyist] copied them: you will find this complete." Now the author of AB (only in the original MS. of 1853) has actually written the seven descendants of Sulṭán and crossed them out: they are, however, still legible and are inserted in the tree of AB (*q.v.*).

As regards the title of the work of el Sháfa'i quoted, the two nouns as written in the original MS. of AB would not be clearly legible, though the adjectives are so, were it not for the aid of the B 1 *nisba*, which (assuming its correctness) gives the whole title, viz. "*El Nafḥat el Sherífa wa 'l Ṭurfa 'l Munífa* (*q.v.* B 1, 1). The copy of AB made for the author's son in 1910 gives only التحفه الشريفة والطرق. Cp. also B 3, I. Or "*Tuḥfat*" instead of "*Nafḥat*" may perhaps be correct.

If by "el Sháfa'i" is meant the Imám Abu 'Abdulla Muḥammad Idrís el Sháfa'i it may be noted that the *Fihrist* (988 A.D.) quotes the names of 109 works by him, of which four or five only survive, and the title quoted is not among them.

MS. 1 gives "Fádin," MS. 2 "Fádni," and later "Fádin."

MS. 3 omits "(or Ḥamayl)"—so spelt in MS. 2.

In para. LXV MS. 3 has omitted a line thus making the DÁŪDÍA descendants of Mashaykh.

LXVI AB (para. CLIII) says "From Muḥammad are descended the MEZANIYYŪN, who are *protégés* to 'Ámir (وهم نصره الي عامر), and the LAḤAWIYYŪN (reading اللحويين for الاحويين), who are *protégés* to 'Ámira (وهم نصره الي عامرة), and the ZUMAYLÁT."

The exact meaning of نصره is obscure, but I think it is represented by "*protégés*" or "*clientes*," *i.e.* not descendants but adherents. 'Ámir may be the individual and ’Ámira be the equivalent of Beni ’Ámir, *i.e.* the tribe; or the text may simply be corrupt. The author’s son could not help me here.

In para. XCIII a different descent is given for the LAḤAWIYYŪN. For “Ruwáḥ’s the RUWÁḤÍA..., etc.,” MS. 3 gives “Dwayḥ’s the DWAYḤA; and Gimayl’s the GIMAYLÁB, a tribe called AWLÁD GIMAYL between el Hind..., etc.” (as text).

LXVII AB (original) gives “And the MUBÁDIRÍA” (والمبادرية); the copy of it made for the author’s son gives “And the BÁDIRÍA” (والبادرية); BA (MS. 2) gives “And the UM BÁDIA” (والام باديه); BA (MS. 1) gives “And the LÁMBÁDIA” (واللام باديه); BA (MS. 3) gives an ingenious emendation, viz. “And the mother was one of the nomads” (والام من الباديه, wa el um min el bádia). The correct version is no doubt “and the Umbádiría”: cp. D 1, XC, and Cailliaud, III, 127, where we get “...des Arabes Qenânehs, Choukryehs [Shukría], Oumbadryehs, Bouadrehs, Kaouâhlehs, habitent les contrées voisines de ces rivières” [the Rahad, Dinder and Atbara]. The name Umbádiría occurs again among the sections of Gilaydát (Dár Ḥámid) of Kordofán (*q.v.*).

LXVIII MS. 1 gives بكرهم by mistake for بكرهن.

LXIX MS. 3 gives “KELLI” (كلي) for “KELB” (كلب) here and in para. LXXXVIII, but later “KELB.”

LXX “FŪL” are the FELLÁTA (see Johnston, *Hist. Coloniz....*, p. 12).

MS. 3 gives “Marṣíṣ” for “Marhíṣ.”

LXXI The author of AB (para. CLII) says that he does not know who were Ráfa’i’s descendants.

For “Zanfal” AB and MS. 3 of BA give “Zanḳal”: the former is correct as the tribe is “ZENÁFLA.”

All three MSS. of BA in this paragraph and the next give “Bashárik” instead of “Shabáriḳ,” but only MS. 3 gives “BASHÁRḲA” for “SHABÁRḲA” in para. LXXII, and the latter is certainly the correct name of the tribe.

LXXII To this group of sub-tribes which, in AB, is prefaced by “It is said that of the seed of Muḥammad were..., etc.,” the “ḤAGÁḤAB” are added by AB. This is an error for ḤAGÁGÁB.

After “the ḲAWÁSMA and” MS. 3 inserts “of Ḥámid” though “Ḥámid” had not been mentioned. Probably Ḥámid ought to be added in para. LXXI to the sons of Ráfa’i.

LXXIII Cp. D 1, XCVIII.

LXXIV MS. 3 omits Fūáḳ and ’Ón here but mentions them some ten paragraphs later.

LXXV, LXXVI For “Dárish” MS. 3 gives “Darásh,” for “KŪÁKÍR” “KŪKÍR,” and for “FOWÁKHIDHÍA” “FOWÁKHIDHA.”

LXXVII For “Durrak” MS. 3 gives (throughout) “Dóka.”

LXXVIII “Ḥamar” and “Ḥamrán” are presumably meant to represent the ancestors of the tribes so named.

MS. 3 gives the descendants of Dasham (*q.v.* paras. LXXXIV, LXXXV) here instead of later, and spells several of the names differently.

LXXIX MS. 3 gives “’Amūr” [illegible] “’Amūd” here and in LXXXI.

LXXXI "Shiblá" is no doubt the "Sabíl" of AB, CLV.

MS. 3 gives "Shibl" here, and in LXXXII "Shibayli."

LXXXII The "MUWÁRIGA" are the "MUWÁḤIDA" of AB, CLV.

After "the 'ISAYLÁT" MS. 3 inserts "and of Ḥakím the ḤAKÍMIA," and after "the ḤASÁNÍA" MS. 3 inserts الثقلي والشبقي اشفل من ابناء حسن ابن عمور.

LXXXIII As descendants of 'Affan MS. 1 gives العقباب او العقاب ("The 'AḲBÁB or 'AḲÁB"); MS. 2 gives العقبان او العفناب; MS. 3 gives merely "the 'AḲBÁB."

LXXXIV MS. 1 gives "Ḥegáz" for "Ḥegázi."

LXXXV MS. 1 gives "ZUHRIYYŪN."

LXXXVI The SHUKRÁB appears again in the next paragraph.

LXXXVII Instead of "and Missír and Ma'atūḳ" MS. 3 has "and Missír the freedman ('ma'atūḳ') of Gurfán." For "Sárib" MS. 3 has "Shárib," and for "SHUKRÁB" "SHUKRÁT." MS. 3 has the whole passage cast in a different form, and adds the "MEZÁLÍṬ" (*i.e.* the Maṣálíṭ of Dárfūr) after the FELLÁTA, and omits 'OḲAYL.

By "TUNGURÁB" are meant the TUNGUR of Dárfūr.

"AFNŪ" is the name given by the people of Bornū to the HAUSSA (see Cooley, pp. 120, 121).

"MADAḲA" may be a corruption of MAḲDISHÓ (see Cooley, p. 127) or of MAGHZÁ (Cooley, p. 131).

LXXXVIII MS. 3 gives here "Dágū" for "Dágir," but "Dágir" later.

XC For "THAḲRA" MS. 3 gives "NAḲRA," and for "ḲUMDAR" "KUMŪRA," and for "DABAYTÍA" "RAYTA."

By the BELŪ possibly are meant the people of that name who formed an aristocracy among the Beni 'Ámir in the East until the Nabtáb section ousted them, and who are mentioned by Munzinger (*Ostafrikanische Studien*, p. 287) as ruling certain territory north of Maṣṣáwa (see Seligman, *Roy. Anth. Journ.* vol. XLIII, 1913, p. 601). Mansfield Parkyns (*Life in Abyssinia*, I, p. 103) also mentions them near Arkíko and gives some account of them.

XCI "BERÁGHÍTH" means "fleas" or, on the coast, "shrimps."

XCIII Contrast para. LXVI for the LAḤÁWIYYŪN.

XCIV MS. 3 says "...and of Dágir the DAWÁGIRA, who are in the east, and the people of el Nūḳ el Bakht are the descendants of Kelb ibn Muḥammad."

XCVI Cp. B 3, VII.

MS. 2 gives "Sabaḳ" here and in XCVII for "Sabíḳ."

MS. 3 gives "Akírit and Adkaym" here and in XCVII.

XCVII MSS. 1 and 3 gives "KIRÁT" for "KURTÁN," but cp. para. CLV. MS. 3 says the GERÁBÍ'A are the children of Ba'asham (and descendants of 'Omrán).

The word GERÁBÍ'A is a plural formed from Girbu'. There is a section of ZAYÁDÍA called AWLÁD GIRBU'; and the name GERÁBA'A also occurs as that of a sub-tribe in Sinai.

XCIX MS. 3 omits "and the ZAYÁDÍA."

C "Sha'ūf" appears in B 1 as "Ashūf," and in ABC as "Shaḳūḳ." Cp. ABC, XXVII.

CI Kabsh is meant as ancestor of the KABÁBÍSH, Ribayḳ of the RIBAYḲÁT, Berára of the BERÁRA, Ḳerri of the ḲERRIÁT, and 'Aṭawi of the 'AṬÁWÍA, all at present sections of the KABÁBÍSH except the ḲERRIÁT ("GERRIÁT"), who are independent.

CII MS. 3 in error writes "Gewár" for "Gerár."

CIII The BENI GERÁR and their sections.

CIV The BAZA'A and their sections. For "Nūrán" MS. 1 gives "Nūlán." MS. 3 says "The sons of Abza'a were Fūr and Nūr and Merwán, and Merwán begot Mál; and as regards el Ḥág Mázin his sons were..., etc."

CVI, CVII Cp. A 3, XXXVII–XXXIX.

I have translated "Baghdád" and "BAGHÁDA," which are obviously intended, but the text of MS. 1 gives (1) بغدار and (2) بعدار, and بقارة (for بغادة), and MSS. 2 and 3 give بغدار and بقارة.

CVIII Contrast D 1, CXXXII.

CX MS. 3 is here confused and inaccurate. These descendants of Ḥámid are collectively known as "DÁR ḤÁMID." For "HABÁBÍN" (which is correct in MS. 1) MS. 2 gives "HABÁNIÍN."

CXI Cp. D 1, CXLVI.

MS. 3 says "The descendants of Ḥammad are ḲOI (*i.e.* AWLÁD AḲOI) and the MEGÁNÍN are descendants of Ḥámid: their father was called 'Magnūn.'"

CXII–CXV MS. 3 puts this earlier and says "Hilál's descendants are HILÁLA and Ḥasan el Hiláli..., etc.," and substitutes "Ūlū el Ghába" for "Ūlū el Gháya."

This concubine, who would be a negress, is apparently invented in order to drag in all the negro tribes of the upper reaches of the White Nile.

CXVI For "ḲÁÍDÁB" and "MAHÍDÁB" and "BÁḲÁB" (MS. 1) MS. 2 gives "ḲÁÍLÁB" and "MAHÍDÁT" and "BALḲÁRA."

MS. 3 says "The descendants of Zayád are the ZAYÁDÍA. The SHUKRÍA are of the stock of Muḥammad ibn 'Ámir Sha'íb; and Sha'íb's descendants are the NÁÍLÁB and the MAHÍDÁT and the 'AḲṢA (?) and the BÁḲÁB and the DÓÁLÍB and the MESÁ'ÍD and the FERÁḲÍD (?) and the ḤAGÍLÁB and the KÁSIRÁB and the SHUKRÁB and the GABÁGIRA and the MA'ÁÍDA, and their subdivisions."

CXVII For this story see Sale's *Koran* (p. 342) and Hughes (p. 601). The Gin was, however, called Ṣakhr.

MS. 3 gives "Khásía" for "Khás," and adds "the FELLÁTA."

Mekáda here means Abyssinia. Cp. D 7 *passim*. The word is used, *e.g.* by the Takárír of Ḳallábát, etc., to denote the Abyssinians: it means "slaves" (see *Angl.-Eg. Sudan*, I, 108).

By the "Khás" are meant the Ḥasa or Khasa of whom Maḳrízi (*Descr. Egypt*, II, 571) speaks as a Muhammadan tribe of Bega inhabiting Sūákin. The name now applies to the strongest division of the Beni 'Ámir and to the language of the whole tribe (see Seligman, *Journ. R. A. I.* vol. XLIII, 1913, p. 600).

CXVIII The Arabic translated "some say they are among the above" is قيل منهم and it seems that "the above" are the group in the preceding paragraph. The generality of *nisbas* gives their ancestor as Zubayr ibn el 'Awwám.

CXIX Cp. A 2, XXXVII; A 11, LXI and D 1, CLIV.

This 'Uḳba ibn Yásir also occurs as ancestor of the Awlád 'Uḳba who are now a section of the KABÁBÍSH, and there is also a traditional connection between the AWLÁD 'UḲBA and the FELLÁTA (see MacMichael, *Tribes*..., pp. 178 *et seq.*). It is just possible that he may have been confused with 'Abdulla ibn Yasín, the Berber holy-man and leader who flourished about 1050 A.D. (see Johnston, p. 63).

CXXI Balḳís is the biblical queen of Sheba.

CXXII "El Gemal" is Sheikh Sulaymán el Gemal, a Ḳuránic commentator. A *ḥáshia* is properly a series of glosses on a commentary. The work of el Gemal was entitled *El Futūḥát el Illáhia*.

The first passage quoted is from Ch. 37 of the Ḳurán, and the second from Ch. 49.

CXXIII Cp. B 1, XXIII and ABC, XXVI. Sóba is the ancient 'Aloa: cp. D 7, V.

CXXIV See Wüstenfeld, T, and cp. paras. LVII and B 1, XXIV.

Zubayr had 14 sons, including an 'Abdulla but not a Ḥasan.

CXXVI MS. 3 gives "Mazayn" for "Merín."

CXXVII There has been no previous mention of this "Khamsín."

CXXVIII MS. 3 reads "The descendants of 'Ámir are the 'AWÁMRA and the...," etc. (as in MSS. 1 and 2), and omits the last sentence.

CXXIX–CXXXII Cp. AB, CLXII–CLXV; A 11, VIII; A 3, X, etc.

The word translated "allied themselves" is تنسب (*i.e. lit.* "traced their genealogy"). Thewords "and [similarly] GUHAYNA were 80 tribes" are omitted in A 1.

MS. 3 omits "and Hilál."

CXXXIII Cp. AB, CLXVI and XXXIX *et seq.*; BA, CCXXVIII; A 2, I; A 3, XV.

MS. 3 gives "Buḍá'a" for "Ḳuḍá'a"; and "Ibráhím el Ga'ali" for "Ibráhím Ga'al"; and "Yemen, the Khazragi on his mother's side, son of 'Adnán" instead of "Yemen son of el Khazrag son of 'Adí"; and "The Ḥimyari on his mother's side, son of Ḥamayd son of Sa'ad the Anṣári on his mother's side" instead of "el Ḥimyari son of..., etc."

The Arabic for "the ...on his mother's side," or "whose mother was descended from..." is ...نسبه لامه من or من جهة امه. This apparent practice of surnaming a man after his mother's tribe is worth noting. Cp. A 9, III (note).

"Son of Ḥimyar" is no doubt an error. A 5, A 6, A 7, A 8, A 10 all give Dhu el Kilá'a el Ḥimyari as son of Sa'ad. "Son of Ḥimyar" was probably at first a corruption of "el Ḥimyari," and then a copyist added "el Ḥimyari" without removing "son of Ḥimyar." The version quoted in para. XXXIX of AB contains the same error. A 2 (alone) gives "son of Ḥudha'a" in place of "son of Ḥimyar."

As a matter of fact I distrust the statement that Dhu el Kilá'a was called "el Ḥimyari" because his mother was of Ḥimyar. Dhu el Kilá'a was a well-known Ḥimyaritic name (see Chaps. XLIII, LXXV and XCIV of Mas'ūdi, and Wüstenfeld, 3), as were also Ḳuḍá'a and 'Adi. There was also a Ḥimyarite king "Masrūḳ" son of Abraha (see Mas'ūdi, Ch. XLIII); and "el Yemáni" and "Yemen" suggest Ḥimyaritic origins. In fact, until one reaches the immediate descendants of el 'Abbás the names given in this paragraph strongly suggest Ḥimyaritic rather than Ismá'ílitic affinities. So, too, the account given by el Mas'ūdi (Ch. XXXI) as that of an old Copt living in southern Egypt, who was interrogated about 260 A.H. by Aḥmad ibn Ṭūlūn, would strongly corroborate a theory of Ḥimyaritic affinities for the GA'ALIÍN. The old Copt said that the NŪBA [*i.e.* the inhabitants of Dongola and thereabouts] used bows of which the pattern had been borrowed from them by the tribes of the Ḥegáz and Yemen, and that "*their kings boast that they are Ḥimyarites*" (وملوكهم تزعم انهم من حمير): see Vol. I, pp. 8 and 168. Of course a late genealogist would not hesitate to graft an Ḥimyaritic branch on to an Ismá'ílitic stem for the sake of exalting the tribe's lineage, and it would appear that this has actually been done. The early (Ismá'ílitic) generations are given correctly in para. CXXXIV.

CXXXIV MS. 3 omits this and the following paragraph altogether.

The pedigree given in CXXXIII is more common than the syncopated one favoured here and by the author of AB, on account of its not containing so many non-Arab names. For Serrár see AB, paras. CLXX and CCXII. Bir Serrár, the old rock-hewn wells at the foot of the hill of the same name near Bára in Kordofán, are said to be named after him.

CXXXV Cp. AB, XXIX; A 1, LII; A 2, III; A 6, III; A 8, IX; B 1, XXVIII.

For this injunction not to trace predigrees beyond 'Adnán (or his son Ma'ad) see Mas'ūdi, Chaps. LXIX and LXX, where the following occur:

(1) ثم قول النبي صلعم كذب النسابون وامر ان ينسب الي معدّ ونهى ان يتجاوز بالنسب الي فوق ذلك لعلمه بما مضى من الاعصار الخالية والامم الفانية

(2) وقد نهى النبى صلّعم على حسب ما ذكرنا من نهيه ان يتجاوز عن معدّ فقد ثبت ان يوفق فى النسب على معّد فقط وقد اختلف اهل النسب على ما ذكرنا فالواجب التوقّف عند امره

(3) وانما ذكرنا هذا النسب من هذا الوجه ليعلم تنازع الناس فى ذلك ولذلك نهى النبى صلّعم عن تجاوز معدّ لعلمه من تباعد الانساب وكثرة الاراء فى طول هذه الاعصار

Caussin de Perceval (Vol. I, p. 183) admits the unimpeachableness of the pedigrees between Muḥammad and 'Adnán and concludes that the birth of 'Adnán cannot be earlier than 130 B.C.

Muḥammad's objection to pedigrees extending beyond 'Adnán was simply that any such must necessarily be guesswork. As he laconically said من هينا كذب النسابون, "Beyond this point the genealogists lie" (quoted by Ibn Khaldūn, Ar. ed. Vol. II, p. 3).

CXXXVI Cp. AB, CLXVI. MS. 3 omits the parenthesis, but adds that [Kerdam] lived "in the land of el Ḥegáz and el Ariáf."

CXXXVII Cp. AB, CLXVII. Tergam's descendants are presumably the TERÁGMA, a subsection of GA'ALIÍN that occur, *e.g.*, at H. el Rekayb on the Blue Nile near el Kámlín. "Terágma" also occurs on the maps as the name of a village in Berber province.

MS. 3 omits "but I do not know of his having any descendants." The Tergam Arabs of Dárfūr and Wadái (*q.v.* Part III, Ch. 3 (1)) may also conceivably have some connection with "Tergam" the brother of Kerdam.

CXXXVIII Cp. AB, CLXVIII; A 2, XIX and A 11, XLV.

In this and the next paragraph MSS. 2 and 3 give "Tomám" for "Tamím."

It appears from the mention of Kūfa that the generations previous to Kerdam lived west of the Syrian desert near Meshed 'Ali on the Euphrates, and that Kerdam or his sons migrated to the Sudan.

CXXXIX Cp. AB, CLXIX and A 11, XI *et seq.*

The singular of SAḲÁRANG is pronounced "Saḳirnyáwi."

CXL This and the following paragraphs, to and including CLXI, are similar to paras. CLXXI to CCIX of AB: points of dissimilarity will be seen from the trees and from the following notes.

AB remarks (CLXXI) that some accounts give only Bedayr and Abu Shayḫ as sons of Samra. In A 1 "Abu Shaykh" is three times given in error for Abu Shayḫ. MS. 3 writes "Bedr" and "Bedría" for "Bedayr" and "BEDAYRÍA."

CXLI According to AB, Ṭerayfi is sometimes called "Turuk, ancestor of the ṬERAYFÍA": he is so called in A 11, XII: refer also to AB, CCXV.

CXLII This is omitted by MS. 3, which by error attributes Mismár's descendants to Samayra.

CXLIII A 1 gives "Ṣubuḥ wa Abu Merkha" by error for "Ṣubuḥ Abu Merkha," a slip which also occurs in A 4, IV. Cp. note to para. CLIV.

CXLIV AB says that some MSS. substitute Fahíd for Ḥammad, but that Fahíd was really son of Ḥammad.

CXLV Of Maḳít AB says that he was also called "'Abd el Ghíth." A 1 gives "Maḳbat" by error.

CXLVI AB for FAḌLIYYŪN gives FAḌÍLIYYŪN (and so also MS. 3), and adds that Faḍl is said also to have been ancestor of the BENI FAḌL.

A 1 by a slip leaves out the words "of Maḳít."

There is a village of Meḳábḍa a few miles north of Old Dongola.

CXLVII A 1 by error gives "Ḥammad" instead of "Selma."

CXLVIII Cp. A 2, XXXIV. MS. 3 gives "GABÁRÁB of Dongola," and after "of Arḳó" adds "with the Khanáḳ and the Island of Náwi (?)."

CXLIX AB notes that Fahíd is sometimes incorrectly called Fuhayd: he is so called in A 11. MS. 3 omits him and makes Guma'a, etc., sons of Ḥammad.

CL A 1 by a slip omits the words "of Guma'a" and leaves a blank in place of "and the Ḥammada."

MS. 3 gives "the Ḥamar and the Aḥámda" as sons of Ḥámid.

CLI Cp. A 2, XIV and A 11, XL. Of "Khanfar" AB says it is sometimes wrongly spelt "Ganfar." A 1 gives "'Aṭía" for "'Abayṭa."

CLII Of Muḳbal and MUḲÁBLA AB says they sometimes occur wrongly as MUḲÁBIL and MUḲÁBILÍA respectively.

CLIII A 1 in place of "are the NEBAH" gives "are the NEBÍH or, as is said, the NEBAH."

CLIV A 1 gives "Ṣubuḥ *huwa* Abu Merkha" ("Ṣubuḥ, that is Abu Merkha"). In place of Ḥamayd el Nawám AB gives "Ḥamayd father of Nawám" and says the accounts which speak of "Ḥamayd el Nawámi" are wrong.

A 2, V also gives Ḥamayd el Nawám, ancestor of the NAWÁÍMA. A 3 XXVIII (*q.v.* note) and A 4, IX speak of "Ḥamayd el Nawám, ancestor of the NAWÁMÍA." Cp. A 11, XVI.

CLV Cp. para. XCVII.

CLVI MS. 2 gives العنجاوية for الفنجاوية.

MS. 3 omits "or Ghanūm."

CLVIII Cp. A 11, XVIII–XX. A 1 by a slip gives "Ghaním" for "Ghánim." MS. 3 adds the GIMÍ'ÁB as descended from Gamū'a.

CLIX MS. 3 omits the words following "ḤASANÁB...."

CLX Cp. A 11, XXI. MS. 3 omits this paragraph.

CLXI Cp. A 2, X and A 11, XXII. AB does not pursue this pedigree beyond 'Armán and Abu Khamsín, except to mention 'Armán's son 'Adlán. A 1 gives "ḌUÁÍBA" as among the reputed descendants of Ḥamaydán, but AB (CCIX) calls them "ḌŪÁBÍA."

CLXII Cp. A 2, V and A 11, XXV.

CLXIII Cp. A 11, XXVI. MS. 3 gives "ḲERRÍÁB" and "KITBÁB" for "ḲARÍBÁB" and "KITÍÁB," and omits the BELÍÁB.

CLXIV Cp. A 11, XXVII.

CLXV Cp. A 2, XI; A 11, XXIV and ABC, XII. MS. 3 omits Tumayr and adds 'Abd Rabbihi, Shabbū, and Būbái. It also alters in the subsequent paragraphs the order in which the descendants of the sons of 'Armán are given.

CLXVII, *et seq*. Cp. A 11, XXIX *et seq*. MS. 3 says "'Abd el 'Ál had 24 sons: they include Muḥammad, ancestor of the KABŪSHÍA and the ḲANDÍLÁB, and 'Abd el Kerím, ancestor of the 'ASHÁNÍḲ, and Ḥasabulla, ancestor of the ḤASABULLÁB, and Ráfa'i, ancestor of the RÁFA'ÁB, and Gádulla, ancestor of the GADÓLÁB, and Khadr, ancestor of the KHADRÁB, and Kaltūt, ancestor of the KALTÍÁB, and Kasr, and Beshr, and Mūsa, and 'Omar, and Tisa'a Kulli, and, the tenth of them, Muḥammad el Nigayḍ, ancestor of the NIGAYḌÁB."

CLXXI It is curious that both BA and A 11 (XXIX) give "Karḳūs" with a ق, but "KARÁKISA" with a ك.

The words inserted in a square bracket have evidently been omitted both in MS. 1 and 2 by error: their insertion makes the total 30 sons correct and squares with paras. BA, CLXXII and A 11, XXIX.

For "'Abūda" MS. 1 gives "'Abūd" here, but "'Abūda" in para. CLXXII. A 11 (XXIX and LXV) gives 'Abūdáb.

MS. 3 from here onwards reads: "'Adlán son of 'Armán had 30 sons: they include the KARÁSIKA (four), whose mother was daughter of 'Ali walad Karkūs walad Shuḳl el Kamál; and the SITNÁB (four); [and] the 'ABDŪTÁB (four), whose mother was daughter of 'Abūd; and Náfa'a, and Nafí'a, and el Malik 'Abd el Dáím, and 'Abd el Ma'abūd, all of them sons of the same mother, namely the daughter of Ádam walad Ḥalayb; and Muḥammad 'Ali, and Abu Selíma and Barakát, all sons of a single mother; and el Malik Muḥammad, ancestor of the MUḤAMMADÁB, son of a different mother [*ferid*]; and Tuayr, son of a different mother; and Abu Bukr, son of a different mother; and el 'Awaḍ, son of a different mother; and 'Abd el Raḥman Bádiḳis, son of a different mother."

MS. 3 then gives a list of descendants, tribal and personal, of Nafí'a and Náfa'a: this entirely differs from any other version, excepting ABC, and is certainly spurious: the writing is so bad and text so corrupt and so obviously a gloss that this passage is not worth an attempt to quote it in full.

The names of the following descendants of Nafí'a (for which cp. ABC) are decipherable: "SIRAYḤAB," "MIRÍÁB," "SHATAYWÁB" (ABC, "SHAṬÍRÁB"), "Mudwás" (*sc.* "sons of"; ABC. "MUDÁWAS"), "MEḲÁBḌA," "Abu el Dūr" (*sc.* "sons of"), "'Abd el Laṭíf" (*sc.* "sons of"), "Abd el Káfi, ancestor of the THAWÁBÍT," "'Abdulla, ancestor of the folk of Walad Abu Zumám," "Abukr, ancestor of the folk of Walad el Nafar," "Bakhít Aswad, who was childless." Among the descendants of Náfa'a appear the "THAWÁWÍÁB" (or "SHAWÁWÍÁB" (?); ABC, "THÁWÍÁB"), and the "'AMAKRÁB," and the "NUGUMÍA" (for whom cp. A 11). The "ḤASÁNÁB" and "ḤADRÁB" of ABC do not appear.

The MS. continues as follows: "El Malik 'Abd el Dáím had 14 sons, 'Ali and Yóiy and Ḥammad, all sons of the same mother, viz. Bukra daughter of his uncle Mukábir; and Abu Ḍaraywa and Abu Baṣrūn and Ḥammád el Haranḳal, sons of a single mother; and Kabūsh; and Muḥammad el Ḳanḳál (ABC, 'el Fiál'), ancestor of the NAFÁFÍ'A at el Dámer; and Shaddū and Ḳaddū, whose descendants are near Berber; and Ḍow and Kena, whose descendants are the KENÁWÍN NÁS WALAD BA'ASHÓM; and el 'Arashkól and Abu Gidád, who had no children.

The descendants of 'Ali include the 'ÁLÍÁB.

The descendants of Ḥammad include the 'ALÁTÍT [who live] near the SABA'ÁNÍA, and the people of el Mádak (Márak?) at el Metemma.

The descendants of Yóiy are the YÓIYÁB at Ḳóz Ba'ara (?).

Abu Ḍawayra [for "Ḍaraywa"] was ancestor of the ḌARWÁB [for "ḌARAYWÁB"] near Bakardash (?). Abu Baṣrūn's descendants are commingled with the ZÁÍDÁB.

Ḥammad el Haranḳal was ancestor of the NÁS WALAD EL ṬARÍḲ [ṬERAYFI (?)] at Metemma.

The descendants of Kabūsh live round Kabūshía.

As for [the sons of] 'Abd el Ma'abūd, 'Abd el Salám el Aṣfar was ancestor of the ṢUFAR and Lakít (?) and el Khadr *and* ["*and*" omitted by ABC] el Fiál, ancestor of the FÁÍLÁB, and Ba'abūsh, ancestor of the BA'ÁBÍSH, and Sa'ad Abu Dabūs.

The sons of Sa'ad Abu Dabūs were 'Abd el Salám and Kanbaláwi and Sanad, and Idrís el Ḳatí'a ancestor of the 'ABDSALÁMÁB, the people of el Buayḍa.

The sons of Sa'ad ABU DABŪS ["Abu Dabūs" error for "ibn Ḍíáb": cp. ABC] were el Burnis[1] and Náṣir and Muḥammad el Ḳuṣayer and 'Ali and Ṣáliḥ. Ends."

"The BÁBSA [for 'ABÁBSA'] are..., etc." (as para. CLXXIII of BA).

Paras. XVIII and XIX in ABC closely correspond to the above.

CLXXII For "Shuḳál" MS. 1 gives "Shuḳálū."

For "the Mek Muḥammad" MS. 2 gives "el mekani Muḥammad" ("who was surnamed Muḥammad"). "Ḳóz Bara" (MS. 3, "Ḳóz Ba'ara") may possibly refer to Bára in Kordofán, a few miles N.W. of which among the sandhills is a *Khór* called Yóiy. *Ḳóz* means a sandhill or ridge.

CLXXIII The first of the 'Abbásids was called 'Abdulla Abu el 'Abbás "el Saffáḥ": it was his elder half-brother and successor, el Manṣūr, who was called "Abu Ga'afir."

For "el Rái..." MS. 3 gives "el Ráma and el Mashhūr."

CLXXIV Cp. A 2, XXVIII, and A 11, LXIV.

The Imám 'Ali had a son Muḥammad who was called "Ibn el Ḥanafía" because his mother was of the tribe of Ḥanífa (see Wüstenfeld, p. 311 and Y).

CLXXV Cp. A 2, XL, and A 11, LXIII; and see note to D 1, CIII.

A 2 gives Ḳuṭáf for Ḳaḥṭán: cp. ABC, XXXI. It is, of course, only the mention of Ḥátim el Ṭai (*q.v.* Wüstenfeld, 6) that suggested (as in A 11, LXIII) the idea of generosity.

CLXXVI Cp. A 2, XXXVIII and A 11, LXII.

Here we have a valuable hint as to the different treatments accorded to the original MS. of "el Samarkandi" by BA, A 2, and A 11, respectively: A 11 simply begins "I heard..., etc." (*i.e.* el Samarkandi heard), but out of spite inserts some remarks of his own.

A 2 is slightly paraphrasing for he begins "The Ḥadárba are a well-known tribe. El Samarkandi says 'I heard...,' etc." BA simply paraphrases the whole without mentioning el Samarkandi.

For Ḥaggág the Thaḳífi see Wüstenfeld, G. He was born in 42 A.H. and died in 95 A.H. He was successively governor of the Ḥegáz and of el 'Iráḳ.

The "ḤAḌÁRMA" are elsewhere called "ḤAḌÁRBA" and "ḤADÁREB" (see D 7, LI in particular). Mansfield Parkyns says (*Life in Abyssinia*, Ch. IV) "The inhabitants of Souàkin and its neighbourhood are called Hadarba and their language Hadandàwy." He regarded them as a branch of the same group as the BISHÁRÍN, and mentions that they were enterprizing traders. For an account of them see Part III, Ch. 13.

CLXXVII Cp. A 2, XXXVI and A 11, LX.

No information beyond that vouchsafed here is given in any of the *nisbas* concerning the GABARTA; but Parkyns (*Life in Abyssinia*, Ch. XL) speaks of a village over the Abyssinian border, east of Ḳeḍáref, as "inhabited by Abyssinian Mohammedans, who are called by their Arab co-religionists, Jibberti." Burckhardt also mentions them as a "class of

[1] reading البرنس for البوس.

Abyssinian merchants" (*Nubia*, pp. 309, 310). Burton (*Pilgrimage*..., I, 177) says "Abyssinian Moslems are called by the Arabs 'Jabarti.'"

Bruce (Vol. III, Bk. III, pp. 43–45) speaks of them as a "tawny" folk, not black, with long hair, and thinks their name signifies "the faithful." They are, he says, "the princes and merchants of this country [*Abyssinia*], converted to the Mahometan faith soon after the death of Mahomet."

CLXXVIII Cp. A 2, XXIX; A 11, LI and C 8, and contrast D 1, CLXV and D 2, XV.

'Omar ibn 'Abd el 'Azíz, of the BENI OMMAYYA, was born in 61 or 63 and died in 101 A.H. He was Governor of Medína.

MS. 3 omits "son of 'Áṭif" and the last eight words of the paragraph.

CLXXIX Cp. BA, CCVII; A 2, XXVII; A 11, LII; D 1, XCII and CIV, etc.

From "Rikáb" to "'Ali ibn Serág" BA agrees practically with D 1, but is less accurate for the earlier generations. Wüstenfeld (Y) gives the following (and cp. D 1):

The Imám 'Ali
|
El Ḥusayn
|
Zayn el 'Ábdín
|
Muḥammad el Báḳir
|
Ga'afir el Ṣádiḳ
|
Mūsa el Káẓim
|
'Ali el Riḍá
|
Muḥammad el Gawád

For "el Ḥalía" MS. 3 gives "el Laḥía" both here and in paras. CCVII and CCVIII.

For Ghulámulla's date see Introduction to Part IV.

CLXXX The Arabic of the quotation is

ابن اخت القوم منهم ومن انفسهم.

CLXXXI For this *et seq.* cp. D 3, 222.

MS. 3 reads "'Abd el Ghani" for "'Abd el Nebi."

CLXXXII "Ḥag" or "Ḥaga" instead of Ḥág is probably correct.

CLXXXIII MS. 3 reads "whose sons were Ak·ḥal and a section (*farḳa*) of the KAWÁHLA..., etc."

CLXXXVI Cp. D 1, CIX.

CLXXXVIII MS. 3 omits "on the Blue Nile."

CXC MS. 3 gives "TUMRÁB" for "TUMAYRÁB."

CXCII For "and Hadhlūl..." (و هذلول) MS. 3 gives "and she was Lūla (و هى لوله) daughter of Malik...."

CXCV MS. 3 omits "Muḥammad."

CXCVIII "...a family of *faḳirs*..., etc.": the Arabic is as follows:

MS. 1. اولاده ذرية فقيري بكنا و طه.
MS. 2. اولاد ذرية فقيري بكنا و طه.
MS. 3. ذريته فقيري و طه.

The copyist of MS. 3 evidently thought, rightly or wrongly, that ي and طه ("Y" and "Ṭ") were symbols of hidden meaning (cp. Hughes, p. 517). For a similar case see MS. C 9, III.

CCII MS. 3 omits "I am not sure of Ḥasabulla's descendants," and "I do not know..., etc."

CCIII MSS. 2 and 3 (and other MSS. I have seen) give "Kenár" for "Kená." MS. 3 omits Selím the son of 'Abd el Rázik̦.

There is a biography of Sheikh Ḥasan wad Belíla in D 3, No. 131.

CCV For Ibráhím el Būlád see AB (LXXXIX, XCIV, etc.).

Various details as to these four famous GÁBIRÁB will be found in D 3, 17, etc. MS. 3 gives "GABÁRÁB" for "GÁBIRÁB."

CCVI MS. 3 gives "Gabríl" for "Merín" (MSS. 1 and 2).

CCVII Cp. para. CLXXIX, and D 1, XCII and CIV, where the relationship between these three Rikábs is given.

MS. 3 omits the generations after 'Áid and the words "called Nowáwa."

A further version of the Rikábia *nisba* will be found in D 5 (*d*), closely resembling BA.

CCIX It is not improbable that with this paragraph (which is omitted by MS. 3) the original copy of the *nisba* by el Sheríf Ṭáhir (*q.v.* in para. CCXXIII) ended. El Sheríf Ṭáhir obviously could not have written the account of the FUNGS which follows because they practically all reigned after his death.

CCX The first quotation is given by Hughes (p. 483, "Quraish"). The Arabic of the second is

قدموا قريشا ولا تقدموا عليها.

The last sentence is

يسبح الله ذلك النور ويسبح الملايكة لتسبيحهم.

The *tasbíḥ* is the saying of *subḥánu 'llahi* ("Glory be to God").

For "the children of Ádam" some copies give "our father Ádam."

CCXI "Abu Nu'aym" is Abu Nu'aym Aḥmad el Iṣfaháni (948–1038 A.D.), the author of *Ḥilyat el Anbiyá* ("Ornament of the Prophets"). See Huart, p. 230.

CCXII It is very hard to decide what are the tribes intended. Probably this list is quite valueless. For "BENI HUZAYL" MSS. 1 and 3 give "BENI HUDAYL."

MS. 3 gives "ḤÁÍ" for "ḤELB," "KHALÁF" for "ḤALÁF," "NÁṢIR" for "NÁḌIR," "GHÁBIḌ" for "ḲÁFIḌ," and adds one other (indecipherable).

"El Ag·hūri" is Sheikh el Islám Abu el Irshád 'Ali ibn Muḥammad ibn Zayn el Dín ibn Sheikh el Islám 'Abd el Raḥman el Ag·hūri, of the Máliki sect. He died in 1066 A.H. (1655–6 A.D.). He wrote three commentaries on "Khalíl" (see Ḥagi Khalfa's *Lexicon*, Vol. V, p. 447). He occurs again in D 3, 22, and his great-grandfather in D 3, 157.

CCXIII Cp. A 2, XXX; A 11, VII and LIII; D 2, I and D 6, XXVI; and cp. note to BA, CLXXIII. See also Vol. I, p. 162, for this migration or its prototype.

Sulaymán ibn 'Abd el Málik ibn Marwán was the name of the seventh of the Ommayyad dynasty, who died in 717 A.D.; but he certainly never went to Abyssinia and the Sudan and he died nine years before "el Saffáḥ" was born. Either the Sulaymán referred to here is another man altogether or, more likely, a confusion has arisen between his name and that of 'Abdulla ibn Marwán, the last of the Ommayyads, who did take refuge in the Sudan.

The first 'Abbásid Khalífa reigned from 750 to 754 A.D.

MS. 3 omits mention of the change of "Ans" to "Ounsa."

CCXIV For "Ounsáb" MS. 2 gives "Unsáb."

CCXV Cp. A 2, XXXII; A 11, LV and D 2, XLI.

CCXVI "FUNG" (فنج) and "FŪNG" (فونج) occur with equal commonness. In D 3 both are used indiscriminately. For the origin of the name see Westermann, pp. lii *et seq.*

910 A.H. (1504 A.D.) is the accepted date for the foundation of the kingdom of Sennár, and there is greater agreement in the numerous extant chronologies of the kings than would be expected.

The points that are worthy of notice here are

(1) That in Bruce and Cailliaud's versions 'Abd el Ḳádir appears as successor instead of predecessor of Náíl, but in BA, D 2, and D 7 (which is the most reliable) 'Abd el Ḳádir is shown as succeeding 'Omára Dūnḳas.

(2) "'Omára Abu Sakínín" (MSS. 1 and 2) should probably be "'Omára Abu Sakákín" (or "Sakaykín" as in MS. 3, D 3, VI and D 7).

(3) Dūda (or Dūra, as in MS. 3) is also given by Bruce and Cailliaud, but in D 2 and D 7 (and as a general rule) he is omitted.

(4) "Ṭanbul" appears in Bruce as "Tiby"; in Cailliaud, D 2 and D 7 as "Ṭabl": MS. 3 also gives "Ṭabl."

(5) 'Abd el Ḳádir and Ounsa appear in transposed order in Bruce, Cailliaud, D 2, and D 7.

(6) The 'Adlán who preceded Bádi Síd el Ḳūm is similarly said by Bruce to have been son of Ounsa and brother of 'Abd el Ḳádir: Cailliaud also calls him brother of 'Abd el Ḳádir. D 2 and D 7 and MSS. in general (*e.g.* D 3, 241) call him "son of Áya": this may be a nickname, or his mother may have been Áya, or there may be a confusion between Áya (written ايه) and Unsa, *i.e.* Ounsa (انة or انسة).

Cailliaud is in error when he speaks of 'Adlán as "Tué par le cheykh Agyb." All the MSS. and all traditions agree that 'Adlán killed 'Agíb, *i.e.* the famous sheikh of the 'ABDULLÁB, known as the *Mángilak*, for whom see D 3 (VI and *passim*) and D 5 (*a*).

As regards the site of the battle, Cailliaud gives it as Karkóg, as do BA, AB and D 3 (No. 241): elsewhere in D 3 (No. 126) it is written "Kargóg" or "Karjój" (كرجوج) by error for Karkóg (كركوج). D 7 gives "Kalkól," and the latter may be correct. The name Karkóg, as generally used, applies to a large and well-known village over 50 miles south of Sennár and it is most improbable that Sheikh 'Agíb would ever have been fighting the FUNG there. His seat was north of Khartoum and the numerous engagements between the FUNG and the 'ABDULLÁB used to take place in the vicinity of el Ḥalfáya, or at least far north of Sennár. Kalkól is close to el Kámlín, some 60 miles south of Khartoum, and a likely spot for a battle to have occurred between FUNG and 'ABDULLÁB. Or again the reference may well be to a small village called Karkóg very close to the south of Khartoum, and a copyist, thinking the southernly Karkóg to be intended, and knowing it to be out of the question, may have substituted "Kalkól."

(7) Nineteen years is too long for Bádi Síd el Ḳūm. Bruce gives 6, Cailliaud 7, D 2 12, and D 7 only 3 years for his reign.

(8) "Bádi, son of Abu Duḳn" (in all three MSS.) should be "Bádi Abu Duḳn."

By "Sídi 'Abd el Ḳádir el Gayli" (in all three MSS.) the author means 'Abd el Ḳádir el Gíláni, the founder of the Ḳádiría *ṭariḳa*, who died in 1166 A.D.

The words translated "was a follower of" are حضر في ديوان.

(9) MS. 3 (only) allots Ounsa son of Náṣir 14 instead of 4 years.

CCXVII–CCXXI Ismá'íl died about 1766 and the total of the preceding reigns mentioned by BA is 310 years. As BA says 'Omára Dūnḳas began to reign in 910 A.H., this would bring us to 1220 A.H., *i.e.* 1805 A.D. It is clear, therefore, that the durations of the reigns have been exaggerated.

There were nominal FUNG kings who succeeded Ismá'íl, and the names that follow here as those of the HAMAG dynasty are really those of the all-powerful HAMAG viziers.

Between Ismá'íl and Náṣir walad Muḥammad there is a gap during which 'Adlán II was nominal king and Bádi walad Ragab and Ragab walad Muḥammad successively viziers. Náṣir succeeded Ragab while 'Adlán was still on the throne. For these kings and viziers see D 7.

In para. CCXIX MS. 3 gives "Muḥammad walad Ragab" for "Ragab walad Muḥammad," and 4 years for 4½.

CCXXII "1230" (١٢٣٠) is no doubt a misprint for "1235" (١٢٣٥). Ismá'íl Pasha took Sennár in June, 1821.

CCXXIII MS. 3 is identical with MSS. 1 and 2 in this paragraph, but for the omission of the words "that was found" and "ibn" (between "Ibráhím" and "el feki") and the substitution of "Gabárábi" for "Gábirábi"; but MS. 3 of the *nisba* ends abruptly with the words "Gábir son of Muḥammad. End" (جابر ابن محمد انتهى). A copy in the possession of the feki Muḥammad 'Abd el Mágid of Omdurmán is identical in this passage with MSS. 1 and 2, but ends abruptly with "and I confide."

Which of the copyists is referred to in the phrase "I found his son..." is uncertain as there is no information available as to the date of el Nūr el Gábirábi.

The date of el Sherîf el Ṭáhir ibn 'Abdulla would be about the end of the fifteenth century A.D., *i.e.* about the time of the foundation of the FUNG kingdom: he was senior to Sheikh el Zayn ibn Ṣughayerūn, whom D 3 (No. 258) says died in 1086 A.H. (1675 A.D.), by five generations, both being descended from 'Áíd; and it appears he wrote the *nisba*, and that from him it passed to Gábir, who was his cousin and junior to him by two generations.

By "his father Gábir" must be meant "his ancestor Gábir."

"*He* copied..." presumably refers to Ibráhím ibn el feki Muḥammad. Cp. the note to D 3, 17.

CCXXV This paragraph and the following three and para. CCXXX are all additions by the latest copyist, the 'Ebayd Muḥammad mentioned. MS. 2 ends with para. CCXXIV and the verse quoted in CCXXIX.

CCXXVIII Cp. paras. CXXXIII and CXXXIV and notes thereon.

El Nūr Bey 'Anḳara was one of the Khalífa's best-known *amirs*. He survived the period of the Dervishes and still resides at Omdurmán. It is very doubtful if he is entitled to claim the ancestry here given: he is said to have been half a black.

"Sáb el Yal" may be an error for "Sáb el Layl."

"Mattí" is the same name as the Biblical Amittai.

CCXXIX Cp. AB, XXX and A 2, XLIII.

MANUSCRIPT AB

Introduction

THE author of AB was Aḥmad ibn Ismá'íl "el Azhari." Both his father and mother belonged to the DAHMASHÍA section of BEDAYRÍA and were therefore ultimately GA'ALIÍN, claiming descent from el 'Abbás the uncle of the Prophet.

Aḥmad "el Azhari" was born at el Obeid in Kordofán, and about 1830–1840 went to Egypt and entered the University of el Azhar. He remained there for twelve years as a student and teacher of the Máliki code, and then returned to el Obeid.

In 1881 he proposed returning to Cairo, but on reaching Khartoum was requested by Ra'ūf Pasha, the Governor-General, to accompany an expedition against the newly arisen Mahdi and attempt conciliation. The party was, however, all but annihilated and "el Azhari" was among the slain.

The original manuscript, written in 1853, is in the keeping of the head of the Ismá'ília *ṭaríḳa*, to which the family of the author all belong, and was lent to me temporarily in 1907 by "el Sayyid" Ismá'íl el Azhari, the son of the author and then Ḳáḍi of el Obeid.

He had borrowed it from the son of that Sayyid el Mekki who had been the head of the *ṭaríḳa* and the Mahdi's foremost adherent in Kordofán. Since then I have seen various other copies and extracts, and probably they are very numerous. The headmaster of el Kámlín school made a copy of the original for the author's son in December 1910, and copies of this copy both for the Director of Education and for me. Having done no more in 1907 than translate the original and not copied out the Arabic I have made frequent use, when in doubt, of the copy made for me.

Of the manner in which the work was composed no more is known than what the author himself states. He seems to have collected a number of current pedigrees, and after eliminating much that he thought worthless to have embellished the remainder with a series of pious aphorisms and arguments, some inferior verses of his own composition, and a wealth of detail as to the present ramifications of his own family. Much of this extraneous matter has been omitted in translation.

I In the name of God....

Praise be to God...(*a long exordium in praise of God and of Muḥammad follows*).

II The servant of his glorious God, el Sayyid Aḥmad ibn el Wali el Sheikh Ismá'íl now speaks. Since the study of the pedigrees of men is one of which the knowledge is useless and ignorance is harmless, and since by expending one's energies on such study one shortens one's days, I paid no attention to it, nor did I feel any tendency to do so, until at last I even became confused as to the exact determination of my relationship to such of my own and my father's generation as were alive. In addition, this confusion existed to such an extent among several of the family that some of them began to vie with others in the length of their pedigrees and to boast of their original ancestors.

III Accordingly, the Imám of the age, the Leader of the Way, the restorer of lawful and true knowledge, the master of his time, my lord and father, el Wali Ismá'íl, by whose agency God granted me to taste the sweetness of the Faith, ordered me to make a genealogical record showing every one of the ancestors from whom were variously descended those that were yet alive, and to point out all the seed of our ancestor el feki Bishára el Gharbáwi and to carry back their pedigrees to him, and his pedigree also to el Malik Náṣir son of Ṣaláḥ son of Mūsa el Kebír, who was known as Masū and in whose person are united all the branches of GA'AL EL DUFÁR now existing, and [he bade me] to mention also how this ancestor was descended from Serrár son of Kerdam, the ancestor of all the GA'ALIYYŪN and to carry back his pedigree to el Sayyid el 'Abbás the uncle of the Prophet, to whom be the blessings of God and salutation, and through el 'Abbás to 'Adnán, and so to arrange all in verse that thereby all our family and suchlike might attain the uttermost of their desire.

IV Then I sought for the books of pedigrees that contain all the tribes of GA'AL EL DUFÁR and suchlike among the Arabs, and by the strength and might of God I was able to obtain numerous manuscripts, including one copied by my maternal grandfather the learned and esteemed and profound sage el Ḥág Muḥammad ibn Bishára from a manuscript which he discovered in God's country, Mekka the noble, in the year of his pilgrimage, written by the hand of el Sheríf Surūr.

V [I also obtained] a copy made—also in the Holy Land—by the learned expert and pious saint el Sheikh Muḥammad ibn 'Ísa ibn 'Abd el Báḳi from a manuscript which he found in possession of the Sheikh el Kámil, the learned genealogist known as "el Moghrabi";

and the latter had copied it from the manuscript of el Sheikh Sálim el Sanhūri.

VI [Again, I obtained] a manuscript which agrees with the two I have mentioned and which is said by its copier to have been also taken from el Sheikh el Sanhūri; and, in addition, more than four other manuscripts.

VII All these manuscripts were examined and their substance extracted, and thereto I added what I ascertained by questioning learned men of high standing, and made of them a genealogical record that will undoubtedly satisfy whoever reads it. This I [completed] on the forenoon of Wednesday the 4th of Gamád el Ákhir in the year 1263 A.H.[1]...

VIII And after I had made this rough copy in that year I continued to study the accuracy of the genealogies which I had collected for several years, and, after ascertaining the truth from the authoritative works of famous Imáms, I rejected whatever was completely inaccurate in certain of the records, and finally accepted as true whatever I had found by the help of God to be correct. Then I set myself to make a fair copy, after having added such words as occasion demanded, [and] I inserted the narrative of various incidents by way of explanation and instruction.

IX Then I named the work "The Complete Compilation of our pedigree to el Sayyid el 'Abbás," and put it into verse, adding extracts quoted on the authority of the Imáms whose names are familiar to all men of education. This I have done in a manner such as I have not seen equalled elsewhere, and I have said all that there is to be said by way of information concerning the ultimate origins and subdivisions [of the tribe]; and I have arranged the result of my researches from the authorities into a complete constellation of five chapters:

X *The first chapter* explains the honour accruing to one that traces his descent to el Sayyid el 'Abbás, and gives some of the virtues of el Sayyid el 'Abbás, and mentions his descendants and what people trace their lineage to them, and shows how honourable is he that is connected with the Prophet, upon whom be the blessing of God, by having Háshim ibn 'Abd Menáf as a common ancestor, and how secure is he that has preserved the record of his pedigree from father to ancestor, and what is ordained for him that disowns them.

XI There is also an appendix enumerating one by one the steps whereby our pedigree is traced to el Sayyid el 'Abbás, God bless him, both in prose and verse, and mentioning all the ways [to grace]

[1] 1846 A.D.

and which of them is the best: it also explains our connection with the Prophet, upon whom be the blessings of God, in that Háshim ibn 'Abd Menáf is our common ancestor, and our lineage as far back as 'Adnán.

XII *The second chapter* explains the duty of studying the profitable part of genealogical records, and shows what part of them is unprofitable.

XIII There is also an appendix giving the rule concerning the observance of ties of blood-relationship.

XIV *The third chapter* gives the descendants of our ancestor the feki Bishára el Gharbáwi and shows how they are related to him.

XV There is also an appendix concerning our ancestor, the feki Bishára, himself.

XVI *The fourth chapter* contains a warning against overweening pride in one's forefathers.

XVII There is also an appendix explaining how the learned and pious man is better than he of noble descent unless the latter be also learned and pious.

XVIII *The fifth chapter* gives some account of the tribes of the Arabs and GA'AL EL DUFÁR.

XIX There is also an appendix giving the pedigree of my maternal grandfather el Ḥág Muḥammad walad Bishára to el Sayyid el 'Abbás, and his connection with the Prophet, upon whom be the blessings of God, through having Háshim ibn 'Abd Menáf as a common ancestor, and the continuation of his pedigree as far as 'Adnán.

XX And now it is time to commence laying before you the result of the work I have done by the help of the Lord of all honour and eternity: so in the name of God, and placing my trust in God and his Prophet, I begin as follows.

(*Here follows Chapter I, a disquisition concerning the honour that accrues to one that traces his descent to el 'Abbás: 2½ pages are omitted in the translation; and then occurs the following, i.e.* para. XXI, *etc.*)

XXI Now as regards the seed of el Sayyid el 'Abbás, God bless him, the genealogists mention that he had two sons, el Faḍl and 'Abdulla, God bless them. The truth, however, is that el Sayyid el 'Abbás had ten sons and three daughters; namely el Faḍl and 'Abdulla and 'Obaydulla and Mushir[1] and 'Abd el Raḥman and Ma'abad and el Ḥárith and Kathír and 'Óf and Tamám and Ámna and Um Ḥabíb and Ṣafía.

XXII After exhaustive search I have not found that el Sayyid Faḍl had any children except Um Kulthūm: the bulk of the tribe [are

[1] reading مشر for قثم.

descended from] el Sayyid 'Abdulla ibn el 'Abbás, and I have found that he had more than three sons, and they include 'Ali and el Faḍl and 'Obaydulla.

XXIII From 'Ali son of 'Abdulla are descended the 'ABÁBSA, and from el Faḍl son of 'Abdulla the GA'ALIYYŪN, and from 'Obaydulla son of 'Abdulla the HILÁLIYYŪN. And their children's children have become scattered in the lands of the East and the West.

XXIV All the sub-tribes of the BENI EL 'ABBÁS who are now in the Sūdán are descended from el Faḍl son of 'Abdulla son of el 'Abbás, whether they be GA'AL EL DUFÁR or not; and this, please God, I will explain in the fifth chapter[1] when enumerating the tribes of the GA'ALIYYŪN, that is of GA'AL EL DUFÁR.

(*The author continues his discourse concerning the immediate descendants of el 'Abbás for* $3\frac{1}{2}$ *pages, and then continues as follows, i.e.* para. XXV, *etc.*)

XXV *Appendix giving the steps whereby our pedigree is traced to el Sayyid el 'Abbás, God bless him, and our connection with the Prophet, upon whom be the blessings of God, in that Háshim ibn 'Abd Menáf is our common ancestor, and our lineage as far back as Adnán.*

XXVI Since it has been shown from what I have said how honour has accrued to us from our connection with the Prophet, upon whom be the blessings of God, and since it has been taught therein that people are to be believed as to their pedigrees, I say praise be to God that I have preserved my pedigree [as handed down] by my ancestors to me and by their ancestors to them.

XXVII And [the truth of] it has been confirmed by such persons as I have found who are advanced in years and are men of weight and reliability, and by questioning them I have verified it, and to what they have told me I have added all the true pedigrees which have come into my hands and been preserved by me, and I have made certain of the truth [of the whole] by enquiries from the learned genealogists.

XXVIII Here then is the course of our pedigree to our ancestor the feki Bishára el Gharbáwi, whereby those of his seed now existing trace their descent, and [an exposition of] the connection with him of any tribes of GA'AL EL DUFÁR now existing, and of his connection with Serrár ibn Kerdam, the ancestor of all the famous tribes of GA'AL, and with our lord el 'Abbás, the uncle of the Prophet, upon whom be the blessings of God, and with his ancestor Háshim ibn 'Abd Menáf, and again with the latter's forefather 'Adnán.

XXIX Indeed I have preserved my pedigree beyond 'Adnán to

[1] reading الفصل for الفضل.

Ádam the father of mankind, God bless him, but I am not permitted to recount it beyond 'Adnán because of the saying of the Prophet as related by the genealogists, "Trace not pedigrees beyond 'Adnán"; and in truth my only desire in giving this record is to show the honour that accrues to me from my connection with the Prophet, for to him [only] do 'Adnán and the rest owe the honour [in which they are held].

XXX Thus the poet has said: "How many a father owes the nobility (which he possesses) to his son even as 'Adnán owes his to the Prophet of God."

XXXI By way of explanation I tell you also that when the GA'ALIYYŪN, that is GA'AL EL DUFÁR, were shown to be descended from el Sayyid el Faḍl son of el Sayyid 'Abdulla son of 'Abbás, and when each one of them began enumerating his ancestors one by one until he reached el Sayyid el 'Abbás, some of the genealogists [were found to] differ in the course of the enumeration owing to inaccuracies of the copyists in altering the spelling of some of the names and omitting others and transposing the position of others.

XXXII But, after making most minute investigations, I adopted [in each case] the version that most often occurred, [and then too] after hearing [the names] from the mouths of them that knew them. Thus my enumeration became authoritative, as you shall shortly see, please God, both in prose and verse.

XXXIII And if the list of ancestors of anyone who claims to be of GA'AL EL DUFÁR does not include Ṣaláḥ, his pedigree is incorrect, for Ṣaláḥ was ancestor of GA'AL EL DUFÁR, and he had seven sons, and his father was Mūsa el Kebír, who was known as Masū.

XXXIV Then the list proceeds from Ṣaláḥ [upwards] to Serrár ibn Kerdam, the ancestor of all the GA'AL, and if any list does not include him its owner is no Ga'ali.

XXXV Now there is a variant account wherein it is said that Ṣaláḥ was son of Muḥammad el Dahmashi son of Bedayr son of Samra, and this is utterly wrong.

XXXVI Another variant says that Ṣaláḥ was son of Muḥammad el Dahmashi son of Bedayr son of Turki son of Bedayr son of Samra, and this also is incorrect.

XXXVII Yet another variant gives Ṣaláḥ as son of Mūsa el Kebír, who was known as Masū, son of Muḥammad son of Ṣaláḥ son of Bedayr son of Samra, and this account is nearer the truth.

XXXVIII The real reliable version is that Ṣaláḥ was son of Mūsa, who was nicknamed Masū el Kebír son of Muḥammad son of Ṣaláḥ son of Muḥammad son of Dahmash son of Bedayr son of Samra son of Serrár.

XXXIX As regards Serrár, the ancestor of all [the GA'ALIYYŪN], some say that he was son of Kerdam son of Buḍá'a son of Ḥarḳán son of Masrūḳ son of Aḥmad el Yemáni son of el Ga'al son of Idrís son of Ḳays son of Yemen son of el Khazrag son of 'Adi son of Ḳuṣáṣ son of Kerab son of Háṭil son of Yáṭil son of Dhu el Kilá'a el Ḥimyari son of Ḥimyar son of Sa'ad son of el Faḍl son of 'Abdulla son of el 'Abbás, but I have not found this true.

XL Others say that Serrár was son of Kerdam son of Abu el Dís son of Buḍá'a son of Ḥaṣín son of Aḥmad el Ḥegázi son of Ibráhím el Yemáni Ga'al el Aswad son of el Faḍl son of 'Abdulla son of el 'Abbás, and this too is given for what it is worth.

XLI Others say that Serrár was son of Kerdam son of Abu el Dís son of Buḍá'a son of Masrūḳ.

XLII Also it is said that Ḥaṣín was son of Aḥmad son of Ḥarḳán, or again that his name was 'Abdulla son of 'Abd el Muṭṭalib son of Háshim. But this account also is feeble.

XLIII The correct account which I have found in the highest authorities and most generally supported and which I have adopted in my version is as follows:

XLIV I say—and God is our help—that I am el Sayyid Aḥmad son of el Sheikh Ismá'íl el Wali son of 'Abdulla son of Ismá'íl son of 'Abd el Raḥím Bábá son of el Ḥág Ḥammad son of the feki Bishára el Gharbáwi son of the feki 'Ali son of Bursi son of Muḥammad son of Kabsh son of Ḥunayn son of el Malik Náṣir son of Ṣaláḥ son of Mūsa, surnamed Masū el Kebír, son of Muḥammad son of Ṣaláḥ son of Muḥammad son of Dahmash son of Bedayr son of Samra son of Serrár, the ancestor of all [the GA'ALIYYŪN], son of Kerdam son of Abu el Dís son of Buḍá'a son of Ḥarḳán son of Masrūḳ son of Aḥmad el Ḥegázi son of Muḥammad el Yemeni son of Ibráhím el Ga'ali, who was ancestor of GA'AL the famous, son of Sa'ad son of el Faḍl son of 'Abdulla son of el 'Abbás, the uncle of the Prophet, upon whom be the highest blessings of God and salutation, son of 'Abd el Muṭṭalib son of Háshim son of 'Abd Menáf son of Ḳuṣai son of Keláb son of Murra son of Ka'ab son of Lūai son of Ghálib son of Fihr son of Málik son of el Nuḍr son of Kenána son of Khuzayma son of Mudraka son of el Yás son of Muḍr son of Nizár son of Ma'ad son of 'Adnán.

XLV Here ends the true pedigree which I have preserved and thereby observed the law.

XLVI I have also put it into verse as an aid to memory to the student in order that he may thereby be enabled to gratify his object to the full.

(*Here follow* 41 *lines of doggerel, eked out with laudatory adjectives and religious remarks and giving the writer's pedigree up to 'Adnán. Then, after* 4 *lines of prose, occurs the following, i.e.* para. XLVII, *etc.*)

XLVII *Chapter II, explaining the duty of studying the profitable part of genealogical records, and showing what part of them is unprofitable, with an appendix thereto.*

XLVIII The study of pedigrees is in part profitable and in part unprofitable. The study of so much as is profitable is obligatory by law upon every Muslim.

XLIX Thus Sídi el Imám 'Omar ibn el Khaṭṭáb, God bless him, said "Ye know from your pedigrees how ye are connected."

L And the Sheikh Tatái says "It is your duty to know from your pedigrees how ye are connected, because of the exhortation ye have received to [keep the record of] your blood-relationships."

LI El Shádhali also says "That which has no other claim to be obligatory than his (*sc.* 'Omar's) [sole] authority is yet obligatory."

LII The above is intended to apply to [the study of the pedigrees of] people between whom [and yourself] there is some relationship; and indeed el Imám Abu el Ḥasan acquiesced in the obligations of such study in the same manner, saying that this applied to blood-relationship, [*i.e.*] to the case of people between whom [and yourself] there is some relationship, and not to [the case of] a man who claims honour by marriage [only].

LIII El 'Adawi also said "Ye know that [the keeping of the record of] your blood-relationships is obligatory"; so he is equally to be credited.

LIV And, look you! Is it not obvious that a man should know from his pedigree the total number of his ancestors in Islam rather than restrict his knowledge to three forefathers [only]?

LV That which is unprofitable in the [study of] pedigrees is the knowledge of the pedigrees of others, that is of those to whom one is unrelated, because the authoritative dictum does not apply to such, and the following saying of the Prophet, upon whom be the blessings of God, about one who was learned in pedigrees bears this out "A knowledge of them is useless and ignorance harmless."

LVI El Tatái says "Such knowledge of pedigrees as 'so and so was son of so and so of the children of so and so, and the children of so and so are connected with the children of so and so by having so and so as a common ancestor' is a [type of] learning that is unprofitable both in this world and the next, and ignorance of it does no harm to him that is ignorant of it, nor does he commit any sin by neglecting it."

LVII On this point too it is to be noted that a noble pedigree confers no merit upon a man from the religious point of view, and pride in such is blameworthy.

LVIII Yūsef ibn 'Omar says "If a man devote himself to the study of what does not concern him[1] in his religion, his labour is impious."

LIX I say that this is the tradition, and if the warning against pride of ancestry is [admitted to have been] proved, then it becomes a matter of knowledge that the study of other people's pedigrees is of no use and unprofitable, since "knowledge of them is useless and ignorance harmless."

LX El Imám Abu el Ḥasan says "He who is ignorant of this should not be called ignorant."

LXI An unprofitable form of genealogical research is the tracing of pedigrees to one's infidel ancestors. Indeed a knowledge of the relationships of infidels is not demanded by the law.

(*The author enlarges on this topic for half a page and then continues*—para. LXII.)

LXII Thus I have shown you from the above what is profitable and what unprofitable in [the study of] pedigrees and the obligation of knowing so much as is profitable, as proved by the saying of el Imám 'Omar quoted above.

LXIII This is supported by the quotation I have found in some genealogical records from the Words of the Prophet...about one who was learned in pedigrees "A knowledge of them is useless and ignorance harmless":

LXIV–LXX That is...(*here follow, word for word*, paras. BA, VII to XI, *followed by a series of quotations from Abu el Ḥasan, etc.*).

LXXI–LXXII (*An explanation of terms used.*)

LXXIII (Identical with BA, XIII.)

LXXIV (Identical with BA, XIV.)

(*The author then continues in the same strain for half a page. Then begins the long third chapter concerning the numerous descendants of el feki Bishára el Gharbáwi. The first* 12 *pages are omitted: then occurs the following, i.e.* para. LXXV.)

LXXV Now our ancestor, the feki Bishára el Gharbáwi, was by origin one of the most noble GA'AL, the dignitaries of high lineage, and he was descended from the children of 'Abbás the uncle of the Prophet ..., and this I dealt with in the first chapter in enumerating my ancestors.

LXXVI Now his forefathers were among the dignitaries of the

[1] reading اذا كان الانسان يحمل نفسه for اذا كان لم يساله على.

kings of the DUFÁR, who were an independent people; and his ancestor in the fifth degree was el Malik Náṣir, son of Ṣaláḥ son of Mūsa "Masū el Kebír," and ancestor of the MALIK-NÁṢIRÍA.

LXXVII This term, which is pronounced "Melkanáṣiría," denotes the stock of our said ancestor and also the other descendants of el Malik Náṣir, with the reservation that our ancestor [Bishára] withdrew apart from the rest, and became so famous for his religious attainments that he came to be regarded by his descendants as founder of a race of his own; and they traced their descent to him and were known among the tribes of GA'AL EL DUFÁR as the GHARBÁWÍNGI (spelt with a *w* and *í* and *n* and then a letter [pronounced] between a *g* and *sh*).

LXXVIII So then you have learnt the facts about him; and if you have regard to his ultimate origin he was an 'Abbási, and if to the tribes of GA'AL, he was a Ga'ali Dufári, and if to the kings of the DUFÁR, he was a Melkanáṣiri.

LXXIX And he lived a life of the greatest godliness and sanctity and purity, and pre-eminent in piety and truth and faithfulness and nobility of character, and ennobled by the greatest virtues.

LXXX Thus finally he became greatly respected among the people and with his children was held in the highest honour by the greatest men of the land.

LXXXI The truth of all that has been said and proved and written of him is shown by the attention and regard paid to him by the kings and the honour and high esteem in which they held him; and they used to write letters patent for him to every one living in their realms directing that no one should interfere with him and his children or with anyone related to him by blood or by marriage among the noble GA'AL that men know so well.

LXXXII And I found a document signed by the learned pious and powerful conqueror the late Sultan Bádi son of the Sultan Nūl, and dated 1145 A.H.[1], and it runs as follows, after the preface...:

LXXXIII "These letters patent I have written for the feki Bishára son of the feki 'Ali son of Bursi that no man interfere with him and his brothers and his sons and his relatives by marriage and his family and any connection of his or any one under his protection: let no one of my subjects interfere with him! And I, the Sultan Bádi son of the Sultan Nūl have confirmed the honours conferred by the Sultan Bádi son of the Sultan Arbáṭ on el feki Bishára son of feki 'Ali son of Bursi, on him and on him that is with him,—honours done to God and His Prophet, a sacred duty.

[1] 1732 A.D.

LXXXIV From whomsoever of his successors hold these letters let no man demand contribution nor first-fruits [*lit.* 'custom'] nor levy nor market due nor impost nor forage-due nor herd-due [*matūrat*] nor anything small or great within the royal realms, either at home or abroad, in the east or in the west.

LXXXV If anyone interferes with him or approaches him let him blame no one but himself [for the consequences]. Beware! I say, beware of disobedience! He who disobeys let him blame no one but himself."

LXXXVI This I have copied from the sealed letters-patent granted to him, word for word, and these letters are now in my possession.

LXXXVII And he had [granted to him] other letters-patent which have been lost in the course of time. It is enough that he relied upon God Almighty.

(*Here follow four pages of laudations of Bishára and his descendants mixed with anecdotes of their lives: then follows* para. LXXXVIII.)

LXXXVIII The reason why our ancestor el feki Bishára was called "el Gharbáwi" ["the Westerner"] was as follows:

LXXXIX When el Sheikh Ibráhím el Būlád ibn Gábir came from Egypt he settled on the island of Tarnag in the country of the SHÁÍḲÍA and taught law [*lit. Khalíl*] and apostleship [*risála*].

XC Now our ancestor el feki Bishára was [still] a child, and his father el feki 'Ali ibn Bursi was a man of religion who observed the Ḳurán and had some knowledge of the sciences, and [the latter] left the circle of his family and devoted himself to religion, and of all his sons he used to urge Bishára in particular to devote himself to religion.

XCI Thus when our ancestor el feki Bishára heard the news of [the arrival of] el Sheikh Ibráhím el Būlád, he crossed the river from their home [at] Ḥósh Már in Dongola and joined el Sheikh Ibráhím at Tarnag Island and sought learning and religious instruction from him, and sat at his feet for a [long] while.

XCII Now the name Bishára was very common among the pupils, so he surnamed our ancestor el feki Bishára "el Gharbáwi," because the home of our ancestor, Ḥósh Már, was to the west of the Island where the Sheikh lived, and our ancestor used to cross the river from the west to the east to visit the Sheikh at Tarnag Island.

XCIII Thus, since the Sheikh Ibráhím named him "el Gharbáwi," he became famous by that name: and the date of his connection with the Sheikh Ibráhím was the eleventh century [of the Hegira].

XCIV So he served him and acquired learning and practical religious instruction from him, for el Sheikh Ibráhím el Būlád was one of the greatest and most pious and learned of sages, [and was] the first to teach law [*Khalíl*] in the land of the FUNG.

XCV I have mentioned the chief points in his biography in what follows: Ibráhím el Būlád was son of Gábir, and his story emits a sweet odour.

XCVI His [full] name was el Sheikh el Imám el Ḥugga Ibráhím son of Gábir son of 'Ón son of Selím son of Rubáṭ, the father of the RIKÁBÍA Sayyids, and he was born at Tarnag, an island in the land of the SHÁÍḲÍA, and went to Egypt and studied under Sídí Muḥammad el Banūfari, and was taught by him the origins and the ends of divinity.

XCVII Then he moved to Tarnag and there taught law [*Khalíl*] and apostleship.

XCVIII He was [also] the first to teach law [*Khalíl*] in the land of the FUNG.

XCIX Many people used to visit him, and he taught the whole science of law [*Khalíl*] from beginning to end seven times and thereby instructed 40 persons, among whom was the virtuous Sheikh 'Abd el Raḥman his brother.

C So his story continues: and it is said that the reason why he was called "el Būlád" was that a certain man swore to divorce his wife if he did not succeed in collecting into his house everything that God had created. Then [el Būlád] decided the matter by placing a Ḳurán on the bed, and explained his action by quoting the following words of God "There is nothing that I have omitted in the Book"; and his Sheikh said to him "You are Būlád el Berr" ["the Steel of the Earth"], and his cognomen of "Būlád" for that reason became famous.

CI His sons were el Ḥág Muḥammad and el Ḥág Ḥammad, both good and virtuous men, and such of his seed as exist now are descended from them.

CII By the help of the Great King, the Almighty, I have now completed all that I promised in this chapter.

CIII *Chapter IV*...(*The title is repeated as in* para. XVI.)

CIV and CV My brethren in God and the Prophet, overweening pride in our forefathers is blameworthy in the law, and it is not the part of an intelligent man to...(*continues as* BA, XVI, *which is slightly expanded*).

CVI So too, the Prophet..., according to the beautiful tradition related by Ibn Dáūd and el Termidhi, said "God hath redeemed you from the brutishness [*ghubiyya*] of the days of ignorance and pride of ancestry.

CVII The faithful are pious and the impious are base. Ye are the children of Ádam, [created] of earth."

CVIII The Imám Abu el Ḥasan in explanation of this tradition says that *ghubiyya* is so spelt and refers to pride and vain-glory, and that the saying was intended to warn people of being boastful as [the people of] the days of ignorance were from pride and suchlike and conceit of ancestry.

CIX For, considering that all men alike were formed from the earth that is trodden underfoot, how shall.... (*Continues as* BA, XLII.)

(*Then follow comments and traditions from el Termidhi and el Kházin on the subject of man's creation* (15 *lines*), *and then a tradition concerning Abu Sufián, ending as follows, i.e.* para. CX, *etc.*)

CX–CXIII Then God revealed this verse and forbade boastful comparisons of pedigrees and competition to amass wealth and disdain of the poor, saying "O people.... (*Continues as* BA, XXII, *the quotations and explanations as given being identical. The same strain continues for* 1½ *pages, and the closing words are as follows, i.e.* para. CXIV.)

CXIV And thus the honour that comes from piety is the greatest, so the pious man is better and nobler in God's sight than the man of noble birth [*el Sheríf*], because God said "The noblest of you in God's sight is the most pious of you."

CXV El Imám el Kházin expounded this verse and showed by virtue of.... (*Continues exactly as* BA, XXXIII.)

CXVI–CXVIII And lastly he quoted Abu Hurayra as saying that the Prophet...was asked "Which.... (*Continues as* BA, XXXVII *and* XXXVIII *down to* "...*of male and female": the only difference lies in a few grammatical variations. Then, after five lines of explanation of terms, Chapter V commences as follows*, para. CXIX.)

CXIX Chapter V, giving some account of the tribes of the Arabs and GA'AL EL DUFÁR, with an appendix.

CXX–CXXIX Know that God...says "And I have made.... (*Here follow* BA, XXIII *and* XXXII *in juxtaposition, followed immediately by* BA, XXIV *to* XXXI. *The copies, but for grammatical variations, are identical with the exceptions noted in* BA.)

CXXX The learned Muḥammad Záíd el Kafūri asked the question "Is the enslavement of all the Arabs permissible or not?" The celebrated answer was that it was [not?] so, and this is the view of Málik and Aḥmad, because slavery implies deterioration.

CXXXI–CXXXII (*As* BA, XLVII *and* XLVIII, *with the exceptions given in the notes.*)

CXXXIII I am not sure of the subdivisions of the seven tribes mentioned because of the variations in the different accounts.

CXXXIV–CXXXV (*These two paragraphs are together identical with* BA, XLIX, *with the exceptions noted in* BA.)

CXXXVI (*As* BA, LI, *with the exceptions there noted.*)

CXXXVII Now there are [also] seven tribes apart from these seven, viz. BAG, BÁGÍG, KHASHBA, KHABRA, ḤARATHA, GHIBRA and 'ÁTHIR. These are of non-Arab [*'agam*] ancestors, blacks and whites.

CXXXVIII–CXXXIX This account is the true one, but in some of the genealogies it is said that the original Arabs are ḤIMYAR and ṬAI.... (*Continues as* BA, L, *with only the exceptions there noted.*)

CXL Now as for the tribes of the Arabs descended from GUHAYNA, taken separately by themselves, according to some genealogies the sons of Dhubián were ten, viz.... (*Continues as* BA, LIX, *with some variations for which see the trees.*)

CXLI–CLIX (*These nineteen paragraphs give the various personal and tribal descendants of Dhubián, and correspond in outline to paras.* LX *et seq. of* BA, *though the latter adds very many details as will be seen by reference to the trees, where all points of difference and additions and omissions can be seen, except such as are specifically mentioned in the notes to* BA. *There is nothing in these paragraphs beyond what is shown in the tree and in the notes to* BA.)

CLX Now Dhubián, whom we mentioned above, was the son of Guhayna son of... (*etc., as in the tree, as far as 'Adnán*).

CLXI This is the end of [the account] which I have accepted, according to what I found in the records dealing with the tribes of the Arabs, but I cannot vouch for its correctness.

CLXII–CLXV Now as regards GA'AL in general the true account is that which I have found given in some of the records, viz. as follows: ...(*Paras.* CLXIII *to* CLXV *are here omitted as being identical with paras.* CXXX *to* CXXXII *of* BA, *q.v.*)

CLXVI Now the man who collected all the tribes of GA'AL together was Kerdam son of Abu el Dís, and whosoever is not enrolled among his descendants is not a Ga'ali.

CLXVII His abode was in the land of el Ḥegáz and the fertile lands, and it is related that his father Abu el Dís had two sons, Kerdam and Tergam; but of Tergam's descendants I know nothing.

CLXVIII As regards Kerdam it is said that his name was the Sultan Ḥasan Kerdam son of Abu el Dís, and that he had ten sons; but those that are known and whose descendants are verified and recorded in the genealogies are three only, viz. Dula and Tomám and Serrár.

CLXIX Dula was ancestor of FŪR and the SAḲÁRANG, and Tomám of the TOMÁM.

CLXX Serrár was ancestor of all [the GA'ALIYYŪN], and had three sons, Samra and Samayra and Mismár. So I will complete what I have to say of the descendants of each of these three in turn, if it please God.

CLXXI–CCIX (*These paragraphs give the descendants of Samra and Samayra and Mismár: the names of all the individuals and the sub-tribes here said to be descended from them will be found in the tree. Any remarks made in passing by the author and not noted in the tree, will be found in the notes to* BA, *q.v.* paras. CXL to CLXI.)

CCX The above are the descendants of Serrár son of Kerdam, the ancestor of all [the GA'ALIYYŪN].

CCXI Some accounts give Bedayr as one of his sons, but this is incorrect: his sons were three, Samra and Samayra and Mismár, and I have given their descendants, all of whom are included in [the term] GA'AL, both the DUFÁR and the others.

CCXII As regards the tribes of GA'AL EL DUFÁR taken separately, their lineage is as follows: their ancestor, from whom they are all variously descended, was Ṣaláḥ son of Mūsa el Kebír son of Muḥammad son of Ṣaláḥ son of Muḥammad son of Dahmash son of Bedayr son of Samra son of Serrár, the general ancestor; and anyone unconnected with him [Serrár] is not a Ga'ali Dufári.

CCXIII The sons of Ṣaláḥ son of Mūsa, known as Masū el Kebír, were seven: [among them] were Naṣrulla, the ancestor of...(*see tree*) ...and Náṣir, ancestor of the...(*see tree*)....

CCXIV All of these are included in the term DUFÁR, being descended from the seven sons of Ṣaláḥ.

CCXV The descendants of Muḥammad were Abukr and the ṬERAYFÍA.

CCXVI–CCXVII (*Gives the sons and grandsons of el Malik Mūsa el Ṣughayr and the tribes descended from them, q.v. in the tree.*)

CCXVIII 'Áíd was the brother of Mūsa el Ṣughayr, the two of them being the sons of Ḥammad[1].

CCXIX 'Áíd was ancestor of the 'ÁÍDÁB, [who are included] among the GA'AL EL DUFÁR.

CCXX This is all I have discovered about the various lines of descent; but I could ascertain nothing definite about [all] the seven sons of Ṣaláḥ and their respective descendants. This suffices.

CCXXI Now you know, from what I have said before, that all whose descent is now traced to el Sayyid el 'Abbás are only the progeny of el Sayyid el Faḍl son of el Sayyid 'Abdulla son of el Sayyid el 'Abbás.

CCXXII–CCXXIII (*Concerning the sons of el 'Abbás, as in* paras. XXI and XXII.)

[1] reading حمد for حماد.

CCXXIV 'Abdulla had a son el Faḍl, who was father of Sa'ad the father of Ibráhím el Ga'ali. Ibráhím begot...(*and so on down to Serrár, as in* para. XLIV).

CCXXV–CCXXVI (*A mere repetition of* para. XXIII.)

CCXXVII I will now give the pedigree, as I have done in the other cases, and I will do so in the course of showing my own ancestry, beginning with my maternal grandfather el Ḥág Muḥammad ibn Bishára, and [showing] how he was descended from el Sayyid el 'Abbás and connected with the Prophet...by a common ancestry from Háshim son of 'Abd Menáf, and I will even go further, back to 'Adnán. Since I have shown you my true and trustworthy lineage on my father's side, I will similarly give the pedigree of my mother's father: it is as follows:

CCXXVIII I am el Sayyid Aḥmad son of el Sheikh Ismá'íl el Wali, and my mother was Zaynab, daughter of el Ḥág Muḥammad son of...(*as in the tree, as far back as 'Adnán*).

CCXXIX This is the record I have kept as ordained by the law, and in the work I have throughout showed the pedigrees, whether through male or female, with intent that the whole should be known, as required by the law.

CCXXX Certain points had been obscure to me, and this fact originally actuated me to write this work; and I have prayed God to give me assistance, for He is Almighty, and I offer to Him praise from first to last; and prayer and homage be to Muḥammad, the foremost of the prophets by his pre-eminence, and [blessings be] upon all his followers. May God forgive my past sins and my future sins, my known sins and my unknown sins, and give me blessing in this world and in the world of eternity, and keep me from all future ill. And may God grant His mercy to all the prophets and apostles; and praise be to God the Lord of the worlds.

CCXXXI This work was finally completed on the noon of Wednesday the 11th of Rabí'a el Tháni in the year 1270[1] after the Hegira or Flight of the last of the prophets, upon whom be the blessing of God...(*the Te Deum of* para. CCXXX *is again repeated*).

[1] 1853 A.D.

AB (NOTES)

II The term "Wali" is a title given to a holy man after death. The reverence paid to them and to their tombs is based on Chapter x (63) of the Ḳurán (see Sell, p. 109, and Hughes, p. 663).

III The term GA'AL EL DUFÁR apparently relates exclusively to those GA'ALIYYŪN who are descended from Ṣaláḥ: see paras. XXXIII and CCXIV.

For the versification of the pedigree see para. XLVI.

IV Only one of the alleged authorities mentioned in this and the two following paragraphs is known to me: this is Sálim ibn Muḥammad el Sanhūri, who was a commentator on the Mukhtaṣar of Khalíl ibn Isḥáḳ el Gindi. He died in 1015 A.H. (1606 A.D.) and is mentioned in Ḥagi Khalfa's *Lexicon* (Vol. v, p. 447). Cp. D 3, No. 195.

It is a common practice of these Sudan genealogists to cull from the works of mediaeval authors certain pious remarks and details of information as to the pedigrees of contemporaries of the Prophet, and, after incorporating this in their own work among innumerable genealogical details derived from entirely different sources, and even from mere hearsay, to quote the mediaeval authors as authority for the whole. The author of AB hovers between this and the more candid policy (paras. VII, VIII, and XXVII).

XXI See Wüstenfeld (W). Two sons are omitted.

XXII Um Kulthūm was el Faḍl's only child.

'Abdulla had eight children, including those given: See Wüstenfeld (W).

XXIII 'Obaydulla and el Faḍl are not shown by Wüstenfeld as having any descendants at all. 'Ali had 17 children.

XXVI Cp. BA, XV and D 5 (*c*), XVIII.

XXIX Cp. BA, CXXXV; A 2, III; A 8, IX.

XXX Also quoted in BA, CCXXIX. The Arabic is:

كم من ابٍ قد علا بابنٍ حوى شرفًا كما علا برسول الله عدنان.

XXXV, XXXVI, XXXVII I have not met with any of these three condemned versions.

XXXIX This, with certain variations, is the account most commonly accepted. Abu el Dís is omitted by error between Kerdam and Buḍá'a. For Buḍá'a a common variant is Ḳuḍá'a. Cp. the trees of BA and MSS. A 1 to A 11, and the note on para. CXXXIII of BA, from which it appears that the version here referred to may be BA or an older copy of BA.

XL I have not met with this version. Ḥaṣín occurs in A 9. Cp. however D 6, II for "Ga'al el Aswad" ("the black").

XLIII, XLIV There is little doubt that the author has chosen this pedigree because he did not like the look of such non-Arab names as Háṭil and Yáṭil, and because, there being many variants of the names between Abu el Dís and Sa'ad he thought the best way would be to omit them all. The result of course is that there are far too few generations between the author and el 'Abbás. His statement that he found this pedigree as it stands "in the highest authorities" is no doubt pure invention.

XLVI The quality of the verse is vile and is on a par with the Elizabethan ballad of John Symon entitled "Pleasant Poesie, or sweete Nosegay of fragrant smellyng Flowers gathered in the Garden of heavenly Pleasure, the holy and blessed Bible, to the tune of the Black Almayne." The following lines from this work (quoted in the *Quarterly Review* of April, 1913) are very similar to the result of our author's efforts, and the very title quoted at once recalls the florid nomenclature of Arabic works:

Isacke was no weede,
Nor Jacob in very deede:
Joseph was a flower of price,
God dyd hym save from cruell device;
Also Moses eke we find;
And Aaron likewyse up we bynde,
Josua is not out of mynd.

XLIX Cp. BA, III and see note thereon.

L Sheikh Tatái was Muḥammad ibn Ibráhím el Tatái, Grand Ḳáḍi of Egypt. He died in 1094 A.H. (1683 A.D.). He is not mentioned by Ḥagi Khalfa.

LI Cp. BA, IV. El Shádhali, the founder of the religious order of the Shádhalía, was Abu el Ḥasan 'Ali el Shádhali ibn 'Abdulla, a descendant of Abu Ṭálib. He was born near Tunis and died in 1258 A.D. He was the author of *Ḥizb el Baḥr* ("the Litany of the Sea") and other works on the duties of worship. (See Huart, p. 278.)

LII Cp. BA, V.

The Imám Abu el Ḥasan is, I think, 'Ali ibn Muḥammad ibn Muḥammad ibn Muḥammad ibn Khalaf el Manūfi. He was born at Cairo in 857 A.H. (1453 A.D.).

LIII El 'Adawi is possibly 'Ali ibn Aḥmad el Sa'ídi, a Máliki doctor. The 'Adawía order was founded by Sheikh 'Adi ibn Musáfir in the second half of the twelfth century A.D.

LV Cp. BA, V.

LVIII Cp. BA, VI, and see note thereto. A Yūsef ibn 'Omar is mentioned in Ḥagi Khalfa's *Lexicon* (Vol. III, p. 413) as a commentator on the *Risála* of el Sháfa'i; and another, surnamed "el Kádūzi," as a commentator on a Ḥanafite *mukhtaṣar* by el Imám Abu el Ḥusayn Aḥmad (*v.* Vol. V, p. 455). The date of neither is given.

LXIV The only difference between this paragraph and para. VII of BA is "el 'Arab" (AB) for "el Anzáb" (BA). See note to BA, VII.

LXXV. This feki Bishára's importance is greatly exaggerated. He is not even mentioned in the *Ṭabaḳát Wad Ḍayfulla* (*i.e.* D 3), although much space is allotted to his contemporaries, the pupils of Ibráhím el Būlád.

LXXVII The word spelt "GHARBÁWÍNGI" is intended to be pronounced "GHARBÁWÍNCHI."

LXXXI "Letters patent" is جاه, *plur.* اجواه. Frequent mention is made in the *Ṭabaḳát Wad Ḍayfulla* of the grant of similar privileges to holy men.

LXXXII Bádi "Abu Shelūkh" reigned 1733–1766 (Bruce) or 1721–1761 (Cailliaud). (See note to D 7, XLVIII for this name.)

LXXXIII Bádi Abu Duḳn reigned 1651–1689 (Bruce) or 1638–1675 (Cailliaud).

LXXXIV "Contribution" is حسب (*ḥasab*), *i.e.* an offering, generally of *dammūr* (cloth) given to anyone who came as friend (*ḥasíb*) of the Sultan. "First-fruits" is عادة (*'áda*), *lit.* "custom." "Levy" is عانة (*'ána*), *lit.* "assistance." "Market-due" is قوار (*ḳuwár*), *i.e.* a due taken on the sale of articles. "Impost" is جباية (*gabáya*). In Dárfūr *Abo gabáyin* under the Sultans was the official responsible for collecting the corn tithes. "Forage-due" is علوق (*'alóḳ*), *i.e.* a gift of corn to feed the beasts of a great man and his retinue when he halted at a village. "Herd-due" is متورت (*matūrat*), *i.e.* the fattest of the flock, for slaughter in honour of a dignitary's visit: Ar. تور, to fatten up (properly of a bull). This list is of interest as showing the local imposts in force under FUNG rule.

LXXXVIII The real reason of the nickname "Westerner" was very probably that Bishára, or his ancestors, came from Borḳu. See D 1, CXLIX.

LXXXIX Ibráhím el Būlád was one of the famous sons of Gábir. He is mentioned in BA, CCV, and in the *Ṭabaḳát*. Also cp. Jackson, p. 26. By race he was a Rikábi.

By "Khalíl" is meant the subjects treated of by Khalíl, viz. Khalíl ibn Isḥáḳ el Gundi, the author of a great compendium (*mukhtaṣar*) of Málikite law. He died in 767 A.H. (1365–6 A.D.). El Sanhūri, 'Abd el Báḳi el Zurḳáni, and el Ag·hūri, all of whom are mentioned by AB or BA (*q.v.* CCXII), were among those who wrote commentaries on Khalíl's work. (See Ḥagi Khalfa's *Lexicon*, Vol. V, pp. 446–7.) Cp. D 3, VI. *Risála* more commonly means "composition" and "the art of letter-writing," but from the context here and elsewhere (and most notably in the couplet quoted in D 3, No. 93), it is clear that by *risála* is meant the office or duty of a *rasūl* or apostle. (See Hughes, p. 545, ii.)

XCVI *Ḥugga* is properly a decisive argument but the term is used to denote a person of incontrovertible authority. For the RIKÁBÍA see the trees to BA and D 1 and D 3, and Part III, Ch. 7. Muḥammad el Banūfari is also mentioned in D 3 (No. 17) as the instructor of Ibráhím el Būlád. Nothing definite is known about him.

XCIX The Arabic phrase is ومدة تدريسه في خليل سبعة ختمات and "seven sealings" means that he lectured on the whole of his subject from beginning to end seven times and on reaching the end of the book (Khalíl's) he each time sealed or signed it in token thereof. Cp. D 3, No. 17. The 40 pupils of the AWLÁD GÁBIR are often referred to in D 3, *e.g.* No. 60.

For 'Abd el Raḥman see D 3, No. 17, and BA, CCV.

C This "divorce oath" is very frequent in the Sudan: a man says "I swear that I will do (or not do) so and so, and if I break my oath I will divorce my wife"—and if he does break his oath he is expected to divorce her, though in practice he often compounds his offence instead.

The passage in the Ḳurán alluded to is in *Sura*, VI (*q.v.* Sale, p. 92).

CVI Cp. BA, XXXVIII.

El Termidhi is Abu 'Ísa Muḥammad el Tirmidhi, author of the Gáma'i, an encyclopaedia of traditions throwing light on the law. He died in 892 A.D. (See Huart, p. 220.)

By Ibn Dáūd is meant Abu Dáūd, one of the six great collectors and recorders of the Sunnite traditions, a contemporary of el Termidhi.

CVII Cp. BA, XLII.

CVIII Cp. BA, XLI.

CIX El Kházin is Sheikh 'Alá el Dín 'Ali ibn Muḥammad ibn Ibráhím el Baghdádi el Ṣūfi "el Kházin." He completed his great work *Lubáb el Ṭáwíl fi ma'áni li tanzíl* (a Ḳuránic commentary) in 725 A.H. (1325 A.D.): see Ḥagi Khalfa's *Lexicon*, Vol. V, p. 298.

CX Cp. BA, XVIII.

CXVI See note to BA, XXXVII. For "...was asked" AB gives قال سئل instead of قال قيل يا.

CXIX See para. III (note).

CXXX The Arabic is as follows:

هل يجوز استرقاق جميع العرب ام لا الجواب المشهور جوازه وهو قول مالك واحمد لان الاسترقاق اتلاف حكما

I cannot help thinking that a negative has dropped out, but the words quoted occur in the original, as in the later copies. The translation given of the last four words represents as nearly as possible the explanation of them offered by the author's son.

"Málik" is Abu 'Abdulla Málik ibn Anas; and "Aḥmad" is Abu 'Abdulla Aḥmad ibn Ḥanbal, *i.e.* two of the four founders of the great orthodox sects of Sunnis.

CXXXI–CXXXII AB gives "Sálim" instead of "Aslam" (BA, XLVIII); and AB gives المشكات القاري instead of المشكات للقاري (BA, XLVIII).

CXXXVII Cp. A 3, XII, where almost all these names are spelt rather differently. "BAG" may refer to the BEGA; but otherwise I have no clue to the identity of these tribes. The original MS. gave KHABRA: later copies taken from it give GABRA. Cp. C 9, 24.

CLXII From here onwards to CCX cp. A 1.

CLXVI Cp. BA, CXXXIII and CXXXVI.

CLXVII Cp. BA, CXXXVII.

CLXVIII Cp. BA, CXXXVII and CXXXVIII.

CLXIX Cp. BA, CXXXIX.

CLXX The phrase "the general ancestor" (جد الكل) is very frequently applied to Serrár (for whom see note to BA, CXXXIV).

CCXIV "Muḥammad" is presumably the son of Ṣaláḥ ibn Muḥammad. In para. CLXXII the Ṭerayfía were given as descendants of Ṭerayf. Cp. BA, CXLI.

CCXVIII Two or three illegible words follow at the end of this paragraph in the original MS.

CCXIX In para. CCXIII these appear as عيداب, but here as عايداب.

MANUSCRIPT ABC

Introduction

THE author of ABC is Ṣadíḳ el Ḥaḍra, a Maḥassi of the village of Salámat el Básha near Khartoum North. He is an old *feki* who has made the study of genealogies his life's work, and is, in fact, in process of completing the compilation of an enormous volume comprizing several hundreds of pedigrees which he has collected. I am afraid that neither his critical faculty nor his educational qualifications can honestly be said to fit him for the adequate presentation of the subject he has so courageously undertaken to elucidate, but he has certainly collected a formidable mass of raw material.

On my showing an interest in his studies he kindly composed for me the monograph here translated: it is in the nature of an abbreviated edition of his *magnum opus*.

The first part deals with that branch of the MAḤASS which is traditionally descended from 'Agam ibn Záíd ibn Muḥammad Maḥsin, *i.e.* with the author's own tribe. The second part is concerned with the Ga'ali group of tribes, the third with those of GUHAYNA, and the fourth with a medley of others. One or two brief biographies are also included.

Ṣadíḳ's method, he informs me, has been to compare various manuscripts (twenty-four in all, he says) and to supplement or check them by personal oral enquiries from other *fekis*. When satisfied as to the truth he has enshrined it in his work. His method, in fact, has been that of the author of AB. It is, however, obvious that he has been unduly credulous, and apt to accept at its face value much information that is worthless: in this respect he falls behind the author of AB. He also shows a distinct tendency to force variant accounts into an unnatural agreement by baldly stating as a fact what is no more than the product of his own imagination.

What then is the value of the work? It is small, but not altogether negligible. In the first place we have in it an example, the only one included in this collection, of a present-day *nisba*, and one that illustrates well the methods followed by native genealogists in dealing with their authorities.

Ṣadíḳ el Ḥaḍra has studied the *Ṭabaḳát* (D 3) and various versions of BA and other such MSS., and we see the result: the presumption is thus created that the authors of some at least of the works to which he referred for his information proceeded on analogous lines.

Secondly, various items of definite fact, otherwise unknown, are to be gleaned as to matters with which Ṣadíḳ is personally conversant. These sometimes help to explain obscure points in the other *nisbas*.

Thirdly, even allowing for inaccuracies and a certain degree of imagination, we get sidelights on native tradition drawn from sources which have been available to Ṣadíḳ in the course of a long life of enquiry, but which do not happen to have come within our ken through any other channel.

It may be added that, though in many cases where ABC differs from other *nisbas*, *e.g.* in the spelling of a proper name, ABC is certainly the less accurate, it is yet quite likely that in some other cases ABC may happen to provide a correct copy of some more accurate MS. than any I have seen.

The appendix is by a different author, for whom see the first note thereto.

I 'Agam was son of Záíd son of ... (*as in Tree* 1)...son of Ka'ab el Khazragi el Anṣári, who died at el Medína the Glorious in 19 A.H. in the Khalífate of 'Omar ibn el Khaṭṭáb, God bless him.

II Sheikh Idrís, whose *ḳubba* is at el 'Ayl Fūng, was son of el Arbáb Muḥammad son of...(*as in tree*, *to 'Agam*). He was born near Shanbát at a place called Shūḥaṭ lying between the railway [and the river], north of Shanbát, opposite the experimental pumping-station. He was born in 910 A.H., and on the death of his parents he moved to 'Aylat el Fūng and lived there until his death. He died and was buried there, after a life of about 149 Arabic years, in 1059 A.H. His mother was Fáṭima, the daughter of the Sheríf Ḥammad Abu Denána[1], who is buried at Abu Delayḳ and was descended from el Ḥusayn ibn 'Ali ibn Abu Ṭálib.

On his father's side Sheikh Idrís was a Khazragi Anṣári descended from Ubi ibn Ka'ab; and [KHAZRAG] are originally Arabs of Yemen descended from Ḳaḥṭán ibn 'Ábir, that is the prophet Hūd, upon whom be peace.

Sheikh Idrís's descendants are [mostly] at el 'Ayl Fūng, and some are in other places.

III El Ḥág Idrís was son of 'Abd el Dáím son of...(*as in tree*, *to 'Agam*) and was born at the Shūḥaṭ mentioned above in 959 A.H. He lived 99 years and died in 1058 A.H. He had seven sons, namely ...(*as in tree*, *which gives their names and descendants*).

[1] reading دنانة for دناه.

IV El Sheikh Khógali, whose *ḳubba* is at Khartoum North, was son of 'Abd el Raḥman son of...(*as in tree, to 'Agam*). He had nine sons and four daughters. These were ...(*as in tree*). Aḥmad and Muḥammad and el Gáz and Um Háni were all children of the same mother, namely, Wanasūna bint 'Omar ibn Ḥammad ibn Muḥammad, so her pedigree meets that of Sheikh Khógali in the person of el Malik Gáma'i. Her tribe was called the MAKANÁB, the children of el Malik Makan. The mother of the remaining seven brothers and two sisters was Bint el Minná bint Ṭá'ulla ibn Sulaymán ibn Abu Mūsa, a Ḳardaḳábía, so her pedigree meets that of Sheikh Khógali in the person of their ancestor, the above-mentioned 'Agam. Their progeny forms several tribes [*ḳabáil*], some of whom live at el Ḳubba, and some round the village called EL KHÓGALÁB after their ancestor Khógali and situated on the east bank opposite Kerreri, and some in the south.

Sheikh Khógali was born on Tūti Island in 1065 A.H. and lived 101 years and died in 1155 A.H.

V The descendants of Ḳardaḳa ibn Felláḥ ibn Sheraf el Dín ibn 'Agam are on Tūti Island: others of them are scattered in Kordofán and the neighbourhood of Gebel el Ḥaráza, in the west, between the two KABÁBÍSH districts of Gabra and el Ṣáfia. They form a considerable number of tribes, about thirty in fact. Others live in the Gezíra of Sennár.

VI Some of the descendants of Marzūḳ ibn Felláḥ ibn Sheraf el Dín ibn 'Agam live at Burri el Maḥass near Khartoum South, namely the children of Ibráhím el Budáni who are called the BUDÁNÁB. With them are other descendants of Marzūḳ surnamed the AWLÁD ḲASŪMA. Other descendants of Marzūḳ are round el Raḳayba on the east bank, opposite el Kámnín, and are called "the MAḤASS." Others of them are at Hillet Balūla, north of el Kámnín, on the east bank. They form various tribes.

VII The descendants of Záíd ibn 'Agam form various tribes. They include the children of Ḥammád ibn 'Abd el Salám ibn...(*as in tree, to 'Ísa*), namely el feki el Sayyid and 'Abd el Salám and el Ḥág Muḥammad Nūr and their sisters Fáṭima and Um Kalthūm: and the children of each of these form a tribe, and they dwell at Shanbát and thereabouts.

They include also the children of 'Agaymi and of his son Aḥmad, some of whom are at Shanbát and some on Tūti Island and some in the Gezíra of Sennár: these form various tribes.

Also the children of Idrís ibn Shakartu ibn...(*as in tree, to 'Agam*).

Also the children of Shakartulla ibn el Ḥág ibn...(*as in tree, to 'Ali 'Ashba*). Some of these are at Shanbát and some round el Mesallamía, which is a government headquarters, and some round Sennár, and all are descended from Idrís ibn Shakartu.

Some of the children of Shakartulla are on Tūti Island, some at Shanbát, and some in the other directions mentioned.

VIII Some of the descendants of Raḥma ibn 'Ali ibn...(*as in tree, to 'Agam*), who are surnamed the SA'ADULLÁB, are on Tūti Island; some are at Shanbát; and some are with the KABÁBÍSH AWLÁD 'UḲBA and are called the AWLÁD ABU SITTA[1].

IX The SA'ADÁB who live round el Ḥinayk, on the west [bank], opposite Gebel Lūla, which is called by the Sudanese Gebel Auli, are the descendants of Sá'ad ibn el feki Ádam ibn...(*as in tree, to 'Agam*), and form various tribes.

With them are the ḤAMMADULLÁB, the inhabitants of Um Ḳaḥf near el 'Ayl Fūng. Some of them too are at el 'Ayl Fūng. Some again are at el Tómát on the Atbara, and at Gíra on the river Sanhít, and at Dóka in the Buṭána.

These people are the children of Maḥmūd walad Záíd. The Arabs who are under their rule, namely ḌUBÁNÍA, trace their descent to GUHAYNA, whereas the descendants of Záíd are SHÁMÍA, descendants of Mazád Abu Sháma ibn 'Agam.

All of these are descended from the ANṢÁR who conquered the Sudan in 43 A.H. during the period of the rule of 'Abdulla ibn Abu Saraḥ, the Companion. After the conquest the KHAZRAG settled in this country and their children multiplied there until the present day. At the time of their coming to conquer the Sudan they numbered about 81,000.

They are Arabs of Yemen and descended from Ḳaḥṭán ibn 'Ábir, that is the prophet Hūd.

Now Ḳaḥṭán is ancestor of all [the tribes of] el Yemen and to him they trace their descent. The children of Ḳaḥṭán were Gurhum and Ḥaḍramaut and Sabá.

X Sheikh Ḥasan ibn Ḥasūna, whose *ḳubba* is in the middle of the Buṭána, between the Blue Nile and the Atbara, was a Sheríf on his father's side. His mother was Fáṭima bint Ḥabashía, whose mother was a Ṣáridía Khamaysía tracing her descent to the ANṢÁR.

Sheikh Ḥasan ibn Ḥasūn visited Egypt and Syria and other lands and performed the pilgrimage. These journeys occupied about twelve years. Then he returned to his own country and became famous among the nomad Arabs for his piety, and his herds of cattle

[1] reading ستة for سنة.

and camels and sheep and his horses and slaves increased in number. And withal he used to give hospitality to travellers, and in one day he gave food to about 15,000, a magnificent performance in those days. He was born on the island called Kagóg, situated on the Blue Nile north-west of Gebel Gária, in 968 A.H., and lived 91 years. He died in 1059 A.H., and was buried in the tomb he built with his own hands. He left no children.

XI The feki Muḥammad el Nūr ibn Ḍayfulla, the author of the *Ṭabaḳát el Awliyá bi 'l Sūdán*, was son of Ḍayfulla ibn 'Ali ibn Ibráhím ibn el Ḥág Naṣrulla, a Ga'ali 'Abbási. His descendants are called the Ḍayfulláb, the children of Ḍayfulla. He died at Ḥalfáyat el Mulūk of the yellow fever known in the Sudan as *el Kik* in 1224 A.H.[1]

XII The Ga'alín (*sic*) who are in the Sudan are the descendants of Ibráhím el Háshimi, nicknamed "Ga'al." The reason of his being so named was that he was possessed of great power and wealth, and in his days a severe famine occurred, and folk came to him from every direction and said "O Ibráhím, make us (*aga'lná*) your folk," and he consented to their wish, and so his people surnamed him "Ga'al" because he "made" (*ga'al*) those who came to him and maintained them until God relieved their distress. He has many descendants in the Sudan: their number may be about 50,000. Among them are the sons of 'Armán, namely Gebel, the ancestor of the Gebeláb, and Gabr, the ancestor of the Gábráb, and 'Abd el 'Ál, the ancestor of the Magádíb and the Ḳandíláb (and in all 'Abd el 'Ál had fourteen sons and from each one of them are descended various tribes), and Shá'a el Dín, the ancestor of the Shá'adínáb (who consist of various tribes), and el Malik 'Adlán ibn 'Armán (who had thirty male children, from each of whom are descended numerous tribes), and Zayd, the ancestor of the Záídáb (who contain many tribes), and Musallam, ancestor of the Musallamáb (who are many tribes), and Mukábir, the ancestor of the Mukábiráb (who are tribes), and Sa'íd, the ancestor of the Sa'adáb and the Nimráb, and Náṣir, the ancestor of the Náṣiráb, and Shai, and Yóiy, the ancestor of the Yóiyáb. These are the twelve sons of 'Armán, and their descendants were even more numerous. Among these descendants were the children of 'Abd el 'Ál ibn el Malik 'Armán, some of whom have already been mentioned, and who were fourteen men in all, and who include the Ḥasabulláb [the children of Ḥasabulla]; and the Ráfa'áb, the children of Ráfa'i; and the Khadráb, the children of Khadr; and the Gódaláb[2], the children of Gádulla; and the Kálíáb, the children of Kali; and the

[1] 1809 A.D.

[2] reading جودلاب for جوداب.

Kitíáb, the children of Kiti; and the Bashíráb, the children of Bashír; and the Mūsíáb, the children of Mūsa; and the 'Omaráb, the children of 'Omar; and Tisa'a Kulli; and the tenth of them, Muḥammad el Nigayḍ, the ancestor of the Nigáḍa.

XIII Among the 'Omaráb was Sheikh Ḥámid Abu 'Aṣa son of Sheikh 'Omar son of Belál son of Muḥammad son of 'Omar son of Muḥammad el Á'war son of 'Abd el 'Ál son of el Malik 'Armán. His mother was a Sheríſía named Ḥalíma, the daughter of el Sheríf Ḥammad Abu Denána who lies buried at Abu Delayḳ. Sheikh Ḥámid Abu 'Aṣa had ten children, namely Muḥammad and Ḥammad and...(*as in tree*).

XIV Náfa'a and Nafí'a were sons of el Malik 'Adlán ibn el Malik 'Armán by a single mother. Among the descendants of Náfa'a are the Tháwíáb and ...(*as in tree*) and many tribes.

XV Among the descendants of Nafí'a are the Serayḥáb and... (*as in tree*).

XVI The sons of el Malik 'Abd el Dáím ibn 'Adlán were fourteen in number, and they included 'Ali and Yóiy and Ḥammad, the mother of all of whom was Bukra the daughter of his paternal uncle Mukábir. The descendants of 'Ali ibn el Malik 'Abd el Dáím are the 'Álíáb: those of Yóiy ibn el Malik 'Abd el Dáím ibn 'Adlán are the Yóiyáb round Ḳózbara: those of Ḥammad ibn el Malik 'Abd el Dáím are round el Metemma. The descendants of Abu Ḍaraywa are the Ḍaraywáb, those of Kabūsh are the Kabūsháb, and those of Ḥammád reside at el Metemma. [Add] also Abu Baṣrūn; and Muḥammad el Fiál, ancestor of the Nafáfí'a; and Shaddū and Ḳaddū, whose descendants are the Waháhíb *el fuḳará*; and Ḍow; and Kena, ancestor of the Kitáwít.

XVII The sons of 'Abd el Ma'abūd were 'Abd el Salám el Aṣfar, ancestor of the Ṣufar el Magháwír [Mafáwír (?)]; and Mūsa, ancestor of the Mūsíáb; and Khadr el Fiál, ancestor of the Fíáíl.

XVIII The descendants of Ba'abūsh are the Ba'ábísh.

The sons of Sa'ad Abu Dabūs included 'Abd el Dáím and Kanbaláwi and Sanad and Idrís el Ḳaṭí'a, the ancestor of the 'Abdsalámáb of el Buayḍa.

XIX The sons of Sa'ad ibn Ḍiáb [were the] Burnis, namely (and?) Náṣir and Muḥammad el Ḳuṣayer and 'Ali and Ṣáliḥ.

XX The sons of Rubáṭ ibn Mismár ibn Serrár ibn Kerdam (*i.e.* the Sultan Ḥasan, Kerdam being a surname) were 'Awad and Ḳuraysh and el Khanfari and Muḳbal and 'Abṭ....(*The descendants of each are given: see Tree 3. Remarks made in passing and not included in the tree are as follows*):

1. *Ḥumayyir and Daḥaysh, ancestors of the* ḤUMAYYIRÁB *and* DAḤAYSHÁB *were full brothers.*

2. *The* MAWWATÁB: "*Among them was Walad Ḍayfa.*"

3. *The* 'AWAḌÍA *sub-tribes:* "*Each one of these tribes has many branches.*"

4. *The* MAḲBŪLÁB: "*Some of them live near Shendi.*"

XXI Mismár ibn Serrár ibn Kerdam had four sons, namely Sa'ad el Feríd, and the three sons of a single mother, Ṣubuḥ Abu Merkha, the above-mentioned Rubáṭ, and Nebíh....(*The descendants of each are given in Tree* 3, *but as remarks not mentioned in the tree are made in passing concerning some of them, these remarks are inserted here, as follows*):

1. *The* ḌUBÁB: "*Among them was Sheikh el Ḥusayn el Zahrá.*"

2. *The* GIMA'A: "*Among them was 'Asákir Abu Kalám.*"

3. *The* ḤAKAMÁB, *or* AWLÁD ḤÁKIM: "*Some of them are in Dongola and others in the* GA'ALÍN *country: among them was the feki Muḥammad ibn el Bedowi, who was Sheikh el Islám.*" "*And Ḥákim also has descendants round Arḳo, called the* MIḤAYNÁB."

4. *The* NÁṢIRÁB: "*Their ancestor Náṣir dwelt on the White Nile near Berayma.*"

5. *Ḥámid Abu Tinka:* (1) "*He of el 'Ayn, which lies west of el Ṣáfia in the* KABÁBÍSH *country.*" (2) The descendants of his son 'Adlán are said to be at el Ḳóz village, those of his other two sons at Um 'Aḍám, and those of his grandson Muḥammad "among the ḤALÁWÍN," *i.e.* all in Mesallamía district.

6. *Marangána (ancestress of the* ḤÁGÁB): "*She of the ridge near Walad Medani.*"

7. *The* RASHÍDÁB: "*Who live on the White Nile near el Ḥanayk.*"

8. *The* MUḲDÁB: "*On the west bank of the White Nile, opposite Gebel Auli.*"

9. *The* NÁÍLÁB: "*They include the sons of el Mek Bábikr who were about* 18 *in all and each of whom had posterity.*"

10. *The* SULAYMÁNÍA: "*On the White Nile, opposite Um Arḍa Island.*"

11. *The* ḤAMAYDÁNÍA: "*Among them was the feki Ibráhím 'Abd el Dáfa'i, the author of the History of the Sudan.*"

12. *The* SHAKÍRÁB: "*Near Um Arḍa Island.*"

13. *The* 'ÍSÁWÍA: "*Some of them are with the* KABÁBÍSH."

14. *The* DUNÍBÁB: "*Who live with the* GIMÍ'ÁB, *and include Ḳuḍur the panegyrist.*"

15. *The* ḤARAYZÁB: "*Who include Sheikh Dafa'alla el Gharḳán*[1], *who lives at Omdurmán.*"

[1] reading الغرقان for القرقان.

16. *The descendants of Fatáḥ the Younger: "They include the 'omda of the* FITÍḤÁB *and the children of Sulaymán ibn el Mek and of his brother Shibayli, and the* ḲUṢAYṢÁB, *the sons of Ḥámid ibn Ḳussa..., etc."* (*as in tree*).

17. *Dardóḳ: "In Dárfūr, and among his descendants were Abó ibn 'Abdulla ibn Gódafát."*

XXII All of the above are ḲURAYSH and descended from el 'Abbás ibn 'Abd el Muṭṭalib ibn Háshim; and all of them are the children of Ibráhím el Háshimi who was surnamed "Ga'al," and the first of their ancestors to come to the Sudan was named Ghánim, surnamed "el 'Abbási." He fled from Baghdád after the Tatar attacked it, in 676 A.H.[1]. Then they (*sic*) came to Egypt and found the Fáṭimites ruling there, but they were unable to settle down with them, so migrated to the Sudan and took up their abode, some on the Blue Nile and some on the White and some in Dárfūr and Dár Wadái (that is Borḳu), and spread in all directions.

XXIII Those that are in Dárfūr are represented by the royal family only. The rest of the Dárfūrians are KUNGÁRA and HILÁLA, and such as are neither are all FERÁTÍT [*i.e.* FERTÍT].

XXIV As regards Borḳu, the royal family are 'ABBÁSÍA, that is ḲURAYSH. The rest are Arabs of Yemen, that is ḤIMYAR, descended from Báriḳ ibn 'Uday ibn Ḥáritha ibn 'Ámir ibn Ḥáritha ibn Tha-'aliba ibn Amrá el Ḳays ibn Mázin ibn el Azd, who are [all of the tribe of] GHASSÁN.

XXV The tribes of MUḌR ibn Nizár and RABÍ'A ibn Nizár. All in the Wádi el 'Arab trace their descent to these tribes, and their pedigrees all meet in Ḳays ibn Ghaylán ibn Muḍr and el Yás ibn Muḍr. RABÍ'A, too, forms one stock with MUḌR. The mother of el Yás ibn Muḍr was el Rubáb bint Ṣayda ibn Ma'ad ibn 'Adnán; and el Yás ibn Muḍr had three sons, Mudraka and Ṭábikha and 'Umayr, and their mother was Khindif, whose [real] name was Layla bint Ḥalwán ibn 'Omrán ibn el Ḥáfi ibn Ḳuḍá'a ibn Ma'ad ibn 'Adnán. Therefore the posterity of el Yás ibn Muḍr were called "KHINDIF," because she was their mother and to her they trace their descent. From 'Adnán branch off all the tribes of the Arabs.

XXVI All of the descendants of Muḍr ibn Nizár who came to the Sudan are the children of Ḳays ibn Ghaylán ibn Muḍr. They include Guhayna ibn Rísh ibn...(*as in Tree* 4, *to 'Adnán*), and, secondly, Guhayna ibn 'Abdulla ibn Anas el Guhani, and thirdly, Guhayna of the tribe of ḲUḌÁ'A, namely Guhayna ibn Zayd ibn...(*as in tree, to 'Adnán*), and, fourthly, Guhayna ibn 'Aṭía ibn Ḥasan ibn 'Abdulla

[1] 1277 A.D.

ibn el Zubayr ibn el 'Awwám ibn Khowaylid ibn Asad ibn 'Abd el 'Uzzá ibn Ḳuṣai ibn Keláb.

All these four, after their arrival in the Sudan, came to an agreement and became one tribe.

The tribes of GUHAYNA are fifty-two in all, not counting those that in the past have entered the Sudan *via* the Nile in the time of the FUNG, and most of them are west of Tūnis and Tripoli [*Ṭaráblus*] and Fezzán and Borḳu. Three of the sons of Baghíḍ came to the Sudan, namely Ḳays and Sufián and Dhubián, and the descendants of Ḳays ibn Baghíḍ were the Guhayna ibn Rísh mentioned above and Guhayna ibn 'Abdulla ibn Anas el Guhani. These are the children of Ḳays.

XXVII The descendants of Sufián ibn Baghíḍ are the KABÁBÍSH, who are the children of Muḥammad ibn Sufián ibn 'Abs ibn Sufián ibn Baghíḍ. They are sometimes surnamed "BENI 'ABS."

Now Muḥammad ibn Sufián had two sons....(*For these and their descendants see tree. Remarks made in passing, and not included in the tree, are as follows:*

1. *The descendants of the sons of Nūr ibn 'Ali.* "*Each of them forms a tribe that defends itself.*"

2. *The descendants of the sons of 'Ali ibn Nūr.* "*Each of them forms an independent tribe that defends the other.*"

XXVIII The sons of Dhubián ibn Baghíḍ ibn Rayth ibn...(*as in tree, to 'Adnán*) were nine in number, namely Watíd and..., *etc.*, *as in tree, which also gives their descendants. Remarks made in passing, and not included in the tree, are as follows:*

1. *The descendants of Muḥammad ibn 'Ámir:* "*Each of them forms a separate tribe, some of them living near el Siūt and others in the deserts of Sennár.*"

2. *Rikáb son of Sulṭán:* "*Not to be confused with Rikáb ibn Ghulámulla.*"

3. *The* SHUKRÍA *descended from Bashír ibn Dhubián:* "*The descendants of Bashír ibn..., etc., are the* SHUKRÍA *and the* NABÁRÍA. *Now all the* SHUKRÍA *trace their descent to Yashkur ibn Wáil ibn...*" (*as in tree, to Nizár*), "*except the* AWLÁD ABU SIN, *who are* ḲURAYSH, *descended from 'Abdulla ibn Ga'afir ibn Abu Ṭálib.*"

4. *The* ḲARÍBÁB: "*Who live on the banks of the Nile opposite Rufá'a.*"

5. *The* KAWÁHLA *descended from Káhil ibn Ḥasan:* "*Not to be confused with the* KAWÁHLA *descended from el Zubayr ibn el 'Awwám.*"

6. *The* KANÁGIRA: "*They include* KUNGÁRA *in Dárfūr, and Borḳu and Bornu and Afnū: others of them are sons of Fellát ibn Kungar, who are partly* FELLÁTA."

7. *The* THAḲRA: "*Some of whom are Muhammadans and the remainder infidels.*"

8. *The* ḲALḲÁLA: "*They are in Tūnis: some of them* [*too*] *live near el Kámnín.*"

9. *The* DAWÁGIRA: "*They live east of Mekka and are the people of el Nūḳ el Bakht.*"

10. *The* SANÁDALÍB: "*Some of whom used to be in Sennár.*"

11. *The descendants of the sons of Hilál ibn Muḥammad:* "*Some of them are at el Hilálía.*"

12. *The tribes descended from 'Áḳil ibn Muḥammad 'Ámir:* "*These tribes live in Upper Egypt. But the* SHÁMÍA *and the* MA'ÁIDA *and the* ḲALÁLÍB *are descended from 'Áid ibn Ḥusayn. Some of them are west of Dárfūr.*"

XXIX The descendants of 'Abdulla ibn Zubayr ibn el 'Awwám are the KAWÁHLA in the Gezíra of Sennár, who are the children of Guhayna ibn 'Aṭía ibn el Ḥasan ibn 'Abdulla ibn el Zubayr ibn el 'Awwám, and also the 'ABÁBDA, who are the children of el Zubayr. These are ḲURAYSH.

XXX The nomads in the Sudan who have been mentioned are all descended from Muḍr ibn Nizár and Rabí'a ibn Nizár.

XXXI The GA'ÁFIRA in Upper Egypt include the descendants of Ga'afir el Ṣádiḳ, and the descendants of Ga'afir el Ṭiár, the brother of the Imám 'Ali ibn Abu el Ṭálib, and the descendants of Ga'afir ibn Ḳuṭáf el Ṭáí, who are of the stock of Ḥátim el Táí, so famous for his generosity and bravery, and the descendants of Ga'afir el Barmaki. All of them live in Upper Egypt.

XXXII The ḤAḌÁRMA were originally nomads in Ḥaḍramaut and moved across to the west bank of the Red Sea [*el Máliḥ*] and settled at Sūákin in the Sudan. They left the east bank in the time of el Ḥaggág ibn Yūsef el Thaḳfi.

XXXIII The GABARTA[1] are by origin Arabs.

XXXIV The MESALLAMÍA of the district so-named are the stock of Musallam ibn Ḥamáz 'Aṭáf the Ommawi. They migrated from Syria in the time of 'Omar ibn 'Abd el 'Áẓíz the Ommawi and settled in the Sudan in the country known after them.

XXXV The inhabitants of Edfu are of different races. Some are ASHRÁF, and some are Arabs, including MANÁḲIRA and KHŪLA and ḤARÁÍZ and KALŪḤ and ḲALÁLÍB and MERÍNÁB, all of whom are GUHAYNA, and the BUṢAYLÍA, the descendants of Ḥammád el Buṣayli, who are Arabs of Ḥegáz tracing their descent to GUHAYNA.

[1] reading الجبرت for الجبرة.

XXXVI The SABÁ'ÍA and the MAṬÁ'ANA are western Arabs, tracing their descent to the MASÁMIDA.

XXXVII The HOWÁRA trace their descent to the BARÁNÍS. They are western Arabs, and their pedigree goes back to ḲURAYSH.

XXXVIII The AWLÁD 'ALI trace their descent to HILÁLA and are GUHAYNA.

XXXIX The ḤEGÁZIYYŪN are eastern Arabs, ḲURAYSH by race.

XL The rest of the inhabitants of Upper Egypt are composed of COPTS [*Aḳbáṭ*], and RŪM, and GUMUSA, the GUMUSA being slaves, and ALEPPANS [*Ḥaleb*], who are children of adultery.

XLI The FAKHRÁNÍA include ASHRÁF on the mother's side.

XLII El Sayyid 'Abd el Raḥím el Ḳenáwi was one of the ASHRÁF of the west, and he is sufficiently famous to need no further description.

XLIII The inhabitants of the Nile [valley] south of Egypt and west of the Red Sea are all 'ABÁBDA, the descendants of 'Abdulla ibn el Zubayr ibn el 'Awwám.

XLIV The inhabitants of Ḥalfa are KANŪZ, the sons of Dowlat el Kanzi, that is NŪBA.

XLV Similarly the original inhabitants of Dongola, all of them, from the Red Sea to the Equator, are descended from the ZING. These came from Neged and el 'Iráḳ.

XLVI The Persians [*Fárisía*] are of the seed of Selmán el Fárisi.

XLVII The original ḤUḌŪR are all GUHAYNA and inhabit the country between Edfu and Aṣwán.

XLVIII The BENI 'ÁMIR, that is UM 'AR'ARA, entered Abyssinia. They are famous for their bravery and courage and stout-heartedness, and are a mighty tribe.

XLIX The facts given above are based on a tree which I found written in the handwriting of el Ḥasan ibn 'Ali, the brother of el Sayyid Aḥmad el Bedowi, and taken from the genealogical tree found by el Sháfa'i 'Ali Ibráhím and the above-mentioned el Ḥasan.

L According to Ibn Khaldūn the tribes of Arabs descended from GUHAYNA came after the Muhammadan conquest of the northern NŪBA in 1318 A.D., and spread over the Sudan, and formed a separate branch.

LI The ḤAMAR Arabs are originally GUHAYNA and trace their descent to that tribe.

LII The TA'ÁISHA and the HABBÁNÍA and the AWLÁD ḤAMAYD and SELÍM are descendants of Ḥammád ibn Gunayd. The ḤAWÁZMA and the Ḥumr and the Messíría and the Rizayḳát are descendants of his brother 'Aṭía. All of them are Guhayna by descent.

Similarly the Beni Helba, who are west of Dárfūr[1] and are a great tribe, trace their descent to Guhayna. So also do the Beni Ḥusayn and the Tergam and Khuzáma and the Máhría (*sic*) and the Masálít and the Koróbát, who live west of Kebkábía.

LIII The Khawábír, who inhabit Wadái[2] in the west, are in some cases merchants and in others nomads. They are Beni Ommayya, Ḳuraysh, by origin.

LIV Some of the descendants of the sons of Abu Bukr[3] el Ṣadíḳ who have immigrated to the Sudan.

They include the sons of Sheikh Muḥammad el Mugelli, who was buried near Esná in the district of Zerníkh, and who was a Sheríf on his mother's side and a Bukri on his father's. With him was his brother Sheikh Aḥmad surnamed "el Yómáni." They came from the direction of el Yemen, from a village in Yemen called Bunda, to Egypt. Thence they went and settled in a village called Zerníkh near Esná, [he] and his sons with him. Among these sons were Sheikh Muḥammad "el Mutargam" ("the Interpreter"), and Sheikh Muḥammad "el Royyán," and Sheikh Muḥammad "el Gharḳadi," and Sheikh Ya'aḳūb. Sheikh Ya'aḳūb proceeded to the Sudan in 1001[4] A.H. and betook himself to the king of the Fung, 'Omára Dunḳas, at Sennár. The latter gave him an order [entitling him] to reside at Ḥalfáyat el Mulūk on the east bank of the Blue Nile, and he lived there for a number of years and died there, and was buried near the [village of the] Izayriḳáb, north of el Ḥalfáya, and his tomb is still there.

LV Sheikh Ya'aḳūb left four sons, Sheikh 'Aṭaalla, Sheikh Mūsa, Sheikh Muḥammad Zámir, and Sheikh Ḥammad, Ḳáḍi of Bandi; and each of these four had numerous children, tribes.

The descendants of 'Aṭaalla live round Bayli and are called the 'Aṭáíáb. The descendants of Sheikh Mūsa are numerous tribes, some round Sennár and some elsewhere, and they are called the Mūsíáb. The descendants of Sheikh Muḥammad Zámir are numerous tribes, some at Ḥalfáyat el Mulūk and some in the Ga'alín (*sic*) country, and they are called the Zamráb. The descendants of Sheikh Ya'aḳūb, who is buried at [the village of] the Izayriḳáb, include Sheikh Ḥammad who is famous as "Um Amiriūm" (*sic*) whose *ḳubba* is at Khartoum North: the latter's [full] name was Sheikh Ḥammad ibn

[1] reading دارفور for داراو. [2] reading وداي for وداعة.
[3] reading ابوبكر for أباكبر. [4] 1592 A.D.

Muḥammad ibn 'Ali ibn 'Omar ibn el Sheikh Máḍi ibn Muḥammad Abu Guayd ibn el Sheikh Ḥammad, Ḳáḍi of Bandi, ibn el Sheikh Ya'aḳūb ibn el Sheikh Muḥammad Mugelli.

LVI [There are] also the sons of Sheikh Aḥmad Abu el Gūd, the brother of Muḥammad Abu Guayd, and these are the ZENÁRKHA who live with the GAMŪ'ÍA.

Similarly the AWLÁD KHAYRULLA near Um Dóm, east of Khartoum.

These form numerous tribes, and all of them trace their descent to 'Abd el Raḥman ibn Abu Bukr el Ṣadíḳ and are ḲURAYSH. They include the MUGELLÍÁB and the ḤAMMATTÍÁB in the GA'ALÍN (*sic*) country, and the MAKTANÁB, and the 'AMŪDÁB, and the DELAYḲÁB, and the ḲERAYDÁB, and the NAḲÁGÁB, and the 'AMÁRNA, some of whom are at Gebel Saḳádi and Móya and the remainder in the east near the Red Sea, at Sūákin and elsewhere.

ABC (NOTES)

I The tribes and persons described in this and the following eight paragraphs are all known as Maḥass at present. It will be seen that the author considers them to be all originally Ḥimyaritic Arabs from southern Arabia, Anṣár of the tribe of Khazrag. One or two of the earlier names given in the tree occur in Wüstenfeld, 16 and 22, but there is no consistent coincidence between the pedigree as given in ABC and that given by Wüstenfeld.

II Cp. D 3, 141 and note thereto for Sheikh Idrís and "el 'Ayl Fūng" (*i.e.* el 'Aylafūn).

For Hūd see Hughes, pp. 181, 182. He is spoken of in Chapters 7, 11 and 26 of the Ḳurán, and was the prophet sent to the contumacious tribe of 'Ád. There is no reason whatever to identify him with Ḳaḥṭán.

III El Ḥág Idrís, as being the ancestor of the Awlád Ḥaḍra (*see Tree* 1), is the author's progenitor. Of el Ḥág Idrís's descendants the author says: "All the descendants of el Ḥág Muḥammad are round Shanbát and, in some cases, near Sennár. Those of el Ḥág Sulaymán are on Tūti Island, including el Khalífa Muḥammad ibn..., etc." (*as in tree*), "and others are round Shanbát, and others near Sennár: they form numerous tribes."

D 3 gives no life of el Ḥág Idrís nor of any of his sons.

IV Cp. D 3, 154 and 19.

The date 1155 A.H. agrees with D 3. Either "1065 A.H." or "101 years" is an error.

V These are the Ḳardaḳáb section of Maḥass.

VI For the Budánáb cp. D 7, CCLIX.

El Raḳayba is generally known as "Ḥillet el Maḥass" or "Maḥass el Raḳayba." For "Kámnín" in place of "Kámlín" see note to D 3, 109, and Vol. 1, p. 341.

The descendants of Marzūḳ would normally be called "Marázíḳ." Sections of that name occur both among the Ḥamar and the Gawáma'a of Kordofán and the Sháíḳía.

VIII There is a section of Awlád 'Uḳba called Sa'adullàb (see MacMichael, *Tribes*..., p. 175).

IX These Ḥammadulláb are a section of Mesallamía (see C 8, XVII and XXIII).

"The Atbara" is spelt in ABC البحر الاتبراوى ("el Baḥr el Atbaráwi").

By "Sanhít" is meant the Setít.

'Abdulla Abu Saraḥ's more common name is 'Abdulla ibn Sa'ad. He made no expedition in 43 A.H. (663 A.D.). The campaign of 651–2 A.D. is no doubt meant.

For the final sentence cp. D 1, LXXI.

X Cp. D 3, 132, according to which Sheikh Ḥasan died in 1075 A.H.

XI This paragraph provides us with the name of the author of D 3 and is corroborated by tradition on the point (see Introduction to D 3). The pedigree, however, differs from that given in D 3 (*q.v.* No. 89) and the latter is more likely to be correct.

For the final sentence cp. D 7, CLXXXV, which corroborates.

XII Cp. BA, CXXXII, etc., for the name "Ga'al."

For the descendants of 'Armán cp. BA, CLXV *et seq.*, A 2, XI *et seq.* and A 11, XXIV *et seq.*, all of which differ to some extent from one another, as a comparison of the trees will show.

The "MAGÁDÍB" are not to be confused with the "MAGÁDHÍB" (*i.e.* AWLÁD EL MAGDHŪB), who are traditionally Ashráf.

"Shai" (شي) appears in A 11 and BA (MS. 3) as "Shabbu" (شبُ) or "Shabbū" (شبو).

As regards "Tisa'a Kulli" and "the tenth of them, Muḥammad el Nigayḍ," there is obviously some error in the texts of ABC, BA, A 11, etc. In ABC the figure "9" is actually written over "Tisa'a," and in the original copy no doubt nine sons were mentioned and after their names the author wrote "nine in all, and a tenth was Negáḍi." Later copyists added other sons and in some cases seem to have converted the "nine in all" and "a tenth" into proper names (see BA, CLXVII and A 11, XXXIX).

XIII Ḥámid Abu 'Aṣa's biography is No. 113 in D 3.

XIV *et seq.* Cp. BA, note to CLXXI.

XVI It will be seen that only 12 of the 14 sons of 'Abd el Dáím are given. See BA, CLXXI, CLXXII for notes.

It is to be assumed that Abu Ḍaraywa was a son of 'Abd el Dáím, as shown in the tree, because he appears as such in BA (MS. 3) and A 11. Similarly, 'Abd el Ma'abūd in para. XVII may, for a like reason, be assumed to be a son of 'Adlán, and Ba'abūsh and Sa'ad Abu Dabūs to be sons of 'Abd el Ma'abūd.

For "el Fíál" (الفيال) BA (MS. 3) gives "Ḳanḳál" (القنقال), and for "KITÁWÍT" (كتاويت), "KENÁWÍN" (كناوين). BA is more likely to be correct in both cases.

XIX These names are not included in the tree. Cp. note to BA, CLXXI.

XX Cp. BA, CLI *et seq.*; A 11, XL *et seq.*, etc.

The names "Ḥumayyir" (*lit.* "little donkey") and Daḥaysh (*lit.* a "donkey's foal") in juxtaposition are curious.

XXI Cp. BA, CXLIII *et seq.*

2. 'Asákir Abu Kalám was the chief of the GIMA'A in the time of the Mahdi (see MacMichael, *Tribes*..., pp. 43, 44).

3. Sheikh el Bedowi was Ḳáḍi of Berber in the Mahdi's time, and at the reoccupation was made President of the Board of 'Ulema in the Sudan.

5. Ḥámid Abu Tinka is a more or less legendary character. Gebel el 'Ayn, between Dongola and Kordofán, is commonly called "'Ayn Wad el Tinka." There is a story current of his having travelled to the DINKA (?) country in the far south and there by accident killed a stork which had built upon the roof of the royal residence—a heinous offence, in conse-

quence of which he fled northwards along the Ḳóz el Ḥágiz to el 'Ayn in the far north, where he died.

9. The NÁÍLÁB are the ruling family of GAMŪ'ÍA, that of Náṣir el Mek.

11. The "History of the Sudan" referred to is without doubt "D 7," of which the introduction should be consulted.

The "AWLÁD EL SHEIKH EL ṬAIB" (*see tree*) are the GAMŪ'ÍA of the village of Sheikh el Ṭaib, *i.e.* Sheikh Aḥmad el Ṭaib el Bashír, for whom see D 7, CCXXXV (and note).

15. Dafa'alla "el Gharḳán" (*i.e.* "the drowned") was a religious recluse living in Omdurmán. Since the Turkish days, *i.e.* for at least 33 years, he never emerged from his room. He was partly paralyzed and only a very select few ever had the *entrée* to his presence. For no other reason than the above he acquired a great reputation for sanctity. He died in 1917.

16. "El 'Anagáwi" (*see tree*) in other versions is "el Fungáwi."

The tribes mentioned as descended from Manṣūr the son of Gamū'a represent the subsections of the GAMŪ'ÍA.

XXII Cp. D 6, XXXIX. D 5 (*c*) speaks of Ṣubuḥ Abu Merkha, Ghánim's grandfather, as the first of the family to settle in the Sudan (paras. I–III). The Tartars took Baghdád in 1258 A.D.

XXIII This accounts for the frequent occurrence in *nisbas* of "FŪR" as descended from Dūla son of Kerdam the Ga'ali. One remembers too the name "Edrisdjal," *i.e.* Idrís el Ga'ali, as grandfather of Sulaymán Solon, one of the early FŪR kings, and how 'Abd el Kerím ibn Gáma'i the founder of the Wadái dynasty is said to have belonged to a Ga'ali family (see Introduction to Chap. I of Part III). Para. XXIV has reference to the second of these traditions.

XXIV See preceding note; and cp. Wüstenfeld, 11. Báriḳ is not mentioned. The remainder are all but correctly given.

XXV See Wüstenfeld, A, D, and J. "Rubáb" (رباب) should be "Ríáb" (رياب) and "Ṣayda" (صيدة) should be "Ḥayda" (حيده).

For Layla see Wüstenfeld, 2. The author seems to nod in representing Ḳuḍá'a as the son of Ma'ad ibn 'Adnán. Otherwise the genealogical facts are correct.

XXVI The accuracy of the first sentence is impugned by the author's own subsequent statements, *e.g.* as to the descent of the fourth tribe of GUHAYNA.

"Ghaylán" is generally written "'Aylán": cp. D 1 *passim*.

For "Guhayna ibn Rísh" see Wüstenfeld, H. "Rísh" (ريش) should be "Rayth" (ريث). The names of this Guhayna's ancestors as given do occur in Wüstenfeld, H, but with altered relationships.

For the second Guhayna see BA, LVIII and note thereto: "Anas" should be "Unays." This Guhayna belonged to the tribe of ḲUḌÁ'A.

For the third Guhayna see Wüstenfeld, 1. "Sawád" (سواد) should be "Sūd" (سود). The family of this Guhayna were neighbours of the family of the Fezára son of Dhubián who was very closely connected with the first Guhayna: see Wüstenfeld, p. 275 (*sub* Leith ben Sa'd).

For the fourth Guhayna cp. BA, LVII and note.

For the 52 tribes of GUHAYNA cp. BA, CXXIII.

The three sons of Baghíḍ according to Wüstenfeld (H) were Dhubián (father of Fezára), Anmár and 'Abs.

XXVII Cp. BA, C. There we get "Sha'ūf" (شعوف) for the "Shaḳūḳ" (شقوق) of ABC. The 'Abs mentioned here obviously represents the 'Abs son of Baghíḍ mentioned in the preceding note.

The genealogy of the NŪRÁB section of KABÁBÍSH is given in a confused manner: for instance, it is expressly mentioned that 'Ali ibn Nūr had "five sons," but reference is subsequently made to a sixth, viz. Kerádim.

On p. 195 of *Tribes...*, I have given a genealogical tree based on the version supplied orally by the chief men of the NŪRÁB themselves: it agrees fairly well with ABC. It will be noticed that the ROWÁḤLA, who are a section of the KABÁBÍSH, do not appear with the NŪRÁB, RIBAYḲÁT and other sections, *i.e.* as descended from Sufián, but among the descendants of Dhubián. There are sections of NŪRÁB called DÁR KEBÍR, DÁR UM BAKHÍT, AWLÁD EL KÍR, and DÁR SA'ÍD: hence the names of the sons of Nūr ibn 'Ali (*see tree*).

Sheikh 'Ali wad el Tóm is the present *náẓir* of the KABÁBÍSH.

XXVIII Cp. BA, LVI and LIX *et seq.*, etc.

In this section the author has several times confused the two men called Dhubián, viz. the son of Baghíḍ and the son of 'Abd: both are descended (*see tree*) from Baghíḍ, and in mentioning the full name of some of the descendants of the former he has, on reaching Dhubián, continued "...son of 'Abd," etc., instead of "...son of Baghíḍ," although he has previously made it clear that, as in all other *nisbas* of the GUHAYNA group, the persons and tribes mentioned are descended from the son of Baghíḍ. I have ignored these errors in the tree.

The name "'Abd el 'Azíz Maḥsin" is an amusing illustration of methods. Other *nisbas* give "'Abd el 'Azíz Maḥass (محس), ancestor of the MAḤASS"; but the author of ABC, himself a Maḥassi, has already provided (*see Tree* I) a better pedigree for his tribe, so he changes "Maḥass" to "Maḥsin" (محسن) by little more than the addition of a dot, and omits mention of the MAḤASS. He even makes mention of two different descendants of Dhubián called 'Abd el 'Azíz Maḥsin. The name Maḥsin occurs again in para. I (*see tree*).

The 'AWÁMRA are given as descendants of 'Omrán, whereas from their name they should clearly be descended from 'Ámir.

One gathers that, in the author's view, there are two different bodies of SHUKRÍA, one descended from Yashkur and one from Bashír. They generally appear in *nisbas* as descended from Bashír. For Yashkur cp. D 7, XI. For the descent of the ruling family of the SHUKRÍA, the AWLÁD ABU SIN, from ḲURAYSH, see C 5.

There is a village called el Ḳalḳála close to el Kámlín.

Cp. BA, XCIV for the DAWÁGIRA.

'Áíd ibn Ḥusayn has not previously been mentioned....

The presentation of the descendants of Dhubián is very inaccurate even if judged by the standard of other *nisbas*. *E.g.* Kungar as ancestor of the "Borḳu, Bornu and Afnu" [*i.e.* Houssa], and with a son "Fellát," is ridiculous; and "Maḳáḳla" for "Ma'aḳla" and "Habbánía" for "Habábín" are really bad mistakes.

xxix Cp. BA, cxxiv.

xxxi Cp. D 1, ciii; and also BA, clxxv and A 2, xl, etc.

xxxii Cp. BA, clxxvi.

xxxiii Cp. BA, clxxvii.

xxxiv Cp. BA, clxxviii.

xxxv "Arabs" here, as so often, means nomad Arabs.

xxxvi "Masámida" I take to represent Maṣámida, *i.e.* Maṣmūda Berbers (see App. to Part II, Ch. 1).

xxxviii The well-known Awlád 'Ali nomads of Egypt are intended.

xliv In the Appendix will be found an account of the Kanūz by one of their number. For "Dowlat el Kanzi," that is Kanz el Dowla, see Part II, Chaps. 1 and 2.

xlv Cp. D 1, clxxxii.

xlvi Cp. BA, xliv. This is an amazing statement! See BA, xliv.

xlviii Cp. BA, ccxv. By "Um 'Ar'ara" are meant the tribe commonly known as Amarar.

l See Vol. 1, p. 138.

lii Practically all the tribes mentioned in this paragraph are Baḳḳára of western Kordofán and Dárfūr. See Part III, Ch. 3; and for the last two named see Vol. 1, pp. 85 and 336 respectively.

liii See Vol. 1, p. 268.

liv The tribes alluded to in this and the following paragraphs are known as Zenárkha and Masháíkha. For the latter, and particularly Sheikh Ya'aḳūb, see D 3, 255.

The name Masháíkha (*sing.* Mushakhi) is said to be complimentary to their nobility of descent, *i.e.* to be properly a sobriquet (cp. Burton, *Pilgrimage...*, 1, 58). Most of the Masháíkha are near Khartoum and others are at Sennár, Abu Ḥaráz, Kabūshía, in the Gezíra, etc. They consist of no more than scattered families. Eleven generations are given as having elapsed since the time of el Mugelli.

The Zenárkha, as the author says, live among the Gamū'ía, to the south of Omdurmán, but are independent and have their own sheikh, though in past days they obeyed the call of the Gamū'ía *naḥás*.

lv The 'Aṭáíáb are in Kassala.

The biography of Ḥammad "ibn Mariam" (or "Wad Um Mariūm," "Um Mariūm," etc.) is No. 124 in D 3, *q.v.* (note) for the nickname.

Bandi is an island between the Shablūka and Shendi.

lvi For the Ḥammattíáb (Ḥammadtuwiáb?) see D 3, 21 and 158.

APPENDIX[1]

The Kanūz

SECTION I

The KANŪZ are divided into two tribes.

Firstly. There are the descendants of el Sayyid Muḥammad Wanas son of Raḥma son of Ḥasan, whose pedigree reaches to el Faḍl son of 'Abdulla son of el 'Abbás. The *amír* Muḥammad Wanas had six sons, and he died and was buried at the burial-place [*gabána*] of Aṣwán.

These sons were:

1. IDRÍS, the eldest, ancestor of el Melik Ṭunbul[2] of Arḳó Island, [whose family] are known as the kings of Dongola.

2. ḤAMDULLA. He had few descendants. Such as exist are at Kalábsha and are known as the WANASÁB EL ḤAMDULLÁB after their ancestor.

3. ARKHI. His descendants are in the Gezíra and the Sudan, and their tribe is called the ARKHIÁB.

4. AD·HAM. [His descendants are] at el Khaṭára and the island of Aṣwán, but most of them are in the Sudan. Branches of them are BELÍLÁB and MUSALLAMÁB.

5. 'ADLÁN. His mother was from the Oases [*el Wáḥát*]. His descendants are at Aṣwán and in the Sudan; and they include the tribe of 'ADLÁNÁB[3] among the SHÁÍḲÍA.

6. KHAYRULLA. His descendants are the KHAYRULLÁB, who are in the province of Aṣwán. Most of them are in the Sudan.

Secondly. We will next mention the noble chieftains called Awlád Tamím el Dár[4] el Anṣári, three in number.

1. The *amír* Sheraf el Dín who had two sons and was buried at Cairo at the Gate of Victory (*Báb el Naṣr*): his sons were Madhnáb, whose tribe is called the ḲURNÁB and resides at Abu Hūr and in the Sudan, and Begū, whose tribe is called the BEGWÁB and resides at Abu Hūr and in the Sudan.

2. Naṣr el Dín Tamím el Dár, whose son was Naṣrulla. The latter's tribe is called the NAṢRULLÁB and resides at Kasengar and [among] the SHÁÍḲÍA.

[1] This brief account of the Kanūz was written for me at Omdurmán in 1914 by el Ṣadíḳ 'Ísa one of the chief men of the tribe residing there.

The Kanūz are now rightly reckoned as one of the main divisions of the Nūbian race living between Dongola and Egypt. They are no doubt a blend of those Awlád Kanz Arabs, who in 1365 conquered Aswán and for some time dominated the surrounding country, and the older Nūbian stock. See Part II.

[2] On the island of Tombos, near Kerma, is "a fortress built by Muḥammad Wad Ṭunbul, king of Arḳô, and here are the tombs of his ancestors" (Budge, II, 372).

[3] For the 'Adlánáb contrast D 5 (*c*), XXVI and XXXIV.

[4] The Awlád Tamím el Dár, however, were Beni Lakhm and not Awlad Kanz at all (see Wüstenfeld, 5, and *Ibid*. I, 441, 442).

3. Tomám, son of Tamím el Dár, [*i.e.*] the *amir* Nigm el Dín ["Star of Religion"], who was buried at Cairo at the Gate of Victory, had four sons, viz.:

(*a*) Um Bárak ibn Nigm el Dín, whose descendants are called the UMBÁRAKÁB and live in Upper Egypt and the Sudan.

(*b*) 'Ónulla ibn Nigm el Dín, whose descendants are called the 'ÓNULLÁB and live in Upper Egypt and the Sudan.

(*c*) Ghulámulla ibn Nigm el Dín, whose descendants are called the ḤARBÍÁB and live in Upper Egypt and the Sudan.

(*d*) 'Ámir ibn Nigm el Dín, whose descendants are called the AWLÁD 'OMRÁN[1] and live in Upper Egypt and Kordofán [in] the Sudan.

SECTION II

The following are said to be the 27 divisions of Kanūz in Upper Egypt and the Sudan[2].

1.	El Wanasáb	At Aṣwán, Khartoum, Omdurman, and Khartoum North		
2.	El Mududáb	"	"	
3.	El Huzayláb	"	"	and el Káwa.
4.	El 'Ónulláb	"	"	and Butri and el Mesallamía.
5.	El Umbárakáb	"	"	and Berber and el Dámer.
6.	Abu Hūr	"	"	and Berber.
7.	El Geraysáb	"	"	and el Kámlín.
8.	Dabód	"	"	"
9.	El Khayrulláb	"	"	and Shendi.
10.	El Ad·hamáb	"	"	and in Dár Fung.
11.	El Ghidaysáb	"	"	
12.	El Naṣrulláb	"	"	
13.	El Bughdaláb	"	"	
14.	El Rífía	"	"	and el Kámlín.
15.	El Sálmáb	"	"	and Berber.
16.	El Ḥawátín	"	"	"
17.	El Felláḥín	"	"	and Shendi.
18.	El Wáznáb	"	"	
19.	El Ṭónáb	"	"	
20.	El Begwáb	"	"	
21.	El Ḥowwasháb	"	"	and Shendi.
22.	El Ṭáyibáb	"	"	
23.	El Gazayra	"	"	
24.	El Ḥagáb	"	"	
25.	El Gharbía	"	"	
26.	El Beláláb	"	"	and Dongola.
27.	El Nuḳdáb	"	"	

[1] *The Beni* [*Awlád*] *'Omrán are a small tribe living among the Bedayria in Kordofán near el Obeid.*

[2] *Nos.* 1, 3 *and* 15 *come from Kalábsha and are sometimes spoken of by that name: these form a majority in the Sudan. The Kanūz are chiefly employed in the workshops of the Steamers and Railways Departments, and as servants. From Section I it seems that Nos.* 9 *and* 10 *and, again, Nos.* 4, 5, 12, 20, *are respectively connected by close ties.*

MANUSCRIPT A 1

Introduction

A FEW years after the reoccupation of the Sudan a Ga'ali named Muḥammad 'Ali Kenán obtained this pedigree from the late Sheikh el Bedowi of Omdurmán, who was Ḳáḍi of Berber in the Mahdía and President of the Board of 'Ulema for some years after the re-occupation.

It corresponds to paragraphs CLXII to CCX of MS. AB, but the relation between AB and Sheikh el Bedowi's copy is not known. Probably paragraphs CLXII to CCX of the former were copied from the latter.

Compare A 5.

I In the name of God....

II—L (*Here follows a replica of the text of* AB *from para.* CLXII *to para.* CCX *inclusive, identical therewith word for word with the exceptions given in the notes to paragraphs* CXXIX *and* CXL–CLXI *of* BA.)

LI (*This paragraph is in nature of a postscript and is written in a different and rougher hand: it commences " This pedigree was asked for by*[1] *Muḥammad 'Ali son of...etc.," as in the tree, and ends "...son of Ma'ad son of 'Adnán."*)

LII Beyond 'Adnán [the tracing of pedigrees] was forbidden by the Lawgiver, upon whom be the blessings of God....

LIII A pedigree from on high, well guarded and indisputable:
There is no pedigree to compare with it.
Pearls heaped high from of old: a pure light
Beyond that of the Heavenly Twins.

A pedigree by whose sweetness the noble ones are known:
The Heavenly Twins encircle it.
Lo here a necklace precious and magnificent,
For Thou art in it: the rarest of all pearls.

[1] *I.e.* Muḥammad 'Ali applied to Sheikh el Bedowi for a copy.

TREE ILLUSTRATING MS. A 1

↑

Ḳuṣai
'Abd Menáf
Háshim
'Abd el Muṭṭalib
'Abdulla
el 'Abbás
'Abdulla
el Faḍl
Sa'ad el Anṣári
Dhu el Kilá'a el Ḥimyari
Yáṭil
Háṭil
Kerab
Ḳuṣáṣ
'Adi
Yemen
Ḳays
Idrís
Ibráhím
Aḥmad
Masrūḳ
Ḥarḳán
Buḍá'a
Abu el Dís

Kerdam
Serrár
Mismár
Sa'ad el Feríd
Ḥákim
Sáíl
Gamíl
Selma
Abu Turki (ancestor of the Ṭerayfía and so named after his father's brother Abu Turki)
Ḥasán
Muṭrab
Sáíl
Bishára
Náṣir
'Ali
Gábir
Ḥusayn
Muḥammad
el Ḥág Ḥusayn
Kenán
Muḥammad 'Ali

MANUSCRIPT A 2

Introduction

THE *nisba* here translated was a copy made for me by Isḥáḳ Muḥammad Sheddád, a Bedayri of Bára in Kordofán, from the copy in his possession.

The latter is alleged to have been copied by Sheikh 'Omára 'Awūda Shakál el Ḳáriḥ (*q.v.* para. XLIV), who lived in Dongola about the middle of the seventeenth century, from the original work of "el Samarḳandi." Compare, however, the introduction to A 3.

This is a true copy of the original pedigree.

I In the name of God...

This is the pedigree of el Sheikh Isḥáḳ ibn el Sheikh Muḥammad Aḥmad Sheddád: Isḥáḳ son of...(*The pedigree is given from son to father, up to el 'Abbás, as in the tree.*)

II And of el 'Abbás the Prophet...said "Nobility pertains to me and to my uncle Ḥamza and to el 'Abbás"; whose lineage finally reaches to 'Adnán.

III And the Prophet...said "Whosoever goes beyond this...etc."

IV *A Copy of the Pedigrees of All the Arabs.*

Verily the noble man begot noble [children].

V–XIII Now Ṣubuḥ...(*From this point to the end of para.* XIII *the text closely corresponds to that of* A 11 (*paras.* XVI *to* XXVII: *all such variations, additions and omissions as occur will be seen from the trees and the notes to* A 2 *and* A 11. *The arrangement is occasionally altered but the source is obviously one.*)

XIV–XXI Rubáṭ had five sons...(*The copyist having omitted the subject-matter of paras.* XXVIII *to* XXXIX *of* A 11, *which are very corrupt, from here onwards to para.* XXI *gives practically the same details as are in paras.* XL *to* XLVI *of* A 11. *For variations see the trees and notes to* A 2 *and* A 11.)

XXII Now the 'ABBÁSIYYŪN, or the 'ABBÁS, are the family of Abu 'Abdulla el Saffáḥ, who is Muḥammad son of 'Abdulla son of 'Ali son of 'Abdulla son of el 'Abbás; and Ibráhím Ga'al is descended from Sa'ad son of el Faḍl son of 'Abdulla son of el 'Abbás; so they [the 'ABBÁSIYYŪN] and the GA'ALIYYŪN have their first common ancestor in 'Abdulla son of el 'Abbás son of 'Abd el Muṭṭalib son of Háshim. Here ends the pedigree of Ga'al.

XXIII The above is what I have found. Now the 'ABBÁSIYYŪN held the power at Isbaḥ'án because they were of the family of Háshim, and the BENI OMMAYYA took it from them, and the 'ABBÁSIYYŪN were impotent until the time of Muḥammad Abu 'Abdulla el Saffáḥ. He then wrested the power from the BENI OMMAYYA, and took it for himself, and slew them there with great slaughter till he had taken their place in the land and put an end to them.

XXIV The KAWÁHLA are descended from el Zubayr ibn el 'Awwám, and their mother was Ṣafía; and according to el Samarḳandi they are the family of Káhil son of 'Ámir son of Khalífa Ibayraḳ son of Muḥammad son of Sulaymán son of Khálid son of el Walíd.

XXV The SHUKRÍA are a great tribe, renowned for their bravery. They are descended from Shukr son of Idrís, and their genealogies are traced to 'Abdulla el Gawád son of Ga'afir son of Abu Ṭálib son of 'Abd el Muṭṭalib (surnamed 'Abd Menáf).

XXVI Similarly the ḤASÁNÍA are [descended] from the family of Ga'afir son of Abu Ṭálib and are the children of Ḥasán son of Gamíl, and their pedigree reaches to 'Abdulla el Gawád son of Ga'afir son of Abu Ṭálib.

XXVII The RIKÁBIYYŪN are the family of Rikáb son of 'Abdulla and their genealogies are traced to el Sheikh Aḥmad el Zíla'i.

XXVIII The FÁDNÍA are the descendants of the noble el Sayyid Muḥammad, son of el Imám 'Ali, known as "Ibn el Ḥanafía."

XXIX The MESALLAMÍA are the family of Musallam son of Ḥegáz son of 'Áṭif el Ommawi, [who] migrated from Syria [*el Shám*] in the days of 'Omar ibn 'Abd el 'Azíz (God bless him), and settled in the Sudan.

XXX The 'AMRIYYŪN (spelt with 'AMR...) are the family of Sulaymán son of 'Abd el Malik son of Marwán the Ommawi. It is said that they ruled the blacks in the Sudan and the country of the HAMAG, and finally [*lit.* "until"] they became assimilated to them in every respect and came to be known as "the FUNG." The reason of their emigration [*i.e.* from Arabia] was thus: Sulaymán fled to the Sudan in the time of the Khalífate of Abu 'Abdulla Muḥammad el Saffáḥ, who was the first of the BENI 'ABBÁS to hold that position, and who wrested the power from Marwán, who is said to have been the last of the BENI OMMAYYA dynasty. Abu 'Abdulla continued laughtering the BENI OMMAYYA and subjecting them till he had taken their place throughout the country. So Sulaymán fled to Abyssinia and settled there for a time. Then news reached him that el Saffáḥ had pursued [?] the BENI OMMAYYA after their dispersion into [various] countries and had finally overtaken Muḥammad ibn el Walíd ibn Háshim in Spain [*el Andalus*] and slain him. Sulaymán therefore fled from Abyssinia to the Sudan and settled there and married the daughter of one of the kings of the Sudan. By her he had two sons, the one named Dáūd and the other Ans. Then [Sulaymán] died, and the names [of his sons] got altered, and Dáūd was called Oudūn, and Ans was called Ounṣ. Ounṣ was ancestor of the OUNṢÁB, and Dáūd of the OUDŪNÁB. These [descendants of Sulaymán] multiplied among the blacks and finally they became fused with them in every respect, and their power flourished and they became those rulers of the Sudan who are known from history. The first king of this stock in Sennár was the Sultan 'Omára, and the power passed from Sultan to Sultan till the time of the Sultan Bádi whose rule ended with the Turkish conquest of Sennár in the Sudan. Ends. This is what we have found.

XXXI As regards FEZÁRA, their pedigree is well known: they are a tribe of BENI TAMÍM, who settled in the Sudan.

XXXII The BENI 'ÁMIR are the family of 'Ámir and occupied Abyssinia and are its rulers.

XXXIII KENÁNA are a great and famous tribe in the Sudan and are the family of Deḳaym el Kenáni, an important[1] and unblemished family: they dwell in the same parts of the country as FEZÁRA.

XXXIV The GÁBIRÍA are numerous in Abyssinia; [but] most of them [are] between the MAḤASS and the well-known [town of] Dongola. They are the family of Gábir son of 'Abdulla el Anṣári. When Dongola was occupied, at the time of its siege, the majority of them assisted the armies of the Muslims in the expedition of 'Amr ibn el 'Áṣi (God bless him).

XXXV RUFÁ'A were settled at the first among the BEGA: then.... They are [one] of the tribes of ḲUṬÁF.

XXXVI The GABARTA[2] are by origin Arabs.

XXXVII FELLÁTA are the children of 'Uḳba; and the writers of genealogies relate that the sheikh who was in Upper Egypt [*Arḍ el Ṣa'id*] and known as el Sheikh Mugelli was one of them[3]. Their pedigree goes back to 'Abd el Raḥman son of Abu Bukr el Ṣadíḳ (God bless him).

XXXVIII The ḤADÁRBA are a well-known tribe. El Samarḳandi says "I heard from el Sheikh 'Abdulla ibn el Wuzír el Ḥadrami that they declare they [came] originally from Ḥaḍramaut and migrated inland

[1] reading وءال راجح for من ءال بحراج.

[2] reading جبرتة for جبرية.

[3] reading فانه منهم for فانهم منهم.

in the time of el Ḥaggág ibn Yūsef and settled with the BEGA till they became [a part] of them and ruled at Sūákin el Gezíra, and settled there on the coasts of the salt sea of the Sudan."

XXXIX The BERÍÁB are ASHRÁF descended from el Ḥusayn.

XL The GA'ÁFIRA are a great tribe: their pedigree goes back to Ga'afir ibn Ḳuṭáf of the tribe of ṬAI, and it is said that Ma'atab ibn Ḥátim el Ṭáí was [one] of them. They are famous by [containing among their number] Kerdam and others whom we have not space to mention. Ends.

XLI Now this pedigree has been transcribed from el Samarḳandi the Great, from the original. As regards the pedigree given as that of the transcriber of it, there is no need to expand it [any further] here.

XLII Now 'Armán and Nimayr and Muḥammad are the sons of 'Abd Rabbihi son of 'Armán son of Ḍūáb son of Ghánim [son of Ḥamaydán] son of Ṣubuḥ Abu Merkha son of Mismár, who is brother of Samra the father of el Bedayri (the ancestor of the BEDAYRÍA); and both of them (Mismár and Samra) are the sons of Serrár ibn Kerdam, as has just been explained from the beginning as far back as 'Adnán.

XLIII And of 'Adnán one has said "How many a father owes the nobility which he possesses to his son, even as 'Adnán owes his to the Prophet of God...."

XLIV This pedigree, which has the authority of past generations, and which was transcribed from [the work of] el Samarḳandi the Great, as we mentioned above, was transcribed by el Sheikh 'Omára el Sheikh 'Awūda Shakál el Ḳáriḥ, and preserved and verified, and upon it are the signatures of the *'omad* and notables and *Khalífas* and learned men whose names appear below.

The signature and seal of el Ostádh Mirghani Sowár el Dhahab, "*Khalífat el Khulafá*" in Dongola and representative of the Khatmía.

El Sheikh Mukhṭár Sáti Muḥammad el Obayyaḍ, and his seal.

The signature and seal of el Sheikh el Ḳáḍi Sáti Muḥammad ibn el Ḳáḍi Muḥammad Ṣáliḥ.

The signature and seal of el Sheikh Muḥammad Ṭáha Muḥammad Nūr el Khuṭ (?), *Khalífa* of Tanḳassi.

The signature and seal of the *Khalífa* 'Abd el Ḳádir Yūsef, the *Khalífa* of el Sheikh 'Awūda el Ḳáriḥ.

The signature and seal of el Sheikh Sáti Muḥammad Muḥammad Ziáda.

The signature and seal of el Sheikh Muḥammad Ḥasan el Sheikh 'Abd el Gelíl Ḥabūba.

El Sheikh Muḥammad Aḥmad 'Ísa.

The signature and seal of the *'omda* Sa'íd Muḥammad Feraḥ, *'omda* of Tanḳassi Island and district.

The *Khalífa* 'Omára Muḥammad 'Ísa, and his handwriting.

The signature and seal of the *Khalífa* Muḥammad Ḥasan Sáti, *Khalífa* of el Ḥág...(*illegible*).

The signature and seal of el Sheikh Ḥámid Muḥammad 'Ísa.

El Sheikh Aḥmad el Ḳurashi Muḥammad Ahmed.

El Sheikh Muḥammad Sulaymán Medani.

El Sheikh Aḥmad Muḥammad Magdhūb.

The *Khalífa* 'Othmán Aḥmad Ḳurashi.

The signature and seal of el Sheikh Ḳumr (?) Idrís Muṣṭafa Maḥmūd.

The signature and seal of el Sheikh Bábikr Sáti Muḥammad el Obayyaḍ.

The signature and seal of el Sheikh Muḥammad Aḥmad el Feki 'Abd el Raḥman.

The signature and seal of el Sheikh Muḥammad Aḥmad 'Abd el Raḥím, *mázūn* of Tanḳassi.

The signature and seal of the *Khalífa* el Sheikh Ibráhím el Dásuḳi.

Seal of el Sheikh 'Abd el Wahháb Aḥmad Ṣughayr, the *Khalífa*, in his handwriting.

El Sheikh Muḥammad Ṭáha ibn *el feki* (?) Aḥmad el 'Álim.

The *'omda* Sináda Muḥammad Feraḥ.

El Sheikh Gerár (?) Muḥammad Feraḥ.

And others.

A 2 (NOTES)

I Cp. BA, CXXXIII (note), A 3, XV, and AB, XXXIX *et seq.*

"Ḥūzabi" is very doubtful: the copyist writes first حيضري ("Ḥaydari") and then over it حوزبي ("Ḥūzabi") or حدزبي ("Ḥadzabi").

II Cp. A 8, V.

III Cp. BA, CXXXV (note).

V–XIII Ṣubuḥ Abu Merkha is here called "Ṣubuḥ Abu Muraḳa'a, but this form does not occur elsewhere. The only emendations made in paras. V–XIII is "Ghaním" for "Ghaníma."

The "MÁÍDÍA" occur also as "MÁGIDÍA" (see note to D 3, 200 and 108).

Para. XI closes with "They" (*sc.* the 13 sons of 'Armán) "died unmarried." This may be a gloss by the latest copyist to save the trouble of giving any more lists of descendants. In para. XLII he actually gives certain descendants of 'Armán by way of a postscript.

Para. XIII opens with "Ḥammad el Bahkarūb begot the NAHKAR" (by slip for BAHKAR), although Ḥammad el Bahkarūb has not been previously mentioned. Presumably he is the "Ḥammad surnamed Kati" of para. XII, and "bi Kati" may be an error for "bi Bahkarūb." A 11 (XXV and XXVII) calls him "el Bahkūr."

XIV–XXI Cp. A 11, XL.

As to Rubáṭ and Sa'ad el Feríd being sons of Mismár see note on the genealogical tree.

"Maḳbuḍ" (مقبض) is an emendation of "Mafḍub" (مفضب).

"SAḲÁRANG" is an emendation of "SAḲÁRAG," and "BORNŪ" of "BORNA."

A 2 (para. XVII) says "Ḥákim begot the ḤÁKIMÁB, the people of Arḳó Island. Gábir begot the MAḤASS, the kings of Khandaḳ and Dongola"; but A 11 omits this.

After "kings of Teḳali" A 2 adds "who are the original royal stock," and after "TOMÁM" adds "in the west": A 11 contains neither of these remarks.

XXII This and para. XXIII are not in A 11, though cp. A 11, LIX.

For "Abu 'Abdulla" see note to BA, CCXIII.

"Is descended from Sa'ad" is given literally as "is son of Sa'ad."

XXIV Cp. BA, CXVIII, CXXIV; A 11, XLVIII; C 1; D 2, XIX and D 1, CXXXI.

The version of D 1 reconciles the two accounts given in A 2. A 11 gives "'Omára" for "'Ámir."

Wüstenfeld (*q.v.* S) gives no "Sulaymán" as son of Khálid: the latter was of the BENI MAKHZŪM.

The name "Ibayraḳ" is clearly connected with "BERÁḲNA," the name of one of the main sub-tribes of the KAWÁHLA.

XXV. Cp. A 11, L and D 2, XXXI.

For 'Abdulla ibn Ga'afir see Wüstenfeld, Y.

'Abd el Muṭṭalib was grandson of 'Abd Menáf.

XXVI Contrast D 1, CLXXI and cp. D 2, XXXIV.

XXVII Cp. BA, CLXXIX, etc.

XXVIII Cp. BA, CLXXIV, etc.

XXIX Cp. BA, CLXXVIII, etc.

XXX Cp. BA, CCXIII, etc.

For a different account of Ounsa and Oudūn see tree of B 1.

XXXI Cp. A 11, LIV, etc.

XXXII Cp. BA, CCXV; A 11, LV and D 2, XLI.

XXXIII Cp. A 11, LVI; D 1, CXL and D 2, XIII.

This paragraph and A 11, LVI originate from the same source but the copyist must be wrong in one case. The reading of A 11 is the better, viz. وءال راجح وءال سليم in place of A 2, viz. من ءال بحراج وءال سليم.

"Deḳaym" should probably be "Deghaym" (see D 2, XIII).

XXXIV Cp. BA, CXLVIII and A 11, LVII.

The reference is to the conquest of Dongola in 652 A.D. by 'Abdulla ibn Sa'ad. I can find no record of 'Abdulla's having a son Gábir.

XXXV Cp. A 11, LVIII and D 2, XIV.

After "then" is written تجري: the meaning is evidently that they migrated (see Part III, Chap. 2 (*a*)). For "ḲUṬÁF" A 11 gives ḲAḤṬÁN.

XXXVI Cp. BA, CLXXVII and A 11, LX.

XXXVII Cp. BA, CXIX and A 11, LXI (and notes).

By "'Uḳba" is meant 'Uḳba ibn Yásir.

For 'Abd el Raḥman see Wüstenfeld, R.

El Sheikh Mugelli is the Mashaykhi mentioned in D 3, 255 and ABC, LIV.

XXXVIII See BA, CLXXVI and D 7, LI.

XXXIX This paragraph appears only in A 2.

XL Cp. BA, CLXXV and A 11, LXIII.

A 2 and A 11 give "Ḳuṭáf" for Ḳaḥṭán (BA): cp. para. XXXV.

XLII See note on paras. V–XIII.

XLIII Cp. BA, CCXXIX and AB, XXX.

XLIV 'Awūda ibn 'Omar Shakál el Ḳáriḥ's biography is in D 3 (No. 66). He was the pupil of a pupil of Ḥasan wad Ḥasūna, who died in 1664, and he was alive in 1659.

Khalífa, literally "a successor," is used to mean the head of a religious sect.

The Khatmía includes the Morghanía *ṭariḳa*.

Tanḳassi Island is close to Debba, in Dongola.

The signatories appear to be mostly GA'ALIÍN (including BEDAYRÍA). This practice of obtaining certificates of authenticity from well-known religious persons is not uncommon: cp. A 8.

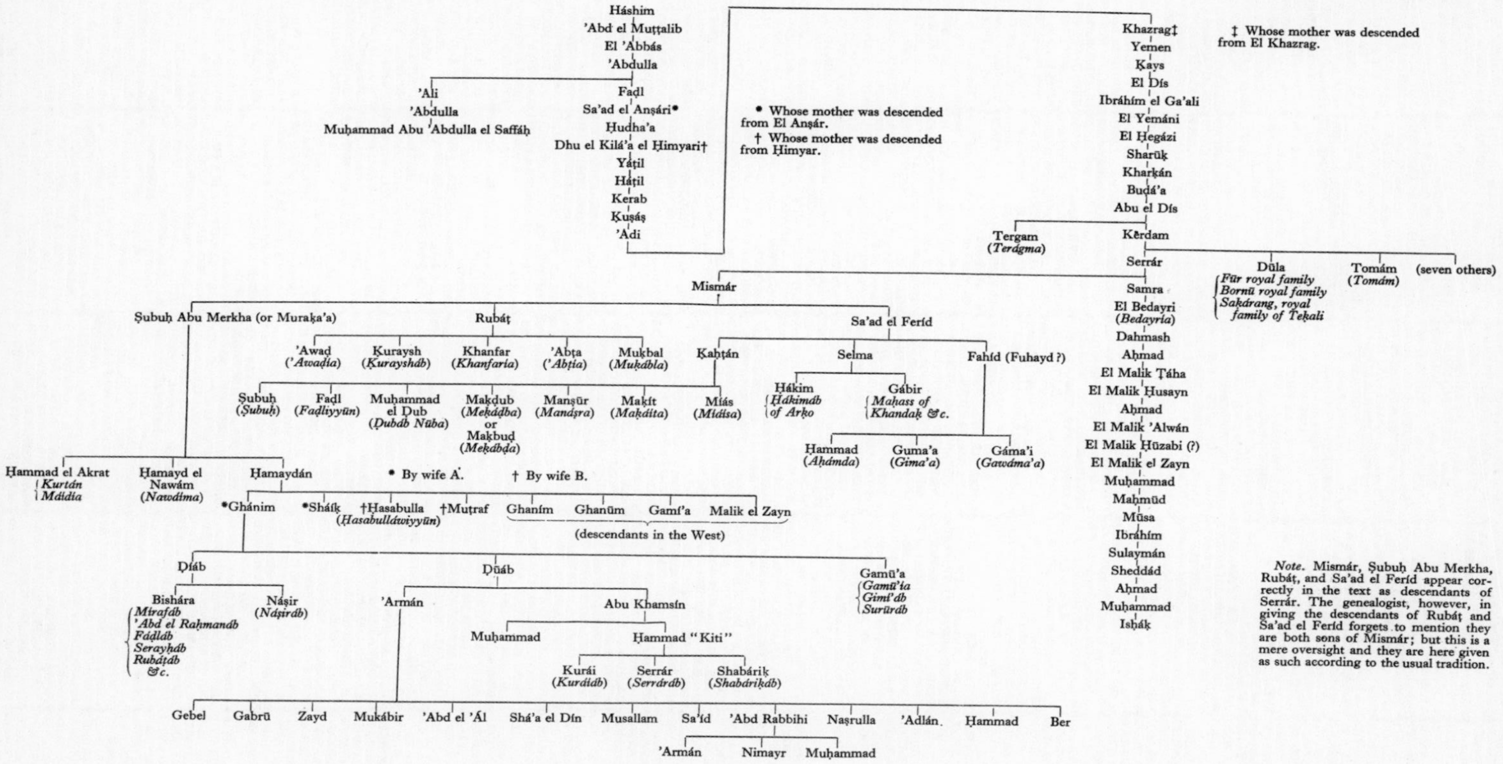

Note. Mismár, Ṣubuḥ Abu Merkha, Rubáṭ, and Sa'ad el Feríd appear correctly in the text as descendants of Serrár. The genealogist, however, in giving the descendants of Rubáṭ and Sa'ad el Feríd forgets to mention they are both sons of Mismár; but this is a mere oversight and they are here given as such according to the usual tradition.

MANUSCRIPT A 3

Introduction

THIS *nisba* was copied for me by el Ṣáfi Sulaymán, *'omda* of the BISHÁRÍA MA'ÁḲLA in Kordofán, in 1909, from the copy in his possession.

From a comparison of paragraphs II of A 4 and XIII of A 3 it seems that both A 3 and A 4 are extracts from the pedigree of Muḥammad ibn 'Ísa Sowár el Dhahab, and that this latter was supposed to have been brought from Mekka by "el Sheikh Kámil el Murshid."

Now Kámil is said to have been a Bedayri, and so was Muḥammad ibn 'Ísa Sowár el Dhahab; and Isḥáḳ Sheddád, whose pedigree we have in A 2, is also a Bedayri, of the same section as Muḥammad ibn 'Ísa. D 3 contains (No. 191) the biography of the last named. He lived, as his descendants still do, in Dongola, and he was a contemporary and friend (see D 3, 191) of that 'Awūda whose son made a copy of A 2 (*q.v.* para. XLIV). Evidently, therefore, A 2, A 3 and A 4, though varying in minor details (*q.v.* in the trees), all represent extracts from a *nisba* which was current in Dongola about the middle of the seventeenth century, and which in one form or another was used by the compiler of AB.

I In the name of God....

[The following is] an extract from the pedigrees of the tribes of the Arabs from the noble tradition as related by el Termidhi and Ibn Nági and el Bokhári and Muslim.

II And [it is related] upon the authority of Abu Hurayra concerning the Prophet...[that he said] "Ye know [from] your pedigrees how ye are connected."

III The Almighty said "And I have made you races and tribes, that ye may know one another. The noblest of you in God's sight is the most pious of you."

IV The tribes whom it is not permitted to enslave are, according to *El Gáma'i el Ṣughayr fí hadíth el bashír el Ḳádir* ["The small encyclopaedia on the tradition of the mighty evangelist"],

ḲURAYSH	MUZAYNA	GHAFÁR[1]
EL ANṢÁR	ASLAM	ḤIMYAR[2]
GUHAYNA	ASHGA'A	KHUZAYMA[3]

[1] reading غفار for عفار. [2] reading حميار for حميارة.
[3] reading خزيمة for حزيمة.

V And the noblest of these...(*continues as* BA, XLIX, *down to* ..."*boast*").

VI And according to the tradition related by Abu Mūsa, ḲURAYSH were, in the time of the Prophet..., eighty[1] tribes.

VII Now GU'UL, considered as a whole, are [descended from]... (*continues as* BA, CXXXII, *down to*...*Háshim*).

VIII The Prophet...said "Carry not your pedigrees beyond 'Adnán."

IX As regards the BENI MA'AMŪR...(*continues as* BA, CXXXI).

X It has been explained that Gu'ul's name was Ibráhím, and he was called Gu'ul because...(*continues as* BA, CXXXII, *i.e.* AB, CLXV).

XI Most of GUHAYNA are...(*continues as* AB, CXXXVI, *for which see* BA, LI).

XII Now there are [also] seven tribes apart from...(*continues as* AB, CXXXVII).

XIII Now this account is the true one, and I was given it from the manuscript of the scribes at Mekka the Noble by el Sheikh Kámil el Murshid. This is the pedigree of the people.

XIV Now the man who collected the whole of the tribe of GU'UL together was Kerdam, and he lived in the Ḥegáz and the fertile lands, and whosoever is not among his descendants is no Ga'ali.

XV The true pedigree is as follows: Kerdam son of Abu el Dís son of Buḍá'a...(*etc., up to Háshim: see tree*).

XVI–XXXV Serrár was ancestor...(*continues like* AB, CLXX*: et seq. The details as given here concerning Serrár's descendants will be found in the tree, which corresponds largely to the tree of* AB).

XXXVI This is what appeared to us and was made clear.

XXXVII The pedigree of MA'ÁḲLA is from GUHAYNA.

XXXVIII Sahal had three sons, 'Ál and Ma'ál and 'Abd el 'Ál: 'Ál begot the MA'ÁLIA, and Ma'ál begot the MA'ÁḲLA, and 'Abd el 'Ál begot the ZAYÁDÍA and the MEGÁNÍN.

XXXIX The MA'ÁḲLA are the descendants of two men, Ḳál and Wál. Ḳál had two sons, Ḥubaysh and Ramaḍán. Ḥubaysh's descendants are the BISHÁRÍA and the SAMÁ'ÍN and KANÁKÍL and AWLÁD BADR. Ramaḍán's descendants are KAGÁBÍL and 'ABÁDÍA and AWLÁD ḤARAYZ.

[1] reading ثمانين for ثمانية.

A 3 (NOTES)

I For "el Termidhi" see AB, CVI.

El Bokhári is the most famous of the Ḳuránic commentators (see Huart, pp. 217–220).

"Muslim" is Abu el Ḥusayn ibn el Ḥaggág, author of a *Ṣaḥiḥ* (see Huart, pp. 218, 219).

"Ibn Nági" may be the Ibn Abu Nágih mentioned by el Maḳrízi (*Kheṭáṭ*, I, 275).

II Cp. BA, III (note).

III Cp. BA, XXIII, etc.

IV Cp. AB, CXXXII and BA, XLVIII. The author of *El Gáma'i el Ṣughayr* was Gelál el Dín el Siūti (1445–1505).

KENÁNA is obviously omitted here by a slip.

VI Cp. BA, CXXX and AB, CLXII.

VII For "GU'UL" (instead of "GA'AL") cp. D 6, XI. The word translated "considered as a whole" is معدودة.

VIII Cp. BA, CXXXV, etc.

XI This paragraph agrees entirely with AB (as opposed to BA) except that the words "in Baṣra and" are omitted after "Ḥimyar."

The word translated in BA, LI, "mixed with" is متخرجة in A 3, ممزوجة in BA, and ممتزجة in AB: the last is probably correct.

XII The spelling here varies from that in AB, CXXXVII: "BAG" in AB is "BEGÁ" in A 3, "KHASHBA" in AB is "ḤASHBA" in A 3, "GHIBRA" (AB) becomes "ḲIBRAT" (A 3), and "'ÁTHIR" becomes "'ÁFIR."

XIII The Arabic of "I was given..." is

قابلتها بنسخة كتبة بمكة المشرفة عن الشيخ كامل المرشد.

For Kámil el Murshid cp. A 4, II.

XIV Cp. AB, CLXVI.

For "the fertile lands" (الارياف) the text of A 3 gives "el 'Iráḳ" (العراق). AB gives الارياف.

XV Cp. AB, XXXIX and BA, CXXXIII *et seq.*

XVI–XXXV The text of these sections contains only what is in the tree. "Suwayḥ" is written for "Shuwayḥ," "ḲODIÁT" for "GHODIÁT," "Ghomar" for "'Omar," and (once) "Ḥamayd" for "Ḥamaydán": these four slips have been corrected in the tree.

The fact that "Ḥamayd el Nawám" is spoken of proves that A 3 was not taken from AB, for AB expressly condemns that version (see BA, CLIV, note). The original of A 3, on the contrary, was evidently used by the author of AB.

The names of 14 sons of Ḥammad el Akrat are given as in the tree, but the form in each case, *e.g.* "Serrárábi," "Náfa'ábi," etc., is not that of a proper name but of a member of a sub-tribe; *i.e.* the son's name would be "Serrár," "Náfa'i," etc., and his descendants (the sub-tribe) would thus be called "SERRÁRÁB," etc., and the singular of such form is "Serrárábi," etc. Though 14 sons are given, the text of the paragraph commences "Ḥammad el Akrat had thirteen sons."

XXXVII This and the following paragraphs, to the end, are only written in pencil in the MS. They may have been copied from a different source but probably represent only vague recollections.

XXXIX The "BISHÁRÍA," etc., are sections of the MA'ÁḲLA.

TREE ILLUSTRATING MS. A 3

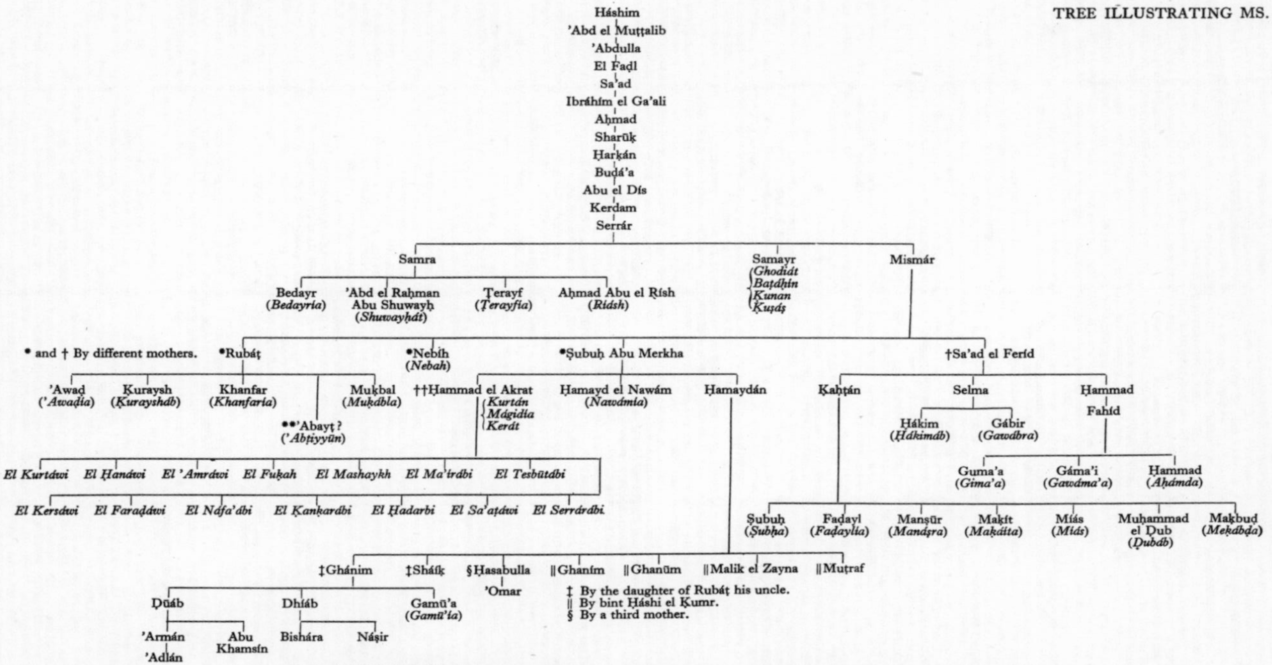

* and † By different mothers.

‡ By the daughter of Rubáṭ his uncle.
|| By bint Ḥáshi el Ḳumr.
§ By a third mother.

** ? Denotes "it is said" in the text.
†† The names given as those of Ḥammad el Akrat's 14 sons are in reality those of sub-tribes, though couched in the singular. *E.g.* "El Náfa'ábi" = a member of the Náfa'áb.

MANUSCRIPT A 4

Introduction

(See Introduction to A 3)

I In the name of God....

The Prophet...said "Ye know from your pedigrees how ye are connected.

II The following is the pedigree which was transcribed by the feki Aḥmad Muḥammad from the pedigree of Sheikh Muḥammad ibn 'Ísa Sowár el Dhahab, [which latter came] from Mekka the Noble, for it was brought [thence] by Sheikh Kámil el Murshid the Bedayri[1]; [and it] gives the pedigrees of the descendants of Ga'al.

III–XII Serrár had three sons...(*for these and their descendants see the tree: no other details are given*).

XIII Here ends the catalogue of the GA'ALIYYŪN.

XIV Now Mismár and Samra and Samayra were the sons of Kerdam son of...(*as in tree*).

A 4 (NOTES)

I Cp. BA, III.

II For Muḥammad ibn 'Ísa see introduction to A 3, and D 3, 191. Cp. A 3, XIII.

III–XII In the tree "Ḳoday" and "ḲODIÁT" have been altered to "Ghoday" and "GHODIÁT" respectively.

[1] reading البديري for البدير.

TREE ILLUSTRATING MS. A

* and † By different mothers.

- El 'Abbás
  - 'Abdulla
    - El Faḍl
      - Sa'ad el Anṣári
        - Ibráhím Ga'al
          - El Yemán
            - Aḥmad el Ḥegázi
              - Sharūḳ
                - Kharḳán
                  - Budá'a
                    - Abu el Dís
                      - Kerdam
                        - [Serrár]
                          - Mismár
                            - *Sa'ad el Feríd
                              - Ḳaḥṭán
                                - Ṣubuḥ
                                - Faḍl
                                - Muḥammad el Ḍub
                                - Manṣūr
                                - Maḳbuḍ
                                - Maḳíth
                                - Míás
                              - Selma
                                - Ḥákim
                                - Gábir
                              - Fihr
                                - Ḥammad (*Aḥámda*)
                                - Guma'a (*Gima'a*)
                                - Gáma'i (*Gawáma'a*)
                            - †Ṣubuḥ Abu Merkha
                              - Ḥammad el Akrat {*Kurtán*, *Mágidia*}
                              - Ḥamayd el Nawám (*Nawámia*)
                              - Ḥamaydán {*Gamū'ia*, *Shaíḳia*, *Dhuábia*, *Bishárab*}
                            - †Rubáṭ
                              - Ḳuraysh (*Ḳurayshia*)
                              - 'Awaḍ (*'Awaḍia*)
                              - Muḳbal (*Muḳábla*)
                              - Khanfar (*Khanfaria*)
                            - †Nebíh (*Nebihát, said to be in the country of the Moghárba*)
                          - Samayra
                            - Ghoday (*Ghodiát*)
                            - Buṭáḥ (*Baṭáḥin*)
                            - Ḳuṣáṣ (*Ḳuṣáṣin*)
                            - Ḳunan (*Ḳunaniyyūn*)
                          - Samra
                            - Muḥammad Bedayr (*Bedayria*)
                            - 'Abd el Raḥman Abu el Shayḥ (*Shuwayḥát*)
                            - Ríásh (*Riáshin*)
                            - Ṭeráf (*Ṭerayfia*)

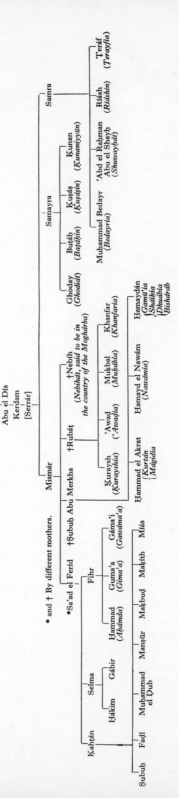

MANUSCRIPT A 5

Introduction

THIS extract is said by the owner, el Hádi, to have been obtained some ten years ago by his uncle Raḥma Muḥammad. He does not know its origin. Probably it is, like A 1, an extract from Sheikh el Bedowi's manuscript, and the variations may be due to the copyist.

Pedigree of the GA'ALIYYŪN.

1 I am el Hádi son of...(*as in tree, no details given*).

TREE ILLUSTRATING MS. A 5

'Abd el Muṭṭalib
El 'Abbás
'Abdulla
El Faḍl
Sa'ad
Dhu el Kilá'a el Ḥimyari
Yáṭil
Háṭil
Kerab
Ḳuṣáṣ
'Adi
Yemen
Ḳays
Idrís
Ibráhím
Aḥmad
Masrūḳ
Ḥarḳán
Buḍá'a
Abu el Dís
Kerdam

Serrár
Mismár
Sa'ad
Ḳaḥṭán
Maḳbuḍ
'Ukásha
Muḥammad
Nuṣr el Dín
Ḥasan
Ḥammad
Raḥma
Faḍlulla
Raḥma
Muḥammad
El Ḥág Aḥmad
El Hádi

MANUSCRIPT A 6

Introduction

THIS pedigree was lent me by Mr H. C. Jackson, who had borrowed it from the famous Zubayr Pasha. The latter, as will be seen from the tree, was one of the GAMŪ'ÍA section of the GA'ALIÍN, being descended from their eponymous ancestor Gamū'a ibn Ghánim. He died in 1913. It is not known from where Zubayr Pasha obtained the pedigree.

(*This pedigree commences with a bald list of* 10 *persons who are related to el Zubayr Pasha, being equally with him descended from Sulaymán ibn Abukr, and then continues as follows*....)

I This is the pedigree of his excellency the late el Zubayr Raḥma Pasha, the great and mighty, to whom are related the persons whose names appear above.

II El Zubayr son of...(*as tree, q.v., as far as 'Adnán*).

III And the Prophet...said "Go not beyond 'Adnán. It is in him that [ye] are united. [The generations] beyond 'Adnán are disputed."

A 6 (NOTE)

III Cp. BA, CXXXV, etc.

TREE ILLUSTRATING MS. A 6

Etc. to 'Adnán
↑
Ḳuṣai
'Abd Menáf
Háshim
'Abd el Muṭṭalib
El 'Abbás
'Abdulla
El Faḍl
Sa'ad[1]
Dhu el Kilá'a[2]
Yáṭil
Háṭil
Kerab
Ḳuṣáṣ
'Adi

Yemen[3]
Ḳays
Idrís
Ibráhím el Háshimi
Aḥmad[4]
Masrūḳ[5]
'Abdulla Ḥarḳán
Budá'a
Abu el Dís
Kerdam
Serrár
Mismár
Ṣubuḥ
Ḥamaydán
Ghánim

Gamū'a
Manṣūr
Gamí'a
Sháhín
'Awaḍ
Abukr
Sulaymán
Ná'am
Sulaymán
Muḥammad
'Ali
Manṣūr
Raḥma
El Zubayr

[1] Whose mother was of El Anṣár.
[2] Whose mother was of Ḥimyar.
[3] Whose mother was of El Khazrag.
[4] Whose mother was from Yemen.
[5] Whose mother was of El 'Abs.

MANUSCRIPT A 7

Introduction

THIS extract is sealed by three sheikhs. It was produced by a woman, who had been born a Teḳaláwía and captured and enslaved in the Mahdía, as a proof of the fact that she was freeborn and not enslaveable.

Apparently it is from the same source as A 10.

This is the pedigree of el Tóm bint Kerayb,
copied from the great original.

I In the name of God....

Praise be to Him who made men races and tribes that they might know one another, and blessings and salutations upon him that said "Ye know from your pedigrees how ye are connected," and upon his family....

II Now the preservation of pedigrees is obligatory, ordained by the law, and to guard them is a duty in the past and in the future.

III The pedigree is as follows: el Tóm daughter of Kerayb son of ...(*as in tree*, *q.v. as far as el Sayyid el 'Abbás*).

A 7 (NOTES)

"The great original" is الام الكبيرة ("The great mother").

I Cp. BA, III, XXIII, XXXII.

III The "meks" mentioned are those of Gebel Teḳali, and it is of interest to notice that they are said to be descended from Gamū'a, *i.e.* to belong to the GAMŪ'ÍA branch of the Ga'ali family.

The name "Gayli" (جيلي) seems to attach to the ruling family at Teḳali from generation to generation. Curiously enough, far to the East, between the Blue Nile and the Atbara, is Gebel Gayli (or "Ḳayli" as it should be written) where a small branch of SHUKRÍA ḤASÁNÁB have their headquarters, and the Sheikh of these people uses the hereditary name of Gayli in place of his father's name; *i.e.* instead of (*e.g.*) "Muḥammad walad Aḥmad" or "Ádam walad el Nūr" he is known as "Muḥammad Gayli" or "Ádam Gayli."

Crowfoot (*Arch. Survey*..., XIX, Mem. p. 24) says Gayli "is a Nubian word meaning 'red.'" Burckhardt (*Nubia*) gives it in Nūba dialect as "geyla" and in Kanzi as "geylem." The Mídóbi for "red" is "Kayli" and the Birḳed "Kaylé."

"'Adnán" for "'Adi" occurs also in A 10.

"Yáṭil" and "Háṭil" are transposed by an error.

TREE ILLUSTRATING MS. A 7

El Sayyid el 'Abbás
|
El Sayyid el 'Abdulla
|
El Sayyid el Sa'ad
|
El Sayyid el Dhu el Kilá'a el Ḥimyari (descended on his mother's side from el Ḥimyar)
|
El Sayyid el Háṭil
|
El Sayyid el Yáṭil
|
El Sayyid el Kerab
|
El Sayyid el Ḳuṣáṣ
|
El Sayyid el 'Adnán
|
El Sayyid el Yemen el Khazragi (descended on his mother's side from el Khazrag)
|
El Sayyid el Ḳays
|
El Sayyid el Idrís
|
El Sayyid el Ibráhím el Ga'ali
|
El Sayyid el Aḥmad el Yemáni
|
El Sayyid el Masrūḳ
|
El Sayyid el 'Abdulla
|
El Sayyid el Ḳuḍá'a
|
El Sayyid el Kerdam
|
El Sayyid el Serrár
|
El Sayyid el Mismár
|
El Sayyid el Ṣubuḥ
|
El Sayyid el Ḥamaydán
|
El Sayyid el Ghánim
|
El Sayyid el Gamū'a
|
El Sayyid el Manṣūr
|
El Sayyid el Ḥamaydán
|
El Sayyid el Ḍiáb
|
El Sayyid el 'Abd el Muna'am
|
Surūr
|
Aḥmad
|
Surūr
|
Maḥmūd
|
El Mek Gayli Abu Gadayn
|
El Mek Gayli 'Omára
|
El Mek Gayli 'Ónulla
|
El Mek Gayli Abu Ḳurūn
|
El Mek Muḥammad
|
Ismá'íl
|
Yásín
|
Kerayb
|
El Tóm

MANUSCRIPT A 8

Introduction

THIS *nisba* is a disreputable looking document nearly two feet long, the lower half covered with signatures and seals: it is badly written, in bad condition, and full of inaccuracies. Obviously several generations have dropped out between Serrár and the present. It was lent me by 'Abd el Ḳádir 'Abdulla, the sanitary barber of el Kámlín and he stated that it was copied for him about 1900 by his relatives, who hold an older copy, in Dongola, viz. at Um Durrag village, near Korti.

He had no knowledge of the origin of the *nisba*, but believed his relatives to have inherited their copy, which, for all he knew, might be the original.

I Praise be to God who created man from a handful[1] of earth and made him races and tribes that the noble and the baseborn might be known apart, and blessings and salutations be upon the noblest of created beings—there is no disputing it—and upon his family and his companions, the good and glorious ones; and the goodness of the ASHRÁF be upon all other noble men, and may the strength of God make their lineage a cause for them to enter into Paradise, as was said by Him who is glorious "Fear God by whom ye beseech one another and [honour] the womb that bore you."

II Now he upon whom be all honour said "Ye know from your pedigrees how ye are connected."

III And according to the agreement between those two quotations it is the bounden duty of every person to know his pedigree and tribe lest perchance he trace his lineage to the ASHRÁF though he be not of them, and so fall into sin, or not know that he is a Sheríf, though being one. For lack of carefulness in this occasions harm.

IV It is thy duty to fear God under all circumstances according to the word of him who is glorious "The noblest of you in God's sight is the most pious of you."

V This is an honourable pedigree, ennobled by the aid of a host[2] of manuscripts, the pedigree of el 'Abbás, of whom it was said by the Lord of the Apostles "Nobility pertains to me and to my uncle Ḥamza and to el 'Abbás."

[1] reading سليلة for سللة. [2] reading حيلة for حليت.

VI Once on a time he upon whom be all honour collected round him his uncle el 'Abbás and his children and threw over them a mantle (or, according to one account a coat) and called to them saying "Verily they are the people of my own kith and kin," and circumcized them.

VII It is said on the authority of el Imám Abu Ḥanífa el Na'amáni "The noblest is the family of 'Ali and the family of el 'Abbás and the family of Ga'afir and the family of 'Akayl and of el Ḥárith ibn 'Abd el Muṭṭalib, and when the origins [of all] are made clear all those who are connected with them are free, of proved lineage."

VIII And here is that pedigree, as you who are learned and intelligent may see: 'Abd el Ḳádir son of 'Abdulla...(*as in the tree*, *q.v.*, *as far as 'Adnán*).

IX The Imám Málik said, "Verily I hate that which carries a pedigree above...; and beyond 'Adnán all is false...."

X This is what has been recorded regarding all who belong to the TUAYMÁB who are in the SHÁÍḲÍA country and the ḤUMAYYIRÁB who are neighbours of the BEDAYRÍA, as is testified by those whose names are written[1] below.

27th el Higga 1319.

(*Here follows a list of some 37 signatories testifying to the truth of the above pedigree.*)

A 8 (NOTES)

I Cp. BA, XLII and XXIII and X.

II Cp. BA, III and XXXII.

III Cp. BA, II and A 11, III.

V Cp. A 2, II.

VIII The text gives "Abu el Kilá'a son of el Ḥimyari" by error for "Dhu el Kilá'a el Ḥimyari."

'Abdulla has been inserted between el Faḍl and el 'Abbás by a later hand.

IX Cp. BA, CXXXV. Two or three words here are illegible.

X The TUAYMÁB are the section of GA'ALIÍN to which the owner of the pedigree belongs. The ḤUMAYYIRÁB are apparently a subsection of them named after the eleventh man on the list.

The signatories are mostly relatives of the owner: they have in many cases added such remarks as "we approve this true pedigree," etc.

[1] reading موضح for موضو.

TREE ILLUSTRATING MS. A 8

'Adnán
⋮
Ḳuṣai
|
['Abd] Menáf
|
Háshim
|
'Abd el Muṭṭalib
|
El 'Abbás
|
'Abdulla
|
El Faḍl
|
Sa'ad el Anṣár
|
El Ḥimyari
|
Abu el Kilá'a
|
Yáṭil
|
Háṭil
|
Kerab
|
Ḳuṣáṣ
|
'Adá
|
Kharūg
|
Idrís
|
Yemen
|
Ḳays
|
Ga'al
|
Aḥmad
|
Masrūḳ
|
Khūda'a
|
Yárith
|
Márith
|
El Yemáni
|
Buḍá'a
|
Maymana
|
Kerdam
|
Abu el Dís
|
Serrár
|
Rubáṭ
|
'Awaḍ
|
El Ḥumayyir el Kebír
|
Abu Serír
|
'Ammar
|
Ḥammad
|
Ibráhím
|
Muḥammad 'Ali
|
Nuṣr
|
Muḥammad el Amín
|
Aḥmad
|
'Abdulla
|
'Abd el Ḳádir

MANUSCRIPT A 9

Introduction

THIS pedigree is that of a certain Muḥammad el Nūr Ḳeṭayna of el Kámlín (Blue Nile). He stated that the original was at Yūnis village in Berber at the mosque of the ḲEṬAYNÁB and that he took his copy thence. The original is known as *nisbat el Ḳeṭaynáb* but its author is unknown.

An attempt seems to have been made here to dovetail together the pedigrees of the GA'ALIÍN and the MAḤASS.

I In the name of God....

God said "O people, I have created you of male and female and made you races and tribes that ye might know one another. Verily the noblest of you in God's sight is the most pious of you."

II And the Prophet...said "Ye know from your pedigrees how ye are connected."

III Here follows the pedigree: Muḥammad son of el Nūr...(*as in tree, q.v., as far as 'Abd el Muṭṭalib*).

A 9 (NOTES)

I Cp. BA, XXII, XXXIII, etc.

II Cp. BA, III.

III The name Ḥaṣín occurs also in AB, XL and XLII.

A note of uncertain authorship following the pedigree states that Sa'ad and Ibráhím were called "el Anṣári" and "el Ga'ali" respectively because their mothers were an Anṣária and a Ga'alía: it is also remarked that Mushayrif's mother was a Maḥassía and that from him were descended the SURŪRÁB, the family of Sheikh Idrís waiad el Arbáb (for whom see D 3, 141), and the 'EBAYDÁB and the MAḤAYSÁB and the 'AWAYḌÁB and the FAḲÍRÁB sections and various MAḤASS.

In D 3, 154, Sheikh Khógali's mother is spoken of as a "Maḥassía Mushayrifía." For these echoes of a matrilinear system see note to BA, CXXXIII.

TREE ILLUSTRATING MS. A 9

'Abd el Muṭṭalib
|
El 'Abbás
|
'Abdulla
|
El Faḍl
|
Sa'ad
|
Ibráhím
|
Ḥarkán
|
'Abdulla
|
Dūla
|
El Dís Sharūḳ
|
El Yemáni
|
Aḥmad el Ḥegázi
|
El Dís
|
'Abdulla
|
Ḥaṣín
|
Buḍá'a
|
Ḍarár
|
'Abdulla
|
Medani
|
Idrís
|
Muḥammad
|
'Abd el Raḥím
|
Mushayrif
|
Serḥán
|
Sharíḥ
|
Muḥammad
|
Abu el Ḳásim
|
Medani
|
Abu el Ḳásim
|
'Abdulla
|
Aḥmad
|
Muḥammad
|
El Nūr
|
Muḥammad

MANUSCRIPT A 10

Introduction

THIS pedigree was sent me by Sheikh el Ṭaib Háshim, the *Mufti* of the Sudan.

His section of GA'ALIÍN is the GÓDALÁB, so named from Gódulla his eleventh ancestor.

1 This is the pedigree of the *faḳír* the *Mufti* of the Sudan, viz. Sheikh el Ṭaib son of Aḥmad son of...(*as in tree*, *q.v.*, *to el 'Abbás*).

A 10 (NOTE)

After "Ibráhím el Ga'ali" is added "and he was ancestor of all the tribes of the GA'ALIYYŪN, and to him do all their numerous tribes trace their descent, and every branch of them is united in his person."

"'Adnán" occurs also in A 7.

TREE ILLUSTRATING MS. A 10

El 'Abbás
'Abdulla
El Faḍl
Sa'ad el Anṣári[1]
Dhu el Kilá'a el Ḥimyari[1]
Yáṭil
Háṭil
Kerab
Ḳuṣáṣ
'Adnán
Yemen el Khazragi[1]
Ḳays
Idrís
Ibráhím el Ga'al
Aḥmad el Yemáni
Masrūḳ
'Abdulla (surnamed Ḥarḳán)
Ḳudá'a
Kerdam
Serrár
Mismár
Ṣubuḥ Abu Merkha
Ḥamaydán
Ghánim
Ḍūáb
'Armán
'Abd el 'Ál
Gódulla
Surūr
Ibráhím
Idrís
Rahma
Idrís
'Ali Ḳumr
Aḥmad
Muḥammad
Háshim
Aḥmad
Sheikh el Ṭaib

[1] So called after his mother's father.

MANUSCRIPT A 11

Introduction

THE particular copy of this *nisba* lent me for translation was the property of one of the family of Ṭalḥa 'Abd el Báḳi, the head sheikh of the BAṬÁḤÍN, a tribe of nomads living east of the Blue Nile.

Its history was unknown, but from internal evidence it would seem clearly to have had the same origin as A 2 and A 3. It has more the appearance of a paraphrase than of an exact copy. The Arabic is somewhat colloquial, the style is disconnected, there are a number of clerical errors, and glosses have been added.

The impression left is that the earliest copyist had access to a lengthy manuscript, possibly the original of "El Samarḳandi," and that he or one of his successors made a hasty transcription without greatly discriminating between the relevant and the irrelevant, at times merely paraphrasing the meaning, at times hurriedly copying a whole passage literally, and at times omitting a few paragraphs.

The glosses were probably added after the BAṬÁḤÍN had acquired their copy, and the latest copyist of all may be entirely responsible for the clerical errors, as for the cramped and crude writing of the text.

I In the name of God....

II Now the knowledge of pedigrees should be pursued with pains and care, for he upon whom be the blessings of God said "Ye know from your pedigrees how ye are connected"; and many reliable men of learning, brilliant savants and geniuses, have given their attention to the study of pedigrees, such as Sídí el Sheikh Abu Sulaymán el 'Iráḳi and Sheikh Maḥmūd el Samarḳandi and Sheikh 'Abdulla ibn Sa'íd el Samarḳandi and Sheikh 'Abd el Raḥman el Baḥráni.

III El Baḥráni, God bless him, used to say "Verily we have undertaken a mighty task, and the pedigrees have fallen into confusion among us. What hero will take them in hand[1] that the Sheríf may be distinguished from other men?...etc."

IV I will mention what is necessary concerning the pedigree of GA'AL, and, God being my aid to the right way, I will tell of the pedigree of the Arabs known as GA'AL. [But as] the tribes of the Arabs are many, I will not deal with them [all]. He that would do so[2]

[1] reading يحملها for يمحلها.   [2] reading الاشتقال for الاستقال.

should [do so by studying] the books of el Samarḳandi the Great and of el Baḥráni el Sheikh[1] 'Abd el Raḥman.

V GA'AL are the ruling race in the Sudan, and they owe their might to the fact of their [descent] from Háshim, and with them is a refuge in times of trouble, and this [has always been] the glory of [the tribes descended from] ḲURAYSH, [even] before the mission of the Prophet. Their poet says:

VI "O thou that travellest from place to place, hast thou not stayed with the family of 'Abd Menáf? Hast thou not visited them and desired their hospitality? They [would] have saved thee from penury and ill. ḲURAYSH was as an egg that is broken and scattered; and as the very essence of the yolk are [the sons of] 'Abd Menáf, that give drink to the thirsty, the protectors of the people, and their guides, that move their encampments in concord and peace, that smite the chieftains [of their foes] in the midst of the pate, that cry 'welcome!' to the guest. 'Amr the mighty apportioned the pottage to his people, what time the men of Mekka suffered from the dearth of food. Happy indeed art thou if thou campedst near to them: verily thou wilt experience generosity and justice."

VII Now the reason of their migration to the Sudan was the outbreak of war between the BENI OMMAYYA and the BENI HÁSHIM. In consequence they migrated to the West, *i.e.* to the Oases, and then returned eastwards, *i.e.* to Dongola, and conquered its people and subdued GUHAYNA, and subsequently Dongola and Berber; and GUHAYNA became subject to GA'AL.

VIII The reason of their being so named was, it is said, that their ancestor Ibráhím ibn Idrís was a generous king, and the feeble tribesmen used to come to him complaining of want of food, and he used to say to them "*ga'alnákum min ahl nafaḳátná*" ["we have made you a part of our household"]; and for this reason he was surnamed "Ga'al." There are also other versions; and God best knows the truth.

IX And his descendants have been famous by this name, viz. GA'AL, until the present.

X We will now take up the thread of our discourse.

XI Serrár had three sons, Samra and Samayra and Mismár.

XII Samra had four sons, Bedayr (ancestor of the BEDAYRÍA[2]) and 'Abd el Raḥman Abu Shayḥ (ancestor of the SHUWAYḤÁT), and Turuk (ancestor of the ṬERAYFÍA), and Ríásh (ancestor of the RÍÁSHÍA).

[1] reading الشيخ for للشيخ.

[2] reading بديرية for بدرية.

XIII From Samayra four [tribes] are descended, the GHODIÁT[1], the ḲUNAN, the ḲUṢÁṢ and the BAṬÁḤÍN.

XIV In the book of el Baḥráni the Great [it is said] that their ancestor was nicknamed Abṭáḥ [after] a *wádi* of that name in the highlands of Mekka, and the nickname passed to his descendants and they were known as the BAṬÁḤÍN.

XV Mismár had four sons, Sa'ad el Feríd, and the three sons by a single [other] mother, Ṣubuḥ Abu Merkha and Rubáṭ and Nebíh.

XVI Abu Merkha had three sons, Ḥammad el Akrat (ancestor of the MÁGIDÍA and the KURTÁN), and Ḥamayd el Nawám (ancestor of the ṢANDÍDÁB[2] and the MANṢŪRÁB[3]), and Ḥamaydán.

XVII [Ḥamaydán] had eight sons, Ghánim and Sháíḳ (whose mother was Ḥamáma the daughter of his father's brother Rubáṭ), and Ḥasabulla (el ḤASABULLÁWIYYŪN) and Muṭraf (whose mother was the daughter of Ḥáshi el Ḳumr el Fungáwi), and Ghaním and Ghanūm and Gamí'a (EL GIMÍ'ÁB) and Malik el Zayn, all four full brothers.

XVIII Ghánim had three sons, Ḍíáb and Ḍūáb and Gamū'a (the GAMŪ'ÍA).

XIX Ḍíáb had two sons, Bishára and Náṣir.

XX Bishára was ancestor of the MÍRAFÁB and the ZAYDÁB and the 'ABDRAḤMANÁB and the FÁḌLÁB and the RUBÁṬÁB and the SERAYḤÁB and the rest of the well-known descendants of Bishára who live from Berber to el Zóra.

XXI The descendants of Náṣir are the NÁṢIRÁB.

XXII Ḍūáb had two sons, 'Armán and Abu Khamsín.

XXIII 'Armán was ancestor of a tribe called the ḲÁMŪS.

XXIV 'Armán had thirteen sons, Gebel and Gabr and 'Abd el 'Áli and 'Adlán and Zayd and Mukábir and Shá'a el Dín and Sa'íd and Naṣrulla and 'Abd Rabbihi and Musallam and Shabbu and Būbáí.

XXV Abu Khamsín had two sons, Muḥammad and Ḥammad el Bahkūr.

XXVI Muḥammad was ancestor of the ḤAMMADÁB and the AWRIḲA[4], the people of el Gerayf, and the ḲERRIÁB, and the BELÍÁB, and the KITÍÁB.

XXVII Ḥammad el Bahkūr begot the WAGÁYÁB, the people of Ádam walad Farag.

XXVIII It is said—and God knows the truth—that the AWRIḲA are descendants of el Bahkūr, as also the ḤURAYRÁB and the ḤUGÁG

[1] reading غديات for قديات. [2] reading صنديداب for صنيداب.
[3] reading المنصوراب for النصوراب. [4] reading الاورقة for الادرقا.

(the *feḳíh's* people): this I was told by some of their descendants, but I am not sure of its truth, and God knows best.

XXIX 'Adlán had thirty sons: four [of them] were the KARÁKISA, whose mother was daughter of 'Ali Karḳūs walad Shuḳl; and four [of them] were the SITNÁB, whose mother was daughter of walad Sinbis[1] (?); and four [of them] were the 'ABŪDÁB, whose mother was daughter of 'Abūd; and four [of them] were the children of Um Ḥalayb; and Náfa'a and Nafí'a the sons of el Fungáwía; and Muḥammad [and] 'Ali, sons of one mother[2], namely the daughter of Karḳūs walad Shuḳl, el Kamálía; and 'Abd el Dáim and 'Abd el Ma'abūd, sons of one mother; and Abu Selíma and Barakát, sons of one mother; and el Mek Muḥammad, only son of his mother; and el 'Awaḍi, only son of his mother; and 'Abd el Raḥman, only son of his mother; and Tór, only son of his mother.

XXX 'Abd el Dáim had fourteen sons, Ḥammád el Hanḳal (?) and Abu el Baṣírūn and el 'Aráshkól and el Kabūsh and Abu el Gidád and el Kenádi [Kenáwi ?] and Ḍow el Ḳidr and el Shaddū and Abu Ḍaraywa and 'Ali and Yóiy and Ḥammad, father of the 'ALÁTÍD, and Muḥammad el Funḳál.

XXXI 'Abd el Ma'abūd's descendants are the SHADŪGÁB and the FÁRISÁB and the DÓGÁB[3] EL WAHÁHÍB, the people of *el feḳíh* Muḥammad son of 'Abd el Wahháb Guayr son of Sulaymán el 'Adhab, and Ḳungár son of Sulaymán el 'Adhab son of Sa'ad son of 'Abd el Salám son of 'Abd el Ma'abūd, for ['Abd el Ma'abūd] had eight sons, Muḥammad el Aṣfar and Balūla el Ḳír and Sinbis and Shuḳl and Katkíb and 'Abd el Salám and Mūsa and el Khuḍayr.

XXXII El Aṣfar begot the ṢUFAR, and Katkíb the KATKITÁB, and Mūsa the ḤAMMÁḌÁ(?) and the TUMÁR, and el Khudayr the FÍÁLÁB and the BA'ÁBÍSH, and 'Abd el Salám begot Musnad, and 'Abd el Dáim, the people of el Ḥófía, and el Kanbaláwi and Sa'ad and Idrís.

XXXIII Sa'ad and Idrís begot the KALÁMÍN, and Abu Bukr begot the Awlád 'Abd el Dáim, [viz.] Ḥaḍbū'a (?) and others.

XXXIV Ḥaḍbū'a (?) begot the people of 'Abdulla walad Delíl; and Abu Ḥasísi [Ḥasín ? Ḥasís ?] (?) begot the people of Ghanáwa [Ghafáwa ?]; and all of these are descendants of Idrís.

XXXV Náfa'a son of 'Adlán had seven sons, Aḥmad Abu Ḥarb and Ḥammád Abu Rikayb and Abu Nó and Muṣṭafa and Samá'ín and 'Ali Abu Zawáíd[4] and Abu Ruays.

XXXVI Among the descendants of Abu Ḥarb are the ḲÁRHÁB and

---

[1] reading سنبس for سسن .   [2] reading اشقاء for اسق .
[3] reading والدوجاب for ولدوجاب .   [4] reading زوايد for زايد .

the Fíla and the 'Amakráb, who are known as the Haḍálíl; and Ḥammád was the father of the Ḥammádáb.

XXXVII Abu Nó was ancestor of the Nowáb, and Muṣṭafa of the Muṣṭafáb, and Samá'ín of the Samá'ínáb[1], and 'Ali Abu Zawáíd of the Nugūmía and the Sheraf, and Abu Ruays of the Ruaysáb.

XXXVIII Nafí'a had twenty sons, [from whom are descended] the Míríáb and the Ṭawíláb and the Ḳabáb and Khaḍímáb and the Shótaláb (?) and the Ḳursháb, etc., as far as is known.

XXXIX 'Abd el 'Áli had twenty-four sons, Ḥammad (who begot el Kabūsh), and Ḳandíl, and Muḥammad, and 'Abdulla el Kabír, and Gabár, and Ḥasabulla, and Mūsa, and 'Omar, and Khiḍr, and Gádulla, and Ráfa'i, and Magzūz, and Kaltūd, and Kashr, and Bashr, and Tisa'a Kulli, and el 'Áshir el Negáḍi whose descendants are with the Baṭáḥín.

XL Rubáṭ had five sons, 'Awaḍ and Ḳuraysh and Khanfar and 'Abdulla and Muḳbal.

XLI Sa'ad el Feríd had three sons, Ḳaḥṭán and Selma and Fuhayd.

XLII Ḳaḥṭán had seven sons, Ṣubuḥ (ancestor of the Ṣubuḥ), Faḍl (ancestor of the Faḍliyyūn), Muḥammad el Ḍub (ancestor of the Ḍubáb), Maḳbuḍ (ancestor of the Meḳábḍa[2]), Manṣūr (ancestor of the Manáṣra), Maḳít (ancestor of the Maḳáíta[3]), and Mimáís (ancestor of the Mimáísa).

XLIII Selma had two sons, Ḥákim and Gábir.

XLIV The sons of Fuhayd were Ḥammad (ancestor of the Aḥámda), and Guma'a (ancestor of the Gima'a), and Gáma'i (ancestor of the Gawáma'a).

XLV Kerdam had ten sons: seven returned to Kūfa, and three bred here, namely Serrár, the ancestor of the whole, and secondly Dūla, the ancestor of the Fūr (the Fūr royal family) and the Saḳárang, kings of Teḳali; and, lastly, Tomám, the ancestor of the Tomám.

XLVI Abu el Dís had two sons, Tergam and Kerdam.

XLVII The pedigree of Serrár leads back to the blessed 'Abdulla son of el 'Abbás the uncle of the Prophet....

XLVIII The Kawáhla[4] are the family of Káhil son of 'Omára son of Khalífa son of Muḥammad son of Sulaymán son of Khálid son of el Walíd.

XLIX Guhayna are well known.

L The Shukría trace their descent to 'Abdulla el Gawád son of Ga'afir son of Abu Ṭálib.

[1] reading سماعيناب for سماعاب. [2] reading مقابضة for مقابض.
[3] reading مقايتة for مقايتية. [4] reading كواهلة for كواهل.

LI The MESALLAMÍA are the family of Musallam son of Ḥegáz[1] son of 'Áṭif el Bukri. He migrated from Syria in the time of 'Omar ibn 'Abd el 'Azíz and settled in the Sudan.

LII The RIKÁBIYYŪN are the family of Rikáb ibn 'Abdulla and trace their descent to el Sheikh Aḥmad ibn 'Omar el Zíla'i, who was of the stock of 'Oḳayl ibn Abu Ṭálib.

LIII The 'AMRIYYUN (spelt 'AMR...) are the family of Sulaymán son of 'Omar son of 'Abd el Malik son of Marwán, and are the ruling race that are known now as the FŪNG.

LIV The pedigree of FEZÁRA is well known. They are one of the tribes of TAMÍM and have dwelt [in the Sudan] since the conquest of el Bahnasá.

LV The BENI 'ÁMIR are the family of 'Ámir ibn el Ḍarab el 'Adwáni, [and] entered Abyssinia.

LVI KENÁNA are the relatives of Duhaym ibn Aḥmad el Kenáni, an important and unblemished family. They dwell in the same parts of the country as FEZÁRA.

LVII The GÁBIRÍA are a numerous body in Abyssinia, [but] the majority of them are between the MAḤASS and Dongola; and it is well known that they are the family of Gábir ibn 'Abdulla el Anṣár[i], who left them [as his posterity] at the time of the conquest of Dongola, after its siege.

LVIII RUFÁ'A used to dwell with the BEGÁ and Abyssinians. Then they migrated to the Nile. They are the family of Ḳaḥṭán; and God knows best.

LIX The 'ABBÁSIYYŪN are of the family of 'Abdulla ibn 'Abbás in the Sudan. They include the family of el Saffáḥ and others.

LX The GABARTA are Arabs by origin.

LXI The FELLÁTA[2] invaded the land of Takrūr. They are the family of Fellát son of 'Uḳba[3] ibn Yásir from el Baṭrayn. Some genealogists say that they trace their descent to 'Abd el Raḥman son of Abu Bukr el Ṣadíḳ: others say they are Arabs. God knows best.

LXII The ḤADÁRBA. I heard el Sheikh 'Abdulla Abu el Wuzír el Ḥaḍrami say that they were from Haḍramaut, and similarly the DELAYḲÁB also, and [that] the cause of their emigration was [their] maltreatment of pilgrims. Then they settled among the BEGÁ at Erkowít and Sūákin, [where they are] till the present day; and some of them have scattered farther afield.

LXIII The GA'ÁFIRA are a mighty tribe, and are descended from

[1] reading حجاز for جماز. [2] reading فلاته for فلات.
[3] reading عقبة for عفقبة.

Ga'afir ibn Ḳuṭáf of the tribe of Ṭai. They are famous for generosity.

LXIV The Fádnía are the descendants of el Sayyid Muḥammad son of the Imám 'Ali, God bless him, and there is much related of them.

LXV The sub-tribes of 'Adlán are seven, the Náfa'áb and the Nifí'áb[1] and the Muḥammadáb and the 'Abūdáb and the Karákisa and the Yóiyáb and the Shaḳálu and the Ḳuruḍ; and the dispute [for the headship ?] is between three of them, viz. the Náfa'áb, the Nifí'áb, and the Karákisa; and it is related that six of these sub-tribes agreed to take the viziership from the Awlád Nimr, but the Náfa'áb dissented and resisted this, because el Arbáb Muḥammad [was] their sister's son. So, when the treaty of Ga'al was concluded, they allotted to the Beni Nimr the rule of the East [bank] to be their own, and [the Náfa'áb] joined the Nimráb instead of joining the six sub-tribes which[2] are collectively called the Sa'adáb; and the treaty was observed until the end of their rule.

(*The following is added in pencil at the close.*)

LXVI Serrár son of Kerdam son of Abu el Dís son of Ḳuḍá'a son of Ḥarḳán son of Masrūḳ son of Aḥmad son of Ibráhím Ga'al, ancestor of the tribe, son of Idrís son of Ḳays son of Yemen son of 'Adi son of Ḳuṣáṣ son of Kerab son of Háṭil son of Yáṭil son of Dhu el Kilá'a son of Sa'ad son of el Faḍl son of 'Abdulla son of el 'Abbás, uncle of the Prophet..., son of 'Abd el Muṭṭalib son of Háshim.

[1] reading النفيعاب for الفيعاب. [2] reading التي for اللتي.

A 11 (NOTES)

II Cp. BA, II and III.

None of the savants mentioned occur either in Ibn Khallikán's or Ḥagi Khalfa's biographical works. For "el Samarḳandi" and "el Baḥráni" see index.

III The full quotation is given in the text of D 6, III, and part of it there translated.

V–VI For the hospitality of ḲURAYSH (the family of 'Abd Menáf) and their lavish entertainment of the pilgrims to Mekka see Muir's *Life of Mahomet* (Introduction, pp. xciv *et seq.*).

The full quotation as given in A 11 is as follows:

يايها الرجل المحول رحله هلا نزلت بآل عبد مناف
هلا مررت بهم تريد قراهم منعوك من ضُر ومن اكفاف
كانت قريش بيضة فتفقت فالمخ خالصه لعبد مناف
اهل السقاية والرعاية والهدى والراحلون برحلة الائلاف
الضاربون الكبش مفرق راسه والقائلون هلم للاضياف
عمر العلا هشم الثريد لقومه ورجال مكة مسنتون عجاف
ثكلتك امك لو نزلت بجنبهم لرايت من كرم ومن انصاف

In "'Amr the mighty apportioned..." there is a play on the word "Háshim." "Háshim's" name was 'Amr (see Wüstenfeld, W), and he was surnamed "Háshim," *i.e.* "He that *hasham* (apportioned)," *sc.* the food and drink. This line is frequently quoted, *e.g.* (1) in the *Tág el 'Arūs* (vol. IX, p. 104), the chief commentary on the great *Ḳámūs*, and (2) in Ibn Hishám's *Síra Sayyıdna Muḥammad...* (p. 87), which was written about 750 A.D., in a quotation from Ibn Isḥáḳ, and (3) in Ibn Dórayd, and (4) in el Mas'ūdi (Chap. XXXIX), and (5) it may also be found in *Lisán el 'Arab* (vol. XVI, p. 94, *sub* "Háshim").

After this penultimate line, which begins with "'Amr" and ends with "food," Ibn Hishám, on page 87 of the *Síra*, adds another in place of the last line given in A 11. On this occasion he only gives two lines in all, but later (ed. Wüstenfeld, vol. I, pp. 113, 114) he quotes seven lines (not including the line about Háshim referred to above), of which the first two are

يا ايها الرجلُ المحوّلُ رحلَه هَلّا سالتَ عن آلِ عبدِ منافِ
هبلَتكَ امك لو حللت بدارهم ضمنوك من جُرْمٍ ومن اقراف

and the other five quite different from A 11. The other works quoted give only the single line; and all but Mas'ūdi (edit. B. de Meynard) commence عمرو العلا. Mas'ūdi begins عمر الذي.

As regards the authorship, the *Lisán el 'Arab* attributes the verses to Háshim's daughter, Ibn Isḥáḳ (*ap.* Ibn Hishám, p. 87) to "one of Ḳuraysh or one of the [other] Arabs," Ibn Hishám (on p. 113, when quoting the seven lines mentioned) to Maṭrūd ibn Ka'ab el Khuzá'i, and the *Tág el 'Arūs* to Ibn el Zaba'ará. Mas'ūdi gives no definite statement on the subject. Again, el Ṭabari quotes separately, in different places, two of the seven lines given in A 11.

The *Kitáb el Amáli* of Abu 'Ali el Ḳáli (vol. I, p. 247) makes Abu Bukr quote five lines to the Prophet of which the first two are:

يا ايها الرجل المحول رحله ألا نزلت بآل عبد مناف

هبلتك امك لو نزلت برحلهم منعوك من عدم ومن اقتار

and the rest quite different from A 11.

The third line of A 11 occurs in el Azraḳi's *History of Mekka* (ed. Wüstenfeld, p. 68) as follows:

كانت قريش بيضة فتفلقت فالمخ خالصها لعبد مناف

This author gives five lines, and, like the *Tág el 'Arūs*, attributes them to Ibn el Zaba'ará: of these five the first is as quoted, the second and third different from anything in A 11, the fourth something similar to the fifth line of A 11, and the fifth reads thus:

عمرو العلا هشم الثريد لمعشر كانوا بمكة مسنتين عجاف

On the whole, however, the nearest parallel I have found is the following from Ibn Wáḍiḥ el Ya'aḳūbi's *History* (ed. Houtsma, 1883), vol. I, p. 282:

يـأيُّها الـرَّجُل المُحَوّل رَحْلَه   هـلّا نـزلت بـآلِ عَبْد منافِ

هبلتْك أُمُّك لو حللتَ بدارِهم   ضمنوك من جوعٍ ومن اقرافِ

عمرو العُلا هَشَمَ الثَّريدَ لقَوْمِهِ   وَرجالُ مَكَّةَ مُسْنِتون عِجافُ

نَسَبُوا اليه الـرِّحْلَتَيْنِ كليهما   عند الشتاءِ ورِحْلَةَ الأَصْيـافِ

الآخذون العهد فـى آفاقها   والـراحلون لـرحـلـة الإيـلافِ

Ibn Wáḍiḥ attributes the verses to "Maṭrūd el Khuzá'i," thus supporting Ibn Hishám (*q.v. supra*). I have to thank Professor Bevan for drawing my attention to this passage. The expression ثكلتك امك (*lit.* "may thy mother be bereft of thee") is explained by Lane (Dictionary) as "an expression of vehement love."

VII Cp. D 6, x, "They" presumably means the alleged Ḳurayshite ancestors of the GA'ALIÍN.

Great numbers of GUHAYNA settled on the Nile and east of it in the centuries following the Arab occupation of Egypt and it is not at all improbable that the forefathers of the GA'ALIÍN of the present day ousted them from considerable areas between Ḥalfa and Khartoum, and even south of that.

Tribes of "Ga'ali" origin have for centuries been predominant over long stretches of country bordering the Nile in the locality mentioned, and the GUHAYNA group of tribes appear to have been to some extent pushed inland, away from the river.

Various branches of GUHAYNA, too, no doubt acknowledged the over-lordship of the Ga'ali *meks*, when the latter, in the seventeenth and eighteenth centuries, were in power round Shendi and Metemma.

For "the oases" (*el Wáḥát*) see Mas'ūdi, Chap. XXXIII. D 6, X in the corresponding passage omits mention of them.

"Eastwards" should rather be "south-eastwards."

VIII Cp. BA, CXXXII; A 3, X, etc.

XI From here onwards cp. BA, CXXXIX *et seq.*

For Serrár's pedigree see para. LXVI.

XIV This story is the one generally accepted by the tribe, and it is interesting because it is well authenticated (*vide, e.g.*, el Mas'ūdi) that in the time of Ḳuṣai, the fifth ancestor of the Prophet, *i.e.* about 400–450 A.D., the tribe of ḲURAYSH were divided into "*el Baṭáḥ*" (*i.e.* "lowlanders" or inhabitants of the valleys) and "*el Ẓuwáhir*" (*i.e.* "highlanders"), and the two divisions were kept apart when Ḳuṣai settled the tribe at Mekka. The "Lowlanders" comprised the Beni 'Abd Menáf, the Beni 'Abd el Dár, the Beni 'Abd el 'Uzza, and the descendants of Zuhra, Makhzūm, Taym, Guma'a, Sahm, and 'Adi—all closely related—and the Beni Ḥanbal ibn 'Ámir. The passage in Mas'ūdi (Chap. XXXIX) runs thus:

ورتب قريشا على منازلها فى النسب بمكة وبيّن الابطحى من قريش وهم
الاباطح وجعل الظاهري ظاهريا فقريش البطاح هى قبائل بنى عبد المناف
etc.

On this matter see also Yaḳūt (*Geogr.* under "El Biṭáḥ"). Whether the BAṬÁḤÍN are really connected in any way with these "Baṭáḥ" can hardly be decided, but the traditional pedigree that unites the GA'ALIYÍN group (including the BAṬÁḤÍN) with ḲURAYSH (*i.e.* the BENI 'ABBÁS) and the co-incidence of the name need not necessarily be dismissed as pure "fakes." It may be that the tribe assumed the name "BAṬÁḤÍN" in order to support the *nisbas* and because they lived in a land of valleys (round Abu Delayḳ and 'Alwán), but I think it improbable that there was not some other reason as well.

XVI–XVII Cp. BA, CLIV–CLVI and A 2, V.

A 2 omits mention of the ṢANDÍDÁB and MANṢŪRÁB, of the name of Rubáṭ's daughter, and of the name of Ḥasabulla's mother. It says of the last four men mentioned that their descendants are in the west, and omits to say they were full brothers.

The names "el Ḥasabulláwiyyūn" and "el Gimí'áb" are written in the text just over the names of Ḥasabulla and Gamí'a.

XVIII–XIX Cp. BA, CLVIII, etc. and A 2, VII, etc.

XX The words "And the rest of...el Zóra" occur word for word in A 2.

By the "'ABDRAḤMANÁB" are meant the Ḥammadtu family (see D 3, 158).

XXI Cp. BA, CLX. A 2, IX, says: "...the NÁṢIRÁB in the west."

XXII Cp. BA, CLXI and A 2, X.

XXIII The paragraph is probably a gloss. It does not occur in BA nor A 2. I have not elsewhere met with "ḲÁMŪS."

XXIV Cp. BA, CLXV and A 2, XI.

XXV Cp. BA, CLXII and note to A 2, V–XIII.

From here the text becomes rather corrupt, and A 2 is no longer of use for checḳing purposes: several names are doubtful.

XXVI I have taken "Awriḳa" (for "Adriḳa") from para. XXVIII, but either or neither may be correct.

"El Gerayf" is Gerayf Ḥamdulla (see BA, CLXIII).

For "ḲERRIÁB" BA gives "ḲARÍBÁB": possibly the ḲERRIÁT are intended.

XXVII Cp. BA, CLXIV. For "WAGÁYÁB" BA gives "AWGÁB."

XXVIII This may be a gloss.

XXIX Cp. BA, CLXVII–CLXXII and notes.

Twenty-eight sons only are given, and the text in this and the following paragraphs is corrupt and differs in many details from BA: the trees may be compared.

Shuḳl should be one of the 30 sons and not father of 'Ali Karḳūs, as is clear from BA, CLXXI and A 11, LXV.

For "Um Ḥalayb" BA gives "Ádam Ḥalayb," which is probably right.

XXX Thirteen names only are given. "Hanḳal" (هنقل) has been corrected in the text by the owner in pencil to هرنعل (*sic*).

"El 'Aráshkól" is the name of a hill near el Dueim on the White Nile: Cp. BA, CLXXII.

For "el Kabūsh" cp. para. XXXIX and BA, CLXVII.

Kabūshía is on the Nile close to the south of the pyramids of Meroe.

XXXII For "el Kanbaláwi" see Part III, Chap. 1 (*k*).

XXXV These are the NÁFA'ÁB section.

XXXVIII These are the NIFÍ'ÁB section.

XXXIX Cp. para. XXX for Kabūsh. Seven sons are missing from the list.

XL Cp. BA, CLI and A 2, XIV. Sections XL–XLVI correspond closely to A 2, XIV–XXI.

XLII "Mimáís" is no doubt the "Miás" of other versions.

XLIII A 2 (*q.v.* note) adds a remark as to the descendants of these two men.

XLV Cp. BA, CXXXVIII and A 2, XIX.

XLVIII Cp. A 2, XXIV and D 6, XII.

L Cp. A 2, XXV and D 6, XV.

LI Cp. A 2, XXIX and D 6, XXIII.

LII Cp. A 2, XXVII and D 6, XXV.

LIII Cp. A 2, XXX and D 6, XXVI.

LIV Cp. A 2, XXXI and D 6, XIII.

The reference is to the conquest of Bahnasá (Oxyrhynchus) in 642 A.D. by 'Abdulla ibn Sa'ad (see Budge, vol. II, p. 184, and Burckhardt, *Nubia*..., p. 528).

LV–LVIII Cp. A 2, XXXII–XXXV and D 6, XXVIII, XXXIII and XXXV.

LIX Cp. A 2, XXII.

LX Cp. A 2, XXXVI.

LXI Cp. A 2, XXXVII; BA, CXIX, and D 6, XLIII.

LXII "I" is evidently el Samarḳandi: see note to BA, CLXXVI. Cp. D 6, LI.

The words "and similarly the DELAYḲÁB also" and "and some of them..." are undoubtedly a gloss by a Baṭḥáni. The BAṬÁḤÍN have a long-standing feud with the DELAYḲÁB as to the ownership of lands near Abu Delayḳ, and so vent their spite by casting aspersions on the antecedents of the DELAYḲÁB.

In D 1, XXVI similar treatment is accorded to the ḤUMR.

For the ḤADÁRBA or ḤAḌÁREB see Part III, Chap. 13 (*b*), and cp. note to BA, CLXXVI.

LXIII Cp. BA, CLXXV and A 2, XL and D 6, LII.

LXIV Cp. A 2, XXVIII and D 6, IV.

LXV Cp. para. XXIX *et seq.*

"Sub-tribes" here is مطارق.

"Ḳuruḍ" (قرض) may be an error for "'Awad" (عوض).

The Arabic translated "When the treaty..." is لما عقدت كلمة جعل. This division of the GA'ALIÍN is referred to and explained in Part III, Chap. 1 (*k*).

TREE ILLUSTRATING MS. A 11

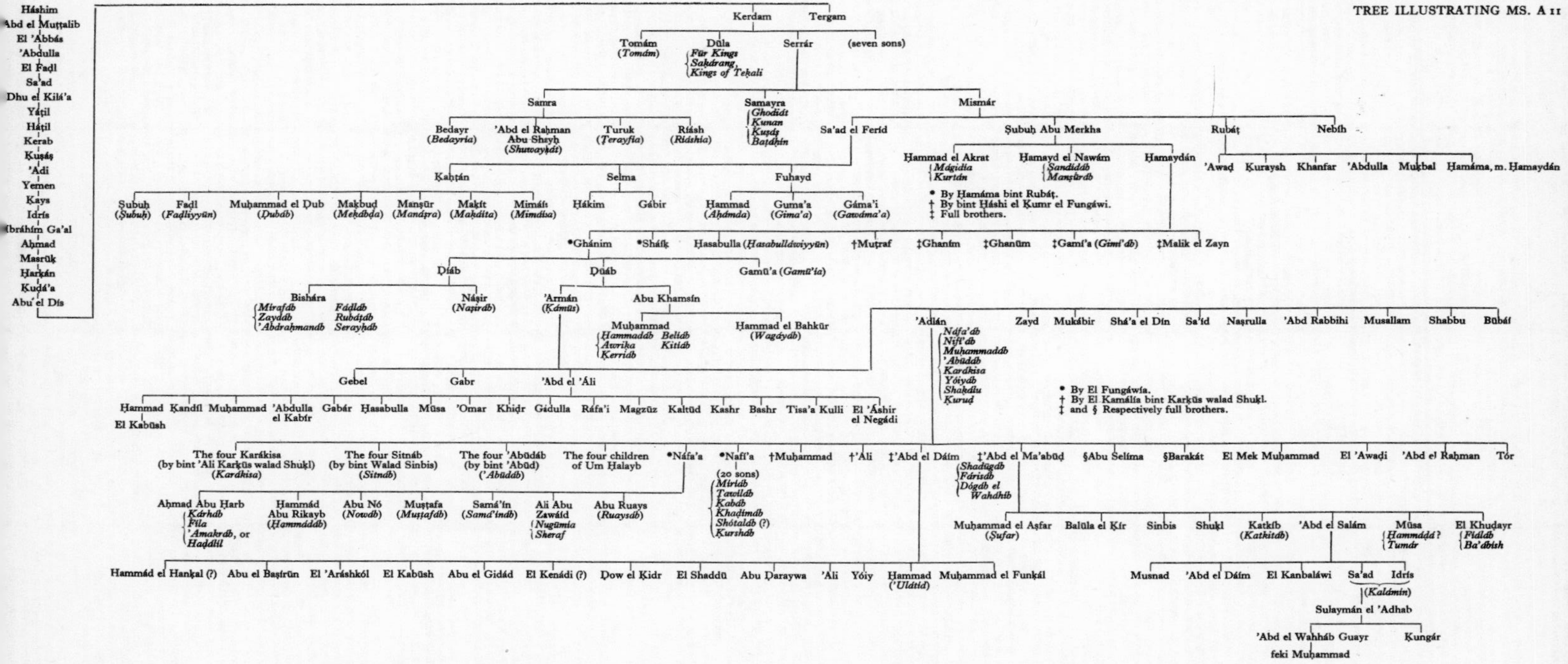

MANUSCRIPT B 1

Introduction

THE copy of this *nisba*, which was lent to me for translation by the *'omda* of the GELÍLÁB at Sa'íd village in el Kámlín district, was taken a few years ago from the copy in possession of el feki Ḥasan walad Muḥammad 'Ísa, a Gelíłábi of Wad el Sha'ír, also in the Blue Nile Province. El feki Ḥasan is said to have inherited his copy from an ancestor, who copied it from some earlier unknown MS.

The GELÍLÁB think (though they have no evidence) that probably their ancestor Sa'íd son of Dáūd son of 'Abd el Gelíl brought the original from the north. He lived nine generations ago (*see tree*) and is said to have built "99" mosques and endowed each with fourteen slaves for service.

It was Ḥegázi Ma'ín the uncle of 'Abd el Gelíl who founded Arbagi about 1475 A.D. (see D 3, IV, and note to D 3, 67, and Jackson, p. 18).

The ultimate source of the *nisba* is obviously the same as that of BA: it no doubt emanated from Dongola two or three centuries ago, and the copyist, being only interested in the part that related to the GUHAYNA group of tribes, omitted the part concerning the Ga'ali group.

I In the name of God...

[The following is] an extract taken from *The Noble Gift and Rare Excellence* [*el Nafḥat el Sharífa wa 'l Ṭurfa 'l Munífa*] of el Sheikh el Imám el Sháfa'í...on the origins of the Arabs.

II Now the [tribes of the] Arabs are ḤIMYAR and ṬAI and THA'ALEB and LAGM and GUDHÁM and HAMDÁN and MA'ÁREF and BÍṢ and ḤUḲNA and KELB EL AZD and MUZAYNA and GUHAYNA. All of these trace their descent to a single ancestor, el Maḥays son of Ḳaḥṭán son of el Maḥays son of Ibráhím...God knows the truth of this, and praise be to Him alone.

III The apostle in the "Traditions" said "Ye know from[1] your pedigrees how ye are connected."

IV And he said of a man who had learnt the pedigrees of the people "A knowledge [of them] is useless and ignorance harmless"—this being in times of mutual love and affection; but...(*continues as* BA, VII *and* VIII, *as far as* "*various nations*").

[1] inserting من.

V And no man neglects it [the study of pedigrees] except the rogue, who is not mentioned when absent nor consulted when present; for it is of benefit to the servants of God in this world and the next, and [whoever ignores it] is a poltroon and a vagabond.

VI–XIX This is the pedigree peculiar to the tribes of GUHAYNA only. Know that Guhayna begot Dhubián, and Dhubián begot.... (*Here follows a genealogical list of the descendants, individual and tribal, of Dhubián. The names can be seen in the tree. No other facts excepting those shown by the tree are given.*)

XX The tribes that may not be enslaved are seven, viz.... (*seven names as in* BA, XLVIII).

XXI Know that GUHAYNA are [to be found] in two different places: [there are in the first place] the descendants of Guhayna el Kabír ibn Hunád of whom the Prophet...said "Through him shall the last of the unbelievers be saved from the fire; whose tribe is from Mekka the noble: there is none of them here: not one of them has come to me excepting 'Abdulla el Guhani, who has come to help me; and Guhayna, all of them, now are the stock of el Zubayr ibn el 'Awwám, the son of my aunt Ṣafía."

XXII The Prophet...referred [also] to him as "my helper" (by "my helper" meaning el Zubayr), and he said too "I am of Guhayna and Guhayna are of me: what pleases Guhayna pleases me, and what angers Guhayna angers me, even though Ḳuraysh be affected." And he prayed for increase for Guhayna for the sake of the stock of el Zubayr.

XXIII [Secondly] their tribe became [*lit.* "reached"] fifty-two tribes in the land of Sóba [under] the rule of the FUNG, but most of them are in the West, namely in Tūnis and Bornūḥ.

XXIV This is a pedigree: Zubayr had two sons, 'Abdulla and Ḥasan. 'Abdulla was ancestor of the KAWÁHLA, and Ḥasan begot 'Aṭía. 'Aṭía begot Guhayna, who begot Dhubián.

XXV This is the pedigree of Zubayr: [he was] son of el 'Awwám son of... (*as in the tree, up to 'Adnán*).

XXVI This is the true and generally agreed upon pedigree. And as a variant, ['Adnán was] son of Ismá'íl...son of Ibráhím...son of Tárikh son of Fárikh son of Náhūr[1] son of Ashra'a son of Rá'ū son of Fáligh[2] son of 'Ámir son of Shálikh son of Fakhshadh son of Sám son of Nūḥ...son of Shíth...son of Barda son of Miháyíl son of Ḳaynán son of Anūsh son of Shíth...son of Ádam...

XXVII This book was completed under the help of God and the

[1] reading ناحور for فاحور. [2] reading فالغ for فالع.

goodness of His grace by the hand of its writer the *faḳír* 'Abd el Gelíl Muḥammad Dafa'alla, who wrote it for his brother Muḥammad son of el Ḥág 'Ali... (*as in tree*, *up to 'Adnán*).

XXVIII This is the true pedigree according to the words of the prophet..."They are liars that trace their pedigree beyond 'Adnán."

XXIX And as a variant—'Adnán was son of Ismá'íl...son of... (*exactly as para*. XXVI, *as far as Ádam*...), and Ádam was created of mud.

XXX In the name of God...

What follows is the pedigree of Ma'ín's own sons. Ma'ín had seven sons... (*see tree*). These are the seven sons begotten of Ma'ín. Muḥammad begot 'Abd el Gelíl, the ancestor of the GELÍLÁB. Ḥegázi was ancestor of the ḤEGÁZÁB, Fáris of... (*etc.*, *as in tree*).

B I (NOTES)

I See BA, LXII–LXV (note) and B 3, I.

II Cp. BA, L. B I and B 3 give "Ma'áref," but BA and AB "Ma'áfir."

III Cp. BA, III.

IV Cp. BA, V.

The latter part of the paragraph is word for word the same as BA, VII–VIII except that for (BA) "...And it is not...a rebel" B I says merely "And he who neglects them is a rebel."

V This is peculiar to B I.

VI–XIX Cp. BA, LIX *et seq.*; B 3, II, etc.

There are one or two mistakes in spelling here, viz.:

مقاربه ("MOḲÁRBA") for مغاربة ("MOGHÁRBA").
فاذنية ("FÁDHNÍA") for فادنية ("FÁDNÍA").
[once] محمد العلاطي ("Muhammad el 'Uláṭi") for حمد العلاطى ("Ḥammad el 'Uláṭi").
حجارة ("Ḥegára") for حجازة ("Ḥegáza").
بقداد ("Baḳdád") for بغداد ("Baghdád").
[once] عول ("Awal") for عوال ("'Awál").

In para. XIII the BASHÁḲIRA are merely mentioned as descendants of Ḥammad el 'Uláṭi, but in para. XVII occurs "Bashḳar was ancestor of the BASHÁḲIRA and 'Isayl of the 'ISAYLÁT," the writer forgetting that he has not previously mentioned Bashḳar specifically as a son of Ḥammad.

XX Cp. BA, XLVIII.

XXI The two divisions of GUHAYNA referred to are apparently (1) those of Arabia, the well-known and ancient Ḥimyaritic tribe, and (2) those in the Sudan round Sóba.

The Arabic for "Of whom the Prophet...said..." is

الذى قال في حقه النبى يخرج ءاخر اهل النار

The meaning is rather obscure, but if the sixth word be pointed يُخْرِ the meaning may be that the most wicked of men may be saved at the personal intercession of GUHAYNA.

"El Kabír" may mean "the great" or "the elder." The whole tradition given here is suspicious.

I can find no Guhayna son of Hunád, nor is it clear why GUHAYNA, a Ḥimyaritic tribe, or 'Abdulla el Guḥani who was also a Ḥimyarite, should ever have been called "the stock of el Zubayr ibn el 'Awwám," who was a Ḳurayshi.

For "'Abdulla el Guhani" see note to BA, LVIII.

Whether the whole of the passage in inverted commas is meant to be included in the tradition, or whether the words from "whose tribe..." to "here" is a gloss by another copyist, is doubtful, but the latter is probable.

XXII The first tradition is well authenticated: el Bokhári (*el Saḥiḥ*, Part II, p. 193) gives it as follows:

حدثنا مالك بن اسمعيل حدثنا عبد العزيز...عن....عن....قال قال النبى
....ان لكل نبى حوارى وان حوارى الزبير العوام

("Málik ibn Isma'íl told me that 'Abd el 'Azíz...told him on the authority of...who had been told by...that the Prophet...said 'Every prophet has a helper, and my helper is Zubayr el 'Awwám.'")

The second tradition I have not traced and it may, or may not, be genuine: the Arabic is as follows:

انا من جهينة وجهينة مني ارضا برضا جهينة واغضب بغضب جهينة حتى قريش

(*lit.* "...as far Ḳuraysh,"—Ḳuraysh being the Prophet's own tribe).

XXIII–XXIV These paragraphs are practically identical with BA, CXXIII, CXXIV: cp. also BA, LVII (note).

XXV This pedigree is very faulty as Zubayr is given as descended from the wrong son of Ḳuṣai (BA, LVII is correct, see Wüstenfeld, T). From Ḳuṣai to 'Adnán is given correctly except that Ka'ab and Murra are transposed. See note to para. XXX.

XXVI No pedigree of any weight ever made 'Adnán son of Ishmael and grandson of Abraham.

For the tree from Abraham ("Ibráhím") upwards to Noah see D I, LXVI, etc. "Tárikh" (Terah) was son of Náhūr (Nahor) and the insertion of "Fárikh" seems to be due to some dim recollection of "Fáris son of Tírash son of Máshūr," the Persian ancestor mentioned in D I, LXV.

The text also gives "Fáhūr" for "Náhūr," "Ashra'a" for "Shárūgh," "'Ámir" for "'Ábir," and "Fakhshadh" for "Arfakhshadh."

"Rá'ū" is another and legitimate form of "Ar'ū" (D I, LXIX).

Between Shem and Adam the text is equally at fault: the father of Noah was Akhnūkh or "Idrís" (Enoch) and not "Shíth"; "Barda" (بردة) should be Lūd (لود) and "Miháyíl" should be Mahaláil: cp. Mas'ūdi, Chap. III (ed. B. de M. vol. I, pp. 68–73).

XXVII The transposition of Ka'ab and Murra (see para. XXV) is here corrected: otherwise the pedigree is the same in paras. XXV and XXVII.

From Muḥammad ibn el Ḥág to Dhubián the direct stem only is given in this paragraph: the other six sons of Ma'ín are added to the tree from para. XXX—the note to which see.

XXVIII Cp. BA, CXXXV.

XXIX The copyist has apparently got into difficulties here as this paragraph is the same as para. XXVI, the very errors being exactly repeated, as far as "Ádam."

XXX From the occurrence again of a formal invocation we may suppose that a copyist added this paragraph from some other source than that of the rest of the *nisba*. By a slip "Ḳalígáb" is written for "Ḳalíngáb." As a matter of fact there is little doubt but that Ḥegázi ibn Ma'ín, the founder of Arbagi, was one of the Ḥuḍūr and had no connection with the Guhayna group whatever (see Part III, Chap. 13).

TREE ILLUSTRATING MS. B 1

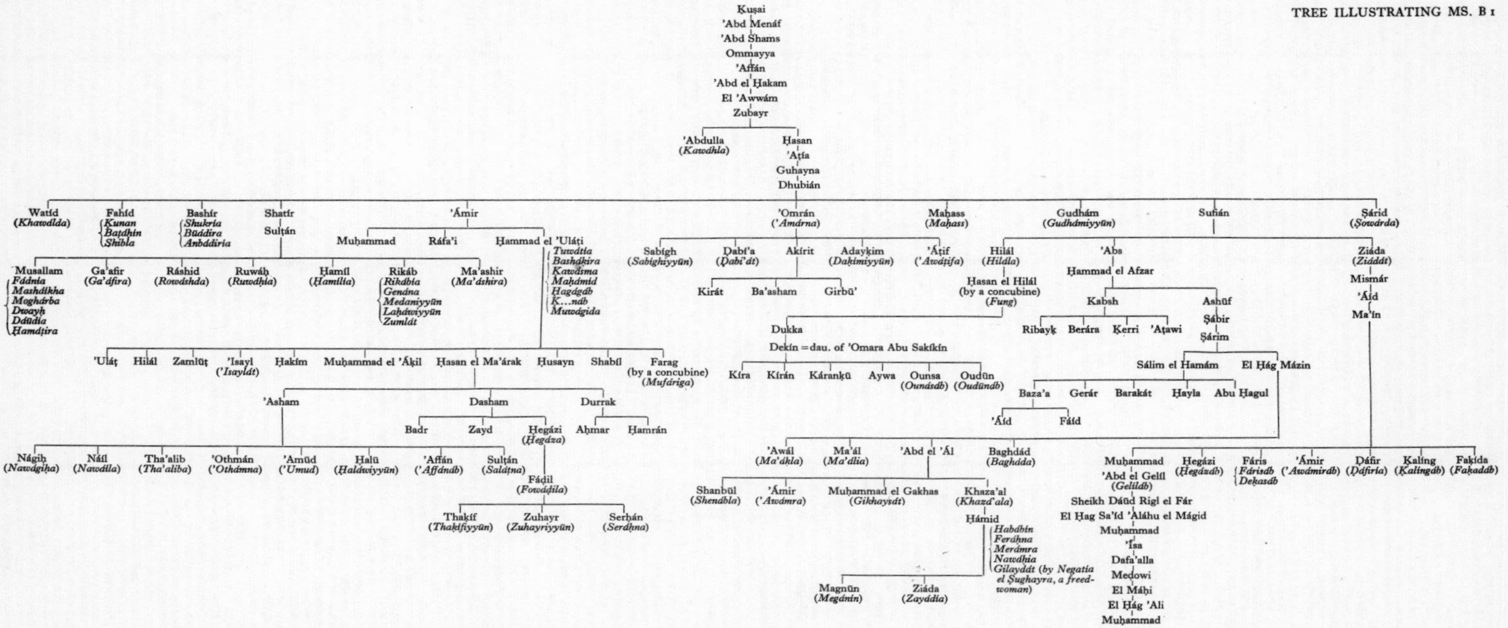

MANUSCRIPT B 2

Introduction

THIS *nisba* was written out for me by Aḥmad 'Omar Sulṭán, the *'omda* of the 'ARÍFÍA, a section of DÁR ḤÁMID in Kordofán, from a copy in his possession. It has little value.

I In the name of God...

This is the pedigree of the 'ARÍFÍA: Aḥmad son of 'Omar son of... (*as in tree*, *up to 'Abd Menáf*).

II Now Mázin the son of Sha'ūf had four sons:...(*as in tree*, *with their descendants*, *as shown therein*).

III These men are the descendants of Mázin son of...(*etc.*, *as in para.* I, *up to 'Abdulla el Guhani*)...'Abdulla el Guhani, the Companion of the Prophet, upon whom be the blessings of God.

IV The MESSÍRÍA and the HABBÁNÍA and the RIZAYḲÁT[1] and the FAYÁRÍN and the TA'ÁISHA are the descendants of Ráshid son of Muḥammad el Aṣla'a son of 'Abs son of Dhubián.

B 2 (NOTES)

I The pedigree from Dhubián to 'Abd Menáf is very inaccurate. The names are all familiar ones, but are jumbled together haphazard.

II "Abza'a," "Gerár," "Dayḥ" [*i.e.* Dwayḥ], and "Shanbūl" are intended as the eponymous ancestors of the BAZA'A, BENI GERÁR, DWAYḤ, and SHENÁBLA, respectively. Cp. BA, CII *et seq.*

[1] reading الرزيقات for الزيقات.

TREE ILLUSTRATING MS. B 2

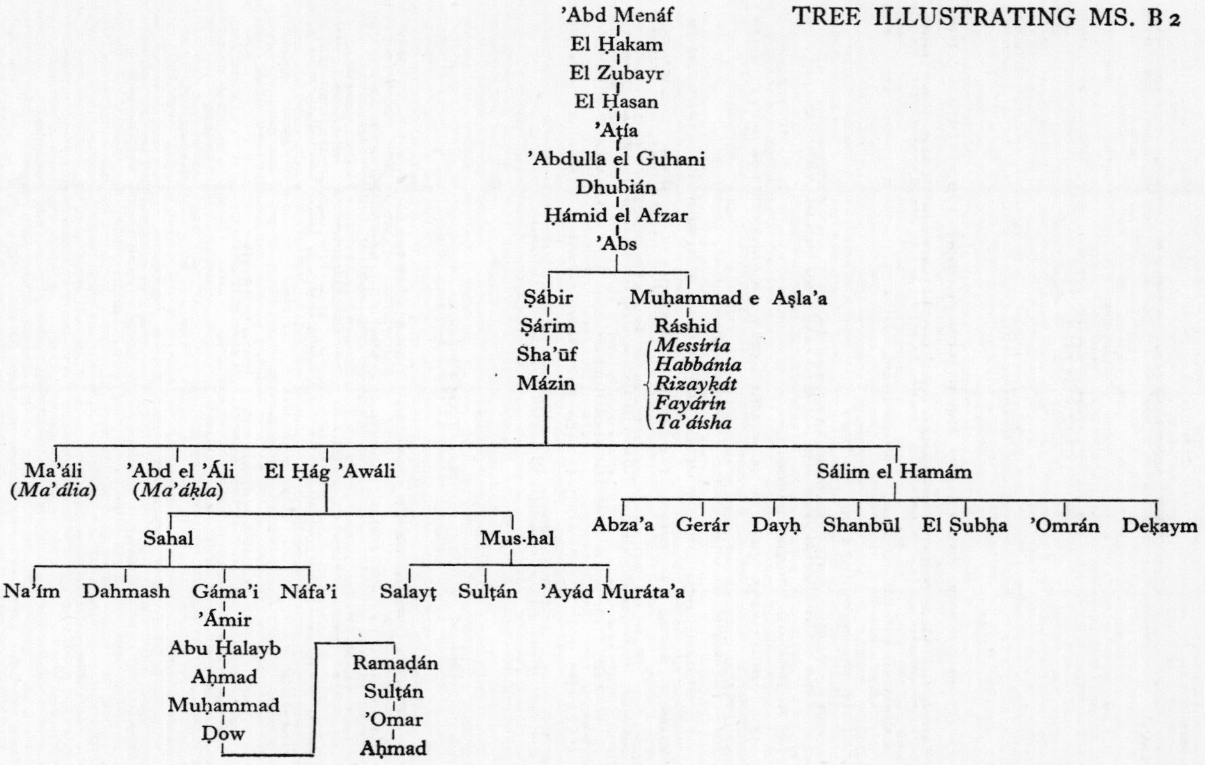

MANUSCRIPT B 3

Introduction

THIS scanty extract was the prized possession of an old *feki* in Dár Ḥamar in Western Kordofán.

It bears a strong family likeness to B I.

I El Imám el Sháfa'i says that the original stock of the Arabs was ḤIMYAR and ṬAI and THA'ALEB and NIGM and GUDHÁM and HAMDÁN and MA'ÁREF and BÍṢAR and ḤUḲNA and KELB EL AZD and MUZAYNA and GUHAYNA,—all of these tracing their descent to one ancestor, viz. Ibn el Maḥays Ḳaḥṭán son of el Maḥays son of Ibráhím; and God knows the truth of this.

II Now as for the tribes of GUHAYNA[1], taken separately: Guhayna[1] begot Dhubián, and Dhubián begot ten sons,—viz....(*as in tree*).

III Ḍabí'a begot the ḌABÍ'ÁT, and Daḳaym the DAḲÍMÍN, and Kírit the KIRÁT, and Ba'ashóm...

B 3 (NOTES)

I Cp. BA, L and B I, I and II.

II Cp. BA, LIX and B I, VI.

III These four men had not been mentioned before. The copyist has omitted the paragraphs preceding this mention of them. From BA, XCVI, we see that they were descendants of 'Omrán son of Dhubián.

With "Ba'ashóm" the *nisba* abruptly ends.

TREE ILLUSTRATING MS. B 3

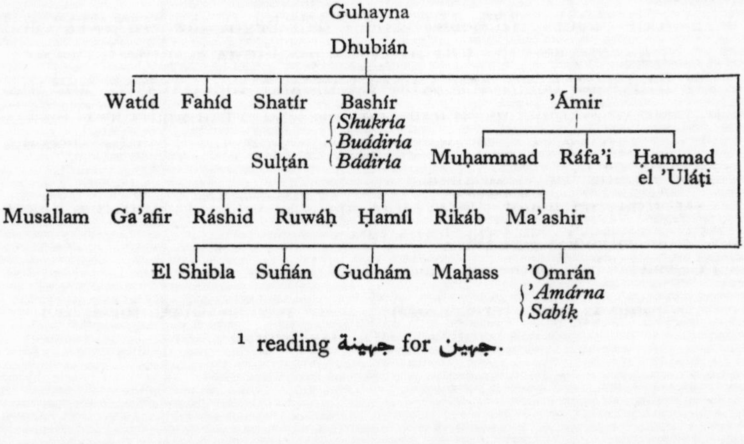

[1] reading جهينة for جهين.

MANUSCRIPTS C 1 (*a*) AND (*b*)

Introduction

THESE two *nisbas* were both found among the effects of Sheikh 'Abdulla Gádulla Balilū, *náẓir* of the KAWÁHLA in Kordofán, in 1909. Their origin is unknown but they were both clearly copies.

C 1 (*a*)

I This is the pedigree of the KAWÁHLA in short.

II Muḥammad Káhil son of 'Ámir son of 'Abdulla (according to Ibn Yaḥya) son of Zubayr son of el 'Awwám; and the mother of Zubayr was Ṣafía daughter of 'Abd el Muṭṭalib. The mother of Muḥammad Káhil was Sikína daughter of 'Ali the Imám son of Abu Ṭálib, whom God bless; and her mother was Fáṭima, the daughter of the Prophet.

III Muḥammad Káhil had thirteen sons: viz. Ḥammad, the eldest, the ancestor of the AḤÁMDA, by el Khaḍría[1]; and Beraḳ and Aswad and Khalífa and Budrán (and also a daughter) by 'Izza the daughter of 'Affán son of 'Othmán, the Imám, whom God bless; and, by the concubine, Sa'íd and Nifayd and Yezíd and Khalbūs and 'Abád; and, by el Fungáwía, Ritayma and 'Akír and Bishára.

IV Khalífa had three sons, el Aḥmar, Muḳwad, and Hilál. The descendants of Hilál are...(*illegible*).

V The descendants of el Aḥmar are the ḤAMAYDÁNÍA and the 'AMRÍA and the KERÁMÍA and the GEBÁLÍA and the LABÁBÍS... (*illegible*).

VI 'Akír begot...(*illegible*); and Ṣaláḥ begot the GHAZÁYA[2] and the...(*illegible*) and the FŪÁÍDA and the SU'ŪDÍA and the KAWÁMLA.

VII Muḳwad begot the ḲURAYSHÁB and the SALÁṬNA and the MUḤAMMADÁB and the NŪRÁB and the RIMAYTÁB and the ḤASÁNÍA and the GIMAYLÍA and the DELAYḲÁB and the 'URWÁB and the SINAYṬÁB and the GHAZALÁB[3].

VIII Ritayma begot the WÁÍLÍA and the GELÁLÍA and the BÁḲÍA and the MUṬÁRFA and the KHALAFÍA.

IX Aswad had two sons, Rashíd and Ḳeláb.

[1] reading الخضرية for الحصرية. [2] reading الغزاية for القزاية.
[3] reading الغزلاب for القزلاب.

X Rashíd's descendants are the...(*illegible*) and the BEḲAYRÁB and the...(*illegible*).

XI Ḳeláb's descendants are the...(*illegible*) and the GELÁLÁB.

XII From Beraḳ, the son of Muḥammad Káhil, are descended the KAMÁLÁB and the KAWÁMLA and the BERÁḲNA and the KIMAYLÁB and the MUDAKÍNÁB and the...(*illegible*) and the MUḤAMMADÍA.

XIII From Budrán the son of [Muḥammad] Káhil are descended the SHARÁ'ANA—all of them—and the BEDÁRIYYŪN, and, it is said, the MÁÍDÍA, and the...(*illegible*).

XIV Bishára was ancestor of the BISHÁRIYYŪN and...(*illegible*) and the BAHKAR and the BAHKARŪN and the MA'ÁLIA and the SUDÁNÍA (?) and the BERAKH (?).

XV 'Abád was ancestor of the 'ABÁBDA, all people of Upper Egypt [*el Ríf*] and owners of the country.

XVI Nifayd was ancestor of the NIFAYDÍA.

XVII Sa'íd his brother was ancestor of the BENI SA'ÍD in the southern mountains.

XVIII Yezíd his brother was ancestor of the YEZÍDÍA and the MA'ÁBDA.

XIX Khalbūs had no descendants.

XX Descendants of Ritayma are at Mekka and Medína...(*illegible*).

XXI Ṣafía the daughter of 'Abd el Muṭṭalib was the aunt of the Prophet.

XXII The [best] known sons of Zubayr ibn el 'Awwám were Bakhít and Muḥammad and 'Urwa and 'Obayḍ and 'Abdulla.

C I (*a*) (NOTES)

I Cp. BA, CXVIII.

II Cp. BA, CXXIV; A 2, XXIV.

No "Muḥammad Káhil" and no "Sikína" appear in Wüstenfeld (*q.v.* T and Y).

III The names of 'Affán and 'Othmán have been transposed. The Imám was 'Othmán ibn 'Affán. "'Izza" is not in Wüstenfeld (*q.v.* U).

The occurrence of "el Fungáwía" (*i.e.* "the Fung woman") suggests that Muḥammad Káhil himself resided in the Sudan.

V The Lababís appear among the subsections of KABÁBÍSH, *q.v.*

VI Cp. para. XII.

XIV "Sudánía" and "Berakh" are doubtful readings.

XVII The mountains of southern Kordofán are meant. Cp. MacMichael (*Tribes*..., p. 202) and Part III, Chap. 5 (*a*).

XIX Contrast C I (*b*), XVIII.

XXII Wüstenfeld (T) does not mention Bakhít or Muḥammad.

TREE ILLUSTRATING MS. C 1 (*a*)

- 'Abd el Muṭṭalib
  - El 'Awwám = Ṣafía
    - Zubayr
      - Bakhít
      - Muḥammad
      - 'Urwa
      - 'Obayḍ
      - 'Abdulla
        - 'Ámir = Sikína
- Abu Ṭálib
  - 'Ali the Imám = Fáṭima
    - Sikína
- MUḤAMMED the Prophet
  - Fáṭima

Muḥammad Káhil = (1) *El Khaḍría, (2) †'Izza bint 'Affán, (3) ‡concubine, (4) §El Fungáwía

- *Ḥammad (*Aḥámda*)
- †Beraḳ
  - *Kamáláb*
  - *Kawámla*
  - *Beráḳna*
  - *Kimayláb*
  - *Mudakináb*
  - *Muḥammadia*
- †Aswad
  - Rashíd (*Beḳayráb*)
  - Ḳeláb (*Geláláb*)
- †Khalífa
  - El Aḥmar
    - *Ḥamaydánia*
    - *'Amría*
    - *Kerámia*
    - *Gebália*
    - *Lababis*
  - Muḳwad
    - *Ḳurayshab*
    - *Ṣaláṭna*
    - *Muḥammadáb*
    - *Nūráb*
    - *Rimaytáb*
    - *Ḥasánia*
    - *Gimaylia*
    - *Delayḳáb*
    - *'Urwáb*
    - *Sinayṭáb*
    - *Ghazaláb*
  - Hilál
- †Budrán
  - *Shará'ana*
  - *Bedáriyyūn*
- †(daughter)
- ‡Sa'íd (*Beni Sa'íd*)
- ‡Nifayd (*Nifaydia*)
- ‡Yezíd
  - *Yezídia*
  - *Ma'ábda*
- §Bishára
  - *Bisháriyyūn*
  - *Bahkar*
  - *Bahkarūn*
  - *Ma'ália*
  - *Sudánia* (?)
  - *Berakh* (?)
- §'Akír
- §Ritayma
  - *Wáilia*
  - *Gelália*
  - *Báḳia*
  - *Muṭárfa*
  - *Khalafia*
- ‡'Abád (*'Abábda*)
- ‡Khalbūs

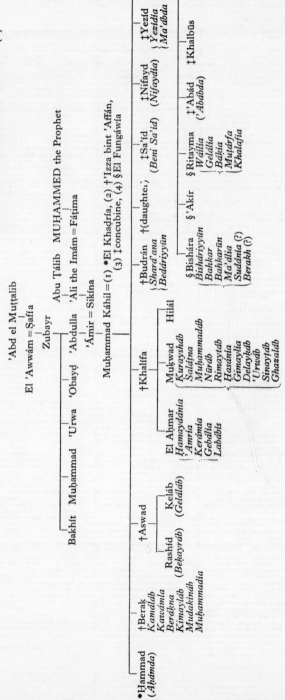

C I (*b*)

I Káhil was son of Mūsa (?) son of 'Abdulla son of Zubayr ibn el 'Awwám, whose mother was Ṣafía the daughter of 'Abd el Muṭṭalib. There is no nobler pedigree among the Arabs but [that of] the BENI HÁSHIM...

II Káhil the son of Mūsa (?) had thirteen sons, who are the ancestors of the KAWÁHLA. Four of them were the sons of the daughter of his aunt, viz. Khalífa and Beraḳ and Aswad and Budrán; and four were the sons of el Fungáwía, viz. Nifayd and Yezíd and Sa'íd and Bishára; and four were the sons of the concubine, viz. Bágíh and Hadi [and] Mudakín (?) and Khalbūs; and one, viz. Ḥammad, was the son of el Khaḍría. These thirteen[1] men are the ancestors of the KAWÁHLA.

III Khalífa had three sons, Muḥammad and Muḳwad and Muḥammad el Aḥmar.

IV Muḥammad was ancestor of the ḤASÁNÍA and the GIMAYLÍA[2] and the SINAYṬÁB and the DELAYḲÁB and the GHAZALÁB[3].

V Muḥammad el Aḥmar was ancestor of the LABÁBÍS and the KERÁMÍA and the 'AMRÍA and the ḤAMAYDÁNÍA, and his sons were Hilál and Ḳedáḥ.

VI Hilál begot 'Abád, the ancestor of the 'ABÁBDA.

VII Ḳedáḥ begot three sons, Shambal and Ṣaláḥ and 'Akír.

VIII The descendants of Shambal are the SHENÁBLA and the ḲURAYSHÁB and the NŪRÁB and the RIMAYTÁB and the SALÁṬNA.

IX The descendants of Ṣaláḥ are the GHAZÁYA[4] and the SHADÁÍDA and the SU'ŪDÍA.

X 'Akír was ancestor of the FŪÁÍDA and the KAWÁMLA[5].

XI 'Abád the second begot the 'ABÁBDA.

XII Beraḳ begot the BERÁḲNA, who [consist of] three sections, viz. the ḤASANÁT [descended from] Ḥasan, and the MUḤAMMADÍA [descended from] Muḥammad, and the BERÁḲNA [proper].

XIII Aswad begot the ASÁWIDA.

XIV Budrán begot the BUDRÁNÍA.

XV Sa'íd[6] begot the KADHÁḲIL (?) NÁS 'ABD EL MUṬṬALIB....

XVI Bishára begot the BISHÁRIYYŪN.

XVII The sons of the concubine were jointly the ancestors of the BEGÁ.

[1] reading 13 for 3.

[2] reading جميلية for جمليه.

[3] reading الغزلاب for القزلاب.

[4] reading الغزاية for القزاية.

[5] reading كواملة for كوامل.

[6] reading سعيد for سعد.

XVIII Hadi begot the...(*illegible*); Khalbūs begot the KHALÁBSA; Mudakín begot the MUDAKÍNÁB; and Hamdán el Khaḍría[1] begot the AḤÁMDA.

C I (*b*) (NOTE)

XI It is not clear what is meant by "the second" (الثاني).

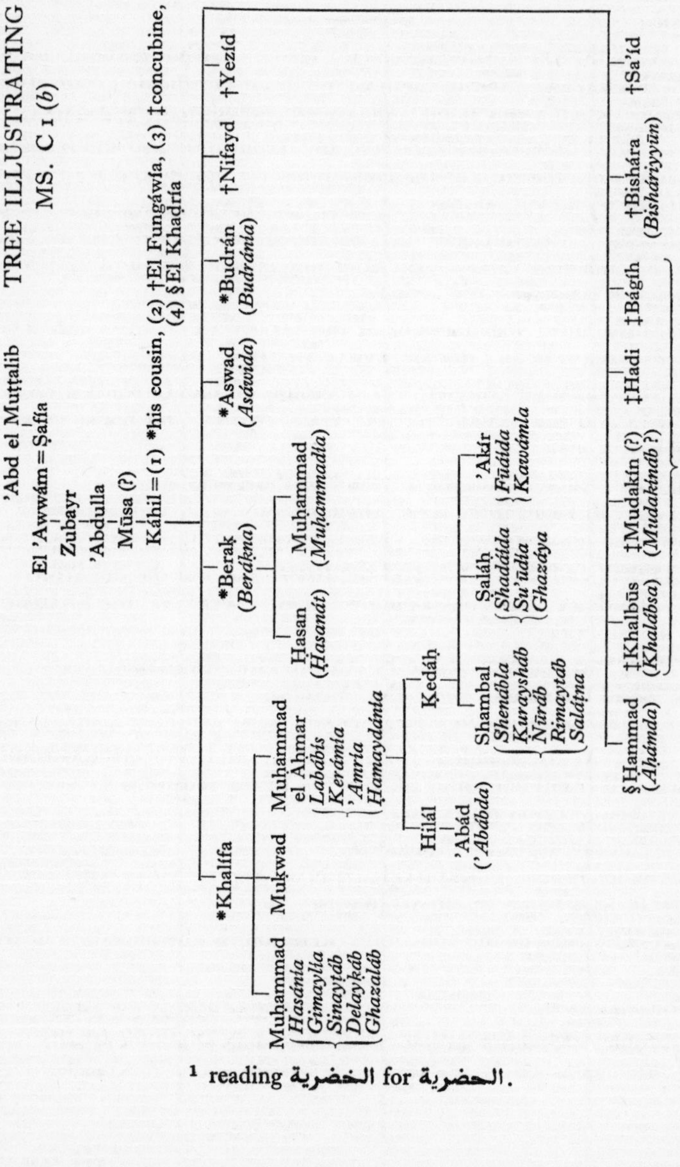

[1] reading الخضرية for الحضرية.

MANUSCRIPT C 2

THIS pedigree was found in the possession of *el feki* Idrís Muḥammad, a Kenáni of el Silayk in Kordofán, in 1908. It consists of nothing more than the series of names shown in the tree. The first five generations are given in Wüstenfeld (Z).

TREE ILLUSTRATING MS. C 2

'Abd Menáf
|
Háshim
|
'Abd el Muṭṭalib
|
Ḥamza
|
Ya'alá
|
El Sayyid el Ṭáhir
|
Sheikh Abu Ḥarayra
|
Sheikh 'Abd el Ghafár
|
Sheikh 'Abd el Mu'aṭi
|
Sheikh Muḥammad
|
Sheikh 'Abd el Gubára
|
Sheikh Háshim
|
Sheikh el Sayyid 'Abd el Munṭalib
|
Ḥanaf
|
Náhūr
|
Sheikh Kenána
|
Sulaymán
|
Sheikh Shahab el Dín
|
El Sayyid Aḥmad Zabad el Baḥr
|
Sheikh Manṣūr
|
Idrís Serág
|
Maṭar
|
El Ḥág el Bashír
|
Abu Ḳurūn
|
Dáūd
|
Dáli
|
Ḥámid
|
Raḥal
|
'Abd el 'Azíz
|
Delíl
|
Tábir
|
'Ísáwi
|
Idrís
|
Muḥammad
|
Idrís

MANUSCRIPT C 3

Introduction

THIS pedigree was copied out for me from his own copy by Ḥámid Muḥammad Gabr el Dár, the hereditary chief of the MUSABA'ÁT of Dárfūr, who lives near el Obeid in Kordofán. He is more negroid in appearance than Arab.

I In the name of God the Compassionate and Merciful.

God Almighty said "Ye people, I have created you of male and female, and made you races and tribes, that ye may know that he is noblest in God's sight who is the most pious"; and God is the source of all learning and knowledge.

II He upon whom be the blessings of God said "Ye know your pedigrees, how ye are descended," and he who knows not his pedigree is a Hamagi.

III The following is the pedigree of the stock of the Sultan Háshim the Musaba'áwi, and it contains the complete pedigree of the tribe of the MUSABA'ÁT.

IV I am el Sulṭán Ḥámid son of el Sulṭán Muḥammad Gabr el Dár son of el Sulṭán Aḥmad el Ga'ali son of el Sulṭán Ḥáshim son of el Sulṭán 'Ísáwi son of el Sulṭán Muḥammad Gunḳul son of el Sulṭán Baḥr son of el Sulṭán Idrís Gerwábukht son of el Sulṭán Muḥammad Tumsáḥ, ancestor of the MUSABA'ÁT and brother of Aḥmad Kūr, ancestor of KUNGÁRA, the two of whom were sons of el Sulṭán Muḥammad Ṣábūn Ga'al son of el Sulṭán Ḥabíb (?) son of el Sulṭán Muḥammad Dáli son of Aḥmad el Ma'aḳūr son of Riziḳ son of Ṣufiál son of el Sulṭán Ga'afir Gurmūn son of Ḳás son of Rufá'a son of Baṭnán son of 'Agíb son of Nagíl son of 'Ísa son of Mámūn son of Idrís son of Hilál son of 'Abd el Salám el Asmar, *Imám* of the people of Baṣra, son of el Nuḍr son of Kenán son of Khuzaym son of Mudraka son of el Yás son of Muḍr son of Nizár son of Ma'ad son of 'Adnán. Ends.

C 3 (NOTES)

I Cp. BA, XXII–XXXIII.

II Cp. BA, III. "Hamagi" is used as a term of opprobrium;—an Arab usage common in the Western Sudan (see Vol. I, p. 275).

III For Háshim's history see MacMichael (*Tribes...*, pp. 12–75).

IV Cp. pedigree XII on p. 585 of *The World's History*, vol. III (ed. Helmolt). Gunḳul (*q.v.* in D 3, 207) is mentioned on p. 545 of the same work and called "Djongol."

The generations from el Nuḍr to 'Adnán are correct, but Wüstenfeld (N) mentions no 'Abd el Salám el Asmar.

References to Muḥammad Dáli, Muḥammad Tumsáḥ, and Aḥmad el Ma'aḳūr will be found in MacMichael (*Tribes...*).

MANUSCRIPT C 4

Introduction

THIS pedigree was translated from a dingy document held by the local *feki* at the MAḤASS village of Kutráng on the Blue Nile.

As an accurate record it is worthless.

I This is the pedigree of the MAḤASS, the five sons of Felláḥ, viz. [*lit.* "of them are..."] Marzūḳ and Ṣubuḥ and Ḳurduḳ and Mūsa and Ḳundur.

II Marzūḳ [*i.e.* his descendants] are settled in Kordofán, Ṣubuḥ among the ḌUBÁÍNA, Ḳundur at 'Aylafūn, Ḳurduḳ at Tūti and el Khartoum, and Mūsa at Kutráng[1].

III The father of Felláḥ was named Sharaf son of Mushayrif[2] son of Záíd son of Mazád son of Dablak son of Ḥamaydi son of Gáma'i son of Sukr son of Kuban son of 'Abūd son of Muḥammad el Máḥass son of 'Abdulla son of Ma'áz son of Gebel son of 'Abdulla son of Ka'ab son of Fihr son of Lūai son of Ghálib son of Kenána.

IV Here ends the pedigree of the MAḤASS descended from Felláḥ.

C 4 (NOTES)

I I have not seen "Felláḥ" mentioned in any *nisba* but this.

II The normal plural to denote "descendants of Marzūḳ" would be "MERÁZÍḲ," and this name does occur as that of a subsection of the GHISHÍMÁT section of the ḤAMAR 'ASÁKIRA and also among the GAWÁMA'A in Kordofán (see Part III, Chaps. I and 4).

'Aylafūn is on the Blue Nile near Khartoum.

Tūti Island lies opposite Khartoum.

Kutráng is on the Blue Nile, south-east of 'Aylafūn.

III The last part of the pedigree is confused and inaccurate. Ka'ab (*q.v.* Wüstenfeld, P) had no son 'Abdulla.

[1] reading كترانج for كتراج.

[2] reading مشيرف for مشريف.

MANUSCRIPTS C 5 (*a*) AND (*b*)

Introduction

THESE two *nisbas* do not coincide with the pedigrees of the A group until Abu Ṭálib. The one coincides with the other at Sa'ūd ibn Waḥsh, but even so they vary in the preceding generations. The first was translated from a copy taken in 1912 by 'Ali walad Ṭai, '*omda* of the NŪRÁB section of SHUKRÍA east of the Blue Nile, from the copy alleged to be in the possession of 'Abdulla Abu Sin the hereditary chief of the SHUKRÍA in Rufá'a district.

The second was taken down for me from the dictation of an old man in Rufá'a district, named Ḥammad el Kaḳam.

Both are clearly inaccurate and rest upon oral tradition rather than documentary evidence. Other forms of the pedigree will be found in the account of the SHUKRÍA.

C 5 (*a*)

These are splendid pedigrees reaching back to Háshim.

I In the name of God...

II Praise be to God who created the human race from water and made it male and female.

III God Almighty said "O people, I have created you of male and female and made you races and tribes that ye may know one another."

IV Again He said...(*text corrupt*).

V And the Prophet...said "He that cuts the connections of blood [*lit.* 'cuts the womb'], God will cut off his hope of salvation."

VI Again the Prophet...said "Ye know your pedigrees, how ye are connected."

VII So this is [written] in obedience to the order of God and His Prophet, and for the preservation of blood-relationships.

VIII I am Sheikh 'Ali son of...(*as in tree*, *up to Háshim*).

IX This was transcribed from el Samarḳandi[1]; and God best knows the truth.

[1] reading السمرقندي for السمرقند.

C 5 (*a*) (NOTES)

III Cp. BA, XXII, etc.
V Cp. BA, XIII.
VI Cp. BA, III.
VII Cp. BA, II and IX.

TREE ILLUSTRATING MS. C 5 (*a*)

Háshim
'Abd el Munṭalib
Abu Ṭálib
Ga'afir*
'Abdulla el Gawád†
'Ón
Ḥasan
'Abd Menáf
Bedr
'Abdulla
Ḥammad
'Ali
Muḥammad
Idrís
Shakír
Zaydán
Waḥsh
Sa'ūd
'Agabi
Tágir
Ḥammad Shóm
Ba'ashóm
'Ali
Bedū
Ḥammad
Ḥámid
Idrís
Tái
Muḥammad
El Sheikh 'Ali

* reading جعفر for جحفر.

† reading جواد for جود.

C 5 (*b*)

I In the name of God...

II And now I will give the pedigree of the Shukría. They are among the most exalted of the Arabs by race, for the Prophet...said "God chose Kenána from among the Arabs...etc. to the end." Therefore Ḳuraysh were among the noblest of the Arabs; and the Shukría are descended from 'Abd el Muṭṭalib.

III This then is the pedigree of el Sheikh Ḥammad ibn Muḥammad, known as "el Kaḳam,"—son of Ḥammad, son of...(*as in tree*, *up to 'Abd el Muṭṭalib*).

IV Now the mother of 'Ón ibn 'Abdulla el Gawád was el Sayyida Zaynab (the daughter of el Imám 'Ali...) whose mother was Fáṭima the Glorious, the daughter of the Prophet....

V The above pedigree from the mouth of one of the Shukría Arabs who knows his pedigree is in accordance with what is in the book of el Samarḳandi the Great, and in that book [the author in speaking of the generations] from Shakír to 'Abd el Muṭṭalib mentions their nobility of character and bravery; and such they have ever maintained, for one of them can meet a thousand foes in war and cope with them without any assistance until they flee in disorder before him.

VI Their characters are pleasant and their conduct good both individually and in their mutual relationships; and were it not that it would take too long I would mention them and their deeds man by man and event after event. Their influence with the rulers of the country has been great because of their skill in affairs of state, and, to sum up, their virtues are many.

VII In addition they are of the family of the Prophet...and that is to be found in the book *Nūr el Abṣár* about the virtues of their ancestress el Sayyida Zaynab, the daughter of the Imám 'Ali..., and the men of learning speak of them from ten different points of view. God best knows the truth.

C 5 (*b*) (NOTES)

III. BA, XLIX.

IV This is incorrect: see Wüstenfeld, Y.

TREE ILLUSTRATING MS. C 5 (*b*)

'Abd el Munṭalib
|
Abu Ṭálib
|
Ga'afir el Ṭiár   El Imám 'Ali
| |
'Abdulla el Gawád = Zaynab
|
'Ón
|
Ḥasan
|
Bedr
|
'Abd Menáf
|
Muḥammad
|
'Ali
|
Idrís
|
Shakír
|
Zaydán
|
Waḥsh
|
Sa'ūd
|
Abu el 'Alá
|
Ranūb
|
Laytát
|
Muḥammad
|
El Ḥág Ṭáí'a
|
Mekki
|
Ḥámid
|
'Abūda
|
Ḥasan
|
'Abd el Gelíl
|
'Abd el Gubár
|
Ḥammad
|
Muḥammad "el Kaḳam"
|
Ḥammad

MANUSCRIPTS C 6 (*a*) AND (*b*)

Introduction

THE former of these two *Sherífi* pedigrees comes from Wad Ḥasūna, between Khartoum and Abu Delayḳ. It is alleged that the original was brought from Mekka by a certain el Ḥág el Sheikh about fifty years ago. This original is in a crabbed but clear hand, written on four small pages. One or two other pages were lost in the Dervish times, but a copy of the whole had previously been taken by Ibráhím el Imám of Wad Ḥasūna. The copy lent to me for translation was made five years ago from Ibráhím el Imám's copy. The grammar and the writing are both bad.

The second version of the pedigree appears to be for the most part a mere variant of the first version, attached to the pedigree of a quite different man. It had evidently been written out within recent years by a copyist. It was given to me by an Inspector but he had forgotten from where he had obtained it. Both the *nisbas* seem quite independent of the A and B groups wherein the authorship is generally ascribed to "el Samarḳandi." They were probably procured by pilgrims from some *soi-disant Sheríf* at Mekka.

It is noteworthy that whereas the former of the two pedigrees makes the Ḥasūna family descendants of el Ḥusayn, *i.e.* ASHRÁF, and though they are commonly regarded as such by many at present, the author of D 3, writing in the latter half of the eighteenth century, had obviously no suspicion that they were ASHRÁF at all.

C 6 (*a*)

I In the name of God, the Compassionate and Merciful. Praise be to God, and blessings and salutation upon the apostle of God, who revealed that which was in darkness, the Prophet, son of 'Abdulla, the last and greatest of the prophets, the mediator for sinners, the disperser of clouds [of doubt], he that made the darkness light: upon him be the blessings of God in every place. Blessings and salutation upon him who revealed that which was in darkness, and all thanks...

II This is the pedigree of the children of el Ḥasan and el Ḥusayn, the sons of Fáṭima the Glorious, God bless her.

III I will commence with the children of el Ḥusayn.

Among them is el Sayyid Ḥasan son of el Sayyid Mekki son of el Sayyid Ḥasan son of el Sayyid Mekki son of el Sayyid Sowár son of el Khalífa Belal el Shayb son of el Sayyid 'Abd el Fattáḥ son of el Sayyid Ḥasūna son of el Sayyid Mūsa el Hárim son of el Sayyid el Ḥág Raḥma son of el Sayyid el Ḥág 'Abdulla son of el Sayyid Maḥmūd son of el Sayyid el Ḥág Ibráhím son of el Sayyid Háshim son of el Sayyid Muḥammad son of el Sayyid Gemál el Dín son of el Sayyid Muḥammad son of el Sayyid Ḥasan son of el Sayyid 'Ali son of el Sayyid Ibráhím son of el Sayyid Idrís son of el Sayyid Ṣáliḥ son of el Sayyid Ḥasan son of el Sayyid Mūsa son of el Sayyid Ibráhím son of el Sayyid Mūsa son of el Sayyid Sháni son of el Sayyid Mūsa el Káẓim son of el Sayyid Ga'afir son of el Sayyid Muḥammad son of el Sayyid Zayn el 'Ábdín son of el Sayyid el Ḥusayn son of el Sayyid 'Ali son of Abu Ṭálib, God bless and honour him.

IV And [God bless] the children of Fáṭima the Glorious, upon whom be the blessings of God, the daughter of the Prophet. In her person are united all the pedigrees of the Sayyids, who are purified of all that is evil,—the abominators[1] of all that are in error or unbelief, the smiters with smiting swords, the pursuers of the right way, the virtuous livers, the forbidders of evil, the arbitrators of mankind.

V In the name of God the Compassionate and Merciful, in whom we put our trust at every time. So long as nights[2] [and days] endure and year succeeds to year praise be to God who chose Muḥammad to be [our] mediator.

VI [Muḥammad] is the one object of love, the eye of [God's] providence, the treasure of gifts, the glory of the resurrection, the bridegroom of the kingdom of God, the tongue of proof, the mediator of all men, the...(*illegible*) of [God's] mercy.

VII God increase the honour of his seed and men's knowledge of them, for they are the noblest and the purest of mankind, the most perfect in goodness, the noblest in rank, the most splendid in power, the greatest in might, the most approved by proofs, the most weighty in the scale, the strongest in faith, the last [*i.e.* greatest] in their coming, the noblest and purest of tribes, the stock of the sons of 'Ali, el Ḥasan and el Ḥusayn, who are the two Sayyids, the fair, the honoured, the brilliant, the noble, the sons of Fáṭima the glorious, the splendid, the magnificent, the Arab, chief of all the faithful women, the daughter of the Lord of the Apostles, even Fáṭima, God bless her. Hear the cry from before God Almighty "O all ye folk[3], veil your eyes until the marriage of Fáṭima is consummated, God bless her, the daughter

[1] reading المبغضين for المبقضين. [2] reading الليالي for اليالي.
[3] reading ياأهل for ياهل.

of the Prophet of God, upon whom be the blessings of God, the chief of all women who are true believers."

VIII It is not permitted to him that trusts in God and the last day to harm a *Sherif*, and if he do so he is a rebel, nor to wrong him, nor to seize him, nor to repulse him, nor to strike him, [and this is] in honour of the Prophet of God, upon whom be the blessings of God, who said "Harm me not in [harming] my family." And they are the flower of mankind, the Sayyids, the sons of Sayyids, and if one of them be ignorant or immoral he is [yet] better than any other ignorant man, and if one of them be learned he is better than any other learned man.

IX If anyone make light of or destroy their honour, or render them odious, or speak them [evil], God will destroy that man's honour on the day of the resurrection, and destroy his kingdom if he be a king, and subvert his empire if he have an empire, and change his wealth to poverty if he have riches, and scatter whatsoever he may have collected together.

X God Almighty said "Say, I ask not of you, for this [my preaching], any reward, except the love of [my] relations," meaning those who are related to the Prophet, upon whom be the blessings of God. Thus he that loves them not is disobedient to Almighty God, and he that injures them and advantages himself shall be punished; and whatever they say must be believed, by virtue of their noble descent, without enquiries as to whether they are liars. And every judge and every chief and every ruler is bound to honour them, and he that would do them evil is [hereby] warned, and every judge and chief and ruler must honour them and ennoble them, for they are Sayyids and sons of Sayyids, the best of men and sons of the best of men.

XI The Prophet, upon whom be the blessings of God, said "Woe, and again I say woe to any that oppose them: their reward shall be [at] the day of the resurrection[1]. He that strikes them with his hand or injures them, I shall oppose him on the day of the resurrection[1], and he is accursed." And he that curses them[2], the Prophet, upon whom be the blessings of God, has ordained that he be slain for having cursed his offspring; his punishment shall be to ride upon an ass, with his face to its tail, and thereon to pass before the gate of the Sultan and the chiefs and the judges and all the people.

XII He that makes light of this pedigree, if he be a king, God will take from him his kingdom, and if he be a chief, God will take from him his chieftainship, and if he be a judge, God will cause him to leave the world without salvation.

[1] reading قيامة for قيمة.

[2] reading لعنهم for لعنه.

XIII He that wrongs the descendants of the Prophet, upon whom be the blessings of God, must receive eighty-seven lashes of the whip; and grief shall fall upon him, and he shall be expelled from the religion of Islám.

XIV But he that honours and respects them and satisfies their needs, shall be honoured by God in this world and the world to come, and his needs shall be satisfied in this world and in the world to come.

XV This is the pedigree of the sons of el Ḥasan and el Ḥusayn, the sons of 'Ali el Kerrár and of Fáṭima the Glorious, the daughter of the Prophet, upon whom be the blessings of God. Praise be to God for the beginning and the end.

24th of *Gemád Tháni* 1327.

C 6 (*a*) (NOTES)

III From Mūsa el Káẓim upwards is correct (see Wüstenfeld, Y), but nothing of the remainder occurs in Wüstenfeld.

Ḥasūna is the father of Ḥasan walad Ḥasūna, for whom see D 3, 132.

X The quotation is from the 42nd chapter of the Ḳurán (see Sale, p. 360).

The word translated "chief" here and later is *muḳaddam*. Its technical meaning is the head or abbot of a *záwia*.

XIII C 6 (*b*) prescribes only 39 in place of 87 lashes. The latter may be merely a misprint: "39" is no doubt correct as "The greatest number of stripes in chastisement is thirty-nine; and the smallest number is three. This is according to Haneefa and Mohammed." (Hamilton's *Hedaya*, p. 204.)

C 6 (*b*)

I (*The first few paragraphs fairly closely resemble paras.* IV–XIV *of* C 6 (*a*)*: they are not worth translating.*)

II This *nisba* was written in the month of Dhu el Ḥigga in the year 485 and its accuracy is testified to by el Sayyid el Sheríf Gemál el Dín [who was ?] also the *muedhdhin* at the mosque of the Moghrabín[1] [Moors] at the city of Fás [Fez]; and verily it is the tree of Idrís ibn Idrís the elder, and the witness thereto is el Sayyid el Sheríf el Ṭaib el Ḥusayn el Sháfa'i, God bless him, as is testified by 'Abdulla Aḥmad, for it was written by the hand of Gemál el Dín.

III Now the blessings of God be on our lord Muḥammad... (*invocations*, *etc.*, *follow*).

[1] reading مغربين for مقربين.

IV This is the pedigree of el Sayyid el Sheríf Muḥammad 'Abd el Wahháb son of Muḥammad son of el Ḍow son of el Nūr son of el Ḥasan son of Sálim son of 'Abdulla son of 'Ali el Ṭaib son of Muḥammad son of el Sháfa'i..., and el Sayyid el Sheríf Muḥammad el Hárib fled [*harab*] from Mekka to the city of Fás and became a devotee [*magdhūb*],...son of Aḥmad son of Gemál el Dín son of Ḥasan...son of Háshim son of Ḳuraysh son of Muḥammad... son of Idrís...son of Khalíl son of Bábikr...son of Muḥammad son of el Zayn el 'Ábdín...son of Khálid...son of Naṣr el Dín...son of Muḥammad...son of el Manṣūr son of Ismá'íl son of Ga'afir son of el Ḥasan son of Fáṭima the Glorious, daughter of the Chosen One... (*there follow praises of Fáṭima, and the pedigree of 'Abd el Muṭṭalib, correctly given, but for two mis-spellings, to 'Adnán*).

V This glorious pedigree, that of el Sheríf Muḥammad 'Abd el Wahháb has now by the help of God been completed by the hand of me its writer Ádam ibn el Sheríf el Zamzami...(*pious remarks follow*).

C 6 (*b*) (NOTES)

II The Arabic is as follows:

وهذه النسبة كُتِبَتْ في شهر الله ذو الحجة سنة خمسة وثمانون واربعماية وشَهِدِه بصحتها السيد الشريف جمال الدين والمُؤَذِّن بجامع المقربين بمدينت (*sic*) فاس وانها شجرت (*sic*) ادريس ابن ادريس الاكبر وشهد بذلك السيد الشريف الطيب الحسين الشافع رضى الله عنه وحضر على ذلك عبد الله احمد لانها كتبت بخط جمال الدين

IV The latter part of the pedigree at least is spurious. Wüstenfeld (Z) mentions no Ga'afir son of el Ḥasan. Each name is preceded in the text by "el Sayyid el Sheríf," and after most of the names follow a few words of praise, such as "protector of the poor," "an observer of the book of God," "God bless him," etc.

MANUSCRIPT C 7

Introduction

THIS document was borrowed from Aḥmad Musá'ad, brother of the *'omda* of the ḤALÁWIYYŪN, who are a section of RUFÁ'A. It was a transcription, and the original had perished.

It is obviously an inferior version of the earlier paragraphs of C 9 (*q.v.*), and is indeed alleged to have been brought from Mekka by "'Abdulla el 'Araki," whose pedigree C 9 represents.

I In the name of God...(*some five lines of laudation follow*).

II When I saw that the records of lineage were being lost in [various] countries and most men's pedigrees in [different] lands, I feared lest my noble pedigree, which connects me with the lord of the apostles, should be lost; for it is not right for one to hide it nor to depart from it without reason; so I wished to record my pedigree, so that all my posterity after me might know it and be quite certain of their own pedigree.

III I am Aḥmad son of el feki Musá'ad son of el Sheikh Aḥmad son of Idrís son of 'Abd el Ḳádir son of Muḥammad son of el feki Shinayna son of the perfect saint el feki Raḥma son of Guma'a son of 'Afíf son of Ibráhím Shakh son of Muḥammad Zaghyū son of Náíl son of Ḥalū son of Ḥammad son of el Sayyid Ráfa'i son of el Sayyid 'Ámir son of el Sayyid Ḥusayn son of el Sayyid Ismá'íl son of el Sayyid 'Abdulla son of el Sayyid Ibráhím son of el Sayyid Mūsa el Káẓim son of el Sayyid el Imám Ga'afir el Ṣádiḳ son of el Sayyid el Imám Muḥammad el Báḳir son of el Sayyid 'Ali Zayn el 'Ábdín son of him that was known as "Lord of the Imáms,...and Commander of the Faithful" el Sayyid 'Abdulla el Ḥusayn, the martyr of Kerbela[1] (which is the name of the place where he was killed), el Ḥusayn the son of Fáṭima the Glorious...(*four lines of laudation of Fáṭima and 'Ali, and the pedigree of the latter up to 'Adnán, correctly given, follow here*).

IV This is transcribed from *El Anwár el Nebawía fí Abái Khayr el Baría* and occurs in the fifth chapter of the *Anwár el Nebawía*: Ibn el Ṣaláḥ mentions it in the commentary on el Bokhári.

V God knows best, and may he bless our lord Muḥammad and his family.

[1] reading كربلة for كربه.

C 7 (NOTES)

II See C 9, IV, which is identical but for the addition of the last eight words in C 7.

III El feki Raḥma may possibly be the "Raḥma el Ḥalawi" of D 3, 221.

"Zaghyū" (زغيوْ) probably corresponds to the "'Azū Rigál" (عزو رجال) of C 9, xv.

The second half of the paragraph, from Ráfa'i onwards, is practically the same as the second half of C 9, v, but there are some variations in the spelling and in the laudations of 'Ali and Fáṭima. Also "el Sayyid 'Abdulla el Ḥusayn" is wrongly given in C 7 for "The father of 'Abdulla, our lord el Ḥusayn" (C 9); and C 7 contains an obvious gloss on "Kerbela."

IV Cp. C 9, xxv. The Arabic in C 7 is as follows:

هذه منقولة من الانوار النبوية في ءاباء خير البرية ومحلها في الفصل
الخامس من كتاب الانوار النبوية ذكره ابن الصلاح فى شرح البخاري

MANUSCRIPT C 8

Introduction

A COPY was made for me of a MS. in the possession of the late Sheikh el 'Abbás Muḥammad Bedr of Um Dubbán, a Mesallami of the Bádráb section, ex-Ḳáḍi of the Khalífa, and later *'omda* of the first *khuṭ* of el Kámlín district.

This copy (called "No. 1" in the notes) was found to be unintelligible in places and I returned it to Sheikh el 'Abbás for verification.

He then produced "No. 2," explaining that the original had been so damaged in the course of years that the copyist—himself not well versed in the subject—had occasionally got into difficulties; but that he had himself revised the whole and made a fresh copy.

The work seems to have been well and carefully done: Nos. 1 and 2 are in close agreement, though the former contains a certain amount omitted in the latter and the order of the paragraphs has been changed in places for the sake of clearness.

Sheikh el 'Abbás thought that the original was written about the time of Idrís Arbáb. The latter (*q.v.* D 3, 141) died about 1650 A.D.

I In the name of God....

II When I, the *faḳír* Mekki Muḥammad, saw how rife were suspicion and incertitude regarding things of importance....

And how ignorant men were concerning the matter of ancestors and pedigrees, I offered my prayers to God and set about clearing the pedigree of Musallam ibn 'Áṭif of doubt and incertitude.

III I took this copy from the *feki* el Amín ibn Delísa, he having taken it from the great book of pedigrees; and it is as follows.

IV Musallam ibn 'Áṭif begot Ibráhím, who begot Muḥammad, who begot Dáūd the elder, who begot Mas'ūd, who begot Dáūd el Ḥáshi. The last named was called "el Ḥáshi" because he used to round up [*yaḥūsh*] the animals on the days when camp was moved.

V Dáūd el Ḥáshi had seven sons, Muḥammad Ḳaṭárish[1], 'Abd el Kháliḳ, 'Arabi, Faza'a, Faragág, Yásir and Sulaymán.

VI Muḥammad Ḳaṭárish begot 'Abd el Kháliḳ, Ḥamṭūr, Hadlūl, Ṣáliḥ, Razūḳ and 'Awaḍ el Kerím.

[1] reading قطارش for غطارش.

VII His brother 'Abd el Khálik begot Dáūd el Gemal, who begot Nebát, who begot Sháwar and Ṣáliḥ.

VIII Sháwar was ancestor of the SHÁWARÁB, and Ṣáliḥ of the ṢAWÁLḤA and the NEBÁTÍA.

IX 'Arabi begot the ḤAḌARÁB.

X The descendants of Faza'a are at Tókar near the Red Sea, and some of them are in the neighbourhood of Gebel Um Meraḥi.

XI Faragág died childless.

XII Yásir begot the DÁŪDÍA NÁS KABANBŪRA, as distinct from the DÁŪDÍA AWLÁD ḤÁSHI, the descendants of Ḥammad el Ḥayḥari.

XIII Sulaymán had six sons, Muḥammad el Munshelakh, Ḥammad el Ḥayḥari, Nebát, Ḥasan and Abu Shelūkh, all by the same mother, and Ibráhím their stepbrother. None of these had any children excepting Ibráhím and Ḥammad el Ḥayḥari.

XIV The above are the seven sons of Dáūd el Ḥáshi and their children. I will now recount the further ramifications of his family in detail.

XV 'Abd el Khálik son of Muḥammad Ḳaṭárish begot 'Abd el Ṣádiḳ, Nigm, Ḥammadulla, Kubgán, 'Anfal, Baḳoi, Abu Sabayka [and Ga'afir].

XVI Ḥamṭūr, his brother, begot the GHUSAYNÁB[1], the MISMÁRÁB, the DELÍLÁB, the KINAYNÁB and the RIḤAYMÁB.

XVII Haḍlūl begot the HAGAḲÁB, the NA'AMÁNÁB[2], the 'AGÍBÁB, the HILÁLTÍT, the ḤASÓBÁB, the BALŪLÁB, the KHALAFULLÁB[3], the ZŪAYNÁB, the KHARŪFÁB, the ḤAMMADULLÁB, the 'ÁHIDÁB and the BÁSHḲÁB.

XVIII Razūḳ begot the RIZḲÁB.

XIX 'Awaḍ el Kerím begot the ṬÁLBÁB.

XX El Ḥág Ṣáliḥ died childless.

XXI 'Abd el Ṣádiḳ son of 'Abd el Khálik son of Muḥammad Ḳaṭárish begot the ṢÁBRÁB.

XXII Nigm, his brother, begot the NIGMÁB, the ḤUSAYNÁB, the MANÍNÁB and the DŪÁLIYYŪN[4].

XXIII Ḥammadulla, his brother, begot the GÁBIRÁB and the ḤAMMADULLÁB.

XXIV Ga'afir, his brother, begot the GA'ÁFIRA and the 'AKÍKÁB.

XXV Kubgán[5], his brother, begot the KABÁGNA and the BAṬṬÁB AWLÁD BAṬṬA.

XXVI 'Anfal begot the 'ANÁFLA.

[1] reading غسيناب for قسيناب.
[2] reading نعماناب for نعماب.
[3] reading خلفلاب for خلفاب.
[4] reading الدواليين for الداوليين.
[5] reading كبجان for لبجان.

XXVII Baḳoi begot the ḤÁSHIÁB, who live at Ḳóz Ragab and the Ḳásh, and who trace their lineage to the ASHRÁF on their mother's side.

XXVIII Abu Sabayka begot the SABAYKÁB.

XXIX Ibráhím the son of Sulaymán son of Dáūd el Ḥáshi begot 'Omar, Ak·ḥal, Faḳad and Baḳoi.

XXX Ak·ḥal and Faḳad died childless.

XXXI 'Omar begot the 'OMARÁB, the BAḲÁÍṢA, the SHÓKÁB, the MITKENÁB and the 'AGAMÁB.

XXXII Baḳoi begot the DELÍSÁB; and among the DELÍSÁB are the ṬERÁRÍF, the people of Idrís Ṭeráf, the father of el Sheikh 'Abd el Raḥman walad Ṭeráf; and the SIRAYRÁB; and the KORŪMÁB, the people of Maḥmūd walad Zaíd.

XXXIII Among the descendants of Ibráhím the elder are the HAGÁNÁB[1], and the BÁDRÁB, the people of el Sheikh el 'Ebayd Muḥammad Bedr.

XXXIV The SHÓKÁB and the 'ASHWÁB and the RIḤAYMÁB are descended from Ibráhím the younger, son of 'Abdulla son of 'Omar son of Ibráhím the elder.

XXXV From Ḥammad el Ḥayḥari son of Sulaymán are descended the ḲUṢAYṢÁB, the TUAYRÁB, and the WANAYSÁB, the stock of el Sheikh Muḥammad walad Abu Wanaysa, and the DŪÁLIYYŪN, the people of Um Ráwía, and the SHAWÁBNA in the Shaybūn country, and the GABÁGIRA, and the NAḲÁḲÍZ and the FAḌLIYYŪN.

XXXVI From him too are descended the MAHÁWASHA, the SHELUKHATÁB[2], the BARṢAḲÁB[3], the 'AWAYDÁB and the ḤAṬÁṬÍB.

XXXVII All of these are branches of the stock of Ḥammad el Ḥayḥari. And here ends the pedigree of the descendants of Musallam ibn 'Áṭif ibn Ḥegáz, who was an Ommawi on the side of his mother Rabí'a el Ommawía; but his father was 'Abd el Ḥamíd son of... (*etc., as in tree, q.v.*). This is the accepted pedigree of the MESALLAMÍA: there is no other reliable one. God best knows the truth, and to Him all men return.

C 8 (NOTES)

II This Musallam is the eponymous ancestor of the Mesallamía.

III El Amín ibn Delísa is said to have been a Mesallami living on the Atbara and a contemporary of Ḥasan wad Ḥasūna (died 1664 A.D.; see D 3, 132). Cp. para. XXXII.

"*He having taken it...*" is كما اخذه من النسب الكبير, but it is not

[1] reading هجاناب for هجناب. [2] reading شلختاب for شختاب. [3] reading برصقاب for برضعاب.

clear what book is meant: the words are no doubt a gloss as they do not occur in MS. No. 1.

IV "*On the days...*" is يوم الظعينة—literally "the day of the howdah," *i.e.* on the day when the women ride in state in their howdahs on the camels from the old encampment to the new. The usual nomad custom is so.

VI No. 1 adds that Ḥamṭūr and Haḍlūl were twins, and calls Ṣáliḥ "el Ḥág Ṣáliḥ."

VII–VIII No. 1 says here "'Abd el Khálik son of Dáūd el Ḥáshi begot the SHÁWARÁB NÁS AWLÁD MAHR as distinct from the SHÁWARÁB" (*i.e.* the rest of the SHÁWARÁB?) "and begot" [*i.e.* was ancestor of (ولد)] "Nebát ibn Dáūd el Gemal"; and later "Nebát ibn Dáūd el Gemal begot Sháwar, ancestor of the SHÁWARÁB, and Ṣáliḥ, ancestor of the ṢAWÁLḤA and the NEBÁTÍA."

In No. 1 there follows this paragraph: "Concerning the BŪÁLDA, the descendants of Būlád Gerri, there is a difference of opinion. Some say they are descended from Būlád son of Musallam, and others that they are GA'AL. God knows the truth about them."

X Um Meraḥi is in Gayli district, north of Khartoum.

XI Not in No. 1.

XII No. 1 adds "And the seed of the sons of Yásir are the BAMBŪNÁB and the WASHKÁB, and the mother of these was one of the NŪBA of el Ḥaráza Um Ḳed, who are descendants of 'Abd el Hádi walad Muḥammad walad Dólíb, who was descended from el Sheikh Rikáb, who was of the stock of el Imám el Zíla'i."

El Ḥaráza is in Northern Kordofán, and 'Abd el Hádi was the father of Nabray (No. 211 in D 3) and probably (see D 3) died about 1750–1800. See MacMichael (*Tribes of N. and C. Kordofan*, Chap. VI). Rikáb is No. 222 in D 3. Cp. note XXXIV and see Chap. 7 in Part III for the RIKÁBÍA.

XIII No. 1 specifies that the five full-brothers were sons of one Merowía el Ḥurra, and Ibráhím of a concubine named Zaynab.

XV No. 1 says 'Abd el Ṣádiḳ and Nigm were twins and inserts Ga'afir (omitted by a slip here in No. 2).

XVI No. 1 adds "the ḲURASHÁB," and gives "KENÁNÁB" for "KINAYNÁB," and says the RIḤAYMÁB were the children of Riḥayma, son of el 'Awayd son of Ḥamṭūr. The descendants of Ḥamṭūr are always spoken of as "ḤAMÁṬIRÍA" to-day.

In a later paragraph No. 1 says "The eldest sons of Ḥamṭūr were Barḳash and Ḳarshan and Thammár and 'Awaḍ el Kerím." These are not mentioned by No. 2; but cp. note XIX.

XVII No. 1 says "The descendants of Haḍlūl, according to what we have copied from the writings of el feki Sherífi ibn el feki Mekki, and according to what has been copied from el feki 'Abdulla ibn el feki el Amín with absolute exactitude, are the SHIŪMÁB, the KHALAFULLÁB, the ḤASANÁB and the MEKKIÁB....The sons of Haḍlūl were Muḥammad and Ḥasan and 'Ali and Khalafulla.

Muḥammad begot 'Agíb, who begot Háltít and Khayr el Síd and Ḥasóba and el Zayn Balūla and Abu Bukr.

Ḥasan begot the HAGAḲÁB and the NA'AMÁNÁB (*sic*) and the KÍÁB.

Razūḳ begot the *feki* Mekki.

Khalafulla begot the HATŪḲÁB (?) and the 'ATWADÁB and the IGÍRBÁB.

'Ali begot Kharūf, who begot the KHARŪFÁB and ḤAMMADULLÁB and the 'ÁHIDÁB and the BASHḲÁB. All of these are the descendants of Haḍlūl."

Perhaps "el Zayn Balūla" should be "el Zayn and Balūla," and by "ZŪAYNÁB" in No. 1 would in this case be meant the descendants of this el Zayn.

There is nothing in No. 2 to correspond to the names of the three sections said in No. 1 to be descended from Khalafulla.

By "'AGÍBÁB" (No. 2) are meant the children of the 'Agíb son of Muḥammad mentioned above (No. 1).

The *feki* Sherífi's *ḳubba* is at Ummát 'Anḳaríb east of el Kámlín. El feki 'Abdulla was also a Mesallami and is said to have been buried near Gebel 'Ísa Ṭálib (near Ummát 'Anḳaríb).

"IGIRBÁB" means "The mangy ones."

XVIII This Razūḳ is not the Razūḳ of the quotation from No. 1 in note XVII, but a son of Muḥammad Ḳaṭárish (so both Nos. 1 and 2).

XIX No. 1, in agreement with No. 2, previously gave an "'Awaḍ el Kerím" as a son of Muḥammad Ḳaṭárish. Later on No. 1 gives another 'Awaḍ el Kerím, "ancestor of the ṬÁLBÁB," as son of Ḥamṭūr. No. 2 has apparently confused the two.

XXVII No. 1 calls them "Our lords the ḤÁSHIÁB," and launches forth into praises of the ASHRÁF, omitted by No. 2.

Ḳóz Ragab is on the Atbara, and the Ḳash to the East.

XXX No. 1 gives the sons of Ibráhím as No. 2, but omits to say Ak·ḥal died childless, and adds "Faḳíd (*sic*) begot the RIZḲÁB."

XXXI For "SHÓKÁB" No. 1 gives "SHAKŪTÁB," and, while giving the 'AGAMÁB as descendants of Ibráhím, does not say that they were so descended through 'Omar.

No. 1 adds among the descendants of Ibráhím one "Muḥammad walad 'Agíb el Shinánábi."

XXXII No. 1 gives "Ṭeráif" for "Ṭeráríf."

After the mention of SIRAYRÁB several lines are added by No. 1 which are incomprehensible and omitted by No. 2. The passage in No. 1 runs thus:

ومن ذرية دليسة السريراب اولاد العراق وابوا دنانة اسمه العراق عبد العال
وابو دنانه حمد اولاد الشيخ عبد الرحمن الكبير بن دليسة الكبير وامهم
الزين فعالوا جارية الحلنقة وولد منها العراق ابو دنانه وخرجوا من الحلنقة
الكبيرة من بحر النيل من بحر ناحية المجاذيب

and may possibly be translated: "And of the stock of Delísa are the SIRAYRÁB AWLÁD EL 'IRÁḲ, and the Abu Denána surnamed 'el 'Irák 'Abd el 'Áli,' and Abu Denána Ḥammad, [these two latter being] the sons of el Sheikh 'Abd el Raḥman the elder son of Delísa the elder; and their mother was el Zayn, called [reading قالوا for عالوا] 'Gáríat el Ḥalanḳa' ['The bondwoman of the Ḥalanḳa']. By her he ['Abd el Raḥman] begot el 'Iráḳ Abu Denána; and they left..., etc." The meaning is apparently that they left the Ḥalanḳa country and settled on the Nile near the MAGÁDHÍB (*i.e.* the AWLÁD EL MAGDHŪB in the vicinity of el Dámer). Cp. D 5 (*c*), XVIII.

For Ḥammad Abu Denána see D 3, No. 141.

For "Maḥmūd walad Záíd" No. 1 has only "walad Záíd."

XXXIII "The people of el Sheikh el 'Ebayd" are the Um Dubbán people under the headship of Sheikh el 'Abbás el 'Ebayd Muḥammad Bedr.

XXXIV No. 1 continues "And of the seed of Ibráhím was 'Awaḍulla Kábū of the AWLÁD BÁṬIL at Gerayfát Omdurmán who are descended from Ibráhím; and the KALÁKLA the children of their [A. BÁṬIL ?] maternal aunt Kalkala el Rubáṭía, who were called KALÁKLA" [emend from "KALÁLKLA"] [*sc.* after] "their mother Kalkala, an 'Awaḍía of the GA'ALIYYŪN 'AWAḌÍA.

The mother of 'Awaḍulla Kábū was one of the NŪBA of el Ḥaráza Um Ḳed who are descendants of 'Abd el Hádi walad Muḥammad Dólíb, and she was ultimately descended from el Sheikh Rikáb. This then is the pedigree of their mother; and all of these were descended from Ibráhím the younger."

Cp. note XII for intermarriage with el Ḥaráza people.

XXXV Muḥammad walad Abu Wanaysa is No. 172 in D 3.

After "DŪÁLIYYŪN" No. 1 adds, in parenthesis, "NÁS WALAD ḤÁSHI": cp. para. XII.

Shaybūn is a hill in the Nūba Mountains: its locality used to be famous in Turkish and pre-Turkish days as containing gold. The people there are entirely distinct, racially, from their neighbours. See note to D 7, CCC.

For "GABÁGIRA" No. 1 gives "ḤABÁGIRA."

In explanation of "the NAḲÁḲÍZ" No. 1 adds "The descendants of Sulaymán el Naḳáz, whose mother was daughter of el Malik Sulaymán the Gamū'i"; and, as regards the FAḌLIYYŪN, No. 1 speaks of them as the descendants of Muḥammad el Faḍl, and includes them among the NAḲÁḲÍZ.

XXXVI No. 1 speaks of the MAHÁWASHA as "descendants of Mahūsh (Mahawwash ?)," and gives the other sections mentioned in this paragraph as descended from "Muḥammad" (*i.e.* Muḥammad el Munshelakh probably).

After this No. 1 continues (omitted in No. 2) as follows: "Muḥammad Musallam had two daughters, Gáíza and el Khiḍayrá. Gáíza was mother of the MOGHÁRBA, and el Khiḍayrá of the FÁDNÍA, who are descended from el Sheríf el Sayyid el Ḥasíb el Nesíb ibn Muḥammad ibn el Imám 'Ali, God bless him, who is known as Ibn el Ḥanafía."

XXXVII In No. 1 Musallam is here called "Musallam el Abwáb son of Áṭif...."

At the close of No. 1 there is added "As for the version that Musallam was descended from Sulṭán, it is not trustworthy: the fact is merely that his mother el Zahra was daughter of Sulṭán, and fame connected him with his [maternal] grandfather because he was his follower and so [his name] became mixed with that of his mother's relations." BA, A 2, A 11, C 9, D 1, and D 6 all agree with C 8. D 2 alone suggests a descent from Sulṭán (who was a descendant of Guhayna).

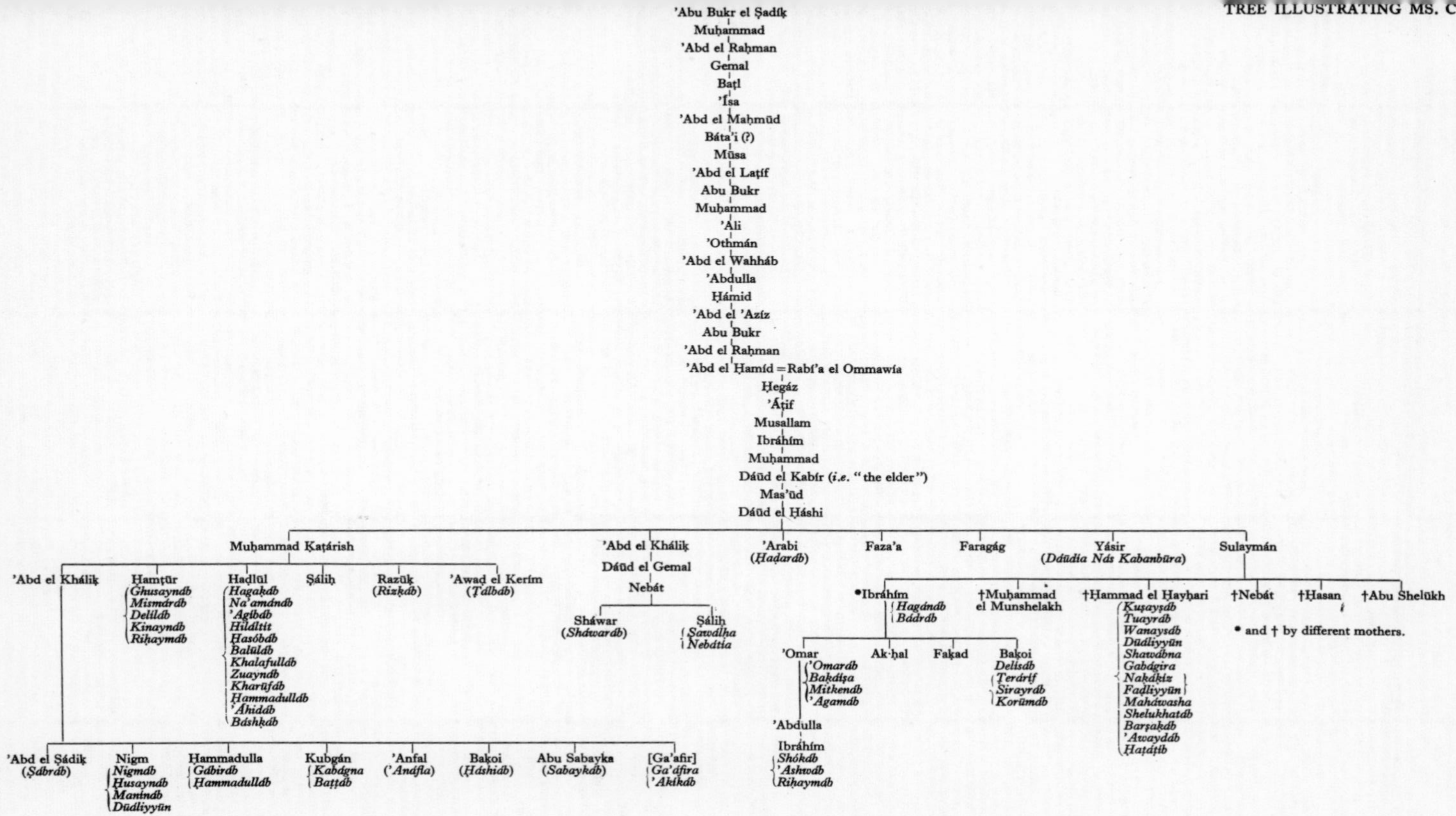
'Abu Bukr el Ṣadiḳ
Muḥammad
'Abd el Raḥman
Gemal
Baṭl
'Ísa
'Abd el Maḥmūd
Báta'i (?)
Mūsa
'Abd el Laṭif
Abu Bukr
Muḥammad
'Ali
'Othmán
'Abd el Wahháb
'Abdulla
Ḥámid
'Abd el 'Azíz
Abu Bukr
'Abd el Raḥman
'Abd el Ḥamíd = Rabí'a el Ommawía
Ḥegáz
'Áṭif
Musallam
Ibráhím
Muḥammad
Dáūd el Kabír (*i.e.* "the elder")
Mas'ūd
Dáūd el Ḥáshi
Muḥammad Ḳaṭárish
'Abd el Kháliḳ
Dáūd el Gemal
Nebát
'Arabi (*Ḥadaráb*)
Faza'a
Faragág
Yásir (*Dáūdia Nás Kabanbūra*)
Sulaymán
'Abd el Kháliḳ
Ḥamṭūr
Ghusaynáb
Mismaráb
Delíláb
Kinaynáb
Riḥaymáb
Hadlūl
Hagaḳáb
Na'amdnáb
'Agíbáb
Hildltit
Ḥasóbáb
Balūláb
Khalafulláb
Zuaynáb
Kharūfáb
Ḥammadulláb
'Áhidáb
Báshḳáb
Ṣáliḥ
Razūḳ (*Rizḳáb*)
'Awaḍ el Kerím (*Ṭálbáb*)
Sháwar (*Sháwaráb*)
Ṣáliḥ
Ṣawálha
Nebátia
•Ibráhím
Hagánáb
Bádráb
†Muḥammad el Munshelakh
†Ḥammad el Ḥayḥari
Kuṣaysáb
Tuayráb
Wanaysáb
Dūdliyyūn
Shawábna
Gabágira
Nakákiz
Faḍliyyūn
Mahámasha
Shelukhatáb
Barṣaḳáb
'Awaydáb
Ḥaṭáṭíb
†Nebát
†Ḥasan
†Abu Shelūkh
• and † by different mothers.
'Omar
'Omaráb
Baḳdíṣa
Mitkenáb
'Agamáb
Ak·hal
Faḳad
Baḳoi
Delisáb
Ṭerárif
Sirayráb
Korūmáb
'Abdulla
Ibráhím
Shókáb
'Ashwáb
Riḥaymáb
'Abd el Ṣádiḳ (*Ṣábráb*)
Nigm
Nigmáb
Ḥusaynáb
Manináb
Dūdliyyūn
Ḥammadulla
Gábiráb
Ḥammadulláb
Kubgán
Kabágna
Baṭṭáb
'Anfal (*'Anáfla*)
Baḳoi (*Ḥáshidáb*)
Abu Sabayka (*Sabaykáb*)
[Ga'afir]
Ga'áfira
'Akikáb

MANUSCRIPT C 9

Introduction

THIS *nisba*, or rather the first five paragraphs of it, purports to be that of the famous Sheikh 'Abdulla ibn Dafa'alla el 'Araki, whose biography is given in D 3 (No. 34).

The actual copy of the *nisba* which has been translated was made for me from his own inherited copy by 'Omar 'Agíb, a descendant of the 'ABDULLÁB viceroys, who were themselves, like the 'Araki family, a branch of RUFÁ'A.

It is interesting to see that Ráfa'i, the eponymous ancestor of the RUFÁ'A, occurs in the B and A groups (which are attributed to "el Samarkandi"), as son of 'Ámir son of Dhubián, ancestor of the GUHAYNA tribes. But in C 7 and C 9 this 'Ámir is called "el Sayyid 'Ámir" and allotted a more noble pedigree, direct to el Ḥusayn, the martyr of Kerbela and grandson of the Prophet.

'Ámir is said to have been the first of the family to settle in the Sudan, and the genealogy of his descendants may be given with approximate accuracy: there is, however, no indication that either of the versions of his ancestry that have been mentioned is correct in any particular. The fact is probably that 'Abdulla el 'Araki went on the pilgrimage and, as in the similar case of C 6, returned with a *Sherífi* pedigree, correct from Mūsa el Káẓim upwards and otherwise spurious.

Mūsa el Káẓim had twelve sons (see Wüstenfeld, Y) and the scribes of Mekka were no doubt prepared to allot him any number more on application.

The RUFÁ'A group as a whole are considered GUHAYNA, but the *Sherífi* descent of the 'ARAKIÍN is never disputed, although they and the RUFÁ'A are allowed to be equally descended from Ráfa'i. For the explanation of this see Chap. 2 (*a*) in Part III.

Paragraphs VIII to XXVI were no doubt added by a later copyist who borrowed them from one of the B group of *nisbas*, and an inferior one at that. They do not even agree with the pedigree given in para. V.

I In the name of God....

II As regards what follows, this is the pedigree of honour concerning the Sheikh of Islám, the Guide [*Murshid*], the Resolute [*Hammám*], 'Abdulla el 'Araki.

III Praise be to God who honoured el Medína with the Prophet of God, and protected it, and chose it above all places, and selected it, and named it "Ṭayyiba" [Sweet] because it was sweetened by the sweetness of the Beloved [*i.e.* the Prophet] and its soil was sweetened. And he bore witness that there is no god but God alone and that He has no partner, but is the God of all created beings and has developed them. And He bore witness that our lord Muḥammad is His servant and apostle, whom His God called "YS" and "ṬH."

IV As regards what follows: when I saw that the records of lineage were being lost in [various] countries and most men's pedigrees in [different] lands, I feared lest my noble pedigree which connects me with the lord of the apostles should be lost, for it is not right for one to hide it nor to depart from it without reason: so I wished to record my pedigree so that all my posterity after me might know it.

V I say then that I am the *faḳír* in God's sight, 'Abdulla son of el Sayyid Dafa'alla son of el Sayyid Muḳbal son of el Sayyid Náfa'i son of el Sayyid Muḥammad "Fala'alah Washm" son of el Sayyid Saláma son of el Sayyid Bedr son of el Sayyid Muḥammad son of el Sayyid Aḥmad son of el Sayyid Ráfa'i son of el Sayyid 'Ámir son of el Sayyid el Ḥusayn son of el Sayyid Ismá'íl son of el Sayyid 'Abdulla son of el Sayyid Ibráhím son of el Sayyid el Imám Mūsa el Káẓim son of el Sayyid el Imám Ga'afir el Ṣádiḳ son of el Sayyid el Imám Muḥammad el Báḳir son of el Sayyid 'Ali Zayn el 'Ábdín son of him that was known as "Lord of the Imáms" and "The Great Captain," whom God proved by [every] kind of trial and test, the Commander of the Faithful, the father of 'Abdulla, our lord el Ḥusayn, the martyr of Kerbela, the son of Fáṭima the Glorious, the queen of the women of the universe, the daughter of the lord of the apostles, our lord Muḥammad...son of 'Abdulla, son of 'Abd el Muṭṭalib son of Háshim [and so on] to his ancestor 'Adnán.

VI At this point ends the authentic and universally accepted pedigree.

VII He upon whom be the blessings of God said "May the curse of God be upon him that intrudes himself upon us without a pedigree or that leaves us without reason."

VIII El Sayyid 'Ámir had three sons, Muḥammad Ráfa'i and Aḥmad el Ad·ham and Ḥammad el Á'líṭ, own brothers.

IX Ráfa'i begot Ḥammad and Muḥammad, own brothers, and also Aḥmad their brother on the father's side.

X Aḥmad begot Bedr; and Ḥammad begot Ḥasan el Ma'árak (the ancestor of the 'ARAKIYYŪN), and Ḥusayn (the ancestor of the BENI ḤUSAYN), and Ḥasán (the ancestor of the BENI ḤASÁN), and Shibayl (the ancestor of the SHIBAYLÁT and father of 'Ayád and el Aṭrash), and Muḥammad el 'Áḳil (the ancestor of the 'AḲALIYYŪN), and Ḥakím, and Zamlūṭ (the ancestor of the KAMÁTÍR), and Ṭowál (the ancestor of the ṬOWÁLIYYŪN), and Mágid (the ancestor of the RÁZḲÍA), and Bashḳar (the ancestor of the BASHÁḲIRA), and Hilál (the ancestor of the HILÁLIYYŪN), and Ḥalū (the ancestor of the ḤALÁWIYYŪN), and 'Isayl (the ancestor of the 'ISAYLÁT), and Farag (the ancestor of the FARAGÁB), and 'Abdulla Ḳerayn (the ancestor of the 'ABDULLÁB[1]).

XI These fifteen were the sons of Ḥammad and [it is written] so in the *Biography* of Ibn Síd [Sayyid ?] el Nás and the work of Ibn 'Abbás upon the origins of the people, and Ibn Ḥaggar verified it with a view to the serious dissensions as to their pedigrees [that might arise] in later days.

XII Now the sons of Muḥammad ibn Ráfa'i, the full-brother of Ḥammad, were Zanfal and Ḥaggág and Ḳásim and Ma'aḍaḍ and Shabraḳ: these are the sons of Muḥammad.

XIII And Muḥammad ['Áḳil] had no children, but Ibn[2] 'Arafa says what is true, namely that the paternal uncle is to be identified with [?] his brother's son.

XIV Ḥasan el Ma'árak had four sons, Ḥammad and 'Asham and Dasham and Daras.

XV Ḥammad begot Aḥmad 'Azū Rigál.

XVI 'Asham begot Nágiḥ and Náíl and Tha'aleb and 'Othmán and 'Amūd.

XVII Dasham begot Bedr and Zayád by [one] mother, and Fáḍil and Ḥaggág [by another], and Ḥammad their brother on his father's side by a concubine.

XVIII Daras begot Aḥmar and el Ḥamrán.

XIX These are the sons of Ḥasan el Ma'árak.

XX Ḥammad el Á'líṭ's [descendants] are the BENI Á'LÁṬ in general.

XXI Ḥammad el Ad·ham's descendants are the ZAMALÁT and the ZIBAYLÁT and the AGAL and the ḲURBÁN and the LAḤAWIYYŪN[3] and the MEZANIYYŪN (who have nothing to do with the MUZAYNA, who were of old an Arab tribe, but are only MUZAYNA descended from Ad·ham the brother of Ráfa'i.

XXII This then is the pedigree of Ráfa'i and his brothers and they were in league with one another; and God best knows the truth.

XXIII The tribes whose members it is not permissible to buy or

[1] reading عبدلاب for عبضلاب. [2] reading ابن for بني.
[3] reading اللحويين for اللمويين.

sell, because they are free, are seven: viz. GUHAYNA and MUZAYNA and ASHGA'A and DASHAM and GHAFÁR[1] and ḲURAYSH and EL ANṢÁR.

XXIV The tribes that have [no ?] pedigrees and whom it is allowable to sell, are seven: viz. the BEGÁ and the BEGÁGÍḤ and GABRA and ḤARATHA and GHIBRA and NAYṢ the ancestor of the Sudanese [*el Sūdán*].

XXV The origin and ancestry of these is non-Arab [*'agam*], of white and black: Ibn el Ṣaláḥ mentions it in the Commentary on el Bokhári: he says this is transcribed from *El Anwár el Nebawia fi Abái Khayr el Baría*, and he says he found it in the fifth chapter of the *Anwár*, which treats of the chosen prophet of God....

XXVI Now el Sheríf Muḥammad el Amín el Hindi has mentioned that the tribes of GUHAYNA here in the Sudan Gezíra are seven, and they are registered in his own handwriting, thus:

M	G	R	M	Ḥ	R	R
MESALLAMÍA	GA'ÁFIRA	RIKÁBÍA	MA'ÁSHIRA	ḤAMAYLA	RUWÁÍḤA	ROWÁSHDA

C 9 (NOTES)

II For 'Abdulla el 'Araki see D 3, 34.

III "...*and named it*...": the Arabic is

وسماها طيبة لانها طابت بطيب الحبيب وطاب ثراها

(See Burton, *Pilgrimage*, I, p. 377, on this subject.)

For "YS" and "ṬH" cp. Hughes, pp. 517, 518. "There are 29 Sūrahs of the Qur'ān which begin with certain letters of the alphabet. These letters, the learned say, have some profound meaning, known only to the Prophet himself...." "YS" is applied to the 36th chapter of the Ḳurán (see Burton, *loc. cit.* I, p. 330). Cp. also BA, CXCVIII.

IV Cp. C 7, II.

V "Fala'alah Washm" (فلعله وشم) is probably an error.

"The Great Captain" is قايد الازمة. The *zumám* (زمام) is properly the small string of leather run through a riding camel's nostril and attached to the rein.

VIII In para. XXI "Ḥammad" is given instead of "Aḥmad."

X Though Ḥasan el Ma'árak is spoken of here as "ancestor of the 'ARAKIYYŪN" 'Abdulla el 'Araki himself was not descended from him according to para. V!

[1] reading غفار for عقار.

XIII Ibn 'Arafa was a Máliki divine in the fourteenth century (see Huart, p. 351), and perhaps he is referred to here. The Arabic of the dictum quoted is

العم يعقل عن ابن اخيه

The phrase has reference originally to liability for a share in blood-money, and there is a play on the word "'Áḳil."

XV Cp. C 7, III.

XXIII Cp. BA, XLVIII, etc.

"Dasham" is an error for Aslam.

XXIV Cp. BA, CXXXVII.

XXV Cp. C 7, IV.

The title of this work means "*The prophetic bouquet concerning the ancestry of the best of men.*"

XXVI Is almost certainly a late gloss. The Hindi family reside in the Gezíra: they are mentioned in D 1, CXXV.

This MGRMḤRR is merely a meaningless *memoriae technica* ("migram ḥarar").

TREE ILLUSTRATING MS. C9

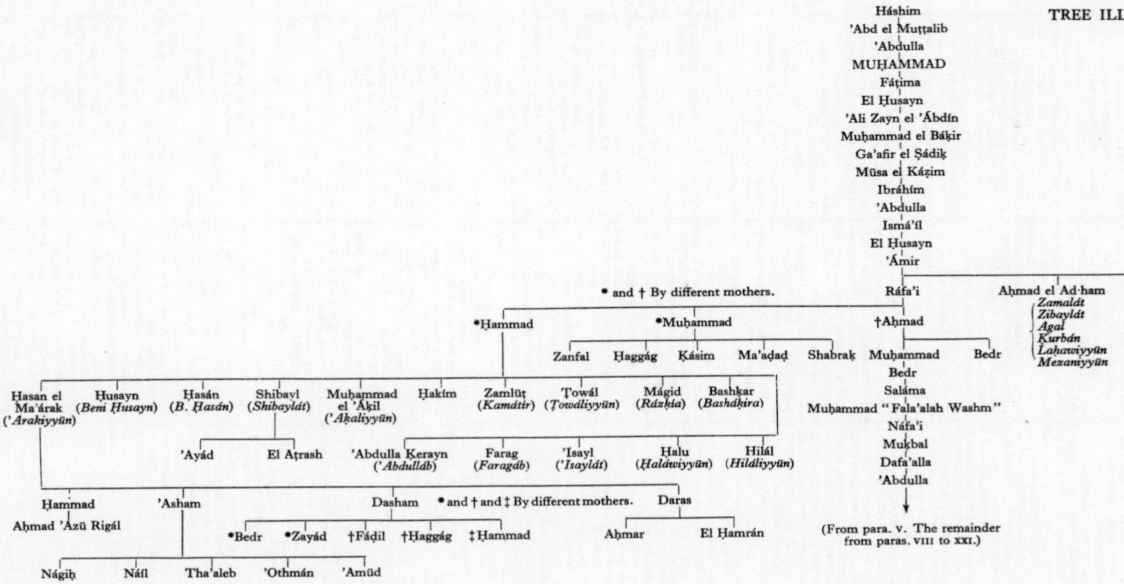

MANUSCRIPT D 1

Introduction

This work, consisting of eighty-five pages of MS., was copied out for me under the direction of Sheikh el Dardíri Muḥammad el Khalífa of Khorsi, the present *Khalífa* of the Tigánía *ṭariḳa* in Kordofán and one of the best known and most respected of the Dóálíb, who are a branch of the Rikábía "Ashráf" of Dongola. It was transcribed from the copy made by el Dardíri in 1884 from the copy taken by his father in 1836 from the oldest copy made in 1738 (see para. ccxvi).

The book falls into three quite distinct portions. The first sixty pages or so are the work of that Sayyid Ghulámulla ibn 'Áíd who was ancestor of the Rikábía and is related to have been a *Sheríf* who migrated to the Sudan from el Yemen and settled in Dongola (see D 5 (*d*)). His date was probably the fifteenth century.

The Sheríf el Ṭáhir who wrote or copied the original of BA was his great-nephew, but their works were quite independent of one another.

Ghulámulla does not concern himself with the Sudan at all: his compilation is cast in the traditional mould, and in arrangement and subject-matter nearly resembles Abu el Fidá's *Historia Ante-islamica*. It is certainly an abridgement of the history of some mediaeval Arabic encyclopaedist (*e.g.* Ibn el Athír), and it deals with the history of the world from the creation to the time of the 'Abbásids.

Several generations later, Ghulámulla's descendant Muḥammad walad Dólíb the Elder, who, as appears from D 3 (No. 187), flourished about 1680 A.D., added a further twenty pages ("Part II"). A portion of the contents of this second part are quotations (or misquotations) from Ibn el Athír—unacknowledged, by the way—the rest is a series of disconnected notes, some on the tribes of Arabia, and some on those of the Sudan. The author was evidently acquainted with the original of BA or extracts from it, as a comparison of paras. lxxxiv *et seq.* with BA shows with sufficient clearness.

His great-grandson the younger Muḥammad walad Dólíb, in the eighteenth century, added another briefer, and probably more original series of notes ("Part III"). It is fairly certain from internal evidence that glosses have been added fairly lavishly both in Part II and in Part III.

A translation of the first part (Ghulámulla's) is not given as it is irrelevant for all practical purposes, but its contents may be summarized as follows before we proceed to the translation of Parts II and III.

It begins:

In the name of God...Now this is a book in which I will collect all that has been verified by the historians and proved by the genealogists, and the fruit of my work shall be that he who has viewed the records of the past and the events of antecedent ages, when he reads of them shall be as it were their contemporary, and when he understands them shall be as it were a spectator of them...And the exposition of pedigrees will show who are exalted and noble by race, and men will learn to know one tribe from another, and by this knowledge shall war become peace and the distant be brought near, and there shall be that observance of the ties of consanguinity ordained by God Almighty....

The author then explains how historical research began in the time of the Khalífa 'Omar and how the Year of the Flight was agreed upon as the basis of Muslim chronology. He then sets to work upon his history, and begins with an account of the creation of the universe, and discusses the planets, the stars, the seasons, etc. Then follow the creation of man, the sojourn in Paradise, the generations that followed Adam, the Flood, and the descendants of Noah.

This leads the author to an account of the ancient tribes of Arabia and the other races of the world, and to the stories of Nimrod, and of Abraham, Job and other prophets, and the foundation of Mekka. Thence we pass to the history of the Israelites, of Persia, of Rome, and of Byzantium, including an account of Christ, and so on to the foundation of Islam.

After a very brief history of the Khalífas and a yet shorter mention of the struggle between the Beni Ommayya and the Beni 'Abbás the work of Sheikh Ghulámulla comes to an abrupt end, and Part II commences, without any preface beyond the single word "*tanbíh*" ("note"), as follows:

I KHUZÁM and the BENI KHUZAYMA are both sub-tribes of SULAYM.

II MAKHZŪM are a sub-tribe of ḲURAYSH and are descended from Makhzūm son of Yaḳẓa son of Murra son of Ka̧'ab son of Lūai son of Ghálib son of Fihr.

III GHATAFÁN are a section of ḲAYS 'AYLÁN and are descended from Ghatafán son of Sa'ad son of Ḳays 'Aylán.

IV BENI ḲUṬAYF are a Syrian people, of the BENI ṬAI.

V There is also a different people called BENI ḲUṬAYF, of [the tribe of] MUDHḤIG[1]: their ancestor is Ḳuṭayf son of Nágia son of Murád [of] the [same] section [as] Farwa son of Musayk the Ḳuṭayfi, the Associate of the Prophet.

VI ZENÁTA are a great tribe in the west and are descended from Zánáti Yaḥya son of Ḍari son of Bermádaghus son of Ḍari son of Zagík[2] son of Mádaghís son of Berr son of Bidyán son of Kana'án son of Hám son of Nūḥ.

VII The MESSÍRÍA Arabs, *i.e.* those originally so called, are descended from Missir son of Tha'aliba son of Naṣr son of Sa'ad son of Nebhán, [and are] a section of ṬAI.

VIII The MAHRÍA are a great tribe descended from Mahra son of Ḥaydán son of 'Amr son of el Ḥáfi[3] son of Ḳuḍá'a; and every Mahri traces his pedigree to him, and the Mahría camels of this tribe similarly owe their name to him.

IX ḤIMYAR are the sons of Ḥimyar son of Sabá son of Ya'arub son of Ḳaḥṭán. Now there are three Ḥimyars among the children of Ḳaḥṭán, viz. the "greater," the "lesser," and the "least." The "least" is Ḥimyar son of el Ghauth[4] son of Sa'ad son of 'Auf son of 'Adi son of Málik son of Zayd son of Sadad son of Zura'a. Ḥimyar the "lesser" is the son of Sabá the "lesser" son of Ka'ab son of Sahal son of Zayd son of 'Amr son of Ḳays son of Mu'áwia son of Gushm[5] son of 'Abd Shams son of Wáil son of el Ghauth son of Hadhár son of Ḳuṭn son of 'Aríb son of Zuhayr son of Aiman son of el Hamaysa'a[6] son of el Ferangag.

Ḥimyar the "greater" was son of Sabá the "greater" son of Yashḥub. Now some of the ḤIMYAR who are in the west belong to the ḤIMYAR of the east.

X The 'AḲALIYYŪN are descended from 'Uḳayl son of Ka'ab son of Rabí'a son of 'Ámir.

XI The MA'ÁḲLA are of the sons of Ma'aḳl son of Málik el Báhili and belong to the BÁHILA Arabs.

XII The RIZAYḲÁT are of the sons of Rizayḳ el Thaḳífi and belong to the BENI THAḲÍF, and there is a section of them in the Sudan.

XIII KHAFÁGA are a sub-tribe of BENI 'ÁMIR.

XIV FEZÁRA are descended from Fezára, the father of a sub-tribe of GHAṬAFÁN. This Fezára was son of Dhubián son of Baghíḍ son of

[1] reading مذحج for مدحج.
[2] reading زجيك for وجيك.
[3] reading الحافى for الحاف.
[4] reading الغوث for القوس.
[5] reading جشم for جسم.
[6] reading الهميسع for الهيسع.

Rayth[1] son of Ghaṭafán. The Beni el 'Ushará and the Beni Shamakh[2] are a part of them.

XV Ḳuḍá'a are descended from Ḥimyar, *i.e.* Ḳuḍá'a son of Málik son of Murra son of Zayd son of Málik son of Ḥimyar son of Sabá.

XVI Kenána are descended from Kenána son of Khuzayma son of Mudraka son of Elyás son of Muḍr, who was the fourth grandfather of our lord the Prophet.

XVII Guhayna is a sub-tribe of Ḳuḍá'a.

XVIII The Karg are a tribe of Rūm living on the frontiers of Adharbígán.

XIX The Tartars are a race living in the far east in the mountains of Ṭafmág on the borders of Ṣín. They are neighbours of the Turk, and between them and the lands of Islam which are beyond the river is a distance of more than six months. It was these people of whom the Prophet said that their features were most hideous.

XX The Khulug... are a tribe tracing their descent from Ḳuraysh. They do not, however, belong to them, but are rather an Arab people with whom 'Omar ibn el Khaṭṭáb has a common ancestor in el Ḥarith son of Málik son of el Nuḍr son of Kenána. It may be added that el Ḥarith was the brother of Fihr.

XXI Ḳuraysh are the descendants of Fihr; and the name of the ancestor of the Khulug was Ḳays.

XXII Zagháwa is a tribe of blacks, an offshoot of the Zing, and the derivative noun is Zagháwi.

XXIII Beni Hubl are a sub-tribe of Kelb and are the descendants of Hubl son of 'Abdulla son of Kenána son of 'Auf son of 'Udhra[3] son of Zayd el Dát son of Rufayda son of Thaur son of Kelb; and they include the descendants of Zuhayr son of Ganáb[4] son of Hubl, and the descendants of 'Abdulla son of 'Abdulla son of Hubl, and the descendants of 'Obayda son of Hubl.

XXIV Hilála are the descendants of Hilál son of 'Ámir son of Ṣa'aṣa'a son of Mu'áwia son of Bukr son of Hawázin. Of this tribe was Maymūna daughter of el Ḥarith, mother of the faithful, and Ḥamayd son of Thaur, the poet and Companion of the Prophet. They also won honourable mention at the battle of Hunayn. The Hilália are descended from them, and of their number was Abu Zayd el Hiláli, so famous for bravery and nobility. There are remnants of them in Egypt and in Morocco.

XXV The Messíría in reality are descendants of Missir (spelt with

[1] reading ريث for مريث.
[2] reading شمخ for شمح.
[3] reading عذرة for عذكرة.
[4] reading جناب for خباب.

an i) son of Tha'aliba son of Naṣr son of Sa'ad son of Nebhán[1], a branch of Ṭai.

XXVI The Ḥumur Arabs (spelt with a u after the Ḥ and the m) are descendants of the Master of the Ass, the Black One, the Liar, the false prophet who appeared in el Yemen, of the tribe of 'Aus; and his name was Aihala[2].

XXVII Bulála, who are between Borḳū and Bárḳirma, are descendants of Belál (Bulál ?) of [the tribe of] el Azd.

XXVIII Ḥamar (spelt with an a after the Ḥ and the m) in origin are descendants of el Aḥmar son of Mu'áwia son of Selím Abu Sha-'abil el Tamími, and they belong to the Beni Tamím.

XXIX The Sulaym Arabs (spelt with vowel-points as in "Zubayr") are descendants of Sulaym son of Manṣūr son of 'Ikrima son of Khaṣafa, a sub-tribe of Ḳays 'Aylán. There are also other Sulaym who are a sub-tribe of Gudhám; and of the former there are branches in the Sudan, and the latter are in the East.

XXX The Bedayría, that is the original Bedayría, are descendants of Bedr son of 'Amr son of Gūayya son of Laudhán[3] son of Tha'aliba son of 'Adi son of Fezára; and they are a section of Fezára.

XXXI Ghaṭafán are a sub-tribe of Ḳays 'Aylán, and their father was Ghaṭafán son of Sa'ad son of Ḳays 'Aylán.

Now Ḳays 'Aylán was the father of a tribe and his [real] name was el Náss (spelt with a double s), and he was son of Muḍr and brother of el Yás; and 'Aylán was a horse belonging to Ḳays, famous among the horses of the Arabs, and Ḳays used to win races upon it. There was too a man of the tribe of Bagíla called Ḳays Kubba after a horse called Kubba and also famous. These two men called Ḳays were neighbours before Bagíla settled in the land of Yemen, so that when anyone mentioned Ḳays he was asked whether he meant Ḳays 'Aylán or Ḳays Kubba.

XXXII Bagíla (shortened into Bagla) are a sub-tribe of Beni Sulaym and trace their descent to their mother, viz. Bagla daughter of Huná son of Málik son of Fahm. The derivative noun is Bagli.

XXXIII The Beni Bagála are a section of Ḍabba; and Bagála was son of Dhuhal son of Málik son of Bukr son of Sa'ad son of Ḍabba.

XXXIV Ḍabba is an Arab tribe and their father was Ḍabba (son of Udd) the uncle of Tamím son of Murr son of Udd son of Ṭábikha son of el Yás son of Muḍr. And Ḍabba had three sons, Sa'ad and Sa'íd and Básil, and Básil was father of the Daylum, and Sa'íd left

[1] reading نبهان for ببهان. [2] reading ايهلة for هبلة.
[3] reading لوذان for الارذان.

no posterity. The children of Ḍabba, excepting the DAYLUM, are included among the BENI SA'AD.

XXXV The DAYLUM are the children of Ḍabba, as I have shown.

XXXVI The BENI ḌUBAYB (spelt with vowel-points as in "Zubayr") are a section of GUDHÁM.

XXXVII GUDHÁM (spelt with vowel-points as in *ghuráb*) are a tribe from el Yemen who settled in the mountains of Ḥismá beyond the Wádi el Ḳurá; and this was the surname of 'Amr son of 'Adí son of el Ḥarith son of Murra son of Udad son of Yashkhub son of 'Aríb son of Zayd son of Kahlán, and Gudhám was brother of Lakhm and 'Ámila and 'Ufayr[1].

XXXVIII The BENI ṢÁHILA are the descendants of Ṣáhila son of Káhil son of el Ḥarith son of Tamím son of Sa'ad son of Hudhayl, and they are tribes and are called the KÁHILIYYŪN.

XXXIX The BENI KÁHIL son of 'Udhra son of Sa'ad Hudhayl[2] are a different tribe.

XL DŪS is a tribe of Arabs.

XLI BAGÍLA is a tribe from el Yemen, from Sabá.

XLII The BENI MUṢṬALIḲ are a section of KHUZÁ'A.

XLIII The KHAṬÁ are a tribe of the Turks.

XLIV The TA'ÁÍSHA Arabs are the descendants of 'Áish son of el Ẓarb son of el Ḥarith son of Fihr Gáhili; and this 'Áish was ancestor of 'Awaymir son of Sá'ada el Bedayri.

XLV The ḤAWÁZMA are a sub-tribe of BAGÍLA and are the children of Ḥázim son of Abu Ḥázim el Bagíli; but a number of Arab and black tribesmen, attracted by the advantages of fellowship and fraternity with them, [joined them], and the original stock and its accretions became indistinguishable.

XLVI KHUZÁ'A are [descended] from EL AZD[3]: that is to say Ḥáritha son of 'Amr Muzayḳiá son of 'Ámir begot Rabí'a, *i.e.* Má-el-Samá, and Rabí'a begot Loḥay and Afṣá and 'Oday and Ka'ab, and from these are descended KHUZÁ'A. Now they were called "KHUZÁ'A" because they separated [تخزعوا] from their [own] people and settled at Mekka; and others went to Syria.

XLVII The HABBÁNÍA are the descendants of Habbán son of el Ḳulūṣ son of 'Amr son of Ḳays, a sub-tribe of BÁHILA.

XLVIII BÁHILA are a tribe of ḲAYS 'AYLÁN, and originally Báhila was the name of a woman of Hamdán[4] who was [married] to Ma'an

[1] reading عفير for صفير.
[2] reading هذيل for هديم.
[3] reading الازد for الاسد.
[4] reading همدان for همذان.

son of Á'ṣir son of Sa'ad son of Ḳays 'Aylán, and Ma'an's descendants were named after her.

XLIX Now if you have studied these genealogical ramifications you must know that in the explanation of pedigrees that follows perhaps one pedigree resembles the form of another, but they are distinguishable from one another, pedigree from pedigree, and tribe from tribe; and the similarity is merely superficial: do not therefore be led astray, for nothing is included in this compilation but what is supported by the authority of trustworthy genealogists, or mentioned by the author of the Dictionary of the Arabic Language, or vouched for by him to the exclusion of any other version. If any genealogies are repeated in a form contradictory to that given previously, [it must be understood that] a variant version is being given.

L The great philosophers are Plato [Iflâṭūn] and Aristotle [Arisṭū] and Ptolemy [Baṭlímūs] and Galen [Gálínūs].

LI The father of the science of the supernatural was Plato, and it is founded upon inductive reasoning from objects of the senses realized by the help of the perceptive faculties.

LII Aristotle is the father of the natural sciences, such as treat of the heavens and the earth and existence and non-existence and meteorology and fundamental laws and botany and zoology, and they are founded upon the use of the perceptive faculties.

LIII The father of astronomy is Ptolemy, and it is founded upon the perceptive faculties and the laws of things perceptible.

LIV The father of experimental medicine is Galen, and it is founded upon the use of the perceptive faculties.

LV The pedigrees found in the works of reliable historians and genealogists are traced to the stock of Nūḥ, who alone among the children of Ádam survived the deluge for ever.

LVI The children of Nūḥ were Sám and Ḥám and Yáfith. [Wahhab ibn Munebbih says that] Sám son of Nūḥ was father of the Arabs and Persians [*Fáris*] and the Romans [*el Rūm*]; [and that] Ḥám was father of the blacks; and Yáfith of the Turks and Yágūg and Mágūg.

LVII Sám begot Arfakhshadh and Ashūdh and Láūdh and Aram.

LVIII From Láūdh son of Ḥám are descended Fáris, and Girgán, and Ṭasm, and 'Amlíḳ, father of the 'AMÁLÍḲ, who were the giants in Syria, who were called the KANA'ÁNIYYŪN[1]; and of them were the Pharaohs of Egypt; and [also] the people of Baḥrayn and 'Omán, and [these latter] were called[2] GÁSHIM: [of them too were the children of Omaym son of Láūdh...].

[1] reading الكنعانيون for اللنعاينون. [2] reading يستمون for يتمون.

LIX ṬASM dwelt in el Yemáma as far as Baḥrayn; and ṬASM and the 'AMÁLÍḲ and OMAYM[1] and GÁSHIM were Arab peoples, speaking the Arabic tongue [. Now 'Abíl reached Yathreb] before it (*i.e.* the town) was built.

LX And most of the 'AMÁLÍḲ settled in Ṣana'á before it was so named.

LXI Aram son of Sám son of Nūḥ begot 'Awaḍ and 'Ábir and Ḥuwayl. 'Awaḍ begot 'Ábir and 'Ád and 'Abíl.

LXII 'Ábir son of Aram begot THAMMŪD and GIDAYS; and they were Arabs, speaking this Egyptian tongue, and the Arabs used to call these nations and GURHUM "the 'Arab el 'Áriba," and the descendants of Ismá'íl they used to name "the 'Arab el Muta'ariba."

LXIII 'ÁD were in Ḥaḍramaut, and THAMMŪD in the rocky country between el Ḥegáz[2] and Syria [as far as Wádi el Ḳurá. GIDAYS] joined ṬASM and lived with them in el Yemáma as far as Baḥrayn. And the name of el Yemáma at that time was Gau. And GÁSHIM dwelt[3] in 'Omán.

LXIV The NEBṬ were descended from Nebíṭ son of Másh son of Aram son of Sám.

LXV The PERSIANS [*el Furs*] are the descendants of Fáris son of Tírash son of Máshūr son of Láūdh son of Sám.

LXVI Arfakhshadh son of Sám begot Ḳaynán[4], and Ḳaynán[4] begot Shálikh, and Shálikh begot 'Ábir, and 'Ábir begot Fáligh and also Ḳaḥṭán and Yūnán; and Ḳaḥṭán begot Ya'arub [and Yuḳẓán,] and Ya'arub begot Yashguḅ [, and Yashgub begot] Sabá, and Sabá begot Ḥimyar and Kahlán and 'Amr and el Asha'ar and Anmár and Murr.

LXVII 'Amr son of Sabá begot 'Adí, and 'Adí begot Lakhm and Gudhám.

LXVIII [Now Ya'arub and] Yuḳẓán settled in el Yemen, and were its earliest inhabitants and the first to be greeted with the words "mayest thou avoid execration."

LXIX Fáligh begot Ar'ū[5], and Ar'ū[5] begot [Sárūgh, who begot Náhūr, who begot Tárikh, in Arabic called] Azar, and Azar begot Ibráhím, (upon whom be the blessing of God).

LXX Arfakhshadh begot Nimrūdh; and [Háshim ibn el Kelbi states that] el Sind and el Hind were the children of Tūkir son of Yuḳṭan son of 'Ábir son of Shálikh son of Arfakhshadh son of Sám.

[1] reading اميم for ايتم. [2] reading الحجاز for الحجار.
[3] reading سكن for كسن. [4] reading قينان for قيقان.
[5] reading ارعو for ارغو.

LXXI Gurhum was descended from Yuḳṭan son of 'Ábir; and Ḥaḍramaut was son of Yuḳṭán. Now Yuḳṭán is Ḳaḥṭán [as is said...].

LXXII The BERBER are descended from Thamílá[1] son of Márib son of Fárán[2] son of 'Amr son of 'Amlíḳ son of Láūdh son of Sám son of Nūḥ.

LXXIII The Romans [*el Rūm*] are the children of Lanṭi[3] son of Yūnán son of Láūdh; and here I speak of the early Romans. The Romans of the Empire, who were numerous and powerful and who were contemporaries of the Prophet (upon him be the blessing of God), and of whom he made it known that their empire would last till the end of the world, were the children of Isḥáḳ son of Ibráhím the Friend of God (upon whom be the blessing of God); and here I speak of the later Romans. And all of them trace their descent to Sám son of Nūḥ.

LXXIV Yáfith begot Gámir and Mū'a and Mūrak and Būán and Fūyá and Máshig and Tírash.

LXXV From Gámir, it is said, were descended the kings of Persia [*Fáris*].

LXXVI From Tírash were descended the Turks and the KHAZAR; from Máshig the ASHBÁN; from Mū'a YÁGŪG and MÁGŪG; and from Būán the ṢAGHÁLIBA[4] and BURGÁN and the ASHBÁN, who in ancient days were in the land of the Romans, before the occurrence of the events connected with the children of el 'Aiṣ son of Isḥáḳ.

LXXVII Ḥám begot Kūsh and Miṣráím and Ḳūṭ and Kana'án.

LXXVIII From Kūsh was descended [Nimrūdh son of Kūsh,—and according to another account he was descended from Sám,—and the remainder of Ḥám's descendants came to live on the coasts as] the NŪBA and the Abyssinians [*Ḥábsha*] and the ZING.

LXXIX Miṣráím [, it is said,] was ancestor of the Copts (*Ḳubṭ*) [and the Berber].

LXXX [It is said that] Ḳūṭ penetrated to el Hind [and el Sind and settled there], and his descendants are there.

LXXXI Kana'án was ancestor of the KANA'ÁNIYYŪN; and some[5] of them went to Syria. Then the BENI ISRÁÍL fought with them there and expelled them and took possession of Syria. Subsequently the Romans attacked the BENI ISRÁÍL and drove them [excepting a few] from Syria to Mesopotamia [*el Iráḳ*]. Then again the Arabs came and conquered Syria.

[1] reading ثميلا for تميلا.
[2] reading فاران for فار.
[3] reading لنطى for نطى.
[4] reading الصغالبة for الصقالية.
[5] reading بعضهم for بعهم.

LXXXII Now it is related on the authority of 'Urwa ibn Misayk el Murádi that when the revelation concerning Sabá was made to the Prophet, a certain man said "O Prophet of God, what is Sabá? Is it a country or a woman?" The Prophet replied "It is neither a country nor a woman, but a man who begot ten [tribes] of the Arabs, and six of them went to Yemen and four of them to Syria: the latter were Lakhm and Gudhám and Ghassán and 'Ámila; and the former were el Azd and el Ash'ariūn and Ḥimyar and Kenda and Mudhḥig and Anmár." Then the man said "O Prophet of God, what is Anmár?" The Prophet answered "Those from whom are descended Khat'am and Bagíla."

LXXXIII Sabá was son of Yashkhub son of Ya'arub son of Ḳaḥṭán, and [his descendants] lived at Márib in the land of el Yemen, and when their villages were laid waste they dispersed into [various] lands: Ghassán occupied Syria, el Azd[1] occupied 'Omán[2], Khuzá'a occupied Teháma, and el Aus and el Khazrag occupied Yathreb, and the first of them[3] was 'Amr ibn 'Ámir, who was ancestor of el Aus and el Khazrag.

LXXXIV Now the tribes of the Arabs are Muzayna and Guhayna and Kenána and Khuzayma and Aslam and Ashga'a and Ghafár, and whoso does not belong to one of these is not an Arab but only a foreigner.

LXXXV Muzayna are to be found on the Nile and in Egypt;
Kenána are at Mekka and in el Yemen and thereabouts;
Guhayna are in the Sudan;
Aslam are in India and Mesopotamia [*el 'Iráḳ*];
Ashga'a are in the west and Persia [*Fáris*] and Morocco [*Marrákesh*]; and
Ghafár are in Spain [el Andalus] and Persia.

LXXXVI The Guhayna who are in the west are the descendants of 'Abdulla el Guhani, son of Anas, the attendant of the Prophet (upon him be the blessing of God!), and also connected with him by birth in that both had a common ancestor in Murra.

LXXXVII This 'Abdulla had two sons namely Dhubián and Sufián.

LXXXVIII Sufián had only one son, who was named Kabsh, and he is the ancestor of everyone who is a Kabbáshi.

LXXXIX Dhubián, the elder son, had ten sons, namely Watíd, Fahíd, Shaṭír, Bashír, 'Ámir, 'Omrán, Maḥass, Afzar, Ṣárid and Agdham[4].

1 reading الازد for الاسد. 2 reading عمان for عماد.
3 reading كان الذى قدم for كان الذين قدم.
4 reading اجذم for اجزم.

XC From Watíd are descended the SHUKRÍA, the BUÁDIRA and the UMBÁDIRÍA; and from Fahíd the ZAGHÁWA.

XCI Shaṭír's only son was Sulṭán, who had three sons, viz. Rikáb, Ma'ashir and Ḥamayd.

XCII Now there are three persons of the name of Rikáb: firstly Rikáb son of Ubi son of Ka'ab, secondly Rikáb son of Sulṭán son of Suhayl of the stock of 'Abdulla ibn Anas el Guhani, and thirdly Rikáb son of Ghulámulla, who was a *Sheríf* tracing his pedigree to el Ḥusayn the son of 'Ali and Fáṭima the daughter of the Prophet of God (the blessing of God upon them!). The mother of Rikáb the son of Ghulámulla was the daughter of Rikáb the son of Sulṭán, and his father named him after his maternal grandfather.

XCIII Rikáb the son of Sulṭán was ancestor of the RIKÁBÍA; and they live in Upper Egypt.

XCIV Ma'ashir was ancestor of the MA'ÁSHIRA, and Ḥamayd of the ḤAMAYDÁT, which is a tribe between el Sind and el Hind.

XCV Bashír was ancestor of the BISHÁRÍA, and 'Ámir of the 'AMÁRNA.

XCVI Maḥass was ancestor of the MAḤASS; and he was called Máḥass because he was a heavy sleeper, and whenever his father called to him his mother would say "má ḥassa" [*i.e.* "he has not awakened"]; so they called him Máḥass.

XCVII The descendants of Afzar are FEZÁRA.

XCVIII Ṣárid was ancestor of the ṢOWÁRDA, and Agdham[1] of the GUDHÁMIYYŪN[2].

XCIX The tribes descended from el 'Abbás are three, the GA'ALIYYŪN on the Blue Nile, the AWLÁD 'ABD EL RAḤMAN in Dár Ṣalíḥ, and the AWLÁD IBRÁHÍM BASHKAL on the White Nile.

C The tribes of the SHÁIḲÍA[3] fall into four divisions;—one is GA'ALIYYŪN, *i.e.* 'ABBÁSÍA, one is BENI OMMAYYA by descent, and one is a remnant of the Barmecides [*el Barámika*], *i.e.* Turkish.

CI The 'ARAKIYYŪN are descended from GUHAYNA, but among them are the children of el Sheríf Aḥmad Muḳbal, who married a wife from among the 'ARAKIYYŪN and begot Dafa'alla the ancestor of their pious *Khalífas*; and the latter's children were Bukr Abu 'Áyesha and 'Abdulla and Ḥammad el Níl.

CII This Ḥammad el Níl's descendants are the 'ÁḲLÁB, including el Sheikh el Ṭerayfi.

CIII The tribes of the GA'ÁFIRA fall into three [groups]; among them

[1] reading اجذم for اجزم. [2] reading جذاميين for جزاميين.
[3] reading الشايقية for الشاقية.

are the stock of 'Ámir and 'Omrán in the neighbourhood of Diráw, and they [are...*a word omitted in the text*]: among them again are the Awlád Ga'afir el Ṣádiḳ, who are ASHRÁF, and the Awlád Ga'afir el Ṭiár who are BENI HÁSHIM; and the DERR, the rulers of Egypt.

CIV The tribes of the RIKÁBÍA are three: the descendants of Rikáb ibn Anas of ḲURAYSH, the descendants of Rikáb ibn Sulṭán of GUHAYNA, and the descendants of Rikáb ibn Ghulámulla. The last named are ASHRÁF of the stock of el Ḥusayn (the blessing of God on him) the son of 'Ali and of Fáṭima the daughter of the Prophet of God (on all of whom be the blessings of God).

CV El Sheikh Ghulámulla had two sons, Rikáb and Rubáṭ.

CVI Rikáb had five sons, 'Abdulla, 'Abd el Nebi, Ḥabíb, 'Agíb, and Zayd el Feríd.

CVII Rubáṭ had one son named Selím.

CVIII Selím had six sons Ruzayn, Dahmash, Muḥammad 'Ón, 'Abd el Rizáḳ, Hadhlūl, and Muṣbáḥ.

CIX 'Abdulla's sons were Ḥaga and Ḥagág.

CX Ḥaga was ancestor of the DÓÁLÍB, the children of el Sheikh walad Dólíb.

CXI Ḥagág was ancestor of el Sheikh 'Ali walad 'Ishayb (the progenitor of the 'ISHAYBÁB), and of el Sheikh walad Ak·ḥal and of a section of the KAWÁHLA at Teḳali and of the ḤADÁḤÍD and of the GENÁNA and of the SIMRIÁB and of many households [living] with the SHUKRÍA.

CXII 'Abd el Nebi had two sons, Máshir and Shakára.

CXIII Among the descendants of Máshir was el Sheikh 'Abd el Ṣádiḳ ancestor of the ṢÁDIḲÁB; and among the descendants of Shakára was Ḥasan walad Shakára and the 'ABÍDÁB and the NŪRÁB [who lived] at el 'Afáṭ in Dongola and left it and joined the KABÁBÍSH and multiplied with them and became nomads.

CXIV The descendants of Ḥabíb are the ṢABÁBÍA.

CXV The descendants of 'Agíb are the stock of el Sheikh Ḥammad[1] Abu Ḥalíma the ancestor of the ḤALÍMÁB.

CXVI The descendants of Zayd el Feríd were the SHABWÁB and the 'AKÁZÁB and the TAMRÁB and the four sons of el Ḥág Mágid.

CXVII Selím, the son of Rikáb's brother, had six sons, as has been mentioned above.

CXVIII The descendants of Ruzayn were the AWLÁD ḤABÍB NESI.

CXIX The descendants of Dahmash were the AWLÁD EL FEKI 'ALI MANÓFAL at el 'Afáṭ.

[1] reading حمد for احمد.

CXX The descendants of Muḥammad 'Ón were the four AWLÁD GÁBIR and the KENÁNÍA.

CXXI The descendants of 'Abd el Rizáḳ were the AWLÁD EL SHEIKH ḤASAN WALAD BELÍL at Kená[1] and the AWLÁD DÁŪD at Abu Tubr.

CXXII The descendants of Hadhlūl were the AWLÁD MAḤMŪD at Gebel el Ḥaráza.

CXXIII The descendants of Muṣbáḥ were the AWLÁD WALAD DÁŪD with the KABÁBÍSH.

CXXIV These are the branches of the RIKÁBÍA who are descended from Ghulámulla and are ASHRÁF.

CXXV *The following are the tribes of ASHRÁF who are in the Sudan:*

The descendants of the aforementioned Ghulámulla.
The MIRGHANÍA, *i.e.* the descendants of 'Othmán el Mírghani.
The AWLÁD EL HINDI in the Gezíra.
The AWLÁD ABU SAḤNŪN at Atbara: they are descendants of el Ḥasan el Muthenni.
The MAR'IÁB EL ḤAMDÁB at Atbara with the nomads: these are ḤUSAYNÍA.
The AWLÁD EL MAGDHŪB at Atbara with the SHUKRÍA.
The AWLÁD EL SHAGERA at el Ḳeḍáref.
The AWLÁD EL SHERÍF ISMÁ'ÍL at el Ḳeḍáref: these are ḤUSAYNÍA.
The AWLÁD BEDR WALAD[2] MASKÍN to the west of el Ḳeḍáref: these are ḤUSAYNÍA.
The SHIBAYLÁT with the BENI ḤUSAYN Arabs, nomads on the Blue Nile.
The KAMÍLÁT in the neighbourhood of Atbara: these are ḤUSAYNÍA.
The AWLÁD BIDAYN in the neighbourhood of el Ḥamda: these are ḤUSAYNÍA.
The AWLÁD BELLA near Karkóg on the Blue Nile: these are ḤASANÍA.
The AWLÁD MUṢṬAFA at Asláng[3] Island.
The AWLÁD 'ABDULLA EL MEKANI at el Táka: these are ḤASANÍA; and some of them are at Kassala and some at Sūákin; and they are of the stock of Abu el Fataḥ.
The AWLÁD ABU RAKHM, near the Rahad, on the Blue Nile: these are ḤASANÍA.
The AWLÁD OBAYḌ near the Dinder: these are ḤUSAYNÍA.
The AWLÁD HAGŪ with the YA'AḲŪBÁB: these are ḤASANÍA.
The AWLÁD ḤAMMAD IBN 'ALI of the ZAGHÁWA hills in Kordofán: these are ḤASANÍA; and they have migrated to Gebel Abu Sinūn and Teḳali and Dárfūr and are known as AWLÁD EL AK·ḤAL. Some of them too are near Erḳud.
The AWLÁD ZAYD EL ABLAG in Dárfūr: these are ḤASANÍA.
The AWLÁD EL SHERÍF HÁSHIM ABU NIMSHA in Dár Borḳū: these are ḤASANÍA.
The BENI ḤUSAYN in Dár Sulá: these are ḤUSAYNÍA.

[1] reading كنا for كنار. [2] reading ولد for و.
[3] reading اسلانج for اسلاج.

CXXVI As regards the tribes of the GAWÁMA'A:—the ḤOMRÁN section consists of

- the AWLÁD GÁMA'Ï
- the SERAYḤÁT
- the ṬERAYFÍA
- the AWLÁD MURG
- the FAḌAYLÍA
- the GHANAYMÍA
- the GAMRÍA

CXXVII The GIMÍ'IA, the cousins of the ḤOMRÁN, consist of

- the GEMÁMLA
- the GA'AFIRÍA
- the AWLÁD BÍKA

CXXVIII All of these [GAWÁMA'A] are descended from Abu Merkha the ancestor of the GA'ALIYYŪN, of the stock of el 'Abbás: and some of them are SHILLUK AWLÁD IBRÁHÍM.

CXXIX GANḲAY are 'ANAG, from among the ZING.

CXXX The KABÁBÍSH are a composite tribe, including some SHÁIḲÍA and GUHAYNA and ḤIMYÁR and ḲURAYSH.

CXXXI The KAWÁHLA are descended from el Zubayr (God bless him) and include some ḲURAYSH and descendants of Khálid ibn el Walíd.

CXXXII The SHENÁBLA are Arabs of Upper Egypt [*el Ríf*] and of Ḥimyaritic descent.

CXXXIII DÁR ḤÁMID are GUHAYNA by descent.

CXXXIV The ḤAWÁZMA[1] include Beduin Arabs from el Ḥegáz and BEDAYRÍA and TAKÁRÍR and scatterlings of other tribes.

CXXXV The MESSÍRÍA and BENI MUḤAMMAD and MÍMA are all of them THA'ALEBA from the BENI THA'ALEB Arabs of el Ḥegáz.

CXXXVI The RIZAYḲÁT are descendants of Gunayd, [and thus] 'ABBÁSÍA.

CXXXVII The ḤUMR are Arabs of Ḥelb in Upper Egypt [*el Ríf*], and the 'AYÁDÍA Arabs of Ḥira.

CXXXVIII The HABBÁNÍA are BENI OMMAYYA by descent.

CXXXIX The BEDAYRÍA who are in the Sudan include some 'ABBÁSÍA and some 'ANAG: they consist of

- SHUWAYḤÁT
- RÍÁSH
- DAHMASH[2]
- AWLÁD MŪSA
- AWLÁD ḤELAYB

[1] reading الحوازمة for الجوازمة. [2] reading دهمش for وهمش.

CXL KENÁNA are Arabs of the East by descent.

CXLI ZAGHÁWA include some BENI TAMÍM Arabs, some MÍMA and some TAKRŪR[1].

CXLII FUNḲUR are 'ANAG.

CXLIII TUNGUR are by descent HILÁLA who ruled Dárfūr.

CXLIV MUSABA'ÁT are also descended from the HILÁLA Arabs.

CXLV The BENI GERÁR are FEZÁRA by descent: their ancestor was Hunád.

CXLVI The MEGÁNÍN and AWLÁD AḲOI are GUHAYNA Arabs by descent.

CXLVII FEZÁRA are among the descendants of Hunád from el Ḥegáz.

CXLVIII Of the ḤAMAR, the TAMÍMÍA, viz. the stock of el Ḥág Muna'am, are BENI OMMAYYA by descent; and

The GHISHÍMÁT[2] are GA'ALIYYŪN, *i.e.* 'ABBÁSÍA; and

The BENI BADR are BEDAYRÍA; and

The TAYÁISA[3] are 'ANAG; and

The DEḲÁḲÍM are partly ḤUSAYNÍA ASHRÁF and partly BENI OMMAYYA: they also include some FŪR.

CXLIX The DANÁḲLA tribes are autochthonous and are all 'ANAG, excepting such strangers as immigrated to their country, namely the RIKÁBÍA AWLÁD GHULÁMULLA, who are ASHRÁF, and the GHARBÁWINGI from Borḳū, who are 'ABBÁSÍA, and the DUFÁRÍA, who are BEDAYRÍA, and the BEKRÁWÍA, who are GA'ALIYYŪN, and the SOWÁRÁB, who are ASHRÁF on the side of their ancestress, the daughter of el Sherif Aḥmad Abu Denána, and the SÁBÁWÍA, who are BEDAYRÍA of the DUFÁRÍA branch. The rest of the DANÁḲLA are 'ANAG and aboriginal autochthons, and there are some remnants of them at the present day who are called the NŪBA.

CL The FŪR are NŪBA with the exception of the royal house which includes Arabs of the BENI HILÁL.

CLI As regards BORḲŪ, the royal house includes AWLÁD 'ABD EL RAḤMAN EL MAGDHŪB the 'Abbásid, but the rest of [the people of] Borḳū are autochthonous 'ANAG, though they include some Arabs, such as the SALÁMÁT and the MAHRÍA, who are descendants of the BENI OMMAYYA.

CLII BORNŪ are Arabs of Ḥimyaritic stock, and include some ḤUSAYNÍA ASHRÁF.

CLIII BÁKIRM are 'ANAG.

CLIV FELLÁTA include ḲURAYSH and ANṢÁR and children of the

[1] reading تكرور for تكرون. [2] reading الغشيمات for الخشيمات.
[3] reading تيايسة for تياسية.

White Gin which deceived the prophet of God Sulaymán (God bless him), and Christian slaves who came to West [Africa] from Aftūriá and conquered it, but were subsequently conquered by Islám and converted, and then multiplied for generation after generation in West [Africa].

CLV The rest of the inhabitants of Kordofán from the banks of the White Nile to Donḳola are 'Anag. The country to the west of it and south of it, and all its mountains, are [peopled by] Nūba.

CLVI Fertít are all Zing by descent.

CLVII The Beni Helba Arabs in the West are descended from the Beni 'Ámir Arabs of the Ḥegáz.

CLVIII So too the Selím Arabs on the White Nile and in the Gezíra and at Teḳali and in the West are descended from the Selím Arabs of the Ḥegáz.

CLIX The Gellába el Howára are from Upper Egypt [*el Ríf*] and descended from remnants of the stock of 'Ád.

CLX The Baza'a are descended from the tribes of el Ḥuḍūr, Arabs of Upper Egypt [*el Ríf*], and are connected in lineage with the Derr.

CLXI The Selímía are Ashráf, and likewise the Awlád el Magmar at Um Gurfa[1].

CLXII The Dágu and the inhabitants of Kága and Katūl are 'Anag.

CLXIII The Ghodiát are Hamag.

CLXIV The people of Sennár are Beni Ommayya by descent.

CLXV The Mesallamía are Bedayría by descent.

CLXVI The Dwayḥ Arabs are Guhayna by descent.

CLXVII The Nūba of el Ḥaráza and Um Durraḳ and Abu Ḥadíd are 'Anag, excepting the Awlád Maḥmūd at el Ḥaráza who are Rikábía Ashráf.

CLXVIII The people of Abu Tubr are partly Mágidía, and partly Rikábía Ashráf.

CLXIX The Nūba of Abu Sinūn are 'Anag by descent.

CLXX The Kurtán are 'Anag by descent.

CLXXI The Ḥasánía Arabs on the White Nile are Guhayna by descent.

CLXXII The Shanáḳíṭ in the West are a medley of Arabs, containing nomad Arabs and Derr Arabs and Arabs of Upper Egypt [*el Ríf*], and there have joined them some Ashráf of the [Beni] 'Abbás and the Ḥasanía and the Ḥusaynía; and the lineage of each is known.

CLXXIII The Moghárba are Arabs of Upper Egypt [*el Ríf*], and

[1] reading جرفة for جرف.

their origin is from the Tartar [*Tatar*] peasants who are in the deserts.

CLXXIV The [people of] FEZZÁN [*el Fayzán*[1]] are also Arabs of Upper Egypt by descent, Tartars.

CLXXV The MOGHÁRBA AWLÁD ZERRŪḲ EL MOGHRABI are ASHRÁF ḤUSAYNÍA in the West; for the ASHRÁF in the days of the BENI OMMAYYA were scattered eastwards and westwards, and similarly the BENI OMMAYYA in the time of the BENI 'ABBÁS reached the western country [*el moghrab*] and conquered it and took possession of it, and their progeny is represented by numberless tribes in the West at present.

CLXXVI Among the ASHRÁF in the West are the stock of Muḥammad el Thauri; and of his stock are Aḥmad el Waráḳ and Zurrūḳ el Moghrabi and Abu el Ḥasan el Shádhali and 'Abd el Raḥím el Bura'i; and they also include the stocks of el Shibli and of Sheikh el Dasūḳi. All of the above are ḤASANÍA in Morocco [*el moghrab el aḳṣá*].

CLXXVII The GAMŪ'ÍA and the GIMÍ'ÁB are GA'ALIYYŪN, *i.e.* 'ABBÁSIA, and similarly most of the SHÁÍḲÍA are GA'ALIYYŪN.

HERE ENDS BOOK II

BOOK III

CLXXVIII The original autochthonous peoples of the Sudan were the NŪBA and the Abyssinians [*el Ḥabsha*] and the ZING.

CLXXIX The first people who subsequently joined them were the BERBER.

CLXXX Every [tribe] that is derived from the HAMAG belongs to the ZING group, and every [tribe] that is derived from the FUNG belongs to the NŪBA group.

CLXXXI The tribes of the Arabs who are in the Sudan, other than these, are foreigners, and have merely mixed with the tribes mentioned above and multiplied with them. Some of them have retained the characteristics of the Arabs, and the element of NŪBA and ZING that is interspersed among them has adopted the Arab characteristics; and on the other hand there have been some Arabs who have become fused with the NŪBA and the ZING and adopted their characteristics; but in each case they know their origin.

CLXXXII The original [home] of the ZING is a mountain inhabited by blacks on the equator and south [of it]. Beyond them are no

[1] reading الفيزان for الفيران.

other peoples; and their country stretches from West Africa [*el moghrab*] to the neighbourhood of Abyssinia, and part of it is on the Nile of Egypt.

CLXXXIII SENNÁR was a famous city of Abyssinia, containing tribes of ZING and NŪBA who were subject to Abyssinia. Subsequently, when they became powerful, they broke away from their allegiance and appointed kings of their own and defended themselves against Abyssinia and protected their lands.

CLXXXIV The BERBER are a nation of people whose tribes are innumerable, descended from the 'AMÁLÍḲ. It was they of whom the saying is related "All that is abominable consists of seventy portions: of these ninety-nine [per cent. ?] is in the BERBER and the [remaining] one in the human race and the Gin."

CLXXXV Most of their tribes are in the west in the mountains of Sūs, etc., and scattered abroad in the neighbouring regions. They include ZENÁTA[1] and HOWÁRA and ṢANHÁGA and NABRA and KETÁMA and LUÁTA and MADYŪNA and SÁNA.

CLXXXVI Another nation of them lives between the Abyssinians and the ZING, on the shores of the sea of the ZING and the sea of el Yemen; and these people[2] are blacks and have strange beasts in their country, nor are there to be found there such animals as the giraffe, the rhinoceros, the hunting leopard, the pard and the elephant. They too it is who cut off men's organs and present them as dowries to their women.

CLXXXVII Their island lies off[3] the coast of Abyan and is connected under the sea with 'Aden from the direction of the point at which Subayl rises to eastwards of that point: opposite to it lies 'Aden and in front of it is Gebel el Dukhán. This island is Soḳóṭrá[4], lying off 'Aden and directly opposite to it.

CLXXXVIII The SALÁMÁT Arabs in the west are [descended] from ḲUḌÁ'A.

CLXXXIX The people of the Sudan are the NŪBA and the Abyssinians [*el Ḥabsha*], as has been stated.

CXC The [descendants of] DAYLUM son of Básil son of Ḥasba son of Udd son of Ṭábikha son of el Yás son of Muḍr are Arabs.

CXCI GURHUM are a people in el Yemen descended from Gurhum son of Ḳaḥṭán son of 'Ámir son of Shálikh son of Arfakhshadh son of Sám son of Nūḥ; and Ismá'íl the son of Ibráhím, the Friend of

[1] reading زناتة for زنانة. [2] reading هم for هو.

[3] reading جزيرتهم قاطعة for جزيرهم فاطعة.

[4] reading سقوطرى for سعوطرى.

God, settled and married among them, and they are his relations by marriage.

CXCII THAMMŪD are the descendants of Thammūd son of 'Ábir son of Aram son of Sám son of Nūḥ.

CXCIII The SULAYM Arabs are said to be [descended] from Ḳays 'Aylán.

CXCIV GHASSÁN are EL AZD. Of them are the BENI GAFNA, the royal family.

CXCV EL AZD are the descendants of Azd son of el Ghauth[1] son of Nabt son of Málik son of Kahlán son of Sabá. They are in Yemen and include all the ANṢÁR.

CXCVI And the children of Asad son of Khuzayma son of Mudraka son of el Yás son of Muḍr are a mighty tribe descended from Muḍr EL ḤAMARÁ; and also the children of Asad son of Rabí'a son of Nizár son of Ma'ad son of 'Adnán are a mighty tribe.

CXCVII The COPTS [*el Ḳubṭ*] are the people of Egypt and its ultimate aboriginals: they are descended from Ḳubṭ son of Miṣr son of Ḳūt son of Ḥám.

CXCVIII The FRANKS [*el Afrang*] are a nation of the Romans [*el Rūm*]. They call the seat of their kingdom Franga, and its king is named "el Fransís."

CXCIX The TURKS [*el Turuk*] are a nation of people descended from Yáfith, and they include the Tartars [*el Tatár*] and Gog and Magog [*Yagūg and Mágūg*]. They are a mighty people:—there is none more numerous excepting the Abyssinians [*el Ḥabsha*]; and there is no more numerous people than the Abyssinians, excepting the Romans [*el Rūm*].

CC The name Christian [*Nuṣári*] is to be traced to Christianity [*el Nuṣránia*], *i.e.* their religion and the faith they follow.

CCI "The JEWS" [*el Yahūd*] is the name of a tribe, and the name is derived from *háda* meaning "to repent."

CCII The ROMANS [*el Rūm*] are descended from el Rūm son of Esau ['Iṣū] son of Isaac [Isḥáḳ] son of Ibráhím the Friend of God, and they are named after their ancestor. It is related that Esau had thirty sons, of whom el Rūm was one; but these Romans have been joined by tribes [*lit.* "branches"] that did not belong to them, namely TANŪKH and NIHD and SULAYM and GHASSÁN: these tribes were in Syria [*el Shám*], and when the Muslims drove them out they entered the lands of the Romans and mingled and multiplied with them and were reckoned as Romans by descent; but they are not Romans and the Roman genealogists know the fact.

[1] reading غوث for غرث.

CCIII NIHD are the sons of Nihd son of Zayd son of Líth son of Aslam son of el Ḥáf son of Ḳudá'a.

CCIV TANŪKH are a tribe from el Yemen. They and the BENI NIMR and the BENI KELB are brethren.

CCV TAKRŪR is the name of a famous city in the Sudan: it lies south and west of the Nile, and its inhabitants are naked blacks. The rule of it is in the hands of the Muslims; and the nobles among these Muslims wear a long shirt, the train [*lit.* "tail"] of which is carried by their servants. Arab merchants travel thither to them with wool and brass and beads, and fetch thence pure gold.

CCVI ABYSSINIA is an enormous country. There was a city under the rule of the Abyssinians called Akhshūm[1], also known as Dhur Taḥná, where the Negus [*Negáshi*] lived; and a number of countries were subject thereto, including the country of Amḥara[2] (which is still so subject) and the country of Sáwa and the country of Dámūt and the country of Lamán and the country of el Sínhū and the country of the ZING and the country of 'Adel el Amrái and the country of Ḥamásá and the country of Bádimyá and the country of Abu Ḥaráz el Islámi and the country of Zíla'a. Each one of these countries has a king [who is] under the Khaṭí (which means Sultan), under whom there is a total of 99 kings, he himself being the hundredth.

CCVII Now all the Sudan used to be in fear of the king of Abyssinia and court him with flattery, in some cases obeying him and in some [merely] flattering him.

Finally they broke away from their allegiance to him, and each mountain became independent, and his rule was restricted to the mountains of the Abyssinians.

CCVIII Subsequently the HAMAG conquered the banks of the White Nile, and the nations of the ZING were divided into numerous sections, of whom some found leaders among their own number, and others were subjected by the tribes of the Arabs who conquered their land.

CCIX Lastly the dominion of Kordofán fell to the FUNG[3] for seven years, then to the GHODIÁT (who are HAMAG by descent) for thirteen years. After the GHODIÁT, the MUSABA'ÁT ruled it for seventeen years: then [the] KUNGÁRA (who are the rulers of Dárfūr) ruled it for thirty-six years.

CCX The Turks took Kordofán from the KUNGÁRA in the year 1233[4], having one year previously taken the dominion of the White Nile from the *Meks* of the GA'ALIYYŪN and the remnants of the HAMAG.

[1] reading اخشوم for اخشرم.

[2] reading امحرة for امجرة.

[3] reading للفونج for للوج.

[4] 1818 A.D.

CCXI God knows the truth, and He is the first and the last, and to Him do all men return.

CCXII Be it known that this compilation is from the histories [*lit.* "history"] of three men.

CCXIII From the beginning to the mention of the Khalífas, and on to the mention of 'Ísa, the prophet of God, is by el Sayyid Ghulámulla.

CCXIV From the first "*tanbíh*," at which point begins the account of KHUZÁM and BENI KHUZAYMA, is by el Sayyid Muḥammad walad Dólíb the elder, up to the second "*tanbíh*."

CCXV From the second "*tanbíh*," at which begins the account of the origin of the Sudanese, up to the end of the book, is by el Sayyid Muḥammad walad Dólíb the younger, who is buried at Khorsi.

CCXVI This work was copied by my father in his handwriting in 1252[1] from the copy made in 1151[2]; and I made this copy on the second of Ramaḍán in the year 1302[3] after the Flight of the Prophet.

[1] 1836 A.D. [2] 1738 A.D. [3] 1884 A.D.

D I (NOTES)

Note that where the reference to Wüstenfeld is marked by a letter the tribe in question is Ismá'ílitic in descent; but where the reference is marked by a figure the tribe is Ḳaḥṭánite.

II Makhzūm to Fihr correct: see Wüstenfeld, R 17.

III Ghatafán to Ḳays 'Aylán correct: see Wüstenfeld, H 8.

IV This Ḳuṭayf is not in Wüstenfeld. The BENI ṬAI are Ḳaḥṭánite.

V See Wüstenfeld, 7. This Ḳuṭayf was son of 'Abdulla son of Nágia... etc.

Farwa was the eighth generation in the direct line from Ḳuṭayf.

VI Cp. Ibn Khaldūn (trans. de Slane, Vol. III, p. 180). He states that genealogists are united in saying that the ZENÁTA are descended from Chana. "Abou Mohammed ibn Hazm écrit, dans son Djemhera: 'quelques uns d'entre eux [*i.e.* Berbers] disent que Chana est le même personnage que Djana fils de Yahya fils de Soulat fils d'Ourçak fils de Dari fils de Zeddjîk fils de Madghis fils de Berr.'" Ibn Khaldūn mentions also a variant given by the same author, viz. Chana (or Djana) son of Yahya son of Soulat son of Ourçak son of Dari son of Chacfoun son of Bendouad son of Imla son of Madghis son of Herek son of Herçac son of Guerad son of Mazîgh son of Herak son of Herîk son of Bedîan son of Kenan son of Ham.

VII See Wüstenfeld, 6. Nebhán was great-grandson of Ṭai, the founder of the great Ḳaḥṭánite tribe of ṬAI. The descendants of Nebhán are correctly given, but for مسِيرِ Wüstenfeld gives مسخر; and "MESSÍRÍA" may thus be a corruption of "MESKHÍRÍA." Cp. paras. XXV and CXXXV and see Part III, Chap. 3, *sub* "ḤAWÁZMA."

VIII Pedigree given correctly, but contrast para. CLI: see Wüstenfeld, 1. The Mahría are a branch of ḲUDÁ'A. Cp. D'Arvieux's *Travels* (p. 345): "Mahrah is a Province in which there are neither Palms nor Cultivated Lands: The Inhabitants have no other Effects than Camels...Alsahah reports that the Camel called Almahrary or of Mahrah is so named from Mahrah the son of Hamdan, the Founder of a tribe." See also el Mas'ūdi (Chap. 16): "They (*i.e.* the people of el Mahrah) have a sort of camel called Mahri camel: it goes as fast as the Bejáwí camel, or even faster as some think."

IX Sabá was son of Yashgub (or Yashḥub) son of Ya'arub: see Wüstenfeld, 1.

The "lesser" and the "least" Ḥimyars are not mentioned by Wüstenfeld, but their alleged ancestors are: see Wüstenfeld, 3.

A confusion has arisen between two men called Zayd: one, the son of Sahal son of 'Amr, was the ancestor of Málik and 'Adi, etc., as given: the other was son of Sadad son of Zura'a son of Sabá "the lesser," who was grandson of the first Zayd (son of Sahal). Sahal and Zayd have been transposed by the copyist: otherwise all is correct from Sabá "the lesser" to el Ghauth.

"Hadhár" is an obvious slip for Gaydán (حذار for جيدان).

"Son of 'Auf" should be inserted before "son of 'Aríb.

"El Ferangag" should be Ḥimyar (*i.e.* the "greater").

By these "three Ḥimyars" are perhaps not meant persons but sections of the great Ḥimyarite tribe, descended from Ḳaḥṭán. It will have been seen that both the lesser branches mentioned are descended from Zayd ibn Sahal, who was the fifteenth descendant, in the direct line, of Ḥimyar the "greater."

The copyist sometimes gives "Yashḥub," sometimes "Yashgub," or even "Yashkhub." Wüstenfeld uses "Yashgub" (and so too Ibn el Athír): Abu el Fidá uses "Yashḥub."

X Pedigree given correctly: see Wüstenfeld, D. 'Ámir was of the tribe of HAWÁZIN.

XI For Báhila see Wüstenfeld, G. "Ma'aḳl" is no doubt an invention.

XII THAḲÍF is a branch of HAWÁZIN: see Wüstenfeld, G. Contrast para. CXXXVI.

XIII Correct: see Wüstenfeld, D. For BENI 'ÁMIR see note to X.

XIV Correct: see Wüstenfeld, H. Contrast para. CXLVII.

XV "Son of 'Amr" is omitted between Málik and Murra: otherwise correct: see Wüstenfeld, 1.

XVI Pedigree correct: see Wüstenfeld, N. "Fourth" is a slip for "fourteenth." Cp. para. CXL.

XVII Correct: see Wüstenfeld, 1.

XVIII The "KARG" are the Georgians: cp. Abu el Fidá (p. 168), and el Mas'ūdi (p. 433).

XIX "Ṣín" is China. "Tafmág" I cannot trace: it is not in Yaḳūt. "The lands of Islam which are beyond the river" are Transoxiana.

XX Two words here are illegible.

The pedigree from el Khulug to Kenána is correct: see Wüstenfeld, N. But Málik, and not el Ḥarith his son, is the first common ancestor of el Khulug and 'Omar ibn el Khaṭṭáb (for whom see Wüstenfeld, P).

XXI See Wüstenfeld, O.

This Ḳays is not mentioned by Wüstenfeld.

XXII "ZING" is used by Arab writers as a generic name for the East African blacks: *e.g.* see el Mas'ūdi (pp. 178, 232, 261, 380) and Abu el Fidá (p. 174). Cp. also note to D 4, XX.

XXIII See Wüstenfeld, 2. KELB is a sub-tribe of ḲUḌÁ'A. "Son of Bukr" has been omitted between Kenána and 'Auf: otherwise the pedigree is correct as far as "Ganáb son of Hubl."

'Abdulla and 'Obayd are among the descendants of Hubl in Wüstenfeld, but are not his sons.

XXIV The pedigree is quite correct: see Wüstenfeld, D.

For Maymūna see Wüstenfeld, F: she was one of the Prophet's wives.

The battle of Hunayn took place in 630 A.D.: at it Muḥammad defeated the BENI HAWÁZIN, of whom HILÁLA (or BENI HILÁL) are a section.

For Abu Zayd el Hiláli see MacMichael (*Tribes*...), *passim*, and Part I, Chap. 4.

XXV This is repeated from para. VII above: contrast para. CXXXV.

XXVI Contrast para. CXXXVII, and see note to A 11, LXII. The vituperative remarks on the ḤUMR were probably added after the Dervish days and as a revenge for some injury done to the Dóálíb by that tribe.

For 'AUS see Wüstenfeld, 7; and for Aihala see Sale (*Prel. Disc.* p. 139). Aihala proclaimed himself prophet the year that Muḥammad died.

XXVII The "BULÁLA" are no doubt meant here. EL AZD are a sub-tribe of KAHLÁN: see Wüstenfeld, 9.

XXVIII For TAMÍM see Wüstenfeld, L. Cp. para. CXLVIII.

XXIX The pedigree is correct: see Wüstenfeld, G. Cp. para. CXCIII.

For GUDHÁM see Wüstenfeld, 5.

XXX See Wüstenfeld, H. The pedigree of Bedr is correct. Cp. para. CXXXIX.

XXXI The pedigree is correct: see Wüstenfeld, G.

For Ḳays 'Aylán see Wüstenfeld, D, where Ḳays is shown as son of 'Aylán son of Muḍr. Others give Ḳays 'Aylán as a single name and son of Muḍr, cp. ABC, XXV *et seq.* Abu el Fidá (*q.v.* p. 194) discusses this question and also mentions the story that 'Aylán was a horse.

Ḳays Kubba was son of el Ghauth: see Wüstenfeld, 9.

XXXII Bagla (whose pedigree is correctly given) was of the tribe of EL AZD (see Wüstenfeld, 10), but she married one of the BENI SULAYM (see Wüstenfeld, G).

XXXIII Correct: see Wüstenfeld, J.

XXXIV All correct: see Wüstenfeld, J.

XXXVI Correct: see Wüstenfeld, 5.

XXXVII "Son of Zayd" should be inserted between Udad and "Yashkhub." The rest is correct: see Wüstenfeld, 4.

XXXVIII Correct: see Wüstenfeld, M.

XXXIX Correct: see Wüstenfeld, 1.

XL Not in Wüstenfeld.

XLII See Wüstenfeld, 11.

XLIII The KHAṬÁ are the people of Chinese Turkestan: see Huart, p. 363.

XLIV From 'Áísh to Fihr is correct: see Wüstenfeld, O. Fihr is the same as Ḳuraysh. 'Awaymir and Sá'ada are not mentioned by Wüstenfeld.

XLV See Wüstenfeld, 9. There was an Abu Ḥázim of the BAGÍLA, but his only recorded son was called Ḳays, not Ḥázim.

XLVI See Wüstenfeld, 11. Má-el-Samá was the name of 'Ámir and not of Rabí'a, and Rabí'a is the same as Loḥay. Loḥay and Afṣá and 'Oday were the sons of Ḥáritha, and their descendants, as stated, are KHUZÁ'A. Ka'ab was grandson of Loḥay.

XLVII These persons are not in Wüstenfeld (*q.v.* G). Cp. para. CXXXVIII.

XLVIII "[Married] to" is literally تحت, *i.e.* "under."

See Wüstenfeld, G and 7. All is correct but that "son of Málik" has been omitted between Ma'an and Á'ṣir.

XLIX صاحب القاموس فى اللغة العربية is the Arabic of "the author... Language."

LI العلم الالهى منسوب الى افلاطون ومبناه على الاستدلال باحول المحسوسات المعلومة بمعاونة الحس

LII ومبناه على الاخد من الحس is "and they are founded upon...etc."

LIII ومبناه على الاحساس واحكام المحسوسات is "and it is founded upon...etc."

LIV ومبناه انه ماخود من المحسوسات is "and it is founded upon ...etc."

LV From the account of the descendants of Noah and the ancient lost tribes of the Arabs, which begins here, to the mention of the conquest of Syria, is quoted, generally *verbatim*, from Ibn el Athír's *Kámil*. Several omissions, which sometimes do not affect the sense, but at other times completely alter it, have been made. The words inserted in square brackets in the translation do not occur in D 1, but as they are essential to the general meaning I have added them from the text of Ibn el Athír. Copies of Ibn el Athír are fairly common in the Sudan. The originals of the passages borrowed by the author of D 1 are to be found on the thirty-fourth and following pages of the first volume of Ibn el Athír (ed. Cairo, 1301 A.H., el Azhar Press). Various other Arab authors give widely divergent accounts of this subject: cp. Sale (*Prel. Disc.* section 1).

LVI *I.e.* Shem, Ham, and Japheth. "Yágūg and Mágūg" are "Gog and Magog." See Ḳurán, Chap. 18. After "Mágūg" Ibn el Athír mentions the origin of the Copts, and gives an anecdote, omitted by D 1, about Ḥám.

LVII Cp. Genesis x. 22: "The children of Shem; Elam, and Asshur, and Arphaxad, and Lud, and Aram." After "Aram" some comments are omitted by D 1.

LVIII "Who were" (الذين هم) should be "among whom were" (ومنهم كانت).

"Them" is the 'AMÁLÍḲ (*i.e.* Amalekites). El Athír gives والفراعنه بمصر: D 1 gives ومنهم فراعنه مصر.

The children of Omaym should not have been omitted as they are referred to in the next line as though previously mentioned. Two lines of Ibn el Athír, about the BENI OMAYM and their tragic fate as unbelievers, are omitted, possibly owing to a superstitious fear: cp. note to LXVI.

LIX Yathreb is the old name of Medína. D 1 appears to have omitted these words merely because 'Abíl had not been mentioned before: in consequence the sense has become nil.

LX Ṣana'á was originally called Ozal (see Sale, *Prel. Disc.* p. 2).

Some remarks by Ibn el Athír about the 'AMÁLÍḲ are here omitted by D 1.

LXII The handiest reference to these lost tribes of the Arabs is Sale's *Prel. Disc.* section 1.

There were two of the ancient tribes called GURHUM: see Sale, *Prel. Disc.* pp. 6, 7, 9. Cp. para. CXCI.

El 'Áriba are the pure original Arabs: el Muta'ariba the insititious Arabs: see Sale, *Prel. Disc.* p. 7. Some remarks of Ibn el Athír are here omitted.

LXIII By الحجر ("the rocky country") is meant Arabia Petraea (see Abu el Fidá, p. 16).

The author of D 1 by omitting the words inserted in brackets has completely altered the sense.

For "Gau" cp. Sale (*Prel. Disc.* p. 4) and Mas'ūdi (ed. B. de M. Vol. III, Chap. XLVII, pp. 276, 288).

LXIV El Nebṭ are the Nabateans. El Mas'ūdi (p. 77) speaks of Nimrod as son of Másh and builder of the tower of Babel and king of the Nebṭ. The term Nebṭ seems to designate vaguely the Chaldean element of Mesopotamia. See Palgrave, *C. and E. Arabia*, II, 158 *et seq*.

LXV "Son of Láūdh" is not in Ibn el Athír. In Abu el Fidá Fáris appears as son of Láūdh.

LXVI Ibn el Athír's remark that Ḳaynán was a sorcerer is omitted by D I: many authors similarly omit his name altogether from the genealogies from superstition: see Abu el Fidá (p. 20) and Ibn el Athír (Vol. I, p. 35) on this point.

Shálikh = Salah: 'Ábir = Eber: Fáligh = Peleg: see Genesis, chap. x. After "Fáligh" D I has omitted Ibn el Athír's note to the effect that "in his days was the earth divided."

Ḳaḥṭán is the ancestor of all the Yemenite Arabs, or 'Arab el 'Áriba, whereas Fáligh, as being forefather of Abraham, is ancestor of the whole Ismá'ílitic stock.

The insertion here of Yūnán is a mistake. Ibn el Athír mentions him later as son of Yáfith. He is the legendary ancestor of the Greeks, who were called Yūnániyyūn before they were subjected by the Romans. The word is the same etymologically as "Ionian."

"*And Ḳaḥṭán begot...*" The text of Ibn el Athír runs فولد لقحطان يعرب ويقظان فنزلا اليمن ("and Ḳaḥṭán begot Ya'arub and Yuḳẓán and they two settled in el Yemen"), but the copyist has transferred from the end of the chapter the names of the descendants of Ya'arub to here, with the result that after the two lines dealing with them he blandly continues ويقظان نزلا اليمن ("and Yuḳẓán settled (*dual*) in el Yemen").

For the descendants of Yashgub and Sabá cp. Wüstenfeld, 5.

LXVII Among the Beni Lakhm were the kings of Ḥíra, who were known as the "Mondars" ("Monádira"): cp. Sale, *Prel. Disc.* p. 9.

LXVIII "*And were...*" Ibn el Athír gives كان (*i.e.* the dual is dropped): D I gives هم (*i.e.* the descendants of Ya'arub and Yuḳẓán).

اول من سلم عليه بابيت اللعن—the formula used in addressing the ancient Arab kings was أَبَيْتَ ٱللَّعْنَ (see Wright's *Arabic Grammar*, Part III, p. 3, and cp. el Mas'ūdi, ed. Sprenger, Chap. III, p. 78, and ed. B. de M. Vol. III, Chap. XLIV, p. 201).

LXIX Ar'ū is the biblical "Reu," Sárūgh "Serug," Náhūr "Nahor," and Tárikh "Terah." Cp. B I, XXVI.

LXX Nimrūdh, or "Nimrod" (*q.v. supra*, note LXIV), appears in el Mas'ūdi (p. 77) as son of Másh son of Aram; in el Ṭabari (p. 127) as son of Kana'án; and in Abu el Fidá (p. 20) as son of Kūsh: the last version is mentioned by Ibn el Athír but omitted by the copyist.

Sind and Hind are intended to represent India. "India" is originally "the land of the Hind," meaning the people of the south and east of the peninsula: generally the people of the north-eastern part were called the

Sind (see el Mas'ūdi, p. 176, note), but Abu el Fidá (p. 174) speaks of the Sind as west of the Hind.

LXXI Yuḳṭán or Ḳaḥṭán is the biblical Joktan.

LXXII Ibn el Athír gives the tribes of ṢANHÁGA and KETÁMA as exceptions. Cp. para. CLXXXIV.

LXXIII No mention of the Romans occurs in this position in Ibn el Athír, who, after dealing with the Berber, passes on to the sons of Yáfith. He later merely mentions that the Romans are descended from Lanṭi son of Yūnán son of Yáfith, but omits the explanatory details given by the copyist. By the "early Romans" (الروم الاول) the copyist means the Romans, the centre of whose power was Rome, and by the "later Romans" (الروم الثانى), the Byzantines.

LXXIV Cp. Genesis, chap. x. 2. Gámir is "Gomer," Máshig "Meshech," and Tírash "Tiras."

LXXVI The KHAZAR are a people on the shores of the Caspian Sea and the Caucasus.

ASHBÁN is the Arabic equivalent for "Hispani," *i.e.* Spaniards: see el Mas'ūdi, p. 369.

For a wonderful account of "Gog and Magog" see el Ṭabari, Chap. VIII.

The "SAGHÁLIBA" are the Slavonians: see el Mas'ūdi, p. 72.

"BURGÁN" is the same as "Bulghár," *i.e.* Bulgarians. The former term is used by el Mas'ūdi (Chap. XXXV).

El 'Aiṣ is "Esau," and Isḥáḳ "Isaac." Some further remarks of Ibn el Athír are here omitted by the copyist. It is here, too, that the mention of the Romans (see note LXXIII) occurs.

LXXVII Cp. Genesis x. 6: "Cush, and Mizraim, and Phut, and Canaan." "Ḳūṭ" (قوط) is the reading both in Ibn el Athír and the copyist, but el Mas'ūdi (Chap. XLVII) gives Fūṭ (as son of Ham)—whence the Biblical Phut. "Ḳūṭ" generally denotes the Goths.

The copyist has very slightly paraphrased the text for the next few lines.

LXXXI The series of quotations from Ibn el Athír breaks off at the end of this paragraph.

LXXXII For Sabá and the dispersion of the tribes, see Ḳurán, Chap. 34, with Sale's notes, and Abu el Fidá, Bk. IV (p. 114) and Bk. V (p. 182). The whole of the following tradition is given in el Mas'ūdi, Chap. XLII.

By LAKHM here is meant those BENI LAKHM who founded the dynasty of the MONÁDIRA (*q.v.* note LXVII) which ruled in Ḥíra and Anbár from about 210 to 634 A.D. (See Van Dyck, p. 24.)

The Kendite dynasty ruled in Negd from 450 to 530 A.D. (see Van Dyck, p. 32); but for "KENDA" el Mas'ūdi gives "KENÁNA" (B. de Meynard's edition).

ANMÁR were a section of EL AZD: for them and KHAT'AM (or KHATH'AM) and BAGÍLA see Wüstenfeld, 9.

LXXXIII Márib was the site of the great reservoir. For the impiety of the local tribes, it was broken down by a great flood, which destroyed most of the inhabitants of the vicinity: see Sale, *Prel. Disc.* p. 8, and text, p. 323.

The Ghassánite dynasty ruled a part of Syria from 37 to 636 A.D.: see Van Dyck, p. 28. Cp. para. CXCIV.

AUS and KHAZRAG were great Kaḥṭánite tribes, descended from EL AZD: see Abu el Fidá, p. 184. They formed the bulk of the "ANṢÁR." Hence some Sudan tribes like to claim descent from them, and especially from Khazrag. Cp. para. CXCV.

'Amr ibn 'Ámir is the 'Amr Muzayḳiá mentioned in para. XLVI.

LXXXIV Cp. BA, XLVIII, XLIX.

LXXXV Cp. BA, LI.

LXXXVI "Anas" [انس] should be "Unays" [انيس] as in BA, LVIII, *q.v.* for an account of 'Abdulla el Guhani.

The "Dhubián" and "Sufián" mentioned in the next paragraph had no connection with the real 'Abdulla "el Guhani." I incline to think that certain members of the tribe of Ghatafán (a division of the Ismailitic ḲAYS 'AYLÁN) were in the author's mind, because among the direct descendants of Ghatafán occur Dhubián, 'Abs, Fezára, Sufián, Mázin, Ṣárid, Dahmán, Ḳays and Rayth (see Wüstenfeld, H), all of which names are closely connected in the Sudanese *nisbas* with 'Abdulla el Guhani. How the confusion arose is not at all clear. See also note to BA, LVIII.

LXXXIX Cp. BA, LIX *et seq.*

XC See note to BA, LXVII.

XCI Cp. BA, LXII, LXIII.

XCII Cp. para. CXXXV and BA, CCVII, CLXXIX; C 6, III, etc.

"Suhayl" should be "Shaṭír."

The pedigree of Ghulámulla, as given by the owner of D 1, the descendant and successor of its author, is as shown in the inset to the genealogical tree that illustrates D 1. The generations from Muḥammad el Gawád upwards are given correctly.

For the descendants of Ghulámulla see BA, CLXXXI, D 3, 222, etc.

XCIV Cp. BA, LXVI.

XCVI This story does not occur elsewhere.

XCVIII Cp. BA, LXXIII.

CI This Dafa'alla's biography is given in D 3 (*q.v.*).

CII The 'ÁḲILÁB are the descendants of Muḥammad Abu 'Áḳla, the father of 'Abdulla el Ṭerayfi. See D 3, 41 and 42.

CIII What the author really means is that the term GA'ÁFIRA is used in three senses. The first group he mentions are meant apparently to be classed as GUHAYNA, 'Ámir and 'Omrán being sons of Sulṭán. Cp. ABC, XXXI. In reality the division is probably quite fallacious and the well-known Upper Egyptian tribe of GA'ÁFIRA are intended in every case. For their settlement between Esna and Aswán see Burckhardt, p. 133. There are a certain number of them in all the bigger towns of the Sudan at the present day.

CIV Cp. para. XCII.

CV *et seq.* Cp. para. XCII; BA, CLXXXI *et seq.*; D 3, 222, etc.

CXI 'Ali walad 'Ishayb is No. 60 in D 3.

"Households" is بيوت.

CXVIII Ḥabíb Nesi is No. 105 in D 3.

CXXI Abu Tubr is a hill in northern Kordofán. *Tubr* is the name of a common convolvulus.

CXXV The term *Sherif* (*pl. Ashráf*) is used indiscriminately for descendants of Ḥasan or Ḥusayn. "In Arabia the Sharif is the descendant of Ḥasan through his two sons Zaid and Hasan al-Musanna: the Sayyid is the descendant of Hosayn through Zayn al-Abidin...." "This word (*s.c.* Sayyid) in the Northern Hijaz is applied indifferently to the posterity of Hasan and Hosayn" (Burton, *Pilgrimage...*, II, pp. 3 and 7, notes).

For the Mirghanía see D 7, CXCII, note.

The best known of the AWLÁD EL HINDI is "el Sheríf" Yūsef el Hindi, a *feki* much respected in the Gezíra and among the nomads: see C 9, XXVI.

For the AWLÁD EL MAGDHŪB see D 3, 123. It is they to whom Burckhardt refers when he says (p. 51): "The few Nubians who know how to write, and who serve the governors in the capacity of secretaries, are taught by the Fokara of Damer...who are all learned men, and travel occasionally to Cairo"; and again (p. 266) he apparently refers to them, when speaking of Dámer, as the "Medja-ydin" religious men or "family of Medjdoule," through whose learning Dámer had acquired a great reputation.

For Bedr ibn Um Bárak walad Maskín see D 3, 76.

For the AWLÁD MUṢṬAFA see D 3, 210.

"AWLAD 'ABDULLA EL MEKANI at el Táka" (اولاد عبد الله المكنى بالتاكة) may be an error for اولاد عبد الله المكنى بال... بالتاكة ("The sons of 'Abdulla nicknamed el... at el Táka").

For the AWLÁD HAGŪ see D 3, 107.

The AWLÁD EL AK·ḤAL are really included among the descendants of Ghulámulla (*i.e.* the first group of ASHRÁF): see D 3, 222.

CXXVIII "Abu Merkha" is "Ṣubuḥ Abu Merkha."

CXXIX The DINKA tribes are meant.

CXXXI Cp. BA, CXVIII.

CXXXII Contrast BA, CVIII.

CXXXIII Cp. BA, CIX, CX.

CXXXIV Cp. para. XLV, *supra*. The BEDAYRÍA and TAKÁRÍR elements are chiefly represented in the ḤALAFA section of the ḤAWÁZMA. See Part III, Chap. 3 (*d*).

CXXXV Contrast VII and XXV, *supra*, and D 2, XXXVIII.

CXXXVI Contrast XII, *supra*.

CXXXVII Contrast XXVI, *supra*.

CXXXVIII Contrast XLVII, *supra*.

CXXXIX Contrast XXX, *supra*.

CXL Cp. XVI, *supra*.

CXLI Cp. XXII, *supra*.

CXLVI Cp. BA, CXI.

CXLVII Cp. XIV, *supra*.

CXLVIII The TAMÍMÍA and the others mentioned are all sections of the ḤAMAR.

CXLIX For the RIKÁBÍA, etc., see index for references.

For Aḥmad Abu Denána see C 8, XXXII (note).

The "NŪBA" here mentioned are those of G. el Ḥaráza and other hills of northern Kordofán.

CL See Part I, Chap. 4.

CLI Cp. paras. CLXXXVIII and VIII.

CLIV Cp. BA, CXIX, etc.

"Aftūriá" (افتوريا) may be an error for "Uruba" (*i.e.* Europe).

CLVI Cp. note to para. XXII.

CLVII Contrast D 2, XXXIX.

CLVIII Contrast D 2, XXXVII.

CLIX See para. LXIII.

CLXI Um Gurfa is a district near to the east of Kagmár in Kordofán.

CLXII See Part I, Chap. 4, *sub* "BIRḲED."

CLXV Contrast D 2, XV; BA, CLXXVIII, etc.

CLXVII See CXXII, *supra*.

CLXVIII See CXXI, *supra*.

CLXIX Abu Sinūn is a hill lying N.W. of el Obeid in Kordofán.

CLXXI Contrast D 2, XXXIV, etc.

CLXXIII "MOGHÁRBA" is the usual plural of "Moghrabi" ("Moor"). The Arabic here is اصلهم من الفلاحين تتر الذين بالبوادي.

CLXXV A Zurrūḳ el Moghrabi is mentioned in Ḥagi Khalfa (Vol. III, p. 418, No. 6222) as a joint author of *Risálat el Ṭuruk*. The MOGHÁRBA of the Blue Nile claim descent from "Aḥmad Zerrūḳ" and speak of him as a *wali* of the Shádhalía *ṭariḳa* in Tunis, and a *Sherif*. See Part III, Chap. 4 (*b*).

CLXXVI Of these ASHRÁF the only ones I have been able to identify are:

1. Zurrūḳ el Moghrabi, for whom see the preceding note.

2. Abu el Ḥasan el Shádhali, for whom see note to para. LI of AB. He died in 1258.

3. El Shibli: viz. Bedr el Dín Muḥammad ibn 'Abdulla el Damashḳi el Terábulusi. He was a Ḥanafite and died in A.D. 1367–8. He wrote *Akám el Margán*, *Maḥásin el Wasáil*, etc. (See Ḥagi Khalfa's *Lexicon*, Vol. I, p. 386, No. 1088, and Vol. v, pp. 453 and 413.)

4. Ibráhím el Dasūḳi was a Ṣūfi Imám of Egypt. He was born in 1240 and died in 1277 A.D. (see Na'ūm Bey, Part I, pp. 130 ff.).

Aḥmad el Waráḳ, Muḥammad el Thauri, and 'Abd el Raḥím el Bura'i I cannot identify either from Yáḳūṭ (*Irshád el Arib*) or Ḥagi Khalfa.

CLXXVIII The Arabic of paras. CLXXVIII and CLXXIX is as follows:

اصل السودان اهل الوطن النوبه والحبشة والزنج ثم اول داخل عليهم البربر

This is taken probably from Ibn Khaldūn (Bk. 2, p. 105), and the remark about the BERBER may be a misunderstanding of Ibn Khaldūn's quotation from Ibn Sa'íd to the effect that next to the Zing are the "Berbera."

CLXXX The FUNG regard themselves as BENI OMMAYYA slightly leavened by negroes. The HAMAG are considered as GA'ALIÍN (*i.e.* 'ABBÁSÍA) leavened by negroes. Where they make a distinction as between BENI OMMAYYA and BENI 'ABBÁS our author, looking rather to the black element, distinguishes only between ZING and NŪBA.

CLXXXIII Menelik II in 1891 wrote to the European powers "En indiquant aujourd'hui les limites actuelles de mon Empire, je tâcherai...de rétablir les anciennes frontières de l'Éthiopie, *jusqu'à Khartoum et jusqu'au lac Nyanza*..." (see *Le Soudan Egyptien*, by Grégoire Sarkissian, Paris, 1913, p. 92). Cp. also Ludolfus (*Hist. of Ethiopia*, trans. Gent, 1684, Bk. I, Chap. XVI): "...Sennar or Fund, governed by its peculiar king, formerly a tributary to the Abessines, but now absolute." See also note to MS. D 7, L.

CLXXXV Several of the Arabic historians (*e.g.* Ibn Khaldūn and el Mas'ūdi, Chap. XLVI) give the subdivisions of the BERBER in North Africa. Some of the names here are corrupt: ZENÁTA, HOWÁRA, ṢANHÁGA, KETÁMA, and LUÁTA are well known. "MADYŪNA" (مديونة) is perhaps "MAṢMŪDA" (مصمودة). "NABRA" (نبرة) is certainly an error for "NAFZA" (نفزة). See Part II, Appendix to Chap. I.

CLXXXVI The people of the modern Berbera are alluded to.

CLXXXVII The Arabic here is at fault: it reads as follows:

وجزيرهم واطعة من حد ساحل ابين ملتحقة في البحر بعدن من نحو
مطالع سهيل الي ما يشرق عنها وفيما حاذى منها عدن وقابله جبل الدخان
وهي جزيرة سعوطري مما يقطع بعدن ثابتا علي السمة

"Suhayl" is Canopus.

Yáḳūt (*Kitáb mu'agam el Buldán*, *sub* "Abín") quotes el Ṭabari as saying "Aden and Abyan were the two sons of 'Adnán ibn Udad," and of the position of Abyan says: وهو مخالف باليمن منه عَدَن.

De Herbelot (p. 329) speaks of Aden as "Aden Abyan."

"Gebel el Dukhán" is the volcanic Gebel Tair (Bruce, Vol. II, p. 232).

CLXXXVIII Cp. para. CLI.

CXC See Wüstenfeld, J. "Ḥasba" (حسبة) is a copyist's error for "Ḍabba" (ضبة).

CXCI, CXCII See para. LXII.

CXCIII See para. XXIX.

CXCIV See para. LXXXIII, and Wüstenfeld, 11 and 12.

CXCV See paras. LXXXII, LXXXIII and Wüstenfeld, 9. "Zayd" is omitted between Málik and Kahlán.

CXCVII Contrast para. LXXIX.

CXCVIII This is practically the same as Abu el Fidá's "...El Afrang who are many nations and the seat of whose kingdom is originally Franga (or Fransa), which borders on the northern frontier of the Andalusian peninsula; and their king is called 'el Fransís'" (see Abu el Fidá, p. 170).

CXCIX Contrast para. LXXVI.

CCI The 3rd pers. sing. pres. tense of *háda* is *yahūdu*.

CCII "The Byzantine Greeks" would perhaps better express the meaning of *el Rūm* here.

CCIII Correct: see Wüstenfeld, I.

CCIV See Wüstenfeld, 2.

CCVI "Akshūm" is Axum, the ancient capital of Abyssinia. Following the rise of the Muhammadan power in the seventh century the frontiers of Abyssinia were forced further westward, and as a result the capital was shifted to Gondar.

Of the provinces mentioned Amḥara is well known, "Sáwa" is Shoa (or Xoa), "Dámūt" is Damota (or Great Damot), "'Adel el Amrái" is Adel, "Ḥamásá" is Hamazen, "Bádimyá" is probably the "Bagemder" of Ludolfus (p. 14), and "Zíla'a" is probably Zeila on the northern coast of Somaliland.

CCIX For the following see MacMichael (*Tribes*..., Chap. 1) and Part I, Chap. 4.

The date 1233 should be 1236.

CCXIII Ghulámulla is the ancestor of the RIKÁBÍA. Mentions of him are very frequent: see BA, CLXXIX, CLXXXI and D 3, 189 and D 5 (*d*).

For this Muḥammad walad Dólíb see D 3, 187.

TREE ILLUSTRATING MS. D 1

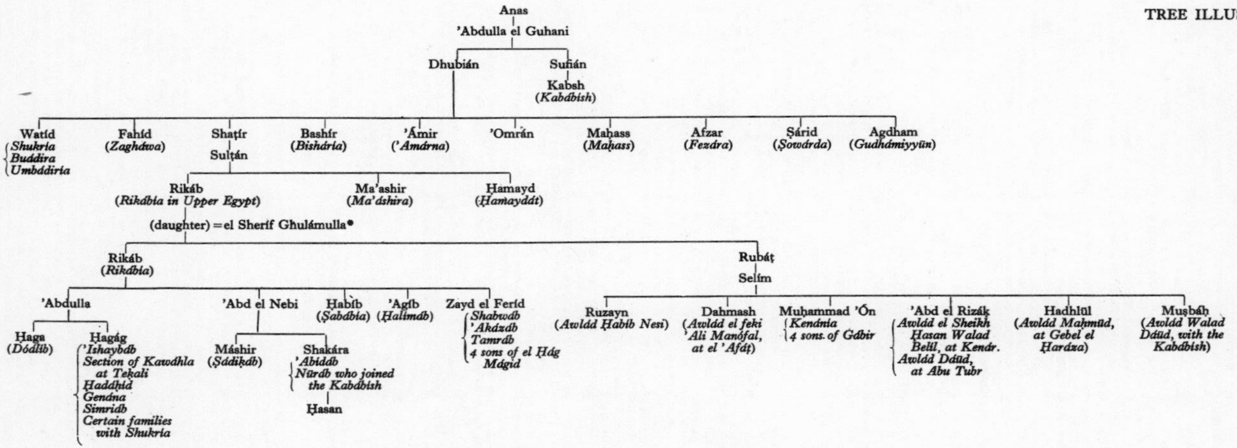

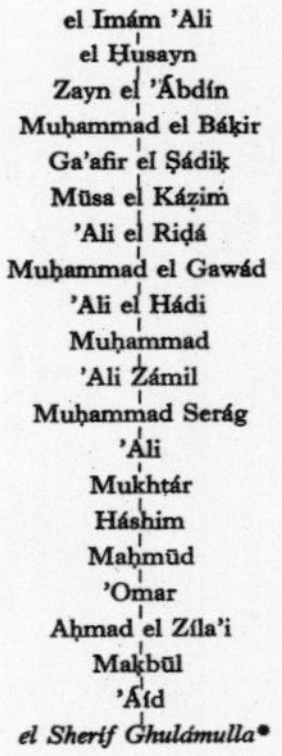

MANUSCRIPT D 2

Introduction

MUḤAMMAD AḤMAD 'OMAR, *'omda* of the second *khuṭ* of el Kámlín district and by race one of the FUNG, wrote out the MS. here translated for me. He based it on documents in his possession, but it is obviously a *précis* rather than a copy, and some of the statements concerning the tribes, however true they may be, may have been added from his own knowledge or recollection and not have occurred in the MS.

I The coming of the BENI OMMAYYA to the Sudan was as follows: Sulaymán son of 'Abd el Malik son of Marwán entered the Sudan and Abyssinia and dwelt in them for a space; and afterwards he migrated to the mountains of the FŪNG and married the daughter of the king Sendál el 'Ág: and they gained the ascendancy over those mountains for a [long] time, and there he begot his sons Ans and Dáūd. Dáūd was surnamed "Oudūn" and Ans "Unsa"; and Unsa begot his son 'Omára Dunḳas, who was the first of the kings of the FŪNG.

II History of the Kings of the FŪNG at Sennár.

910, 1236, 1505.

1.	From	910[1]	to	940	King	'Omára Dunḳas himself.
2.	"	940	"	950	"	'Abd el Ḳádir, his son.
3.	"	950	"	962	"	Náíl, his brother.
4.	"	962	"	970	"	'Omára Abu Sakákín.
5.	"	970	"	985	"	Dekín, son of Náíl.
6.	"	985	"	997	"	Tabl.
7.	"	997[2]	"	1007	"	Unsa.
8.	"	1007	"	1013	"	'Abd el Ḳádir II.
9.	"	1013	"	1020	"	'Adlán, son of Áya.
10.	"	1020	"	1032	"	Bádi, known as Síd el Ḳūm.
11.	"	1032	"	1052	"	Rubáṭ, his son.
12.	"	1052	"	1088	"	Bádi Abu Duḳn.
13.	"	1088	"	1100	"	Ounsa II.
14.	"	1100	"	1127	"	Bádi el Aḥmar, his son.
15.	"	1127	"	1130	"	Ounsa III.
16.	"	1130	"	1136	"	Nūl, son of Bádi Nūl.
17.	"	1136	"	1175	"	Bádi Abu Shelūkh.
18.	"	1175	"	1182	"	Náṣir.

[1] 1505 A.D. [2] reading ٩٩٧ for ٩٨٧.

19.	From	1182	to	1191	King	Ismá'íl.
20.	„	1191	„	1203	„	'Adlán II.
21.		1203	—		„	Ṭabl.
22.		1203	—		„	Bádi V.
23.		1204	—		„	Ḥasab Rabbihi.
24.	From	1204	to	1205	„	Nowár.
25.	„	1205	„	1236[1]	„	Bádi VI, son of Ṭabl.

Total 26 (*sic*)

[This list] is undisputable.

III [Thus] the Fūng ruled, and after them there came into power the Hamag, their viziers, until [in] 1236 A.H., on the 9th of Ramaḍán, Ismá'íl Pasha, the Egyptian Khedive, son of Muḥammad 'Ali Pasha, the Viceroy, came into power.

IV *The Tribes of the Arabs.*

The Arabs form the bulk of the population of the Sudan. They came to it by way of Egypt and the Red Sea, and gradually gained the power over it and settled on its lands and founded in it a number of kingdoms.

V The Sháíḳía. Among them are the 'Adlánáb and the Sowáráb and the Ḥannakáb and the 'Omáráb.

VI The Dwayḥía. They are of the stock of 'Abd el Raḥman wad Ḥág, who came from Mekka.

VII The 'Ónía and the Manáṣír. Their place is the neighbourhood of Abu Ḥammad and among them are the Wahhábáb and the Kebána and the Sulaymánía and the Kagūbáb and the Khubará and the Rubáṭáb, and among them are the Bedría and the Feráníb and the Ḍa'ífáb and the Mírafáb, who live at Berber, and among them are the Ṣiám and the Muṣṭafiáb and the Labíáb and the Raḥmáb.

VIII The Ga'aliyyūn. The most famous of the tribes of the Arabs in the Sudan. Among them are the 'Omaráb and the Magádhíb[2] and the 'Abábsa and the Ráskía and the Sa'adáb and the 'Awaḍía and the Hamag, the viziers of the Fūng, and the Nifí'áb and the Náfa'áb and the Mukábaráb and the Inḳerriáb[3]. Their locality is between Abu Ḥammad and el Khartoum and el Dámer and the desert of Ḳerri.

IX The Gimí'áb. Between Ḳerri and el Sheikh el Ṭaib.

X The 'Ábdulláb. Their place is el Ḥalfáya, and they are a branch of the Ḳawásma. They are called 'Ábdulláb after their ancestor 'Abdulla Gemá'a.

[1] 1821 A.D. [2] reading مجاذيب for محاذيب.

[3] reading انقرياب for انقرباب.

XI Now the GAMŪ'ÍA and the SURŪRÁB and the GIMÍ'ÁB and the GA'ALIYYŪN and the MÍRAFÁB[1] and the RUBÁṬÁB and the SHÁÍḲÍA are all descended from the same ancestor, viz. Abu Merkha, who was ultimately descended from el 'Abbás.

XII The ḤASANÁT. Their place is round el Ḳeṭayna.

XIII The DEGHAYM and KENÁNA are the sons of 'Omar, and live at Gema'án near Abbá Island.

XIV The SELÍM and the RUFÁ'IYYŪN are GUHAYNA by descent.

XV The MESALLAMÍA are GUHAYNA by descent, and their place is in the Gezíra.

XVI The MEDANIYYŪN. Their place is at Medani.

XVII The 'ARAKIYYŪN. Their place is Abu Ḥaráz and 'Abūd.

XVIII The KHAWÁLDA are round 'Abūd, and they are GUHAYNA by descent.

XIX The KAWÁHLA are round 'Abūd and Wad Medani, and they trace descent to Zubayr ibn el 'Awwám, and among them are the ḤASANÁT and the SHENÁBLA.

XX The YA'AḲŪBÁB[2] are said to trace their descent to the GA'ALIYYŪN.

XXI The 'AḲALIYYŪN. Their place is between the Dinder and the Blue Nile.

XXII The ḤAMMADA are between the Dinder and the Rahad.

XXIII The ḲAWÁSMA reside north of Sennár.

XXIV The KAMÁTÍR. Their place is Karkóg.

XXV The LAḤAWIYYŪN are mostly nomads and live on the east of the White Nile between el Káwạ and el Gebelayn.

XXVI The BENI ḤUSAYN are spoken of as "AWLÁD ABU RÓF," and most of their nomads are from Gebel Saḳadi and Móya to Khor el Dulayb.

XXVII The MARḲŪM are a large tribe.

XXVIII The 'ULÁṬIYYŪN are mostly nomads: and all the six tribes are descended from GUHAYNA.

XXIX The FŪNG are they who founded the ancient kingdom of Sennár with the 'ÁBDULLÁB, and they were the greatest power in the Sudan, and their descent is from the BENI OMMAYYA.

XXX The HAMAG were the viziers of the FŪNG, and their descent is from the GA'ALIYYŪN.

XXXI The SHUKRÍA are GUHAYNA by descent.

XXXII The BAṬÁḤÍN are GA'ALIYYŪN by descent.

XXXIII The ḌUBÁNÍA are GUHAYNA by descent.

[1] reading ميرفاب for مريفاب. [2] reading يعقوباب for يقوباب.

XXXIV The Ḥasánía are Kawáhla by descent.

XXXV The Howára are Ḥuḍūr by descent.

XXXVI The Gima'a are composed of various tribes, and most of them are Ga'aliyyūn.

XXXVII The Ta'áisha and the Habbánía and the Awlád Ḥamayd and Selím are the descendants of Ḥammád son of Gunayd, [and live] round el Kalaka.

XXXVIII The Ḥawázma and the Ḥumr and the Messíría and the Rizayḳát are the descendants of 'Aṭía, the brother of the Ḥammád mentioned above, and all of them are Guhayna.

XXXIX The Beni Helba are Guhayna by descent.

XL The most important of the sources from which pedigrees are traced are the Beni Ommayya and the Beni 'Abbás and Guhayna, as was pointed out by the two sheikhs Ibn Khaldūn and Ibn el Athír in their respective works.

XLI The 'Awámra are all descendants of 'Ámir son of Ṣa'aṣa'a son of Dhubián son of Ḥuṣfa son of Ghílá son of Muḍr son of Nizár[1] son of Ma'ad son of 'Adnán son of Ud son of Udad [etc.] up to the prophet el Sayyid Ismá'íl son of our lord Ibráhím, the Friend of God, upon both of whom be the blessings of God.

XLII Now Ismá'íl son of Ibráhím was ancestor of the Arabs, and Isḥáḳ son of Ibráhím was ancestor of the non-Arabs [*el 'agam*]; and God knows best. The mother of the Arabs was Hágar the Copt [*el Ḳubṭía*], and the mother of the non-Arabs was Sára the Israelite [*el Isráíla*].

D 2 (NOTES)

I Cp. BA, CCXIII; A 11, LIII, etc.

"Oudūn" is أُوْدُون and "Unsa" is أُنسة. In the following paragraph we have "Unsa" in some places and "Ounsa" (أُونسة) in others.

II "1505" is the Christian year corresponding to 910 A.H.

V "'Omáráb" is an error.

XI "Abu Merkha" is "Ṣubuḥ Abu Merkha."

XVI See D 3, 93 note.

XXVII The Marghūmáb are meant.

XXVIII By "The six tribes" is meant the last six tribes mentioned.

XXX Cp. D 7, XLIX and para. VIII above.

[1] reading نزار for نذار.

MANUSCRIPT D 3

Introduction

The remarkable work known as the *Ṭabaḳát wad Ḍayfulla* ("Ḍayfulla's Series") was written, as we gather from biography No. 154, in 1805.

The author, "Wad Ḍayfulla," was Muḥammad el Nūr walad Ḍayfulla walad Muḥammad of the FAḌLIÍN section of the GA'ALIÍN. He lived at Ḥalfáyat el Mulūk, and died in 1809 (see D 7, CLXXXV and ABC, XI).

The whole book would normally cover something over two hundred medium-sized pages of closely written Arabic MS. The particular copy from which the following extracts were taken is the property of el Amín walad Muḥammad walad Ṭáha walad el Sheikh Khógali, the *Khalífa* of his great-grandfather, Sheikh Khógali, whose tomb is near Khartoum North and whose biography is included in the text (No. 154).

The family of Wad Ḍayfulla, who are now known as the ḌAYFULLÁB, still live at Ḥalfáyat el Mulūk close to the KHÓGALÁB, and though the latter are MAḤASS and the former was a Ga'ali, there has been considerable intermarriage between the two groups during the last few generations.

It is practically certain that the KHÓGALÁB copy was taken direct from the original, which is believed to be held by the *Khalífa* of the ḌAYFULLÁB, and both internal evidence and the inherent probabilities of the case suggest that the copy is a reasonably exact and accurate one.

Other copies are known to exist; *e.g.* one belonged to the late Zubayr Pasha, one is owned by Sheikh Aḥmad el Sunna of Wad Medani, one by the BARRIÁB who live south of Wad Medani, and one by the *Khalífa* of Sheikh Idrís Arbáb of 'Aylafūn.

The subject-matter of the book is the biographies of the holy-men of the Sudan for about 300 years, beginning from about the first decade of the sixteenth century—in other words, during the period of the FUNG kingdom. The domed *ḳubbas* of most of these holy-men have survived to the present, and a fair number of additional *ḳubbas* have been built subsequently to commemorate the *fekis* of subsequent generations.

The author does not concern himself with lengthy genealogies of dubious authenticity, but casual details of the inter-relationship of various families are very rife, and are the more worthy of confidence in that they are purely incidental to the main purpose and mutually corroborative.

The biographies contain, as a rule, details of the place of birth, characteristics, education, career and death of each holy-man, with special mention of his manifestations of profitable and miraculous powers, his teachers, those taught by him, and any remarks made concerning him by other holy-men. In fact the method is very much that of el Mas'ūdi's panegyrics.

But though the form is to some extent stereotyped and modelled on more classical prototypes, the style of writing is distinctly original.

The Arabic is Sudanese colloquial and presents a very interesting study. No dictionary would alone enable one to deduce the meaning of all the words and phrases: one has to read them aloud and imagine a Sudanese is speaking.

The narrative as a rule is vivid and fresh: the tale is seldom spun out tediously, and there are occasional gleams of humour. In fact it is in the descriptive narrative of action that Wad Ḍayfulla shines, and the biographies numbered 52, 60, 63, 66, 74, 143, 153 and 207 are particularly picturesque and realistic.

The grammar is bad, the spelling indifferent, and the style loose; but there is art galore, and even a jumble of personal pronouns referring indiscriminately to two or three different people cannot obscure the fact.

The value of the book is not merely that it tells one for whom the majority of the *ḳubbas* that stud the Sudan were built, but that one gains some insight into the ways of living and thinking and speaking of the people of the land in the seventeenth and eighteenth centuries. Many of their beliefs and customs, their superstitions and practical ideas, are revealed; and the fact that the author is not aiming at any such effect must obviously enhance the value of the information gained.

Where any test of the accuracy of dates and statements of fact is possible by cross-checking, it is surprising how seldom Wad Ḍayfulla is found nodding. There are no attempts either to record conversations or to specify dates in the lives of the more remote generations of *fekis*. When our author knows a date he inserts it: when he does not he omits it. He leaves the impression of a kind-hearted but perspicacious old man of careful and thorough habits, devoting his unusual gifts of memory and narration to the cause of religion, and at the same time taking a real pleasure in regaling his contemporaries and posterity with the records of the holy-men of the past.

It is not unlikely that he drew many of his facts from the library of that Ḥasan 'Abd el Raḥman Bán el Nuḳá mentioned in D 7, CXC. Ḥasan's father was a pupil of an ancestor of Wad Ḍayfulla (see biography No. 89).

As regards the plan followed in the translation, it must be explained that only portions of the text have been selected. There are in the original many pages containing uninteresting records of movements from village to village, list of pupils, and remarks made by one holy-man as to the excellence of another. In addition, the text is frequently so blurred and blotched or torn that it is impossible to be sure of the meaning of the whole of a passage. I have therefore only translated word for word such portions as are reasonably clear and as describe some incident of interest from the historical or sociological point of view, and have noted in brief paraphrase such points as seem worthy of mention in the remainder.

Word for word translation is shown in inverted commas, paraphrase in smaller type.

N.B. 1. Such facts as are given in the English text of any biography may be taken to occur similarly in the Arabic of the same biography, and where relevant information concerning some holy-man occurs in the untranslated part of the Arabic text of the biography of someone else, it is always included in the notes to the biography of the former.

2. Dates of birth and death are not infrequently given in the course of the Arabic text. Where this is the case the dates are placed, in the English text, immediately after the name of the subject of the biography, whatever may have been their position in the Arabic MS.

3. The English equivalents of Arabic dates, notices of textual emendations, and references to the numbers allotted to the English biographies or to the genealogical trees, are placed in the textual footnotes of the translation.

4. The genealogical trees which form an Appendix to the work are compiled from the scattered remarks that occur at random in the course of the book.

I The first page consists of a fragment of three and a half lines, viz. "In the name of God the Compassionate and Merciful. The Sheikh, the learned *feki*, the sage Muḥammad Ḍayfulla, my father and lord, said 'Praise be to God, the Mightiest of the most mighty....'"

II The second page, which is in part torn, gives a brief account, on back and front, of the story of Iblís, Noah, the prophet Idrís, Abraham, Isaac, Jacob, Job, Moses and Aaron.

III The third page, also fragmentary, commences with mentions of Jesus and Mary and the Jews. Praises of Ḳuraysh follow, and quotations from the Ḳurán. On the back of this page, after an invocation to God, commences the historical portion of the work, as follows:

IV "Know that the FUNG possessed and conquered the land of the NŪBA early in the tenth century, in the year 910[1]. And [then] the town of Sennár was founded by King 'Omára Dunḳas. The town of Arbagi was founded thirty years previously by Ḥegázi ibn Ma'ín.

V And in these countries neither schools for learning nor Ḳurán were in vogue; and it is said that a man might divorce his wife and she be married by another man on the selfsame day without any period of probation (*'idda*), until Sheikh...(*word missing*)... el Ḳuṣayer el 'Araki[2] came from Egypt and taught the people to observe the period of probation and dwelt on the White [Nile] and built himself a castle, which is now known as 'the castle of Maḥmūd' (*Ḳuṣr Maḥmūd*).

VI And early in the second half of the tenth century the Sultan 'Omára Abu Sakaykín appointed Sheikh 'Agíb el Mángilak, and in the early days of [the latter's] rule Sheikh Ibráhím el Būlád came from Egypt to the SHÁÍḲÍA country and there taught law [*Khalíl*] and apostleship [*risála*]; and learning spread throughout the Gezíra.

VII Then after a short time came Sheikh Tág el Dín el Bahári[3] from Baghdád and introduced Ṣūfiism into the FUNG court.

VIII Then came el Telemsáni el Moghrabi; and he inspired Sheikh Muḥammad[4] ibn 'Ísa Sowár el Dhahab, and instructed him in dogma, and taught him what pertains to the sphere of faith, and the interpretation of the Ḳurán, and its correct recital, and the methods of reading it and its syntax.

IX And the doctrine of the Unity of God and the art of reciting the Ḳurán spread throughout the Gezíra, for 'Abdulla el Aghbash[5], and Nuṣr father[6] of the *feki* Abu Sinayna[7] at Arbagi, were his pupils in Ḳuránic teaching.

X Then arose Sheikh Idrís[8], who was not inspired by any other sheikh. Some say he was instructed by the Prophet, and others that a man from the west [*el moghrab*], called 'Abd el Káfi, whom he met by the way, deputed him.

XI Shortly afterwards arose Sheikh Ḥasan[9] walad Ḥasūna by the will of the Prophet of God, upon whom be the blessings of God.

XII Then came Sheikh Muḥammad ibn...(*word missing*)...[to] the Berber country and introduced there the tenets of el Sháfa'i; and these tenets spread in the Gezíra.

[1] 1504 A.D. [2] No. 157. [3] No. 67.
[4] No. 191. [5] No. 31. [6] reading والد for ولد.
[7] No. 51. [8] No. 141. [9] No. 132.

XIII Then came the MASHÁÍKHA, and the town of el Ḥalfáya was founded...." (*Page ends.*)

One or more pages are missing here. The next page extant begins with the education and rise of Sheikh Idrís[1] wad Arbáb of 'Aylafūn (*q.v.*), and from here onwards the book is complete and no pages are missing: the key-words that should connect one page with the next and that have so far failed to do so, from here onwards connect every page.

Here follow in turn extracts from the biographies of all the holy-men mentioned by the *Ṭabaḳát*. In the Arabic the names are arranged in a rough alphabetical order, and as not only are there lapses from this system but the order, when observed, is that of the Arabic alphabet, I have re-arranged the order in which the biographies are given to suit the English alphabet.

A

1. "'ABD EL BÁḲI WALAD KUWAYS, el Kahli."

Born and buried at el Shará'ana...."He was one of the forty pupils of Sheikh Dafa'alla[2]."

2. "'ABD EL BÁḲI EL WÁLI."

"He was one of the four contemporaries by whose lives the world profited, namely Sheikh Bedr[3] ibn el Sheikh Um Bárak in the east, Sheikh Muḥammad[4] ibn el Ṭerayfi and Sheikh Khógali[5] in the north, [and fourthly himself 'Abd el Báḳi]."...His "Sheikh" was el Mesallami[6]...."He died at Móya, a well-known hill in the south, in the days of King Bádi walad Nūl."

3. "'ABD EL DÁFA'I."

He lived in the south and was a pupil of Sheikh Ya'aḳūb[7] ibn el Sheikh Bán el Nuḳá. "They were five in number who were pupils of Sheikh Ya'aḳūb, viz. Mūsa[8] and Marzūḳ[9] his two sons, and Hagū[10] son of his sister Batūl, and 'Abd el Ráziḳ[11], and 'Abd el Dáfa'i."

4. "'ABD EL DÁFA'I EL ḲANDÍL ibn Muḥammad ibn Ḥammad, el Gamū'i" (b. 1100 A.H.[12]; d. 1180 A.H.[13]).

He was born at el Ḥalfáya and was a follower of Sheikh Khógali [ibn 'Abd el Raḥman]....He was taught by the *feki* Shukrulla el 'Ūdi[14] (his "Sheikh") and the *feki* Belál[15] and Abu el Ḥasan[16]....He created a record by teaching for 58 years and performed the pilgrimage....His death occurred at Sennár but his body was taken to el Ḥalfáya for burial.

[1] No. 141. [2] No. 84. [3] No. 76. [4] No. 177.
[5] No. 154. [6] No. 172. [7] No. 254. [8] No. 209.
[9] No. 159. [10] No. 107. [11] No. 27. [12] 1689 A.D.
[13] 1767 A.D. [14] No. 240. [15] No. 79. [16] No. 47.

5 "'Abd el Ḥalím ibn Sulṭán ibn 'Abd el Raḥman ibn el feki Muḥammad Baḥr, el Moghrabi el Fási."

His grandfather came to the Sudan with a merchant from Egypt....He himself was born at el Ḥalfáya, and his mother's name was Síáḳa....He was taught by Sheikhs Ṣughayerūn[1] and Idrís[2].

6. "'Abd el Ḳádir el Bakkái ibn el Ḥág Fáíd."

He was born at Shendi, and had a brother named Ḥammūda....He was a disciple of Sheikh Muḥammad el Meḍowi[3] ibn el Miṣri....He was buried at Abu Ḥaráz.

7. [4]"'Abd el Ḳádir ibn el Sheikh Idrís."

He was the youngest son of his father[5], and was born at Abyaḍ Díri.... His mother was Ṭáhira bint walad Abu 'Aḳrab, a Maḥassía....He had a son, Idrís.

8. "'Abd el Kerím ibn 'Agíb ibn Korūma, el Kahli."

He learnt Ṣūfiism from the *feki* Náfa'i el Fezári, who died at el Bashá-ḳira, and who was taught it by Mukhṭár[6] walad Abu 'Anáya, el Gáma'i [*i.e.* of the Gawáma'a tribe], who was taught it by Ṭáha[7] walad 'Omára, who was taught it by Sheikh Dafa'alla[8] ibn el Sháfa'i, who was taught it by el Ḥág 'Abdulla[9] el Ḥalanḳi, the disciple of Sheikh Dafa'alla[10]....

The *feki* Muḥammad ibn Medani was one of his pupils. He went on the pilgrimage but was never heard of again.

9. "'Abd el Laṭíf el Khaṭíb ibn el Khaṭíb 'Omára[11]."

He was born at Sennár and in time succeeded his father as preacher.... He was profoundly learned, and performed the pilgrimage....His death, at the hands of el Malik Ṣubr, was avenged upon the latter by King Bádi.

10. [12]"'Abd el Mágid ibn Ḥammad el Aghbash" (d. 1121 A.H.[13]).

He was taught by his father Ḥammad[14], and, in his turn, taught the *feki* Mekki walad Serág el Magdhūb, and the *feki* Walad Abu 'Aṣída, and the *feki* Samíḥ el Tamírábi, and the latter's two sons Sa'ad and Ḥammad.

11. [15]"'Abd el Maḥmūd el Nófalábi."

An 'Araki of the stock of Maḥmūd[16] "Rágil el Ḳuṣr."...He was born at el Ḳūbía and attained very great fame....He was a contemporary of Sheikh Khógali[17], whose daughter he married....He was a party to a famous "*cause célèbre*," described as follows:

'Abd el Maḥmūd had married a Ga'ali woman called Ḥusna and by her had two daughters: she then demanded a divorce from him, "and he said to her 'Settle your dowry upon my daughters'; and when she had done so he divorced her. Then she went to the *feki* Ḥammad[18] and offered herself to him, forgoing her right to a dowry; and he married her. And she said to him 'I have been unjustly treated by 'Abd el Maḥmūd: he robbed me of my stipulated right,

[1] No. 241. [2] No. 141. [3] No. 165. [4] Tree 4.
[5] No. 141. [6] No. 206. [7] No. 248. [8] No. 83.
[9] No. 33. [10] No. 84. [11] No. 219. [12] Tree 2.
[13] 1710 A.D. [14] No. 118. [15] Tree 7. [16] No. 157.
[17] No. 154. [18] No. 124.

and I want you to get it back for me from him.' And the *feki* Ḥammad believed her story and complained against 'Abd el Maḥmūd to the troops encamped at Abu Zaríba; but they said to him 'We will not interfere in your affairs.' Then the *feki* Ḥammad wrote to him a letter on a tablet and the contents were as follows: 'From Ḥammad ibn Mariam to 'Abd el Maṭrūd. God Almighty said "Give the women their dowry freely," and you have disobeyed the book of God and robbed the woman of her dowry. You are no 'Abd el Maḥmūd [*lit.* "Slave of Him that is praised"], you are 'Abd el Maṭrūd [*lit.* "Slave of the expelled one"]!'—that is the devil. This letter he gave to a Fezári *faḳír*; and ['Abd el Maḥmūd] said to him 'You are my disciple [*ḥowári*] and I have educated you, and do you bring me a letter like this?' And God caused that *faḳír* to die the very same day. [Meanwhile] the *feki* Ḥammad was staying in his village, which is at Omdurmán, when fire broke out and consumed all his rooms and surrounded the room in which he was on every side. And the people said to him 'Come out'; but he replied 'I won't! Shall I leave my books?' Then Aḥmad ibn 'Ali el 'Ónábi went in after him and brought him out, bed and all. Then they rebuilt the rooms with stone but the fire blazed up in the stone. And indeed we have seen written in the handwriting of the *feki* Ḥammad the following: 'After I escaped from the fire all and sundry believed in him and were amazed at him, and,' he added, 'el Ḥusna has done all this: she said he robbed her of her dowry,—may God call her to account!'"

12. "'ABD EL NŪR IBN OBAYḌ."

He was a follower of Sheikh Muḥammad[1] walad Da'ūd el Luḳr, and was buried at Abu Ḥaráz.

"'ABD EL RAḤÍM IBN EL SHEIKH SULAYMÁN EL ZAMLI" (*vide sub* "Wadád," No. 251).

13. [2]"'ABD EL RAḤÍM[3] IBN EL SHEIKH 'ABDULLA[4] EL 'ARAKI."... He was known as "Ibn el Khaṭwa."...He was born in the Ḥegáz.

14. [5]"'ABD EL RAḤMAN 'ABU FÁḲ' ibn Medani[6] walad Um Gadayn."

He was born and buried at Nūri in the SHÁÍḲÍA country, but spent part of his life at el Abwáb.

15. [7]"'ABD EL RAḤMAN IBN ASÍD" (d. 1127 A.H.[8]).

His mother was Sitt el Dár the daughter of Sheikh 'Abd el Raḥman[9] ibn Ḥammadtu, and his father Asíd, a Sháíḳi of the AWLÁD UM SÁLIM section....He was born at Nūri....He was taught law [*Khalíl*] by his

[1] No. 186. [2] Tree 9. [3] reading عبدالرحيم for عبدالرحمن.
[4] No. 34. [5] Tree 10. [6] No. 164. [7] Tree 10.
[8] 1715 A.D. [9] No. 21.

maternal uncle and "Sheikh," Muḥammad[1] walad Um Gadayn, and was instructed in the Ḳurán by Sheikh 'Abd el Raḥman[2] ibn el Aghbash.... In 1107 A.H. [1695 A.D.] he left the SHÁIḲIÁ country with his mother's relatives, the AWLÁD UM GADAYN[3], for el Abwáb.... Among his followers were the noble *feki* Walad Baḥr, Sheikh ibn Medani, Málik[4] ibn 'Abd el Raḥman, Ḥammad[5] ibn el Magdhūb, and Muḥammad ibn Bakhít el Muḥammadábi.

16. [6]"'ABD EL RAḤMAN IBN BELÁL" (d. 1155[7] A.H.).

He was the fifth successor of Sheikh Ṣughayerūn[8].... His instructors were his father[9] and his maternal uncle the *feki* Abu el Ḥasan[10]; and among his pupils were the *feki* Ḳumr el Dín and his brother el Zayn, the three sons of the *feki* Ḥammad el Tūd [Tór ?], the *feki* Serḥán[11] walad Ṭeráf, the *feki* Sanhūri[12] walad Madthir, and others.

17. [13]"'ABD EL RAḤMAN IBN GÁBIR[14]."

He was one of the most famous *savants* of the Sudan.... He was taught by his brother Ibráhím el Būlád and by Sídí Muḥammad el Banūfari.... "He taught the science of law [*lit. Khalíl*] from beginning to end forty times, and he had under him three mosques, in the SHÁIḲÍA country, at Korti, and among the DUFÁR respectively: in each of these he used to teach (*lit.* 'read') for four months."... Among his pupils were such famous men as 'Abdulla[15] el 'Araki, 'Abd el Raḥman[16] ibn Masíkh el Nuwayri, Ya'aḳūb[17] ibn el Sheikh Bán el Nuḳá, el Mesallami[18] walad Abu Wanaysa, Luḳáni el Ḥág[19] (maternal uncle of Ḥasan Ḥasūna), and 'Ísa[20], the father of Muḥammad ibn 'Ísa Sowár el Dhabab.... "The four sons of Gábir were like the four elements, each one of them having his peculiar excellence. The most learned of them was Ibráhím, the most virtuous 'Abd el Raḥman, the most pious Ismá'íl, and the most zealous 'Abd el Raḥím[21]; and their sister Fáṭima, the mother of the son[22] of Serḥán, was like unto them in learning and religion. And their mother was named Ṣáfia."... They were buried at Tarnag in the SHÁIḲÍA country.

18. "'ABD EL RAḤMAN IBN ḤÁG EL DWAYHI."

He was born in the SHÁIḲÍA country and was a pupil of 'Abd el Raḥman[23] ibn Asíd.

19. [24]"'ABD EL RAḤMAN IBN EL ḤÁG KHÓGALI[25]."

"He devoted himself entirely to the service of God: no one ever saw him eat or drink or laugh or tell a tale or talk of what concerned him or what concerned him not or uncover his head."

[1] No. 203. [2] No. 20. [3] Nos. 14, 164, 203.
[4] No. 158. [5] No. 123. [6] Tree 1.
[7] 1742 A.D. [8] No. 241. [9] No. 79.
[10] No. 47. [11] No. 234. [12] No. 227.
[13] Tree 1. [14] No. 96. [15] No. 34.
[16] No. 23. [17] No. 254. [18] No. 172.
[19] No. 156. [20] No. 144. [21] reading عبدالرحيم for عبدلرحمن.
[22] No. 241. [23] No. 15. [24] Tree 7. [25] No. 154.

20. [1]"'Abd el Raḥman ibn Ḥammad el Aghbash[2]."

He was taught by his father and 'Ísa walad Kanū[3].

21. [4]"'Abd el Raḥman ibn Ḥammadtu el Khaṭíb."

He was taught by Sheikh Ismá'íl ibn Gábir and visited Sheikh el Banūfari....His sons by one wife were Medani el Nátiḳ[5] and the *feki* Sheikh el Á'sir[6]; and, secondly, by Um Gadayn, Muḥammad and Medani; and, thirdly, Málik[7] and Abu Duḳn.

22. [8]"'Abd el Raḥman ibn Ibráhím walad Abu Maláḥ."

He was born at Debbat 'Antár, and was named by his mother after her maternal uncle 'Abd el Raḥman[9] ibn Masíkh el Nuwayri....As a boy he was taught by Muḥammad[10] ibn 'Ísa Sowár el Dhahab. Subsequently he visited Egypt and took lessons from Sheikh el Islám 'Ali el Ag·hūri....He was the father of Sheikh Khógali[11].

23. [12]"'Abd el Raḥman ibn Masíkh, el Nuwayri."

He was a close companion of Sheikh 'Abdulla el 'Araki[13], and "one of the forty disciples of Walad Gábir."..."He was, too, one of the four whom Sheikh 'Agíb appointed [*walá*] by order of King Dekín 'Síd el 'Áda.'"...He was buried at el Fuḳara behind Arbagi.

24. [14]"'Abd el Raḥman ibn Muḥammad ibn Medani."

He was known as "Anūnírán."...He was taught by the *feki* Muḥammad[15] ibn Ibráhím, and held in great respect by the Danáḳla and Sháíḳía.... He was murdered by his cousins out of envy.

25. [16]"'Abd el Raḥman ibn el Sheikh Ṣáliḥ[17] Bán el Nuḳá" (b. 1121 or 1122[18]).

He was taught by the *fekis* Ḍayfulla[19], and 'Abd el Hádi (a disciple of Muḥammad ibn Medani), and 'Abd el Báḳi ibn Faḳa, the disciple of el Khaṭíb 'Abd el Laṭíf[20] of el 'Egayga, and Ismá'íl ibn el feki el Zayn, and others. ...Among his pupils were 'Abdulla[21] ibn Ṣábūn and 'Ali el Sháfa'i[22] and Feraḥ ibn Taktūk[23]....

He used to have visions.

26. "'Abd el Raḥman ibn Ṭeráf."

A Mesallami by origin, born at el Ḥukna on the Atbara....He and his family migrated thence to Sóba on the Blue Nile....He was a friend and follower of Sheikh Idrís[24] wad el Arbáb, who "taught him medicine; and he instructed the people accordingly. And he used to cure devils by A. B. T. Th. G. H. Kh. etc."

He was buried close to Sóba, in the desert.

[1] Tree 2.
[2] No. 118.
[3] No. 143.
[4] Tree 10.
[5] No. 163.
[6] No. 236.
[7] No. 158.
[8] Tree 7.
[9] No. 23.
[10] No. 191.
[11] No. 154.
[12] Tree 7.
[13] No. 34.
[14] Tree 10.
[15] No. 252?
[16] Tree 8.
[17] No. 226.
[18] 1708–9 A.D.
[19] No. 88.
[20] No. 9.
[21] No. 38.
[22] No. 63.
[23] No. 95.
[24] No. 141.

27. "'ABD EL RÁZIK ABU KURŪN" (d. 1070 A.H.[1]).

He was by race a Rufá'i....He was a follower of Sheikh Ya'akūb[2] ibn el Sheikh Bán el Nuká, who sent him to teach at el Abwáb, and a contemporary of Sheikh Idrís[3] wad el Arbáb and Sheikh Ḥasan[4] Ḥasūna and Sheikh Ṣughayerūn[5] and Sheikh Maskín[6] el Khafí....He had twelve sons....

He worked several miracles, of which the following is an example. "And there came to him a slave girl, the wife of King 'Adlán, and said to him 'My lord, my children have died; I prithee beseech God to recompense me for them with others.' He said to her 'I grant it, I grant it' five times, and she bore five children; and they became the ancestors of the 'ADLÁNÁB."...

He died at Muays and was buried at Meshra el Aḥmar, "and his tomb is plain to see and should be visited with becoming humility and gravity...and the news of his death reached Sheikh Ḥasan walad Ḥasūna...."

28. "'ABD EL ṢÁDIK IBN ḤUSAYN WALAD ABU SULAYMÁN, EL HOWÁRI."

He was born, died and was buried at Um Dóm....The *feki* el Zayn[7] taught him law [*Khalíl*] and Sheikh el Meḍowi[8] apostleship [*risála*].

29. "'ABD EL WAHHÁB IBN EL FEKI ḤAMMAD[9] EL NEGÍD, EL GAMŪ'I."

He was *Imám* of the mosque at Asláng, and was buried on the hill to the west of it...."And when the *feki* Ḥammad[10] went forth with Sheikh 'Agíb the Great to war against the king of the FUNG he said 'After me my son Bekri shall read in the mosque, and after him this boy 'Abd el Wahháb.'"

30. "'ABD EL WAHHÁB WALAD ABU KURBI."

Born at Asláng Island, and buried west of it.

31. [11]"'ABDULLA EL AGHBASH, EL BEDAYRI EL DAHMASHI."

He was born at Berber and taught by Muḥammad[12] Sowár el Dhahab and Walad Gábir[13]....He propagated [*lit.* "lit the fire of"] the Kurán at Berber.

32. "'ABDULLA IBN EL 'AGŪZ."

A pupil of Sheikh Muḥammad el Mesallami.

33. "'ABDULLA IBN 'ALI EL ḤALANKI."

He was born at Táka and finally buried there....He was taught by Sheikh Dafa'alla[14] and, in his turn, taught Sheraf el Dín[15] walad Barri, and

---

[1] 1659 A.D., reading سبعين for سبعه .   [2] No. 254.
[3] No. 141.   [4] No. 132.   [5] No. 241.
[6] *v. sub* No. 250.   [7] No. 258.   [8] No. 165.
[9] No. 126.   [10] No. 126.   [11] Tree 2.
[12] No. 191.   [13] No. 17?   [14] No. 84.
[15] No. 237.

Dafa’alla[1] ibn el Sháfa’i of the ’ARAKIÍN....He lived for some time at Abu Ḥaráz.

34. [2]“’ABDULLA IBN DAFA’ALLA EL ’ARAKI.

He was born at Abyaḍ Díri. His mother was Hadía bint ’Aṭíf of the GIMI’ÁB....’Abd el Raḥman[3] el Nuwayri accompanied him when he went to the SHÁIḲÍA country to visit ’Abd el Raḥman[4] [ibn Gábir].... “In his days came Sheikh Tág el Dín[5] el Bahári from Baghdád.”...

Among his pupils were his two brothers Abu Idrís[6] and Ḥammad el Nil, Muḥammad[7] walad Dáūd el Luḳr and Sheikh Sheraf el Dín[8].... He performed the pilgrimage 24 times....His sons were Manófali and ’Abd el Raḥman Abu Shanab and ’Abd el Raḥím[9] ibn el Khaṭwa and others....He was buried at Abu Ḥaráz.

35. [10]“’ABDULLA IBN ḤAMMAD IBN EL FEKI ’ABD EL MAGÍD[11].”

A nephew of Musṭafa [’Abd el Magíd].

36. “’ABDULLA WALAD ḤASÓBA EL MOGHRABI.”

His father came as a stranger to the land and settled at Sóba and attached himself to Sheikh Idrís[12] [wad el Arbáb]. ’Abdulla himself was born at Sóba, and migrated later to Um Leban on the White Nile, where he died and was buried....His sons were Tágūr[13] el Naḥási, Muḥammad el Bekri, and el Ḥág.

37. “’ABDULLA IBN MŪSA ‘EL MUSHAMMIR.’”

A Begáwi by race; born at Um Ḥurfa....Sheikh Idrís[14] nicknamed him “el Mushammir” [“One who tucks up his clothes”].

38. “’ABDULLA IBN ṢÁBŪN.”

He was by birth a slave [*mamlūk*], the property of a woman of el Ḳalay’a....Though offered a wife he refused and died unmarried.

40. “’ABDULLA EL SHERÍF.”

He was nicknamed “Tuwayl el Ḥalfáya.” He was born in Fás....

He was a follower of Aḥmad ibn Náṣir, and died at Sennár.

41. [15]“’ABDULLA ‘EL ṬERAYFI.’”

His father was Sheikh Muḥammad Abu ’Áḳla[16] el Káshif....He was a pupil of Sheikh Dafa’alla[17].... He went on the pilgrimage but died on the road....His sons were named Aḥmad[18] and Muḥammad[19]....

“He was called ‘Ṭerayfi’ from the beauty of his features [*aṭráf*], namely his face and his forearms and his feet.”

42. [20]“‘’ABU ’ÁḲLA.’”

His real name was Muḥammad....’Áḳla was his daughter and hence he was called “father of ’Áḳla.”...He was a follower of his father’s brother Sheikh Abu Idrís[21]....His sons were ’Abdulla “el Ṭerayfi[22],” Shams el Dín, Abu Idrís, and Ḥammad Abu Ḳurn.

[1] No. 83. [2] Tree 9. [3] No. 23. [4] No. 17.
[5] No. 67. [6] No. 48. [7] No. 186. [8] No. 238.
[9] No. 13. [10] Tree 2. [11] No. 10. [12] No. 141.
[13] reading تاجور for تاحور, No. 246. [14] No. 141.
[15] Tree 9. [16] No. 42. [17] No. 84. [18] No. 56.
[19] No. 177. [20] Tree 9. [21] No. 48. [22] No. 41.

43. "'ABU 'ÁḲLA' IBN EL SHEIKH ḤAMMAD."

His grandfather [*gidhu*] was Sheikh Dafa'alla....Among his followers was Sheikh Ismá'íl[1] ibn Mekki el Daḳaláshi...."And when he died, God bless him, there arose from his tomb a scent sweeter than pinewood and the camphor tree. And his sons were Ḥammad el (Ḥasíb?) and Sheikh Ḳismulla; and all the stock of Sheikh Dafa'alla is descended from these two."

44. "ABU BUKR."

"The holy-man of Ḥagar el 'Asal, a Takagábi by origin. He it was that guided Sheikh Ḥasan[2] ibn Ḥasūna and revealed to him the mysteries."

45. "ABU BUKR WALAD TUAYR."

A pupil and follower of Sheikh el Zayn[3].

46. [4]"ABU DELAYḲ."

"He was paternal uncle of Sheikh Bedowi[5] and a follower of Sheikh Selmán el Ṭowáli[6]. He was entirely devoted to religion and went clothed in patches and rags [*dulḳán*]. He was called 'Abu Delayḳ' ('Father of Rags') and also 'Dhanab el 'Aḳrab' ('Scorpion's Tail') because he will not suffer deeds of darkness, but is swift to strike [such as do them].

He guided and instructed [the people], and among his followers was his brother's son Sheikh Bedowi[7]. His children were Ḥusayn and 'Áyesha; and when he was nigh unto death, the people said to him 'Who is to be the *Khalífa* after you?' And he said ''Áyesha my daughter.' And Sheikh Bedowi married her and begat by her el Nuḳr and Sheikh Meḍowi[8] and 'Abdulla and Tág el Dín. He died, and was buried at el Nigfa and his tomb is plain to see."

47. [9]"ABU EL ḤASAN IBN ṢÁLIḤ, EL 'ŪDI" (b. 1070[10] A.H.; d. 1133[11] A.H.).

His mother was Ḥósha, the daughter of Sheikh el Zayn[12].

48. [13]"ABU IDRÍS."

His full name was Sheikh Muḥammad ibn el Sheikh Dafa'alla[14] ibn Muḳbal el 'Araki....He was *Sheikh el Islám* and very famous....He was buried with his brother Sheikh 'Abdulla[15].

49. [16]"ABU EL ḲÁSIM 'EL GUNAYD.'"

The son of Sheikh 'Ali el Níl[17].

50. "ABU EL ḲÁSIM EL WADIÁNÁBI, EL MESALLAMI."

A pupil of Sheikh Idrís.

[1] No. 145. [2] No. 132. [3] No. 258. [4] Tree 12.
[5] No. 74. [6] No. 230. [7] No. 74. [8] No. 167.
[9] Tree 1. [10] 1659 A.D. [11] 1720 A.D. [12] No. 258.
[13] Tree 9. [14] No. 84, reading دفعالله for دفع.
[15] No. 34. [16] Tree 1. [17] No. 62.

51. "ABU SINAYNA."

His full name was Muḥammad ibn Nuṣr, el Tergami el Ga'ali. He was born at el Buwayḍ.

"His father Nuṣr was instructed in the Ḳurán and its teachings by Sheikh Muḥammad[1] ibn 'Ísa; and it was the latter who advised him to marry the mother of 'Abu Sinayna.' And it was thus: Sheikh Muḥammad saw her when she was young and said to him 'You shall marry this girl and she shall bear to you a pious son.' [Nuṣr] replied '[Then] she will bear [one like] you yourself.' And thrice or four times [Sheikh Muḥammad] said 'She shall do so.' And it came to pass that her people journeyed from Dongola to el Buwayḍ in the region of el Abwáb, and [Nuṣr] went after her and married her, and there was born to him 'Abu Sinayna.'...Subsequently ['Abu Sinayna'] settled at Arbagi and taught the people there."...

He was buried at Arbagi.

52. "ABU SURŪR, EL FAḌLI."

He was born at el Ḥalfáya....His mother was Kanūna bint el Ḥág 'Ali of the FAḌLÍA tribe....He was taught law [*Khalíl*] by Sheikh el Zayn[2] and the articles of faith [*el 'aḳáid*] by the *feki* 'Ali[3] walad Barri. ...After teaching awhile at el Ḥalfáya he went to Dárfūr and taught there....He was finally murdered in Dár Ṣalíḥ, "and the cause of his death was that while he was asleep his concubines killed him by smashing his skull with stones; may God be their enemy!"

53. "ABU ZAYD[4] IBN EL SHEIKH 'ABD EL ḲÁDIR."

He was a follower of Sheikh el Zayn[5]....He travelled to Dárfūr and Borḳū in the days when Sultan Ya'aḳūb reigned in the latter....He died in Dárfūr....His sons were Ṣubáḥ and 'Abd el Ḳádir and 'Ali and Ḥegázi[6].

54. [7]"'ABŪḌI."

A disciple of el Mesallami[8]....His sons were Muḥammad[9], Aḥmad, el Mesallami, 'Abd el Ḥafíẓ and Ibráhím[10], all of them *fekis*...He died at el Ferár.

55. [11]"'EL 'AGAMI' IBN ḤASŪNA."

His real name was Muḥammad....His mother was Fáṭima bint Waḥshía whose father was a Mesallami Ḳabayṣi and whose mother was a Ṣáridía Khamaysía[12]....He went on the pilgrimage and died in the Ḥegáz.

56. [13]"AḤMAD IBN EL SHEIKH 'ABDULLA EL ṬERAYFI."

A follower of Sheikh Dafa'alla Aḥmad, in whose charge Sheikh 'Abdulla left his sons when starting for the pilgrimage....He died in *sannat el gidri* ("small-pox year"), as did some sixteen of his relatives also.

[1] No. 191. [2] No. 258. [3] No. 58.
[4] reading ابوزيد for ابزيد. [5] No. 258.
[6] No. 133. [7] Tree 11. [8] No. 172.
[9] No. 179. [10] No. 135. [11] Tree 5.
[12] reading خميسية for حميسية. [13] Tree 9.

57. "'Ali walad Abu Duḳn."

His father was a Dongoláwi....His mother's name was Siáḳa....His burial-place was el Ruays near el Ḥalfáya....Sheikh Idrís[1] visited his tomb.

58. [2]"'Ali ibn Barri" (b. 1010 to 1013 A.H.; d. 1073[3] A.H.).

His mother was Umháni bint el Wali 'Ali ibn Ḳandíl el Ṣáridi.... Various laudations of him are quoted, including one by the *feki* Ṣughayerūn[4] el Shaḳaláwi, who said "I knew Sheikh Idrís[5] and Walad Ḥasūna[6] and 'Abd el Ráziḳ[7] and Básbár[8], but I found none of them as quick in his answers as this boy, 'Ali ibn Barri."...

Among his pupils was the *feki* Arbáb el Khashan[9]....His "sheikh" was Básbár, and the famous case of Básbár and the Ḥammadía woman is related in the biographies of both master and pupil....'Ali also had a dispute with Mismár el Ḥalashi of Ḳerri about a cow and foretold the resultant deposition of Mismár by the King of Sennár, in favour of 'Ali ibn 'Othmán. "And they have been deposed [from their power] until this present day. His son Khidr held the sheikhship after el 'Agayl for six months and was then deposed; and Mismár the son of Walad[10] 'Agíb [ruled] for two months after Sheikh 'Abdulla, and was then deposed."

59. "'Ali walad Dhiáb, el Ḳurayshábi."

He was born at Asláng Island and taught by *fekis* Belál[11] and Abu el Ḥasan[12]....He visited Sennár, and finally died at Ḳóz walad Barakát where he had started a school....Muḥammad el Nūr Ṣubr and other descendants of Ḥammad[13] ibn Mariam were among his pupils.

"'Ali ibn Ḥammūda" (*vide sub* "Baḳádi," No. 68).

60. "'Ali walad 'Ishayb."

"He was born at Dongola. He was taught by Sheikh Muḥammad el Banūfari in Egypt and excelled in learning. Then he settled in the south, and Sheikh 'Agíb the Great built him a mosque, and the king of the Fung granted him many lands on the east bank and in the Gezíra [*el Hūoi*] and in the rainlands, and he acted as a judge and did justice therein and gave judgements according to the accepted standards and to the [more] valid arguments in the dispute.

And he was the companion of Sheikh Ibráhím el Būlád ibn Gábir in the quest after learning in Egypt; and it is said that each of the two prayed a prayer against the other and obtained his desire therein: Sheikh 'Ali walad 'Ishayb prayed against Sheikh Ibráhím el Būlád saying 'May God shorten your life [that you may die] in your youth'; and the whole incident[14] is explained in *The*

[1] No. 141. [2] Tree 3. [3] 1662 A.D.
[4] No. 242. [5] No. 141. [6] No. 132.
[7] No. 27. [8] No. 73. [9] No. 65.
[10] reading ولدولد for ولدولده. [11] No. 89. [12] No. 47.
[13] No. 124. [14] reading المسألة for المسلة.

Biographies (?). And Sheikh el Būlád said to him 'May God make your learning useless.' And verily [the period of] el Būlád's teaching was seven years [only] and in it he taught 40 persons, and then he died; and as for Sheikh 'Ali we have never heard of his having engaged in teaching of any importance, but only that he judged cases. And he was buried at el 'Aydai, and his tomb is plain to see; and all the 'ISHAYBÁB are his descendants."

61. "'ALI EL LABADI."

A Moghrabi by origin, born at Sennár...."His father was one of God's chosen."...His sister was given in marriage to 'Abd el Ḥafíẓ el Khaṭíb, the father of el Khaṭíb 'Omára[1]....His sons were Ahlulla, Gháb 'Ain, and Mekki....A miracle related of him is that he dipped his stick (*'ukáz*) into a jar (*zeer*) full of water, pronouncing these words "In the name of God the Compassionate and Merciful A. B. T. Th. G. Ḥ. Kh.," and immediately the water was turned into yellow clarified butter (*samn*)....He was buried at Sennár.

62. [2]"'ALI 'EL NÍL' IBN EL SHEIKH MUḤAMMAD[3] EL HAMÍM."

He was the third successor (*Khalífa*) of Sheikh Tág el Dín[4] in the country of the FUNG....He was a follower of his father in religious matters....He was called "el Níl" ("the Nile") because of the floods of knowledge that he poured in the dry wastes of the people's minds,—the sobriquet being given him by Sheikh Dafa'alla[5]....His father, whose "Sheikh" was Tág el Dín el Bahári, lived at Mundara; and it was there 'Ali was buried....On his deathbed he appointed Sheikh "el Gunayd[6]" his successor....He lived in the reign of King Rubáṭ of Sennár.

63. "*El feḳír* 'ALI WALAD EL SHÁFA'I."

A pupil of *feki* 'Omára[7], and a follower of Sheikh Dafa'alla[8]....He composed religious poetry, "and if he heard his poetry recited by anyone else he used to weep and fly in the air: this was witnessed several times." He was buried at Sennár.

64. [9]"'ARAKI IBN EL SHEIKH IDRÍS[10]."

His father named him after Sheikh 'Abdulla el 'Araki[11]....He died of small-pox.

65. "ARBÁB IBN 'ALI IBN 'ÓN" (d. 1102[12] A.H.).

He was called "el Khashan el Khashūna."...Among his pupils were el Ḥág Khógali[13], the *feki* Ḥammad[14] ibn Mariam and Sheikh Feraḥ[15] walad Taktūk....He died at Sennár.

66. "'AWŪḌA IBN 'OMAR, 'SHAKÁL EL ḲÁRIḤ.'"

He was a pupil of Mūsa Feríd, the disciple [*ḥowár*] of Sheikh Ḥasan walad Ḥasūna....

[1] No. 219. [2] Tree 1. [3] No. 190. [4] No. 67.
[5] No. 84. [6] No. 49. [7] No. 219. [8] No. 84.
[9] Tree 4. [10] No. 141. [11] No. 34. [12] 1690 A.D.
[13] No. 154. [14] No. 124. [15] No. 95

Several miracles are recorded of him:

(1) "Sheikh Muḥammad[1] ibn 'Ísa was nigh unto death, and his wife, the daughter of el Malik Ḥasan walad Kashásh[2] the king of Dongola, and mother of Ḥiláli[3] his son, said to him 'Your elder sons you have guided [in the right way]; but who is to look after my son?' And he said to her 'You must [apply to] el Ḥaḍari.' Then she came and brought her bracelets and anklets and said to him (*i.e.* el Ḥaḍari) 'I want you to make my son to sit in the seat of his father.' He replied [to her son] 'Son of my Sheikh, sit on my prayer-mat': so he sat there. Then [el Ḥaḍari] arose and ran round the room [*khalwa*] and came and knelt before him and took hold of his hand and kissed it, saying 'I have made you to sit in the seat of your father.' And indeed Ḥiláli attained[4] great eminence among the FŪNG and the Arabs and acted as a judge and a teacher of all kinds of knowledge."...

(2) "There came to him a certain man called Ibn 'Abád, who was addicted to evildoing[5], and said to him 'I have a flourishing water-wheel and give you a quarter [share] in it.' And he replied 'What do you want from me?' The man answered 'I want the grace[6] of God.' ['Awūḍa] said 'I give you a quarter of God's grace.' Then the man repented and asked pardon of God. Afterwards he came again and said 'I have made it up to a half'; and ['Awūḍa] said 'And I grant you half of the grace of God.' And the man improved more and more: and finally he came and said 'I give you the whole water-wheel'; and ['Awūḍa] said to him 'I give you the whole of God's grace'; and the man fell down in a faint [and remained so] for some days, but finally he became a paragon and one of the saints [*auliyá*] of God."...

(3) "Mismár walad 'Araybi in his journey to Dongola in the year 1070[7] wrought havoc among the men of rank and dignity[8]; and the people appealed to him ['Awūḍa] for help, and he said to them 'His destruction will be at the hands of the short pale bald man; and as for me, I am your security that the Sheikh of Ḳerri shall not enter Dongola: if he comes, [and if] 'Awūḍa is alive, strain some beer for him and he will drink it; and if he be dead pour it over his tomb.' I say that most of these events connected with the Sheikh ['Awūḍa] are fully corroborated, and are compatible with the Book and the Law [*sunna*] and the Unanimities[9]."

He went on the pilgrimage, and met Sheikh 'Ali el Ag·hūri *en route*.

[1] No. 191. [2] reading كشاش for كشكش. [3] No. 134.
[4] reading حظي for حطي. [5] reading حوارج for حوارح.
[6] reading اليل for الليل. [7] 1659 A.D.
[8] reading اجواه for احواه. [9] reading اجماع for احماع

B

67. "'El Bahári,' *i.e.* Tág el Dín, el Baghdádi."

"His actual name was Muḥammad. 'El Bahári' was a surname due to the saying 'a shining [*báhir*] moon has passed,' and he was so called from the light of his countenance,—sweet is the odour of his story. He was the *Sheikh*, the *Imám*, the divine *Ḳuṭb*, the immortal *Ghauth*, the successor of Sheikh 'Abd el Ḳádir el Gíláni. He was born at Baghdád, and went on the pilgrimage, and thence to the Sudan by leave of the Prophet of God...and of Sheikh 'Abd el Ḳádir el Gíláni. He came with Dáūd ibn 'Abd el Gelíl, the father of el Ḥág Sa'íd, the ancestor of the people of el 'Aydag[1], early in the second half of the tenth century, at the beginning of the rule of Sheikh 'Agíb; and he dwelt with Dáūd at Wád el Sha'ír behind Um 'Aẓám."...

He married in the Gezíra and lived there for seven years...."He was the instructor of five famous men, viz. Sheikh Muḥammad el Hamím[2], and Sheikh Bán el Nuḳá 'el Ḍarír[3],' and Ḥegázi the founder of Arbagi and its mosque, and Shá'a el Dín walad Tuaym the ancestor of the Shukría, and Sheikh 'Agíb the Great."

It is said he taught 40 persons including the *feki* Ḥammad el Negíḍ[4] the head of Aslang mosque, and the *feki* Raḥma[5] the ancestor of the Ḥaláwiín, and the *'omda* Walad Abu Ṣádiḳ, and Bán el Nuḳá "el Ḍarír[6]" ["the blind"]....It is also said he journeyed to Teḳali and there instructed 'Abdulla el Gamál, the ancestor of Sheikh Ḥammad[7] walad el Turábi.

68. "'Baḳádi.'"

His real name was 'Ali ibn Ḥammūda, el Kahli el Aswadi. He was born at el Shará'ana and was a pupil of Ḥámid Abu Mūna.

69. "Baḳdūsh ibn Surūr, el Gamū'i."

A pupil of Sheikh Muḥammad[8] walad 'Ísa....He was appointed by Sheikh 'Agib the Great.

70. [9]"'Bán el Nuḳá' walad el Sheikh 'Abd el Rázıḳ."

His father called him "Bán el Nuḳá" after his grandfather[10]...."He died at about the age of 40, or rather more."

71. [11]"'Bán el Nuḳá' ibn Ḥammad ibn el Sheikh Idrís, el Faḍli."

His actual name was Muḥammad....His mother was a Sudanese.... "He was called 'Bán el Nuḳá' because his mother said 'My purity [*nuḳái*] (that is innocence) has been revealed [*bán*].' He was a staff of support to King Náíl."...He was acquainted with Sheikhs Tág

[1] written العيدْى.
[2] No. 190.
[3] No. 71.
[4] No. 126.
[5] No. 221.
[6] No. 71.
[7] No. 125.
[8] No. 191.
[9] Tree 8.
[10] No. 71.
[11] Tree 8.

el Dín el Bahári[1] and Muḥammad el Hindi....He died and was buried at el Wa'ar.

72. [2]"BARAKÁT ḤAMMAD IBN EL SHEIKH IDRÍS."

He was a follower of el Imám 'Ali ibn Abu Ṭálib and of his own grandfather Sheikh Idrís[3]....Among his disciples were the *fekis* Meḍowi[4] ibn Medani and Muḥammad ibn Yūsef....He had ten sons, including Meḍowi[5], Arbáb, 'Araki, 'Abd el Raḥman and Ḥammad.

73. "BÁSBÁR 'EL SHUKRI.'"

By birth he was a Ga'ali 'Óni....He was named Básbár by his mother. ...He was born at el Mekayna and was a follower of Sheikh Sheraf el Dín[6]....

Among his pupils were the two Awlád Barri[7], Ḥamayd el Ṣáridi[8] and the Awlád[9] el Ḥág Fáíd....

"It is related that Sheikh Básbár married a woman of the AḤÁMDA ['a Ḥammadía'] and divorced her. Then there came to her a son of her father's brother, a Ḥammadi, a disciple [*ḥowár*] of Sheikh 'Abd el Rázik Abu Ḳurūn, and married her, in spite of [Básbár's] warning to him. And [the Ḥammadi] said to his 'Sheikh' ['Abd el Rázik] 'You must protect me from him'; and [the Sheikh] replied 'Do not go near the river.' [Now these AḤAMDA] were riverain folk. And it is said that that man never went near the river for years; until finally his wife became pregnant and bore a child. Then he went close to the river for the shaving-ceremony of his child; and the moment he put his foot into the water a crocodile seized it and bit him that he died. Then [the crocodile] cast him upon the river bank. Then Básbár, who was [sitting] under the acacia trees, cried out 'He got him, he got him, did my boy 'Ali.' Now 'Ali at that time was a small boy, [still] with a tuft on his head."...

Básbár's sons were el Bedowi and Medani and 'Abd el Ḳádir Abu Ḳurūn.

74. [10]"BEDOWI WALAD ABU DELAYḲ" (d. 1118[11] A.H.).

It is said that his father was named 'Abdulla, and that his mother's name was Gawádi, and that he was by origin a Kahli...."Sheikh Khógali[12] once said 'The fire of 'Abd el Ḳádir, after [the death of] Sheikh Idrís[13], was with Sheikh Bedowi.'"...

Several traditions and remarks concerning him and a number of verses are quoted. One story is as follows: the scene is at Wad Ḥasūna. "And I was in doubt whether to light the fire on the higher plateau or whether to go down to the river and do so at Sellama. Then I saw the Prophet of God...and he said to me 'Dwell in the red country with the red people'; and 'the red country' is the hill of el Nigfa,

[1] No. 67. [2] Tree 4. [3] No. 141.
[4] No. 168. [5] No. 166. [6] No. 238.
[7] Nos. 58 and 136. [8] No. 129. [9] No. 6.
[10] Tree 12. [11] 1706 A.D. [12] No. 154. [13] No. 141.

and 'the red people' are the BAṬÁḤÍN. So I built a retreat [*khalwa*] and in front of it a porch [*rákūba*]. [And it happened that] a man of the MARGHŪMÁB[1] had slain a son of Sheikh Na'ím el Baṭḥáni[2] and by chance came to me; so I put him inside the retreat and sat myself in the porch. [Then the avengers] came and entered [the retreat] after him and slew him and said to me 'Sheikh Na'ím farts warnings, and you are making trouble for yourself.' [Then] they set fire to the retreat, but it would not take hold. And I said 'These are no people [for me], I won't live with them.' And again I saw the Prophet of God, and as I was sitting before him I perceived many black ants making for him from the four quarters; and I said, 'My lord, the Prophet of God, what are those ants [doing]?' And he said 'They are come to you [for protection]; stay where you are; let no one interfere with [*lit.* come to] them.' [And so] here am I [*lit.* you see me[3]], O Sheríf, in this place, eating my food [*lit.* my blessing] and awaiting my end....

And when he drew nigh unto death he said 'O ye women of the KAWÁHLA, I will be your [strong] rock[4] on the day of the resurrection'; and he died in the year 1118[5]; and in that same year el Samíḥ made war on Shendi."

75. "BEDR IBN EL SHEIKH SELMÁN IBN YÁSIR."

"He embraced the tenets of Ṣūfiism like his father, and was a follower of his father Sheikh Selmán, and instructed the people. His clothes were always of wool [*ṣūf*], and he was held in high esteem by the kings, and by the tribes of the Arabs from Berber to Upper Egypt....

His sons were el Amín and Sheikh Muḥammad and Abu Ṣáliḥ, and 'Ali the son of the Bisháría woman."...

He was buried with his father.

76. "BEDR IBN EL SHEIKH UM BÁRAK IBN EL SHEIKH MASKÍN, EL KHAFÍ."

All the MASKÍNÁB, except a very few, are descended from him.

77. "BEKRI IBN EL SHEIKH 'ABDULLA[6] IBN ḤASÓBA."

His *ḳubba* is at Sóba Bekri, but he died and was buried at Um Leban on the White Nile "with his father Sheikh 'Abdulla."

78. "BEKRI WALAD EL FEKI IDRÍS."

He was born at Gedíd, where his *ḳubba* now stands...."He had the prophetic gift and was a friend of my grandfather the *feki* Muḥammad walad Ḍayfulla."

[1] reading مرغوماب for مرقوماب.
[2] No. 213.
[3] reading تراني for تران.
[4] reading جبلكن for جبلكا.
[5] 1706 A.D.
[6] reading عبدالله for عبدالرحمن.

79. [1] "BELÁL IBN EL FEKI MUḤAMMAD[2] EL AZRAḲ IBN EL SHEIKH EL ZAYN[3]."

He was taught by his father, and in his turn taught the *feki* Muḥammad[4] ibn 'Abd el Raḥman, and Sa'ad and Ḥammád the sons of the *feki* Samíḥ el 'Armáni, and the *feki* Shammar[5] walad 'Adlán, and Meḍowi[6] ibn el Sheikh Barakát of the MAḤASS, and others.

80. [7] "BERR 'ABD EL MA'ABŪD IBN EL SHEIKH 'ABD EL RAḤMAN[8] EL NUWAYRI."

He was a follower of his mother's father Sheikh Muḥammad[9] walad Maḥmūd el 'Araki.

81. "BERR WALAD NA'ÍM[10] 'ABD EL SHERAKA."

A pupil of Sheikh Dafa'alla[11].... Born and buried at el Kerrada.

82. "BURT EL MESALLAMI."

He was the disciple [*ḥowár*] of Sheikh Selmán[12] el Ṭowáli and, together with Abu Delayḳ[13], learnt from him the tenets of Ṣūfiism.... "He had supernatural powers [of prophecy], and said to Sheikh Ṣáliḥ[14] walad Bán el Nuḳá 'You shall be a great man: the saints shall come to you, the saints shall come to you; and they shall make you be seated [in their presence], and you shall light the fire of 'Abd el Ḳádir.' And his tomb is in the open country between Walad Ḥasūna and Walad Abu Delayḳ, and over it is a *ḳubba*."

D

83. "DAFA'ALLA IBN 'ALI[15] 'EL SHÁFA'I.'"

Born at Arbagi.... He was taught by Sheikh 'Abdulla el Ḥalanḳi[16].

84. [17] "DAFA'ALLA IBN EL SHEIKH MUḤAMMAD[18] ABU IDRÍS[19]" (b. 1003[20] A.H.; d. 1094[21]).

The best man of his epoch.... His mother was Fáṭima Um Ḥasón[22] bint el Ḥág Saláma el Ḍubábi.... He was born at Ḍubáb behind Um 'Aẓám and was taught by his father.... Sheikh Ṣughayerūn[23], Belal el Shayb ibn el Ṭálib, el Ḥág Khógali[24], and Muḥammad[25] ibn el Ṭerayfi all spoke in praise of him.... 'Abdulla[26] el 'Araki was his father's brother.... He settled at Abu Ḥaráz.... He founded a number of mosques in the Gezíra and endowed them with land and slaves.... During all his life he never went to Sennár: if King Bádi walad Rubáṭ wished to speak to him he (the king) used to go to Abu Ḥaráz on purpose....

[1] Tree 1. [2] No. 204. [3] No. 258. [4] No. 175.
[5] No. 235. [6] No. 166. [7] Tree 7. [8] No. 23.
[9] No. 192. [10] No. 212. [11] No. 84. [12] No. 230.
[13] No. 46. [14] No. 226. [15] No. 63. [16] No. 33.
[17] Tree 9. [18] No. 48. [19] reading ابو ادريس for ابو دريس.
[20] 1594 A.D. [21] 1683 A.D.
[22] reading حسون for حسين. [23] No. 241.
[24] No. 154. [25] No. 177. [26] No. 34.

He died, aged 91, in 1094[1] A.H. "and in 1095[2] commenced *Um Laḥm.*"

85. [3]"DAFA'ALLA IBN MUḤAMMAD, el Kahli el Hadhali" (d. 1121[4] A.H.).

His mother was Ría bint Mūsa walad Hatūna, "and she called him Dafa'alla after Sheikh Dafa'alla el 'Araki[5] because the latter was the 'Sheikh' of her father."...He was born and resided at el Ḥalfáya, and was taught law [*Khalíl*] by Muḥammad[6] el Azraḳ ibn el Sheikh el Zayn, and was the companion in Ṣūfiism of Bedowi walad Abu Delayḳ. ...He was often called "Walad Ría."..."When on his deathbed and surrounded by his relatives he said 'Be of good cheer, O ye women of the HATŪNÁB[7] (?), I will be your [strong] rock on the day of the resurrection'; just as Sheikh Bedowi[8] walad Abu Delayḳ said 'Be of good cheer, O ye women of the KAWÁHLA, I will be your [strong] rock on the day of the resurrection.'" He died in 1121[9] A.H.

86. [10]"DAFA'ALLA IBN MUḲBAL, 'EL 'ARAKI.'"

"He came from the west country, from near Bir Serrár, and was accompanied by the *feki* Muḥammad walad Fakrūn, the father of the MASHÁÍKHA, the people of Anḳáwi; but I do not know if they were relations or merely brethren in Islam. He settled at Gerf el Gimí'áb and married Hadía bint 'Áṭif in the GIMÍ'ÁB country and by her begot his five famous sons, the just ones, Ḥammad 'el Nîl' and 'Abdulla[11] and Abu Idrís[12] and Abu Bukr Abu 'Áyesha and el Magdhūb. He was known as 'el 'Araki' because of his descent from the well-known tribe of 'ARAK."

87. "DÁŪD IBN MUḤAMMAD IBN DÁŪD IBN ḤAMDÁN."

He was born and buried at Kuthra, and educated at el Ḥalfáya by Dafa'alla[13] "walad Ría."...

"The great men of his epoch trusted him greatly, and especially Sheikh Muḥammad Abu el Kaylak."

88. [14]"ḌAYFULLA IBN 'ALI IBN 'ABD EL GHANI IBN ḌAYFULLA, el Faḍli" (d. 1095 A.H.[15]).

He was born at el Ḥalfáya....Sheikh el Zayn[16] taught him law [*Khalíl*] and apostleship [*risála*]; Sheikh Dafa'alla[17] ibn el Sheikh Abu Idrís taught him the tenets of Ṣūfiism [*taṣūf*]; and the *feki* Ḥamayd[18] el Ṣáridi taught him the doctrine of Unity [*tawḥid*] and grammar [*naḥu*]. ...He was a great teacher at el Ḥalfáya, and died in the year *Um Laḥm*[19].

[1] 1683 A.D. [2] 1684 A.D. [3] Tree 6. [4] 1709 A.D.
[5] No. 84. [6] No. 204. [7] reading هتونابيات for هنونابيات.
[8] No. 74. [9] 1709 A.D. [10] Tree 9. [11] No. 34.
[12] No. 48, reading ابو ادريس for ابو داريس. [13] No. 85.
[14] Tree 6. [15] 1684 A.D. [16] No. 258. [17] No. 84.
[18] reading حميد for احمد, No. 129. [19] 1684 A.D.

89. [1]"ḌAYFULLA IBN MUḤAMMAD IBN ḌAYFULLA[2]" (d. 1182 A.H.[3]). His father named him after his grandfather[4].... He was taught by the *fekis* Belál[5] and Abu el Ḥasan[6] and Idrís ibn Bella el Kenáni and Sheikh Khógali[7].... The last named was his "Sheikh" and taught him Ṣūfiism.... "Everyone agreed that he was the most learned man of his age in religious subjects, and there is a saying 'After the *feki* Ibráhím[8] el Ḥág [was] the *feki* Abu el Ḥasan, and after the *feki* Abu el Ḥasan [was] the *feki* Ḍayfulla.'"...

Among his pupils were the *feki* Ismá'íl, Sheikh of el Ḳóz, and Sheikh 'Abd el Raḥman[9] Bán el Nuḳá, 'Abd el Raḥman ibn Arbáb and others....

He began teaching in 1130[10] A.H. and continued till his death in 1182[11] A.H.

90. [12]"'DÓLÍB NESI.'"

"His name was Muḥammad el Ḍarír ibn Idrís ibn Dólíb, and the meaning of 'Nesi' in the language of the DANÁGLA is 'son's son.' He was a man of extraordinary energy and used to enter the square retreats [*khalwát*] for the performance of religious ceremonies [*dhikr*] and devotion ['*ibáda*]. Now the place where there are 40 retreats is Gebel Burṣi, and each of them is a forty-days'-retreat; and el Burṣi is a hill between the SHÁÍḲÍA country and Dongola. The people of Dongola say 'O God, bless us with the devotion of Dólíb Nesi and the generosity of Ḥabíb Nesi[13] and the learning of Walad 'Ísa.' His sons were Sheikh Muḥammad el Níri[14] (for whom see under M) and the *feki* Idrís, a reader of the Ḳurán and its judgments, and Mekki and Medani,—all of them good men.

He was buried at el Debba and all the DÓÁLÍB are his descendants."

91. "ḌOW EL BAYT IBN AḤMAD EL SHÁFA'I."

He was born at Berber and trained by Sheikh 'Ísa[15] ibn Kanū and Muḥammad[16] walad Sháfa'i.... He resided among the ZAYDÁB at Gerf 'Agíb.

92. "ḌOWAYN AḤAYMER."

His mother was the daughter of el Khaṭíb 'Omára[17].... He was born at Sennár and began life as a merchant. He was a pupil of Sheikh Khógali[18].

93. "DUSHAYN, 'ḲÁDI EL 'ADÁLA' ['The Just Judge']."

He was born at Arbagi and was a Sháfa'ite...."He was one of the four judges appointed by Sheikh 'Agíb by order of King Dekín when he came from the east. He ordered Sheikh 'Agíb to appoint the judges, and ['Agíb] appointed Sheikh 'Abdulla el 'Araki[19],

[1] Tree 6. [2] reading ضيفالله for ضيف. [3] 1768 A.D.
[4] No. 88. [5] No. 79. [6] No. 47. [7] No. 154.
[8] No. 139. [9] No. 25. [10] 1718 A.D. [11] 1768 A.D.
[12] Tree 1. [13] No. 105. [14] No. 187. [15] No. 143.
[16] No. 180. [17] No. 219. [18] No. 154. [19] No. 34.

and Sheikh 'Abd el Raḥman[1] ibn Masíkh el Nuwayri, and the *feki* Baḳdūsh[2] for the GAMU'ÍA country, and el Ḳáḍi Dushayn for Arbagi and the Sháfa'ites in general."...

He died and his tomb is at el Dákhila....

The following couplet is quoted of him:

ابن دشين قاضي العدالة الما بيميل بالضلالة
نسله نعم السلالة الاوقدوا نار الرسالة

F

94. "FERAḤ IBN EL FEKI ARBÁB[3]."

He and his brother Busáṭi taught the doctrine of Unity [*tawḥid*] after their father's death....He had a son named Arbáb.

95. "FERAḤ WALAD TAKTŪK, el Baṭháni."

A pupil of the *feki* Arbáb[4]....He was the author of a poem beginning "Where are the days of the sons of Gábir," and of the saying:

الموت الياب الموت يبشر بالموت

("Death! He that defies death may yet assure himself that he shall die.")

G

96. [5]"GÁBIR and GABRULLA."

The sons of 'Ón ibn Selím ibn Rubáṭ ibn Ghulámulla, el Rikábi.... Gábir was the father of the four famous men, the AWLÁD GÁBIR[6], and their mother was named Ṣáfia....The descendants of Gabrulla, the brother of Gábir, are the AWLÁD UM SHEIKH of Hilália mosque.

97. "GÁD EL NEBI and GUBÁRA."

"They came from el Yemen and their home was in Ḥaḍramaut."... Gád el Nebi settled at Delíl.

98. "GÁDULLA."

The disciple [*ḥowár*] of the *feki* Ḥammad ibn Mariam.

99. "GÁDULLA OF ḤÁDULLA."

Gádulla el Shukayri died at Sennár.

100. "GAMÍL IBN MUḤAMMAD."

He was taught by Sheikh el Zayn[7], and learnt Ṣūfiism [*el taṣūf*] from Ḥasan[8] walad Ḥasūna.

101. [9]"GHÁNIM ABU SHIMÁL, el Gáma'i el Kordofáli."

He was a pupil of 'Ali[10] ibn Barri and the *feki* Arbáb[11]...."He came [*ḳadam*] from Dár Kurun with his wives and his children and settled at Gebayl Auli on the White Nile."..."He married 'Áyesha el Faḳíra, the daughter of the pious Walad Ḳadál, and by her begot Busáṭi ibn el Faḳíra."

[1] No. 23. [2] No. 69. [3] No. 65. [4] No. 65.
[5] Tree I. [6] No. 17, etc. [7] No. 258. [8] No. 132.
[9] Tree II. [10] No. 58. [11] No. 65.

102. "Gódatulla and Góda."

"They were both learned men of Kordofál.... The former was one of the Beni Muḥammad and lived at Zalaṭa in the north [*dár el riḥ*] and was taught by el Ḳadál[1] ibn el Faraḍi."... Góda and Edóma were by origin of the Beni 'Omrán and were taught by Sheikh el Zayn[2].

"Gubára" (see *sub* "Gád el Nebi").

103. "El Gunayd or Ḥunayd."

He was the son of Sheikh Muḥammad...(*lacuna*)...ibn el Sheikh 'Abd el Rázik[3].... He embraced Ṣūfiism and died at el Ḥalfáya.

104. "El Gunayd walad Táha[4] ibn 'Omára."

He embraced Ṣūfiism, and was a follower of Sheikh Dafa'alla[5] walad el Sháfa'i.... He died in the Ḥegáz.

H

105. [6]"Ḥabíb Nesi, el Rikábi."

"He dwelt in Dongola Ḳashábi and was one of the great holy-men [*awliyá*] of the Rikábía, and many miracles were vouchsafed to him." The people of Dongola in his day used to say "O God, bless us."...(etc. as in No. 90).

"Ḥádulla" (see *sub* "Gádulla," No. 99).

106. "Hagá ibn 'Abd el Laṭíf ibn el Sheikh Ḥammad[7] walad Zurrūḳ."

He was born at Shanbát.... Many miracles, to which Sheikh Khógali[8] testified, were vouchsafed to him: *e.g.* when he was being buried and the sun was about to set, it suddenly went back to the east again to give more time for the burial.

107. [9]"Hagū ibn Batūl el Ghubsha[10]."

His father was a Ḥamráni named Ḥammád.... He was educated by his mother's brother Sheikh Ya'aḳūb[11].... He was buried at Um Ma-wákiḥ.

108. "Hagyū ibn el feki Sálim ibn el Máídi."

He was a pupil of 'Abd el Raḥman[12] ibn Belál, and, after the death of 'Abd el Raḥman, of the *feki* Ḍayfulla[13].

109. "'Ḥaláwi,' el Ḥagágabi el 'Ámri."

His real name was Muḥammad ibn Gemál el Dín.... He was born at el Kámnín, and was a pupil of Sheikh Muḥammad[14] ibn 'Isa Sowár el Dhahab.... He visited Egypt, and died and was buried at el Ḳóz.

110. "Ḥamd el Síd ibn Bella."

He was born at el Ḥalfáya.... His sons were the *fekis* Muḥammad and Ḥammad, and 'Abd el Raḥman.

[1] No. 147. [2] No. 258. [3] No. 27? [4] No. 248.
[5] No. 83. [6] Tree 1. [7] No. 127. [8] No. 154.
[9] Tree 8. [10] reading الغبشة for القبشة. [11] No. 254.
[12] No. 16. [13] No. 89. [14] No. 191.

111. [1]"Ḥamdán ibn Ya'aḳūb[2]."

He was called "el Baṭrán," and was born at el Ḥumr....He died in the year *el Wada'a* ("the year of tranquillity").

112. "Ḥámid el Layn ibn el feki Sulaymán ibn el Sheikh Ḥámid[3]."

He was taught by Sheikh el Zayn[4] and was a great collector of books. ...He was the first to introduce from Egypt the commentary of 'Abd el Báḳi on Khalíl....He was a friend of the author's father.

113. "Ḥámid ibn 'Omar, el Bádiri."

He was known as "Abu el 'Aṣá" ["Father of the Stick"], because he always carried a stick....He was born at Saḳádi and embraced Ṣūfiism.... He was a follower of Muḥammad el Manṣūr....His sons were Ḥammad, Ibráhím, Sulaymán and Sheikh 'Ali....He was buried at el Gebayl.

114. [5]"Ḥammad ibn el feki 'Abd el Mágid[6]."

He succeeded his father....Among his pupils was the *feki* Ḥammad[7] walad el Magdhūb[8].

115. "Ḥammad ibn 'Abd el Raḥím, el Mashayrífi."

He was known as "Ḥatík el Maḥassi."...He was born at el Khartoum and taught law [*Khalíl*] by Muḥammad "el Azraḳ[9]" ibn el Sheikh el Zayn....He was buried at Abu Nagíla.

116. [10]"Ḥammad Abu Ḳurūn ibn el Sheikh Muḥammad[11] el Hamím."

117. "Ḥammad ibn Abu Zayd, el Haḍri el Buṣaylábi."

He was born at Arbagi and educated by the *feki* Muḥammad walad Ḥegázi....He was buried at Arbagi.

118. [12]"Ḥammad ibn el Aghbash."

He was a pupil of Sheikh 'Abd el Raḥman[13] ibn Ḥammadtū....His father was Sheikh 'Abdulla[14] el Aghbash....He was born and buried at Berber....His sons were 'Abd el Mágid[15], 'Abd el Raḥman[16], 'Abdulla, 'Ali, Ḥusayn and Abu Ḳerayn.

119. [17]"Ḥammad 'el Asḍá' ibn el Sheikh Dafa'alla[18]."

He succeeded his father and taught law [*Khalíl*] and apostleship.... Muḥammad walad el Ṭerayfi[19] was his spiritual guide. "Sheikh el Gunayd[20] walad Ṭáha told me that Sheikh Dafa'alla said to Sheikh Muḥammad walad Dafa'alla[21] ibn el Sháfa'i 'Take advantage of the days of Sheikh Dafa'alla[22] [while] you are young'; and [again] he said to Sheikh Muḥammad 'You were instructed by

[1] Tree 8. [2] No. 254. [3] No. 113.
[4] No. 258. [5] Tree 2. [6] No. 10.
[7] No. 123. [8] reading المجذوب for المحذوب.
[9] No. 204. [10] Tree 1. [11] No. 190.
[12] Tree 2. [13] No. 21. [14] No. 31.
[15] No. 10. [16] No. 20. [17] Tree 9.
[18] No. 84. [19] No. 177. [20] No. 104.
[21] reading ولد دفع الله for ولد فع الله, No. 83. [22] No. 84.

my son Ḥammad[1]'; and to Dafa'alla walad el Sháfa'i[2] he said 'You were taught by Sheikh 'Abdulla[3].'"

120. "ḤAMMAD IBN ḤAMAYDÁN, el Ga'ali."

A pupil of Sheikh Dafa'alla[4].... He taught at el Ḥalfáya, and among those whom he instructed were "my grandfather [*gid*] the *feki* Muḥammad ibn el feki Ḍayfulla[5], and the *feki* Idrís ibn el Izayriḳ."

121. [6]"ḤAMMAD IBN ḤASAN 'ABU ḤALÍMA' IBN EL FEKI[7], el Rikábi."

A friend of Sheikh Idrís[8] and a pupil of Sheikh Muḥammad[9] ibn 'Ísa Sowár el Dhabab.... He was held in great respect by Sheikh 'Agíb the Great.

122. [10]"ḤAMMAD IBN EL SHEIKH IDRÍS[11]."

He succeeded his father as *Khalifa*.

123. "ḤAMMAD IBN EL MAGDHŪB[12]" (b. 1105[13] A.H.; d. 1190[14]).

He was a pupil of the *feki* Ḥammad[15] ibn 'Abd el Mágid and a follower of Sheikh 'Ali el Dirávi, the disciple of Sídí Aḥmad ibn el Náṣir el Shádhali.... He died, aged 85, in 1190, and his tomb is at el Dámer.... He performed the pilgrimage.... He had a son, Aḥmad, born in 1159[16] A.H.

124. [17]"ḤAMMAD IBN MUḤAMMAD IBN 'ALI, el Mashaykhi" (b. 1055[18]; d. 1142[19]).

"He was commonly known as Ḥammad 'ibn Mariam,' his mother being Mariam. The latter's mother was a Maḥassía Mashayrifía, a daughter of Walad Ḳadál[20] 'el Wali'; and her father was Walad Kishayb[21], one of the holy-men [*awliyá*] of Abu Nagíla whose tombs are visited, a Mesallami by origin."

Ḥammad was born on Tūti Island in 1055[22] A.H.... He was a pupil of the *feki* Arbáb[23] Khashan, but quarrelled with him.... He died in 1142[24] A.H. aged 87.... His sons were Muḥammad el Nūr, Muḥammad el Maḳbūl and Muḥammad el Shafíḥ....

There are some five pages of anecdote, praise and poetry on this man. "El Sayyid walad Dólíb said of him

ما امثله الا بعمر بن الخطاب

(*I.e.* "I can compare him to no one but 'Omar ibn el Khaṭṭáb.")

125. [25]"ḤAMMAD EL NAḤLÁN IBN MUḤAMMAD, el Bedayri" (d. 1116[26] A.H.).

[1] No. 119. [2] No. 83. [3] No. 34.
[4] No. 84. [5] No. 88. [6] Tree 1.
[7] No. 149. [8] No. 141. [9] No. 191.
[10] Tree 4. [11] No. 141.
[12] reading المجذوب for المجدوب. [13] 1693 A.D.
[14] 1776 A.D. [15] No. 114. [16] 1746 A.D.
[17] Tree 11. [18] 1646 A.D. [19] 1730 A.D.
[20] No. 147. [21] No. 208? [22] 1646 A.D.
[23] No. 65. [24] 1730 A.D. [25] Tree 9. [26] 1704 A.D.

"He was known as 'Ibn el Turábi.' His mother's name was Ḳáía. He studied law [*Khalíl*] under the *feki* Muḥammad[1] ibn el Tanḳár at Muays and excelled therein, having taken the course ten times [*lit.* 'took ten sealings']. Then he embraced Ṣūfiism and devoted himself entirely to God and renounced the world, following the teaching of Sheikh Dafa'alla[2]; and [the latter] guided him....

And when he was nigh unto death he said to the people 'The world has lost its *faḳír* and its commander and they will never repair the loss.' Those who benefit from his teaching are the rulers of the present generation....

He died, God bless him, in the year 1116 after the Flight of the Prophet."...

126. "Ḥammad el Negíḍ, el 'Awaḍábi el Gamū'i."

He was a follower of Tág el Dín el Bahári[3] and was born at Aslang Island...."He was a man of power and rank at the court of Sheikh 'Agíb and went to war with him, and was killed at Karkóg[4] in the battle against the Fung: and Sheikh 'Agíb built for him the mosque which is still standing, and devoted lands to its endowment."... He had a son, 'Abd el Wahháb[5].

127. "Ḥammad walad Zurrūḳ."

He and the *feki* Gád[6] el Nebi[7] came [together ?] from Ḥaḍramaut.... His sons were 'Abd el Salám, 'Abd el Laṭíf and two others....'Abd el Salám begot Abu Delayḳ, and 'Abd el Laṭíf begot Hagá[8]....

"'Abd el Salám was known as 'Sawáḳ el Raká' ['the Jug-Driver'], for when they [his women ?] went down to the river to fill his jug, he would drive them both along with a stick....

And Abu Delayḳ was called 'Yalám el Asad' ['the Lion's Roar'], because, while he was studying as a pupil of Sheikh Maskín el Khafí and had gone out one day to collect firewood, a lion killed his donkey."

128. "Ḥammadnulla walad Malák."

He was born at Khartoum, and was a follower of Sheikh Khógali[9].... His sons were Muḥammad and Muḥammadayn.

129. "Ḥamayd el Ṣáridi."

"And Ṣárid is a [sub]-tribe of Gudhám." He was born at el Kubr, and was a follower of Básbár[10]. "My paternal ancestor, the *feki* Ḍayfulla el Fadli[11], was taught by him the doctrine of Unity [*tawḥíd*] and Arabic."

[1] No. 202. [2] No. 84. [3] No. 67.
[4] reading كركوج for كرجوج. [5] No. 29.
[6] reading جاد for جار. [7] No. 97. [8] No. 106.
[9] No. 154. [10] No. 73. [11] No. 88.

130. [1]"Ḥammūda ibn el Tanḳár, 'Giáb el 'Agwa' ['the Bringer of Dates']."

His mother was Ámna bint Serḥán[2], and he was a follower of Sheikh Idrís[3]. The reason of his nickname, "Giáb el 'Agwa," was as follows: "His mother's brother, Sheikh Muḥammad[4] ibn Serḥán fell sick, and it was said to him, 'The remedy for you is dates'; and as there was a dearth of them in the country, Ḥammūda, God bless him, brought some from Upper Egypt [*el Ríf*], and they cured the malady.

He wrote a useful commentary in the form of marginal notes on Khalíl, copied from that of his mother's brother and the Awlád Gábir[5]."

131. [6]"Ḥasan walad Belíl, el Rikábi."

He dwelt at Dongola el 'Afáṭ and was a follower of Ḥabíb Nesi[7].... He performed a number of miracles....He had a son, Ḳurayshi.

132. [8]"Ḥasan ibn Ḥasūna ibn el Ḥág Mūsa" (d. 1075[9] A.H.).

"[Mūsa] came from Morocco [*el moghrab*], from el Gezírat el Khaḍrá, from the land of Andalus, and married one of the Mesallamía and begot Ḥasūna; and he said 'I have put my seed in the source when I am sprung.' And Ḥasūna married the daughter of his mother's sister, Fáṭima bint Waḥshía, the sister of el Ḥág Luḳáni[10], [Waḥshía's] mother being a Ṣáridía Khamaysía; and by Fáṭima Ḥasūna had four children, Sheikh Ḥasan and el 'Agami[11] and Sowár and el Ḥága Nafísa. These four sons of Fáṭima all died childless. Sheikh [Ḥasan] was born at the island of Kagoi [Kagóg], and his story breathes a sweet odour."...

Several pages follow, all concerning visions and wonders, dreams and miracles and manifestations of God's favour to Ḥasan walad Ḥasūna.... After completing his religious education he performed the pilgrimage and travelled for some twelve years in the Ḥegáz, Egypt and Syria in company with various other persons, including Abu Ḥamayda and Aḥmad Tūd the Dongoláwi....He finally returned to the Sudan, "and then, when his herds had become numerous, he went up to el Durūrba and Ḳanṭūr el Ḥomár ['Donkey's Dam'] and dug his reservoir [*ḥafír*] of Um Ḳanáṭír ['Mother of Dams']. He amassed slaves and mounted them on horseback and said 'I will guard my flocks with them'; and the tradition among the people is [that he had] 500 slaves, each one of whom bore a sword with scabbard-tip and plate and pin of silver: they consisted of a commander and troops [under him]; and [they also carried] clubs. And they used to trade in their swift horses to Teḳali and Dár Borḳū (?)[12] and Dárfūr and Sennár and [the country

[1] Tree 1. [2] No. 233. [3] No. 141. [4] No. 241.
[5] No. 17, etc. [6] Tree 1. [7] No. 105. [8] Tree 5.
[9] 1664 A.D. [10] No. 156. [11] No. 55. [12] reading برقو for يبق.

of] the AWLÁD 'AGÍB. And his slaves became [whole] villages; and so many[1] were the visits paid to him that they made an enclosure for the firstborn [of the flocks and herds offered to him]. The enclosure which Sheikh Ḥasan built for his house was as large as that of the King of Sennár...."

The following is one of the miracles related: "A girl died and her mother came to him [Ḥasan] and said, 'My lord, my daughter has died, and the property of her father is ill-gotten; I prithee shroud her for me.' And Sheikh Ḥasan went to her and looked upon her and said 'Your daughter is well: she has not died. Arise!' And lo! her breath returned to her, and she arose and lived...."

A second miracle relates how a man was drowned and remained three days in the river: then came Ḥasan Ḥasūna and said "Arise!" and the drowned man returned to life, was married, and begot a son.... Yet again, a man brought Ḥasan two dead birds, and Ḥasan took them from him, "and placed the sleeve of his shirt upon his head, and the birds flew away."... He was held in high honour by the FUNG king Bádi walad Rubáṭ who, on an occasion of their meeting, granted every request of Sheikh Ḥasan.

"Now his sister, the daughter of Ḥasūna, was named Fáṭima, and one of the SHUKRÍA married her, and when he wished to transfer her [to his home] he brought for her a camel with its howdah ['*utfa*] and gave her four handmaidens [*ferkhát*, *lit.* 'chickens'] and a herd of camels and a herd of cattle and a herd of sheep....

And when he drew nigh unto death he summoned his brothers, the sons of Ḥasūna, 'Abd el Fattáḥ and 'Abd el Ḳádir and Mánid and said to them 'My successor is Belal el Shayb the son of 'Abd el Fattáḥ'; and [then] he shaved [Belal's] head with his finger, using no razor; and he bequeathed a third of his wealth to five poor men [*fuḳará*] and each of them thereby received 36 head of slaves; and their masters[2] drove off the weak and the strong [together], some of them going down to Sennár and others going to Rás el Fíl."...

Among Sheikh Ḥasan's followers were his brother el 'Agami[3], and el Kūfi, and el Ḥág 'Abd el Salám el Begáwi, and the *feki* Muḥammad[4] walad Surūr, "and from among the Danágla, Sheikh Mūsa Feríd[5] and Sheikh Munowwar and Aḥmad Tūd....

He reared a crocodile in the reservoir, and it did much harm, so he shot it with a rifle, and the charge exploded backwards and caused his death. He died in the year 1075[6] A.H.; and in his death he rose as a Star of Religion."

[1] reading كثرة for كثرت.
[2] reading سيادهم for سادهم.
[3] No. 55.
[4] No. 210.
[5] reading فريد for قريد.
[6] 1664 A.D.

133. "Ḥegázi."

He was son of Abu Zayd[1] ibn el Sheikh 'Abd el Ḳádir...."He died in the prison of Náṣir, of hunger and thirst."

134. "Ḥiláli ibn el Sheikh Muḥammad[2] ibn 'Ísa Sowár el Dhahab."

His mother was the daughter of *Mek* Ḥasan walad Kashásh, the *malik* ["king"] of Dongola.

"Ḥunayd" (see *sub* "el Gunayd").

I

135. [3]"Ibráhím ibn 'Abūdi 'el Faraḍi.'"

His mother was the sister of el Mesallami[4] and daughter of Abu Wanaysa....He was taught first by el Mesallami, his "Sheikh," and then by 'Abd el Raḥman[5] walad Ḥammadtu....

"He compiled the marginal commentary known as *el Faraḍia* on the study of what is obligatory [*el Fariḍ*], and was nicknamed 'el Faraḍi' because he was a great authority on obligation."...He married the daughter of his maternal uncle el Mesallami but subsequently divorced her.

136. [6]"Ibráhím walad Barri."

He was born at Nasri Island, and his mother was Umháni bint 'Ali walad Ḳandíl, a holy-man of the Ṣowárda....He read law [*Khalíl*] under Sheikh Ṣughayerūn[7] and learnt what pertains to the sphere of faith [*'ilm el kalám*] from the *feki* Ḥusayn Abu Sha'ar the disciple of Muḥammad[8] ibn 'Ísa Sowár el Dhahab....He was the companion[9], in Ṣūfiism, of Sheikh Muḥammad[10] walad Dáūd....He performed the pilgrimage, and died, aged 120 years, in *Sannat el Wada'a* ("the year of tranquillity").

137. "Ibráhím ibn Nuṣr."

"A learned man of Sennár, and its legal adviser [*mufti*]."... He was a pupil of el Ḳadál[11] walad el Faraḍi.

138. "Ibráhím el Sa'ūdi."

He was a Sháfa'ite, and the preacher [*Khaṭib*] of Sennár.

139. [12]"Ibráhím ibn el Sheikh Ṣughayerūn[13]."

140. "Ibráhím ibn Um Rabí'a."

He was a Takagábi, born at Baḥr el 'Asal, and a pupil of 'Abd el Raḥman[14] ibn Gábir.

141. [15]"Idrís ibn Arbáb."

[The earlier part of this biography, the first given, is missing. The first intelligible statements concerning Sheikh Idrís make mention of a

[1] No. 53. [2] No. 191. [3] Tree 11. [4] No. 172.
[5] No. 21. [6] Tree 3. [7] No. 241. [8] No. 191.
[9] reading صحب for صحت. [10] No. 186. [11] No. 147.
[12] Tree 1. [13] No. 241. [14] No. 17. [15] Tree 4.

certain Moghrabi, Sheikh Mūsa el Ḳaylūbi, and the date 981 A.H. (1573 A.D.), and of an exchange of presents between Idrís and Sheikh Ṣughayerūn[1].]

"Sheikh Khógali[2] said 'The first to light the fire of Sheikh 'Abd el Ḳádir was Sheikh Idrís.'"...

He was a most eminent teacher and a pillar of religion. One of his disciples [*ḥowár*] was Sheikh 'Ísa el Ṭálib.

He foretold many important events. "For example, his prophecy to Sheikh 'Agíb when [the latter] applied to him for a prediction regarding the war with the FUNG: Sheikh ['Agíb] said 'The FUNG have oppressed us' [*lit.* 'changed the customs upon us']: [Idrís] replied 'Do not make war upon them for they will kill you and subject your seed afterwards until the day of Resurrection.' And it happened as he had said. Again, his prophecy to King Bádi Abu Rubáṭ when he was Master of the Household [*Síd Ḳūm*] to King 'Adlán walad Áya and [they] proposed making war on Sheikh 'Agíb. Now this Bádi was a disciple [*ḥowár*] of Sheikh Idrís and enquired of him concerning the matter and [the Sheikh] replied 'Ye shall kill Sheikh 'Agíb and be victorious, and thou shalt return to Sennár as king, and the kingdom shall be in the hands of thy descendants after thee.' And it happened as he had said, and five [of Bádi's descendants] ruled, Rubáṭ, and Bádi his son, and Ounsa walad Náṣir, and Bádi his son, and Ounsa his son; and the period of their rule was 110 years.

Again, his prophecy that the kingdom of the FUNG would come to an end: and the reason that it did so was that they fought among themselves and divided themselves into two parties, each of which fought the other until their kingdom was lost."

142. "'ÍSA WALAD ABU SAKAYKÍN."

He was born at Abyaḍ Dírí....Both a Maḥassi and a Mesallami married his mother in turn and claimed 'Ísa as their son.....

His *ḳubba* is on the road between 'Aylafūn and Gebel el Maylakít.

143. "'ÍSA WALAD KANŪ."

A most holy man, the disciple and pupil of Sheikh Muḥammad[3] ibn Ísa Sowár el Dhahab....He was born at Dongola el 'Agūz ("Old Dongola"), and was by birth a Ḥaḍari....He instructed 'Abd el Raḥman[4] ibn el Aghbash and the *feki* Ḍow el Bayt[5] in the art of Ḳuránic reading [*tagwíd*]....One of the miracles related of him is that "he was in prison, and the house in which he was imprisoned caught fire; but when the fire reached him, it died out: and in the corner of the house was a hen; and she ran hurriedly to drag her eggs to him, and he was

[1] No. 241. [2] No. 154. [3] No. 191.
[4] No. 20. [5] No. 91.

heard to say 'I am 'Ísa to my hen' [*i.e.* 'the hen knows that I am the great 'Ísa Kanū']."

144. "'ÍSA IBN ṢÁLIḤ, el Bedayri."

He was the father of Sheikh Muḥammad[1] Sowár el Dhahab, and a pupil of 'Abd el Raḥman[2] ibn Gábir.

145. "ISMÁ'ÍL ṢÁ...(*torn*)...IBN EL SHEIKH MEKKI[3] EL DAḲALÁSHI."

His mother was Khayra, a Saḳarnáwía, who was given to Sheikh Mekki as a present by the Sultan of Teḳali and bore to him el Nūr and Ismá'íl.

146. "'IZZ EL DÍN WALAD NAFÍ'A."

He was born at el Manáḳil, and was a follower of Sheikh Dafa'alla, and later of Muḥammad walad Medani and Muḥammad walad 'Awayḍa.

K

147. [4]"'EL ḲADÁL' MUḤAMMAD."

He was the son of Ibráhím ibn 'Abūdi "el Faraḍi" by the daughter of el Mesallami[5] walad Abu Wanaysa, and was surnamed "el Ḳadál" because he was an upright man....His father taught him law [*Khalíl*] and apostleship....He was born on the White Nile, and went to Kordofán to visit his pupil Gódatulla[6], and was given a present of 50 camels by the king of the KUNGÁRA. He lived in the reign of Ounsa walad Náṣir, and died at Um Ṭalḥa after a residence there of four months, and was buried with "el Faraḍi" and el Mesallami....He is fabled on one occasion to have flown to the Gezíra [*el Huoi*] on his bedstead.

148. [7]"ḲÁḲUMR IBN EL ḤÁG IBRÁHÍM[8] IBN BARRI IBN 'ADÍLA IBN TIMYA."

He was taught by his father's brother the *feki* 'Ali[9], and was a contemporary of Básbár[10].

149. [11]"ḲASH IBN SIDR IBN 'ABD EL NEBI IBN 'AGÍB IBN RIKÁB IBN GHULÁMULLA."

He begot Ḥasan, the father of the *feki* Ḥammad[12] and of Ḥalíma, and Ḥusayn, the father of 'Ali; and 'Ali married Ḥalíma and by her begot the *feki* 'Othmán "Síd el Ruaykiba" and another....His son Ḥasan was nicknamed "Abu Ḥalíma" ["Father of Ḥalíma"] after his daughter Ḥalíma....As he lived among the MOGHÁRBA he was buried among them.

150. "KERRÁR IBN EL SHEIKH SELMÁN[13] EL ṬOWÁLI."

151. "KHALÍL IBN 'ALI, el Ṣáridi el Khamaysi."

He was born at Kagoi Island and was a contemporary of Sheikh Ḥasan[14] walad Ḥasūna.

[1] No. 191. [2] No. 17. [3] No. 169.
[4] Tree 11. [5] No. 172. [6] No. 102.
[7] Tree 3. [8] No. 136. [9] No. 58.
[10] No. 73. [11] Tree 1. [12] No. 121.
[13] No. 230. [14] No. 132.

152. "KHALÍL IBN BISHÁRA, el Dwayḥi."

He was known as "Abu Sayf 'Ūd" or "Sayf el 'Ūd."...He was born at Shanbát and was a pupil of Sheikh Muḥammad[1] walad el Ṭerayfi.... He dwelt and died at Ṭalḥa.

153. "KHALÍL IBN EL RŪMI."

He was a Dongoláwi Gábri by race, and migrated southwards to Surkum where he dwelt, living a holy life, for some years. Then he went, at el Ḥág 'Omára's request, to Dádūn and built mosques. Several wonders and miracles are related of him; such as the following:

"There came to him a man, saying 'A slave-woman of mine ran away a year ago: pray God to return her to me.' [Khalíl] said 'Fetch a jar of servants' beer and a gelded cock'; and the man fetched two jars of servants' beer and two gelded cocks: then they strained the beer and drank it, that is he [*sc.* Khalíl] and his DANÁGLA who were with him. Then came the man and said to him 'Where is my slave-woman?' He replied 'Go among the trees and say "O Bakhita[2]!" three times.' And the woman appeared, carrying a waterskin with the ropes of it [trailing] over her face; and she said 'My master, what has brought you here? This is the river Atbara.' Her master answered her 'This is Sennár.' Then he drove her with him and came [to Khalíl] and [Khalíl] from afar off said to him 'Be off with you[3].'"...

Again, "when the troops all revolted against the king of the FUNG at Ḳerri and Sennár and el Ís, and the soldiers had surrounded him on every side, and had killed all who were with him, so that none were left but thirty horsemen, and when [the king] had hidden from them in the courtyard of Kimayr bint el Mek, his sister, Kimayr went to Sheikh Khalíl and said to him 'My lord, my brother is losing his kingdom and we fear his destruction at the hands of his slaves.' And he said to her 'Your brother is the wrongdoer and the mischief-maker.' She replied 'Let him come to you, and he will repent at your hands of his wrongdoing and mischief-making.' He said 'Bring him to me.' And she went to the king and brought him muffled and disguised in woman's raiment; and when he came before the Sheikh he said 'I repent of what you prohibit.' [The Sheikh] replied 'The FUNG have taken your crown [*lit.* "turban of the king"] from you, but here is my turban for you, and I guarantee to you the kingdom of your father until you die; but if you go forth to battle, take me with you and I will bring [or, "and take with you"] el Ḥág 'Omára [*sc.* to your aid].' And in the morning he went forth against those armies with his thirty horsemen, and took with him the Sheikh and el Ḥág 'Omára, as the Sheikh had commanded him, and he routed

[1] No. 177. [2] reading بخيتة for بخية.

[3] reading امش for امس.

them by the blessing of the Sheikh, and slew them with most dire slaughter, and remained king until he died. Now the king mentioned was Bádi el Aḥmar ibn Ounsa walad el Malik Náṣir."

154. [1]"KHÓGALI IBN 'ABD EL RAḤMAN IBN IBRÁHÍM" (d. 1155[2] A.H.).

"His mother's name was Ḍowwá bint Khógali; and his father 'Abd el Raḥman was a Maḥassi Kabáni, and his mother a Maḥassía Mushayrifía. His grandfather Ibráhím was one of the disciples of the AWLÁD[3] GÁBIR and a follower of Muḥammad ibn el Sheikh Ibráhím el Būlád, as I have seen it written. Sheikh Khógali was born on Tūti Island, and was first taught to write by 'Áyesha el Faḳíra bint walad Ḳadál. He learnt what pertains to the sphere of faith [*'ilm el kalám*] and Ṣūfiism[4] from the *feki* Arbáb[5], and studied law [*Khalíl*] under Sheikh el Zayn[6] walad Ṣughayerūn....He went on the pilgrimage to the holy house of God, and followed the teaching of Sheikh Aḥmad el Tabankatáwi el Felláti, the divine saint [*kuṭb*] who resided at Medína."

His life and character are then treated of from three aspects (*nuẓar*). Firstly are given records of things said by him, and of him by various eminent holy-men; secondly a description of his character and personal appearance; thirdly miracles performed by him. The following are quotations from parts two and three respectively.

(1) "It was characteristic of him that he held to the Book and the Law [*sunna*] and followed [the precepts and example of] the Shádhalía Sayyids as to word and deed. And he used to wear gorgeous raiments, such as a green robe of Baṣra, and upon his head a red fez [*ṭarbūsh*], and [round it] as a turban rich muslin stuffs. For footwear he wore shoes [*ṣarmūga*]; and he fumigated himself with India-wood [*el 'ūd el hindi*], and perfumed himself, and put Abyssinian civet on his beard and on his clothes. All this he did in imitation of Sheikh Abu el Ḥasan el Shádhali, for all blessings come from God Almighty and he was thankful to Him for the same. And it was remarked to him that the Ḳádiría only wear cotton shirts and scanty clothes, and he replied 'My clothes proclaim to the world "We are in no need of you," but their clothes say "We are in need of you."'

It was also characteristic of him that he never rose up to salute any of the great ones of the earth, neither the AWLÁD 'AGIB, the rulers of his country, nor the kings of GA'AL, nor any of the nobility,

[1] Tree 7.
[2] 1742 A.D.
[3] No. 17, etc.
[4] reading التصوف for الصوق.
[5] No. 65.
[6] No. 258.

excepting only two men, the successor [*Khalífa*] of Sheikh Idrís and the successor of Sheikh Ṣughayerūn.

El Sha'aráwi says that such superiority, namely [that shown by] his not rising up, has not occurred among any [other] sheikhs, not even in the case of Sheikh 'Abd el Ḳádir, for the latter, if the 'Abbásid Khalífa came to see him, used to rise up. [The only exception is furnished by] Sheikh Muḥammad el Ḥanafi el Shádhali in Egypt, who used not to rise up for any one, neither for Pashas nor for Sanjaks."...

(2) It is related that a sandbank formed off Tūti Island and greatly impeded the working of the water-wheels of the MAḤASS. The latter appealed to Khógali, pointing out that they would have to migrate elsewhere, since they were shut off from the water at low Nile; so Khógali mounted his donkey and went to the bank and dipped his staff in the river and said "In the name of God the Compassionate and Merciful! O Sheikh Aḥmad ibn el Náṣiri!"—and the sandbank disappeared: "and this miracle has lasted until our own day, this year of 1219[1]. Now his staff was of iron." He was, in addition, a great healer of the sick. "I and the King of Death," said he, on one occasion, "have contended together for the life of the daughter of 'Ebayd, and he has left her to me."...

His final exploit is related thus: "When the Sultan Bukr, Sultan of [the] KUNGÁRA, heard of some abusive remarks of King Bádi he swore that he would enter Sennár, and tear up its trees, and dam its river [so that] cavalry might ride over its bed. Then he made his preparations and set forth till he reached the outskirts of the country on the east side; and he was at el Mefáza when he saw Sheikh Khógali; and the Sheikh had in his hand a staff and rapped him with it on the finger-tips[2]. And his hand swelled up and became paralysed [*lit.* 'died'], and this was the cause of his death, for the Sultan of the FUNG had besought the mediation of Sheikh Khógali, and said to him 'The Sultan of [the] FŪR is coming against us.'—Then the Sultan Bukr, the Sultan of [the] KUNGÁRA, enquired of the river folk saying 'There came to me a dark man wearing a green robe and rapped me with a staff,' and described him to them as he had seen him; and they replied 'That was Sheikh Khógali.'"...

Elsewhere we find the following:

"As regards his original faith, the foundation thereof was Ḳádirism, but in his methods of daily readings of the Ḳurán [*awrád*] and in his rules of personal conduct he was a Shádhali, and indeed his 'Sheikh' was a pupil of Sheikh Muḥammad el Náṣir the Shádhali."...We

[1] 1805 A.D.

[2] reading اظلافه for اضلاعه.

are also told the date of his death: "He died, God bless him, on the forenoon of Sunday the 18th of Gamád el Thåni in the year fifty-five[1]; and his son the *feki* Aḥmad succeeded him by his father's direction, and was a pious servant [of God] and followed in his father's footsteps in all purity of heart; and the period of his holding office [as *Khalífa*] was six years."

155. [2]"ḲURNI IBN EL FEKI MUḤAMMAD[3] ABU SABÍB IBN EL FEKI 'ALI IBN BARRI."

He was a follower of el Ḥág 'Abdulla[4] el Ḥalanḳi.

L

156. [5]"LUḲÁNI."

The brother of the mother of Sheikh Ḥasan[6] ibn Ḥasūna and a pupil of Sheikh 'Abd el Raḥman[7] ibn Gábir. He was one of the 40 disciples all of whom attained the rank of *Ḳuṭb*.

M

157. [8]"MAḤMŪD EL 'ARAKI, 'RÁGIL EL ḲUṢAYER.'"

"He was born on the White [Nile], and went for instruction to Egypt and was the pupil of el Náṣir el Luḳáni and Shams el Dín el Luḳáni; and he was the first to order the people to observe the period of probation [after divorce]. Before his time a woman could be divorced by her husband and married by another, all in one day or on successive days. He settled on Gezírat el Huoi on the banks of the White Nile and built himself a mansion, which is now known as Ḳuṣayer Maḥmūd....

Now his coming was before that of the AWLÁD GÁBIR[9]: the latter studied under el Banūfari, and el Banūfari under 'Abd el Raḥman el Ag·hūri, and Sheikh 'Abd el Raḥman el Ag·hūri was a follower of Shams el Dín and Náṣir el Dín, the two Luḳánis. His coming was in the time of the FUNG, and Sheikh Khógali[10] said that from el Khartoum to el Ís there were seventeen schools, all of which were destroyed by SHILLUK and *Um Laḥm*."...

He died and was buried at el Ḳuṣayer.

158. [11]"MÁLIK IBN EL SHEIKH 'ABD EL RAḤMAN[12] WALAD ḤAMMADTU."

He lived at el Zóra, and built a mosque wherein law [*Khalíl*] was taught....His son was 'Abd el Raḥman, the father of the *feki* Ḳarbáwi and Málik...."Among his pupils were the *fekis* Aḥmad and 'Abdulla,

[1] 1743 A.D. [2] Tree 3. [3] No. 178. [4] No. 33.
[5] Tree 5. [6] No. 132. [7] No. 17. [8] Tree 7.
[9] No. 17, etc. [10] No. 154. [11] Tree 10. [12] No. 21.

the sons of the *feki* Ḥammad[1] ibn el Magdhūb, and the *feki* Khógali, the *Khalífa* of the GHUBUSH, and the *feki* Muḥammad ibn Ḥámid el Mitkenábi, and Ṭáhir the grandchild [*sabṭ*] of Ḥammad[2] ibn Mariam, and 'Abdulla walad Mekka the grandchild of Sheikh Muḥammad[3] ibn el Ṭerayfi."

159. [4]"MARZŪḲ IBN EL SHEIKH YA'AḲŪB[5]."

He succeeded his brother Mūsa[6]....He was buried with his father and his brother at el Ḥumr.

160. [7]"MÁZRI IBN EL TANḲÁR."

He was a pupil of his mother's brother, el Ḥág Muḥammad[8] ibn Serḥán, and a follower of Sheikh Idrís[9].

161. [10]"MEDANI 'EL ḤAGGAR' IBN 'OMAR IBN SERḤÁN."

He was the nephew of Sheikh Ṣughayerūn[11] and was taught by him, and so proficient did he become that he was nicknamed "el Ḥaggar" ["the Rock"]....When Ṣughayerūn died, [his successor] Sheikh el Zayn[12] invited him to assist him with the teaching in the mosque until Ibráhím[13] was grown up....He was buried at el Ḳóz, and his tomb is known as *ḳubbat el Ḥaggar*....His sons were Ḳuṭbi and Nūrayn, the former father of the *feki* Ibráhím, and the latter of Muḥammad "ibn el Rayda." "[This Muḥammad's] mother was Burra bint el Sheikh el Zayn and the mother of his father Nūrayn was Rábi'a bint el Sheikh Ṣughayerūn; and he was taught by the *feki* 'Abd el Raḥman[14] ibn Asíd; and when he died he was buried at el Ḳóz in front of the *ḳubba* of his grandfather Medani."...

162. [15]"MEDANI IBN MUḤAMMAD[16] IBN MEDANI EL NÁṬIḲ."

He was taught by his father, and also by his grandfathers (*i.e.* grandfather and great-great-uncles), the Awlád Um Gadayn, Muḥammad[17] and Medani[18]....Among his pupils was the *feki* Ḥammad[19] ibn el Magdhūb.... He was buried at Nūri with his fathers...."And the *feki* Sheikh ibn Medani said 'The MEDANIYYŪN are the gold and we the silver.'"... He taught the Ḳurán to Básbár[20].

163. [21]"MEDANI EL NÁṬIḲ IBN EL SHEIKH 'ABD EL RAḤMAN[22] WALAD ḤAMMADTU."

He was called "el Ṭiár" ["the Aviator"]....The reason why he was called also "el Náṭiḳ" ["the Oracle"] was that after his death a quarrel arose as to his successor, and a *feki* appealed to him at his tomb, "and he replied to him [*náṭiḳahu*] from the tomb 'The *Khalífa* is Sheikh': now Sheikh[23] was his full-brother."...After considerable wranglings Sheikh was duly appointed and was known thereafter as "Sóṭ

[1] No. 123. [2] No. 124. [3] No. 177. [4] Tree 8.
[5] No. 254. [6] No. 209. [7] Tree 1. [8] No. 241.
[9] No. 141. [10] Tree 1. [11] No. 241. [12] No. 258.
[13] No. 139. [14] No. 15. [15] Tree 10. [16] No. 194.
[17] No. 203. [18] No. 164. [19] No. 123. [20] No. 73.
[21] Tree 10. [22] No. 21. [23] No. 236.

Medani" ["the Voice of Medani"]....His son was Muḥammad....Among his pupils was Básbár[1].

164. [2]"MEDANI WALAD UM GADAYN."

He was the son of Sheikh 'Abd el Raḥman[3] ibn Ḥammadtū. "Now Medani[4] el Náṭiḳ died during the lifetime of his father Sheikh 'Abd el Raḥman, so he [walad Um Gadayn] was called Medani after him in the hope that he would be like his brother, and indeed God fulfilled this hope."...

His sons were 'Abd el Raḥman Abu Fáḳ[5], 'Abd el Raḥím, Sheikh ibn Medani and Ḥammadtu ibn Medani of Dongola....He had great influence with the kings of Dongola and the SHÁÍḲÍA.

165. "'EL MEḌOWI'" (d. 1095 A.H.[6]).

His full name was Muḥammad ibn Muḥammad el Kadáwi[7] ibn el Sheikh Muḥammad[8] el Miṣri.... He was taught by his grandfather el Miṣri....He visited Sennár and stayed there with the *feki* 'Omára[9], who introduced him to King Ounsa ibn Náṣir before all the court. On this occasion the king at once dismissed his court and rose up to greet him.... While at Sennár he was frequently received by the king and loaded with presents....He died at Ḳóz Ragab in the year *Um Laḥm*.

166. [10]"MEḌOWI IBN BARAKÁT ibn Ḥammad[11] ibn el Sheikh Idrís."

He was a pupil of the *fekis* Belál[12] and Abu el Ḥasan[13], and highly spoken of by Sheikhs Khógali[14] and Ṣáliḥ[15] Bán el Nuḳá....He "lit the fire of the Ḳurán" at three places, viz. el 'Ayl Fung, Gedíd and Elti....He had a son, the *feki* Muḥammad.

167. [16]"MEḌOWI IBN EL SHEIKH BEDOWI[17]."

He succeeded his father, and was succeeded by his son Sheikh Náṣir el Dín.

168. "MEḌOWI IBN MEDANI ibn 'Abd el Dáim ibn 'Ísa, el Anṣári el Khazragi."

He was born at Kutráng, and was a follower of el Ḳadál[18] ibn el Faraḍi. ...He was taught by Sheikhs Barakát[19] ibn Ḥammad and Sheraf el Dín[20] walad Barri.

169. "MEKKI EL DAḲALÁSHI."

He lived between el Sheḳayḳ and 'Id el Gima'a and was a pupil of Sheikh Dafa'alla[21].

170. "MEKKI EL NAḤŪ, el Rubáṭábi."

He was a pupil and disciple of Sheikh Muḥammad[22] el Miṣri. Among his pupils were Sheikh Mūsa[23] walad Ya'aḳūb "Abu Ḳussa," el Sherif 'Abd el Raḥman, and the *fekis* Ḥámid el Layn[24] and Ḥamayd[25] el Ṣáridi....

[1] No. 73. [2] Tree 10. [3] No. 21. [4] No. 163.
[5] No. 14. [6] 1684 A.D. [7] reading الكداوي for اكداوي.
[8] No. 195. [9] No. 219. [10] Tree 4. [11] No. 122.
[12] No. 79. [13] No. 47. [14] No. 154. [15] No. 226.
[16] Tree 12. [17] No. 74. [18] No. 147. [19] No. 72.
[20] No. 237. [21] No. 84. [22] No. 195. [23] No. 209.
[24] No. 112. [25] No. 129

"His large commentary on the Senūssía consisted of 40 pamphlets [*kurási*], and his smaller commentary of 10 pamphlets. He also wrote a commentary on articles of faith concerning apostleship [*'aḳídat el risála*] and, it is said, a commentary on apostleship [*risála*], but of this I am not sure."

171. [1]"EL MESALLAMI."

He was a disciple of el Ḳadál Muḥammad[2], his "Sheikh" and paternal uncle, and was taught by him. His companion in Ṣūfiism was Sheikh Dafa'alla el 'Araki[3] the son of Sheikh Abu Idrís....He was buried at el Ḳubía with his "Sheikh" el Ḳadál and his grandfather el Mesallami[4].

172. [5]"EL MESALLAMI WAD ABU WANAYSA."

"[Abu Wanaysa's] father was 'Ali el Faḳír, and Wanaysa was his daughter."...El Mesallami was a follower of Sheikh 'Abd el Raḥman[6] ibn Gábir and lived on the White Nile, and was finally buried between that river and el Kharū'a....Among his contemporaries as pupils of Sheikh 'Abd el Raḥman were Sheikhs Ya'aḳūb[7] ibn el Sheikh Bán el Nuḳá and 'Abdulla[8] el 'Araki and 'Abd el Raḥman[9] el Nuwayri and el Ḥág Luḳáni[10] and 'Ísa[11], the father of Muḥammad walad 'Ísa "Sowár el Dhahab."

"'EL MIṢRI'" (*vide sub* "Muḥammad 'el Miṣri,'" No. 195).

173. "MUḤAMMAD IBN EL 'ABBÁSI."

He was a pupil of Muḥammad[12] ibn 'Ísa "Sowár el Dhahab." His son was the *feki* Mūsa.

174. "MUḤAMMAD IBN 'ABD EL DÁFA'I[13]."

A follower of Sheikh Khógali[14]....He was the successor of Sheikh Muḥammad[15] walad Dáūd el Lukr. He was buried at Ḥilla 'Agíb.

175. [16]"MUḤAMMAD IBN EL FEKI 'ABD EL RAḤMAN IBN EL AGHBASH."

He was taught by the *fekis* Belál[17] and Abu el Ḥasan[18] and Busáṭi and Feraḥ[19] walad Arbáb, and succeeded his father...."He united learning and good works."

176. [20]"MUḤAMMAD IBN 'ABDULLA[21] IBN ḤAMMAD."

He was called "el 'Álim" ["The Learned"] and "Ṣáḥib el Ḥáshia" ["The Commentator"]....He was taught by his paternal uncle the *feki* 'Abd el Mágid[22] and by the *feki* Muḥammad el Azraḳ[23], and followed in his life the precepts of Sheikh Bedowi[24] walad Abu Delayḳ....He died at Berber.

177. [25]"MUḤAMMAD IBN EL SHEIKH 'ABDULLA[26] EL ṬERAYFI."

When Sheikh Dafa'alla[27] el 'Araki died, Muḥammad's paternal uncle

[1] Tree 11. [2] No. 147. [3] No. 84. [4] No. 172.
[5] Tree 11. [6] No. 17. [7] No. 254. [8] No. 34.
[9] No. 23. [10] No. 156. [11] No. 144. [12] No. 191.
[13] No. 4. [14] No. 154. [15] No. 186. [16] Tree 2.
[17] No. 79. [18] No. 47. [19] No. 94. [20] Tree 2.
[21] No. 35. [22] No. 10. [23] No. 204. [24] No. 74.
[25] Tree 9. [26] No. 41. [27] No. 84.

Shams el Dín married him to his daughter 'Ankólíba....He had a son, Yūsef[1]....He was buried at Abu Ḥaráz.

"MUḤAMMAD 'ABU 'ÁḲLA'" (*vide sub* "Abu 'Áḳla," No. 42).

178. [2]"MUḤAMMAD ABU SABÍB ibn Timya, el Ṣáridi."

"Sheikh Ḥasan[3] appointed him to succeed his father[4], and the reason for this was that the Sheikh's sons were in disagreement, some of them wanting 'Araki and some this Muḥammad. Then the question was put to their father's brother el Ḥág Ibráhím[5] as to who was to be the *Khalífa*, and he said 'I will not say to one of the sons of 'Ali[6] "Come forward" and to the other "Remain behind." Will they go to Sheikh Ḥasan?'

So they[7] set out to see him, but 'Araki and his brethren reached the Sheikh first; and [the latter] condescended to them and slaughtered a sheep for them: then came this Muḥammad and his brethren, and [the Sheikh] condescended to them and said 'Fetch the matting for the successor [*Khalífa*] of Walad Barri[8].'"...

179. [9]"MUḤAMMAD IBN 'ABŪDI[10] 'Waḳámir (?).'"

A pupil of his father....A description of his clothes follows.

180. "MUḤAMMAD IBN 'ADLÁN, el Sháfa'i el Hóshábi."

He was a pupil of 'Abdulla el Moghrabi, a learned man of Medína.... Subsequently he went to Tanḳási in the SHÁÍḲÍA country and taught there. ...He also did missionary work in Bornū and Hausaland [*Afnū*].

Among his pupils were Ismá'íl ibn el feki el Zayn el Sherífábi, Muḥammad walad Feraḥ, Muḥammad walad Sulaymán and Sa'ad walad Gódulla.

"MUḤAMMAD 'EL 'AGAMI' IBN ḤASŪNA" (*vide sub* "el 'Agami," No. 55).

181. "MUḤAMMAD IBN 'ALI IBN ḲARM EL KÍMÁNI, el Miṣri el Sháfa'i."

He entered the Sudan in the early days of the FUNG rule and took up his residence at Arbagi, Sennár and Berber, in turn. He died and was buried at Berber. "He was one of God's own miracles, for all the Sheikhs were taught by him knowledge and the laws of obligation [*el feriḍ*], as for instance Sheikh 'Abdulla[11] el 'Araki and el Ḳáḍi Dushayn[12] el Sháfa'i and Sheikh 'Abd el Raḥman[13] walad Ḥammadtu and Sheikh Ibráhím el Faraḍi[14]...and Sheikh Muḥammad[15] el Miṣri."...His sons were el Shakák and Sháfa'i and Mekki and Medani.

[1] No. 256. [2] Tree 3. [3] No. 132.
[4] No. 58. [5] No. 136. [6] No. 58.
[7] reading سافرا for سافر. [8] No. 58.
[9] Ṭree 11. [10] No. 54. [11] No. 34.
[12] No. 93. [13] No. 21. [14] No. 135.
[15] No. 195.

182. "MUḤAMMAD IBN ANAS."

He was a follower of Sheikh Khógali[1] and the *fekis* 'Abd el Raḥman[2] ibn Asíd and 'Abd el Rázik el 'Awaḍi.

183. "MUḤAMMAD IBN ARBÁB[3]" (d. 1170 A.H.[4]).

A follower of el Ḥág Khógali[5], as were his brothers Busáṭi and Feraḥ[6]. ...He was buried at el Basháḳira.

184. "MUḤAMMAD IBN 'AWAYḌA."

A pupil of el Ḳadál[7] ibn el Faraḍi.

"MUḤAMMAD 'EL AZRAḲ'" (*vide sub* "Muḥammad ibn el Sheikh el Zayn").

"MUḤAMMAD 'BÁN EL NUḲÁ'" (*vide sub* "Bán el Nuḳá," No. 71).

185. [8]"MUḤAMMAD IBN EL SHEIKH DAFA'ALLA[9] ibn el Sheikh Abu Idrís."

He was taught by, assisted and succeeded his father....He was a contemporary of the *feki* Medani walad Dushayn.

"MUḤAMMAD EL ḌARÍR IBN IDRÍS" (*vide sub* "Dólíb Nesi," No. 90).

186. "MUḤAMMAD IBN DÁŪD EL LUKR[10], el 'Ūdi."

His mother was Keríta bint el Ḥág Teḥámíd, and he was born at Bayba between Elti and Um 'Uḳud....He was a pupil of Sheikh 'Abdulla el 'Araki[11], who, on his deathbed, appointed him his successor....He died at Ḥilla 'Agíb on the Dinder.

187. [12]"MUḤAMMAD WALAD DÓLÍB."

His father was Muḥammad el Ḍarír[13] ibn Idrís ibn Dólíb el Rikábi, and his mother was named Zaynab....He was born at Debba, educated there and died there....He lived in the reign of King Ounsa walad Náṣir....Among the miracles related of him are the following:

(1) He was attacked by a scorpion and spat upon it, and it died....

(2) A dog barked at him and he turned round upon it, and it died....

188. "MUḤAMMAD IBN FÁID EL SHERÍF."

He was born on the shore of the Bitter Sea [*Baḥr el Murr*]....He was a pupil of Sheikh Idrís[14].

"MUḤAMMAD IBN GEMÁL EL DÍN" (*vide sub* "Ḥaláwi," No. 109).

189. [15]"MUḤAMMAD IBN ḤÁG ḤABÍB ibn Ḥabíb Nesi[16], el Rikábi."

He lived at Ḳashábi Island in Dongola....It is related of him that when "King Dekín of Kordofál" presented him with 50 head [*sc.* "of slaves," or "of cattle"] he said that he did not deserve so much and asked that they should be given instead to Sheikh Ziáda[17] ibn el Nūr who did deserve them....He was a descendant of Sheikh Ghulámulla, whose *ḳubba* is at Dongola el 'Agūz....He himself was buried at Ḳashábi.

[1] No. 154. [2] No. 15. [3] No. 65. [4] 1756 A.D.
[5] No. 154. [6] No. 94. [7] No. 147. [8] Tree 9.
[9] No. 84. [10] reading اللقر for الاغر. [11] No. 34.
[12] Tree 1. [13] No. 90. [14] No. 141. [15] Tree 1.
[16] No. 105. [17] No. 259.

190. [1]"MUḤAMMAD 'EL HAMÍM' IBN 'ABD EL ṢÁDIḲ IBN MÁSHIR, el Rikábi."

He was nicknamed "el Hamím" ["the Earnest"] because the wife of his "Sheikh" sent him to buy a dish of bread [*kisra*], and, on his return, he found she had left the village, so he followed her with the dish of bread from Arbagi to Sennár and thence to Ḳūbia....He was a pupil of Sheikh Tág el Dín el Bahári[2] and a contemporary of Sheikhs Idrís[3] and Bán el Nuḳá el Ḍarír[4], and the latter wrote some verses in his honour....He died and was buried at el Mundara.

"MUḤAMMAD IBN ḤAMMAD ibn el Sheikh Idrís" (*vide sub* "Bán el Nuḳá," No. 71).

"MUḤAMMAD 'WALAD EL BAḤR' ibn el Sheikh Ibráhím el Faraḍi" (*vide sub* "Walad el Baḥr," No. 252).

191. "MUḤAMMAD IBN 'ÍSA IBN ṢÁLIḤ, el Bedayri, 'Sowár el Dhahab' ['The Bracelet of Gold']."

His mother was Ḥaḳíḳa....Among his pupils were 'Ísa[5] walad Kanū, 'Abdulla[6] el Aghbash the father of the GHUBUSH, Nuṣr el Tergami, and 'Abd el Raḥman Abu Maláḥ the father of Sheikh Khógali[7]; and among his friends were Sheikh 'Awūḍa[8] Shakál el Ḳáriḥ, el Ḥág 'Abdulla the holy-man[9] of Gerri, Muḥammad[10] walad el 'Abbási, and Ḥammad[11] walad Abu Ḥalíma the holy-man of Sharáū....He lived in the reign of Bádi ibn Rubáṭ...."He ruled the seven kings of the Gin, and the FUNG and the kings of GA'AL obeyed him."...He was buried at Dongola.

"MUḤAMMAD 'EL ḲADÁL'" (*vide sub* "'El Ḳadál' Muḥammad," No. 147).

"MUḤAMMAD EL ḲANÁWI" (*vide sub* "Muḥammad 'el Miṣri,'" No. 195).

"MUḤAMMAD 'WALAD ḲŪTA'" (*vide sub* "Muḥammad ibn Musallam," No. 196).

192. [12]"MUḤAMMAD IBN MAḤMŪD[13] EL 'ARAKI."

He was a most learned and pious man, and was buried with his famous father at el Ḳuṣayer.

193. "MUḤAMMAD IBN MEDANI ibn Dushayn[14] 'Ḳáḍi el 'Adála.'"

"Sheikh 'Izz el Dín[15] walad Nafí'a el 'Araki said 'After Sheikh Dafa'alla the man who had intimacy with God was the *feki* Muḥammad ibn Medani.'"...Among his contemporaries were Sheikhs Mūsa[16] walad Ya'aḳūb and Ḥammad ibn Dafa'alla, and among his pupils the *fekis* Dafa'alla ibn 'Abd el Ḥafíẓ and Khidr the holy-man [*rágil*] of el Nūba and 'Abd el Hádi the holy-man of el Ruays...."He was buried in the village which is famous by his name."

[1] Tree 1. [2] No. 67. [3] No. 141. [4] No. 71.
[5] No. 143. [6] No. 31. [7] No. 154. [8] No. 66.
[9] reading راجل for راحل. [10] No. 173. [11] No. 121. [12] Tree 7.
[13] No. 157. [14] No. 93. [15] No. 146. [16] No. 209.

194. [1]"MUḤAMMAD IBN MEDANI[2] EL NÁṬIḲ ibn el Sheikh 'Abd el Raḥman walad Ḥammadtu."

He was taught by his father's brother the *feki* Sheikh[3] el Á'sir[4], whom he succeeded...." And the *feki* Ḥammad[5] ibn el Magdhūb told me that Muḥammad walad Sálim el 'Adawi said to him 'When I went to Egypt I found no one whose knowledge [*lit.* "who could read"] of law [*Khalíl*] equalled that of Muḥammad ibn Medani, excepting el Khadáshi.'...

Now the Muḥammads who shared one name and one father and one epoch were three, Muḥammad[6] ibn Medani ibn Dushayn and Muḥammad[7] ibn Medani ibn 'Abd el Raḥman ibn Ḥammadtu and Muḥammad ibn Medani ibn el 'Álim el Sháfa'i."

195. "MUḤAMMAD 'EL MIṢRI.'"

Also called Muḥammad el Ḳanáwi [Fatáwi ?].

He was taught by Sheikh Sálim el Sanhūri[8] and Yūsef el Razḳábi walad 'Abd el Báḳi....He visited the land of the FUNG, *e.g.* Sennár and Arbagi, "in the second half of the tenth century, in the days of Sheikh 'Agíb."...He finally died at Berber.

"MUḤAMMAD IBN MUḤAMMAD EL KADÁWI" (*vide sub* "el Meḍowi," No. 165).

196. [9]"MUḤAMMAD IBN MUSALLAM."

He was generally called "Walad Ḳūta" after his mother Ḳūta the daughter of Ámna bint Fáṭima bint Gábir, [Fáṭima] being the sister of the four *Imáms*[10]....His father was a Ḥalanḳi of the Nás walad Sída.... He was taught by his mother's brother the *feki* Muḥammad[11] ibn el Tanḳár. He first taught at el Ḳóz and then moved his residence to el Ḥilálía.

197. "MUḤAMMAD EL NUḲR ibn el Sheikh 'Abd el Rázik[12] Abu Ḳurūn."

He was taught by his father and the Awlád Ya'aḳūb[13].

198. [14]"MUḤAMMAD IBN EL ḤÁG NŪR ibn el feki Ḥammad[15] walad Abu Ḥalíma, el Rikabi."...

He was born at Sharáū, and was taught by Ḥammad[16] ibn Ḥamaydán and Sheraf el Dín[17] walad Barri....He instructed Ibráhím the son of his brother Ḳalíng....His sons, the *fekis* Nūr and Medani, succeeded him in turn.

"MUḤAMMAD IBN NUṢR EL TERGAMI" (*vide sub* "Abu Sinayna," No. 51).

[1] Tree 1. [2] No. 163. [3] No. 236.
[4] reading الاعسر for اللعسر. [5] No. 123.
[6] No. 193. [7] No. 194.
[8] reading السنهوري for السنهور. [9] Tree 1.
[10] No. 17, etc. [11] No. 202. [12] No. 27.
[13] No. 254. [14] Tree 1. [15] No. 121.
[16] No. 120. [17] No. 237.

199. "Muḥammad ibn 'Omrán."

He was taught what pertains to the sphere of faith [*'ilm el kalám*] and logic [*el munṭiḳ*] at Shendi by el Meḍowi[1] ibn el Miṣri.

200. "Muḥammad ibn el feki Sálim, el Máídi."

He was a follower of the *feki* Belál[2] and his son 'Abd el Raḥman[3] and Sheikh Khógali[4].

"Muḥammad ibn Serḥán" (*vide sub* "Ṣughayerūn," No. 241).

"Muḥammad walad el Shuḳl" (*vide sub* "Walad el Shuḳl," No. 253).

201. "Muḥammad ibn Surūr ibn el Ḥág Ghanáwa."

A follower of Sheikh Ḥasan[5].

"Muḥammad Tág el Dín" (*vide sub* "el Bahári," No. 67).

202. [6]"Muḥammad ibn el Tanḳár, el Ga'ali el Bishárábi."

His mother was Ámna bint Fáṭima bint Gábir, and he was taught by her brother Ṣughayerūn[7]....

He was a follower of Sheikh Idrís[8] and would have liked to be his successor but was prevented by Sheikh 'Abd el Rázik[9]. He then settled at el Muays and built a mosque there, and subsequently went south to el Burṣi, where he died....Among his pupils were Muḥammad "walad Kūṭa[10]" and Sheikh Ḥammad[11] ibn el Turábi.

203. [12]"Muḥammad 'ibn Um Gadayn' ibn el Sheikh 'Abd el Raḥman[13] ibn Ḥammadtu."

He was taught by his brother the *feki* Sheikh[14], whom he eventually succeeded, and by his brother's son Ibn Medani[15]....Among his pupils were 'Abd el Raḥman[16] ibn Asíd and Medani[17] ibn Muḥammad ibn Medani....He was buried with his brother Medani[18] at el 'Egayga....His sons were 'Abd el Raḥman, Ḥammadtu and Ibráhím....Muḥammad, the son of the last-named, succeeded the Awlád Um Gadayn as *Khalífa*.

204. [19]"Muḥammad ibn el Sheikh el Zayn, 'el Azraḳ'" (d. 1108 A.H.[20]).

He was taught by his father and his paternal uncle Ibráhím "el Ḥaggar[21]." The latter died in 1098 A.H.[22] The *feki* Sálim el Máídi was one of his pupils....One of his miracles is related thus: "The late Sheikh Ismá'íl ibn Belál told me that one of the Ḥuḍūr was in a boat on the Salt Sea, and a storm arose so that the boat was almost swamped, and the man called upon Muḥammad ibn el Zayn, and saw him come flying through the air with his staff; and the sea became calm and the boat was saved."...He died in the year *Um Ḥinaydil*, viz. 1108.

[1] No. 165. [2] No. 79. [3] No. 16. [4] No. 154. [5] No. 132. [6] Tree 1. [7] No. 241. [8] No. 141. [9] No. 27. [10] No. 196. [11] No. 125. [12] Tree 10. [13] No. 21. [14] No. 236. [15] No. 194. [16] No. 15. [17] No. 162. [18] No. 164. [19] Tree 1. [20] 1696 A.D. [21] No. 139. [22] 1686 A.D.

205. [1]"MUḤAMMAD EL ZAYN IBN EL SHEIKH MARZŪḲ[2]."

He was taught by his father's brother Mūsa[3] and by Sheikh Ṣughayerūn[4]....His sons were Sheikh Ya'aḳūb and Marzūḳ and Meḍowi.

206. "MUKHṬÁR WALAD ABU 'ANÁYA."

A follower of Sheikh Ṭáha[5] ibn 'Omára....Sheikh Ismá'íl el Daḳaláshi[6] and the *feki* Náfa'i were among his pupils.

207. "MUKHṬÁR IBN MUḤAMMAD GÓDATULLA[7]."

His father was a disciple of el Ḳadál[8] ibn el Faraḍi, and he himself was born at el Zalaṭa in Northern Kordofál...."He died a martyr's death at the hands of Gunḳul the Sultan of FŪR—both he and his pupils—and their possessions were confiscated; and the reason was that [Mukhṭár] ordered [the Sultan] to do the right, and warned him against wrongdoing. [For the Sultan] advanced from el Káb with 1000 horse to make war upon King Dekín, and [Mukhṭár's] disciple the *feki* Náfa'i el Fezári said to him[9] 'Send me[10] to him'; and [Mukhṭár] replied 'Tell him not to fight the FUNG in their country: if he does so God and the Prophet will be on their side, and I also.' And when [the Sultan] heard that he said 'Raise the sword,' and when they had done so he said 'Please God I will kill the *feki* Mukhṭár, and we will bury him among ourselves, and [then we shall be able to] visit [his tomb]!' And he set off to attack them (?) and found the *feki* together with his disciples reading, and he killed both the *feki* and his disciples and his compatriots and confiscated their goods. Then through the grace of the *feki* in those days was Gunḳul slain, and [he died] leaving about fifty sons, and these have been killing one another even up to this present day. That any one of them should die in his bed, as for instance el 'Ísáwi did, has been a rare occurrence."

208. [11]"MŪSA WALAD KISHAYB, el Ga'ali el 'Armánábi el Mesallamábi."

One of his ancestors settled on the White Nile with the ḤASANÁT; and, later, the KAWÁHLA and others rendered Mūsa obedience....

He was a pupil of Sheikh el Zayn[12] and a contemporary and equal of Sheikh Khógali[13]....He was succeeded by his son the *feki* Meḍowi.

209. [14]"MŪSA IBN YA'AḲŪB[15]."

His mother was named Marḥab....He was a famous saint and miracle-worker, and was taught by his father. He lived in the reign of Bádi ibn Rubáṭ....It is said that a stray slave-woman was found who could not communicate in any known tongue with any one, but Mūsa at once understood all she said....He was buried at el Ḥumr.

[1] Tree 8. [2] No. 159. [3] No. 209. [4] No. 241.
[5] No. 248. [6] No. 145. [7] No. 102. [8] No. 147.
[9] reading تلميذه for لتلميذه. [10] reading ارسلني for ارسكني.
[11] Tree 11 (?). [12] No. 258. [13] No. 154. [14] Tree 8.
[15] No. 254.

210. "Muṣṭafa el Sheríf, el Moghrabi el Sūsi."

"He embraced Ṣūfiism and followed Sheikh Muḥammad[1] ibn el Ṭerayfi."...He was buried west of Asláng Island.

N

211. [2]"Nabray ibn el feki 'Abd el Hádi ibn el Sheikh Muḥammad[3] walad Dólíb...."

He was born at el Ḥalfáya and educated by the *feki* Dafa'alla, and by the *feki* Ḍayfulla[4], and by his father's brother the *feki* Ṣughayerūn in Dongola....He was buried at el Ḥalfáya.

212. "Na'ím ''Abd el Sheraka' ibn el Ḥág, el Ga'ali el Nawámi."

He was born at el Kerrada and buried near el Ḥilália...."He was called ''Abd el Sheraka' ['Servant of the Partnership'] because he divided his year into two halves: during one half he would serve Sheikh Idrís[5], and during the other he would serve Sheikh Abu Idrís[6]."

213. "Na'ím el Baṭḥáni."

He was the disciple [*ḥowár*] of Sheikh Idrís[7]...."His tomb is in the desert in front of Walad Abu Delayḳ."

214. [8]"Nanna ibn el Turábi."

He was the brother of Sheikh Ḥammad[9] el Naḥlán.

215. "Nowáw ibn el Sheikh Ḍow el Bayt[10]" (d. 1176[11] A.H.).

He was a Sháfa'ite....His son the *feki* Muḥammad, a follower of Sheikh Khógali[12], was taught by 'Abd el Raḥman[13] walad Belál and died in 1171[14], in his father's lifetime, and was succeeded by his son the *feki* el Ṭáhir.

216. [15]"Nūr el Dín Abu Shimla ibn el Sheikh Muḥammad[16] el Hamím."

He was brother of Sheikh 'Ali el Níl[17]....Their father migrated from Rufá'a to Mundara, and it was there his sons were buried....It is related that Sheikh 'Ali sent his sons to the country south of Mundara, to fetch wood from the country of the *dolayb* palms, for re-roofing his mosques, and gave them twenty-four camels for the purpose. The party, however, met some elephants which frightened the camels by their trumpeting so that they bolted. The sons accordingly returned and reported to Sheikh 'Ali, who was about to borrow other camels when Nūr el Dín said "'I swear by Sheikh Tág el Dín el Bahári the animals that caused our beasts to bolt shall bring [the wood] in their place.' Then he addressed an assistant of his father named Abu Sa'ad and said to

[1] No. 177. [2] Tree 1. [3] No. 187. [4] No. 89.
[5] No. 141. [6] No. 48. [7] No. 141. [8] Tree 9.
[9] No. 125. [10] No. 91. [11] 1762 A.D. [12] No. 154.
[13] No. 16. [14] 1757 A.D. [15] Tree 1. [16] No. 190.
[17] No. 62.

him 'Ab' Sa'ad!' and he replied '[Yes], master of Ab' Sa'ad's mother!' Then [Nūr el Dín] said 'Tell the animals which made our beasts to bolt that Sheikh 'Ali's order to them is "Come and carry in their place."' And the elephants came, and they were four in number, and carried the load of the twenty-four camels."

217. [1]"EL NŪR IBN EL SHEIKH MŪSA[2] 'ABU ĶUSSA.'"

His mother was a slave-woman, and his father's brother was Sheikh Muḥammad walad Marzūķ....He was buried at Mugaḍḍala.

218. "NŪRAYN WALAD EL ĶUBGA."

He was born at el Ķóz, his mother being the daughter of Sheikh Sheríf the disciple of Sheikh el Zayn[3]....He taught at Arbagi....His son was the *feki* Senūssi[4]. He was buried at el Matassi (?).

O

219. "'OMÁRA IBN 'ABD EL ḤAFÍẒ el Khaṭíb."

His mother was the daughter of el Labadi[5], and he was born at Sennár. ...In *Ramaḍán* 1177 A.H.[6] he left Sennár and arrived in Egypt in *Safar* 1178 A.H.[7] After staying at el Azhar university he proceeded to the Ḥegáz. In 1180[8] he returned to Egypt....In 1189[9] he again performed the pilgrimage....He married Fáṭima bint Sálim, a merchant's daughter....He was a contemporary of Sheikh 'Izz el Dín[10] walad Nafí'a of Manáķil, the disciple of el Ķadál[11] ibn el Faraḍi.

R

220. "RÁDULLA IBN DELÍLA, el Ṣáridi el Khamaysi."

He was born at Shanbát and was taught by *fekis* Belál[12] and Abu el Ḥasan[13]. Later he went to el Burṣi and el Ṭurfáya, and died at the latter.

221. "RAḤMA EL ḤALÁWI."

A pupil of Tág el Dín[14] el Bahári.

222. [15]"RUBÁṬ and RIKÁB."

"They were the two sons of Ghulámulla. RUBÁṬ was one of God's chosen [*ragul magdhūb*]. The ṢOWÁRDA married a slave-girl of theirs to him, and deceived him about her, and she bore to him[16] Selím. Then they confessed to him their deceit and said to him 'She is a slave.' So he complained of them to the Ķáḍi, and the latter gave judgment for him that his son was free and bound him to pay the

[1] Tree 8. [2] No. 209. [3] No. 258. [4] No. 232.
[5] No. 61. [6] 1764 A.D. [7] 1765 A.D. [8] 1767 A.D.
[9] 1776 A.D. [10] No. 146. [11] No. 147. [12] No. 79.
[13] No. 47. [14] No. 67. [15] Tree 1.
[16] reading له سليم for لسليم.

value of the mother. This occurred in the time of the Fung. Now Selím sought the daughter of his uncle Rikáb in marriage, and her name was Ganíba: but she refused him because of [the taint of] slavery. Then it happened that Ḳandíl el 'Óni had a daughter who was sick, and he referred her case to Selím, and she recovered, so [Ḳandíl] married her to him, and she begot 'Ón. And 'Ón begot Gábir, the father of the four Sheikhs. Again, Malik el Kanísa [*lit.* 'The king of the Church'] had a sick daughter, and she was cured, and he married her to [Selím], and she bore to him Hadhlūl. Then Ganíba bint Rikáb regretted her refusal, for he was a man of piety and popular among the people; so he married her and she bore him four sons, Ruzayn and 'Abd el Rázik and Dahmash and Miṣbáḥ. Ruzayn was ancestor of the Nás Ḥabíb Nesi[1], and 'Abd el Rázik of Nás el Sheikh Ḥasan walad Belíl, and Dahmash of the Ruaydáb, the people of Abyaḍ Díri, and Miṣbáḥ of the Rikábía of el 'Afáṭ. Ends.

Rikáb ibn Ghulámulla had four sons, 'Abdulla and 'Abd el Nebi (by a single mother), and Zayd el Feríd, and Ḥabíb and 'Agíb (by a single mother). 'Abdulla begot Ḥág and Ḥagág. Ḥág begot the Dóalíb, and Ḥagág begot the Nás walad Ak·ḥal. 'Abd el Nebi begot the Ṣádiḳáb, and Zayd el Feríd the 'Akázáb and the Tamráb and the Shabwáb, and 'Agíb the Sidráb, the Nás walad Abu Ḥalíma. Here ends the genealogical tree of the Rikábía."

S

223. "Sa'ad el Kursani."

He was a Sháiḳi and taught at Nūri....His teacher was 'Abd el Raḥman[2] ibn Asíd.

224. "Sa'ad walad Shūshái, el Moghrabi."

He was buried near Shendi and north of it....A contemporary of Sheikh Ṣughayerūn[3].

225. "El Ḥág Sa'íd ibn Muḥammad el 'Abbási."

He lived at el Takáki and was taught apostleship [*risála*] by el Mesallami[4] walad Abu Wanaysa....He visited Berber, Shendi and Sennár.

226. [5]"Ṣáliḥ ibn Bán el Nuḳá[6]" (b. 1092[7]; d. 1167[8] A.H.).

"He was the third of the *Khalífas* who lit the fire of Sheikh 'Abd el Ḳádir in the land of the Fung."

His biography is divided into three chapters; firstly, the evidence of his contemporaries as to his character, etc.; secondly, an account of his teaching and career, and thirdly praises of his virtues and some account of his miracles.

[1] No. 105. [2] No. 15. [3] No. 241. [4] No. 172.
[5] Tree 8. [6] No. 70. [7] 1681 A.D. [8] 1753 A.D.

The following is from the second chapter: (Ṣáliḥ speaks)

"Now Sheikh Ḥammad el Samíḥ, when he invaded Shendi, killed the king of the GAMŪ'ÍA and more than 100 men, and ravaged the country and looted our slaves and our cattle and our sheep and camels....Then I and my cousins went to ask for them back and he returned a part to us...and promised the remainder. And that night I saw Sheikh 'Abd el Ḳádir sitting on a bed...and I said to him 'Ḥammad has looted my camels...etc.'"

The following is from the third chapter:

"Sheikh Ṣáliḥ related that there came to him the divine message giving him leave to light the fire [of religion] after the death of Sheikh Bedowi. Now this was in the year '18[1], and in that same year el Samíḥ attacked Shendi. His son, Sheikh 'Abd el Raḥman[2], was born in the year '22[3]. And in those days the court gave him a share in the river-lands and the rain-lands; and he lit the fire [of religion] and lived honourably according to his obligations and the divine laws and commandments[4]; and there was no house, whether of a true believer or otherwise, over which he had not influence. And he divided the land granted him by the court among the people as though it had been a banquet....

And he died in the year '67[5] aged 75...and his place was taken by his son Sheikh el Zayn, acting for Sheikh 'Abd el Raḥman[6] his brother, and [el Zayn] lit the fire like his father and executed all that his father had done at all times and places [*lit.* 'both when in a state of presence and of absence']. At the same time he never relaxed his reading of the Ḳurán, and especially [read it] during the last third of the night[7]. He died in the year '89[8] aged 70, and his place was taken by his son Sheikh Bán el Nuḳá."

227. [9]"SANHŪRI IBN MADTHIR ibn Sanhūri ibn Ḥammūda[10] ibn el Tanḳár."

228. "SELÍM, the holy-man [*rágil*] of el Sayál...."

He was a Khálidi, and was much praised by Sheikh Ḥammad ibn el Turábi....He died at el Sayál.

229. "SELMÁN EL 'AWAḌI" (d. 1121 A.H.[11]).

He was taught, as a child, by Sheikh 'Abd el Rázik[12], and when grown up by Sheikh Muḥammad el Nuḳr[13]....He died in the same year as the *feki* 'Abd el Mágid[14], viz. 1121 A.H.

[1] 1706 A.D. [2] No. 25. [3] 1710 A.D.
[4] reading مندوباته for منذوباته. [5] 1753 A.D.
[6] No. 25. [7] reading الليل for اليل.
[8] 1775 A.D. [9] Tree I. [10] No. 130.
[11] 1709 A.D. [12] No. 27. [13] No. 197.
[14] No. 10.

230. "Selmán el Ṭowáli, 'el Zaghrát[1].'"

He was a follower of Sheikh Muḥammad el Hamím[2], and among his pupils were Sheikhs 'Abd el Ḳádir[3] ibn el Sheikh Idrís, Abu Delayḳ[4] and Burt[5] el Mesallami....He died at the age of 120.

231. "Senūssi ibn el feki Mekki ibn el Sheikh 'Ali ibn el Sheikh Ḥámid" (d. about 1117[6] A.H.).

A follower of the *feki* 'Abd el Raḥman[7] ibn Belál....He died at el Gebel about the year 1117[8].

232. "Senūssi walad Nūrayn[9]."

He was born near Arbagi....His mother was one of the Ghodiát[10].

233. [11]"Serḥán ibn el Ḥág Muḥammad ibn Serḥán."

He was born at Arḳo Island, and had a son named Idrís....He quarrelled with his cousins and migrated to the Sháíḳía country and settled to the east of the island on which the Awlád Gábir dwelt, and married their sister Fáṭima, and begot el Ḥág Muḥammad[12] and el Ḥág 'Omar and el Ḥág Abu el Ḳásim and Ámna, "the mother of el Tanḳár's children."...He performed the pilgrimage.

234. "Serḥán ibn el feki Ṣubáḥ walad Ṭeráf."

He was born at Gerf Ḳumr, died in 1206[13] aged about 90, and was buried at his birthplace....He was a follower of 'Abd el Raḥman[14] ibn Belál.

235. "Shammar ibn Muḥammad ibn 'Adlán, el Sháíḳi."

He was born at Arbagi....He was taught by the *fekis* Belál[15] and Abu el Ḥasan[16] and Busáṭi ibn el feki Arbáb[17]...."He became a *mufti* [jurisconsult] in the sects of both Málik and el Sháfa'i and a teacher of the doctrine of both. The people of Arbagi called him 'The Indian Boat' [*Markab el Hind*]."...He was buried at Arbagi.

236. [18]"Sheikh el Á'sir[19] ibn 'Abd el Raḥman ibn Ḥammadtu."

He was born and resided at Nūri, and was taught by his father and his brother Medani[20]....When the latter died a dispute arose as to whether Sheikh or Málik[21] should be his successor, and the choice fell upon Sheikh. ...Among his pupils were 'Abd el Mágid[22] ibn el Aghbash and 'Abd el Ḳádir[23] ibn el Sheikh Idrís...."And miracles were vouchsafed to him, one being as follows: He guaranteed to 'Othmán walad Ḥammad that he should be victorious in war against the Fung: and the circumstances were as follows: [Sheikh] fell ill and was told that his remedy lay in the fat of storks [*rahū*], and 'Othmán shot a stork with a rifle and brought it to him, and his illness left him. Then [Sheikh]

[1] reading الزغرات for الزقرات.
[2] No. 190.
[3] No. 7.
[4] No. 46.
[5] No. 82.
[6] 1705 A.D.
[7] No. 16.
[8] 1705 A.D.
[9] No. 218.
[10] reading غدوية for قدوية.
[11] Tree 1.
[12] No. 241.
[13] 1790 A.D.
[14] No. 16.
[15] No. 79.
[16] No. 47.
[17] No. 65.
[18] Tree 10.
[19] reading الاعسر for العسر.
[20] No. 163.
[21] No. 158.
[22] No. 10.
[23] No. 7.

prayed for him that he should [always] hit the mark when shooting; and indeed it was only by rifle-fire that the FUNG were defeated, for of a truth they [*sc.* rifles] do not miss[1] their mark. Now when 'Othmán had defeated the foe he came out of his retreat [*khalwa*] wearing a shirt of rough wool. [And] the armies parted and each went their way [*lit.* 'the horses parted, tail from tail'], and Sheikh 'Ali walad 'Othmán sent to King Bádi walad Rubáṭ and informed him of the defeat and demanded of him his kingdom. Then King Bádi told his troops the following: 'At midday, after the doors had been closed[2] and he that was inside was cut off [from the outer world] there came in to me a left-handed [*á'sir*] man wearing rough woollen clothes and like a eunuch[3] in appearance, and said to me "[If] you send forth an army to Kagabi I will do so and so to you."' And the SHÁIḲÍA horse-traders said to him 'That was the *feki* Sheikh, and indeed 'Othmán was putting his faith in him.'"

237. [4]"SHERAF EL DÍN IBN 'ABDULLA el 'Araki ibn el Sheikh 'Ali[5] ibn Barri."

His mother was 'Agabat bint el Ḥág Ibráhím ibn Barri....He was born at Nasri Island and taught by his mother's brother Muḥammad Ḳáḳumr[6]....He performed the pilgrimage, and instructed many people of the Ḥegáz....He died at el Ḥigayr....He was a contemporary of the author's father: "My brother in God, el Ḥág 'Abd el Ḳádir walad Ṣa'íd, told me that in his pilgrimage in the year '64[7] he met a great sheikh who said to him 'I became a follower of the Way in the footsteps of Sheikh Sheraf el Dín when he came on the pilgrimage.' My father[8] also told me saying 'In the year that the small-pox raged I and the *feki* 'Abd el Dáfa'i[9] and the *feki* Idrís walad Nuṣár were sitting in front of the mosque, when there came up to us Sheikh Sheraf el Dín riding a mare....'"

238. "SHERAF EL DÍN ABU GEMÁL EL DÍN."

The holy-man [*rágil*] of Anḳáwi....He was the son of Muḥammad ibn Fakrūn, whose tomb is at el Ḥilália....He was born at Muays and then moved to Anḳáwi....He was taught by Sheikh 'Abdulla el 'Araki[10] and himself taught Sheikh Básbár[11]....He was buried east of Anḳáwi.

239. [12]"SHERAF EL DÍN IBN EL FEKI 'ALI walad Ḳūta."

He died at Ḳóz walad Ḍíab.

240. "SHUKRULLA IBN 'OTHMÁN ibn Bedowi el 'Ūdi."

He was born at Shanbát; was taught by Ḥammad[13] ibn Ḥamaydán,

[1] reading تخطي for تخصي.
[2] reading التسديد for السديد.
[3] reading كالخصي for كالحصي.
[4] Tree 3.
[5] No. 58.
[6] No. 148, reading قاقمر for قاقم.
[7] 1751 A.D.
[8] No. 89.
[9] No. 4.
[10] No. 34.
[11] No. 73.
[12] Tree 1.
[13] No. 120.

and was a contemporary of Sheikhs Ḥammad el Samíḥ and Ḥammad ibn el Turábi[1]....His pupils were very numerous and included the *feki* 'Abd el Dáfa'i[2]....He died aged between 40 and 50 and was buried at Shanbát.

241. [3]"'ṢUGHAYERŪN,' *i.e.* Sídí Muḥammad ibn Serḥán el 'Ūdi."

"His mother was Fáṭima bint Gábir ibn 'Ón ibn Selím ibn Rubáṭ ibn Ghulámulla, nor has such fruit been born save from such a tree. He was called 'Ṣughayerūn' because his mother's relatives, the AWLÁD GÁBIR, used to call him Muḥammad el Ṣughayer ['the Small,' or 'the Lesser'], and this was perverted into 'Ṣughayerūn.' He was born, God have mercy on him, on Tarnag Island in the SHÁÍḲÍA country, and was, God bless him, one of those who united learning and Ṣūfiism. He excelled in learning under his mother's brother Sheikh Ismá'íl ibn Gábir, who gave him leave to teach. Then he transferred himself to Sheikh Muḥammad el Banūfari and studied a certain amount of law [*Khalíl*] with him, and Muḥammad said that it benefited one's teaching. And God blessed him and he sat in the seat of his mother's brothers after them. He was one of the most ascetic of sages, one of the greatest of saints, and, in Ṣūfiism, the lover of Sheikh Idrís ibn el Arbáb. The reason of his coming to Dár el Abwáb ['Land of the Gates'] was that the sons[4] of his father's brother were at violent enmity with him because he usurped their greatness and followed his mother's relatives in learning and piety. So they incited Zimráwi the king of the SHÁÍḲÍA against him and bid him slay him. Then [Zimráwi] mounted his horse and came to him [Ṣughayerūn] while he was in the mosque, and found his mother, the daughter of Gábir, with him; and she said 'O Zimráwi, you have come to kill Muḥammad'; and they lowered him from his horse in a fainting condition and he began [to groan] saying 'Ḥak! Ḥak! The cattle of el Ḥág Muḥammad have butted me.' Then they came to [Ṣughayerūn] and interceded with him for [Zimráwi], and he replied 'This thing is not my doing but that of my mother's brothers[5].' Then he put a spell upon him and he recovered. And [Zimráwi] said to him 'I bestow upon you four *sáḳias*, each of them 40 *'ūds* of the length of a spear [in breadth], and four brood mares and four head [of slaves].' But [Ṣughayerūn] replied 'It would be impious for me to receive anything from you or to live in your country.'

Again, it is said that King Bádi Abu Rubáṭ, who was Master of the Household [*Síd Ḳūm*] to King 'Adlán walad Áya, put his trust in [Ṣughayerūn]; and when King 'Adlán, after killing Sheikh 'Agíb

[1] No. 125. [2] No. 4. [3] Tree 1.
[4] reading اولاد for اولا. [5] reading اخوالي for احوانالي.

at Karkóg, moved with his army to Dongola province and reached Meshwa (?), the FUNG deposed him and appointed Bádi the Master of the King's Household. Then [Bádi] requested [Ṣughayerūn] to accompany him to the south, and [Ṣughayerūn] said 'I will join you,' and he proceeded after [the king] to the south with his mother and his brethren and his wives and his children. And when he came to el Deríra the holy men [*fuḳará*] of the south and of the north disputed among themselves, the former bidding him dwell in the south and latter in the north; and he said to them 'God decide the matter!' And he took his ablution-jug and went into the desert and foregathered with el Sayyid el Khiḍr, God bless him; and el Sayyid told him 'Your dwelling-place shall be Ḳóz el Mutraḳ, opposite the plain of Um Wizín.' And [Ṣughayerūn] went thither and found it rough land and forest, so he went on to el Figayga and found it was an open site clear of trees, and he said 'This is el Figayga [*i.e.* 'The Little Clearing'] where the brethren of Sheikh 'Abd el Raḥman[1] walad Ḥammadtu stop'; and this was why it was called 'el Figayga.' Then Sheikh[2] ibn Serḥán sent to King Bádi at Sennár and informed him of his arrival and requested him to grant him a site on the unoccupied land[3] to dwell in and a watering-place on the river. And the king sent for his henchman and said to him 'Give him all the land he wants and mark the boundaries for him'; and [the Sheikh] replied 'Beyond a site of unoccupied land[4] and the watering-place for the holy men and a place for burial I want nothing': and this was characteristic of his self-restraint and asceticism in all earthly matters. Then the Sheikh, God bless him, built the mosque founded under the auspices of el Khiḍr, upon whom be the blessings of God; and it is said that with his own noble hand he set up[5] the central pole [that supports the roof], [at the foot of] which the Sheikhs give their lessons: and men flocked to him from every quarter and camels were heaped upon him galore, and he found favour in the eyes of all men.

Among his famous followers were Sheikh Dafa'alla[6] ibn el Sheikh Abu Idrís, and the *feki* 'Abd el Ḥalím[7] walad Baḥr, and the sons of Barri (the *feki* 'Ali[8] and el Ḥág Ibráhím[9]), and Tór el Matan el Kahli el Berḳáni (who was buried in front of his tomb), and the three sons of el Tanḳár (the *feki* Muḥammad[10] and Ḥammūda[11] and Mázri[12]), and Medani[13] el Ḥaggar the son of el Ḥág 'Omar his brother, and Muḥammad the son of el Ḥág Abu el Ḳásim his brother, a pious

[1] No. 21. [2] No. 241. [3] reading خلا for حلا.
[4] reading الخلا for الحله. [5] reading غز for قز.
[6] No. 84. [7] No. 5. [8] No. 58. [9] No. 136.
[10] No. 202. [11] No. 130. [12] No. 160. [13] No. 161.

and good man, who died about the same time as his uncle leaving no children excepting his daughter Ḥága the mother of the *feki* Belál[1]. And the son of Serḥán begot the *feki* el Zayn[2] and Ibráhím el Ḥaggar[3] and Abukr and five daughters, viz. Rábi'a, who was married by Medani el Ḥaggar[4] the son of [Ṣughayerūn's] brother 'Omar, and Ḥága, who was married by Muḥammad[5] ibn el Tanḳár the son of [Ṣughayerūn's] sister Ámna, and Zaynab, who was married by Muḥammad the son of el Ḥág Abu el Ḳásim, [Ṣughayerūn's] brother. Now the length of time he was teaching at el Abwáb [may be gauged by the fact that] he completed the course thirteen or fourteen or fifteen times [*lit.* 'sealings']. He was buried at el Ḳóz, and his tomb is to be visited: through its medium the rainfall is obtainable for the crops."

242. "Ṣughayerūn el Shaḳaláwi."

He was born at el Shaḳál near Shendi, and lived and died at Um el Raḥi....He was taught by Ṣughayerūn[6] the son of Serḥán, and was a follower of Sheikh Idrís[7], and a friend of Sheikh Ḥasan[8] and 'Abd el Rázik[9] and Básbár[10] and 'Ali[11] ibn Barri.

243. [12]"Ṣughayerūn walad Abu Wagíba."

He was a Zarnakhi, born at Abu Hashím, and educated in the Sháíkía country...."He was at the fight between 'Othmán walad Ḥammad and the Fung."...He taught his brother's son Sheikh Ṣáliḥ[13] Bán el Nuḳá. He died the year after "small-pox year."

244. "Sulaymán el Zamli."

His village was el Sayál....He was taught by Raḥma[14] el Ḥaláwi, the pupil of Tág el Dín[15] el Bahári....His son was 'Abd el Raḥím "Wadád Síáti[16]."

245. "Surūr el Ṣáridi."

He was born and died at el Khasháb, and was a pupil of Ḥasan[17] ibn Ḥasūna.

T

"Tág el Dín el Bahári" (see "el Bahári").

246. "Tágūr el Naḥási ibn el Sheikh 'Abdulla walad Ḥasóba."

A learned and pious man.

247. [18]"Ṭáha ibn el Ḥág Luḳáni."

A follower of Sheikh Ḥasan[19] walad Ḥasūna.

[1] No. 79. [2] No. 258. [3] No. 139.
[4] No. 161. [5] No. 202. [6] No. 241.
[7] No. 141. [8] No. 132. [9] No. 27.
[10] No. 73. [11] No. 58. [12] Tree 8.
[13] No. 226. [14] No. 221. [15] No. 67.
[16] No. 251. [17] No. 132. [18] Tree 5. [19] No. 132.

248. "Ṭáha ibn 'Omára el Fūrayn (el 'Aurayn ?)."

Born at el Ḳugr....A pupil of Dafa'alla[1] ibn el Sháfa'i. His brother was called "el Akhrash."...He died near Sennár.

249. "Tayrgum el Rufá'i."

Born and buried at el Ḥilália....A pupil of Sheikh Dafa'alla[2].

U

250. "Um Bárak ibn el Sheikh Maskín."

W

251. "'Wadád' ibn el Sheikh Sulaymán el Zamli."

His name was 'Abd el Raḥím....He lived at el Sayál in the Ḥaláwiyyūn country, and was buried there.

252. [3]"'Walad el Baḥr.'"

His name was Muḥammad ibn el Sheikh Ibráhím[4] el Faraḍi....He was a pupil of his brother Muḥammad el Ḳadál[5]....His sons were the *fekis* Ibráhím and el Berr; and the former begot the *feki* Aḥmad el Fezári.

253. "'Walad el Shuḳl.'"

His name was Muḥammad....He was a pupil of el Ḳadál[6] ibn el Faraḍi....He lived "near to the north of Um Ṭalḥa at el Á'dáū."

Y

254. [7]"Ya'aḳūb ibn el Sheikh Bán el Nuḳá[8]."

He was a pupil of 'Abd el Raḥman[9] ibn Gábir, and one of the forty disciples, all of whom attained the rank of *Ḳuṭb* He was buried at el Ḥumr.

255. "Ya'aḳūb ibn el Sheikh Mugelli, el Mashaykhi."

He was born in Upper Egypt [*el Rif*], and entered the Gezíra in the early days of the Fung rule.

"And the king entertained him and gave him his daughter in marriage and apportioned to him in the neighbourhood of el Ḥalfáya as much land as his horse could encompass[10] eastwards and westwards and southwards [*lit.* 'right'] and northwards [*lit.* 'left'], and conferred it upon him fully and freely[11], and it remains so to the present day."..."He was buried half a mile [*míl*] from el Ḥalfáya and his tomb is plain to see and should be visited."

[1] No. 83. [2] No. 84. [3] Tree 11.
[4] No. 135. [5] No. 147. [6] No. 147.
[7] Tree 8. [8] No. 71. [9] No. 17.
[10] reading يسور for يشور. [11] reading السبل for السل.

256. [1]"Yūsef ibn el Sheikh Muḥammad[2] ibn el Ṭerayfi." A pupil of his father.... Before his death he appointed his son Sheikh Muḥammad to succeed him.

Z

257. "Zayn el 'Ábdín ibn el Sheikh 'Abd el Raḥman ibn el Sheikh Dafa'alla."

A follower of Sheikh el Gunayd[3].

258. [4]"El Zayn ibn el Sheikh Ṣughayerūn[5]" (d. 1086 A.H.[6]). He was born in the Sháiḳía country.... His mother was Ḥóḍa, one of the Ṭerayfía. He followed the teaching of his father, and died in 1086 A.H.

259. "Zíáda ibn el Nūr ibn el Sheikh Muḥammad walad 'Ísa." He was the *Khalifa* of Sheikh Muḥammad[7] 'Ali and, like all the pupils of that famous man, the recipient of favours from King Bádi walad Rubáṭ. King Dekín too sent him on one occasion 50 head [of slaves]. He died at Dongola el 'Agūz [Old Dongola], and was succeeded by his son Aḥmad.

On the back of the last, *i.e.* the 220th page, is written in a rough and different hand:

"The ownership of this *Tabaḳát* has been transferred to Muḥammad ibn Aḥmad Ḥammad el Níl el Rayyaḥ. He has not... (*illegible*)... nor changed it."

[1] Tree 9. [2] No. 177. [3] No. 49.
[4] Tree 1. [5] No. 241. [6] 1675 A.D.
[7] No. 181 (?).

D 3 (NOTES)

I On the back of this fragment is written in a crude scrawl, in no way resembling the body of the text, "This is the Ṭabaḳát walad Ḍayfulla. In the name of God...(*invocation*)...I lie at the door of Sheikh Khógali... (*praises of the Prophet*)...."

Khógali ibn 'Abd el Raḥman (No. 154), who died in 1155 A.H. (1742 A.D.), lived and was buried at el Ḥalfáya, the birthplace of the author's family (see No. 88).

The words "*my father*" must be taken to mean "my grandfather." The author's father was Ḍayfulla walad Muḥammad walad Ḍayfulla (see No. 89). In No. 120 (*q.v.*) Muḥammad Ḍayfulla is actually called "my grandfather."

It must be noted that the word "*Sheikh*" is, with very few exceptions (*e.g.* "Sheikh 'Agíb"), used throughout in the technical sense as denoting not temporal power but the spiritual authority of a superior of a religious order. For the exact meaning of the term see Hughes, pp. 556 and 571, and Sell, pp. 104, 110, 111.

The word "*feki*" (or "*feḳih*") means properly one learned in jurisprudence or dogmatic theology (see Hughes, pp. 106 and 128), but is used commonly to mean merely a learned man, or a cleric. It must not be confused with "*faḳir*," a term used properly of one who is poor in the sight of God, *i.e.* a "dervish."

II It is impossible to say whether any pages are missing between this and the page on either side of it.

III This page also contains a reference to the tradition (see Hughes, p. 475) from the *Mishkát* (Bk. XXIV, Chap. 1, Part 3) that there were in all 124,000 prophets, "but those mentioned in the Ḳurán are enough."

IV For the Arabic of the following passage and textual emendations see Appendix 1. The date, and the name of the founder of the FUNG dynasty of Sennár, are given correctly. For the chronology of the FUNG kings see D 7.

Arbagi was, until late in the eighteenth century, one of the chief towns of the Sudan, but it was then destroyed by the SHUKRÍA and 'ABDULLÁB and has now disappeared (cp. D 7, XC). It is said to have been largely peopled by Ḥuḍūr. For the foundation of Arbagi about 1474 A.D. by Ḥegázi ibn Ma'ín, cp. Jackson, p. 18. It was visited by Poncet in 1699: he calls it (p. 17) "the Town of Harbagy." The earliest mention of it ("Arbatg") is in Ludolfus (Bk. IV, Chap. VI). He also mentions "Gerri" (Ḳerri) and "Helfage" (Ḥalfáya). The GELÍLÁB of Wad Ráwa claim that their ancestor was 'Abd el Gelíl the nephew of Ḥegázi ibn Ma'ín (cp. *sub* No. 67).

V The "*'idda*" of Muhammadan law is "the term by the completion of which a new marriage is rendered lawful." (See Hamilton's *Hedaya*, Vol. I, Chap. XII, p. 128, *sub* "Edit.")

"*Sheikh...el Ḳuṣayer*" is Maḥmūd el 'Araki (No. 157). The missing word (the page is chipped) is no doubt "*rágil*" a term used apparently to denote "the holy-man of...": other examples of this use of the word are to be found in Nos. 44 and 191. Maḥmūd is in No. 11 called "*Rágil el Ḳuṣr*" ["the Holy-man of the Castle"], and so "*Ḳuṣayer*" may be taken to be a diminutive form: it is used also in No. 157.

It is not clear what was the relationship between Maḥmūd and the rest of the 'Araki family of holy men whose biographies are given, *e.g.* Abu Idrís, Sheikh Dafa'alla, etc. (for whom see Tree No. 9 and D 1, CI).

The word translated "came" is قدم (*ḳadam*) and has a technical flavour: it is frequently used by the author in speaking of the advent of holy men. The technical word "*muḳaddam*" (a sort of abbot or legate, see Sell, pp. 104–107) is formed from the same root. So, too (*e.g.* paras. VIII and X), the phrase قدم علي (*ḳaddam 'alá*) in the transitive sense is used, and I have there translated it "inspired."

"*Dwelt on the White [Nile]*" is in the Arabic سكن الابيض, and "dwelt at el Obayḍ" would be the normal translation: but it is probable from No. 157, and certain from D 7, II (*q.v.*), that the White Nile is meant and the words "*el baḥr*" (the Nile) have here and in No. 157 been left out. In addition, el Obayḍ ["el Obeid"] was not built until about 1760 (see MacMichael, *Tribes...*, p. 12). For the whole passage cp. D 7, II.

VI Abu Sakaykín (or Abu Sakákín) was the fourth of the FUNG kings and reigned about 1551–1559 (Bruce).

The term *Mángilak*, or *Mangil*, may roughly be rendered Viceroy. It was especially the title of those 'ABDULLÁB sheikhs who ruled the country round el Ḥalfáya for the FUNG kings. These 'ABDULLÁB were a section of the ḲAWÁSMA branch of the RUFÁ'A, and it was their Sheikh 'Abdulla Gemá'a who was the ally of 'Omára Dunḳas (see para. IV) and assisted him to found his empire (see Budge, Vol. II, pp. 200 and 204; Jackson, pp. 17–22; D 5 (*a*); and, in particular, the Appendix to Chap. 2 (*a*) of Part III).

'*Agíb el Mángilak* was the son of 'Abdulla Gemá'a, and he is occasionally called 'Agíb Káfūt (see Budge, *loc. cit.*, Jackson, p. 24, and Part III, *loc. cit.*).

For *Ibráhím el Būlád*, one of the famous AWLÁD GÁBIR, see Nos. 17 and 23 and AB, LXXXIX, and cp. Jackson, p. 26.

For the terms "*Khalíl*" and "*risála*" see AB, LXXXIX (note).

VII The text gives el Bahár for el Bahári. This syncopation is very common throughout in proper names, *e.g.* we get 'Omár for 'Omára, el Ḥamr for el Ḥamra, el Káf for el Káfi, el 'Ūd for el 'Ūdi, etc. I have not noted these particular alterations every time they occur as it would be unnecessary.

For *Ṣūfiism* see Hughes, pp. 608–622 (including a bibliography), and Sell, pp. 1–45 (*The Mystics of Islam*). A large number of the technical terms used by the author are borrowed from the Ṣūfi vocabulary, *e.g* "*ṭaríḳa*," "*sálik*," "*dhikr*," "*záhid*," "*wali*," "*magdhūb*," etc.

For this and following paragraphs, cp. D 7, XXI *et seq.*

VIII No biography of el Telemsáni is given.

"*Instructed him in dogma*" is سلكه طريق القوم (*sallakhu ṭaríḳ el kūm*), a Ṣūfi phrase. Human life being considered as a journey, the "*ṭarik*" or "*ṭarika*" is the road to be followed, the "*sálik*" is one who follows it, and "*sallak*" is to cause another to follow it. By "*ṭarik el kūm*" (*lit.* the road of the people) is meant particularly "*ṭarik el fukará*," *i.e.* the road of the holy men (cp. Appendix 5, etc., *passim*).

"*'Ilm el kalám*" is the same as "*'akáid*" (*q.v.* No. 52) and relates to matters of faith in contradistinction to "*'ilm el fekih*" which relates to matters of practice, *i.e.* jurisprudence. Cp. No. 136; and see Hughes, pp. 106 and 286.

"*The interpretation of ...syntax*" is in the Arabic

علوم القرآن بتجويد وروايات و نحوها

Cp. Hughes, p. 517: "The recital of the Qur'ān has been developed into a science known as 'Ilmu 'l Tajwīd...,' which includes a knowledge of the peculiarities of the spelling of many words in the Qur'ān; of the...various readings;...of the various divisions, punctuations, and marginal instructions; of the proper pronunciation of the Arabic words; and of the correct intonation of different passages."

IX "*The doctrine of...Kurán*" is "*el tawḥid wa el tagwid.*" For the latter see para. VIII (note). For *tawḥid* see Hughes, p. 629; but the word is also used technically by the Ṣūfis to denote the final identification of the saint with the Supreme Being by absorption (see Sell, p. 110).

X "*Arose*" is ظهرت ولاية, or, literally, "appeared the saintship of." For the term "*wali*" see Sell, p. 109, and Hughes, p. 663, and AB, II.

For *'Abd el Káfi* cp. Jackson, p. 27.

XII Probably Sheikh Muḥammad ibn 'Ali (No. 181).

The repetition of the word قدم in the text is obviously a slip.

El Sháfa'i is the *Imám* Muḥammad ibn Idrís, the founder of one of the four orthodox Sunni sects (see Hughes, p. 570).

XIII The *Mashdíkha* are a small section who claim to be descended from the Khalífa Abu Bukr el Ṣadíḳ. They are related to the MESALLAMÍA.

In this particular context are meant Muḥammad walad Fakrūn (see No. 86), Sheraf el Dín (No. 238), Ya'akūb ibn Mugelli (No. 255) and Ḥammad ibn Mariam (No. 124).

El Ḥalfáya, now called Khartoum North, is on the right bank of the Blue Nile opposite Khartoum. Previous to the Turkish conquest it was one of the most important towns in the Sudan and the seat of the power of the 'ÁBDULLÁB. With the founding of Khartoum its importance waned.

Poncet visited it in 1699 and calls it "Alfaa, a large village built with square stone, where the men are tall and comely" (p. 17).

NOTES TO THE BIOGRAPHIES

1. "*El Shará'ana*" is properly the name of a sub-tribe of KAWÁHLA, but is here used for their village.

2. *Gebel Móya* lies about 20 miles east of Sennár.

This *'Abd el Báḳi el Wáli* is the eponymous ancestor of the WÁLÍA section of KAWÁHLA, and is regarded by the family of the *'omda* of the

Baṭáḥín, among others, as their "Sheikh," *i.e.* it is his tomb to which they pay their "visits" (*ziára*) and which they help to maintain, and to him that they would have recourse for any supernatural assistance: in other words they regard him as the particular medium through which they may approach Providence. If they lost a camel by theft they would enquire at his tomb, or if a woman was barren she would appeal at his tomb—the guardian thereof benefiting proportionately. Cp. note to No. 73, and see Jaussen, p. 309, on the subject of *ziáras* and tombs.

'Abd el Báḳi's tomb is not at Gebel Móya but at Um Ḳarḳūr, some 40 miles N.N.W. of it.

Bádi walad Nūl ruled at Sennár from 1733 to 1766 A.D. (Bruce). He is generally known as Bádi "Abu Shelūkh" (for which name see note to D 7, XLVIII).

4. No. 174 is this man's son.

6. *Abu Ḥaráz* is five miles north of Wad Medani, on the Blue Nile. It was the home of the 'Araki family.

7. *Abyaḍ Díri* is north of Khartoum near Wad Ramla station. Cp. Nos. 34 and 142. This man's descendants and those of his brother Muḥammad (see No. 141, note) are at Wáwissi, north of Khartoum.

8. *El Basháḳira* is a village on the Blue Nile about 45 miles above Khartoum.

"*Was taught it by*..." is in each case اخذه من or اخذه عن, *i.e.* literally, "took it from."

Which of the three men named Muḥammad ibn Medani (for whom see No. 194) is meant here is not clear.

Náfa'i el Fezári occurs again in Nos. 206, 207.

9. "*Succeeded his father*" is ولى الخطابة مكان ابيه.

The "*khaṭíb*" is the preacher who recites the "*khuṭba*" in the Friday service at the mosque (see Hughes, p. 472).

"*King Bádi*" must be Bádi "Abu Shelūkh" (1733–1766, Bruce) as 'Abd el Laṭíf's father (*q.v.*) flourished about 1767. "Ṣubr" I cannot identify.

From No. 25 (*q.v.*) we know No. 9 lived at el 'Egayga.

For the circumstances of his death cp. D 7, LVII.

10. We know the date of his death from No. 229 (*q.v.*).

For the word "*el Magdhūb*" see note to No. 61.

Feki Samíḥ and his two sons are again mentioned in No. 79 (*q.v.* note).

11. *El Ḳūbía* is spelt "el Ḳubía" in No. 171.

"*And he said to her*...." The Arabic of the whole of this passage will be found in Appendix 2. The word used for dowry here is "*ṣadáḳ*" which is properly the gift of the bridegroom to the bride, as opposed to "*mahr*," which is the purchase price paid to the bride's parents. (See Jaussen, *Coutumes des Arabes*..., p. 49.) If a man divorce his wife she can by Muhammadan law "demand the full payment of the dower" (see Hughes, p. 91). Since, however, it was the wife, and not the husband, who sought the divorce, and since she would not be able to effect this object legally, she would, as the price of her husband's compliance, be compelled to forgo her right to receive the full dower. 'Abd el Maḥmūd, however, instead of keeping the dowry himself, arranged for it to be given to the children of the marriage. When she married Ḥammad she demanded from him no dowry for herself, because, whereas it is customary in the Sudan for the second husband before marriage to repay to the first husband the amount of the dowry previously paid by the latter, in the case in point the woman cunningly represented 'Abd el Maḥmūd as not having yet paid her her dowry. She apparently let Ḥammad think that 'Abd el Maḥmūd had divorced her on his own initiative and denied receipt of her dowry, but at the same time did not mention that it had been transferred to the daughters.

"*God Almighty said....*" The quotation is from the 4th chapter of the Ḳurán (beginning): see Sale, p. 53.

For "*faḳir*" see note to para. 1, *supra*.

Omdurmán (or "Um Durmán," correctly). I know of no evidence to show the existence of this village at any earlier date than that of Ḥammad ibn Mariam. From No. 124 we know he was born in 1646 and died in 1730, and here we have Omdurmán spoken of as "his village." It is not at all improbable that he and his relatives founded it. It was a small village of no importance at all until the Mahdía. Then the Khalífa massed whole tribes there, and it has now become the native capital of the Sudan. On the above evidence we may perhaps date its foundation about 1680–1700. Browne mentions it ("Emdurmân") in 1794 (*q.v.* p. 459, App. II).

"*His rooms*" is "*khalwát*." A "*khalwa*" is properly a place of retreat, and is used also to mean the act of retirement by a holy man from the world (see Hughes, pp. 122 and 271). The term is now often used of the guest-houses or rest-houses provided in a village for strangers and attached, as a rule, to the mosque: it is often also used in its proper sense of a place of retreat for meditation: cp. note to No. 90.

13. He is here called 'Abd el Raḥman, but in the biography of his father (No. 34) the names of two of the latter's sons are given as 'Abd el Raḥman Abu Shanab and 'Abd el Raḥím ibn el Khaṭwa, and "'Abd el Raḥím" is therefore obviously correct.

14. *Nūri* is a few miles north of Merowi in Dongola.

El Abwáb ["the Gates"] is another name for the Kabūshía district, about 80 miles south of Berber. It was so called because it formed the meeting point of many roads, viz. the two river roads, the road to Napata, the old caravan route that ran from Kabūshía N.N.E. to the Atbara and the Red Sea, and the route that ran S.S.E. through the cultivable valleys to Abu Delayḳ and Ḳayli (see *Arch. Survey of Nubia*, XIXth Memoir, by Crowfoot).

15. For *Nūri* see *sub* No. 14.

For "*Khalíl*" see AB, LXXXIX (note) and cp. Jackson, p. 26.

We are told here that the year 1107 A.H. was called "*Um Ḥinayḍil*" ["Mother of little melons"], but in No. 204 that name is given to 1108 A.H.

No. 161 (*q.v.*) was a pupil of No. 15.

"*Sheikh ibn Medani*" is the son of Medani walad Um Gadayn (Tree 10); *q.v. sub* Nos. 164 and 162.

17. '*Abd el Raḥman* is one of the famous AWLÁD GÁBIR, whose

descendants are called GÁBIRÍA or GAWÁBRA. He flourished about 980 A.H. (1572 A.D.), as can be gathered from para. VI, *supra*, which roughly fixes the date of his elder brother, and from a rather obscure remark in the biography of Ibráhím ibn Um Rabí'a, one of his pupils (No. 140), mentioning "the year 982" *apropos* of a *nisba* written by one of the four brothers ("وكتبه الفقير ابن جابر الجهني فى العرب نسبا"), *i.e.* "And the *fakir* Ibn Gábir el Guhani wrote it as a *nisba* on the Arabs." Whether this *nisba* has any connection with the original of BA (*q.v.* para. CCXXIII and note) I cannot say. Ibn Gábir is called "el Guhani" here because his ancestor Ghulámulla's wife was of GUHAYNA origin (see Tree to D 1 and Tree 10 of the *Ṭabaḳát*).

'Abd el Raḥman is mentioned in BA, CCV.

"*He was one of....*" The actual words of the Arabic are:

فهو القطب الربانى والغوث الصمدانى شيخ الاسلام والمسلمين

i.e. literally, "He was the divine *Ḳuṭb* the immortal *Ghauth*, the Sheikh of Islám and the Muslims." "*Ḳuṭb*" and "*Ghauth*" are both high titles of sanctity: the former (see Hughes, p. 531) means literally an axis, and the latter a mediator or sin-bearer of the faithful (see Hughes, p. 139; and, for both terms, Sell, p. 108).

For *Ibráhím el Būlád* see para. VI, *supra*, AB, LXXXIX *et seq.*, and BA, CCV.

Muḥammad el Banūfari (for whom see also No. 157) is also mentioned in AB, XCVI.

"*He taught...forty times*," *i.e.* in Arabic بلغت ختماته في خليل اربعين ختمة, or, literally, "his sealings in Khalíl reached forty sealings." For the explanation of this see note to AB, XCIX; and for Khalíl see AB, LXXXIX. "He" in this passage ought, I think, to be understood to mean not 'Abd el Raḥman but Ibráhím his brother: see No. 23 and No. 60, and AB, XCIX.

The DUFÁR are BEDAYRÍA: see AB, note III.

"*The four sons of Gábir....*" For the Arabic of this passage see Appendix 3. By a slip the name of 'Abd el Raḥman is repeated twice: that in one of the two cases, probably the second, the reading should be "'Abd el Raḥím" is clear from BA, CCV (*q.v.*), where the other brothers also are mentioned.

19. "*He devoted...God*" is انقطع الي الله.

21. For *Ismá'íl* and *el Banūfari* see *sub* No. 17.

This No. 21 is the head of the large Ḥammadtu family of Dongola. From ABC, LVI, it seems they are ZENÁRKHA or MASHÁÍKHA by tribe.

22. *Ibráhím walad Abu Maláḥ* was one of the disciples of the AWLÁD GÁBIR (see No. 154).

In No. 157 is mentioned 'Abd el Raḥman el Ag·hūri as the teacher of el Banūfari, and el Banūfari taught No. 17 who in his turn taught 'Abd el Raḥman ibn Masíkh, the great-uncle of this No. 22. The 'Ali el Ag·hūri mentioned here (and in No. 66) was great-grandson of 'Abd el Raḥman el Ag·hūri (see note to BA, CCXII), and is known to have died in 1066 A.H.

(1655–6 A.D.). As Khógali, the son of No. 22, is said (see No. 154) to have died in 1742 A.D., there is no discrepancy in the dates.

At the end of biography No. 22 the text contains a reference to some book "written at the end of *Dhu el Ḥigga* of the year 1030 by 'Ali ibn Muḥammad, who was known as 'Zayn,' son of 'Abd el Raḥman el Ag·hūri el Máliki"; and here our author seems to be a little at fault, not in the date, but in the name: 'Ali was son of Muḥammad ibn Zayn el Dín ibn 'Abd el Raḥman el Ag·hūri (see note to BA, CCXII). The book was no doubt one of the commentaries 'Ali is known to have written on *Khalíl*.

23. *Dekín "Síd el 'Áda"* (cp. Cailliaud, II, p. 255, "Ṣáḥib el 'Áda") was the fifth FUNG king. Bruce gives his date as 1570–1587. Sheikh 'Agíb is the same as he mentioned in para. VI. The appointments mentioned were judgeships as will be seen from No. 93, where the names of all four will be found. No. 23 is said to have been an 'Araki by race, but his connection, if any, with those in Tree 9 is not known. "Walad Gábir" is not No. 17 ('Abd el Raḥman) but Ibráhím el Būlád, as we know from No. 60 and AB, XCIX. The famous 40 are mentioned frequently, *e.g. sub* Nos. 156, 254, 60, etc. It may be noted that Ibráhím's contemporary, Tág el Dín el Bahári (*q.v.* No. 67), is also said to have had 40 pupils: for this number 40, cp. Nos. 17 and 90.

25. In his biography the date of his birth is given as 1121 A.H.; but in that of his father (No. 226) as 1122. He had a son, Ḥasan, who, as appears from D 7, CXC, was the possessor of a library of books.

26. For this casting out of evil spirits by means of the alphabet, cp. No. 61. The Arabic from "*taught him*..." is as follows:

وادله في الطب ودل الناس عليه وكان يطب الشياطين بالف ب ت ث
ج ح خ الخ

His *ḳubba* is shown on the map very close to Sóba.

27. 1007 in the text must be a slip for 1070 in order to agree with the dates of the other persons mentioned here.

"*And there came to him*..." For the Arabic see Appendix 4.

'*Adlán* is 'Adlán I of Sennár (1610–1615, Bruce).

"*Five times*" is literally "five knots," *i.e.* each time he made the promise he tied a knot (*sc.* in a piece of fibre or such-like) to signify that he was binding himself to the performance.

Muays is about four miles from Shendi.

"*And his tomb*..." is وقبره ظاهر يزار عليه سكينة ووقار.

There is a reference in the text to "GA'AL and its kings" (جعل وملوكها). This use of GA'AL for GA'ALIYYŪN (the later form) is common in *nisbas*. Cp. AB, *passim*, and No. 154.

That No. 27 was a man of wealth is evidenced by a remark in the text that he killed 60 sheep in honour of an important visitor.

An anecdote is also related of how he restored to health a broken-down donkey.

Meshra el Aḥmar is near Shendi.

28. *Um Dóm* is an Island between Khartoum and Sóba on the Blue Nile.

29. "*Imám*," *i.e.* "precentor," is in the Arabic here "*ṣáḥib*," *i.e. lit.* "master."

Asláng is an island in the river about 22 miles north of Khartoum.

The "*King of the* FUNG" is 'Adlán I (1610–1615, Bruce): *vide sub* No. 126. "*'Agíb the Great*" is "'Agíb the Mángilak" of para. VI, *supra* (*q.v.*).

32. I am told he was a Ga'ali Ḥasabulláwi and was buried at Gebel Saḳadi Móya, west of Sennár.

33. *Táka* is the district round Kassala.

Abu Ḥaráz is close to the north of Wad Medani.

For this biography cp. No. 8.

34. This man's pedigree is given in C 9.

36. "*Attached himself to*" is "*ṣaḥiba*."

There is a site near Sóba called "Wad Ḥasóba" to this day.

Um Leban is an island on the White Nile between Dueim and Káwa.

38. *El Ḳalay'a*: there is a place of this name in the Gezíra some 22 miles north-west of el Manáḳil.

40. *Fás* is Fezzán.

41. This man is mentioned in D I, CII.

42. His descendants were called the 'ÁḲLÁB (see D I, CII).

43. "*Among his followers was...*" is ممن اخذ عليه طريق القوم (cp. para. VIII, *supra* and note).

The "*Sheikh Dafa'alla*" mentioned here cannot be, as is usual, No. 85, because it would be quite incorrect to say that all the stock of the latter were descended from No. 43's two sons: see Tree 9, which shows numerous other well-known descendants of Sheikh Dafa'alla el 'Araki.

44. "*Holy-man*" is "*rágil*": see note to para. V, *supra*.

Ḥagar el 'Asal is between Khartoum and Shendi.

"*He it was...*": the Arabic is:

هو الذي دل الشيخ حسن بن حسونة وكشف له الحجاب

46. The entire Arabic of this biography is given in Appendix 5.

"*Patches*" is "*gibab*" (*sing.* "*gibba*"): this word "*gibba*" (or "*jibbeh*") became very familiar in the Mahdia, being used for the patched shirts worn by the Dervishes in obedience to the Mahdi's orders.

The simile involved in the nickname of "Scorpion's Tail" is "as a man stung by a scorpion dies at once, so he who swears falsely on the tomb of Abu Delayḳ will die at once." On this subject see Jaussen, pp. 311, 312.

The district and village of Abu Delayḳ, the headquarters of the BAṬÁḤÍN, lying about 90 miles east of Khartoum, is called after this man. His real name was 'Ali and he is generally said (cp. *sub* No. 74) to have been a Kahli, but his descendants are always called DELAYḲÁB.

El Nigfa is a low hill close to the south-west of the village of Abu Delayḳ: the tomb of Abu Delayḳ is on this hill and is still much used by the Arabs for the taking of oaths.

48. The text gives some three pages of praises and poetry in honour of "Abu Idrís."

50. "*A pupil of...*" is سلك طريق القوم علي.

51. "*His father... the people there.*" The Arabic is given in Appendix 6. The dialogue is more than typically difficult.

El Tergami, *i.e.* one of the TERÁGMA. It will be seen from the Ga'ali Trees that Tergam was brother of that Kerdam from whom the great majority of the tribe claim descent.

"*Dongola*" is here written "Donḳola" (دنقلة) but the author often elsewhere calls it "Ḍonḳola" (ضنقلة), *e.g.* in Appendix 9.

52. *El 'aḳáid*, which embrace all matters of faith, are in contradistinction to *'ilm el feḳih*, which relates only to matters of practice. See Hughes, pp. 106 and 286, and also note to para. VIII, *supra*.

"*And the cause....*" For the Arabic see Appendix 7.

For the use of رضحا for رضخن cp. note to No. 74 (end).

By *Dár Ṣaliḥ* is meant Wadái.

53. *Ya'aḳūb* was Sultan of Wadái from 1681 to 1707. He engaged in war with Dárfūr and was defeated by the Sultan Aḥmad Bukr at Kebkebía (see Schurtz, pp. 542 and 545).

54. "*'Abūḍi*" is written عبوض: see note to para. VII, *supra*.

55. "*Sáridia*": *i.e.* a woman of the ṢOWÁRDA.

"*El 'Ágami*" is written العجم: cp. note to No. 54.

The AWLÁD EL 'AGAMI live at Berber, and there are a few of them on Bundi Island. 'Agami is of course the brother of Ḥasan wad Ḥasūna (No. 132).

56. The date of *sannat el gidri* is not stated.

58. For *Wali* see note to para. X, *supra*. For "Ḳandíl el Ṣáridi," see note to No. 222.

For the "*famous case*" referred to *vide sub* No. 73.

Mismár el Ḥalashi was one of the 'ABDULLÁB *Mángilak* family of Ḳerri. For lists of these 'ABDULLÁB see Budge, II, p. 204, and Cailliaud, III, p. 96, and Jackson, p. 105, and Part III, Chap. 2 (*a*) above; and see note to para. VI, *supra*. The names here given as those of sheikhs of Ḳerri will not square with the above lists, but the explanation is probably that those sheikhs who were deposed after only a few months' reign are not mentioned in the lists quoted by Cailliaud, etc. The Arabic of this final passage is given in Appendix 8 and it will be seen that owing to the indiscriminate use of personal pronouns it might be translated in several different ways: it is clear, however, that the author is not giving a consecutive list of sheikhs but only mentioning examples of such as were deposed after very short terms of power.

For *'Ali ibn 'Othmán* see No. 236; and for Mismár No. 66.

"*Walad 'Agib*" and "*Sheikh 'Abdulla*" are the same person.

60. For the Arabic of the whole of this biography see Appendix 9. The village of Wad 'Ishayb lies about four miles below el Kámlín on the east bank of the Blue Nile, and its people are called 'ISHAYBÁB: they are a section of RIKÁBÍA and the descendants of this No. 60.

For *el Banūfari* see No. 17.

'Agib the Great is the *Mángilak* of para. VI.

"*The Gezíra*" is in the Arabic here "*el Huoi*." The full name of the Gezíra, *i.e.* the land enclosed between the White and the Blue Niles, was

"Gezíra Sennár" or "Gezírat el Huoi." The people of the Blue Nile region more often use "el Huoi" than "el Gezíra." The word *Hūoi* is often pronounced almost as though it were *Hóg*, and the fact is that there is no exact English equivalent to this final consonant, which is quite different from the soft *g* of, *e.g.*, Karkóg, or the usual hard initial or medial *g*. The same letter occurs in another word in this same biography, viz. "'Aydai," as it is here written, or "'Aydag" (maps "Eidag") as it is often pronounced (cp. *sub* No. 67). Other examples of this case are "Kagoi" in No. 132, "Fóga" (in western Kordofán), which is pronounced almost like "Foiya" by most natives, and "Fung" or "Funye" (*q.v.* in Westermann, p. lii). Cp. also notes to Nos. 108 and 200 for another case in point. Père Jaussen's remarks on the pronunciation of "*gím*" as "*yei*" among the Arabian tribes will be found on pp. 6, 7 of his book, and I may quote the following editorial from *Sudan Notes and Records* (No. 2, 1918): "We believe that ج in the mouth of a Sudan Arab has a sound which is intermediate between hard *g* in *go* and *j* in *just*. The sound also exists in Nubian (Berberine) and has been recorded as occurring in other Arabic dialects (Landberg, *Etudes*..., I, p. 539: 'Quelquefois et dans quelques contrées en Ḥaḍramaut ج est prononcé avec un son entre ğ (j) et g. Ce n'est ni l'un ni l'autre'). The sound in question is articulated in the 'front,' *i.e.* it is formed by the front part of the tongue and the hard palate; it is therefore nearly related to both *d* and *y*, and we agree...that it very nearly corresponds to *dy*."

'Aydag is close to the north of Wad 'Ishayb.

For *Ibráhím el Būlád* see para. VI and No. 17, *supra*, and note to No. 23, and AB, XCIX.

In No. 121 there is a passing mention (omitted in the translation) to "the *feḳír* Muḥammad Ḳandíl ibn el feki Ḥammad ibn el Sheikh 'Ali walad 'Ishayb."

61. "*His father was*..." is ابوه رجلا مجذوبا.

"*Magdhūb*" is a Ṣūfi term (see note to para. VII, *supra*): it is explained by Hughes (*q.v.* pp. 116, 301, 310, 612) as meaning "abstracted" or "attracted," "one chosen of God for Himself": "rapt" in English also suggests the meaning implied. For miracle-working by reciting the alphabet cp. No. 26.

62. The statement that 'Ali "el Níl" was the successor of Tág el Dín implies that he succeeded to the Sheikhship of the Ḳádiría *ṭariḳa* (*vide sub* No. 67). In No. 216 we have his brother Nūr el Dín swearing by Tág el Dín. The story of the *dolayb* palms (*q.v. sub* No. 216) is given at length both in No. 62 and 216.

63. "*A follower of*...," *i.e.* he embraced Ṣūfiism as taught in the first instance by Dafa'alla el 'Araki. See No. 8, where we have 'Ali's son Dafa'alla el Sháfa'i instructing Ṭáha the son of that 'Omára whom we have here teaching 'Ali walad el Sháfa'i.

"*And if he heard*...." For the Arabic see Appendix 10. I understand the meaning to be that if any other aspiring poet after 'Ali's death recited, as his own composition, lines he had borrowed from 'Ali, the spirit of the latter would be heard wailing and his wraith be seen in the air.

65. A Maḥassi by race.

66. "*'Awūda*" is sometimes spelt by the author عُوض and sometimes عووض and sometimes عوضة.

Mūsa Ferid is mentioned in No. 132.

"*Sheikh Muḥammad....*" The Arabic is given in Appendix 11. The text here gives "Kashkash" for "Kashásh," but the correct form occurs in No. 134.

"*El Ḥaḍari*," *i.e.* one of the ḤUḌŪR: very probably 'Ísa Kanū (No. 143) is meant. The bracelets and anklets would be an offering to the *feki* in return for his services. For the prayer-mat cp. No. 178.

"*FUNG*" is here and elsewhere spelt فونج but the author also often uses the form فنج.

"*The grace of God*," *i.e.* in Arabic اليل الله: this is pronounced "*alil ulla*." "*Alil*" means "what belongs to": "*hádha líli*" ("this is mine") in the Sudan is thus the same as the more common "*hadha biṭái*." "*Líli*" is probably an abbreviation of "*ili li*," the colloquial Arabic for "which is mine" (*lit.* "to me"), and "*alil ulla*" would similarly be short for "*ili li ulla*" ("that which is to, or belongs to, God"). It will be seen that in this passage the author spells it اليل thrice and الليل once.

The "*Sheikh of Ḳerri*" is Mismár, one of the 'ABDULLÁB *Mángils*. I do not know who is the "short pale bald man" unless it be 'Ali ibn Barri (No. 58, *q.v.*). In No. 58 Mismár is called "el Ḥalashi."

"*Strain some merissa for him* [*i.e.* '*Awūḍa, i.e. the speaker*]...." That is to say, "He will be everlastingly disgraced by drinking the forbidden beverage." Cp., however, No. 153.

"*Pour it over his tomb...*," *i.e.* as an insult to his memory.

For "*the Book and the Law*, etc...." cp. BA, IX.

For '*Ali el Ag·hūri* cp. No. 22.

'*Awūḍa* is mentioned in A 2, XLIV.

67. *Tág el Dín* is wrongly called "el Bokhári" in Jackson, p. 27.

"*His actual name....*" The Arabic is given in Appendix 14. For the meaning of the terms "*Sheikh*," "*Imám*," "*Ḳuṭb*," "*Ghauth*" see Sell, pp. 104–112. "*Imám*" may be translated "Precentor" or "Leader" or "Pattern" (see Hughes, p. 202); "*Ḳuṭb*" is literally an axis (see Hughes, p. 531); and "*Ghauth*" is literally a mediator (see Hughes, p. 139).

'*Abd el Ḳádir el Gíláni* was the founder of the Ḳádiría order and died at Baghdád in the second half of the twelfth century (see Hughes, p. 2, and Sell, p. 116). The Arab nomads of the Sudan chiefly belong to the Ḳádiría *taríḳa*, but their allegiance is somewhat nominal. For the successive *Khalífas* of this order see note to No. 226. The influence of the Ḳádiría received a great impulse early in the nineteenth century, when Aḥmad ibn Idrís sent missionaries from the Ḥegáz to the Sudan. The Senussi himself was a member of the order, and intellectually the Senussía and the Ḳádiría have close affinities. The latter's influence now extends from India to Algiers. Its propaganda is essentially peaceful.

'*Abd el Gelíl*, the father of Dáud, is the eponymous ancestor of the GELÍLÁB, and nephew of Ḥegázi ibn Ma'ín, the founder of Arbagi. Ḥillat Sa'íd, a few miles north of el Kámlín and the chief village of the Wad

Ráwa district, is named after the Ḥág Sa'íd here mentioned. Cp. note to para. IV, *supra*, and B I, XXX. 'Aydag is also in the Wad Ráwa group of villages (cp. note to No. 60).

The GELÍLÁB still own lands at Wad el Sha'ír, which lies west-south-west of Rufá'a in the Blue Nile Province.

"*He married in the Gezíra*...." From a remark in the biography of No. 190 we know he married a woman of the 'AKK and by her had two daughters. The 'AKK were an Arabian tribe very largely represented at the conquest of Egypt by the Arabs in 640 A.D. (see Butler, *The Arab Conquest*...). They were Ḳaḥṭánites.

Shá'a el Dín walad Tuaym is said to have lived eleven generations ago. The subsections of the SHUKRÍA all claim him or his father Tuaym as a common ancestor.

"40 *persons*." See note to No. 23.

Teḳali is a mountain in southern Kordofán (see MacMichael, *Tribes*..., *passim*).

68. Presumably a relative of No. 1 (*q.v.*). He is said by natives to have been buried at el Ḳáb between Sennár and Wad Medani. He died in 1803 (see D 7, CLXII).

69. Cp. No. 93.

70. "*He died*..." is

وتوفي رحمة الله تعالى وهو في حدود الاربعين سنه او نيف يسير

This branch of the family is omitted in Jackson's Tree (*Yacubabi Tribe*) as living not near Sennár but in the north near Shendi.

71. He is the head of the great Bán el Nuḳá family, of which one branch live in the north near Shendi, and the other, the YA'AḲŪBÁB, near Sennár. They are generally believed to be RÁZḲÍA by race: Jackson (*Yacubabi Tribe*) speaks of them as "originally Shaigi."

"*He was called*..." is

وسمي بان النقا لان امه قالت بان نقاءي اي صفاي وكان عكازا عند الملك نايل

King Náil was the second of the FUNG kings: his date was 1534–1551 (Bruce).

No. 71, called elsewhere "el Ḍarír" ["The Blind"], is given in Jackson's Tree (*Yacubabi Tribe*) as son of Ḥamdán Abu Duḳn son of 'Abūd, and there appears as "Bennaga Derair."

72. "*He was a follower of*" is سلك الطريق علي.

El Imám 'Ali was the Prophet's son-in-law.

'*Araki*, like No. 64, was evidently so named after 'Abdulla el 'Araki.

73. Básbár's descendants are known as the BASÁBÍR. "El Sḥukri" was probably only a nickname. He is always said now to have been a Sháiḳi, and as the SHÁIḲÍA are by origin GA'ALIÍN and 'Ón was son of Sháiḳ (see D 5 (*c*), IV), the term "Ga'ali 'Óni" is quite explicable.

"*It is related*..." For the Arabic see Appendix 15.

This story is also related in almost the same terms in No. 58. The latter adds that it was for seven years that the Ḥammadi abstained from going to the river; and in place of لعقيقة ولده ("for the shaving ceremony of his child") gives ورد البحر يجيب الما لسماية ولده ("went to the river to fetch water for the naming of his child"). No. 58 also adds that Básbár, who was sitting under the acacia trees, was engaged in trimming a tablet (يصلح لوحا), *i.e.* the board used by *fekis* as a schoolmaster uses a slate. The point of the story of course is that Básbár's son in revenge translated himself into a crocodile.

Most of the AḤÁMDA are not riverain folk, hence the note that the particular Ḥammadi in question lived on the river, the implication being that it was very hard for him to avoid visiting the river for years.

As regards the shaving ceremony see Hughes, p. 554: "At the birth of a child it is incumbent upon the Muslim father to sacrifice a goat (one for a girl and two for a boy) at the ceremony called 'Aqīqah, which is celebrated on either the 7th, 14th, 21st, 28th, or 35th day after birth, when the hair is first shaved and its weight in silver given to the poor." On the Blue Nile the father names his child on the 7th day after birth and gives a party in honour of the event and kills a sheep or goat for the guests. The water fetched from the river, in this story, would, if it is really the naming ceremony that is referred to, be merely water wherewith to fill the jars from which the guests would drink. Elsewhere, however (p. 17), Hughes says: "'Aqīqah. A custom observed by the Arabs on the birth of a child; namely, leaving the hair on the infant's head until the 7th day, when it is shaved, and animals are sacrificed..."; and again (pp. 50, 51) "The naming of the child should, according to the Traditions...be given on the 7th day....On this, the 7th day, is observed also the ceremony of 'Aqīqah, established by Muḥammad himself....It consists of a sacrifice to God, in the name of the child, of two he-goats for a boy, and one he-goat for a girl...," which sacrifice is eaten by the friends assembled: while they eat they offer the prayer "O God! I offer to thee instead of my own offspring, life for life, blood for blood, head for head, bone for bone, hair for hair, skin for skin. In the name of the Great God do I sacrifice this goat."

It would appear therefore that the father went to fetch water for the "'aḳíḳa" proper, *i.e.* for shaving the boy's head, and that it is not strictly accurate to say he wanted it for the naming of the boy, although it is true both functions took place on the same day and presumably on the same occasion.

The occasion of the naming of a child is also celebrated among some Sinaitic tribes (see Jaussen, p. 16 note). For the *'aḳíḳa* as the ceremony of shaving the head of a child, cp. Jaussen, p. 94; and cp. Nachtigal (*Voy. au Ouadaï*, p. 88) for the same custom as practised in Wadái, and Crowfoot, *Customs of the Rubáṭáb* (pp. 122 and 130), where the naming ceremony is described.

In the Sudan, when the child's hair is first cut, which is, by the way, often some four months after birth, a long tuft (the "*'uruf*" mentioned here) is left growing on that part of the head which was first visible at the time of birth. Now previous to the child's birth it is customary for the parents to dedicate this tuft to some famous saint ("Sheikh"), to whose *ḳubba* the "visits" mentioned in note to No. 2 are paid, vowing at the same time some gift, such as a sheep or a camel or some money to the saint in case of their hopes being fulfilled. When the child has reached the age of about 4 or 5 years the parents, in fulfilment of their vow, take him (or her) to the *ḳubba* of the saint and discharge their vow. One of the guardians of the shrine, *i.e.* a descendant of the "Sheikh," then cuts off the tuft of hair. The tuft is as a rule left in the *ḳubba*, but, at Wad Ḥasūna for instance, it is hung up on a tree sacred to the Sheikh just outside the *ḳubba*, and remains there till some accident happens to remove it: see note to No. 132. The technical word for this dedication is حوّر ("*ḥowwara*"): *e.g.* نحوّر رلولد للشيخ means "we dedicate the boy (*i.e.* his hair) to the Sheikh." Cp. the word "*ḥowár*," "a disciple," explained in Hughes, p. 169, *q.v.* There is a mention of the cutting of the tuft in biography No. 132 (*q.v.*).

That the origin of these customs is of ancient date is clear when one reads in Herodotus (Bk. II, § 65) "The inhabitants of the various cities [of Egypt], when they have made a vow to any god, pay it to his animals in the way which I will now explain. At the time of making the vow they shave the head of the child, cutting off all the hair, or else half, or sometimes a third part, which they then weigh in a balance against a sum of silver; and whatever sum the hair weighs is presented to the guardian of the animals."

It will not be out of place here to describe the votive offerings and such like which I saw in November 1913 hung on the gnarled old *hegliḳ* tree standing in front of the *ḳubba* of Sheikh Ḥasan walad Ḥasūna (No. 132) at the village that bears his name.

1. Many small tufts of hair from children's heads ("*'uruf*"); some of these were wrapped in little bags.

2. Large bunches of women's hair. These had been left by women whose hair had begun falling out and who looked to the saint to restore it.

3. Several little bundles of the shin-bones of sheep and goats which had been sacrificed at the time of the naming ceremony ("*samáia*").

4. Several miniature shepherd's crooks of this shape 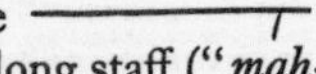. These were about a foot long and were imitations of the long staff ("*maḥgan*") of the same shape which the Arabs use for shaking down pods ("*'ulayf*") from the acacia trees for their goats to browse upon. The dedication of these sticks is the equivalent of a prayer that the boy may become a good herdsman.

5. Some bundles of big bones, chiefly camels'. It was explained that these had belonged to animals which had died of some disease, and the owners had dedicated the bones to the Sheikh in the hope that he would stay the disease from the rest of the herd.

6. Many camels' hobbles ("*'uḳal*"). These were deposited by the owners of camels which had strayed or fallen sick, in the expectation of the aid of the Sheikh in finding or healing the beasts.

7. There were several articles such as a hair-tent, bowls, grindstones, etc., left temporarily by Arabs in charge of the saint until their return at the end of the season. These were not in any way dedicated to the Sheikh but only entrusted to him for the time being. For this cp. Crowfoot, *Customs of the Rubáṭáb* (p. 123).

The other objects specified were left permanently.

The following quotations from Père Jaussen's *Coutumes des Arabes au pays de Moab* show that the tree-cult underlying the practices described is not necessarily of African origin, although so widely spread through Africa, *e.g.* among the BASA on the Abyssinian frontier, who have a "sacred tree" (see James, *Wild Tribes...*, p. 193), and in Dárfūr and Wadái (see Chap. 4 of Part I):

(1) P. 36. "À d'autres sanctuaires on fait une simple visite, relevée d'une offrande, et on laisse un souvenir en attachant à l'arbre sacré qui ombrage la cour, ou aux barreaux des fenêtres de la *qubbeh* quelques morceaux d'étoffe."

(2) P. 310. "En témoignage de confiance un bédouin arrache quelques crins à la queue de sa chamelle, et les attache en ex-voto à une branche de tamarisc dressée au milieu des pierres de la sépulture."

(3) P. 334. "Les arbres sacrés...se présentent sous un double aspect: ils sont joints à un sanctuaire ou bien ils sont isolés. Dans le premier cas, ils ne paraissent pas avoir une origine indépendante du lieu saint qu'ils ombragent, ni un rôle distinct de l'influence attribuée au *wély* [*wali*] qui les a fait croître, qui les vivifie et les protège....La seconde catégorie d'arbres sacrés ne jouit pas du bénéfice de la proximité d'un sanctuaire; ils se dressent isolés, près d'une source, sur une colline, ou au sommet d'une montagne...."

(See also Plate V to Jaussen's book.)

Cp. also Zwemer, p. 284, for remarks on what he calls "these rag trees" in Arabia.

74. The KAWÁHLA themselves accept the DELAYḲÁB as distant relatives.

'Abd el Ḳádir is 'Abd el Ḳádir el Gíláni the founder of the Ḳádiría order: cp. note to No. 67. The phrase "the fire of 'Abd el Ḳádir...was with..." is the equivalent of "the mantle of so and so descended upon...." For this succession of *Khalífas* of the Ḳádiría see note to No. 226.

"*And I was in doubt...*": for the Arabic see Appendix 16. "To light the fire" is here again used in the metaphorical sense. Sellama is probably Sellama el Ḥág Yūsef near east of Khartoum.

The word "*'ugub*" (عجب) is commonly used in the Sudan to mean "again."

This direction to Bedowi to settle "in the red country with the red people" is fastened upon by the BAṬÁḤÍN of Abu Delayḳ as proving conclusively that the country round el Nigfa and Abu Delayḳ was occupied by them before the advent of the DELAYḲÁB, and as disproving the latter's claim to own those parts. Most of the BAṬÁḤÍN are of the red-brown colour that generally distinguishes the nomad Arab.

For "*khalwa*" see note to No. 11.

The *MARGHŪMÁB* are a branch of KAWÁHLA; some of them still graze round Abu Delayḳ with the SHUKRÍA. "O Sheríf" is addressed to the man to whom Bedowi is telling the tale.

No. 86 used the same words as Bedowi on his deathbed: the Arabic is يا كاهليات انا جبلكا يوم القيامة. For this incorrect form جبلكا, *i.e.* جبلكًا for جبلكن, cp. Appendix 7, where we have رضخا for رضخن.

"*El Samiḥ*" is Ḥammad el Samíḥ, the fifth of the 'ABDULLÁB *Mángils* of Ḳerri. Cailliaud (vol. III, p. 96) gives his name correctly, Budge (vol. II, p. 204) and Jackson (p. 105) wrongly as Ḥámid (or Ḥamed) el Shemík. His attack on Shendi is again mentioned in No. 226.

75. This *feki* is reported to have been a Ga'ali and to have been buried near Ḳóz Na'ím in the direction of Shendi. Probably he is the son of No. 229, the 'AWAḌÍA being GA'ALIÍN.

"*He embraced...*" is انتحل مذهب الصوفية; and "*Was a follower of*" is اخذ الطريق من.

The wearing of wool was a sign of asceticism. Whether "*Ṣūfi*" is derived from "*ṣūf*" (wool) is doubtful (see Hughes, p. 608).

76. This *feki* is reported to have been buried near J. Arang between Wad Medani and el Ḳeḍáref, east of the river Rahad. His descendants are mentioned in D 1, CXXV, as among the ASHRÁF of the Sudan, being descended from Ḥusayn.

For his date see No. 2, where it is mentioned that Sheikh Khógali, who died in 1742, was his contemporary.

77. He was brother of No. 246. The site of his *ḳubba* is shown on the map as on the Blue Nile, close south of Khartoum, near Sóba. As he was buried elsewhere it is presumably his placenta or afterbirth that is marked by the *ḳubba*: cp. No. 78. This custom, which had its place, too, in ancient Egypt, is common in the Sudan, and among the Arab tribes appears to be varied according to whether the river is available or not. In the latter case the afterbirth is buried outside the threshold of the house, close in front of the door. With it, in the case of the Blue Nile tribes, are buried a date (if available), a thread of red silk, and a seed of corn (*dhuraia*): a tuft of a few branches (*za'af*) from the crest of a palm-tree, still connected together at their base, as they grew, is stuck in the ground over the spot where the afterbirth is buried, the upper half of the tuft projecting visibly. If the river is close at hand the afterbirth is (in the case of the Blue Nile tribes) first placed in a dish and carried round the village by a band of boys and girls, soliciting alms, and then, after being weighted with a stone, thrown into the river together with the date, the silk and the seed. The benefits supposed to arise from the date and the seed are good growth and a long and prosperous life to the child: the benefit from the silk thread (which presumably represents the umbilical cord) is said to be to the mother, it being hoped that no ill effects will follow as a consequence of her not being entirely rid of the afterbirth. A similar custom is said to be observed both at the time of circumcision (the foreskin being substituted for the afterbirth) and when the boy is married; but in the latter case, instead of being buried or thrown into the river, the date, silk and seed are placed in a forked stick on the right side of the lintel.

For the whole subject of the importance of the afterbirth and the rites connected with the disposal of it see Seligman (*Hamitic Problem*, pp. 658 *et seq.*) and cp. Crowfoot, *Customs of the Rubáṭáb* (p. 129).

78. For a *ḳubba* at the birthplace instead of at the burialplace see note to No. 77.

"*He had the prophetic gift*" is كان من اهل الكشف (*lit.* "he was of the people who revealed, *sc.* the future").

79. His pupil, No. 4, died in 1767, and his own father (No. 204) in 1696. The *feki* Samíḥ is, in No. 10, called "el Tamírábi."

80. He is said to have been a Rázḳi, and if so would be connected by birth with the Bán el Nuḳá family.

81. A Ga'ali by race (*vide* No. 212). El Kerrada is said to be near el Ḥilálía, *i.e.* south of el Kámlín.

82. "*He had supernatural...*": for the Arabic see Appendix 17.

"*The saints* (*Awliyá*) *shall come to you*": *sc.* "to visit you."

يجلسوك may mean, as I have translated it, "they shall make you be seated," *i.e.* absolve you from standing up as a sign of respect in their presence; or, possibly, "they shall make you sit [in a position of authority]": cp. the use of قعد in No. 66 (Appendix 11).

For "*light the fire of 'Abd el Ḳádir*" cp. notes to Nos. 74 and 67.

"*His tomb....*" The site is shown on the maps as "'Id Burta" because there is now a well close by. The *ḳubba* has disappeared, but the tomb exists: it lies a few miles west of Abu Delayḳ.

83. From No. 33 we know he was an 'Araki. Cp. No. 8.

84. This is the famous "Dafa'alla el 'Araki" or "Sheikh Dafa'alla." Um 'Aẓám is about 15 miles south-west of Rufá'a. Note that he was born at his mother's village: her name has been changed from "Um Ḥusayn" to "Um Ḥasón" because it is known to the family as the latter at present. The Ḍubáb are a debased semi-negroid tribe (*q.v.* Vol. I, p. 207).

Bádi walad Rubáṭ reigned from 1651–89 (Bruce) or 1642–77 (MS. D 7).

"*Um Laḥm*" ("Mother of meat") by a euphemism denotes a year of famine. See D 7, XLI.

85. "*Be of good cheer...*" is as follows in the Arabic:

ابشرن يا هنونابيات [for هتونابيات] انا جبلكا يوم القيامة

I read "Hatūnáb" for "Hanūnáb" because Dafa'alla's mother's grandfather is given above as "Hatūna" and not "Hanūna." For the quotation cp. note to No. 74.

86. D 1 (*q.v.* CI) says "The 'Arakiyyūn are descended from Guhayna, but among them are the children of el Sheríf Aḥmad Muḳbal, who married a wife from among the 'Arakiyyūn and begot Dafa'alla, the ancestor of their pious *Khalífas*; and the latter's sons were Bukr Abu 'Áyesha and 'Abdulla and Ḥammad el Níl."

"*The west country*" ("*Dár el Gharb*") is Kordofán: the phrase is often used on the Blue Nile in this sense.

Bir Serrár is about 30 miles north-north-east of Bára.

Muḥammad walad Fakrūn was father of No. 238 (*q.v.*).

The Gimi'áb country is a little north of Khartoum.

It is curious that the author only gives the biography of two of the five sons of Dafa'alla. The el Magdhūb here mentioned must not be confused with el Magdhūb the father of No. 123. No. 123 was born in 1693 A.D., whereas the grandson (No. 84) of No. 86 died as early as 1683.

"*He was known as*..." is in the Arabic:

ونسبه مشهور بالعركي نسبه الي عرك قبيلة معروفة

but I know of no tribe called 'Arak: the name 'Arakiyyūn at present certainly only applies to the generations subsequent to No. 86.

The whole of the text of this biography is given.

87. *Muḥammad Abu el Kaylak* was the famous vizier of Sennár, who died in 1776 A.D. after a career of king-making and conquest. Information concerning him will be found in MacMichael (*Tribes*..., pp. 10–13 and 211) and Jackson, pp. 50–59, and in MS. D 7 *passim*.

88. This is the author's great-grandfather.

For "*Um Laḥm*" see No. 84.

89. This is the author's father: cp. No. 120. Contrast ABC, XI.

90. For the Arabic see Appendix 18: the whole biography is quoted.

This *Dólib* is a descendant of the Ḥág ibn 'Abdulla ibn Rikáb mentioned in No. 222, but the exact degree of relationship is not specified by the author. The intermediate generations as given from memory by one of the Dóalíb are given in MacMichael, *Tribes*..., p. 93; but they may be inaccurate.

For "*khalwa*" see note to No. 11. For "*dhikr*" (pronounced "*zikr*") see Hughes, pp. 703–710; and for "*'ibáda*" see Hughes, p. 612.

"*A forty-days'-retreat*" (Ar. خلوة الاربعين) is a common expression for one of these retreats to which a recluse retires for meditation for 40 days. For this number 40 cp. No. 23 (note).

"*O God, bless us*..., etc." occurs again in No. 105.

"*Walad 'Ísa*" is probably No. 191.

91. The Zaydáb country is in Berber province, a little south of el Dámer.

93. For these four judges see Nos. 23 and 69: the Arabic here is

وهو احدي القضاة الاربعة الذين قضاهم الشيخ عجيب....

Dekín reigned from 1570 to 1587 A.D. (Bruce).

There are two villages of "Dushaynát" and one called "Wad el Ḳáḍi," all about 15 miles south-south-west of el Manáḳil.

This No. 93 is grandfather of No. 193, the founder of Wad Medani. It is said that he was by race a Buṣayl ábi from Upper Egypt.

The translation of the couplet is: "Son of Dushayn, the Just Judge, who does not err into error: his offspring are good men and true, who lit the fire of apostleship." Cp. note to No. 117.

95. He belonged to the 'Abádla section of Baṭáḥín and his *ḳubba* lies close to the east of Sennár (*vide* maps, "Sheikh Feraḥ").

The sons of Gábir are No. 17 and Ibráhím el Būlád and their two brothers. Many similar apothegms to that quoted are attributed by the Arabs to Feraḥ: such are the following:

1. (of the rain) شنْ جانا نازل شنْ لنا بالمنازل, *i.e.* "if it descend upon us what matter to us the houses [we have built]."

2. (also of the rain) ان جانا صاب شِنْ لنا بالسحاب, *i.e.* "if it pour down upon us what matter the clouds to us."

The idea in both cases is that the primary consideration is that rain should fall: whether its coming is foretold by clouds or whether the houses are rainproof are secondary matters. Note the play on words in the first quotation.

96. These two brothers are only allotted four lines in the text: they lived at a date rather beyond our author's ken, *i.e.* about the middle of the sixteenth century.

Ḥilália (*sic*) is between el Kámlín and el Rufá'a on the east bank.

97. *Gád el Nebi* is mentioned again in No. 127. The text gives no further details.

99. The title is جادالله وحادالله but the و should be interpreted as "or" instead of "and"; or او may be read. An exactly similar case arises in No. 103; and the inference is that the author was copying the names from a MS.: the writing of G and Ḥ only differs by a single dot, whereas the sound of the two letters is absolutely distinct. The text here and in No. 103 speaks as though one man and not two was intended.

101. "*El Gáma'i el Kordofáli*," *i.e.* one of the GAWÁMA'A of Kordofán (or Kordofál): for the spelling of the latter word see MacMichael, *Tribes*..., p. 223, and cp. No. 102.

Auli is a hill about 26 miles south of Khartoum.

Busáṭi was no doubt so named after the son of Ghánim's teacher el Arbáb (see No. 94).

"*Walad Ḳadál*" is perhaps son of No. 147; but see notes to Nos. 124 and 125. 'Áyesha is mentioned again in No. 154.

102. There is nothing in the text, which is translated practically complete, to show who Edóma was.

Gódatulla in No. 207 is called "Muḥammad Gódatulla."

103. Cp. note to No. 99.

105. For the meaning of "*Nesi*" see No. 90. Cp. D 1, CXVIII.

106. *Shanbát* is a few miles north of Khartoum.

107. Here note an instance of the common occurrence of a man being known not by his father's name but his mother's: cp. *sub* Nos. 17, 46 and 85. Note also the almost universal mistake of writing a ق for an غ (القبشة for الغبشة). In the Sudan the ق is pronounced in ordinary dialect like a hard *g* but any one desirous of being thought learned pronounces it deliberately as *gh* (غ), and hence the *fekis* being used to pronounce the ق as *gh* generally spell proper names really containing a غ with a ق.

This *Hagū* is called Hagū "Abu Ḳurn" in Jackson (*Yacubabi Tribe*) and appears to have been one of the most famous of a famous family. His mother Batūl appears as such in Jackson's Tree, but Ya'aḳūb (No. 254), the eponymous ancestor of the YA'AḲŪBÁB, is there shown as Hagū's brother, and son of Batūl, instead of brother of Batūl. Jackson's Tree being based on oral information is probably wrong, and the detailed consistency of the *Ṭabaḳát* is probably correct. The YA'AḲŪBÁB too told Jackson that Batūl's husband Ḥammad was a *Sherîfi* (descendant of the Prophet) and it is more likely the *Ṭabaḳát* is correct also on this point. Jackson speaks of Hagū's *ḳubba* being at el 'Azáza (some 15 miles north-west of Sennár and ten miles south of a well and village shown on the map as "Hagu Abu Garn"), and "Um Mawákiḥ is presumably thereabouts. According to Jackson's Tree Hagū had four sons, Sheikh el Tóm, Ḥaggar, 'Abd el Ḳádir and Ṭai el Dín.

108. "*El Máidi*" (المايدي) is now generally pronounced "el Mágdi." There is a village called "Wad el Mágdi" a few miles south of el Kámlín: cp. No. 200.

109. "*El 'Ámri*," *i.e.* one of the 'AWÁMRA.

"*El Kámnin*" (for which cp. ABC, VI) is the old, and more correct, form of "el Kámlín": cp. Poncet (p. 17), who speaks of "Camin" in 1709, and Trémaux (vol. II, p. 71), who in 1862 calls it "Kamnyn." The word is connected with "*kamna*," an ambuscade, the root being كمن [to hide oneself]: the site is so called because it lies very low and is invisible from a distance.

"*El Ḳóz*" is probably the place of that name west of Shendi [maps, "el Góz"].

111. Cp. No. 159. "*El Baṭrán*" means "petulant" or "insolent." His *ḳubba* is near Sabíl in Sennár Province.

"*Sannat el Wada'a*" is also mentioned in No. 136.

El Ḥumr is near Sennár.

112. "*'Abd el Báḳi*" is 'Abd el Báḳi el Zurḳáni, for whom see note on AB, LXXXIX and BA, XLVIII.

113. "*Bádiri*," *i.e.* one of the BŪÁDIRA.

This man is great-grandfather of No. 231 who died about 1117 (A.H.), *i.e.* 1705 A.D., and the two were buried at the same place (assuming el Gebel to be the same as el Gebayl). "*El Gebayl*" is Gebayl Um 'Ali near Kabūshía in Shendi district.

The 'OMARÁB, who include the well-known religious family of the AWLÁD 'ABD EL MÁGID, are descended from and named after 'Omar, the father of No. 113. They are reckoned GA'ALIÍN, but on the mother's side claim to be ASHRÁF owing to "Abu el 'Aṣá" having married a daughter of the Sheríf Ḥammad Abu Denána (*q.v.* in No. 141, note). See also ABC, XIII.

114. One of the GHUBUSH of Berber.

115. "*El Mashayrifi*," *i.e.* a Maḥassi (cp. *sub* No. 124). He is evidently connected with Tree II (note his tribe and place of burial). Abu Nagíla is at Khartoum North, opposite Tūti Island.

117. Evidently some connection of No. 93 (*q.v.* note).

119. "*Take advantage of*...": for the Arabic see Appendix 19.

121. In No. 191 this man is called "The holy-man of Sharáū."

123. A contemporary of the author: see No. 194 and note to D I, CXXV.

For "*el Magdhūb*" see note to No. 61.

This man is mentioned in Jackson (p. 64) and in No. 15, *supra*: in the latter he is spoken of as "el Rihaywábi of Abḥaráz" [*i.e.* Abu Ḥaráz]: *i.e.* he was a Ga'ali.

"*Was a pupil of*" is حفظ الكتاب علي; "a follower of..." is سلك الطريق علي (see note to VIII, *supra*).

124. A story of this man is in No. 11, *q.v.*

The Arabic of this biography down to "...by origin" is given in Appendix 20.

Abu Nagila: cp. No. 115.

By "*Walad Kishayb*" I think No. 208 is meant: note that the latter's ancestor settled on the White Nile and that Ḳadál "el Wali" (No. 147), whose daughter (?) "Walad Kishayb" married, was born on the White Nile. No. 208, in his biography, is called a Mesallamábi, and "Walad Kishayb" is here called a Mesallami.

For "*a daughter of Walad Ḳaddl*" I think "a daughter of Ḳadál" should probably be read: see note to No. 125 on this superfluous "*walad*" or "*wad*." If the mother of Mariam was a grand-daughter of Ḳadál chronological difficulties arise owing to the excessive number of generations between 'Abūdi and No. 124 (see Tree 11).

"*Visited*" is the technical term: see note to No. 2.

This No. 124 was probably (see note to No. 11) the founder of Omdurmán: his *ḳubba* is to the south of Khartoum and is called "Wad Um Mariam" ("*Wad Um*" being equal to "*ibn*," a curious periphrasis). His descendants are called the MARIŪMÁB, "Mariūm" being a colloquial corruption of "Mariam": similarly "*ḥarūm*" is a corruption of "*ḥarím*" ("women") in some parts of the Sudan.

For No. 124's pedigree and nickname see ABC, LV. He was a descendant of No. 255.

125. "*He was known...*" is المشهور بان الترابي: this must be wrong, and as he is always known as "Wad el Turábi," and as his brother Nanna (No. 214) is called "ibn el Turábi" I have read بابن for بان. As a matter of fact he was not "son of el Turábi" at all but "el Turábi" himself, if his own descendants are to be trusted, and they are very positive. It is true that this colloquial "*wad*" does sometimes creep in where it has no place, and this has happened, I think, in No. 124 (*q.v.* note). Ḥammad was called "el Turábi," it is said, because when at Mekka he was asked "What is your race?" and replied "Turábi"; and again when asked "Whence come you?" he replied "Min el turáb" (*note*, "*turáb*" means "earth" or "soil" and his reply was therefore, as it were, "I am of the earth, earthy"). As a matter of fact, however, "Abu Tūráb" was the sobriquet of the *Imám* 'Ali, whose veterans used the war-cry of

الجنة الجنة الى التورابية

("Paradise, paradise for the Tūrábía"), and it is very likely that "el Turábi" means no more than "the followers of 'Ali": see Mas'ūdi (ed. B. de M.), vol. v, Chaps. 87 and 94 (pp. 80, 217, 261). There is no evidence of any connection with the TURÁBIÍN who live north of Nekhl in the Sinai Peninsula.

His *ḳubba* is a few miles north-west of el Kámlín and is much in vogue at the present day.

His descendants declare his father's name was 'Abd el Raḥman, and not Muḥammad. His mother Ḳáía was the daughter of el Ḥág Saláma el Ḍubábi (*q.v.* in No. 84) and he was thus, it is said, connected with the 'Araki family.

The name "*Naḥlán*" is a corruption of "*wahalán*" ("dirty," "unkempt"): he is said to have remained for thirty-six months shut up in his *khalwa* in a course of asceticism and retirement.

The present *Khalífa* is the eighth in descent from him, the names being as follows: Abu 'Áḳla (present *Khalífa*), ibn Ḥammad, ibn Muḥammad, ibn Ḥammad, ibn el Sayyid, ibn el Na'ím, ibn 'Abd el Ḥabíb, ibn Ḥammad.

"*He studied....*" For the Arabic see Appendix 21.

Muays is close to Shendi.

"*Took ten sealings*": see note to AB, XCIX.

"*Sulṭana*" ("*rulers*") here probably means spiritual rulers or *fuḳara*.

The text mentions that he, like No. 241 (*q.v.*), met "el Sayyid el Khiḍr," and followed his teaching. For el Khiḍr see note to 241.

Some six pages are devoted to the biography of No. 125. He is mentioned in D 7 (*q.v.* XLIII) but is there called Aḥmad instead of Ḥammad: D 3 carefully dates his death as in سنه ستة عشر بعد المائة والالف and the dates of his contemporaries corroborate the accuracy of this. He is also mentioned in Budge (vol. II, p. 202). Jackson by confusing Bádi el Aḥmar with Bádi "Síd el Ḳūm" has antedated "Wad el Turábi" by about a century.

126. Cp. No. 29 (his son).

Karkóg. The word is here written "Kargóg" (كرجوج), and the same spelling occurs incidentally in No. 117 (not in the translated text). For remarks upon the accuracy or otherwise of this spelling see note to BA, CCXVI.

127. "'*Sawáḳ el Raká*,' *for when...donkey*": for the Arabic see Appendix 22. The "*raká*" is the leathern jug used by Muhammadans for their ablutions.

Maskín is the father of No. 250.

129. By "*GUDHÁM*" here is not meant the Arabian tribe of that name but the descendants of Gudhám (or Agdham), who appears in the GUHAYNA pedigrees as brother of Ṣárid, the ancestor of the ṢOWÁRDA (cp. *e.g.* D 1, XCVIII).

"*My paternal...*" is

واخذ عليه التوحيد والعربية جدي لابي الفقيه ضيف الله الفضلي

130. "'*Agwa*" are properly dried dates of best quality, pressed in baskets.

"*His mother's brother...Gábir*": for the Arabic see Appendix 23.

131. Cp. D 1, CXXI. D 3 does not mention the exact connection of Belíl with the rest of the RIKÁBÍA but see No. 222 and BA, CCIII.

132. This is the famous "Wad Ḥasūna," founder of the village of that name about 27 miles west of Abu Delayḳ, and eponymous ancestor of the ḤASŪNÁB. The present inhabitants of Wad Ḥasūna claim to be ASHRÁF (see C 6 and cp. ABC, X), but many are of very mixed descent. Sheikh Ḥasan

is reputed to have owned all the surrounding country and some sixty-four *ḥafírs* [reservoirs, dug to hold the rain water] and innumerable slaves. The brand he used for his animals was ١١٨, *i.e.* 118, that being the total arrived at by adding together the numerical values of the consonants of his name (HSN), but his descendants of the present day use ١٧١, *i.e.* 171, as their brand: see Hughes, p. 3, *sub* "Abjad."

The *ḳubba* of Sheikh Ḥasan is one of the most highly venerated in the Sudan and liars are very chary of swearing upon it, for "it kills." Just outside it is the "tree of the Sheikh" covered with votive offerings (see note to No. 73).

For the Arabic of the first portion of the biography see Appendix 24.

"*Andalus*" is southern Spain: the author probably regarded it as a part of Morocco.

"*I have put my seed...*": there is a play on "*nasl*" and "*aṣl*": it is implied that the ancestors of Mūsa were originally connected with those of the MESALLAMÍA: the latter consider themselves descendants of the Khalífa Abu Bukr el Ṣadíḳ (see C 8).

"*And by Fáṭima....*" Ḥasūna had other children by another wife, as will be seen later from the text. For "Waḥshía" ABC, x, gives "Ḥabashía."

"*Kagoi*" (so pronounced as a rule) is spelt "Kagóg" [كجوج]: cp. note to No. 60, and No. 151. It lies between Khartoum and Shendi (maps, "Koggug").

"*He went up to el Durūrba...*": for the Arabic see Appendix 25.

"*El Durūrba*" is a hill near to the north-west of Wad Ḥasūna.

"*Donkey's Dam*" was so called, it is said, because Sheikh Ḥasan killed a wild ass there.

"*Plate and pin of silver*": on the sling of a sword is hung a circular plate of silver ("*miḥáḥir*," *sing.* "*muḥára*"), through which the leather passes. This is held in position by a long silver pin ("*ibzaym*") which is welded on to the plate thus (the shaded part being the leather):

"*Commander*" is "*sid ḳūm*." The same phrase was used at the FUNG court to denote the marshal or "mayor of the palace," whose prime duty was in early times the ceremonial slaying of a king when, through age or impotence, it was considered that he should for the good of the state be superseded: see Vol. I, p. 50.

"*Troops*": the word is "*gundi*," and the plural "*gunūd*" means troops. It is possible "*gundi*" here denotes some officer of rank.

"*The property of her father...for me*": the Arabic is ابوها ماله مال حرام كفنها لي. The father was presumably a thief and the expenditure of illgotten money on a shroud would be regarded with abhorrence; "*ḥarám*" is the Latin "*nefas*."

"*And* [*then*] *he shaved...*": for the Arabic see Appendix 26.

The reference is to the cutting of the "'*uruf*" (see note to No. 73).

The "*'uṭfa*" is a howdah, with framework of wood, fixed on the saddle of a camel. It is used on state occasions, such as a "*raḥíl*" (moving the bride to the bridegroom's house) or the moving of camp, for the women-folk. They are shrouded from view by the hangings and are surrounded by a display of all their household valuables fastened to the saddle outside: see illustrations in MacMichael, *Tribes...*, pp. 192, 193.

Rás el Fíl is on the Blue Nile, south of Roṣayreṣ.

The tomb of the "Ḥág 'Abd el Salám el Begáwi" here mentioned is close to Wad Ḥasūna (see maps).

Músa Feríd is mentioned in No. 66.

"*He reared a crocodile...*": for the Arabic see Appendix 27. The reservoir mentioned was Um Ḳanáṭír. It is said at Wad Ḥasūna that the crocodile was brought from the river by Sheikh Ḥasan's slaves.

Eight pages of MS. are devoted to this biography.

ABC gives Sheikh Ḥasan's date as 968–1059 A.H. (ABC, x).

133. For this man see D 7, CI, CXXI and CCVII, and cp. Jackson (p. 65), who says he was of the family of Idrís wad el Arbáb.

Náṣir was the HAMAG vizier who ruled the FUNG kingdom from 1787 onwards: he was son of Muḥammad Abu el Kaylak (see D 7, CI *et seq*.).

134. Cp. No. 66 (para. 2). See also note to No. 187.

135. The ancestor of the "FARAḌIYYŪN."

"*Farḍ*" is "a term used for those rules and ordinances of religion which are said to have been established and enjoined by God Himself, as distinguished from those which are established upon the precept or practice of the Prophet, and which are called '*sunna*'" (Hughes, p. 124).

"*He compiled...*": for the Arabic see Appendix 28. The fact of his marriage and divorce is taken from No. 252.

136. Cp. No. 58.

For "*'ilm el kalám*" see note to para. VIII, *supra*.

"*Sannat el Wada'a*" is also mentioned in No. 111.

Ibráhím had a son Yūsef, as is mentioned incidentally in No. 33.

137. For "*mufti*" see Hughes, pp. 58 and 367.

139. Cp. Nos. 89 and 204. He was called "el Ḥaggar" and died, as we know from No. 204, in 1098 A.H. (1686 A.D.).

140. See note to No. 17. "Baḥr" may be an error for "Ḥaggar" (بحر for حجر).

141. See postscript to para. XIII, *supra*.

Sheikh Idrís (*q.v.* also in D 7, XXI) is one of the most famous of all the "saints" of the Sudan. His *ḳubba* is at el 'Aylafūn and his family (MAḤASS) reside there: cp. note to A 9, III. ABC gives his pedigree in full.

The present generation is the eighth after him, thus: Muḥammad ibn Barakát ibn Ḥammad ibn Muḥammad ibn Barakát ibn Meḍowi ibn Barakát ibn Ḥammad ibn el Sheikh Idrís.

His descendants state that the mother of Idrís was Fáṭima, surnamed "Ṣulḥa," the daughter of el Sheríf Ḥammad Abu Denána (*q.v.* C 8, note XXXII), and that he was born in 913 A.H. (1507 A.D.) and died in 1060 A.H. (1650 A.D.) aged 147 [lunar] years. This information is derived from their copy of the *Ṭabaḳát wad Ḍayfulla*: cp. also ABC, II; Jackson, p. 27; and D 7, III.

Idrís belonged to the Ḳardáḳáb section of Maḥass and was granted land at el 'Aylafūn by the Fung king. Previous to his coming, which was soon after the commencement of the Fung dynasty, the land had been occupied by slaves of the Fung, and hence its name, "'*ayla*" being, it is said, a Sudanese word for "slaves," and "fūn" being the same as "Fung": cp. No. 166, and ABC *passim*, where the village is called "el 'Ayl Fūng" and "'Aylat el Fūng."

The people of el 'Aylafūn are chiefly descendants of Barakát (see Tree 4), and with them are a few Sháíḳía (Ḥannakáb), Rikábía and Ga'aliín.

The biographies of three of Sheikh Idrís's sons are given, viz. Ḥammad, 'Araki and 'Abd el Ḳádir: he had also three other sons, viz. Muḥammad, Ramli and Belál. The first and second were by one mother, the third and fourth by another, and the fifth and sixth by another.

"*The first to light the fire....*" See Nos. 74 and 226 and notes thereto, and cp. No. 67. The present generation are followers of the Khatmía branch of the Ḳádiría *ṭariḳa*.

Sheikh 'Ísa el Ṭálib, is ancestor of the Ṭálbáb Bedayría now under the '*omda* of the Shukría Ḳadūráb. He was a cousin of the Bedayri "Wad el Turábi" (No. 125). His *ḳubba* is near the hill named after him, between el Kámlín and Gebel Ḳayli.

"*For example, his prophecy...*": for the Arabic see Appendix 29. This passage is full of valuable information: it gives us the cause of the war between the Fung and the 'Abdulláb of Ḳerri, and its result, the manner of the accession of Bádi "Síd el Ḳūm," and the duration of his dynasty and its limitations.

For the war with the 'Abdulláb see No. 126 and D 7, XX, and Jackson, p. 26.

'Adlán walad Áya reigned from 1610 to 1615 A.D. (Bruce), and Bádi "Síd el Ḳūm" from 1615 to 1621 (Bruce).

The reigns of Bádi's five descendants according to Bruce occupied from 1621 to 1729 (109 years), according to Cailliaud from 1611 to 1717 (107 years), and according to Trémaux's computation from 1623 to 1729 (107 years): the last named agrees most closely with the 110 (lunar) years of the text. Ounsa walad Bádi "was the last of the true royal family to rule" (cp. Jackson, p. 37).

142. The Bedayría of Wad el Turábi claim 'Ísa as a Bedayri and cousin of No. 125.

Nos. 7 and 34 were born at the same place.

143. "*A Ḥaḍari*": *i.e.* one of the Ḥuḍūr: cp. No. 66.

"*He was in prison...*": for the Arabic see Appendix 30.

145. He is mentioned also in No. 43, *q.v.* The obliterated word is probably "Ṣábūn," a not uncommon sobriquet, or "Ṣáḥib...."

By "*Saḳarnáwia*" is meant one of the Saḳárang of Teḳali (cp. BA, CXXXIX).

146. He is one of the 'Araki family, but lived some four generations later than Dafa'alla el 'Araki (see Nos. 193 and 219).

147. "*El Kaḍál.*" قَدَل is a word used in the Sudan to mean "he walked in a dignified manner."

Ounsa walad Náṣir reigned at Sennár from 1689–1701 (Bruce).

148. For "*Timya*" see No. 178.

149. "*Was nicknamed...*" is وبها كُنّي [جاب...حليمة...].

151. For *Kagoi*, spelt "*Kagóg*," see No. 132 and note.

Sheikh Ḥasan Ḥasūna was born at the same place, and his mother's maternal grandmother was, like No. 151, a Ṣáridía Khamaysía (*i.e.* one of the Ṣowárda).

152. The nickname means "Father of the Swordstick," or perhaps "Father of the sword of wood."

Shanbát is just north of Khartoum.

There is a "*Ṭalḥa*" between el Kámlín and Rufá'a, but the name is common. "*Dwayḥi*" denotes his tribe.

153. *Surkum* is a hill a few miles north of Omdurmán.

"*Gábri*," *i.e.* one of the Gawábra or descendants of Gábir.

"*There came to him...*": for the Arabic see Appendix 31.

"*Servants' beer*": Arabic "*merisa shalátít.*" "*Shalátít*" (*sing.* "*shaláti*") is, I am told by natives, a term for servants, whether freemen or slaves; and "*merisa shalátít*" might mean either "beer, the unclean drink of servants" (and cp. note to No. 66), or (more likely here) "such coarse beer as servants are given to drink." In either case the difference of opinion between Nos. 66 and 153 as to beer-drinking is noteworthy. The story ends as abruptly in the text as in the translation.

"*When the troops...*": for the Arabic see Appendix 32.

Another account of this rebellion, of which the leader was el Amín Arádib walad 'Agíb, will be found in D 7, xlii. The difference between the clerical and lay versions is worth noticing.

Note that "*Fung*" in this story is once spelt فنج and once فونج: the variation is common.

Bádi el Aḥmar ruled from 1701 to 1726 (Bruce).

Ḳerri, north of Khartoum, was the centre of the 'Abdulláb domain, and el Ís (Káwa) the headquarters of Fung power on the White Nile. El Ís, Bruce's "el Aice," is also Browne's "Allais, on the Bahr-el-abiad, the place which the ferry-boats frequent" (p. 452).

By "*slaves*" is meant the soldiery: the Fung army was almost entirely recruited from slaves drawn from such localities as Teḳali and Daier in southern Kordofán (cp. Bruce, *passim*).

El Ḥág 'Omára was apparently the patron saint of Khalíl el Rūmi.

154. *Khógali* is one of the most famous holy-men of the Sudan, and his *ḳubba* at el Ḥalfáya is very well known. For his biography and pedigree cp. ABC, iv.

For "*'ilm el kalám*" see note to para. viii, *supra*.

'Áyesha was the wife of No. 101, *q.v.*

"*It was characteristic...*": for the Arabic see Appendix 33. For the Shádhalía order see note to AB, li. For the different types of clothing affected by the religious orders see Hughes, p. 119 (*sub* "Faqir") and pp. 92 *et seq.* (*sub* "Dress").

"*Cotton shirts*" ("*gibba*"). An allusion to the patched shirt of the *fakir* that became so familiar at a later date, in the Mahdía.

"*The kings of* GA'AL," *i.e.* the *Meks* of the GA'ALIÍN. See note to No. 27.

Khógali's rising to greet the successor of Sheikh Idrís Arbáb would be in compliment to Sheikh Idrís as having been the representative of the Ḳádiría order (see No. 141), and (incidentally perhaps) as being of the same tribe (MAḤASS) as Khógali. Ṣughayerūn (*q.v.* No. 241) was the "lover" in the Ṣūfi sense of Sheikh Idrís and the successor of the AWLÁD GÁBIR, whose disciple and follower Khógali's grandfather Ibráhím had been: his successor was Sheikh el Zayn (No. 258).

The text later mentions in the following terms

ومن اخلاقه تعظيمه واجلاله اولاد المراتب مثل الركابية والمشايخة

that Khógali paid considerable respect to the RIKÁBÍA and MASHÁÍKHA "nobility" and others. The whole of this passage describing the attitude of superiority assumed by Khógali suggests a suspicion that interested parties may have obtained the insertion of these qualifying exceptions in the interests of their own prestige, or that a later copyist did not wish to give offence; otherwise "el Sha'aráwi's" remarks are somewhat inapposite.

"*Sheikh 'Abd el Ḳádir*" is of course "el Gíláni."

"*Aḥmad el Náṣiri*" is later on called "Muḥammad el Náṣir" (but see note to para. VII, *supra*). This story of the sandbank gives us the only intimation in so many words of the date of the composition of the *Ṭabaḳát*.

"*When the Sultan Bukr...*": for the Arabic see Appendix 34. Bukr reigned in Dárfūr from 1682 to 1722 (see Schurtz, p. 545). The story ends abruptly as in the translation.

"*As regards his original faith...*": for the Arabic see Appendix 35.

The "*awrád*" (*sing.* "*wird*") are portions of the Ḳurán set aside for daily reading.

"*He died...*": for the Arabic see Appendix 36.

Where the date is in the twelfth century the author as a rule omits the first two figures: if the eleventh or thirteenth century is intended he always inserts them.

155. "*Abu Sabíb*" is here written ابسبيب ("Absabíb").

156. "*The 40 disciples*": *sc.* of Ibráhím el Būlád (cp. Nos. 23 and 254).

The holy-men whose names begin with M are divided into two groups by the author, the northern and the southern: the following are the southern group: Nos. 157, 159, 166, 168, 169, 174, 177, 179, 182, 183, 184, 185, 186, 188, 190, 192, 193, 198, 200, 201, 205, 209, 210. The last two of these to be treated of by the author are Nos. 157 and 192 (Maḥmūd el 'Araki and his son Muḥammad), and at the close of the latter's biography, and before commencing the northern group, the author says:

فلما فرغنا علي ما يسره اسر لنا من فضل اعيان الصعيد انتقلنا نتكل علي
اعيان السافل من حرف الميم

("Having completed the pleasurable task of relating the virtues of the notables of the south, we transfer our attention to the notables of the north whose names begin with M.")

All the M's, excepting the numbers quoted, above fall into the northern group. The dividing line between the two is, roughly speaking, the latitude of the junction of the White and Blue Niles.

157. "*Born on the White* [*Nile*]" (مولده بالابيض). See note to para. v, *supra*, for remarks upon this, and "period of probation" ("'*idda*"), and "*Rágil*."

Practically the whole of this biography is here translated, but Maḥmūd lived too early for the author to know much about him: he is mentioned in Jackson, p. 22.

For *el Banūfari* see No. 17 and for *el Ag'hūri* No. 22.

"*Studied under*" is تعلموا عند; "*was a follower of*" is اخذ عن.

"*Sheikh Khógali said*..." is

قال الشيخ خوجلي كان من الخرطوم الي اليس سبعة عشر مدرسة كلها خربتها شلك وام لحم

For *el Ís* cp. 153 (note); and for "*Um Laḥm*" No. 84. We may infer from this passage that there was a successful raid made by the SHILLUK from the upper reaches of the White Nile between about 940 A.H. (Maḥmūd's approximate date: see paras. IV to VI, *supra*) and 1095 A.H. (*i.e.* 1533 to 1684 A.D.).

158. For *Zóra* see BA, CLIX and A 11, XX.

The GHUBUSH are the AWLÁD EL AGHBASH (Tree 2).

159. Cp. Nos. 111 and 3.

161. "*The former father of*...": the Arabic is فولد قطبي والد الفقيه ابراهيم, and this would make Ḳuṭbi grandfather of Ibráhím. The addition of ه to the first word makes the sense more correct.

"*El Rayda*" is presumably the name of Muḥammad's mother. The pronouns in this passage are characteristically vague, but the meaning is clear.

El Ḳóz is the "Goos" of Bruce's map, lying some miles east-north-east of the junction of the Atbara with the Nile.

162. This *Sheikh ibn Medani* is son of No. 164, called, apparently, after his father's half-brother (No. 236): cp. Nos. 164 and 15.

"*The* MEDANIYYŪN *are*..." is as follows: المدنيين الذهب ونحن الفضة. The MEDANIYYŪN are the descendants of Medani el Náṭiḳ (*i.e.* Nos. 194, 162, etc.), and "we" denotes the descendants of Um Gadayn, *i.e.* of a different mother.

163. He was no doubt called "el Ṭiár" because of his supposed power of transporting himself through the air from place to place. For his death see No. 164.

164. *Um Gadayn* was evidently the mother's name.

"*Now Medani el Náṭiḳ died*...": for the Arabic see Appendix 37.

165. *Ounsa ibn Náṣir* reigned from 1689 to 1701 A.D., according to Bruce; and as "el Meḍowi" died in 1684 Cailliaud's date (1675–1687) is probably nearer the truth.

166. "*El 'Ayl Fung*" (العيل فنج) is now called "el 'Aylafūn" (maps, "Eilafun"): see No. 141 (note).

Gedíd is on the west bank of the Blue Nile opposite el 'Aylafūn: as there are three villages there now they are generally called, in the plural, "el Gedáid."

Elti is on the same bank as, and south of, Gedíd.

167. His tomb is with that of his father at Abu Delayḳ.

168. *Kutráng* is a village on the east bank of the Blue Nile above el 'Aylafūn. This man's tomb is at Wad Digays, south of Um Dubbán, east of Kutráng.

169. *El Sheḳayḳ* is west of the White Nile between el Dueim and Omdurmán.

170. "*His large commentary*...": for the Arabic see Appendix 38.

"*The Senūssia*" is a work on *tawḥid* ("doctrine of unity"). For *sharaḥ* ("commentary") see Hughes, p. 572.

171. "*His companion*..." is

وصحب في التصوف الشيخ دفع الله العركي

For *el Ḳubia* see No. 11.

172. Cp. No. 17.

174. See No. 186.

175. "*He united*...": the Arabic of this common phrase is

كان ممن جمع بين العلم والعمل

The author mentions in this biography that one of Muḥammad ibn 'Abd el Raḥman's disciples gave him the information he has written in the *Ṭabaḳát* concerning him.

177. The author states that one of this man's disciples, *faḳir* Musṭafa ibn Abu Sháma, gave him the information retailed here. See No. 2.

178. Cp. No. 148. Timya was not literally the father but the great-great-grandfather of No. 175. The name Timya is here written تِمْيَه [for تَمِيَّه], but in No. 148 it is once written تيمة and once تميه.

"*His father*" is 'Ali ibn Barri, and "'*Araki*" is 'Abdulla el 'Araki, father of No. 237, and brother of No. 178.

"*The matting*" ("*el bursh*") would be for the *Khalífa* to sit upon (cp. No. 66).

For the Arabic of the text see Appendix 39.

180. *Tanḳási* Island is near Debba in Dongola Province.

181. "*He was one of*...": for the Arabic see Appendix 40.

183. The *ḳubbas* of this man and of his son 'Abd el Raḥman are close to Basháḳira West: they are of red brick and unplastered.

185. *Medani* is father of No. 193.

186. The form "*el Luḳr*" occurs in Nos. 12 and 174, though here "el Ághir" is used.

Um 'Uḳud [maps, "Um Mughud"] and *Elti* lie on the west bank of the Blue Nile below el Kámlín.

187. *Ounsa walad Náṣir* reigned 1689–1701 (Bruce).

This Muḥammad is given the surname of "el Níri" in No. 90 (*q.v.*).

In the text of No. 134 mention is made of "Ṣughayerūn and 'Abd el Hádi, the sons of Sheikh Muḥammad walad Dólíb."

189. "*Ibn Ḥág*" is qualified by قيل (*i.e.* "said to be son of, etc.").

"*King Dekín of Kordofál*" is الملك دكين من دار كردفال. See note to No. 207.

For *Ghulámulla* see No. 222.

There occur in this biography the words "...What my grandfather, Mūsa walad Ría, told me..." (ما حدثني به جدي موسي ولد رية), and it would appear therefore that the author's mother was probably the daughter of this Mūsa and a Kahlía by race: see No. 85.

190. "*His Sheikh*": *i.e.* Tág el Dín el Bahári.

El Mundara is a hill about halfway between el Kámlín and the Atbara: the tomb of No. 190 is to be seen there.

191. A very famous holy-man of the DAHMASHÍA section of BEDAYRÍA. His present *Khalífa* resides at Omdurmán and is a merchant held in considerable respect. See Jackson, p. 27, but "'Ali" is there an error for "Muḥammad." The fabled reason of his nickname is that he was born with a bracelet of gold on his wrist, but see Vol. I, p. 177.

For "*holy-man*" ("*Rágil*") see No. 44, note.

Bádi ibn Rubáṭ reigned 1651 to 1689 (Bruce).

"*He ruled...*": this phrase occurs elsewhere in the *Ṭabaḳát in toto*.

For the *Gin* see Hughes, pp. 133–138.

193. The town of Wad Medani, capital of the Blue Nile Province, is so named after this man. He was a Buṣaylábi from Upper Egypt, and so far as one can deduce from the *Ṭabaḳát* he probably died about 1700 A.D.

El Nūba is a village on the Blue Nile a short distance above Khartoum: it is reputed to have been founded by some NŪBA from el Ḥaráza in Kordofán.

"*He was buried..., etc.*" is دفن في حلته المشهورة به.

194. "*Now the Muḥammads...*" is

والمحمدون الذى اشتركوا فى اسم واحد وفى ابوا واحد وعصر واحد ثلاثة

By "*one father*" is meant "fathers of the same name."

195. Cp. Jackson, pp. 26, 27.

For *Sálim el Sanhūri* see note to AB, IV. He died in 1606 A.D.

196. "*El Ḳóz*" is "Ḳóz walad Ḍiáb" (cp. No. 239).

198. Cp. No. 191, *re* Sharáū.

200. For *Sálim el Máídi* see also No. 204; and cp. No. 108.

"*Máídi*" is now often pronounced, and spelt, "Mágdi": see note to No. 60 on this point. A few miles south of el Kámlín is a village called "Wad el Mágdi" and it is probable this was the home of No. 200 or of No. 108.

202. *Ámna* is mentioned also in No. 196.

204. "*One of his miracles...*": for the Arabic see Appendix 41.

For "*Um Ḥinayḍil*" see note to No. 15.

Of the year 1098 the text says "The year of the Nile which collected the people after the dispersion of *Um Laḥm*, viz. 1098"

(سنة النيل اللمّم الناس من نجعة ام لحم وهي سنة ١٠٩٨)

Um Laḥm, the famine year, was 1095 (see No. 84), and presumably in 1098 there was a high Nile which relieved the distress caused by 1095.

205. Jackson (*Yacubabi Tribe*) gives Medani as son of Muḥammad el Zayn.

206. From No. 8 we know this man was a Gáma'i by tribe. For Náfa'i see Nos. 207 and 8.

207. "*He died...*": for the Arabic see Appendix 42.

Gunḳul was king of the MUSABA'ÁT, a branch of the FŪR who ruled in Kordofán. In the reign of Mūsa ibn Sulaymán (Schurtz, 1637–1682) Gunḳul laid claim to the throne of Dárfūr. For his pedigree, etc., see MacMichael, *Tribes...*, p. 55 (note): he was the father of the 'Ísáwi mentioned later; and the latter was father of the famous Háshim.

King Dekín is mentioned again in No. 189: he appears to have been the FUNG representative in Kordofán, and the seat of his power would be near Teḳali and Daier, the locality intended by "their country."

Náfa'i is mentioned *passim*, *e.g.* in No. 206. The author probably means to denote by "He said 'raise the sword'" that Náfa'i was executed on the spot, but this is not certain.

I do not know what قبقب عليهم means, but have translated it "set off to attack them."

208. See note to No. 124.

"*Rendered obedience*" is انقادت له, *i.e.* he was their *Sheikh*.

209. This *Mūsa* is generally known as "Abu Ḳussa," and was one of the chief of the YA'AḲŪBÁB: see Nos. 170 and 217. He and his brother (No. 111) have a *ḳubba* at Sabíl (see No. 111, note).

"*Marḥab*" is Marḥaba bint Faḍl (see Jackson, *Yacubabi Tribe*).

211. The *feki* Ṣughayerūn mentioned here is claimed as ancestor by the DÓÁLÍB in Kordofán (see MacMichael, *Tribes...*, p. 93).

212. For *el Kerrada* see No. 81.

"*He was called...*": for the Arabic see Appendix 43.

213. "*In front of*" is "east of," *i.e.* 15 miles north-north-west of Gebel Rera, between Abu Delayḳ and the Atbara.

214. This man has a conspicuous white *ḳubba* at el Ḥilália. See note to No. 125. Nanna is said to have had a son Mūsa. His name is spelt in D 3 نَنّ.

216. The "*dolayb*" palm is *Borassus flabellifer*.

"*I swear by Sheikh...*": for the Arabic see Appendix 44. Tág el Dín was the *Sheikh* of this family: cp. No. 62, where the anecdote here related is also given.

221. Cp. C 7, III.

222. For the Arabic of the first part of this biography see Appendix 45.

For the genealogical items given in this biography cp. D 1, paras. CIV to CXXIV and BA, CLXXXI *et seq.*

Ḳandil el 'Óni is possibly the "Ḳandíl el Ṣáridi" of No. 58. 'Ón was a descendant of 'Ámir ibn Dhubián, one of whose brothers was Ṣárid (ancestor of the Ṣowárda) and another was Shatír the ancestor of Rikáb and Rubáṭ (see BA). If these two Ḳandíls are one man it may be noted that the Barri family (No. 58, etc.) were related on their mother's side with the Rikábía of Dongola.

"*The four Sheikhs*" are No. 17 and his three brothers.

"*Nás*" means, and is often translated, "the people of...," *i.e.* (here) "the descendants of."

"*El Feríd*" denotes literally an only son.

226. "*He was the third...*" apparently Tág el Dín (No. 67) is not counted. The other two were Bedowi wad Abu Delayḳ and Idrís Arbáb (see No. 74 and note).

It is mentioned incidentally in this biography that Ṣáliḥ's paternal uncles were named Ṣáliḥ Abu Náíb and el Zayn respectively; and from No. 27 (*q.v.*) we know there were also two others, Bedowi and Ḥegázi.

The invasion of Shendi alluded to was in 1706 A.D. (see No. 74).

"*I saw Sheikh 'Abd el Ḳádir...,*" *sc.* "el Gíláni, in a vision."

"*Sheikh Ṣáliḥ related...*": for the Arabic see Appendix 46.

228. For *el Sayál* see No. 251. It is in the Gezíra.

"*A Ḳhálidi,*" *i.e.* one of the Khowálda.

230. "*El Zaghrát*" means one who makes the "*zagharít,*" *i.e.* the shrill cry of "loo-loo-loo" generally used by women. It is said that Selmán when alone in the wilds would make this noise and the wild gazelle and ariel would come to him to be milked. He was a Ga'ali, and was buried at Wad Sáḳ Órṭa near Rufá'a. A number of his descendants live at Abu 'Ushara and el Sellama, on the Blue Nile, south of el Kámlín.

The "*zagharít*" is not purely African. Burton speaks of it at Mekka. (See *Pilgrimage...*, II, 159.)

233. He is elsewhere called Muḥammad Serḥán el 'Ūdi.

234. *Gerf* (or Gerayf) *Ḳumr* is on the east bank of the Blue Nile, just outside Khartoum.

235. "*He became...*": for the Arabic see Appendix 47.

236. *Málik* was one of the Awlád Um Gadayn and a half-brother of Sheikh el Á'sir.

"*And miracles...*": for the Arabic see Appendix 48.

'Othmán walad Ḥammad was the liberator of the Sháíḳía from the yoke of the Fung. A traditional account of this incident is in Nicholls ("*The Shaiḳiya*"), pp. 10–14, from which it would appear that the Sháíḳía about 1690 (I should say a few years earlier) quarrelled with the 'Abdullábi viceroy, defeated him by a ruse, and obtained their independence.

Poncet was at Korti in 1699 and says (p. 15): "Whereas the People who are beyond Korti upon the River Nile are in Rebellion against the King of Sennár, and that they Pillage the Caravans..., they are forced to keep at a Distance from the Banks of the River and...to enter into the Great Desert of Bihouda...": the reference is certainly to the Sháíḳía, who were notorious freebooters. See Vol. I, p. 216. 'Othmán is mentioned again in No. 243 (*q.v.*).

The account given by Nicholls varies from that of D 3 as to the name of the FUNG king and of the 'ABDULLÁB sheikh: D 3 is much more likely to be right.

'Ali walad 'Othmán, who occurs again in No. 58, was one of the 'ABDULLÁB of Ḳerri. The Arabic is very vague and confused, but it may be the SHÁÍḲÍA defeated the army of the 'ABDULLÁB and that the leader of the latter then sent word of the defeat to his FUNG suzerain at Sennár and (possibly) seized the opportunity to join forces with the SHÁÍḲÍA against the FUNG.

"*He came out of his retreat*": "he" must refer to Sheikh although the Arabic hardly admits of it as it stands: cp. note to No. 12. The whole story is somewhat confused.

Kagabi is in the SHÁÍḲÍA country.

"*Small-pox*": cp. No. 243.

238. A Mashaykhi. A section of MASHÁÍKHA called themselves SHERAFELDINÁB after him. For his father see No. 84.

239. *A Halanḳi*, see No. 196.

240. For *Ḥammad el Samiḥ* see No. 226.

241. This biography is given in its entirety in Appendix 49 (in Arabic).

For the AWLÁD GÁBIR and their sister Fáṭima see Nos. 17 and 222 and notes.

"*The lover of el Sheikh Idris*": see note to No. 154.

"*Four sáḳias*": *i.e.* the land of 4 *sáḳias*, *i.e.* about 40 acres of riverain land. An '*ūd* is a variable measure. The word for a spear here is "*ṣaláṭia*," *i.e.* the long broad-bladed spear used by horsemen and not the smaller, generally barbed, throwing spear. Grants of land merely mention a given breadth parallel to the river, and the grantee can push his cultivation as far inland, within this limit, as the levels of the ground and the nature of its soil and the water-raising capacity of his water-wheel permit. An average water-wheel cultivates perhaps seven acres, but under favourable conditions ten acres can be watered.

Karkóg: see note to No. 126.

For "*el Sayyid el Khiḍr*" see Hughes, p. 272. He is a mysterious prophet. "Some say he lived in the time of Abraham and that he is still alive in the flesh, and most of the religious and Ṣūfi mystics are agreed upon this point, and some have declared that they have seen him." He is sometimes confounded with Elias, sometimes with Phineas, sometimes with St George of England! He is generally supposed to have drunk of the fountain of life. See also Sell (pp. 106, 107): he is said to be the intermediary between God and the founder of a religious order, and to exercise great influence with holy-men and to unveil the future to them and give them supernatural powers.

El Berḳáni: *i.e.* of the BERÁḲNA section.

"*Five daughters*": only three are mentioned by name.

"*sealings*": see note to No. 17.

"*the rainfall...*": see note to No. 2.

242. "*Taught by*": تفقه على; "*was a follower of*" سلك الطريق علي.

243. For the "*fight*" mentioned cp. No. 236.

"*The year after small-pox year*": cp. No. 237: the Arabic is توفي عقب الجدري.

244. *El Sayál*: cp. No. 251.

246. The brother of No. 77.

248. "*El Fūrayn*": the text here gives العورين, but in No. 206 we have الفورين.

250. The father of No. 76. He is said to be buried near Gebel Arang in Mefáza district.

252. The application of a tribal name, "el Fezári," as a nickname to a member of the MAḤASS tribe, which is totally distinct from the FEZÁRA, is analogous to the use of "el Guhani" in the case of 'Abdulla el Guhani (see BA, LVIII).

254. Cp. No. 156. This Ya'aḳūb is the eponymous ancestor of the YA'AḲŪBÁB (see Jackson, *Yacubabi Tribe*).

255. A section of the MASHÁÍKHA are called MUGELLIÁB after this man's father. Mugelli is said to have died in Egypt in Zerníkh Island and to have been a descendant of the Khalífa Abu Bukr. Cp. No. 238, and see A 2, XXXVII and ABC, LIV.

"*And the king*...": for the Arabic see Appendix 50.

It is a not uncommon expression to say that a courtyard, *e.g.*, is "big enough for a horse to gallop in," and the phrase "as much land as his horse could encompass" probably means, as it has been explained by natives, "as much land as a horse could gallop round."

The word "*míl*" means properly a distance as far as one can see under normal circumstances. Burton (*Pilgrimage*..., II, 63) defines a "*mil*" as 1000 paces.

256. He died in 1802 (see D 7, CLII).

259. *Bádi walad Rubáṭ* reigned from 1651 to 1689 (Bruce).

For *Dekin* see note to No. 207.

APPENDIX I

(Paras. IV to XIII)

اعلم ان الفنج ملكت ارض النوبه وتقلبت عليها اول القرن العاشر سنة عشرة بعد التسعماية وخطت مدينه سنار خطاها الملك عمارة ...قس[1] وحطت[2] مدينه اربجي قبلها بثلاثين سنه خطاها حجاز بن معين ولم تشتمر[3] فى تلك البلاد مدرسة علم ولا قرءان يقال ان الرجل يطلق المراة ويتزوجها غيره في نهارها من غير عدة حتي قدم الشيخ ...[4] القصير العركي من مصر وعلم الناس العدة وسكن الابيض وبنا له قصر يعرف اءلان بقصر محمود وفي اول النصف الثاني من القرن العاسر[5] ولي السلطان عماره ابو سكيكين الشيخ عجيب المانجلك ففي اول ملكه قدم الشيخ ابراهيم البولاد من مصر الي دار الشايقية ودرس فيها خليل والرسالة وانتشر علم الفقيه فى الجزيرة ثم بعد يسير قدم الشيخ تاج الدين البهار[6] من بغداد وادخل طريق الصوفية في دار الفنج ثم قدم التلمسانى المغرب[7] على الشيخ محمد بن عيسي سوار الذهب وسلكه طريق القوم وعلمه علم الكلام وعلوم القرءان بتجويد[8] وروايات ونحوها وانتشر علم التوحيد والتجويد في الجزيرة لانه اخذ عليه القرءان عبدالله الاغبش ونصر ولد[9] الفقيه ابو سنينه في اربجي ثم طهرت ولايه الشيخ ادريس من غير شيخ قدم عليه قيل اخذ من الرسول وقيل قدم عليه رجل من المغرب بالخطوة اسمه عبد الكاف وبعد يسير طهرت ولاية الشيخ حسن ولد حسونه بمدة من رسول الله صلى الله عليه وسلم ثم قدم الشيخ محمد بن قدم دار بربر وادخل فيها مذهب الشافعى وانتشر مذهبه فى الجزيرة ثم قدمت المشايخة وخطت مدينه الحلفاية

[1] for دنقس (page torn).
[2] for خطت.
[3] for تستمر.
[4] *sc.* راجل.
[5] for العاشر.
[6] for البهاري.
[7] for المغربي.
[8] written بجوتيد.
[9] for والد.

APPENDIX 2

(From No. 11)

و قال لها اكتبي صداقك لبناتي فلما فعلت ذلك طلقها فذهبت الي الفقيه حمد اوهبت له نفسها وعفت من صداقها وتزوجها وقالت له انا مظلومة من عبد المحمود غصب شرطي بدورك ترد لي شرطي منه فان الفقيه حمد صدقها في قولها وشكاه على الجنود فى نزولهم في ابو زريبة قالوا له ما بندخل في حديثكم وكتب له الفقيه حمد كتابا فى لوح وصورته من عند حمد بن مريم الى عند عبد المطرود اما قال الله تعالى وءاتوا النسا صدقاتهن نحلة وانت خالفت كتاب الله وغصبت صداق المرة[1] انت ماك عبد المحمود عبد المطرود هو ابليس فاعطا الكتاب لفقير فزاري [قراري؟] فقال له انت حواري وخرجتك تجيب لي مثل هذا الجواب والفقير توفاه الله في يومه والفقيه حمد نازل في حلته الفى ام درمان انطلقت النار اكلت جميع خلواته والخلوة الذى فيها احاطت النار بجميع جهاتها قالوا له الناس امرق قال ما بمرق اترك كتبي فدخل عليه احمد بن على العونابي فشاله بعنقريبه مرقه ثم بنوا الخلوات بالحجر فسرجت النار في الحجر وقد راين[2] بخط الفقيه حمد قال بعد مروقي من النار اعتقدته العوام ونفسه تعجبت منه قال والشي هذا كله سوته الحسنه قالت غصب صداقي الله حسيبها انتهي

[1] for المراة.   [2] for راينا.

APPENDIX 3

(From No. 17)

اولاد جابر الاربعة كالطبايع الاربعة كل واحد له خاصية اعلمهم ابراهيم واصلحهم عبد الرحمن واورعهم اسماعيل واعبدهم عبدالرحمن[1] واختهم فاطمة ام بن سرحان نظيرتهم في العلم والدين

[1] for عبدالرحيم.

APPENDIX 4

(From No. 27)

وجاءته زوجة الملك عدلان وقالت له يا سيدى وليداتي مات بدورك تسئل الله يعوضنى اياهم قال لها اديتك واديتك الي خمسة عقد فولدت خمسة عيال هم اجداد العدلاناب

APPENDIX 5

(No. 46)

ابوا دليق عم الشيخ بدوي سلك طريق القوم علي الشيخ سلمان الطوالي وانقطع الي الله ولبس الجبب والدلاقين وسمى ابو دليق وسمى ذنب العقرب لكونه لايحتمل امور الظلمة سريع العضب لهم وسلك وارشد وممن اخذ عليه طريق القوم بن اخيه الشيخ بدوي وله من الاولاد حسين وعايشة ولما دنع الوفاة قالوا له من الخليفه بعدك قال عايشة بنتي وتزوج بها الشيخ بدوى وولد منها النقر والشيخ مضوي وعبدالله وتاج الدين وتوفي ودفن فى النجفة وقبره ظاهر

APPENDIX 6

(From No. 51)

ابوه نصر قرا القرءان واحكامه على الشيخ محمد بن عيسي واشار له بتزويج ام ابوا سنينة وذلك ان الشيخ محمد رءاها وهي صغيرة فقال له تزوج هذه البنية تجيب لك ولدا صالحا قال له تجيبك انت فقال في الثالثة او الرابعة تجيبني وذلك ان اهلها يسافروا من دنقلة الي البويض بارض الابواب فلحقها وتزوج بها فولد له ابو سنينة ثم سكن مدينة اربجي و درس بها الناس

APPENDIX 7

(From No. 52)

وسبب وفاته قتلته سراريه فرضخا[1] راسه وهو نايم بالحجارة قاتلهن الله

[1] for فرضخن.

APPENDIX 8

(From No. 58)

فعزلوا من الدرجة الي زماننا هذا فان خضر ولده شاخ بعد العجيل ستة شهو ر ثم عزل ومسمار ولد ولده عجيب شهران بعد الشيخ عبدالله ثم عزل

APPENDIX 9

(No. 60)

علي ولد عشيب مولد ببندر ضنقله وطلب العلم عند الشيخ محمد البنوفري بمصر وبرع فيه فسكن دار الصعيد وبنا له الشيخ عجيب الكبير مسجد وتصدق عليه ملك الفنج بديار كثيرة في الشرق والهويْ وفي دار المطر وولى القضا وعدله فيه وحكم بالمتفق عليه والقوي من الخلاف وكان رفيق الشيخ ابراهيم البولاد بن جابر في طلب العلم بمصر ويقال كل منهما دعا علي صاحبه دعوة فاستجبت فيه فدعا الشيخ علي ولد عشيب علي الشيخ ابراهيم البولاد فقال له الله يقصر عمرك صبي جميع المسلة[1] السلوك تجيب فيها وقال له البولاد الله لاينفع بعلمك فان البولاد تدريسه سبعة سنين وعلم فيها اربعين انسانا ثم توفاه الله والشيخ علي لم يبلغنا له تدريس له بال الا ان عندهم[2] القضا ودفن بالعيدي وقبره ظاهر والعشيباب كلهم ذريته

[1] for المسالة. [2] for عنده.

APPENDIX 10

(From No. 63)

وكان اذا سمع شعره ينشده غيره يبكي ويطير في الهوى وقد شوهد ذلك منه مرارا

APPENDIX 11

(From No. 66)

الشيخ محمد بن عيسي لما دنع الوفاة قالت له زوجته بنت الملك حسن ولد كشكش[1] ملك ضنقلة ام حلالي ولده اولادك الكبار رشدتهم اما وليدي من ليه[2] قال لها عليك بالحضري جاءت وجابت اسورتها وحجولها وقالت له مرادي تقعد وليدي في محل ابوه فقال له ولد شيخي اقعد فوق سجادتي نقعد فقام حام الخلوه ثم جاء برك في وجهه فاخذ يده فقبلها وقال له قعدتك في مكان ابوك فان حلالي حطي[3] عند الفونج والعرب حظا وافرا وولي القضا وتدريس جميع فنون العلم

[1] for كشاش. [2] for له. [3] for حظي.

APPENDIX 12

(From No. 66)

جاءه رجل يقال له بن عباد كان فاسقا بالحوارح[1] كلها قال له عندي ساقية معيشة اعتيك فيها ربع قال له ايش تدور عندي قال بدور الليل[2] الله قال له اعطيتك ربع اليل الله فان الرجل تاب واستغفر ثم جاءه ثانيا قال له كملت لك النصف الاخر قال له اعطيتك نصف اليل الله فمشا في الخير والزيادة ثم جاءه قال له اديتك الساقية كلها ثم قال له اديتك اليل الله كله فوقع مغشيا عليه ايام حتي فاق فصار من اولياء الله تعالى

[1] for حوارج. [2] for اليل.

APPENDIX 13

(From No. 66)

وان مسمار ولد عريبي في سفره الي ضنقلة سنة سبعين بعد الالف خرب المراتب وكسر الاحواه[1] فاستغاث به الناس وقال لهم خرابه علي يد الرجل الاصفر القصير الاصلع اما انا ضامن لكم شيخ قري ما بج[2] في ضنقلة فان جاء عوضة حي صفوا له المريسة يشربها وان مات صبوها فوق قبره قلت فهذه الوقايع من الشيخ كثيرهم بلغ مبلغ التواتر وهي جايزه كتاب وسنة واحماع[3] انتهي

[1] for اجواه. [2] for بيجي. [3] for اجماع.

APPENDIX 14

(From No. 67)

اسمه محمد والبهاري نعته ماخوذ من قولهم قمر باهر مضي وسمي بذلك لضيا وجهه ريحانة من اخباره هو الشيخ الامام القطب الرباني والغوث الصمداني خليفة الشيخ عبد القادر الجيلاني مولده ببغداد وحج الي بيت الله الحرام ومن[1] قدم بلاد السودان باذن من رسول الله صلى الله عليه وسلم والشيخ عبد القادر الجيلاني وقدم مع داوود بن عبد الجليل ابو الحاج سعيد جد ناس العِيدَيْ وقدومه اول النصف الثانى من القرن العاشر اول ملك الشيخ عجيب وسكن مع داوود في واد الشعير ضهرت[2] ام عظام

[1] for منه. [2] for ضهرة.

APPENDIX 15

(From No. 73)

وحكى ان الشيخ باسبار تزوج بامراة حمدية وطلقها ثم جاء ابن عم لها حَمَدِي تزوجها وكان حوار الشيخ عبد الرازق ابو قرون فنهاه من ذلك ولم ينتهن وقال لشيخه انت تكافيه مني فقال له لا تقرب البحر الناس بحريين يقال ان ذلك الرجل لم يقرب البحر سنين حتي ان زوجته حملت فولدت وورد بالقرب لعقيقة ولده اول ما ادخل كراعه في البحر اختطفه تمساح فوضه حتى مات ثم رماه في ساحل البحر وباسبار تحت السدرات صاح شاله شاله علي ولدي وعلي يوميذ ولدا صغير له عُرُف انتهي

APPENDIX 16

(From No. 74)

ترددت في النار هل اوقدها في الضهرا او ادلي البحر اوقدها في سلمة عجب رايت رسول الله صلى الله عليه وسلم قال لي اسكن الارض الحمرا مع الناس الحمر والارض الحمرا قلعت[1] النجفة والناس الحمر البطاحين بنيت خلوة قدامها راكوبة رجلا من المرقوماب[2] قتل ولد الشيخ نعيم البطحاني والرجل وقع عندي وادخلته في الخلوة وقعدت في الراكوبة دخلوا عليه قتلوه قالوا الي الشيخ نعيم يزرط العبرات وانت مسوي لك وقاعة طلقوا النار في الخلوة ابت ما تاكلها قلت ما الناس ما بسكن معاهم[3] رايت الرسول ثانيا انا قاعد في وجهه رايت رايت نملا كثيرا من الجهات الاربعة يمشي طالبه قلت يا سيدنا يا رسول الله ايش هذا النمل قال وقاعك اقعد في مكانك ما يجيهم احد تران[4] يا شريف في هذا المكان ناكل رزقنا ونرجي اجلنا

[1] for قلعة.
[2] for المرغوماب.
[3] for معهم.
[4] for تراني.

APPENDIX 17

(From No. 82)

وكان من ارباب الاحوال وقال للشيخ صالح ولد بان النقا يكن لك شان عظيم يجوك الاوليا يجلسوك وتوقد نار عبد القادر

APPENDIX 18

(No. 90)

دوليب نسي هو محمد الضرير بن ادريس بن دوليب ومعني نسي في لغة الضناقلة هو ولد الولد وكانت مجاهدته فوق الحد وكان يدخل للذكر والعبادة الخلوات المربعات ومحل اربعين خلوة فى جبل البرص وكل خلوة اربعين يوما والبرص جبل من بين دار الشايقية وضنقلة وناس ضنقلة يقول اللهم ارزقنا عبادة دوليب نسي وكرامة حبيب نسى وعلم ولد عيسي وله من الاولاد الشيخ محمد النيري وسياتى في حرف الميم والفقيه ادريس وهو مقري القرءان واحكامه ومكى ومدني [مدين ?or] وهما فاضلين ودفن بالدبة وجميع الدواليب نسله انتهى

APPENDIX 19

(From No. 119)

أدركوا زمن الشيخ دفع الله صغارا فقال للشيخ محمد ارشادك على يد حمد ولدي وقال لدفع الله ولد الشافعي مددك على يد الشيخ عبدالله انتهى

APPENDIX 20

(From No. 124)

حمد بن محمد بن علي المشيخي المشهور عند الناس بامه مريم امها محسية مشيرفية من بنات ولد قدال الولي وابوها ولد كشيب من اوليا ابو نجيلة الذين تزار قبورهم وهو مسلمي الاصل

APPENDIX 21

(From No. 125)

قرا خليل على الفقيه محمد بن التنقار في مويس وبرع فيه فاخذ عشر ختمات ثم انتحل مذهب التصوف وانقطع الي الله وتزهد وسلك علي الشيخ دفع الله وارشده...... ولما دنع الوفاة قال للناس الدنيا انفقدب[1] فقيرها واميرها ما بيرقعوها التاخذ منه السلطنة الحية

[1] for انفقدت.

APPENDIX 22

(From No. 127)

عبد السلام مشهور بسواق الركا يوردوه بالركا للبحر يسوقهما بالمطرق . . . وابو دليق ولد عبد السلام مشهور بيلام الاسد وذلك انه بيقرا عند الشيخ مسكين الخفي وفزع للحطب فقتل الاسد حماره

APPENDIX 23

(From No. 130)

خاله الشيخ محمد بن سرحان مرض قيل له شفاك في العجوة وكانت مفقودة فى البلد فجابها لهم حمودة رضي الله عنه من الريف وكانت سبب شفاوه وشرح على خليل حاشية مفيدة صورة خاله واولاد جابر انتهي

APPENDIX 24

(From No. 132)

حسن بن حسونة بن الحاج موسي قدم من المغرب من جزيرة الخضرا من [دا]ر الاندلس تزوج في المسلمية فولد حسونة وقال وضعت نسلي في اصلي وحسونة تزوج بنت خاله فاطمة بنت وحشية اخت الحاج لقاني وامها صاردية خميسية وولد حسونة من فاطمة اربعة الشيخ حسن والعجمي وسوار والحاجة نفيسة واولاد فاطمة الاربعة عقروا ما ولد وولد الشيخ بالجزيرة كجوج ريحان من اخباره

APPENDIX 25

(From No. 132)

طلع الي الدرووبة وقنطور الحمار حفر ام قناطير حفيره وسعي العبيد وركبهم الخيل وقال بحرس بهم سعيتي والمتواتر عند الناس خمسماية عبد كل واحد شايل سيف قبعه وابزيمه ومحاحيره فضة وليهم[1] سيد قوم وجندي وعكاكيز وان الخيل المعدات يجلبوها الي تقلي ودار برق[2](?) ودارفور وسنار واولاد عجيب ورقيقه سار حلالا ومن كثرت[3] الزيارات زربوا المهار

[1] for ولهم. [2] written يبق. [3] for كثرة.

APPENDIX 26

(From No. 132)

وزينه باصبعه بلا موس واوصي لخمسة فقرا بثلث ماله كل فقير جاءه ستة وثلاثين راس في رقيق الخدمة الرقيق الاعيان والفرسان ساقوا سادهم[1] بعضهم ادلوا سنار وبعضهم شالوا راس الفيل

[1] for سيادهم.

APPENDIX 27

(From No. 132)

وكان من قضاء الله وقدره ربا تمساحا في الحفير وكثر ضرره فضربه ببندق فانعكس الشرار عليه وكان سبب موته وتوفي سنة خمسة وسبعين بعد الالف وفي ذلك طلع كوكب الدين

APPENDIX 28

(From No. 135)

والف الحاشية المشهورة بالفرضية فى علم الفريض ولقب بالفرض[1] لانه كان له باعا طويلا فى الفريض

[1] for بالفرضي.

APPENDIX 29

(From No. 141)

ومنها اخباره للشيخ عجيب حين شاوره علي حرب الفنج قال الشيخ الفنج غير العوايد علينا قال له لاتحرب عليهم فانهم يقتلوك ويملك ذريتك من بعد الي يوم القيامة فكان الامر كما قال ومنها اخباره للملك بادي ابوا رباط حين جاء سيد قوم للملك عدلان ولد اية طالبين قتال الشيخ عجيب وبادي المذكور حوار الشيخ ادريس فساله عن امره فقال له تقتلوا الشيخ عجيب وتنتصروا وانت ترجع الي سنار ملك ويكون الملك فى ذزيتك من بعدك فكان الامر كما قال وقد ملك منهم خمسة رباط وبادي ولده واونسة ولد ناصر وبادي ولده واونسة ولده ومدت ملكهم ماية سنة وعشر سنين ومنها اخباره ان ملك الفنج ينقضي وسبب انقضايه انهم يتحاربون ينقسمون الي قسمين تقاتل كل طايفة الاخرى حتي يضيع ملكهم

APPENDIX 30

(From No. 143)

منها انه في حالة السجن البيت المسجون فيه انطلقت فيه النار فالنار لما قابلته ماتت وفي كوع البيت دجاجة مركضة[1] تجر في بيضها اليه وسمعوه يقول انا عيسي عند دجاحتي[2]

[1] for فركضت. [2] for دجاجتي.

APPENDIX 31

(From No. 153)

[ظهرت له كرامات وخوارق عادات منها] انه جاءه رجل وقال له شردت لي خادم من ذو عام وقال له اسل الله يردها لي فقال له جيب برمة مريسة شلاتيت وديكا خصي فجاب الرجل برمتين شلاتيت وديكين خصيان فصفوا المريسة وشربوها هو وضناقلته الذين معه ثم جاءه الرجل وقال له اين خادمي فقال شيل الشجر وقل يا بخية[1] ثلاث مرات فجاءت الخادم شايل قربة ماء وحبالها على وجهها وقالت يا سيدي ان جابك هنا هذا بحر اتبرة وهو قال لها هذه سنار فساقها واتاه بها وقال له من بعيد امس[2]

[1] for بخيتة. [2] for امش.

APPENDIX 32

(From No. 153)

ومنها ان ملك الفنج لما خرجت عليه العساكر بجميعها من قري وسنار وأليسْ واحاطت به العساكر من كل جانب وقتلوا جميع من كان معه وما بقي له الا ثلاثين فرسا واختفي منهم في حوش كمير بنت المك اخته فذهبت كمير المذكورة الي الشيخ خليل وقالت له يا سيدي ان اخي فارقه ملكه ونخشي عليه من الهلاك من عبيده وقال لها اخوك الظالم المفسد فقالت اتيه اليك ويتوب علي يدك من الظلم والفساد فقال ءاتيه اليّ فاتت الي الملك وجاءت به مختفيا والبسته ثوب امراة فلما حضر بين يدي الشيخ قال انا تبت مما تنها مني عنه فقال له الفونج اخذوا عمامة الملك منك فهاك عمامتي وضمنت لك ملك ابيك الي ان تموت ولكن اذا خرجت للقتال احضرني واحضر حاج عمارة فلما اصبح خرج الي تلك الجيوش في ثلاثين فرسا واحضر الشيخ والحاج عمارة كما امره الشيخ وهزمهم ببركة الشيخ وقتلهم اشر قتلة وبقي فى ملكه الي ان مات والملك المذكور بادي الاحمر ولد اونسة ولد الملك ناصر انتهي

APPENDIX 33

(From No. 154)

ومن اخلاقه تمسكه بالكتاب والسنة ومتابعة الساده[1] الشاذلية في اقوالهم وافعالهم وكان يلبس الاثياب الفاخرة مثل البصراوي الاخضر وعلى راسه الطربوش الاحمر ويتعمم بالشيشان الفاخرة ويتنعل الصرموجة ويتبخر بالعود الهندي ويتعطر ويجعل الزباد الحبشي في لحيته وثيابه ويفعل ذلك اقتداء بالشيخ ابوالحسن الشاذلي والمهار[2] النعمة الله تعالي ويحمد الله علي ذلك وقيل له ان القادرية انما يلبسون الجبب والمرمقات قال ثيابي تقول للخلق انا غنية عنكم وثيابهم تقول انا مفتقرة اليكم ومن اخلاقه انه لايقوم يسلم علي احد من الجبابرة لا اولاد عجيب سلاطين بلده ولا ملوك جعل ولا لاحد من المراتب الا الاثنين خليفة الشيخ ادريس وخليفة الشيخ صغيرون قال الشعراوي هذه المرتبة يعني ترك القيام ما وقعت من المشايخ ولو الشيخ عبد القادر فانه اذا دخل عليه الخليفة العباسي يقوم له الا الشيخ محمد الحنفي الشاذلي بمصر فانه لا يقوم لاحد لا البواشات ولا السناجك

[1] for السادة. [2] *sic* for مهار ?

APPENDIX 34

(From No. 154)

ومنها ان السلطان بلر سلطان كنجارة حين بلغه سبة من الملك بادى حلف ليدخلن سنار ويقلع الشجر ويسد البحر وتمشي الخيل عليه فلما تجهز وصار حين بلغ طرف الدار من جهة الصبح وبقي علي المفازة فرا الشيخ خوجلي وبيده عصا فوكزه بها في ءاخر اضلاعه[1] فانتفخت يده فماتت فكان سبب موته لان سلطان الفنج استغاث بالشيخ خوجلي وقال له سلطان فور قادم الينا ثم ان السلطان بكر سلطان كنجارة سال اولاد البحر وقال لهم جاءني رجل ازرق وعليه قميص اخضر فوكزني بعصا و وصفه لهم كما رءاه وقالوا له هذا الشيخ خوجلي انتهي

[1] for اظلافه.

APPENDIX 35

(From No. 154)

واما اصل طريقته فالاساس قادري والاوراد والاخلاق شاذلي فان شيخه تلميذ الشيخ محمد الناصر الشاذلي

APPENDIX 36

(From No. 154)

وتوفي رضي الله عنه ضحوة الاحد نهار ثمانية عشر في جماد الثاني سنة خمس[1] وخمسين وجلس في مكانه ابنه الفقيه احمد باشارة من ابيه وكان عبدا صالحا قام مقام اباه في جميع صفاته ومدت[2] حلافته[3] ستة سنين

[1] for خمسة. [2] for مدة. [3] for خلافته.

APPENDIX 37

(From No. 164)

فان مدني الناطق توفي في حيات[1] ابوه الشيخ عبدالرحمن فسماه مدني عليه رجاء ان يكون مثل اخاه وقد حقق الله رجاه

[1] for حياة.

APPENDIX 38

(From No. 170)

شرحه الكبير علي السنوسية في اربعين كراس[1] وشرحه الصغير في عشرة وشرح عقيدة الرسالة ويقال انه شرح الرسالة ولم اقف عليه

[1] for كراسي.

APPENDIX 39

(From No. 178)

وخلفه الشيخ حسن بعد ابيه في مكانه والسبب في ذلك ان اولاد الشيخ اختلفوا فطايفة مسكت عركي وطايفة مسكت محمد هذا وقيل لعمهم الحاج ابراهيم الخليفة منه فقال اولاد علي ما بقول لهذا تقدم وللاخر تاخر هل يمشوا للشيخ حسن فسافر[1] اليه فسبق عركي واخوانه الي الشيخ فرحم لهم وذبح لهم شاه ثم قدم محمد هذا واخوانه فرحم لهم وقال جيبوا البرش لخليفة ولد بري

[1] for سافرا?

APPENDIX 40

(From No. 181)

والشيخ محمد بن قرم فهو ءاية من ءايت[1] الله لان جميع الشيوخ كلها اخذت منه العلم والفريض

[1] for آيات.

APPENDIX 41

(From No. 204)

ومنها ما اخبرنى به الشيخ اسماعيل بن بلال رحمه الله تعالى قال رجلا من الحضور في مركب المالح هاجت عليهم الريح كادت المركب تغرق قال يا محمد بن الزين شافه جاء طايرا بعكازه فهبط البحر سلمت المركب

APPENDIX 42

(From No. 207)

وقتل مظلوما شهيدا قتله جنقل سلطان فور هو وطلبته وسبي اموالهم والسبب في ذلك انه امره بمعروف ونهاه عن منكر انه قدم من الكاب فى الف جواد لقتال الملك دكين قال لتلميذه[1] الفقيه نافع الفزاري ارسكني[2] اليه قال قولوا له لا تقاتل الفونج في دارهم ان قاتلتهم الله والرسول معاهم وانا معاهم فلما سمع ذلك قال ارفعوا البتير فلما رفعوه قال ان شاءالله الفقيه مختار اقتله وندفنه عندنا نزوره فقبقب عليهم فوجد الفقيه فى المجلس وحيرانه في المطالعه فقتل الفقيه وحيرانه واهل بلده وسبي اموالهم فببركة الفقيه جنكل في تلك الايام قتل وترك نحو خمسين ولدا هذا يقتل هذا الي زمننا هذا اليموت علي الفراش فيهم قليل مثل عيساوي

[1] for تلميذه? [2] for ارسلني?

APPENDIX 43

(From No. 212)

وسمي عبد الشركة لانه قسم السنة نصفين نصفا يخدم الشيخ ادريس ونصفا يخدم الشيخ ابو ادريس

APPENDIX 44

(From No. 216)

وحاط الشيخ تاج الدين البهاري الحيوان الجفل زملنا يجي يشيل في مكانهن كلم حوارا لابيه اسمه ابوا سعد فقال له ابسعد فقال له سيد ام ابسعد فقال له قل للحيوان الجفل زملنا الشيخ علي قال لك تعال شيل فى مكانها فجاءت الفيلة وهي اربعة فشالت حملة اربعة وعشرون جمل

APPENDIX 45

(From No. 222)

رباط وركاب ابنا غلام الله اما رباط كان رجلا مجذوبا فزوجوا الصوارد امة لهم غروه بها فولدت لسليم[1] ثم اقروا له بالغرور وقالوا له هي خادم فشكاهم للقاضي فحكم له بحرية ولده والزمه قيمة امه وهذه الواقعة في زمن الفنج فان سليم خطب ابنت[2] عمه ركاب اسمها جنيبة فابته لاجل العبودية ثم ان قنديل العوني عنده ابنة مرضانة فعزم لها سليم فوفيت فزوجه اياها فولدت عون وولد عون جابر ابوا المشايخ الاربعة وايضا ملك الكنيسة عنده بنتا مرضانة فشفيت فزوجه اياها فولدت له هذلول ثم جنيبة بنت ركاب ندمت علي امتناعها لكونه رجلا صالحا والناس رغبوا فيه فتزوجها فولدت منه اربعة عيال

[1] for له سليم. [2] for ابنة.

APPENDIX 46

(From No. 226)

الشيخ صالح ذكر انه اتاه المدد الالهي بالاذن له في وقود النار بعد وفات[1] الشيخ بدوي وذلك سنة ثمانية عشر وفى تلك السنة قتل السميح شندي وولد ولده الشيخ عبد الرحمن سنت[2] اثنين وعشرين فحينيذ شاطرته السلطنة في ديار البحر والمطر فوقد النار وقام بالكرم بفرايضه وسننه ومندوباته فما من[3] بيت من بيوت الدين وغيرها الا وله عليه يد فدار السلطنة قسمها علي الناس مثل الوايمة......وتوفي سنه سبعة وستين عن خمسة وسبعين سنة......وقام بعده ابنه الشيخ الزين بوكالة من الشيخ عبدالرحمن اخيه واوقد النار مثل ابيه ونفذ جميع ما فعله ابوه فى حالة الحُضور والغيبة ومع ذلك مداوما لتلاوة القرءان لايفتر عنه وخصوصا ثلث اليل[4] الاخر

[1] for وفاة. [2] for سنة.
[3] في? [4] for الليل.

APPENDIX 47

(From No. 235)

فصار مفتيا في مذهب مالك والشافع ومدرسا فيهما وسموه ناس اربجي مركب الهند

APPENDIX 48

(From No. 236)

حصلت له كرامات منها انه ضمن لعثمان ولد حمد النصر على حربة الفنج والسبب في ذلك انه مرض وقالوا طبه في دهن الرهوْ فضرب عثمان رهوة بالبندق اتا بها اليه فزال منه المرض فدعا له بالاصابة فى بندقه وما كسر حربة الفنج الابضربة البندق فانها لا تخصي[1] وان عثمان لما كسر الحربة خرج من خلوته لابس قميص الشملة الخيل ديل انفصلا من ديل وان الشيخ على ولد عثمان ارسل الي الملك بادي ولد رباط اعلمه بكسر الحربة وطلب منه الملك فان الملك بادي اخبر العسكر قال لهم نصف النهار بعد ما جروا السديد[2] وانقطع الداخل دخل علي رجل اعسر لابس شملة انه كالحصي[3] قال لي تمرق حربة لكجبي افعل بك كذا وكذا فان الشايقية الجالبين الخيل قالوا له هو الفقيه شيخ فان عثمان معتقدا فيه

[1] for تخطي. [2] for التسديد? [3] for كالخصي.

APPENDIX 49

(No. 241)

صغيرون وهو سيدي محمد بن سرحان العودي وامه فاطمة بنت جابر بن عون بن سليم بن رباط بن غلام الله فما طابت تلك الثمرة الا من تلك الشجرة وسمي صغيرون فان اولاد اخواله اولاد جابر يقولوا له محمد الصغير فقلب على صغيرون ولد رحمه الله بالجزيرة ترنج من دار الشايقية وكان رضي الله عنه ممن جمع بين الفقيه والتصوف وبرع فى الفقيه على خاله الشيخ اسماعيل بن جابر وجازه بالتدريس ورحل الي الشيخ محمد البنوفري وقرا عليه شيا من خليل وقال محمد هذا يصلح للتدريس فجعل الله بركة فيه وجلس فى مجلس اخواله بعدهم وكان من زهاد العلما وكبار الصالحين ومحب في التصوف الشيخ ادريس بن الارباب وسبب قدومه الي دار الابواب اعدوا له اولا[1] عمه عداوة شديدة لكونه حاز منصبهم وقام مقام اخواله فى العلم والصلاح وساقوا عليه الملك زمراوي ملك الشايقية وامروه بقتله فركب جواده وجاءه وهو في المسجد فوجد امه بنت جابر معه فقالت له يا زمراوي جيت تقتل محمد فنزلوه من الجواد مغشيا عليه فجعل يقول حك حك بقر الحاج محمد نطحني فجاءوه فشفعوا به

[1] for اولاد.

وقال لهم الشي هذا ماه مني من اخوانالي[1] فعزم له فشفي وقال له اعطيتك اربعة سواقي وكل ساقية اربعين عودا بعود الصلطية واربعة فروس ولادات واربعة روس فقال له مالكم حرام عليَّ وسكن بلدك حرام عليّ وقيل ان الملك بادي ابوا رباط وكان سيد قوم الملك عدلان ولد اية وكان معتقدا فيه فان الملك عدلان بعدما قتل الشيخ عجيب فى كركوج سافر بجيوشه دار دنقلة فلما جاء في مشوه عزلوه الفنج من الملك وولوا بادي سيد القوم الملك فحينيذ[2] ظلب منه ان يسافر معه الي الصعيد فقال له بلحقك ثم قدم بعده الي ارض الصعيد بامه واخوانه وزوجاته واولاده فوقع فى الدريرة فاختلف فقراه ناس الصعيد امروه سكن الصعيد وناس السافل امروه يسكني السافل فقال لهم اختار الله علي ذلك فاخذ ركوته وشال الخلا فاجتمع بالسيد الخضر عليه السلام قال له مسكنك قوز المطرق مقابل سهلت[3] ام وزين فسار اليه ووجده شجرا ووعرا فمشا الي الفجيجة فوجدها فجة ساهلة من الشجر وقال هذه الفجيجة ينزل فيها اخوان الشيخ عبد الرحمن ولد حمدت وهذا سبب تسميتها بالفجيجة ثم ان الشيخ بن سرحان ارسل الي الملك بادي بسنار واعلمه بالقدوم وطلبه ان يعطيه بقعة الحلا[4] للمسكن والمشرع للورود فان الملك جاب زوله له وقال له اعطه جميع الدار اليدورها وحددها له وقال له بلا بقعة الحلة[5] والمشرع للفقرا وموضع موضع[6] المقبرة ما ندور شي وهذا فى حقه رحمه الله تعالي من الوراعة والزهد في الدنيا ثم ان الشيخ رضي الله عنه بنا المسجد بتاسيس الحضر عليه السلام ويقال ان الشعبة الوسطي التي هي موضع التدريس للمشايخ قزه[7] بيده الكريمة وشدت اليه الرحال من سير الاقطار وضربت اليه اكباد الابل واتفقت به الناس وممن اخذ عليه من الاجلا الشيخ دفع الله بن الشيخ ابو ادريس والفقيه عبد الحليم ولد بحر واولاد بري الفقيه على والحاج ابراهيم وتور المتن الكاهلي البرقاني فهو مدفون امام قبره واولاد التنقار الثلاثة الفقيه محمد وحموده ومازري ومدني الحجر بن الحاج عمر اخيه ومحمد ولد الحاج ابوا القاسم اخيه وكان صالحا فاضلا وتوفي بدور عمه وليس له

[1] for اخوالي.
[2] for حينئذ.
[3] for سهلة.
[4] for خلا.
[5] for خلا?
[6] *dele.*
[7] for غزه.

عقب الا بنته حاجة فولدت الفقيه بلال وولد بن سرحان الفقيه الزين وابراهيم الحجر وابكر وله من البنات خمسة رابعة تزوجها مدني الحجر بن اخيه عمر وحاجة تزوجها محمد بن التنقار بن اخته ءامنة وزينب تزوجها محمد بن الحاج ابو القاسم اخيه ومدت[1] تدريسه فى الابواب هل ثلاثة عشر ختمة او اربعة عشر او خمسة عشر ودفن بالقوز وقبره يزار يستسقي بقبره العيش انتهي

[1] for مدة.

APPENDIX 50

(From No. 255)

وحضاه الملك وزوجه ابنته وقطع له في الدار بنواحي الحلفاية قدرما يشور[1] جواده شرقا وغربا يمينا وشمالا وجوهها له من جميع السل[2] فهي الي الان كذلك

[1] for يسور. [2] for السبل.

MANUSCRIPT D 4

Introduction

THE full work of which a *précis* and part translation[1] follows contains about forty pages of Arabic MS. It was written so recently as 1911 by Dáūd Kubára ibn Sulaymán, a Berberi of Ḥalfa, and is a medley of history and tradition. Much of it relates to such irrelevant facts as the names of village sheikhs and the kinds of vegetables grown in different parts. The account given of the intestine troubles of Nūbia in the eighteenth century is of some interest, and the record of what is presumably the traditional belief of the people as to the origin of the Nūbian race is of distinct value.

I The author of the work is Dáūd Kubára ibn Sulaymán of Ḥalfa town.

II In his prefatory remarks he states that, being moved by enthusiasm to learn the history of Nūbia, he consulted "the learned men of the NŪBIANS (النوبيين) and the Turks whose ages were about a hundred years and more" on the subject, and from their statements compiled this work, which he calls "*The Precious Pearls of Useful Knowledge*" or "*A Compendium of the History and Geography of EL NŪBA* (النوبة), *and the Reasons of the Coming of the Turks in the Time of the Sultan Selím I and in the Time of Muḥammad 'Ali Pasha, the Founder of the Khedivial Dynasty, until the Present Day.*"

III The opening remarks are an eulogy of the ancient glories of the NŪBIANS (النوبة), with special reference to "the city of Barkal, the first capital of the NŪBIANS (النوبيون)," and "the city of Donḳola el 'Agūz, the seat of the power of King Donḳol," and el Khandaḳ, and Arḳó, and Sáí, and Wádi Ḥalfá, and "Faraṣ, which was the capital of the famous kingdom of King Kaykalán," and Ibrím.

IV The work proper now begins, and the first chapter is headed "*The Capital of the Kingdom of the NŪBA*," and straightway proceeds as follows:

"Its capital was Gebel 'Abd el Hádi, which lies between Dongola

[1] So much as is a *précis* is given in small type. Actual quotation only (in inverted commas) is in ordinary type.

and Kordofán, and various other hills. Now the cities and hills of the NŪBIANS were dense with troops and horsemen, and when their power had become firmly established in the Sudan a great army was assembled, under the leadership of King Ṭahráḳ and of Sebákh the King of Abyssinia, to make war on the kingdom of Egypt; and after much fighting and great slaughter Egypt was conquered."..."Then the Assyrians conquered Egypt as far as the first cataract, that is the Sudan cataract, after ejecting the armies of the NŪBIANS (النوبيين) and the Abyssinians."...The Egyptians then recovered their power and not only expelled the Abyssinians but overran "the lands of the NŪBA (النوبة) and the Sudan, and set up mighty monuments."

V Subsequently the Romans conquered Egypt and "the land of the NŪBA" (النوبة). Then followed a period of dire oppression, and the people were reduced to extremities when the torch of Islam was first lighted.

VI Egypt was conquered in the Khalífate of 'Omar ibn el Khaṭṭáb by 'Amr ibn el 'Áṣi, and its people, excepting a few Jews and Copts, were converted.

The armies of the Muhammadans also penetrated "to the furthest limits of the land of the NŪBA, to Dábat el Dólíb and the hills of the NŪBA," and left garrisons there to keep the peace.

VII "Finally the civil war between the BENI OMMAYYA and the BENI HÁSHIM broke out in the Ḥegáz; and when they considered the armies which had settled in the land of the NŪBA, they took up their abode there and mingled with the NŪBIANS, and took their women to wife, and intermarried with them, and made the land of the NŪBA their home, and dwelt in complete concord with the NŪBIANS: and this is the sole reason of the presence [in the Sudan] of the ASHRÁF and Arabs of the Ḥegáz; and in the course of time they multiplied and formed a great proportion of the inhabitants of the country of the NŪBA."

VIII This chapter, the second, is in praise of the Nūbian character, its nobility, piety and courage.

IX We are now told that the power in Egypt passed from hand to hand until the time of "Ṭóman Bái, the last of the GERÁKISA dynasty," when the 'Othmánía Turks prepared to invade the country; and a long description is given of the means whereby the Sultan Selím finally overcame Ṭomán Bái on January 22nd, 1517 A.D., and conquered Egypt and founded a dynasty which remained in power for some 139 years.

X Selím gradually extended his conquests up the river till he reached Ḥalfa, and there "he imposed a tax on the water-wheels and the palms, payable in cash and cloth and produce, and made the seat of his power the city of Aswán and Ibrím."

XI Subsequently "Hamám Abu Yūsef el Ṣa'ídi, the chief of the tribe of the HOWÁRA revolted [*sc.* against the *Mamlūk* rule] and became Sultan of Upper Egypt and part of the NŪBA country as far as Wádi Ḥalfá, and these parts became subject to him. It was part of this man's policy to sell the right of ruling the lands of the NŪBA to anyone who wanted it for fixed sums; and this system continued for a long time, and as a result it caused greedy competition between the various Turks, that is the *Káshifs*. On this account the tribes of Ibrím formed an alliance, viz. the IBRÁMÁB[1] and the MAGRÁB and ÁGHA ḤUSAYN and the SAKRÁB (?) and the KÍKHIÁB and the ṬUBASHÍA and the ḤAMDŪNÁB and the KARÁÍÁB, with a view to making war on four other tribes, viz. the DÁŪDÁB and the DABÁBÍA and the MANDŪLÁB and the AZRÍḤÁN (?).

XII And when these four tribes saw that they could not compete with their foes at Ibrím, they moved to the vicinity of el Derr, which lies ten miles to the south of Ibrím, and made their preparations there for carrying on the conflict; but before fighting actually took place a settlement was arranged between the parties by the mediation of the learned and sensible elders among the NŪBIANS on the following conditions: the tribes of Ibrím who had settled at Ibrím were to be allotted six places to rule, viz. Ibrím and 'Aníba and Ganíba and Maṣmaṣ and Tūshki East and Tūshki West; and the four tribes were to take fifteen places, viz. Armaná and Farayḳ and Balána and Ḳusṭal and Arnadán and Faraṣ and Faraṣ Island and Sarra East and Sarra West and Dabayra and Ashkít and Arḳayn and Dabarūsa and Anḳash and Ḥalfá Deghaym. Thus the settlement was effected, and this state of affairs continued for a long time without any tribe encroaching on another.

XIII And the *Káshifs* coalesced with the NŪBIANS by intermarriage until it came to pass that most of the tribes of *Káshifs* were descended from NŪBA mothers; and thus the *Káshifs* became partners of the NŪBIANS in their possessions, and the tribes became closely connected for the preservation of order, and lived together in peace.

XIV Finally there arose two persons, one from the tribe of the MANDŪLÁB, and the other from the DÁŪDÁB, and went to King Hamám Abu Yūsef, the King of Upper Egypt (*el Ṣa'íd*), and gave him many presents with a view to obtaining from him appointments as rulers of the part of Nūbia lying between the first and the second cataracts, *i.e.* from Wádi Ḥalfá to the cataract of Aswán, for one year.

[1] reading ابراماب for ابراصاب.

This appointment he granted to them for the period of one year; and on their arrival at Derr they appointed employées and assistants for their rule, and started from Derr for Wádi Ḥalfá to collect the taxes. But when they reached the neighbourhood of Ferayḳ they fell to disputing as to which of them was chief, and the two of them remained there, each enrolling the names of his fellow tribesmen. Then the two tribes met there, and a great fight took place, and the army of the MANDŪLÁB was defeated.

XV After this an alliance was formed between the MANDŪLÁB and the ASHRÁF, *i.e.* the DABÁBÍA, and the AZRÍḤÁN, against the DÁŪDÁB, and there was war between them for a long space, and all the chieftains and horsemen of both parties were slain...."

XVI The author then gives the names of the *Káshifs* who were the heads of the four tribes mentioned, and the names of certain of their descendants, and the places where the latter severally reside at present.

XVII The next chapter deals very briefly indeed with the career of Muḥammad 'Ali Pasha and his successors up to 1882 A.D. Nothing of interest is recorded.

XVIII This chapter mentions by name those whom the author considers to be the most learned or noteworthy personages of the present generation in Nūbia. The list contains thirty-one names, chiefly of *Ḳáḍis*, Sheikhs and Dervish *amirs*.

XIX Following the above is the heading "*Learned Men*," but our author states there is not room to include a list of these, but "I pray Almighty God," says he, "that our Government may see fit to educate our sons, for the children of to-day are the men of the future."

XX The author now passes to the geography of Nūbia. Its boundaries on the Nile are, he states, from the north of Aswán to Dábat el Dólíb on the northern frontier of the SHÁÍḲÍA country, "not counting the hills of the NŪBA lying between Dongola and Kordofán, and the hills of the ZING NŪBA in southern Kordofán."

XXI He next proceeds to mention all the places of interest in Nūbia, dividing the country for this purpose into a series of districts and taking them one by one from north to south.

The first ten districts are on the river: the tenth reaches on the south to "Dábat el Dólíb, near Old Dongola."

The eleventh district comprises "the hills of the NŪBA between Dongola and Kordofán."

The twelfth comprises "the hills of the ZING NŪBA in southern Kordofán."

The thirteenth is Gebel Barkal.

XXII These thirteen districts are then subdivided into smaller areas, generally villages, and a few remarks are given concerning natural features or any point of interest.

Under "Korosko," the alphabet of the local *rotána*, spoken from Korosko to Dár Maḥass, is given: it is stated to be a mixture of Arabic, Turkish and Nūba, and is as follows:

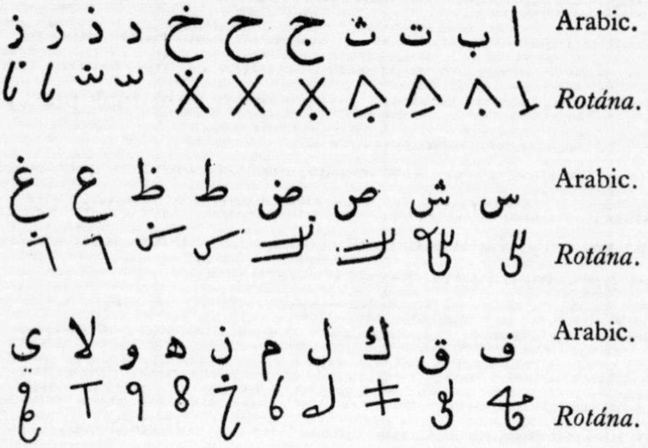

XXIII The eleventh district is not subdivided, but the author says of it "The Nūba hills lying between Dongola and Kordofán are many in number, and in them are tribes innumerable. The best known of them is Gebel 'Abd el Hádi, the capital (عاصمة) of the hills of the Nūba: its inhabitants are Nūbians (نوبيون)." They cultivate, says the author, by raincrop, have considerable flocks and herds, and are iron-workers, and some of their women make pottery.

XXIV Of the twelfth district (the hills of southern Kordofán) little is said. *Gebels* Teḳali, el Daier, and Marra (which, by the way, is in Dárfūr) are mentioned, as also the fact that each *gebel* speaks a different language.

XXV The work was completed on the 4th of *Ramaḍan* 1330 A.H. (1911 A.D.).

D 4 (NOTES)

II The Arabic for the title is

كتاب الدر الفريد فى الاخبار المفيدة المحتوي علي ملخص تاريخ الامة النوبية وجغرافية بلادها واسباب دخول الاتراك في مدة السلطان سليم الاول ومدة محمد علي باشا مؤسس العائلة الخديوية الي زمننا هذا

The words "NŪBA" and "Nūbian" are used by the author indiscriminately to denote the people of what is known now, as in past times, as Nūbia, as well as the inhabitants of the hills of northern Kordofán. He includes the mountaineers of south Kordofán (Nūba Mountains Province) in his category of NŪBIANS or NŪBA, but differentiates them as "ZING NŪBA": see note to para. XX.

III Barkal, or Napata, was the seat of the Nūbian kingdom which is known to have risen to power between 600 and 700 B.C. Piankhi reigned about 721 B.C. (see Breasted, pp. 367–8, and Budge, vol. II, pp. 1–2). For the ruins at Barkal see Crowfoot (*Arch. Survey of Nubia*, XIXth Mem. p. 31).

Donḳola el 'Agūz ("Old Dongola") was the capital of northern Nūbia for some 600 years: it took the place of Napata (see Budge, vol. II, pp. 297, 299, 372).

Of "King Donḳol" nothing is known. An older form of "Donḳola" was "Domḳola" (*e.g.* see Yáḳūt, *Geogr.* مدينة النوبه اسمها دمقلة).

Faraṣ was "certainly one of the leading cities of Lower 'Nūbia'" and should probably be identified with the mediaeval Begrásh (see *Egypt. Expl. Fund Report* 1910–11, and Budge, vol. II, p. 303). I can find no mention of "King Kaykalán."

IV "*Its capital was...*" is as follows in the Arabic:

اما عاصمتها فهي جبل عبد الهادى الواقع ما بين دنقلا وكردفان و حلافها من الجبال لا تحصى

Gebel 'Abd el Hádi is Gebel el Ḥaráza in northern Kordofán. 'Abd el Hádi was the most famous of its chiefs, and was a Dólábi by race, *i.e.* by origin a Rikábi from Dongola. Pallme met him in 1838 (see Pallme, pp. 96 and 240, and MacMichael, *Tribes*..., pp. 93, 94). Cp. Cuny (p. 138), "Le Djebel Haraza, ou Djebel Abd-el-Kadi" [misprint for Hadi], "du nom de son chef récemment décédé" (1857). Cp. also Rüppell, p. 125.

The word عاصمة here translated "capital" must mean the ancient headquarters, if not the cradle of the race, as distinct from its more obvious meaning of "capital" in para. XXIII.

The suggestion that el Ḥaráza was once the headquarters of the present Nūbian stock is extremely interesting and significant. If one re-read in the light of this passage the well-known quotation given by Quatremère anent the expedition of Ḳaláūn against King Any (*q.v.* in vol. I,

p. 185), it at once seems probable that, when Any fled away to the "'ANAG country" across a desert waste, it was at el Ḥaráza, as would be natural, that he sought refuge. Traditions of the 'ANAG as being the ancient inhabitants of el Ḥaráza are universal and there is no doubt whatever that from an early period there was intercourse between the riverain "NŪBIANS" and the settlers in the western hills. I incline to think that this intercourse is far older than has been supposed, and there is no reason why it should not date back at least to the seventh century B.C. It is of course more probable that emigrants from the river should have colonized el Ḥaráza, Um Durrag, etc., than that the opposite process should have occurred, but it is often overlooked that there was in early times an enormous nomad population of Hamitic affinities, who roamed the inland country west of Dongola and the junction of the Niles, the "desert of Gorham" and the neighbourhood of el Ḥaráza that is, and who were partly of BERBER origin, and whom Marmol (vol. III, ed. Perrot), in speaking of their wars with "the prince of Dongola," calls "ceux de Gorhan, qui est une espèce d'Egyptiens qui courent par les déserts."

The modern Nūbian or Berberi may owe nearly as much from the genealogical point of view to these nomads as to their riverain congeners. (See vol. I, pp. 27 *et seq.*)

"King Ṭahráḳ" is of course Taharka, "who flourished in the second quarter of the seventh century before Christ and was the second Sudani conqueror of Egypt" (see Budge, vol I, p. 482. Breasted gives his date as about 688–663 B.C.).

By "Sebákh" may be meant Shabataka, the Ethiopian monarch who succeeded Shabaka about 700 B.C. Manetho calls him Sebichos and mentions that he was killed by Taharka, who succeeded him (see Breasted, *Hist.* pp. 377–8).

The Assyrian invasion by Esarhaddon was about 670 B.C.

V The NŪBIANS first had dealings with Romans about 30 B.C. when a prefecture was established in Egypt. From then for a period of 500 years the BLEMYES and NOBATAE (*i.e.* the NŪBIANS) were more or less continually in touch with them.

VI 'Amr's conquest of Egypt was in 641 A.D.

Dábat el Dólíb, mentioned again in para. XXI, is immediately south of "Debba" (*i.e.* Dába), on the eighteenth degree of latitude.

VII This is in agreement with the usual Sudanese tradition: the main immigration to the Sudan of 'Abbásid tribes, as represented by the Ga'ali group, and of Ommayyad tribes, as represented by the FUNG, is generally represented as contemporaneous with the civil war in the middle of the eighth century between the 'Abbásids and the Ommayyads in Asia.

IX The date January 22nd, 1517, is quite correct. Ṭóman Bái was put to death by Selím I (see Lane-Poole, *History*..., p. 354; and Muir, *Mameluke Dynasty*..., Chaps. XX, XXI).

"GERÁKISA" is the same as Circassian.

XI For Hamám and the period of HOWÁRA rule in Upper Egypt and Nūbia see Burckhardt's *Nubia*, and Part III, Chap. 8 above.

The HOWÁRA had held considerable power since 1412 A.D., when they took Aswán from the BENI KANZ, but the period of their greatest power was the eighteenth century, when, under Hamám, they "had assumed the whole government of Upper Egypt south of Siout and the Mamelukes had been obliged to cede it to them by treaty" (Burckhardt).

The names of tribes mentioned in the latter part of the paragraph are doubtful.

XIII The *Káshifs* were minor officials appointed by the Turks to administer villages or small groups of villages: they were nominally subject to the Beys who were responsible for the larger provinces (see, *e.g.*, Norden, *Travels*..., vol. I, pp. 58–62).

XX Cp. para. II (note) for "ZING NŪBA" (النوبة الزنوج), and D I, CLXXXII. Broadly speaking "ZING" seems generally to denote blacks whose original home was south, south-east and south-west, as distinct from the Nilotic negro proper.

MANUSCRIPT D 5 (*a*, *b*, *c* and *d*)

Introduction

THE following is a series of four translations. The Arabic text was sent by the native headmaster of Manáḳil school to an Inspector in the Education Department in 1913 as being of some interest. They are referred to as (*a*), (*b*), (*c*) and (*d*) respectively. The first (*a*) is evidently not copied from any original manuscript but is merely an oral tradition. It is headed simply "This is the history of the 'ÁBDULLÁB."

The second (*b*) is a short note of eight lines about the 'ARAKIÍN, based, one would say, on some casual verbal information, and by no means accurate, but headed "This is copied from the *nisba* of the 'ARAKIYYŪN in possession of the Khalífa of the 'ARAKIYYŪN, Sheikh 'Abdulla."

The third (*c*) is headed "This was copied from the *nisba* in possession of el Ostádh el Sheikh 'Ali Muḥammad, Imám of the mosque of el Manáḳil and educated there. He took it from the *History of Dongola* word for word (اخذه من تاريخ دنقلة مصححا)."

To the end of para. XXVII may be, and probably is, an extract copied from a manuscript. The remainder is probably from oral tradition: it agrees in some points and differs in others from the account given by Nicholls (*The Shaiḳíya*), but from the latter it is obvious that there is no really authoritative version.

The fourth (*d*) is headed "This is copied from the *nisba* of the RIKÁBÍA in possession of el feki el Bashír ibn el feki Muḥammad." It is merely a variant of the accounts given in BA and D 1.

D 5 (*a*)

The 'Ábdulláb

I Among the most famous and bravest of the tribes of the Sudan is the 'ÁBDULLÁB.

II This tribe used to rule from Ḥagar el 'Asal to the old kingdom of Ḳerri. They were viziers of the FUNG.

III Serious fighting occurred between them and the SURŪRÁB west of Ḥalfáya el Mulūk at a spot called nowadays Fásher el Sheikh 'Agíb el Ḥág, [that being the name of] the ancestor of the tribe.

IV The cause of the fight was as follows: the SURŪRÁB attacked the 'ÁBDULLÁB at el Ḥalfáya; and in old days fighting was done only with swords and spears, and it was customary in warfare that the opposing armies should stand aside and the fighting be begun by the kings. They were followed by the viziers, and the latter by the rest of the armies.

V In this particular engagement the Sheikhs of the 'ÁBDULLÁB and the SURŪRÁB respectively came forth to battle, and the first to begin the fight were the Sheikh of the 'ÁBDULLÁB and the king of the SURŪRÁB. Then the former stood up on his steed and said to the latter "Hit the leather" ("shew your strength"), and [the king of the SURŪRÁB] hurled at him a spear of the kind called by them *el ṣalaṭía* so that it came out at his back. And when [the Sheikh of the 'ÁBDULLÁB] knew his end had come he drew his sword and smote the king of the SURŪRÁB with it, and they two both died. And the Sheikh of the 'ÁBDULLÁB did not fall from his mare, though dead, and no one knew that he was dead till the end of the battle. And when the SURŪRÁB knew that their king was slain they fled in utter disorder, and complete victory rested with the 'ÁBDULLÁB.

VI One of their customs was that their chief man was liable to death at any time whatsoever, for if any one of the sons of his father's brother wished to slay him he would inform him of the fact and appoint a date for him; and the chief would reply "yes" for fear that report should become current that he was afraid. So he prepares himself to meet the demand of his cousin and shaves his head and gets out his sword and places it in front of him and prostrates himself twice in prayer and seats himself to await [his cousin's] coming. Then his cousin arises and takes his sword and goes to find the king we have mentioned and orders the chamberlain to procure him permission [to enter] from the king. Then the chamberlain informs him by knocking at the door, and he gives [his cousin] leave to enter. The latter enters drawing his sword and stands behind the king, who is facing southwards, and strikes him on the neck without the king's saying so much as a word. Afterwards the great men [of the tribe] gather together and place the king's hat on his [*sc.* the slayer's] head and appoint him their ruler. Such were their customs of old.

D 5 (*a*) NOTES

IV The SURŪRÁB belong to the Ga'ali group of tribes, and are a branch of the GAMŪ'ÍA.

V "*Hit the leather...etc.*" is (اظهر قوتك) دُقّ الجِلْد.

VI "*Chief man*" is ريس ("rais"); "*sons of his father's brother*" is ابنا عمه, and "*his cousin*" ابن عمه; "*chamberlain*" is حاجب ("ḥágib"); "*hat*" is قلندسوة.

It would appear that we have in this paragraph a reference to the well-known African cult of the Divine King, the belief that the king incarnates the divine spirit and that he should be periodically killed with a view to the appointment of a successor whose virility has not suffered from retention in an ageing body. The custom is practised by the DINKA and by the SHILLUK, and the killing of the king is a matter of high ceremony and reverence. The same custom was held among the FUNG at Sennár, where Bruce relates that "It is one of the singularities of this brutal people that the king ascends his throne under an admission that he may be lawfully put to death by his own subjects or slaves, if the great officers in council assembled decree that it is not for the advantage of the state that he should be suffered to reign any longer. There is one officer of his own family who alone can be the instrument of shedding the blood of his sovereign and kinsman...." The officer was called the "*Síd el Ḳūm*." The FUNG were largely SHILLUK by origin (see Westermann) and the 'ABDULLÁB rose to power in alliance with the FUNG: it is not therefore surprising to hear of a form of the belief in the Divine King as existing among the 'ABDULLÁB. (For this subject see Seligman, *Hamitic Problem*..., pp. 664, 665, and vol. I, p. 50 above.)

"*Who is facing southwards*" is وهو متقبل القبلة.

D 5 (*b*)

The 'Arakiyyūn

I The pedigree of these tribes goes back to our lord el Ḥusayn ibn 'Ali. Their ancestor was Muḥammad Abu Idrís el 'Araki son of Dafa'alla son of Aḥmad. The tribe is connected by descent with the BÁDRÁB, whose *Imáms*, Sheikh 'Abdulla el 'Araki and his brother Sheikh Muḥammad, gave instruction to many folk.

II Their number includes many holy men that visited the holy sanctuary and Medína...(among their holy men the following are mentioned:

(1) Sheikh 'Abdulla walad Ḥusayn.
(2) 'Ali walad Nafí'a.
(3) His son Fáliḥ ibn 'Ali.
(4) 'Abdulla walad el Ḳuṣayer).

D 5 (*b*) NOTES

I Cp. C 9 and D 3, Tree 9. From these it would appear that the information given is inaccurate. The biographies of Muḥammad Abu Idrís, of his father Dafa'alla, of 'Abdulla el 'Araki, and of Muḥammad ibn Dafa'alla, are given in D 3 under Nos. 48, 86, 34, and 185 respectively. The Bádráb seem out of place here altogether.

II None of these holy men occur in D 3: they would seem to have lived at a later date and to have been of negligible importance.

D 5 (*c*)

The 'Abbásia now living in the Sudan

I The 'Abbásía now living in the Sudan are descended from Ṣáliḥ surnamed "Ṣubuḥ" and nicknamed "Abu Merkha." He was the first to come to the Sudan, [viz.] after the decay of the Beni 'Abbás and at the beginning of the 'Othmáni dynasty, which are described by the historians in their works. He was a pious man, and the Sudan was honoured by his presence in it as the lands of Irák had been honoured by the presence of his ancestors.

II The vulgar saying of the people of the Sudan that Ṣubuḥ Abu Merkha was a foolish man who used to wipe himself upon *merakh* bushes is nonsense, and unpardonable in the sight of God: possibly it may be due to the Nūba on account of their enmity to his descendants, who conquered them.

III He was son of Muḥammad el Mutawakkil 'ala Alla son of Ya'aḳūb son of 'Abd el 'Azíz el Khalífa el Mutawakkil 'ala Alla, the last of the 'Abbásid Khalífas. This 'Abd el 'Azíz was son of Ya'aḳūb son of Ga'afir el Mutawakkil 'ala Alla. The last named was killed by the Tartars, and at his death Baghdád was sacked, and then the power of the 'Abbásid dynasty waned and gradually disappeared like all other dynasties: glory be to God. Ga'afir was son of Hárūn el Wáthik son of el Mu'taṣam son of the Commander of the Faithful Hárūn el Rashíd son of el Mahdi son of Abu Ga'afir el Manṣūr son of Muḥammad son of 'Ali son of 'Abdulla the ancestor of the nation, the translator of the Ḳurán, son of our lord el 'Abbás the uncle of the Prophet....

The Tribes of the Ḥasanáb

IV These tribes are descended from Ḥasán son of Zayn el Dín son of 'Ón son of Sháiḳ. Ḥasán was the youngest son of Zayn el Dín son of 'Ón, and his mother was Fáṭima daughter of Sheikh Ḥasán, the Sheikh of the ḤASÁNÍA; and he was called after his grandfather.

V When Zayn el Dín died and his son Ḥasán was grown up he came to his brothers and his first cousins on the father's side and desired them to give him some of the properties and lands of his father, which were in their possession; and they refused because [though ?] he was their brother, the son of their father, and the [cultivable] lands of the SHÁIḲÍA consisted of only a very narrow strip of shelving river bank; and at that time the river bank was where at the present day runs the road known as *Darb el Sulṭán*.

VI And when he saw their unwillingness he went away and devised a scheme, and said to them "We will meet, if it please God, on horseback." And they laughed at him and said "By whose aid will you do it, considering that we are your first cousins ?"

VII Now at that time the strong among them used to prey upon the weak, and looting was rife; and the sons of 'Ón ibn Sháiḳ lived at Kórti West and thereabouts. Then Ḥasán went and married a wife in the country of his brothers and she bore him four sons and one daughter.

VIII One of the sons he called Fahd ("Leopard"), another Sima'a ("Wolf-hyaena"), a third Ḥaníd (?), and a fourth Ḍurbán ("Porcupine") after the names of beasts and birds of prey, his intention being that they should thereby affright their foes, as was the custom of ḲURAYSH. And his daughter he named Maḳásh (?).

IX And he taught his sons to ride on horseback, to fight with the sword, to use the spear and to shoot with arrows; and when they had attained the proficiency in warfare that he desired he collected them and his daughter and made them swear that never would they be taken prisoners but would rather fight until all died or all were victorious. Especially upon his daughter did he enjoin that she should fight until she died and not let her cousins capture her to marry her, and she acquiesced.

Then they prepared themselves for death and attacked their cousins and slew many of them; and after this they crossed the river at the ford of el Karafáb on the east bank, and Ḥasán ibn Zayn el Dín swore an oath that their horses should not be unsaddled until he found a country for his children to inhabit whether [other folk] liked it or no, or else had all been killed.

X And when they reached the Wádi el Maḥfūr there met him the sons of his [great-] uncle, that is the sons of el Ḥág Muḥammad the brother of 'Ón, and they greeted him and were overjoyed, for they desired his aid against their foes and to secure that he and they should be as one single hand against all others.

XI And they said to him "The lands that contain us will contain you." He replied "What will contain me and my sons will only be the distance that contains me on my horse." They said "That shall be so"; and he galloped his horse from the landing-place of the village of el Ḥág Muḥammad to the landing-place of Shilluk, now known as "Ṭaraf Baḳárish," and again from this to the landing-place of Ḳubbat el Sheikh el Nuwábi.

XII Then he set up a stone as boundary between himself and the lands of the king of the BÁZA, king 'Aḳil, the master of Kardáfil (*sic*), and this stone is called "*el Shaykhūn*" and is still standing in the middle of the road.

Now this road was then the river frontage, and the site [of the stone] was the [summit of the] shelving bank, which was stony and of little value.

XIII So Ḥasán and his sons became entirely separated from all intercourse with their cousins, the stock of 'Ón ibn Sháiḳ, the KANŪDÁB and the 'AMRÁB, and became united in life and in death with the children of their [great-] uncle el Ḥág Muḥammad.

XIV This is the story of Ḥasán ibn Zayn el Dín and what happened between him and his cousins the 'ÓNÍA in the year in which died the king of the BÁZA, namely the year 900[1].

XV And the above is taken [منقول] from the *History of Old Dongola* ("*Donḳola el 'Agūz*"). But the NŪBA and the BÁZA did not know the [true] date and took their reckoning from the years in which their famous men died.

The Tribes living in the Sháiḳia Country

XVI The tribes living in the SHÁIḲÍA country are of various races. The greater part of them are NŪBA, and these live in certain definite places, some of them at el Ḳadír and Massáwi Island, and some in the vicinity of Nūri and el Bellal and Kenána (as far as the limits of el Daḳáit), and others at el Kásingar and its vicinity eastwards and westwards, and [the] islands. These are the habitations of the NŪBA.

XVII Another of the tribes among the SHÁIḲÍA is the BÁZA, who live near el Zóma.

1 1498 A.D.

XVIII Another is the 'IRÁḲÁB, who live at el Nūri. Their ancestor, el 'Iráḳi, came from el 'Iráḳ, and it is said they are ASHRÁF, and God knows best; but people are to be believed as to their pedigrees and what good is apparent in them, for their progenitors were learned and pious men, as were also the ḤAMMATTUWIÁB.

XIX Among the SHÁIḲÍA too are the DWAYḤÍA. Their ancestor was DWAYḤ, of the stock of el Ghulám el Rikábi; and they and the RIKÁBÍA have a common descent to our lord 'Oḳayl ibn Abu Ṭálib.

XX Among the SHÁIḲÍA too are the ṬERAYFÍA, the inhabitants of el Gharíba and Kórti and the neighbourhood. Their ancestor el Ṭerayfi came from Dárfūr as a trader and settled in the country [of the SHÁIḲÍA] and begot there his offspring.

XXI Among the SHÁIḲÍA, again, are the ḤALANḲA, the inhabitants of Um Bakól. Their ancestor came from el Táká and settled here.

XXII The BEDAYRÍA are of the stock of Abu Merkha, the ancestor of the 'ABBÁSÍA, SHÁIḲÍA and others, and every genealogical record mentions them.

XXIII Living in the SHÁIḲÍA country too are the FELLÁLÍT, the sons of Felláti. Their ancestor came from the FELLÁTA country as a pilgrim, and settled near Uska on the west of the SHÁIḲÍA country.

XXIV Other tribes are the SHELUFÁB and the SHIRAYSHÁB, and the TAKÁRÍR who live near el Ghazáli and el Duaym, west of Merawi.

XXV The ancestor [of these TAKÁRÍR] came from Hausaland and settled in the country [of the SHÁIḲÍA] and mingled with the people of the land and adopted their habits (تزيوا بزيهم), and their complexions changed from very black to brown (*samra*) by reason of intermarriage (*lit.* "women").

XXVI The remnants of all tribes we have mentioned are still occupying these regions, excepting the tribe of FUNG. These latter have disappeared and left no trace excepting the sons of their daughters, the 'ADLÁNÁB[1], the sons of Muḥammad "the younger" (*el ṣughayr*) son of Sháiḳ.

XXVII The kings of the FUNG were bold and cunning, oppressive and unjust, and when the SHÁIḲÍA came and established their power the authority of the FUNG was dispersed, their kingdom brought to nought and their rule destroyed, and they and their progeny went away altogether by reason of the cry of the oppressed...(there follow a few pious reflections)....

XXVIII The above is what I have found and copied and heard, and God knows best the truth, and to Him do all men return.

[1] reading عدلاناب for عدلناب.

XXIX The 'Ón who was mentioned above was 'Ón son of Sháiḳ, and he had three sons, Zayn el Dín and Kanūd (Katūd ?) and 'Amr, [whose descendants were] surnamed KANŪDÁB (KATŪDÁB?) and 'AMRÁB and ZAYNELDÍNÁB and ḤASANÁB; and the best known tribal names are 'ÓNÍA and ḤASANÁB.

XXX Such descendants of el Ḥág Muḥammad ibn Sháiḳ, 'Ón's full-brother, as are to be found to-day are the stock of Yūsef, MANÁTÁB and ḲŪTÁB and MAḤMŪDÁB: these were the sons of his own begetting. But the allies (الموالى) who are mixed with them are for the most part SOWÁKIRA and SHELLÁLÍL and others.

XXXI The mother of Sowár ibn Sháiḳ was one of the TUNGUR of Dárfūr. He had no full-brother. He had six sons, Ḥamdulla and Tamalayk and Nimr and 'Áíd and Waṣíf and Gádát.

XXXII The sons of Ḥamdulla are 'AKŪDÁB and AMÍNÁB, of Tamalayk TAMÁLAYK, of Nimr 'ANAYNÁB and ḤAMARTŪDÁB, of 'Áíd 'ÁÍDÁB, and of Waṣíf ẒILAYṬÁB.

XXXIII The sons of Muḥammad Kadunḳ[1] ibn Sháiḳ are the KADUNḲÁB[2], and these fall into three divisions, BANÁDIḲA, ṢUBḤÁB and 'AYNÁB (?)[3].

The KADUNḲÁB[4] used to be the most numerous of the SHÁIḲÍA, but they were continually intermarrying [with others], like every [other] tribe with a few rare exceptions.

XXXIV Muḥammad "the younger" ibn Sháiḳ was full-brother of Muḥammad Kadunḳ[5], and was ancestor of the 'ADLÁNÁB; but the ancestresses of this section were all daughters of the FUNG, for they lived close to the latter at Merawi. And they acquired the characteristics of the FUNG; for the latter in those days were the ruling power and gave to the 'ADLÁNÁB a share of their dominion as being the children of their daughters. Thus you see the 'ADLÁNÁB have lost their brown complexion and their natural love of the open air.

XXXV Ḥowwash ibn Sháiḳ had no full-brother. He was ancestor of the ḤOWWASHÁB, and the ancestresses of these were nomad Arabs. They used to marry whatever they found, good or bad, among the races of mankind, and in consequence their natures are invariably evil.

XXXVI Náfa'a ibn Sháiḳ was ancestor of the NÁFA'ÁB. He had no full-brother.

1 reading كدنق for كندق.
2 reading كدنقاب for كندقاب.
3 reading عيناب for عياب.
4 reading كدنقاب for كندقاب.
5 reading كندق for كدنق.

XXXVII Sálim ibn Sháíḳ had four sons, Khálid and Serayḥ and Ya'aḳūb and Ráshid.

XXXVIII Khálid's descendants are the KHÁLIDÁB, Serayḥ's the SERAYḤÁB, Ya'aḳūb's the YA'AḲŪBÁB, and Ráshid's the RISHAYDÁB.

D 5 (*c*) NOTES

I–III The author's knowledge of history is so hopeless that it is not easy to guess at the date at which it is suggested that Ṣubuḥ immigrated to the Sudan.

From Hárūn el Wáthik to el 'Abbás the generations are correct; but Ga'afir was Hárūn's brother, not his son. Ga'afir ruled from 847 to 861 A.D. and was not killed by "the Tartars" at all. The author seems to have gloriously confused the Saljūḳ Turks, the Mongols or Tartars, and the Ottoman Turks.

The last of the 'Abbásids, 'Abdulla el Musta'ṣim was killed by Hulagu the Mongol in 1258 and the sack of Baghdád followed; but no less than twenty-six Khalífas ruled, at least nominally, for a total period of nearly 400 years, at Baghdád, between the death of Ga'afir el Mutawakkil and the accession of 'Abdulla el Musta'ṣim.

The probability is that the author means to suggest that Ṣubuḥ came to the Sudan about the middle of the thirteenth century. Cp. ABC, XXII, where Ghánim, Ṣubuḥ's grandson, is spoken of as being the first immigrant, *i.e.* in 1277 A.D.

"*Merakh*" is *Leptadenia Spartium*, a switch-like shrub without leaves.

IV The connection of the Ḥasanáb with the rest of the SHÁÍḲIA, according to the version given by the author of D 5 (*c*) in the following paragraphs, if given in the form of a genealogical tree, would be as follows:

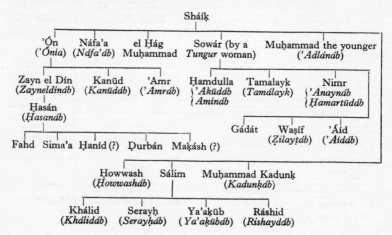

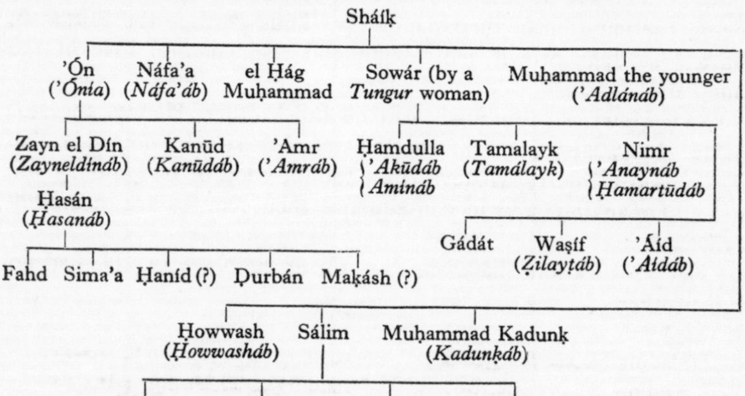

VIII "*Sima'a*" (سمع) is a mongrel beast, the offspring of the wolf begotten from the hyaena (so Lane's *Dictionary*).

The meaning of "*Ḥanid*," if that be the true reading, is unknown: the same applies to "*Maḳásh*."

IX For other mentions of this participation of SHÁÍḲÍA women in battle see Cailliaud (Chap. XXV) and Nicholls, pp. 10, 21 and 31.

XI The custom of granting a man as much land as he could gallop round is said to have been not uncommon.

XII Báza (or Básа) lies east of Kabūshía. The name is an old one: see Quatremère, who, quoting a mediaeval Arab historian, speaks of the king of "the Gates" [*i.e.* Kabūshía] and "the Princes of Barah (Bazah), el Takah...etc.": this in 1286 A.D. See vol. I, p. 183 and cp. D 6, XLI.

XVIII See C 8, XXXII (note) for 'IRÁḲÁB.

"*People are to be believed...*" is

الناس مامونون على انسابهم والخير فيهم ظاهر لان اسلافهم كانوا علماء و صلحاء و كذلك الحمتّوياب

For this cp. AB, XXVI and BA, XV and D 6, XL.

The ḤAMMATTUWIÁB or ḤAMMADTUWIÁB are the descendants of Ḥammadtu, for whom see D 3, 21 and 158.

XIX By "*Ghulám*" I presume Ghulámulla ibn 'Áíd is meant. Cp. Nicholls, p. 39.

XX Cp. Nicholls, p. 19.

XXIV In Nicholls (Appendix II) the SHELUFÁB and SHIRAYSHÁB are given as being themselves SHÁÍḲÍA.

XXVII Cp. Nicholls, Chap. II.

XXX "*SOWÁKIRA*" is the plural of "*sókari*," a word used on the river for the village watchman who is chosen by the villagers to take charge of stray goats, etc., that are found damaging their cultivation. He is, in return, paid so much a head by the owner for each animal so impounded.

"*SHELLÁLÍL*" are inhabitants of the cataracts ("*shellál*").

XXXI Cp. Nicholls, p. 50. The descendants of Sowár are generally known as SOWÁRÁB.

XXXII "*ḤAMARTŪDÁB*" (حمرتوداب) may possibly be an error for "*ḤAMMADTUWIÁB*" (حمدتوياب or حمتوياب), *q.v.* para. XVIII.

XXXIII In the name "*KADUNḲÁB*" or "*KANDUḲÁB*" we probably have, not a mere misprint, but an instance of the very common Sudanese-Arabic habit of inverting syllables. Similar examples are "'*ADNÁLÁB*" often used for "'*ADLÁNÁB*," "*istibália*" for "*isbitália*" (a hospital), "*góz*" for "*zóg*" (a husband), "*laḥbaṭ*" and "*ḥalbaṭ*" (to mix up), etc.

XXXIV Others give the 'ADLÁNÁB a Kanzi origin (see Appendix to ABC).

D 5 (*d*)

The Tribes of the Rikábia

I The ancestor of these tribes was Sheikh Ghulámulla. He was born on an island called Nowáwa after his father had come from the land of Yemen.

II He begot two sons on one of the islands of the Red Sea, called Siákía, and thence he proceeded with them to the land of Dongola, which, when he arrived there, was utterly sunk in error owing to the lack of learned men. When he arrived there he built a mosque and taught the Ḳurán and the sciences.

III Now his two sons were Rikáb and Rubáṭ.

IV Rikáb had five sons, 'Abdulla, 'Abd el Nebi, Ḥabíb, 'Agíb and Zayd el Feríd.

V Rubáṭ had six sons, Ruzayn, Dahmash, Muḥammad 'Ón, 'Abd el Rázik̇, Miṣbáḥ and Hazlūl.

VI Ruzayn's descendants were [the family of] Ḥabíb Munesi; and Dahmash's were [those of] the *feki* 'Ali Manófali at Dongola.

VII Muḥammad 'Ón begot the AWLÁD GÁBIR, the great men of learning.

VIII The descendants of 'Abd el Rázik̇ were [the family of] Sheikh Ḥasan walad Belíl at el Kenára.

IX The sons of Miṣbáḥ are among the KABÁBÍSH and consist of many subdivisions.

X The descendants of Hazlūl are at el Ḥaráza.

XI The sons of 'Abd el Nebi were 'Abd el Ṣádik̇, ancestor of the ṢÁDIK̇ÁB, and Shakára, the ancestor of Ḥasan walad Shakára at Dongola.

The descendants of Ḥabíb are the people of el Ṣabábi.

XII The descendants of 'Agíb are (*sic*) Sheikh Muḥammad walad Abu Ḥalíma.

XIII The descendants of Zayd el Feríd are (*sic*) Walad Ḥág Mágid.

XIV Ḥág Mágid's descendants are the BAHÍGÁB and the 'AKÍZÁB.

D 5 (*d*) NOTE

For the whole of this extract cp. BA, CLXXIX *et seq.* to CCVIII; D I, XCII and CIV *et seq.*

MANUSCRIPT D 6

Introduction

THIS work was written in 1860, almost certainly by a certain Aḥmad ibn el feki Ma'arūf. From internal evidence one would say that he was a Fádni.

He devotes much space to the FÁDNÍA, who are not a very important tribe, and is obviously anxious to glorify their origin and exploits.

It is also clear that the author wrote from the north-eastern Sudan. His explanation of the word "*Ga'ali*" (para. XI) is the one that could only be current in the north, and he speaks (para. XII) of the KAWÁHLA as a southern tribe. That he did not live on the river is suggested (*a*) by his vagueness as to Dongola and Berber (paras. LIX and LX), and (*b*) by his interest in and knowledge of the tribes of nomads living between the Nile at Kabūshía and the Abyssinian frontier. As regards the sources of the information given, it is obvious that they are much the same as those of A 11 and A 2, and that we have here another of the "Samarḳandi" group of *nisbas*; but though the opening paragraphs are apparently copied almost word for word, the author soon breaks away and gives various details drawn, in all probability, from purely oral sources.

The actual manuscript translated, which consists of seven folios, is frayed and stained and may well be the original text of 1860. It came into the possession of the Education Department of the Sudan Government in 1913, but in what manner or from what direction is not known. The Arabic is indifferent and the style loose and disconnected.

I In the name of God....

II I have composed this essay to explain the origins of the Arabs each in their turn to whoso wishes to know them.

III I say, and God is my help, that I have heard from our lord Abu Sulaymán el 'Iráḳi and Abu Maḥmūd el Samarḳandi that they heard our Sheikh Abu Sulaymán el Baḥráni say in some of his retreats (*i.e.* schools, "*khalwát*") "We have undertaken a mighty task. Verily pedigrees have fallen into confusion. What hero will take them in hand that the *Sherif* may be known from the pretended *Sherif*?" Then he would correct himself and say "But to contradict one who calls himself a *Sherif* is a large and difficult matter and a pure heart cannot encompass it, for men are of different classes: some are modest..." (several lines, showing the difficulties to be encountered owing to men's different characters and motives, follow).

IV I must now return to my subject, namely the mention of the Arab tribes that are occupying the land of the Sudan—in our day that is; and God knows best what the future may be.

V The first of them to be mentioned is the family of the noble Sherif el Sayyid Maḥmūd son of Muḥammad son of Sulaymán son of Ga'afir son of 'Abdulla, and his pedigree goes back to Muḥammad ibn el Ḥanafía.

They include numerous tribes, almost innumerable, known as the FÁDNÍA, or, as they were originally called after the manner of Arabic, "the FAWÁDANI." These include the family of Ḥasan ibn Bá Fádni ibn Muḥammad, among whose descendants was a man called Barakát ibn Ḳásim ibn Maḥmūd ibn Mūsa ibn Ḥusayn ibn Ḳatáda ibn Ḥasan ibn Bá Fád (*sic*). This man was a powerful personage and married the daughter of 'Anḳá ibn 'Áṭif, who bore to him a son and a daughter; and [the former] was named Ibn Gebel ibn Barakát ibn Ḳásim. And when he saw the condition of 'Anḳá's family and knew their ways he feared lest his son should become like them, so he worried him saying "Join your people" and "You will see me on your tracks." So he joined his people at Wahayn, which lies north of the city of el Abwáb, which is a great city said to contain stone images of such beasts as lions and wolves and snakes; and it has seen much of the ravages of war and the blessings of peace in the days of Islam and the days of ignorance.

VI [The FÁDNÍA] also include the family of Mas'ūd ibn Bá Fád (*sic*), who has descendants still tracing to him their parentage.

VII They include also the family of Sálimayn ibn Bá Fád whose descendants are well known on account of their condition and their good characters to this day.

VIII They include also the family of Mas'ūd ibn Bá Fád, and of Sa'íd ibn Bá Fád, whose stock has died out.

IX Chapter giving an account of the Arabs known as GA'AL, they being still the ruling power of that country. Their pedigree is to Sa'ad el Anṣári, but I am not sure of their ramifications—only that it is to Sa'ad that the great majority of the pedigrees are traced.

X The reason of their migration to the Sudan was their quarrel with the OMMAWÍA at the time of the quarrel between the BENI OMMAYYA and the BENI HÁSHIM. So they migrated to the west, and then returned to Dongola and conquered its people, and advanced by degrees till they overcame GUHAYNA.

XI The reason of their being called by this name was that they had an ancestor who was black and hideous to look upon, and so his father's sister called him "Beetle" (*Gu'al*), and the tribe was called after him.

XII The KAWÁHLA. They include the family of Káhil son of 'Omára son of Khalífa son of Ibayraḳ son of Muḥammad son of Selím son of Khálid son of el Walíd. And they include innumerable tribes in various places, all in the South. Most of them live in the desert of the BEGA and seldom come down to the Nile; nor do they pass the site at Sóba called Balūla.

XIII FEZÁRA. A well-known sub-tribe of TAMÍM. They have been settled in the Sudan since the conquest of el Bahnasá. Their story is well known.

XIV GUHAYNA. They are famous among the tribes of the Arabs and there is no need to relate wherein their fame lies. In the Sudan they include the family of Sa'íd ibn Gamíl, and the family of Mádir ibn 'Ámir, and the family of Musá'ad ibn Kelayb, and the family of Baṭḥán ibn Dágna.

The reason of their emigration (خروجهم) was that 'Aṣám el Moghrabi, king of Berbera, slew a number of their merchants; and God knows best. Then they went out against him and conquered his country and looted its wealth; and so they continued until, as mentioned above, GA'AL came and defeated them and conquered the country; and GUHAYNA became a subject people therein, and they entered the island of Anágíl the Begáwi after his stock had died out and his rule come to an end.

XV The SHUKRÍA are the family of Shukr ibn Adrak, and their pedigree goes back to 'Abdulla el Gawád son of Ga'afir el Ṭíár son of Abu Ṭálib.

They are a great tribe and their stock continues to the present day. I do not know what was the reason of their emigration.

XVI The ḤASÁNÍA are similarly descended from Ga'afir el Ṭíár. They are the sons of Ḥasán ibn Gamíl and their pedigree goes back to 'Abdulla el Gawád ibn Ga'afir el Ṭíár. Their pedigree and that of the children of Shukr meet in the person of 'Ali el Zayni.

XVII The 'ÁNIMÍA are the descendants of 'Ánim ibn Gawád el Ya'arebi, a very small tribe. Of their number was a certain clever man called 'Ali, who in the time of Barakát was his companion. Now he loved making mischief and stirred up Barakát and his people to revolt; and the nomads offered prayers against him, and Almighty God caused him to be overcome, and they took him prisoner and enslaved him for a time. Then Barakát attacked them and rescued him, and he used to say in praise of Barakát and his people... (here follows a page or so of rhymed prose and poetry).

XVIII The Ḥamrán are one of the tribes of Ḥarb, who are nomads living between Mekka and Medína.

Of their number in the Sudan are the families of Ḥamál and of Musá'ad ibn Gárulla and of Sálim Bá'áíd, and Ibn Lohay. I am not sure of the real reason of their emigration, but it is said that it was their fight with Muzayna.

XIX The Beni 'Ámir are the descendants of 'Ámir ibn el Ṭufayl. They entered Abyssinia and were its rulers. They are famous for their bravery and courage. A story is told about this 'Ámir and the Prophet...(short story follows).

The reason of their emigration to Abyssinia was that they killed their Sheikh Fá'asi ibn 'Abdulla. They wander about the borders of Abyssinia.

XX The Beni Aḥmar are a tribe of Beni Ommayya. They were in Abyssinia, but most of them have disappeared and only a few remain.

XXI The Rawágiḥ are the descendants of Rágiḥ ibn Sa'ad el Thaḳfi. Their stock[1] still exists.

XXII The 'Awáṣim are the descendants of 'Áṣim ibn 'Ámir ibn Naṣír el 'Omari, a descendant of 'Omar ibn el Khaṭṭáb. It was he who first settled them in Egypt: then they invaded the Sudan in the days of el Ẓáhir Abu Barri.

XXIII The family of Musallam, namely Musallam ibn Ḥegáz[2] ibn 'Áṭif el Ommawi. He moved from Syria in the time of 'Omar ibn 'Abd el 'Azíz, God bless him, and settled in the Sudan, and he has left many descendants.

XXIV The Aṭáía are nomads descended from Aṭa ibn Zaím el Ḥimyari. I am not sure either of the reason of their emigration or of their ramifications, but it is said that they are the people who aided el Ḥaggág in the slaying of Ibn el Zubayr...*etc.*

XXV The Rikábiyyūn are the descendants of Rikáb ibn 'Abdulla, and their pedigree goes back to Sheikh Aḥmad ibn 'Omar el Zíla'i, the descendant of 'Oḳayl ibn Abu Ṭálib, God bless him. It is probable that they are the children of Rikáb el Guhani.

XXVI The 'Amriyyūn (so spelt) are the descendants of 'Amr ibn Sulaymán the Ommawi. It is said that they are at present the ruling people in the Sudan. They and the people of Lūlūh, one of the Hamag districts, have intermarried to such an extent that they have become like these people in every respect, and they are known as the Fūng.

[1] reading العقب for القعب. [2] reading حجاز for حجار.

XXVII The Ḥamzát are the descendants of Ḥamza ibn 'Abd el Muṭṭalib. There are a number of them on the bank of the Kádimía near el Khór.

XXVIII Kenána are a great tribe belonging to the famous Kenána of el Yemen. In the Sudan they include the families of Duhaym el Kenáni and of Rágiḥ and of Selím. They live in the same locality as Fezára.

XXIX The Rowási are the descendants of Rási el Ḳaḥṭáni. They were in Abyssinia but most of them disappeared. In Abyssinia they contain a number of Beni Ba'alá. A number of them apostatized.

XXX The Ḳálla are by origin Arabs. In Abyssinia they are infidels. They are a nuisance to the Abyssinians, killing them and capturing their women and children. There is a difference of opinion as to their origin, some saying they are descended from Ḳaḥṭán and some from Ḥimyar and some from the Beni Ghassán, and the last is true.

XXXI Thaḳíf. A very small community and unimportant among the Arabs...(some depreciatory lines by Ibn el Moghrabi about them are quoted).

XXXII The Ṣaláḥiyyūn are the descendants of Ṣaláḥ ibn Gábir ibn Ghassán. They are numerous, and most of them live in Abyssinia towards the coast.

XXXIII The Gábiría in Abyssinia are a considerable tribe, but most of them are between the Maḥass country and Dongola the famous. They are the family of Gábir ibn 'Abdulla el Anṣári, who begot them at the time of the conquest of Dongola, when it was destroyed and God gave the Muslims the victory in the invasion of 'Amr ibn el 'Áṣi, God bless him.

XXXIV The Gerátima are the family of Geratím ibn 'Uḳba el Rabí'i of the tribe of Rabí'a. They live between Abyssinia and the Begá.

XXXV Rufá'a. They lived at first in Abyssinia and [among] the Begá[1], and then they moved to the Nile lands. They are one of the Ḳaḥṭánite tribes in the Sudan. Our Sheikh Abu Nuṣr Muḥammad el Shádhali[2] said "I do not know exactly how they are descended, beyond that it is certain they are descended from Ḳaḥṭán."

XXXVI The Zenárkha are the family of Zerníkh ibn Á'gif of the Beni Lám, the famous tribe in Neged[3] el Ḥegáz.

XXXVII The 'Awáṣi are the family of 'Áṣi ibn Gamá'a el Mukhalladi, the Mukhallad being also an Arab tribe.

[1] reading البجا for البحا. [2] reading الشاذلى for السادلى.
[3] reading نجد for نحد.

XXXVIII The YERÁBÍ'A are also Arabs and descended from Ḥimyar. They originally lived at Ṣana'á in el Yemen. They settled in the Sudan in the time of 'Abd el Malik ibn Marwán.

XXXIX The 'ABBÁSIYYŪN are descended from el Faḍl ibn 'Abbás. In the Sudan they include the family of el Saffáḥ. They are a mighty tribe and more of them are in the Sudan than elsewhere. The reason of their emigration thither was the rise to power of the Fáṭimite dynasty in Egypt, and they declined with it and dispersed into the Sudan.

XL The GABARTA are originally Arabs, it is said ḲURAYSH, but I do not vouch for this and know only that people are under this impression. I have enquired from some of their learned men saying "I hear from the people of el Táka that you are descended from ḲURAYSH," and they replied "We also say so"; and I think it is [true], but God knows best, and we assume that pedigrees are [properly] kept.

XLI The 'ÁDILIYYŪN are the family of 'Ádil ibn 'Azíz the Sa'adi. They fall into two divisions: some live in the district of Ousa near the GABARTA, and the others live in the strongholds known as el Táka, west of the hills of the BÁZA. And it is said that beyond these strongholds, and between them and Abyssinia, is a great mountain called el Lós, where they suppose the Companions of the Cave are, and they live in these strongholds and are known as the ḤALANḲA. It is therefore possible that they are the family of Ḥalayḳ el Sa'adi son of Dhulayma son of Bardhal son of Amal son of 'Ámir son of Hawázin son of Mas'ūd son of Sa'ad son of Bukr, or that they are descended from Ḥaláḳ el Mundabi (?); and the former is more correct.

They contain numerous tribes that cannot be enumerated. They have intermarried with the BEGÁ so much that they have become assimilated to them. It is said that their language resembles that of the BEGÁ [and is] a branch of it.

XLII The 'ALÁMIYYŪN are the descendants of 'Alám ibn Sa'ad el Ziáti and are known as the "House of 'Alám." Most of them live near the TUNGUR in the districts of el Takrūr.

XLIII FELLÁTA settled in the land of el Takrūr. They are the family of Fellát son of 'Abdulla son of 'Uḳba son of Yásir.

XLIV The BEKRIYYŪN are numerous in the land of el Takrūr, and in Egypt they form the well-known House of el Bekri. And the genealogists make mention of the Sheikh who was descended from the said Sheikh [el Bekri], and who lived in Upper Egypt (*arḍ el ṣa'íd*), and who was a very great man and one of the saints famous for piety; and it is a remarkable thing that his descendants remember nothing important about him: yet by the grace that is given him he has facilitated the granting of their prayers, and their holy men and their tribe [itself] are called el Mashaíkh[1].

XLV The Ṣawáíl are the family of Ṣáíl ibn Yerbū'a el Muzani and are a sub-tribe of Muzayna who migrated from near Jedda. There are many of them in Egypt. They left el Yemen at the same time as Humayl el Selmi.

XLVI Sulaym are a well-known tribe of the Ḥegáz. Most of them live between the Holy Places, and some of them settled in the Sudan, and these latter are the Yuásifa.

XLVII The Masha'ala are the family of Masha'al ibn Ya'aḳūb el Gaḥadli, and are a branch of the Gaḥádla, who again are an Arab tribe, partly sedentary and partly nomad, residing to the right hand of Mekka, and represented in the Sudan by the family of Masha'al ibn Gaḥdal.

XLVIII The 'Agárifa are the family of 'Agraf ibn Ma'amir el Khuzá'i, Khuzá'a being the well-known tribe at Mekka and thereabouts, who are represented in the Sudan by the family of 'Agraf only. They are a moderate sized community. The reason of their immigration to the Sudan was the ill-treatment they received from el Ḥaggág at the time when he [re-]built the temple. God and the Prophet know best.

XLIX The 'Arágín are the people of those countries, and were not Arabs of the Ḥegáz. They were extremely skilful and versatile. It is said that among them was a man called 'Azíz the Poet...(some verses follow).

L The Senábla are the family of Sanbal ibn Gabr. They are a large Arab tribe.

LI The Ḥadáreb. I was told by Sídi 'Abdulla Báwazíz el Ḥaḍari that they came originally from Ḥaḍramaut, and were said to be a branch of the Ḥamūm, who are nomads in Ḥaḍramaut, and that they emigrated thence to the Sudan in the days of el Ḥaggág ibn Yūsef, and settled among the Begá until they became exactly as if they were Begá themselves, and took up their abode at Sūákin, the well-known island on the coast of the Sudan near Abyssinia; and [he said that] they were called "the Ḥaḍárem," deriving the name from "*ḥaḍra*," but from ignorance the ḍ was changed into d and the m into b, as can be understood, and they became the "Ḥadáreb."

LII The Ga'áfira are a great tribe. Their descent is from Ga'afir el Ṭái, and it is said that their ancestor was Ḥátim el Ṭái. They are famous for their generosity, as he was.

LIII The Mūsiyyūn are the family of Mūsa ibn Sa'íd el Thaḳfi.

[1] reading المشايخ for المسايخ.

They are a branch of THAḲÍF and numerous. In the Sudan they live like [nomad] Arabs.

LIV Among them was a powerful man called 'Ali ibn Gubára, and there is a story of him and the kings of the Arabs. It is said that Abu Ya'aḳūb, one of the Arab Sultans, sent him to the king of el Takrūr with a letter written as follows, "In the name of God the Compassionate and Merciful, this from Abu Ya'aḳūb to the Sultan of el Takrūr. If you want to preserve your self-respect and maintain your honour, submit to me: otherwise I will most surely equip[1] against you an army like locusts in swarm, who will lay waste your lands and loot your goods and take captive your sons and make an end of your women. So when you read this letter, you will have a correct idea of my dominion, and if you desire relief from ill and survival from annihilation, then subject yourself to me as I order you."

LV When this letter reached the king of el Takrūr he told his servant to beat him [*sc.* 'Ali ibn Gubára] and impale his companions. This was done; and that very night the Sultan heard [*sc.* one] say "If you slay this man, [*sc.* he will be avenged]"; and his vizier said to him "It is not the custom of kings to kill envoys nor punish them," so he ordered him to be released.

LVI Then, after releasing him, he mounted him on a horse and said to him "Go, tell yon Sultan that when Gog and Magog have obeyed him I will obey him: his wits are wandering: does he order me to obey him before I order him to do anything at all? He is one of those that carves the mountains with his fingernails." And when this message reached the king of the Arabs he turned to his troops and said "Is there any one of you I can send to deal with him?" And 'Ali ibn Gubára said "I have a prior right in this matter over all."

LVII Then [the king] equipped a force, to go with him, of 3000 cavalry and 2000 riflemen and 1000 bowmen and 1000 swordsmen using the short Moorish sword, and the expedition started.

LVIII And when they reached the land of el Takrūr, the two armies met, and God gave the victory [to 'Ali] and he returned in joy and happiness [from the field of battle]; and God the Almighty made him ruler of el Takrūr, and to this day the Sultans of el Takrūr are his descendants.

LIX Chapter mentioning the wonders of that land and its chief places.

BERBER is an immense village. It has had many rulers, including the giant dynasty of which each king began his reign as a true believer

[1] reading جهزت for جهرت.

and ended it a pagan. West of it is a great mountain called Gebel el Ruūs, where there are marvels that it would take too long to relate.

LX DONGOLA is a great place and its story is well known. It was conquered by 'Amr ibn el 'Áṣi.

LXI The people of Berber were converted by the people of Dongola; and there are there (*i.e.* in Dongola) great cities and islands encompassed by walls, and a great mosque built by 'Amr ibn el 'Áṣi and known as "the mosque of 'Amr," and the entrenchment (*khandaḳ*) made by Ibn 'Uḳba el Gábiri el Anṣári in the time of Ayyūb.

LXII Here ends the history of the Arabs who settled in the Sudan.

This history is the property of the *faḳír* Aḥmad ibn el feki Ma'arūf, and I finished writing it in *Gemád* 1277[1].

D 6 (NOTES)

III Cp. A 11, II and III.

"*The pretended Sherif*" is المشروف.

V The Arabic begins ...اول ما يذكر منهم من هناك السيد but this is clearly corrupt, and should, I think, read ...اول ما يذكر منهم آل السيد.

Compare BA, CLXXIV for these FÁDNÍA. "Fawádin" would be the normal Arabic plural formed from Fádin, the name of their ancestor.

The Arabic translated "*He worried him...tracks*" is

ازعجه ان الحق بقومك وسترانى باثرك

For el Abwáb see D 3, 14 (note).

IX "*That country*" (ذلك الاقليم) is presumably the [northern] Sudan.

X Cp. A 11, VII. Contrast para. XXXIX later.

XI This version of the origin of "Ga'al" is not, it is almost needless to say, in vogue among the GA'ALIÍN themselves, though not uncommon in Dongola. Cp. A 3, VII, and see Robertson Smith, p. 196.

XII Cp. A 11, XLVIII. Balūla is the name of a village and ferry situated on a bend of the Blue Nile a mile or two below el Kámlín.

XIII Cp. A 11, LIV.

XV Cp. A 11, L.

XXIII Cp. A 11, LI.

XXV Cp. A 11, LII.

XXVI Cp. A 11, LIII.

XXVIII Cp. A 11, LVI.

XXX *i.e.* the "GALLA."

XXXIII Cp. A 11, LVII.

XXXV Cp. A 11, LVIII.

XXXVII Cp. BA, CXXVI for MUKHALLAD.

XXXVIII "YERÁBÍ'A" is a plural from Yerbū'a, which name occurs later in para. XLV.

[1] 1860 A.D.

'Abd el Malik ibn Marwán was the fifth Ommayyad Khalífa and died in 705 A.D. after reigning twenty years.

XXXIX Cp. AB, XXIII and CCXIII and ABC, XXII.

"*'ABBÁSIYYŪN*" is used here practically as the equivalent of "GA'ALIYYŪN." Contrast para. X.

The Fáṭimites conquered Egypt in 969 A.D. and were supplanted by the Ayyūbites in 1171 A.D.

XL Cp. A 11, LX and AB, XXVI.

XLI "*And it is said...*" is as follows in the Arabic, which appears corrupt:

ويقال ان فى طرف تلك الاجمة بينها وبين الحبش جبل يقال له اللوس جبل عظيم وهم يتهمون فيه باصحاب اهل الكهف وهم اهل تلك الاجمه يشتهرون بالحلنقة

The Companions of the Cave (*Aṣḥáb el Kahf*) are the legendary "Seven Sleepers of Ephesus." Muḥammad borrowed the story from Christian traditions and introduced it as a revelation into the Ḳurán (*q.v.* Chap. XVIII. See also Sale's notes thereto, Hughes, p. 24, and Gibbon's *Decline and Fall...*, Chap. XXXI).

El Lós is Gebel Kassala. See Werne (p. 217). "In former times the race of the Hallenga had, at the foot of the hill of Kassela-el-Lus, a great city....The true name of the hill is el Lus, and the word Kassela is the name of a sainted Sheikh. The rock-dome of Kassela is surrounded by six pillar-like rocks; and hence the saying 'Kassela-el-Lus saba Rus' (Kassela-el-Lus of the seven heads)." Again of the caves in Gebel Kassala Werne (p. 245) says: "They are said to be inhabited by men of ancient days, spirits, and ghosts."

"*Ḥalayḳ*" may be a misprint for "Ḥalanḳ." The proper names following are probably corrupt.

XLII Dárfūr and westwards are meant.

XLIII Cp. A 11, LXI.

XLIV The MASHÁÍKH or MASHÁÍKHA are meant. They claim descent from Abu Bukr el Ṣadíḳ, the first Khalífa of Islam. The unnamed Sheikh is probably Mugelli (*q.v.* A 2, XXXVII and D 3, 255).

XLVI YUÁSIFA is a plural formed from Yūsef, *i.e.* "sons of Yūsef."

XLVIII El Ḥaggág ibn Yūsef's date was 42–95 A.H. It was in 74 A.H. (693 A.D.) that he pulled down the temple of Mekka and restored it to its old pre-Islamic form. For this and the cruelties he perpetrated at this period see Ockley (p. 480).

XLIX It is not clear what "*those countries*" refers to: the Arabic is ...العراجين من تلك الديار واهلها. From para. LIX it seems the northern Sudan is meant.

L "*Sanbal*" and "*SENÁBLA*" are probably misprints for "Shanbal" and "SHÉNABLA."

LI Cp. A 11, LXII, from which it seems "*Báwaziz*" (باوزيز) is an error for "Abu el Wuzír" (ابو الوزير).

LII Cp. A 11, LXIII.

LIV There is little clue as to what war is referred to in this story. There is no historical Sultan named Abu Ya'aḳūb. In para. XLII "*el Takrūr*" is apparently meant to represent any of the western states of the Sudan, and if the same is the case here the reference may conceivably be to the incident of 'Abd el Kerím, the first Muhammadan ruler of Wadái, the grandfather of the Sultan Ya'aḳūb and the conqueror of the TUNGUR. He reigned 1635–55 and was of a Ga'ali stock from near Shendi (see vol. I, pp. 68 and 198).

The Arabic translated "*you will have a correct idea of my dominion*" is اعلم انك قد وقفت على صراط ملكي—the word *ṣirát* being literally "the [right] way" (see Hughes, p. 595).

LV The Arabic of this passage is as follows:

فلما وصل الكتاب الى ملك التكرور امر خدامه ان يضربوه وان يخرقوا
رفقه فعلوا فلما كان ذات ليله سمع السلطان يقول لو قتلت هذا الرجل
فقال له وزيره ما جرة عادة الملوك ان يقتلوا الرسل ولا يعذبوهم فامر باطلاقه

LIX "*It has had...pagan*" is

ولها ملوك كثيرة وكان فيها ملك جبار يعبد كل منهم جديد ويكفر باخر

LX Cp. A 2, XXXIV; D 4, VI, etc.

LXI By "*the mosque of 'Amr*" is perhaps meant the mosque superimposed at Old Dongola upon the ruins of an ancient Christian church (see Budge, II, p. 372 and *Anglo-Eg. Sudan*, I, p. 31). At Khandaḳ there is an old brick fort in the middle of the town, which may be alluded to here (see Gleichen, p. 29).

LXII The Arabic of this paragraph is

انتهي انساب العرب المموءون (*sic*) بالسودان و مالكها الفقير الى الله احمد
بن الفقه (*sic*) معروف وقد فرغت من تحريره فى جماد ١٢٧٧

MANUSCRIPT D 7

Introduction

VERSIONS of this work, which represents the only known attempt by a native historian to give a detailed chronological account of the FUNG and Turkish days, are by no means uncommon. General Gordon possessed a copy and presented it in 1881 to the British Museum, where it is numbered "Arabic 2345." It was no doubt from this same copy that Colonel Stewart had obtained most of the historical facts given in the *Report on the Sudan* which he wrote at Khartoum in February 1883.

Professor Budge similarly made use of this MS. in writing *The Egyptian Sudan*, and Na'ūm Bey Shuḳayr must have had access to this or another copy.

Mr Jackson has paraphrased yet another copy, and, by adding facts drawn from other sources, has woven the whole into the narrative he has entitled *Tooth of Fire* (published 1912). In the introduction he says he knows of eight copies in all, and mentions that one copy is in the Imperial Library at Vienna.

My own acquaintance with this work dates from 1907, when Sir F. R. Wingate, the Governor-General, showed me the rough translation of a copy found in Sennár by Sir R. von Slatin, the Inspector-General.

Notes I took from this MS., which I referred to as "*The Sennár History*," were incorporated in *The Tribes of Northern and Central Kordofán* (published 1912).

The particular copy here translated was made for me at Omdurmán in 1914 from the MS. belonging to *Mek* 'Adlán of Sennár, the lineal descendant and heir of the FUNG kings. This had been temporarily borrowed for me by Mr S. A. Tippetts, the Senior Inspector of Sennár Province.

While engaged on editing this copy I found another in possession of the *feki* Muḥammad 'Abd el Mágid of Omdurmán. One of his pupils had made this copy for him in the *Mahdía* from the MS. in possession of the respected *feki* Hagyū wad Masía, the Ya'aḳūbábi, of Sennár Province.

The original work, to which there is no reason to attribute other than a single authorship, was undoubtedly based, so far as the FUNG period is concerned, on those chronologies of the FUNG kings which were shown at Sennár to Bruce in 1772 and to Cailliaud in 1821. The former was shown an "undoubtedly authentic" list by the *Síd el Ḳūm* ("Master of the Household"). The latter says "Je m'étais procuré, chez les érudits de la ville [Sennár], plusieurs listes chronologiques des rois Foungis du Sennâr: mais, en les comparant entre elles, je doutais de pouvoir arriver à un travail satisfaisant: enfin, par l'entremise d'Ismâyl, j'en obtins une du roi Bâdy lui-même. Je puis donc garantir que la chronologie que je donne ici est plus exacte que celle de Bruce" (vol. II, 255).

The main difference between these two lists is that Bruce dates the accession of 'Omára Dūnḳas, the first FUNG king, in 1504, and Cailliaud in 1484. The discrepancy is explained in an appendix, and the date 1504 may be taken as correct.

With one or more of these chronologies as a basis, and with the *Ṭabaḳát wad Ḍayfulla* (MS. D 3) for occasional reference and quotation, the original of the work which is here translated was probably compiled gradually during the *régimes* of successive Turkish rulers and completed about the time of Mumtáz Pasha (1871–1873).

Its author is unknown and its exact date is doubtful. The British Museum copy, it is said, "consists of 108 octavo pages and was written, and perhaps also composed, by Muḥammad Abû Bakr Makkî Aḥmad in 1879" (Budge, Preface, p. xi). It ends with the year 1871. One would suppose that Muḥammad Abu Bakr would have carried the history down to his own date had he been the composer and not merely a copyist.

Mr Jackson says that all the copies he has seen "seem to be derived from the account put together by Abd el Dafaa and an abstract of this, with a few alterations and additions, made by Zubeir wad Dawwa." He does not say to what year the narrative is in each case carried down. By "'Abd el Dafaa" he means Ibráhím 'Abd el Dáfa'i the elegist, who is twice mentioned in D 7 in the third person. Of this Ibráhím more anon.

The copy found by Sir R. von Slatin was made, as is stated at the close of it, on the 19th of *Sha'bán* 1322 A.H. (October 30, 1904 A.D.). The copy I have translated consists of 110 octavo pages and gives an account of events down to 1288 A.H. (1871 A.D.). That of Muḥammad 'Abd el Mágid ends abruptly with 1865.

None of these gives any direct indication as to the author's name, and *Mek* 'Adlán's evidence is practically worthless: he fluctuates between vague reminiscences of the *Ṭabaḳát wad Ḍayfulla* and "an unknown scribe" who may have lived in the lifetime of *Mek*

'Adlán's father 'Othmán or in the time of 'Adlán II, *i.e.* in the eighteenth century. He does not even know his own family history and has not the faintest idea whether the book was written by one man or half a dozen.

There is, however, internal evidence which makes it easy to guess at certain probabilities. In the first place, the author only describes in detail events that occurred in the Gezíra, from Sennár to Khartoum, and he is familiar with the geography of this region and the details of its administration.

It is also evident that he was frequently in Khartoum, for he is interested in the various buildings that were erected there, knows various junior officials, tells of visitors from Egypt, and knows exact dates of arrivals and departures.

Similarly he shows far more knowledge of the Blue Nile than of the White. Kordofán, Berber, Dongola, Kassala and other more distant provinces hardly come within his ken at all.

Again he speaks with exaggerated respect of Sheikh 'Abd el Ḳádir wad el Zayn, the Ya'aḳūbábi, and represents him as having an almost supreme influence. Here there must be considerable exaggeration, for whereas several of 'Abd el Ḳádir's contemporaries are mentioned by travellers, I have seen no reference to 'Abd el Ḳádir, and his name is not universally remembered. No other secular Sheikh is spoken of in similar terms.

Another man upon whom the author heaps titles of respect is Sheikh Aḥmad el Ṭaib, the introducer of the Sammánía *ṭariḳa*, who lived a day's journey north of Omdurmán. Other holy men receive no more than passing words of praise.

He also indulges in gross adulation of Ga'afir Muẓhar Pasha, and abuses his successor Mumtáz Pasha with an almost equal lack of proportion. Other Governor-Generals are treated very leniently.

One also notes the author's familiarity with Turkish ranks and titles.

For the FUNG and the HAMAG he holds no particular brief, and of the history of the 'ABDULLÁB of el Ḥalfáya and the SA'ADÁB of Shendi he expressly mentions his ignorance. The successive Sheikhs of Khashm el Baḥr, near Sennár, are, on the other hand, fairly well known to him.

From a consideration of the above facts and other minor points one would say that the author of this history was perhaps by birth one of the YA'AḲŪBÁB of Sennár, and by training a follower of the Sammánía *ṭariḳa*. He had an education better than the average, and was much in touch with the Turkish officials—as were the successive heads of his family. Probably he throve most successfully in the times of Mūsa Pasha and Ga'afir Muẓhar Pasha, and was employed at Khartoum in some minor administrative position, or else was one of those tactful "vicars of Bray" who were always to be found attached to the suites of the secular dignitaries.

From his expressed opinion of Mumtáz one would hazard the opinion that he fell into disfavour during that Pasha's *régime* and completed his history after passing beyond his reach.

On the other hand, the author of ABC (para. XXI), speaking of the Ḥamaydánía section of the Gamū'ía, says "Among them was the *feki* Ibráhím 'Abd el Dáfa'i, the author of the *History of the Sudan*"; and one notes that the family of the much belauded Sheikh el Ṭaib (*q.v.* in ABC, *Tree* 3) are very closely related to the Ḥamaydánía. The history mentioned may certainly be assumed to be the one under discussion. Na'ūm Bey Shuḳayr, in his *History of the Sudan*, also speaks of "Sheikh 'Abd el Dáfa'i, author of the Fung chronicle" (Part II, Bk. IV, Chap. 1, p. 73).

Thus, in support of the theory that Ibráhím 'Abd el Dáfa'i wrote it, we have (1) the tradition recorded by Mr Jackson and Na'ūm Bey and quoted above, (2) the express statement in ABC, and (3) the close relationship between Ibráhím and the founder of the Sammánía *ṭaríḳa*.

On the other hand, (1) the history is carried up to a date between 1870 and 1880, and yet Ibráhím was composing elegies in 1809 and 1823 (see paras. CLXXXV and CCXXXV). (2) One would expect more references to the Gamūí'a and their *Meks* from a Gamū'i author, and a larger interest in the affairs of the Gamūí'a country along the west bank of the White Nile. (3) The tradition that Ibráhím 'Abd el Dáfa'i is the author is not by any means universal: my acquaintanceship with it is limited to the two quotations made above. (4) The general setting of the two passing references to Ibráhím in paras. CLXXXV and CCXXXV does not seem quite to suit the theory that Ibráhím was speaking of himself.

There is of course the possibility of a divided authorship, but there is no particular evidence to support such theory.

One can only leave the question of authorship doubtful, and say that, all things considered, the history is a very creditable piece of work. It is written in a simple and straightforward way, with a reasonable sense of proportion; and the author never loses the thread of his discourse.

Of the Turkish days he writes as a courtier, but it would have been unsafe, and less lucrative, to do otherwise: in fact he is at times unexpectedly critical. He has rescued from oblivion the scanty records of many events that happened in the reigns of those kings of Sennár of whom little more than the names are recorded by Bruce and Cailliaud, and he has given us the only extant account of the Sudan in Turkish days as regarded from a native point of view. In addition, so far as I am aware, he provides the only connected narrative from which we can learn the names and dates of the successive Turkish Pashas and Beys who ruled the country, and he alone draws our attention to the experiments that were made in administrative decentralization between 1857 and 1862.

The account of Sóba in pre-FUNG days (see para. I) is evidently taken from the passage of Ibn Selím el Aswáni preserved by el Maḳrízi and quoted above in Part II, Chap. 2.

I In the name of God the Compassionate and Merciful. Praise be to God....

Now this is a history of the lands of the NŪBA and relates who ruled them, beginning with the kings of the FŪNG, and what happened in their time [and] until this present day, and who succeeded them, and how their kingdom came to an end; but God Almighty best knows and judges of that which is hidden.

It is related in the histories which I have seen that the first of the kings of the FŪNG who was invested with the royal power was King 'Omára Dūnḳas, who founded the city of Sennár in 910 A.H.[1]

Previously to his date the FŪNG had overthrown the NŪBA and made the city of Ṣóbá (*sic*) their metropolis; and in that city were beautiful buildings and gardens and a hostel occupied by the Muhammadans. Its site was on the east of the Nile, near to the confluence of that river with the White Nile; and the chief food of its inhabitants was the white *dhurra* known as *el ḳaṣṣábi*. Their religion was Christianity, and they had a bishop appointed by the prelate of Alexandria, as had the NŪBA before them. Their books were in Greek (*Rūmía*) but they used to commentate upon them in their own language.

II These people were overthrown in the ninth century, and in those days there were no schools for the Muhammadans who lived among them and no observance of the Muhammadan law, so that it is even said that a woman might be divorced by her husband and married by another man on the same day without any purificatory period. This state continued until the coming among them of Maḥmūd el 'Araki from Egypt. He taught them some of the elements of Muhammadan law: he also built himself a hostel on the White Nile

[1] 1504 A.D.

between el Ís[1] and the ḤASÁNÍA, and lies buried there at the present day.

III Previous to this man's time there were certain learned men in the country, such as the AWLÁD ḌAYFULLA, whose tombs near Abu Ḥalíma, east of the Blue Nile, are well known, and Sheikh Idrís walad el Arbáb, who was born in 913[2].

IV Islám first entered the land of the NŪBA in the Khalífate of Hárūn el Rashíd el 'Abbási, but, as we mentioned, there was no real observance of the law (*el sharí'a*).

V Let us now return to our subject. The commencement of the reign of 'Omára Dūnḳas was at the beginning of...(a line of the text has been inadvertently omitted here, it appears)...the people collected round him and ceased not visiting him where he lay at Gebel Móya, which is east of Sennár; and finally there came to him 'Abdulla Gemá'a of the ḲAWÁSMA Arabs, the father of Sheikh 'Agíb el Káfūta the ancestor of the AWLÁD 'AGÍB; and they determined to make war upon the 'ANAG, the kings of Sóba and el Ḳerri.

VI So 'Omára and 'Abdulla Gemá'a with their men went and made war upon the kings of Sóba and el Ḳerri and defeated them and slew them.

VII Then their people agreed that 'Omára should be king in place of the king of 'Aloa, that is Sóba, because he was the more powerful ["elder" ?], and that 'Abdulla Gemá'a should take the place of the king of el Ḳerri.

VIII So ['Abdulla] went and founded the town of Ḳerri, which is by Gebel el Royyán on the east bank, and made it the seat of his kingdom; and likewise 'Omára founded the town of Sennár, [so called because] previously a woman called Sennár lived there, and made it his capital. This was in 910[3].

IX Now 'Omára and 'Abdulla lived like brethren, but 'Omára's rank had precedence over that of 'Abdulla if they were together in the same place; but if 'Omára were absent 'Abdulla had exactly the same powers as were vested in 'Omára; and this system remained in force among their respective descendants until the end of their rule.

X After the victory of the FUNG over the NŪBA, the latter scattered and fled to Fázoghli and Kordofán, with the exception of a few of them who were converted to Islam and mixed with the Arabs settled in their country. These at present are few in number and live in the neighbourhood of Shendi and Gerayf Ḳumr; and not many people

[1] reading اليس for الليس.

[2] 1507 A.D.

[3] 1504 A.D.

know that these men are by origin NŪBA, for their language has become Arabic and their complexion assimilated to that of the Arabs as a result of cross-breeding with them.

XI And indeed the immigration of Arabs to the Sudan increased greatly, most of them belonging to the tribes of ḤIMYAR, RABÍ'A, BENI 'ÁMIR, ḲAḤṬÁN, KENÁNA, GUHAYNA, BENI YASHKUR, BENI KÁHIL, BENI DHUBIÁN, BENI 'ABS (viz. the KABÁBÍSH), FEZÁRA and BENI SELÍM.

XII And King 'Omára continued living at Sennár, carrying on the affairs of state, until he died in the year 940[1] after a reign of 30 years.

XIII He was succeeded by his son 'Abd el Ḳádir, who reigned ten years and died in 950[2].

XIV After him reigned his brother King Náíl, and he resided at Sennár like his father and brother, carrying on the government for twelve years. He died in 962[3].

XV His successor was King 'Omára Abu Sakaykín, one of the royal family, and in his days died 'Abdulla Gemá'a, and in his place 'Omára appointed his son Sheikh 'Agíb el Káfūta as Sheikh of Ḳerri. And 'Omára continued at Sennár, carrying on the government, until his death in 970[4] after a reign of eight years.

XVI King Dekín walad Náíl then came to the throne. He was one of the greatest of the kings of the FUNG. He reorganized the administration in the best possible manner, and made fixed laws that no one of all the people of his kingdom might transgress; and to every district of his kingdom he appointed a chief; and to such as were wont to be seated in his presence he gave a definite order of precedence when they were so seated in the council chamber; and he ceased not to devote himself to the organization of his realms until, afte rreigning fifteen[5] years, he died in 985[6].

XVII He was succeeded by King Ṭabl, who followed in the footsteps of King Dekín until his death in 997[7] after reigning twelve years.

XVIII Ṭabl was succeeded by King Ounsa, who reigned ten years.

XIX Then King 'Abd el Ḳádir reigned for six years, and died in 1013[8].

XX He was succeeded by King 'Adlán walad Áya, and in his reign Sheikh 'Agíb rebelled, and the king sent a large army against him and a battle was fought near Kalkól, and Sheikh 'Agíb was slain and his hosts routed, and his family fled towards Dongola. Then the king

[1] 1533 A.D. [2] 1543 A.D. [3] 1554 A.D.
[4] 1562 A.D. [5] reading "fifteen" for "twelve."
[6] 1577 A.D. [7] 1589 A.D. [8] 1604 A.D.

sent to them Sheikh Idrís Muḥammad Aḥmad, who was noted for his piety, with a promise of immunity, and when they returned he lavished favours upon them and appointed the eldest of them, el 'Agayl, Sheikh of Ḳerri as his father had been.

XXI King 'Adlán continued reigning at Sennár until his death in 1020[1] after a reign of seven years; and in his reign flourished a number of holy men, such as Sheikh Idrís, whom we mentioned. This latter attained a remarkable age, for he was born in 913[2] and died in 1060[3], and so lived 147 years. He was instructed by Sheikh 'Abd el Káfi el Moghrabi.

XXII So too, in the reign of King 'Adlán, there came [to the country] Sheikh Ḥasan walad Ḥasūna el Andalūsi. He had been visiting the Holy Places and Egypt and Syria for about twelve years, and then settled where he now lies buried; and his tomb is well known and much visited. His was, God bless him, an austerity of the first order though he was blessed with this world's goods in abundance.

XXIII During this king's reign too came Sheikh Ibráhím el Būlád from Egypt. He was the first to introduce and teach the *Mukhtaṣar* of Sheikh Khálil el Máliki into the land of the FUNG, and through him God manifested many miracles.

XXIV There also came Sheikh Muḥammad el Miṣri and visited Sennár and Arbagi, and then he returned and settled at Berber and there taught all the sciences, and was made a judge, and as such conducted himself with continence and rectitude.

XXV Sheikh Tág el Ḍín el Bahári too came from Baghdád, and Ṣūfiism obtained great fame in the land of the FUNG through him.

XXVI And a certain Moghrabi of Tlemsan, too, inspired Sheikh Muḥammad walad 'Ísa Sowár el Dhahab, and from him this Sheikh obtained direction in the right way, and taught others many of the branches of knowledge.

XXVII After King 'Adlán King Bádi Síd el Ḳūm came to the throne, and reigned three years, and died in 1023[4].

XXVIII He was succeeded by el Rubáṭ, who continued living at Sennár until his death in 1052[5].

XXIX After him reigned his son King Bádi Abu Duḳn. He was a man of bravery and generosity and high purpose. He raided the White Nile and engaged its inhabitants, who are called SHILLUK, and he invaded the mountains of Teḳali that lie west of the White Nile some two days' march. The reason of his invading Teḳali was

[1] 1611 A.D. [2] 1507 A.D. [3] 1650 A.D.
[4] 1614 A.D. [5] 1642 A.D.

that the king of Teḳali had attacked one of his friends who journeyed thither, and plundered his goods, and when told that the victim was a friend of the king of Sennár had replied "If the king of Sennár wants me on his account and crosses the wastes of Um Lamá'a, then let him do what he will."

XXX Now the desert spoken of by the king of Teḳali is difficult to cross owing to lack of water, but must be passed by one going from Sennár to Teḳali. And when the man returned to his friend the *Mek* Bádi he told him how his possessions had been plundered and what the king of Teḳali had said, and [Bádi] at once equipped his troops and said to his friend "When we reach the wastes of Um Lamá'a, let me know." And when they arrived there the man told him, and the king and all his men dismounted from their horses and crossed over on foot. Then they remounted and rode on until they reached the hills of the NŪBA; and there they slew many and took numerous prisoners and so proceeded until they came to Teḳali and laid siege to it.

XXXI And the king of Teḳali had fortified it against them, and he used to come out to meet them by day, and send them provisions by night; and when the king of Sennár saw the generosity of his spirit he made terms with him on the basis of a fixed tribute payable yearly by the king of Teḳali.

XXXII Then he returned to Sennár with the prisoners taken from the NŪBA and Teḳali, and on arriving there built a village for each different race of prisoners; and these villages surrounded Sennár like a wall to the east and west, and the inhabitants acted as troops for the aid and protection of the realm, and they bred and multiplied until the fall of the FUNG kingdom. Now each village was named after the race inhabiting it, for instance "Teḳali" and "el Kadero" and "el Kanak" and "el Kárku."

XXXIII And this king was a man of continence and piety and paid great respect to the men of learning and religion, and he used to send presents with the guide Aḥmad walad 'Alwán to the learned men of el Maḥrūsa; and his virtues became so famous among them that they celebrated him in many poems, including that in which Sheikh 'Omar el Moghrabi says...(thirteen lines of poetry follow)...This poem is a long one, consisting of about seventy lines.

XXXIV And the same Sheikh also said of him...(nine lines of poetry follow); and this also is a long poem of about sixty lines.

XXXV Similarly all the best men of el Maḥrūsa sang thus in his praise, and the evidence of these learned men is sufficient honour.

XXXVI Among the praiseworthy monuments he left are the great mosque he founded at Sennár, and the royal palace. The latter consisted of five stories on the top of one another, and a number of buildings adjoining them for the storage of government equipment, such as arms and the like. He also built two halls [*díwánayn*] where he might sit in council, one of them outside the palace and the other inside its enclosure, and round the whole he built a vast wall and made therein nine gates, and to each of the great men of his kingdom he appointed a special gate for entry or exit thereby.

XXXVII Likewise he made a special hall for the great men of the kingdom, wherein they might sit to consider their business; and if one of them [*lit.* "this chief"] wished to enter the hall [*díwán*] of the king he must enter alone, unaccompanied by any of his people. But the ninth gate was reserved for the king himself, and no man might enter with him or go out by it, save only the king and Walad 'Agíb the king of Ḳerri.

XXXVIII All these gates opened from the same frontage of the wall, which formed a straight line, and in front of them was a roofed area supported by two pillars, and under it a high bench [*musṭaba*] called "Dakka man Nádák" ("The bench of him that hath called upon thee").

XXXIX These buildings survived until the time of the late Effendína Ismá'íl Pasha the son of Effendína el Ḥág Muḥammad 'Ali Pasha; but in his days the palace fell and all traces of it disappeared. All glory be to Him whose kingdom continueth for ever!

XL King Bádi continued at Sennár like his predecessors, applying himself to the work of his kingdom and to doing good until he died in 1088[1] after a reign of thirty-six years.

XLI After him his brother's son Ounsa walad Náṣir came to the throne, and in 1095[2], during his reign, there occurred a great famine, so that men ate dogs; and they called this year "*Um Laḥm*" ("Mother of Meat"), and many folk died, and certain districts were devastated owing to the famine and small-pox.

And King Ounsa remained at Sennár until his death in 1100[3] after a reign of twelve years.

XLII He was succeeded by his son the *Mek* Bádi el Aḥmar ("The Red"), and he was the first FUNG king against whom a section of his people revolted; for el Amín Arádib walad 'Agíb rebelled with about a thousand men of the FUNG and others, and appointed over them as *Mek* one named Awkal. And they designed to depose the *Mek* Bádi el Aḥmar and made ready for war, but he, though having only about forty-five horsemen, met them and routed them and drove them

[1] 1677 A.D. [2] 1684 A.D. [3] 1688–9 A.D.

to a place called el 'Aṭshán, and slew el Amín Arádib, and returned victorious.

XLIII And in his days lived the pious saint Aḥmad walad el Turábi. And Bádi reigned, honoured and respected, until his death in 1127[1] after a reign of twenty-seven[2] years.

XLIV After him came to the throne his son Ounsa; and he gave himself up to frivolous amusement and the practice of immorality, until the news of his doings reached the FUNG in the south, namely the troops of Lūlū, and they determined to depose him, for it is they who depose and appoint whatever king they choose without any slaying.

XLV And when they reached their decision they moved northwards until they reached el Kabūsh near Sennár, and then appointed Nūl to rule as king, and sent word to king Ounsa saying "If you put your vizier to death we will confirm you in your old position and not oppose you." Then Ounsa did as they bid him, and after some demur slew his vizier and sent the herald and some of the chief men ['*omad*] of Sennár to request forgiveness in accordance with their promise. But they paid no attention to these and maintained their resolve to depose him; and when he had abandoned all hope he begged for immunity for himself and his family, and this they granted him, and his reign came to an end.

XLVI This was in 1130[3], and he was the last of the line of FUNG kings who belonged to the royal family.

XLVII He was succeeded by King Nūl, a connection of the OUNSÁB family on the mother's side. He did not belong to the stock of the kings who preceded him, but his appointment was merely agreed upon because he was a sensible man and an orthodox follower of the Faith. And indeed the common opinion of him was justified, for he showed himself just and steady in his conduct, and in his days the people had complete rest, so that they called him "El Nóm" ["Sleep"] because he was so just. He reigned until his death in the eighth month of 1135[4].

XLVIII After him ruled his son King Bádi "Abu Shelūkh"; and he was the last of the kings who were powerful, for at the close of his reign the Sheikhs of the HAMAG overcame him, and the constitutional appointment of kings became a farce, and all power, whether of loosing or of binding, passed into the hands of the HAMAG.

XLIX Now the HAMAG are a section of those Arabs who are descended from the ANWÁB [*i.e.* NŪBA], or, as another account says, a branch of

[1] 1715 A.D.
[2] reading ٢٧ for ٢٢.
[3] 1718 A.D.
[4] 1723 A.D.

the GA'ALIYYŪN EL 'AWAḌÍA, who are of the seed of our lord el 'Abbás ibn 'Abd el Muṭṭalib; but God knows best.

L In the reign of Bádi "Abu Shelūkh" the Abyssinians advanced to the number of about 100,000, and the king made ready the troops of Islam against them with all their equipment and their arms complete, and begged the men of piety and learning to strive in prayer for the victory of Islam, and [appointed] over the army el Amín and some of the great men of the realm who were noted for their strength and skill.

LI There also joined them Khamís, the chief of the FŪR troops, with a large army; and in command of the cavalry was Sheikh Muḥammad Abu el Kaylak, the chief of the HAMAG.

LII Then they set forth with Islamic resolve and ardour, and the engagement took place east of the river Dinder, near 'Agíb, and a furious combat ensued, and men innumerable were slain; but God gave the victory to the troops of Islam and the Abyssinians suffered a terrible defeat.

LIII And the Muhammadans took great booty and a quantity of rifles and cannon and tents and horses, etc., and the fame of this victory spread throughout the world of Islam, so that embassies came [to Sennár] from the Ḥegáz and el Sind and el Hind, and people [immigrated] from Upper Egypt and Morocco and settled there.

And owing to the terror of this victory the Abyssinians never attacked or raided Sennár [again].

LIV [The news of] the victory of the Muhammadan troops also reached the [Sultan of] the Sultans of Islam and the Emperor of the mighty Emperors, and he rejoiced exceedingly, and his heart dilated with pleasure.

LV After the victory the army returned to Sennár and held festivities and thanksgivings, and the king gave alms to the poor and needy and showed humility and abasement before God Almighty.

LVI Now this battle befel in *Ṣafar el Khayr* 1157[1].

LVII And King Bádi reigned for a long time, and in the early and middle years of his reign he had a good and devout vizier who managed the affairs of state excellently until death overtook him, but then the king undertook the ruling of affairs, and his first act was to slay the remainder of the OUNSÁB; and he changed many of the laws and the established customs, and invoked the aid of the NŪBA, and appointed them chiefs in place of the old nobility, and consented to an evil policy of plunder and slaughter, even going so far as to connive at the murder of (?) the well-known man of learning el Khaṭíb

[1] 1744 A.D.

'Abd el Laṭíf. And, not content with the wrongs he inflicted himself, he let his sons also commit deeds of injustice and malice. So in general the atrocities which he committed alienated the hearts of his people, and especially those of the FUNG nobility and others.

LVIII While things were thus he made ready a great army to fight the MUSABA'ÁT, and in command was his vizier Walad Tóma, and among the chiefs was 'Abdulla walad 'Agíb, and among the famous warriors was Sheikh Muḥammad Abu el Kaylak. Thus he set forth with his army until he reached the MUSABA'ÁT, and a battle took place at a place called Ḳiḥayf in the year 1160[1], and the commander-in-chief Walad Tóma and 'Abdulla walad 'Agíb were killed and the army took to flight. But Sheikh Muḥammad Abu el Kaylak rallied them and exhorted them and put strength into their hearts, and they returned and met the MUSABA'ÁT a second time, and a furious struggle ensued, and Shammám walad 'Agíb and el 'Agayl his son were slain.

LIX Then the king was informed of all that had taken place in both encounters and of the determination and patience of Sheikh Muḥammad Abu el Kaylak and how he had rallied the soldiers, and he sent word appointing him commander-in-chief in Walad Tóma's stead.

LX And when he had learnt of his appointment Abu el Kaylak returned to war against the MUSABA'ÁT and used all his endeavours until God gave him the victory over them and suffered him to turn them out of Kordofán; and this was in the early part of the year.

LXI Now there were with Abu el Kaylak a number of the FUNG nobles, and news reached them that during their absence the king had ill-treated their dependants, so they came before Sheikh Muḥammad and voiced their grievance against the king and asked for his consent to their deposing Bádi and appointing another. And after discussion he consented to their plan and took up the matter in complete accord with them.

LXII The same day he struck camp and set out for Sennár with such troops and great men of the FUNG, that is slaves of the king, as were with him. This was in 1174[2]. And after he had crossed the White Nile he camped at el Ís[3] and sent to Náṣir, the son of the *Mek* Bádi, saying that if he came to him he would appoint him king.

LXIII And Náṣir came secretly to Sheikh Muḥammad at el Ís[4], and they took the [usual] oaths and assurances from him, and set out for Sennár taking him with them.

LXIV On arriving there they besieged the *Mek*, and [finally]

[1] 1747 A.D.
[2] 1760 A.D.
[3] reading باليس for بالليس.
[4] reading باليس for بالليس.

granted him immunity for his person and safe conduct to Sóba; and he left Sennár in abasement.

LXV And when they knew he had left they entered Sennár unopposed and fulfilled their promise to the *Mek* Náṣir and made him king. This was in 1175[1].

LXVI In these days the power of the FUNG dissolved and the power, whether of loosing or binding, passed to the HAMAG, and Sheikh Muḥammad Abu el Kaylak subdued the king and put to death numbers of the great men of the FUNG.

LXVII And *Mek* Náṣir remained *Mek* at Sennár until 1182[2], but Sheikh Muḥammad then deposed him and exiled him to the village of Buḳera beyond el Támayn.

LXVIII After his expulsion the *Mek* Náṣir sent to some of the FUNG and asked their aid to make war upon Sheikh Muḥammad; so [the latter] sent his brother's son Bádi walad Ragab and Aḥmad walad Maḥmūd, the Sheikh of the FŪÁRI, and a detachment of troops, and they came in unto [Náṣir] and slew him; and they had found him with the Ḳurán on his right hand and his prayer-mat on his left, for he was a learned man, and his handwriting was beautiful, God have mercy upon him!

LXIX Náṣir's death was in 1182[2], and thereupon Sheikh Muḥammad appointed his brother Ismá'íl, son of the *Mek* Bádi, king at Sennár; but all power remained in the hands of Sheikh Muḥammad Abu el Kaylak.

LXX And [Ismá'íl] removed abuses and acted justly by his people and treated well the men of religion, so that in return they prayed for him, and God blessed him in his lifetime and his seed after him.

LXXI And in this year there befel a great famine, and it was known as "*Sannat el Kabsa*" ("The Year of Pressure"); and in 1185[3] the river rose to a great height, and likewise in 1189[4].

LXXII In 1190[5] Sheikh Muḥammad Abu el Kaylak died, may God have mercy upon him! And Sheikh 'Adlán walad Ṣubáḥi, the Sheikh of Khashm el Baḥr, also; and between these two there had been great affection.

Now [the latter] was a continent and temperate man, honourable and pious.

LXXIII After the death of Sheikh Muḥammad the Sheikhs appointed Sheikh Bádi walad Ragab, the son of Sheikh Muḥammad's brother, and when this was done the FUNG collected and came before the *Mek* Ismá'íl seeking to be relieved of Sheikh Bádi. But when

[1] 1761 A.D. [2] 1768 A.D. [3] 1771 A.D.

[4] 1775 A.D. (reading ٨٩ for ٨٣). [5] 1776 A.D. (reading ١١٩٠ for ١١٩٨.)

Bádi heard of this he exiled the *Mek* Ismá'íl to Sūákin and put the *Mek* 'Adlán upon the throne in his stead.

LXXIV And the viziership of Sheikh Bádi was successful, and he treated the people justly and extended all the boundaries of the realm, and even surpassed his uncle Sheikh Muḥammad in boldness and might and strength and bravery.

LXXV In his days the SHUKRÍA Arabs rebelled, so he made ready his army and marched against them and killed Sheikh Abu 'Ali, the Sheikh of the SHUKRÍA.

LXXVI Then he sent Sheikh 'Agíb walad 'Abdulla and Sheikh Ḳandaláwi to Táka to make war upon the ḤALANḲA Arabs, and they did so, and Sheikh 'Agíb and 'Ísáwi were killed. Ḳandaláwi returned, but the SHUKRÍA opposed him on his way and slew him. This was in 1193[1].

LXXVII And Sheikh Bádi remained at his home, the village of Rufá'a, east of the Nile, until the SHUKRÍA had been brought into subjection. And while there he beat Náṣir the son of Sheikh Muḥammad Abu el Kaylak violently with whips, and deposed Sheikh Muḥammad el Amín and sent him to el Ḳerbayn; and he also deposed Sheikh Aḥmad walad 'Ali[2], the Sheikh of the district of Khashm el Baḥr, and appointed [in his place] Ṣubáḥi walad 'Adlán.

LXXVIII Then his cousins, the sons of Sheikh Muḥammad, changed their attitude towards him on account of his having beaten their brother, and asked him for permission to go to Sennár for the treatment of the illness which had resulted to their brother from the beating. And he gave them leave, and when they reached Sennár they began plotting war and entered into an agreement with the *Mek* 'Adlán and some of the great men of the FUNG whose attitude Sheikh Bádi had caused to change.

LXXIX There also joined them Sheikh Aḥmad walad 'Ali, the Sheikh of Khashm el Baḥr district, and Sheikh Muḥammad el Amín, the Sheikh of Ḳerri; and they all assembled at Sennár and made known their rebellion, hitherto covert, against Sheikh Bádi, and took all the horses and arms they could find from the Arabs, and marched for el Dákhila against Sheikh Shanbūl and Sheikh Ṣubáḥi, whom Sheikh Bádi had sent to collect the tribute of the RUFÁ'A Arabs.

LXXX The forces met at el Dákhila and fought, and Sheikh Shanbūl was killed and Sheikh Ṣubáḥi taken prisoner alive, and all the horses and the arms that had been with them were captured.

[1] 1779 A.D.

[2] reading احمد ولد على شيخ for محمد ولد شيخ.

LXXXI Now as soon as ever they had resolved upon rebellion the news thereof had reached Sheikh Bádi, but he had not bothered himself until he heard that Sheikh el Amín walad 'Agíb was privy to the plot, but hearing this he said "Now it is war," for he knew that Sheikh el Amín was a match for him in bravery and strength; and he started at once and crossed the Nile and paused not, not even at Sennár, in his eagerness against them, until they met in battle.

LXXXII The commander of his troops was his son, and after a fierce battle his army and his son fled; and when he saw that he drew his sword and plunged into the [enemies'] army alone, and he asked every man he met [his name], and he would reply "So and so," and Bádi would pass on, until finally there met him Sheikh el Amín, and when questioned [as to his name] the latter replied "Muḥammad el Amín"; and when Bádi had made sure of this he struck him three blows, but they did him no hurt because his mail was strong and Sheikh Bádi struck blindly from the excitement of his anger.

LXXXIII Then Sheikh el Amín struck Bádi a single and surer blow, for his sword was sharp and his knowledge of warfare complete, and Sheikh Bádi tried to keep his balance upon his horse's back but could not, and fell to the earth.

LXXXIV And lying thus he called for his uncle's sons, Ragab and Náṣir and Idrís and 'Adlán and their other brothers, that he might give them his last instructions. Then Sheikh Aḥmad walad 'Ali said to him "Are you even yet alive?" and smote him on the mouth with his sword, and he died.

LXXXV But when the sons of his uncle Abu el Kaylak came up they were exceedingly wroth with Sheikh Aḥmad walad 'Ali for striking their brother as he lay on the ground, and thus were laid the foundations of the enmity between the sons of Abu el Kaylak and those of Aḥmad.

LXXXVI The death of Sheikh Bádi was in 1194[1], and he was succeeded as Sheikh and vizier by Sheikh Ragab walad Muḥammad, and the king, if he could be so called, was 'Adlán.

LXXXVII And Sheikh Ragab went to Kordofán and remained there besieging the mountains, and he sent his brother, Sheikh Náṣir, with about 700 horsemen to the Gezíra to give battle to Sheikh el Amín at el Hilálía, which lies east of the Blue Nile.

LXXXVIII And when they came upon Sheikh el Amín he had with him only sixteen horsemen of his own family and slaves, but a fierce engagement took place and the troops of Sheikh Náṣir were routed and driven into the river.

[1] 1780 A.D.

LXXXIX When Sheikh Náṣir had established himself in the Gezíra he summoned Bádi walad Mismár, the brother of Sheikh el Amín, and made him Sheikh in the place of his brother.

XC This was in 1198[1]; and when Sheikh el Amín learnt that it was the people of Arbagi by whose influence his brother Bádi had been appointed, he betook himself to the SHUKRÍA and enlisted their aid, and with them attacked the town of Arbagi and put its fighting men and such as were scattered in different parts to the sword, and razed it to the ground and left it desert, though it had been the fairest town in the Gezíra, populous and prosperous in trade, with fine buildings and schools of learning and religion, inhabited by men of wealth and well stocked with provisions. But from that day forward it lay waste until now.

XCI While all this was happening Sheikh Ragab was in Kordofán, and his brother Ibráhím, who was known as "Walad Saláṭín," at Sennár with the king, acting for his brother, in charge of all his possessions.

XCII Then 'Adlán bethought himself of how the HAMAG had treated his father the *Mek* Ismá'íl and his grandfather the *Mek* Bádi, and sent for Sheikh el Amín and the AWLÁD NIMR; and they came before him, and he mustered his courage and arrested Ibráhím walad Muḥammad by their advice, for when he had sought their alliance they had said to him "We will not agree unless you arrest Ibráhím."

XCIII So he arrested him and the HAMAG who were with him and Sheikh Aḥmad walad 'Ali and el Zayn walad Hárūn and el Amín walad Tiktak and Walad Ḳandaláwi and slew them all in the *fásher*, that is in the market-place (*sūḳ*).

XCIV Then he fetched out the daughters of Sheikh Muḥammad and distributed them to the chiefs of the troops as slaves. This was in 1199[2]. Now el Na'ísan, the famous poet, was living at Sennár at this time, and the king designed to put him to death because of his inclination towards the children of Abu el Kaylak, and menaced him with angry words; and he, seeing his death was intended, fled away to Kordofán; and so soon as he saw Sheikh Ragab he wept and sobbed and recited a number of woeful elegies wherein he described the slaying of Ibráhím and the enslavement of the daughters of Muḥammad.

XCV And when Sheikh Ragab heard of the murder of his brother and learnt how he had been dishonoured, he set forth straightway with his troops; and there were with him the *Malik* Sa'ad ibn el Mek Idrís walad el Faḥl and el Ḥág Maḥmūd el Magdhūb, the worker of miracles.

[1] 1784 A.D. [2] 1785 A.D.

XCVI And Ragab pushed forward until he reached the village of Shádli. And as they marched Sheikh Maḥmūd el Magdhūb used to say "O Sennár the flames have come upon thee!" and at times "The flood has quenched the flame!"; and on the eve of the battle he said "I and thou!"—referring to the [impending] death of himself and Sheikh Ragab.

XCVII And the armies met at a place called el Teras and fought, and Sheikh Ragab and el Ḥág Maḥmūd were slain.

XCVIII Now the sons of Sheikh Ragab were Muḥammad and Dóka and Bádi and Ḥasan and 'Ali and Ibráhím and Kamatu.

XCIX And it is said of el Ḥág Maḥmūd that after he had been buried the call to prayer used to be heard nightly at his tomb, for in his lifetime he was a *muedhdhin* ("one who calls to prayer").

C And when Sheikh Ragab had been killed his troops fled in disorder and reached the village of 'Abūd, and when they had camped there they were all of different minds and some said one thing and some another, but in the end they decided to scatter in flight.

CI Then the *feki* Ḥegázi Abu Zayd sent to them and bade them be of good heart and promised them victory and said he would inspire them; so they were reassured and made Sheikh Náṣir walad Muḥammad their Sheikh. This was in 1202[1].

CII And Sheikh Náṣir remained at el Tómát for two years and then moved to Ṭaiba Ḳandaláwi for a space.

CIII Meanwhile King 'Adlán was being treated for his illness, and [on his recovery] he prepared a mighty host and appointed to command it el Amín Raḥma walad Katfáwi, with whom were Muḥammad walad Khamís Abu Ráda and a number of the great men of the FUNG.

CIV The armies met at a place called Inṭaraḥná and a fierce battle followed. The troops of the king were routed, but among the HAMAG was slain 'Ali walad Saláṭín, the son of Sheikh Muḥammad and brother of Ibráhím, a man renowned for his bravery.

CV And there was great slaughter among the troops of the *Mek*, and some of them were drowned in the river. And Sheikh Náṣir's men pursued them and drove them into Sennár. Then the *Mek* was exceedingly sorry that he had not accompanied his troops in person, and so great was his grief that he survived but a few days and then died.

CVI But Sheikh Náṣir encamped with his army at el Labayḥ and closely besieged the *Mek's* troops, and the population fell into dire straits, so that finally the *Mek's* army sallied forth to give him battle; but they were discomfited before any fighting actually took place,

[1] 1787 A.D.

and Náṣir and his men entered Sennár and made great havoc there, and pursued the routed army to el Sáli, and then returned.

CVII This was in 1203[1], and from now onwards the FUNG ceased to have any authority or leadership, and their king was quite powerless: in fact the kings were like prisoners in the hands of the HAMAG, even as one of the 'Abbásid Khalífas said when their rule had fallen into decay and their power gone, "Ah! Is it not wonderful that one like myself should see even the least thing forbidden him, and, though the whole earth was once dependent upon him, have nought whatever of it in his hands?"

CVIII And in the same year Sheikh Náṣir appointed Awkal king, but after a short space he replaced him by Ṭabl, and proceeded with the latter northwards to fight against Sheikh el Amín and Abu Rída.

CIX The armies met at a place near Shendi and *Mek* Ṭabl was slain and the Sheikh suffered a severe defeat.

CX Then he appointed Bádi king, and he too was killed at el Ḥalfáya, and at the same time was killed *Mek* Rubáṭ, the nominee of Sheikh el Amín and Abu Rída. *Mek* Ḥasab Rabbihi was then appointed, but he too died.

CXI All this occurred in 1204[2], and in the same year Sheikh Náṣir returned to Sennár.

CXII And in 1205[3] Sheikh Muḥammad el Amín walad Mismár was killed by Abu Rída because the former had severely flogged Sheikh 'Abdulla walad 'Agíb. [Sheikh Muḥammad] was residing at the village of Walad Bán el Nuḳá, and all his sons were away; so when they saw him all alone they determined to kill him, but they dared not openly attack him because he was known to be a man of great bravery and courage. But they went to work secretly and climbed on to the top of his house and pulled off the roofing and stoned him from a distance until he was dead.

CXIII The same year Sheikh Náṣir made Nowwár king. And Nowwár remained at Sennár, and Sheikh Náṣir perceived that he was a man of sagacity and strength, so he grew afraid of him and made haste to put him to death.

CXIV He then appointed *Mek* Bádi walad Ṭabl, who reigned until the time of the late Ismá'íl Pasha, the son of Effendína Muḥammad 'Ali Pasha.

CXV Now at the time of his accession *Mek* Bádi was very young, but as all the power [of the FUNG kings] was now merged in that of the HAMAG I have not mentioned the exact length of time [each reigned].

[1] 1788 A.D. [2] 1789 A.D. [3] 1790 A.D.

CXVI Sheikh Náṣir was fond of amusement and play, and very capricious. It is even said that he never touched gold with his hand, excepting on one occasion, when it befel that one of his friends came to him and told him that he proposed going to the Ḥegáz; and Náṣir opened his coffer and filled both his hands with gold to give it to the man, and he intended the man to hold out the flap of his robe so that he might bestow upon him lavishly; but the man held out [only] his two hands, so Náṣir gave him what was in his own hands and no more.

CXVII And many tales are told of his generosity, and it is said that four kings who were all famous for their generosity lived at the same time, namely Náṣir at Sennár, and the Sultan 'Abd el Raḥman in Dárfūr, and Murád Bey in Egypt, and Aḥmad Pasha el Gazár in Syria, and each of the latter three had a larger empire than Náṣir.

CXVIII And between him and el Ḥág Sulaymán walad Aḥmad existed complete friendship and trust, and when the latter came to him he used to honour him and bestow on him bountiful gifts; and he was, God have mercy on his soul, a man held in honour and respect.

CXIX Náṣir continued in residence at Sennár, and Muḥammad walad Khamís Abu Rída at el Ṭurfáya, east of Sennár, paying no heed to Náṣir but occasionally entering Sennár alone, by night and secretly, to have discourse with his friends, and then leaving it.

CXX Things remained thus for some time, and in 1211[1] Náṣir crossed the river with his troops, accompanied by his brother 'Adlán, to attack Abu Rída; and a fight ensued and Abu Rída was killed and the villages on the east bank were looted and laid waste. But with all his generosity Sheikh Náṣir was an oppressor and held not his hand from taking the possessions of true believers, but enriched one man by impoverishing another.

CXXI And in his time the *feki* Ḥegázi died of thirst in prison. A number also of the ḤADÁRMA were slain by the hand of his brother Ḥusayn. But subsequently he turned upon this brother and seized all the possessions and herds he had.

CXXII In his time, too, died the *feki* 'Abd el Raḥman Abu Zayd, the pious and learned saint, and also that other holy man the *feki* Muḥammad Nūr Ṣubr.

CXXIII During the days of his rule, again, the Sultan Háshim walad 'Ísáwi and the sons of Sheikh el Amín, supported by FEZÁRA and BENI GERÁR, advanced into the Gezíra; and Náṣir went out against them and met them near Sírū. And they came to terms and all returned to Sennár excepting the BENI GERÁR, who went back

[1] 1796 A.D.

whence they came after Náṣir had honoured them and given presents to their chiefs.

CXXIV Now Sheikh Náṣir had entrusted the management of the kingdom to his vizier el Arbáb Dafa'alla, while he himself devoted his time to frivolity and amusement; and he had become infatuated with his slaves, and they took to oppressing the people without any hindrance from him, for he had given them orders that none of his brethren nor the chief men of the kingdom were to have access to him until they had applied to his vizier el Arbáb Dafa'alla.

CXXV And [the nobles] were thereby irritated, and the hearts of the people were alienated by the oppression they suffered; and his brethren for the same reasons threw off their allegiance to him and defied him. So they openly rebelled, and collected at 'Abūd and thereabouts, and were joined by all those whose purpose it suited that Náṣir's rule should come to an end.

CXXVI This was in 1212[1]; and when Náṣir learnt of it he went out to fight them, and camped at el Sabíl and tried to win them over by the medium of men of learning and rank. He likewise sent to them their sisters the daughters of Abu el Kaylak; but they would have no truck with him at all on any condition save that he should resign the sheikhship. And when he saw there was no hope of winning them back to allegiance he returned to Sennár; and his brethren quitted 'Abūd and followed him until they reached el Buḳera, a village near Sennár. And when Náṣir saw they were at el Buḳera he took some of his treasures and fled to the southern districts by night. And news of his flight reached them the following morning, and on receipt of it they entered Sennár.

CXXVII Then Idrís remained at Sennár, and 'Adlán followed in [Náṣir's] tracks as far as the village of Sírū, which lies west of the Nile, but failed to overtake him, and, hearing that he had made for Deberki on the river Dinder, and despairing of coming up with him, he returned to Sennár.

CXXVIII And Náṣir remained near Deberki for a time and then moved northwards to seek protection with Sheikh 'Abdulla walad 'Agíb.

CXXIX And when Náṣir arrived Sheikh 'Abdulla gave him protection, and he stayed with him at el Ḥalfáya, and after a while he crossed the Nile and took up his abode at the village of 'Abūd.

CXXX But when his brethren heard of his whereabouts they set forth from Sennár and went to the village of Abu Ḥaráz, which lies east of the Nile, and camped there. And Idrís remained at Abu

[1] 1797 A.D.

Ḥaráz and sent on 'Adlán with his slaves and some of the troops, but he took the precaution of including no HAMAG or FUNG among them for fear of disaffection.

CXXXI And when el Arbáb Dafa'alla, the vizier of Náṣir, got the news of 'Adlán and the dissension among the troops, he took his helmet off his head and went to meet 'Adlán's army and sought peace for himself.

CXXXII And Náṣir was captured without any bloodshed and taken back by 'Adlán to Abu Ḥaráz and handed over to Ṣubáḥi walad Bádi to be slain in revenge for the slaying of the latter's father Bádi walad Ragab. And Ṣubáḥi slew him and buried him at Abu Ḥaráz close by the tomb of Sheikh Dafa'alla el 'Araki. This was in the early part of 1213[1].

CXXXIII Idrís was then chosen to be Sheikh. He was a patient and brave man, kind of heart and just to the people, and by nature he loathed thieves and never inflicted upon them any other punishment than death, so that in his days the crime of theft was stamped out, and men left their possessions and their wares spread out in the market-place all night and all day with no one to guard them, and yet nothing whatever was taken, and there was no fear unless it were that a dog might take some meat.

CXXXIV And complete contentment reigned, and Idrís was assisted by his brother 'Adlán in organizing his kingdom and quelling such Arab tribes as were rebellious and seditious; and indeed 'Adlán undertook no expedition but he returned victorious.

CXXXV Most of their efforts were directed against the nomad Arabs with a view to weakening their power of revolt, and in consequence the inhabitants of the villages enjoyed a period of peace.

CXXXVI Among the viziers of Idrís were el Arbáb Ḳurashi and el Arbáb Zayn el 'Ábdín walad el Sayyid el feki 'Abd el Gelíl walad 'Ámir and the *feki* el Amín walad el 'Ashá, but he did not entrust them with the management of his kingdom as his brother Sheikh Náṣir had entrusted it to his vizier el Arbáb Dafa'alla, preferring to direct affairs himself.

CXXXVII In consequence his position was strengthened, as the poet has it of a man who does his work in person...(a few verses follow).

CXXXVIII Then, when everything had been settled, Sheikh Idrís went in person to el Ḥalfáya, towards the close of 1214[2], to war upon Sheikh 'Abdulla walad 'Agíb on account of certain words the latter had been reported as having uttered in favour of their brother Sheikh Náṣir.

[1] 1798 A.D. [2] 1799 A.D.

CXXXIX And the armies met and a fierce battle ensued, until finally Sheikh 'Abdulla walad 'Agíb was slain and his troops routed.

CXL Then Sheikh Idrís offered them peace and appointed over them Sheikh Náṣir walad el Amín, who was still in power in the time of the late-lamented, the dweller in Paradise.

CXLI Now Sheikh 'Abdulla was a just ruler, an ardent follower of the faith and an observer of the Ḳurán; and during his rule he ordered that when women were married smaller dowries should be paid, and the result was an increase in the number of marriages and consequently of births.

CXLII It was he, too, who bade everyone in the market, even the butchers, when they heard the call to prayer, to assemble at the mosque for public worship; and this became a general custom and continued even after his death.

CXLIII Among his praiseworthy acts, again, was the extirpation of the robbers who were known as "el 'Akálít": he caught them band by band and cut off their heads, and so stamped out theft and robbery in his days.

CXLIV Sheikh Idrís remained at el Ḥalfáya and sent his brother 'Adlán with a troop of soldiers to the neighbourhood of Shendi, and 'Adlán, on reaching Walad Bán el Nuḳá, wrote to the *Mek* Muḥammad walad Nimr promising to sanction his appointment as king of the country of the GA'ALIYYŪN,—for the *Mek* Sa'ad had died.

CXLV And when the letter reached the *Mek* Muḥammad walad Nimr he was surprised at it and forgot how he and his brothers had acted in the time of King 'Adlán the Fungówi in the matter of enslaving the daughters of Muḥammad Abu el Kaylak, for in the hour of his fate he was blinded.

CXLVI So he and a number of his brothers and cousins and his son Idrís, who was still small, went out [to meet 'Adlán]; but Sa'ad and Nimr refused to go with them and fled away by themselves.

CXLVII And when King Muḥammad and his brothers and cousins and his son Idrís presented themselves, ['Adlán] imprisoned all of them, and *Mek* Muḥammad died in prison from the grievous weight of chains heaped upon him. And as for the *Mek's* son Idrís, his mother came and ransomed him for 300 *wuḳias* of gold. But of the rest of the prisoners only el Fahl was released, and he only at the intercession of el Ḥág Sulaymán walad Aḥmad.

CXLVIII 'Adlán then started for el Ḥalfáya with the other captives, keeping Nimr and his companions, who offered no resistance, surrounded; but when it was dark Nimr and his companions escaped.

CXLIX Then the chiefs of the MAGÁDHÍB intervened to the end

that 'Adlán should return to Shendi; and at Shendi he appointed Musá'ad as *Mek*, and, this done, returned to his brother Sheikh Idrís at el Ḥalfáya with the rest of the captive AWLÁD NIMR. And after he had reached el Ḥalfáya and met his brother they proceeded to Sennár and there executed the prisoners.

CL In 1216[1] war broke out between the *Mek* Nimr and the *Mek* Musá'ad, and this war was called "The war of the 'AWÁLÍB," and during its course 'Adlán went west and fought with the *Mek* 'Ísáwi and defeated him and brought him back captive to Sennár, where he died in prison.

CLI In 1217[2] occurred the war of the BAṬÁḤÍN and the SHUKRÍA, and Sheikh 'Awaḍ el Kerím Abu Sin, Sheikh of the SHUKRÍA Arabs, was killed.

CLII In the same year died el Ḥág Náṣir walad Matassi, a man of piety, and also the *feki* Miṣri walad Ḳandíl, a student of the Ḳurán and a pious man; and also Sheikh Yūsef the son of Sheikh Muḥammad walad el Ṭerayfi. He too was a pious man, and the *feki* Aḥmad walad el Ṭaib and others composed elegies upon him.

CLIII We will now return to the history of the Sheikh. The historian states that Sheikh Idrís followed in the steps of his father Muḥammad Abu el Kaylak in justice and beneficence until he died in the month of *Gemád el Ákhir* 1218[3].

CLIV He was succeeded in the Sheikhship by his brother 'Adlán, but the latter neglected his kingdom and exercised no vigilance in its affairs and gave himself up to pleasure. But he only ruled for the rest of *Gemád* and *Ragab* and *Sha'abán*, and on the 16th of *Ramaḍán* he was slain.

CLV And the manner of his death was thus. As soon as he became distracted from the affairs of state and ceased to give his attention to them, his foes roused themselves, and their ambitions were excited. The first to make a plot for his downfall was Muḥammad walad Ragab walad Muḥammad, who conspired with Kamtūr and the *Mek* Ránfi and some of the FUNG and some of Sheikh 'Adlán's own entourage. These dared not yet openly proclaim their revolt, but lay quiet awaiting an opportunity; and finally God willed the consummation of their hopes, for Muḥammad walad Náṣir "Abu Rísh," who was in great need of corn, moved from the village of el Kubr; and this man had had a brother named 'Ali, who was bold and reckless and used to abuse roundly all that 'Adlán did, and it was said —and God knows the truth—that 'Adlán had poisoned him: so then "Abu Rísh" left el Kubr and joined Muḥammad walad Ragab and

[1] 1801 A.D. [2] 1802 A.D. [3] 1803 A.D.

the others who have been mentioned above, and their hearts were fortified and their backs strengthened because of their knowledge of the temerity and enterprise of Muḥammad "Abu Rísh" in all matters of difficulty. Now on the night agreed upon by the conspirators 'Adlán was being wed to the daughter of Walad Guma'a and was filled with happiness and joy, and there was with him a clever man to whom news had come of the conspiracy, and this man quoted to him the following lines as a warning against being taken unawares... (two lines of poetry follow: the author then recounts how 'Adlán was none the less surprised and wounded, but got on his horse and rode off with his son Muḥammad, but fell dead at Sennár from his wounds)...And when the conspirators received news of this they went thither [to Sennár] and bore him into a compound that belonged to him and buried him there.

CLVI Then King Ránfi and Sheikh Kamtūr and Muḥammad walad Náṣir all agreed to the appointment of Muḥammad walad Ragab, and he was made Sheikh, but the real power lay with Muḥammad "Abu Rísh."

CLVII And the *Mek* Ránfi and Sheikh Kamtūr and Walad Ragab[1] and Muḥammad "Abu Rísh" all remained at Sennár, but they were no longer of one mind, and, as God Almighty said, "You deem them to be together but their hearts are far apart."

CLVIII And the month of *Ramaḍán*, in the middle of which 'Adlán had been slain, had not passed before they were at open enmity. The KAMÁTÍR (*i.e.* family of Kamtūr) formed one party and the sons of Muḥammad [walad Náṣir "Abu Rísh"] the other, and they came to blows...(the author gives details of the fighting: Muḥammad walad Náṣir and Muḥammad walad Ragab were ranged against Kamtūr; Kamtūr proved victorious; Walad Ragab was imprisoned at Sennár; Walad Náṣir was wounded; and Kamtūr's followers took to looting at Sennár. Then the *'Ulema* tried to effect a reconciliation and Kamtūr was persuaded to return the loot and release Muḥammad walad Ragab, but Muḥammad walad Náṣir "Abu Rísh" refused the overtures and gave battle to Kamtūr, late in 1218[2], and drove him across the river)....

CLIX And when Walad Náṣir had won the victory he entered Sennár and put to death the *feki* el Amín walad el 'Ashá, the vizier of his uncle Sheikh Idrís.

CLX And the sheikhship was confirmed to his cousin Muḥammad walad Ragab in name, but in actual fact [Muḥammad "Abu Rísh"] directed affairs entirely.

CLXI And [the latter] prepared to reside at Kassala, but when all was quiet again and the fighting had ceased, he entered Sennár and

[1] reading وولد رجب for ولد رجب.

[2] 1803 A.D.

put to death the *Mek* Ránfi and sent for the *Mek* Bádi, whom his uncle, Sheikh Idrís, had deposed, and appointed him king. And Bádi remained king until the coming of the late Ismá'íl Pasha the son of Effendína.

CLXII And in this same year 1218[1] died the famous and learned *feki* 'Ali Baḳádi.

CLXIII Then Sheikh Kamtūr gathered together such of his family and relatives as remained with him and set out for Khashm el Baḥr, that is the east bank of the Nile, and settled there until the year '19[2], and in the latter part of that year he moved northwards.

CLXIV And when Walad Ragab heard of this he had Kamtūr pursued until he was forced to cross the Nile. And Kamtūr stopped at Omdurmán, and the *'Ulema* and men of religion intervened and prevented Muḥammad's people [from touching Kamtūr], so they returned to el Gedíd, while Kamtūr crossed over to the east bank and went back.

CLXV Meanwhile, Walad Ragab was camped at Walad Medani, and Walad Náṣir went to Kassala [and stayed there] till the beginning of 1221[3].

CLXVI Then Walad Ragab and Walad Náṣir fell out until they came to be actually at war, and their forces met at a place called el Harába and attacked each other, and the *feki* Zayn el 'Ábdín walad el Sayyid was killed, and Walad Ragab was routed and driven to el 'Aylafūn. But Walad Náṣir, instead of pursuing him, went home to Kassala and appointed as Sheikh his uncle Sheikh el Ḥusayn walad Muḥammad, while he himself with his slaves remained at Kassala enjoying and amusing himself.

CLXVII And Walad Ragab entered into correspondence with Sheikh Kamtūr and the family of Sulaymán ("Awlád Sulaymán"), and Sheikh Kamtūr and his brethren came and camped at Abu Ḥaráz, and with them the Awlád Sulaymán and the Awlád Shanbūl, excepting Sheikh 'Adlán; and Walad Ragab met them there, and they entered into a compact to war upon Walad Náṣir, and appointed as their king one called 'Agbán.

CLXVIII (The author describes how in the middle of the year both Walad Náṣir and his brother died suddenly on the same day. The slaves of Walad Náṣir and of [his uncle] 'Adlán [walad Muḥammad Abu el Kaylak] then fell to quarrelling together, as Walad Náṣir had only left a small son and 'Adlán's slaves preferred their master's son Muḥammad. The two factions fought and 'Adlán's slaves fled and joined Muḥammad Walad Ragab and Kamtūr. With this new addition to his forces Walad Ragab then attacked

[1] 1803 A.D. [2] 1804 A.D.
[3] 1806 A.D. (reading ١٢٢١ for ١٢١٢).

Walad Náṣir's slaves, but he was defeated at Ṭaiba Ḳandaláwi and el Ḥág Sulaymán walad Aḥmad was killed. Walad Ragab then fled to 'Aylafūn and Kamtūr to Abu Ḥaráz, and Walad Náṣir's slaves retired again to Kassala, via the village of Walad el Magdhūb, and made one Tayfara their ruler.)

CLXIX And among the sons of their masters the slaves had with them Muḥammad walad Ibráhím walad Muḥammad Abu el Kaylak; and when they were returning after their victory this man asked their leave to make a raid on [the] Baḳḳára, and they gave him leave: so he parted [from them at] Walad el Magdhūb and raided [the] Baḳḳára and took some spoil, which he sent to the slaves at Kassala.

CLXX Then he met [the] Fezára and entered into league with them to fight the slaves and accompanied them to el Khartoum, where they looted as they willed and slew Ibráhím ibn el feki Muḥammad walad Ali, the *khalífa* of the *feki* Arbáb.

CLXXI Muḥammad walad Ibráhím then went to 'Abūd and stayed there. The slaves meanwhile remained at Kassala in impiety and drunkenness and villainy; and all power, for loosing or for binding, was in their hands for eight months.

CLXXII (The author then tells how Muḥammad walad Ibráhím was joined by many of the notables and made his plans. The slaves being apprised of this went to Sennár and put the family of Ragab in chains and took them to Kassala. Muḥammad then attacked them and killed a number and captured the rest. He put all the prisoners to death excepting Tayfara, who during his brief rule had done no harm in word or deed.)

CLXXIII Thus the power passed to Walad Ibráhím, and he resided at Ṭaiba Ḳandaláwi for a time and then moved to Um Ḍaraysa.

CLXXIV Meanwhile Muḥammad walad Ragab had been at el 'Aylafūn, but he now moved to Abu Ḥaráz and looted the Fádnía Arabs.

CLXXV Then the 'Arakiyyūn came to him and told him that the loot had not belonged to the Fádnía but to themselves. He, however, refused their request and reviled them, wherefore they named him "The Rough-tongued," and affairs came to such a pass that he attacked them and slew Sheikh Dafa'alla walad el Ṣámūta and Abu 'Áḳla ibn el Sheikh Yūsef, though he had but few troops with him; and his victory was so complete that they fell into[1] the grain pits (*maṭmūra*) and hid therein and were put to the extreme of shame.

CLXXVI Then Sheikh Muḥammad walad Ragab relented and left the 'Arakiyyūn and went towards el Ṭurfáya to meet Sheikh Kamtūr and seek his protection, and Kamtūr accorded it him because of the fear of Walad Ibráhím that was in his heart; or rather, as soon as

[1] reading سقطوا for سقوا.

ever Walad Ibráhím made representations to him, he seized him [Walad Ragab] and sent him to him [Walad Ibráhím]. And when he arrived Walad Ibráhím handed him over to Muḥammad walad 'Adlán to be slain in revenge for his father ['Adlán]. So he was put to death, God have mercy upon him!

CLXXVII And when Walad Ibráhím had settled his affairs and got all the power into his own hands he rested awhile without any quarrels; but on hearing that Muḥammad walad 'Adlán had entered into an agreement with el Arbáb Dafa'alla walad Aḥmad and the *feki* Medani walad el 'Abbás and others to attack him and throw off his sway, he seized the *feki* Medani and put him to death; but el Arbáb Dafa'alla received news of the execution and fled eastwards to Sába'a Dólíb.

CLXXVIII Then Walad Ibráhím, with his vizier el Arbáb Ḳurashi and a body of his men, wẹnt to the village of Walad Bahá el Dín and sent for Muḥammad walad 'Adlán from the village of Borḳū; and when he arrived Walad Ibráhím and his vizier Ḳurashi took him into the *khalwa*, that is the place of worship of that pious man, and Ḳurashi began addressing him with rude and offensive words. Walad 'Adlán, however, replied in conciliatory and gentle terms, so finally Walad Ibráhím bade his brother cut his throat.

CLXXIX Now the slaves of Náṣir who were following Walad Ibráhím were standing outside the *khalwa*, and as soon as they heard the "cut his throat" they cast earth upon the heads of the slaves of 'Adlán, who had come with Muḥammad walad 'Adlán, and the latter at once drew their swords and took up their position at the door of the *khalwa*. And the slaves of Walad Ibráhím and the slaves of Náṣir wavered, for they were not averse to the appointment of [Walad] 'Adlán and detested Walad Ibráhím on account of his having handed over the charge of affairs to Ḳurashi. And the slaves of 'Adlán demanded Walad Ibráhím from them and threatened them and frightened them by saying they would loose their master Walad Ibráhím upon them or else burn them and him together in a fire.

CLXXX And Ḳurashi was very nervous and blustered greatly and showed his disquietude and fear; and finally they brought out Walad 'Adlán; and Walad 'Adlán saw the gulfs of death yawning before him and was terrified, and his breath was choked with the imminence of the destruction that was upon him, and he stood fascinated.

CLXXXI Now the horse of Walad Ibráhím with the king's caparisons upon it was standing near, and Abu Sulaymán the slave of 'Adlán shouted to him [Walad 'Adlán] "Why are you stupified? Mount the mare and plunge your sword into the hearts of these dogs who wished to kill you!" And when Walad 'Adlán heard him and realised what was before him he sprang upon the mare as it stood and drew his sword.

CLXXXII Then the slaves of Náṣir at once gathered round him, and he regained his confidence and ordered them to fetch out Walad Ibráhím and Ḳurashi from the *khalwa* after taking away from them their swords. And the soldiers rallied to Walad 'Adlán and took Walad Ibráhím and his vizier Ḳurashi to the village of Borḳū; and on arrival [Walad 'Adlán] at once slew Ḳurashi, in accordance with the wishes of Náṣir's slaves who were following him, and proceeded to Sennár accompanied by all the soldiers, and there imprisoned Walad Ibráhím in the house of his father's sister Mahayra.

CLXXXIII This all occurred in 1223[1], and the rule of Walad Ibráhím, which had lasted for sixteen months beginning from *Ragab* '23 ['22?], came to an end; and the power passed to Muḥammad walad 'Adlán, who slew all the sons of Ragab except Ḥasan, who was in the end destined to cause his death.

CLXXXIV He also put to death Muḥammad walad el Sheikh Idrís, and many people who rebelled against him, and Muḥammad walad Ibráhím who had been held captive near el Manáḳil, and then he went in the direction of the White Nile and collected the remnant of the slaves of Náṣir and a young son of his and slew them all... (The author adds further remarks as to the severe measures taken by Walad 'Adlán to consolidate his power)...

CLXXXV And in the days of Walad 'Adlán, in '24[2], an epidemic was caused by yellow fever, and many people perished; and this illness was called by the natives "*el kik*," and among the notables who succumbed to it was el Ḥág Muḥammad walad Nūrayn of the stock of Sheikh Ḥámid walad Abu 'Aṣá, and the *feki* Muḥammad Nūrayn of el Ḥalfáya, the author of the *Biographies* (*lit.* series) *of the Saints of the Sudan* ("*Ṭabaḳát el Awliyá bi'l Sūdán*"), who was mourned by Sheikh Ibráhím 'Abd el Dáfa'i in a very beautiful elegy of about twelve lines, beginning as follows: "Let the eye weep all its days with grief for the running of the river dry. He was rich in learning, a pontiff and son of a pontiff, a guest of God's own. Verily he has won prestige and glory in the earth."

CLXXXVI Early in 1225[3] Muḥammad 'Adlán moved northwards to war against Sheikh Náṣir walad el Amín, and the latter heard of his coming and fled to Shendi. And Walad 'Adlán reached el Ḥalfáya and stayed there awhile accompanied by the *Mek* Bádi and his uncle Sheikh Ḥusayn and all his troops.

[1] 1808 A.D. [2] 1809 A.D. [3] 1810 A.D.

CLXXXVII Then he returned to Sennár without having fought. In '26[1] occurred a war between the SA'ADÁB and the GIMÍ'ÁB in which was killed el Arbáb Bánuḳá [*i.e.* Bán el Nuḳá], a brave and noble and pious man; and a number of his cousins fell with him, and the remainder took to flight; and as a result of this war the power of the GIMÍ'ÁB was greatly enhanced and their heads were raised over the kings of the GAMŪ'ÍA and Walad 'Agíb.

CLXXXVIII In '27[2] Walad 'Adlán set out to collect tribute from the RUFÁ'A Arabs in the vicinity of Gebel Moya; and el Labayḥ fled from him but was pursued by the troops and overtaken, and some of his people were killed and much booty taken.

CLXXXIX In '28[3] Walad 'Adlán went to el Ṭurfáya and stayed there awhile, and there came to him Sheikh Khalífa with a certain Effendi. And in the same year there appeared a comet, which was followed by a severe famine; and that year was called "The Year of Hardship" ["*Sannat el Gibiṣ*"].

CXC In '29[4] died Sheikh Ḥasan ibn el Sheikh 'Abd el Raḥman walad Bán el Nuḳá. He was the possessor of a library of books, all of which were lost at the time of Nimr's revolt in the Turkish days. There also died the pious el Ḥág Dafa'alla walad Ḍayfulla this year at el Ḥalfáya...

CXCI (The author describes how in the same year Walad 'Adlán, who was at 'Abūd, prepared to attack Náṣir walad 'Agíb, the 'Abdullábi, at el Ḥalfáya. He was interrupted by news that the *Mek* Bádi was starting from Sennár against him and had enlisted the KAMÁTÍR, *i.e.* the AWLÁD KAMTŪR, to assist him. Walad 'Adlán therefore turned south and besieged the *Mek*, but a friendly agreement was soon reached and Walad 'Adlán visited the *Mek* at Sennár and was received with due honour. In 1231[5] Walad 'Adlán resumed the offensive against Náṣir walad 'Agíb and replaced him by Náṣir walad 'Abdulla. This however was only a temporary move, as, on his return to Sennár, Walad 'Adlán ordered the reinstatement of Náṣir walad 'Agíb.)...

CXCII And in 1232[6] the most learned and pious Sheríf, the noble el Sayyid Muḥammad 'Othmán el Mírghani el Mekki, visited Sennár and met its rulers and called upon all men to follow his *ṭaríḳa*; but only a few people did so, and the rulers paid no heed to him but wished to test him by examination; so they brought forward the *feki* Ibráhím walad Baḳádi, one of the most brilliant of the *'Ulema*, to examine him. And the *feki* Ibráhím arrived at Sennár with a racking headache, and the pain increased until he died,—and this before he had ever met the Sheríf.

[1] 1811 A.D. [2] 1812 A.D. [3] 1813 A.D.
[4] 1814 A.D. [5] 1816 A.D. [6] 1817 A.D.

So the Sherif left Sennár; and at that time his age was twenty-five years.

CXCIII In 1233[1] there was a very high Nile and the village of el Basháḳira on the east bank was swept away. This Nile was known as "The Nile of Abu Sin" because Ḥammad[2], the son of Sheikh 'Awaḍ el Kerím Abu Sin, was killed the same year by the BAṬÁḤÍN[3]. And the latter took refuge with the *Mek* Nimr, and Sheikh Muḥammad Abu Sin advanced against them with all his Arabs in a great army and prepared to make war on *Mek* Nimr. But the *'Ulema* and religious Sheikhs intervened and prevented their fighting, so they returned to their own country.

CXCIV In 1234[4] el Arbáb Muḥammad walad Dafa'alla walad Sulaymán was treacherously murdered by Muḥammad walad 'Adlán in order that he might marry his widow, who was very beautiful.

CXCV In 1235[5] Walad 'Adlán plotted the death of Kamtūr in revenge for his father's death...

(The author tells how Walad 'Adlán fell suddenly upon Kamtūr, who was almost undefended, and slew him and the *feki* Aḥmad walad el Ṭaib. He then returned to Sennár rejoicing at having now achieved his revenge on all who had participated in his father's death. Kamtūr's brothers then appointed Ḍerrár as Sheikh in place of Kamtūr and, in 1236[6], while Walad 'Adlán was out collecting tribute from the Arabs, they attacked him by night in the house where he was. They were, however, detected by Walad 'Adlán's men and a fight ensued in which the latter lost heavily. Aided by the darkness Walad 'Adlán and his women broke through the wall of the house and escaped, and meanwhile great confusion prevailed among the combatants. In the morning, when it was light, the scattered forces of both parties reassembled and the fight was continued.)...

CXCVI And the party of Walad 'Adlán was victorious, and sent tidings of the victory after him; but he paid no heed, for he was consumed with shame at his flight. However el Arbáb Dafa'alla walad Aḥmad Ḥasan, who had been one of those who stayed behind and brought the news of the victory, had speech with him and told him "There was no fighting like that which took place while you were there," and "They were only routed by fear of you," so that Walad 'Adlán was reassured by skilful arguments and took his men and went to Sennár.

CXCVII And after they had settled down at Sennár certain tidings reached them of the advance of Ismá'íl Pasha the son of Effendína into their country; and they were thrown into great perturbation, and

[1] 1818 A.D.
[2] reading حمد for احمد.
[3] reading بطاحين for بحطاجيون.
[4] 1819 A.D.
[5] 1820 A.D.
[6] 1821 A.D.

each man began to look after his own interests, and the soldiers scattered in the attempt to prepare themselves for eventualities, so that Muḥammad walad 'Adlán was left at his village with only el Arbáb Dafa'alla walad Aḥmad and a few men.

CXCVIII Then Ḥasan walad Ragab seized his opportunity and fell upon Walad 'Adlán by night with only five horsemen and a few of his relatives, and broke open the door and entered his house. And Walad 'Adlán came out and fought fiercely against them alone, and three times he repulsed them, but finally one of the relatives [of Ḥasan Ragab] struck him and cleft his leg while his attention was elsewhere. And when he collapsed they fell upon him with their swords and dispatched him and buried him in his house.

CXCIX Now the days of Walad 'Adlán were days of prosperity excepting only the "Year of Hardship"; and after his death they had no settled rule, and their councils were divided, and they fought among themselves in revenge, and scattered, and broke away from all control; but glory be to Him whose kingdom has no end and whose rule is everlasting!

CC Now as regards the Sheikhs of Khashm el Baḥr, among them was Sheikh 'Adlán walad Ṣubáḥi who was with Sheikh Muḥammad Abu el Kaylak and died a few days after him.

CCI After him his brother's son, Sheikh Aḥmad walad el Sheikh Kamtūr, succeeded.

CCII He was deposed by Sheikh Bádi walad Ragab, who appointed Ṣubáḥi walad 'Adlán in his place.

CCIII Then Sheikh Aḥmad, who had been deposed, succeeded again and remained in power until Sheikh 'Adlán deposed him.

CCIV After him ruled Sheikh Muḥammad Kamtūr, who was killed by Walad 'Adlán. He was a gentle man, who never showed anger nor was insolent nor abusive; but if his anger was aroused he would curse the Devil. He had numerous brothers, all of whom were noble of character and withal brave and generous and well versed in their religion.

CCV And Sheikh Kamtūr was succeeded by one of them, namely his brother Sheikh Ḍerrár, in whose days the period of their eminence came to an end.

CCVI Of the successive rulers among the AWLÁD 'AGÍB and the kings of the SA'ADÁB I have no knowledge.

CCVII The kings of the FUNG who were possessed of power began with 'Omára Dūnḳas and ended with the *Mek* Bádi walad Nūl, and after the reign of the latter all power, whether of loosing or of binding, was in the hands of Sheikh Muḥammad Abu el Kaylak and his family until '36[1]. Then Muḥammad walad 'Adlán was slain and their influence ceased and they no longer directed affairs, and it was even as Sheikh Idrís walad el Arbáb had said, "In the end they will be divided and fight[2] among themselves and their rule will disappear and the Turks will conquer the country." So, too, the *feki* Ḥegázi walad Abu Zayd, of the family of Sheikh Idrís, foretold by shaking letters together that the days of the sons of Muḥammad [Abu el Kaylak] would end with Muḥammad walad 'Adlán.

CCVIII Now after the death of Walad 'Adlán dissension was rife, and they continued quarrelling during *Ragab* and *Sha'abán* until the country passed under the sway of Effendína Ismá'íl Pasha, the son of the late Muḥammad 'Ali Pasha.

CCIX Now [Ismá'íl Pasha] arrived in the latter part of *Sha'abán* and camped on the west [bank] opposite el Ḥalfáya; and Sheikh Náṣir walad el Amín met him and submitted to him and was granted peace and presented with a splendid robe and left in his own country; but Ismá'íl Pasha took with him on his march to Sennár Náṣir's son el Amín and the kings of the SA'ADÁB, namely the *Meks* Nimr and Musá'ad. And he camped with all his forces and the boats which were accompanying him by river at Omdurmán. Then he crossed the river and camped at el Khartoum, and was met by the *feki* Muḥammad walad 'Ali, the *khalífa* of the *feki* Arbáb, and treated him with honour and granted him peace; and he did not stretch forth his hand against the districts which he crossed excepting only to obtain provisions.

CCX And [Ismá'íl Pasha] started from el Khartoum for Sennár on the last day of *Sha'abán*, accompanied by the *Ḳádi* Muḥammad el Assiūṭi, and el Sayyid Aḥmad el Baghli, the *Mufti* of the Sháfa'ites of the Sudan, and el Sayyid Aḥmad el Saláwi, the *Mufti* of the *Sayyids* of the Máliki sect, and camped at a village west of el Mesallamía. Here he was met by some of the notables and granted them peace; and, after he had started, there met him Ragab walad 'Adlán and el Arbáb Dafa'alla walad Aḥmad and tendered their submission, and to these also he granted peace and gave robes as he had done previously in the case of the kings of the GA'ALIYYŪN.

CCXI And before he reached Sennár the *Mek* Bádi and some of the HAMAG came and tendered their submission...

(The author mentions that honours and presents were heaped upon Bádi and his nobles by Ismá'íl, who entered Sennár on the 12th of *Ramaḍán*. A proclamation was then issued nullifying all complaints based on events previous to the conquest. Ismá'íl acted with the utmost fairness and won

[1] 1821 A.D.

[1] reading يقاتلون for يتقالون.

all hearts by his justice, "for he heard the plaint of the poor man in person without any intermediary." Ragab walad 'Adlán was then sent with troops to chase Ḥasan walad Ragab, and caught him and brought him and some of his supporters back as prisoners: several of the latter were put to death at Sennár.)...

CCXII Then he sent Muḥammad Sa'íd Effendi with a force of soldiers and Sheikh Raḥma walad Raḥála against *Mek* Idrís el Miḥayna, the *Mek* of the GAMŪ'ÍA, because the latter had not met him and he had heard of his looting villages. And they came upon him at his house on the White Nile and slew him and took his possessions and returned to Sennár.

CCXIII And, when affairs were settled satisfactorily, the first taxes were imposed by the issue of an order for the classification of houses[1] [into three groups, namely] high, medium and smaller. Then he had lists made of slaves and flocks but did not impose any tax upon them; and he took nothing from the country except fodder for his horses. Early in '38[2] arrived His Highness Effendína Ibráhím Pasha... (The meeting is described. The author says that in *Rabí'a Awal* both went south, but Ibráhím "returned in a few days and went to el Maḥrūsa." Ismá'íl meanwhile proceeded to Fázoghli, where he captured the local chiefs and "expelled the merchants who resided there and imposed a tax of gold upon them.")...

CCXIV And while he was away in the *Gebels*, Díwán Effendi Sa'íd [imposed] taxation on the people with the compliance of the *mu'allim* Ḥanná el Mubáshir and el Arbáb Dafa'alla walad Aḥmad. On each head of slaves they made the tax fifteen *riáls*, on each head of cattle ten *riáls*, on each sheep (شاة) and donkey five *riáls*. Meanwhile a false rumour spread that Ismá'íl Pasha had been killed in the *Gebels*... (The author describes how some showed sorrow and some joy and some withheld judgment. When Ismá'íl returned safe and was told of this he "punished no one for what he had done, but treated them with gentleness and mercy, as was the custom of his late-lamented father, and he put no one to death except Walad 'Agayláwi, whom he impaled.")...

CCXV And Ismá'íl Pasha, on his arrival, found that Díwán Effendi and el Mubáshir had apportioned the collection of the taxes to various employés, and appointed clerks, and arranged the assessments, and issued ledgers, and sent these employés out to the villages to collect the money. And from his compassion for the folk he was dipleased at what had been done and called in the ledgers for alteration; but it was found that el Mubáshir had sent them to el Maḥrūsa.

So he sent Sheikh Sa'ad 'Abd el Fattáḥ after them, to bring them back, but Sa'ad failed to overtake them...(The author explains how Ismá'íl Pasha, since he had been unable to alter the amounts in the ledgers,

[1] reading منازل for منار.

[2] 1822 A.D.

ordered special leniency in the collection of taxes. We are also told that as a result of the amount of fever in Sennár, Ismá'íl Pasha, in 1237[1], moved with his court to Wad Medani. In 1238[2] troops were sent for Ḥasan walad Ragab, but he decamped. Several of Ismá'íl's suite died this year.)...

CCXVI In *Safar* 1238[3] His Excellence moved northwards by boats, and when he reached Shendi the *Mek* Nimr and the *Mek* Musá'ad met him, and he requisitioned from them many things, and they were unable to provide them all and were afraid. So they made outward show of obedience to his orders, but asked for an extension of time, and engaged to fulfil his requirements before the time limit he appointed. They also begged him to leave his boats and honour them with his presence in the town. Accordingly he landed and camped in one of the houses at Shendi, unaccompanied by anyone except his *Mamlūks*. Then they fell upon him in the night and set fire to the house, and Ismá'íl Pasha [*lit.* "the late-lamented one"] and his *Mamlūks* were burnt to death within. And, oh! To what deeds was the way thus prepared! Their act was the cause of the devastation of the land and the death of true believers, the shedding of their blood, the plunder of their goods, the dishonouring of their wives, the general ruin of the countryside, the captivity of the women and the children and the dispersal of the people into other districts.

CCXVII When the news reached Muḥammad Sa'íd Effendi el Kadakhdár at Walad Medani, he collected his scattered forces, and fortified himself at Walad Medani, and sent Shama'dán Agha and Muṣṭafa Káshif with some mounted men to verify the report; and they reached el Khartoum and then returned to him with the facts.

CCXVIII Then el Arbáb Dafa'alla fled from Walad Medani and camped at 'Abūd, and bands of men rallied to him there...

(The author describes how an expedition was then sent from Wad Medani to 'Abūd but found the bird flown; so they laid the village waste and killed the local *khalífa*, Muḥammad walad 'Abd el 'Alím, and returned.

El Arbáb had, meanwhile, gone south and joined Ḥasan walad Ragab, and the two of them collected an army at Abu Shóka. Muḥammad Sa'íd then sent a second expedition, composed of SHÁÍḲÍA and *Delatía*, which gave battle to the rebels at Abu Shóka and defeated them with great slaughter. Ḥasan Ragab, his uncle Ḥusayn and his son Muḥammad were among the slain. Much booty was taken, and the force returned triumphantly to Wad Medani.)...

CCXIX Now when the news of the murder of Ismá'íl Pasha reached Muḥammad Bey Defterdár, who was at the time in charge of Kordofán, he at once started with some of his troops and a certain number of FŪR for el Abwáb, and [thence] proceeded, slaying and looting

[1] 1822 A.D. [2] 1822 A.D. [3] 1822 A.D.

unceasingly, to el Metemma. There he found a number of people collected, and some of them came and asked him for peace, and he granted it to them. Then one of these same people sprang at him and wounded him with a spear that was in his hand.

Seeing this, the Defterdár ordered them all to be slain; but a few escaped. Then he went to the *feki* Aḥmad el Rayyaḥ in his *khalwa* and ordered all [there] to be burnt.

CCXX He next moved to Shendi and found the *Mek* Nimr had fled, so he returned along the east bank to look for Walad 'Agíb at el Ḥalfáya.

So far from finding them, however, he found el Ḥalfáya deserted; so he burnt it and passed on to Ḳubbat el Sheikh Khógali, but similarly found no one there. Then he crossed the river to Tūti Island and there slew many people.

CCXXI After this he went to el 'Aylafūn. Now he had been preceded there by some of his Fūr soldiery, and the people of el 'Aylafūn had come out and given battle to them. So when the Bey arrived he slew them all and burnt down the village and took prisoner slaves and freemen alike.

CCXXII Thence he marched along the east bank to Walad Medani. Now Walad 'Agíb was at this time living at Kutráng, and, as soon as he heard of what had happened at el 'Aylafūn, he quitted the village and left the river and camped at el Ḳubba and thence crossed over to Omdurmán with his men.

And there joined him the remnant of the Hamag, who had survived the battle at Abu Shóka.

CCXXIII The Bey, meanwhile, went to Walad Medani with the captives of el 'Aylafūn and stayed there a short time and gave orders to Ḥusayn Agha el Gókhadár to proceed to the White Nile.

CCXXIV On his way thither Ḥusayn Agha passed through the villages of el 'Ádayk, and when he reached Walad el Turábi he turned eastwards, away from the river, and looted camels and sheep from the Shukría, and then went across to the White Nile and stopped at the camp of the Ga'aliyyūn. And the troops raided the camps and took what booty they wanted. Then some [of the Arabs] begged for peace, and he granted it and ordered their flocks to be returned to them after they had accepted his conditions.

CCXXV Afterwards there came to him one of the soldiers and told him that the *feki* Faḍlulla, from the camp of the 'Aḳáḳír on the White Nile, was one of those who had raised their heads and stretched out their hands to slay the soldiers, for his brother had been killed.

So el Gókhadár enquired for the *feki* Faḍlulla, but could not find him; and, having with him 72 men from the encampment of the GA'ALIYYŪN, he ordered their hands to be cut off; and the sentence was carried out on all of them, and in consequence some died, and others survived. Then he moved elsewhere.

CCXXVI The Defterdár, for his part, went to Kordofán, and then returned the same year to the country of the GA'ALIYYŪN.

CCXXVII And while the Defterdár was on his way to Kordofán, Walad 'Agíb and the HAMAG refugees who were with him were on the west bank at Omdurmán, and they were attacked there by 'Ali Agha el Buṣayli and some SHÁÍḲÍA and MOGHÁRBA troops, and they fled before them to the neighbourhood of Shendi and joined the *Mek* Nimr, and remained with him until they heard that the Defterdár was advancing from Kordofán.

Then they scattered, and some of them settled down at el Hilália. And news of this reached el Kadakhdár Muḥammad Sa'íd, and he sent troops in boats who came upon them at early dawn and killed a number of them and put the rest to flight.

Then the soldiers returned to Walad Medani with the loot they had taken.

CCXXVIII And when the Defterdár Bey reached the country of the GA'ALIYYŪN, the *Mek* Nimr fled and camped at a place called el Naṣūb in the desert, but the Bey overtook him with a troop of Turkish and SHÁÍḲÍA soldiery, and a fight took place. And after many of the *Mek's* men had been killed he was put to flight. This was a great battle, and much plunder was taken and many women and children captured.

CCXXIX Then the Bey returned with his loot and prisoners to Um 'Arūḳ and camped there; and so numerous were the captives that he made a thorn-enclosure for them and supplied it with water by means of a trench; and some of them died from the severity of the conditions and some were ransomed by Sheikh Bashír walad 'Aḳíd, and others were sent to el Maḥrūsa.

CCXXX The survivors of the battle of el Naṣūb had, in the meanwhile, scattered in every direction, and the Bey now advanced from Um 'Arūḳ to fight them, that is Musá'ad and Walad 'Agíb.

CCXXXI And on his way he seized the *feki* Ibráhím 'Ísa, and with him one called 'Agíb walad Deḳays, and beat them and took them with him towards Abu Ḥaráz and kept them prisoners awhile and then released them.

CCXXXII And he continued the pursuit of the refugees until he overtook Musá'ad at a place called Makdūr, between the Dinder and the Rahad, and there he inflicted great slaughter upon them and took much booty and many captives. Now among the slain was Sheikh

Ṣáliḥ, one of the Awlád Bán el Nuḳá, and their possessions were looted and the books of Sheikh Ḥasan were scattered [and lost]. This occurred early in 1239[1].

CCXXXIII The Defterdár now moved to Sabderát, and on his return thence directed the captives, both the freemen and the slaves, to be sent to el Maḥrūsa, and instructed Muḥammad Sa'íd el Kadakhdár also to proceed to el Maḥrūsa with such as were left of the entourage of Effendína the late Ismá'íl Pasha and all his belongings.

CCXXXIV And he appointed Ḳólali el Ḥág Aḥmad to act for him, and dispatched him to Walad Medani, while he himself returned to Um 'Arūḳ with el Sayyid Aḥmad Effendi el Saláwi and remained there.

And el Ḥág 'Abd el Rázịḳ was his clerk at this period.

CCXXXV On the 17th of *Ragab* of this year there passed away the Leader in the Way, the Authority on Sacred Law and Truth, the Leader of the Zealous, the Guide of the Seekers after Knowledge, Sheikh Aḥmad el Ṭaib ibn el Bashír, upon whom be the mercy of God; and Sheikh Ibráhím 'Abd el Dáfa'i composed a long elegy upon him, which contained the following lines:...(six lines of poetry follow)....

CCXXXVI At the end of that year the Bey ordered all the slaves whom he had acquired by requisitioning them from the people to be sent to el Maḥrūsa, and himself prepared to go northwards also, having heard of the coming of 'Othmán Bey Barungi to the Sudan. He stayed at Um 'Arūḳ until the arrival of 'Othmán Bey, and then proceeded to el Maḥrūsa, taking with him el Sayyid Aḥmad el Saláwi.

CCXXXVII This was in *Muḥarram* 1240[2]; and in *Ṣafar* of the same year 'Othmán Bey reached Omdurmán with his *Gehadía* troops—and this was the first time that the *Gehadía* entered the Sudan—and the *mu'allim* Mikháyíl Abu 'Ebayd as a *Mubáshir*.

CCXXXVIII Then he crossed over to el Khartoum and was met by Sheikh Shanbūl[3] walad Medani, and bestowed upon him honours and robes and appointed him Sheikh over all the lands from Ḥagar el 'Asal to the hills of the Fung.

CCXXXIX There also met him Sheikh 'Abdulla walad 'Omar, and him he blew from a cannon's mouth.

CCXL He then left el Khartoum for Walad Medani, after appointing 'Othmán Ágha el Khūrbaṭli, the Director of Military Supplies, to act for him, and ordering the *feki* Arbáb walad el Kámil to be blown from a cannon also. On his arrival at Walad Medani he put a large

[1] 1823 A.D. [2] 1824 A.D. [3] reading شنبول for شبول

number of people to death with the cannon, and ordered el Sayyid Aḥmad el Baghli, the *Mufti* of the Shafa'ite Sayyids, to depart to el Maḥrūsa.

These evil acts excited great discontent among all the people, and their hearts were alienated from him, and they loathed this occupation of the country.

CCXLI Then he ordered the payment of the taxes...

(The author describes the distress that followed: soldiers were sent out to collect the taxes, and in consequence most of the people fled far afield. Some fled to el Ḳeḍáref, and the officer who was sent after them overtook them there and shot them down in heaps. A drought and an epidemic of small-pox then both occurred and the people were reduced to eating dogs and donkeys, and corn rose to a piastre for a *roṭl*. Thus "half the population perished by the sword and sickness and famine." 'Othmán Bey is described as quite pitiless, and curses are hurled at him by the author.)...

CCXLII And el Khūrbaṭli 'Othmán remained acting as vice-governor, but his rank was that of a lieutenant whereas in the army were *Ḳáimaḳáms* [Colonels] and *Beyḳbáshis* [Majors] and *Yūzbáshis* [Captains], and these paid no attention to his orders or prohibitions, and each man acted as he pleased. Thus the people were ruined, for they had no ruler to care for them.

CCXLIII However this state of affairs did not last long, for God in his goodness relieved the people by the destruction of 'Othmán Bey and the advent of Maḥḥi Bey. 'Othmán Bey died in the middle of *Ramaḍán* 1240[1], and his lieutenant [el Khūrbaṭli] hid the fact of his death until he sent for His Excellence Maḥḥi Bey from Berber; and the latter came secretly, and camped on the east of the river near the village of Ḥammad for a few days, and then returned to Berber, and, after a short stay there, came back with all his troops and took up his residence at el Khartoum and stationed his men at el Ḳubba. This was in 1241[2].

CCXLIV Maḥḥi Bey cancelled the taxation and prohibited the *Gehadía* troops from the aggression they had practised in the time of 'Othmán Bey, and then he sent for the *'omdas* and notables and such religious leaders as were left in the Gezíra, and, when they arrived, he consulted them as to how best to serve the interests of the people and secure their means of livelihood and persuade them back to their lands. And each of those present gave his views, but he agreed only with the opinion of Sheikh el Zayn, who was at the time Sheikh of a *khuṭ* (*i.e.* district); and him he honoured before all of them and gave a splendid robe, and bestowed on him the sheikhship of the

[1] 1825 A.D. [2] 1826 A.D.

district of el Kū'a, and took him with him to the neighbourhood of el Ḳeḍáref to consult with him as to the necessary measures.

CCXLV And when Maḥḥi Bey entered el Ḳeḍáref he ordered corn to be sent to the Gezíra, as there was none whatever there... (The author describes how this saved the situation and how blessings were called down upon Maḥḥi Bey's head. He adds, however, that the soldiery, who were known as *el Bayraḳia*, and who were camped at Ḳubbat Khógali, were bad characters and destroyed the tomb and everything near it. He adds a list of several *fekis* who died this year owing to an outbreak of small-pox: they include "Muḥammad Nūr, the *khalífa* of Sheikh Khógali.")...

CCXLVI And in the month of *el Ḳa'ida* of that year His Excellency Khūrshid Agha arrived as ruler of the Sudan; and Maḥḥi Bey met him at Omdurmán, and they stayed there awhile together...

(The author mentions a few unimportant circumstances of Maḥḥi Bey's departure and enlarges on the excellence of his rule, the soundness of his policy of repatriating those who had fled before the extortions of 'Othmán Bey, and his courtesy to the natives.)...

CCXLVII And in *el Ḥigga* 1241[1] plentiful rains fell, at which the people rejoiced greatly, and counted it of good augury, and hastened to sow the crops.

CCXLVIII The same month Khūrshid Agha went up the White Nile and captured some booty and returned in safety. Then he went to Dár el Abwáb and arrested Sheikh Bashír walad Aḥmad 'Aḳíd and his brother Musṭafa and extorted great wealth from the former.

CCXLIX Now before his expedition up the White Nile he sent Sheikh 'Abd el Ḳádir with a promise of peace to Sheikh Idrís 'Adlán in the south; and Idrís was given safe conduct and brought back by Sheikh 'Abd el Ḳádir to meet Khūrshid Agha at Berber.

And Khūrshid Agha reassured Sheikh Idrís and bestowed great honour upon him, for since the time of Effendína Ismá'íl Pasha Sheikh Idrís had met none of the rulers of the land, and had only come to him under promise of peace. Therefore Khūrshid Agha paid particular attention to him and invested him with the sheikhship of the FUNG mountains and gave him permission to remain there.

CCL Then Khūrshid Agha returned to el Khartoum and made an expedition against the Arabs of Walad el 'Igba round Sírū and returned in safety.

CCLI After this he collected the Sheikhs at el Khartoum to fix the official taxation, and bade them choose one who should be invested with the sheikhship over all of them and so be the medium between him and themselves. And they unanimously chose Sheikh 'Abd

[1] 1826 A.D.

el Ḳádir, and Khūrshid Agha at once issued a *firmán* to him making him Sheikh over all the other Sheikhs from Ḥagar el 'Asal to the far end of the FUNG mountains, and gave him a splendid robe and a sword of honour.

CCLII And when he had finished all he wished he fixed the amount of taxation per *feddán* with the universal consent of the Sheikhs.

CCLIII In *Muḥarram* 1243[1] he made an expedition against the DÍNKA, and thence proceeded to the FUNG mountains...

(The author mentions the death there of one of Khūrshid Agha's *mu'áwins*, and speaks of them as an experienced company whose advice the Governor-General always took.)...

CCLIV In the same year trouble was caused by Sheikh Khalífa el 'Abádi walad el Ḥág, who showed himself disobedient and rebellious and came to Berber and attacked the troops stationed there.

And when the news reached Khūrshid Agha he at once started with a force of *Gehadía* in boats, and when he reached Berber he found the soldiers had killed Khalífa and the trouble had died down; so he returned.

CCLV In '44[2] he attacked the FUNG mountains in person and slew some of [the people of] Gebál Abu Ramla, and the hearts of the people of el 'Aṭísh were filled with respect for him, and some of those who had fled returned.

CCLVI Then Sheikh 'Abd el Ḳádir advised him to exempt the chief men among the people from taxation in order to obtain their goodwill in the development of the country. And he did so, and the result of this policy was apparent, for, as an example, if he exempted one of the *fekis* or chiefs from payment on ten *ḳada'as*, the man so exempted at once reassured the people and persuaded them to return to their lands, so that Khūrshid Agha obtained from them [the taxes on] one or two hundred *ḳada'as* or more: thus owing to his wisdom and the farsightedness of his advisers the development of the country progressed and the population increased.

CCLVII In 1245[3] there was such a high Nile that the people were afraid of being drowned on their lands.

CCLVIII The same year Sheikh Aḥmad el Rayyaḥ el 'Araki came from Dár el 'Aṭísh...(The author tells how the Governor-General honoured him and sent him back with letters, to reassure the people of his district, and to promise them that he was coming to visit them shortly, and that such as came down from the hills he would pardon and such as did not he would put to death. He then went to el 'Aṭísh district and collected the people, many of whom came to meet him and others of whom he compelled to come in by force, and sent them, to the number

[1] 1828 A.D. reading ١٢٤٣ for ١٢٤٧. [2] 1829 A.D. [3] 1830 A.D.

of 12,000 souls all told, under escort to their lands; and when the people saw that he was consulting their welfare they ceased all resistance and became loyal subjects.)...

CCLIX Then Khūrshid Agha returned to el Khartoum and began the building of the mosque in the same year, and ordered the people to build houses, for most of them lived in tents of hair-matting and cowhide and there were no buildings of brick, excepting those of the family of the *feki* Arbáb near the mosque and those of the families of the *Ḳáḍis* and of the *feki* Ḥammadnulla and those of the BUDANÁB[1].

CCLX Similarly he ordered work to be started on barracks for the troops and storerooms for the equipment of the *Gehadía*. The Government buildings, that is the present *ḥakimdária*, had been begun by Maḥḥi Bey...

(The author speaks of the energy shown in building the mosques and dwelling-houses. Some unimportant changes of personnel in the Government are also mentioned.)...

CCLXI In 1246[2] Khūrshid Agha made an expedition in boats against [the] SHILLUK and inflicted upon them such slaughter as had never been seen since the time of the *Mek* Bádi Rubáṭ.

CCLXII In the same year died the *feki* 'Abd el Ḳádir walad Ḍayfulla.

CCLXIII In 1247[3] Khūrshid Agha made the Sabderát expedition and hemmed them in so strictly that they desired to submit and asked for peace: and Khūrshid Agha granted them peace and returned... (certain transfers of personnel are mentioned)....

CCLXIV The same year occurred a great earthquake, and the excellent Muḥammad el Magdhūb Ḳumr el Dín, son of Sheikh Ḥammad walad el Magdhūb, died and was buried at el Dámer; and el Khurbaṭli Ḥasan Káshif, the ruler of el Ḥalfáya district and the White Nile, also died and was buried at Ḳubbat el Sheikh Khógali.

CCLXV In 1248[4] Khūrshid Agha went to Kordofál and returned... (In 1249[5], the author says, Khūrshid Agha was promoted in rank by Muḥammad 'Ali Pasha: great rejoicings and festivities in the Sudan are said to have followed the receipt of this news.)...

CCLXVI In 1250[6] Khūrshid Agha went to Kordofán and returned in safety. Then he visited Shendi, accompanied by the Grand *Ḳáḍi*, with a view to the settlement of the disputes that had arisen between Sheikh Bashír Aḥmad 'Aḳíd and the GA'ALIYYŪN people about the lands which the former had occupied. And His Excellence sent for all the Governors of Provinces, and they all assembled at Shendi and

[1] reading بدناب for بدتاب.
[2] 1831 A.D.
[3] 1832 A.D.
[4] 1833 A.D.
[5] 1834 A.D.
[6] 1835 A.D.

held a meeting there at the end of *Dhū el Ḥigga*, that is at the end of the year '50, and then he sent them back to their provinces...

CCLXVII (The author adds that early in 1251[1] Khūrshid Agha visited Dongola and thence proceeded to Egypt and met the Viceroy and came back again as Governor-General. As soon as he reached Khartoum he sent for all the *Káshifs* and *Mámūrs* and Sheikhs, and they came and waited his will with great trepidation having heard rumours of conscription.)...

And their fears increased as he kept silence for two days, for he was closeted with Sheikh 'Abd el Ḳádir and insisting upon taking the Arabs for the *Gehadía*, while the Sheikh was begging him not to do so for fear the people would disperse and the land lie waste. And finally they agreed to call for the slaves, and when His Excellency had accepted this compromise he summoned the officials and Sheikhs who had come to el Khartoum and promised them that freemen should be exempt and decided the number of slaves which each district was to produce for the *Gehadía*, according to its capacity.

CCLXVIII So all men were then reassured and ceased to fear, and began bringing in the slaves needed for the *Gehadía*.

CCLXIX This same year the sun was eclipsed after the evening prayer and its light disappeared and it was divided into two halves, one dark and the other not, and it remained so until near sunset and then shone brightly again.

CCLXX The same year again His Excellency visited the southern mountains with his troops and busied himself there and collected many slaves, some of whom he enlisted in the *Gehadía* to serve the Government, and others of whom he distributed to the *Mámūrs* or sent elsewhere.

CCLXXI Then he returned to el Roṣayreṣ and there awaited Muḥammad Effendi, whom he had sent with the *Gehadía* to Dár el 'Aṭísh as he had heard that the MAKÁDA had come down accompanied by Ragab walad Bashír and killed the pious Walad 'Áruḍ and many people; and when the troops had arrived in Dár el 'Aṭísh God had moved the hearts of the inhabitants not to fight, so Ragab walad Bashír was taken prisoner and the troops returned in safety.

CCLXXII And in the same year Muḥammad Effendi was granted the rank of *Míralái* and went with the Sudanese troops to the Ḥegáz.

CCLXXIII In '52[2], in *Ṣafar*, a violent wind blew for two successive days. On the first day it blew red; and this was after the time of the evening prayer, and it became very dark and then suddenly light again. On the second day the wind blew black and the air was darker

[1] 1835 A.D. [2] 1837 A.D.

than on the previous day: this too lasted from the time of the evening prayer until the sunset.

CCLXXIV In the same year occurred a serious drought, and corn of any kind was unobtainable; but His Excellency the Ḥakimdár issued a hundred *ardebs* of *dhurra* at his own expense to the poor and needy, and ordered a hundred *ardebs* from the Government store to be sold in the market to help the people. He also ordered prayers to be made for rain and attended them in person.

CCLXXV And in this year too the people were visited by cholera, which was known as "The yellow wind" [*el ríḥ el aṣfar*], and so great was the mortality that in el Khartoum itself more than twenty corpses were taken out [for burial] daily.

CCLXXVI And when the epidemic was at its height the Ḥakimdár went to Shendi and stayed there for some time. And from there he sent Ragab walad Bashír to el Khartoum, where he was put to death by being impaled.

CCLXXVII Now the notables who perished by this novelty were the *feki* el Senūssi ibn el feki Baḳádi, and the *feki* el Nakhl, the reader of the holy Ḳurán at the village of Baḳádi, and the *feki* Muḥammad ibn el Ḥág el Ṭaib, the *Imám* of the mosque at el Khartoum, and the *feki* Muḥammad 'Ali walad el 'Abbás, and Sheikh el Ṭerayfi ibn el Sheikh Yūsef, and Sheikh Muḥammad ibn el Sheikh Ḥasan walad Bán el Nuḳá, and Sheikh Sa'ad 'Abd el Fattáḥ el 'Abádi, and Sheikh Muṣṭafa, the *khalífa* of Sheikh Dafa'alla el 'Araki.

CCLXXVIII This same year His Excellence pulled down the mosque which he had begun to build in '45[1], because it was too small: so, when el Khartoum increased in size as a settlement and the population multiplied, he demolished it down to its foundations, and began building on its site the present mosque, which is much more spacious.

CCLXXIX In *Ramaḍán* of this year Aḥmad Káshif, the ruler of el Ḳeḍáref, made an expedition in the direction of the lands of MAKÁDA, and slew many of them, and sent the captives to el Khartoum.

CCLXXX The same year appeared a great star in the middle of the day and sparks flew from it. Also an epidemic of fever broke out, which the people called "*Um Saba'a*" ("Mother of Seven"), and caused great mortality; and among the notables who died was el 'Awag el Darb el feki Muḥammad Barakát, a man well known for his generosity, descended from Sheikh Idrís. The fever was called "Mother of Seven" because most of those who were stricken by it died on the seventh day, and if one survived the seventh day he was saved.

[1] 1830 A.D.

CCLXXXI In 1253[1] Muṣṭafa Bey came as Governor of the whole of the Gezíra of Sennár. He had previously been in Kordofán.

CCLXXXII In the same year there was an eclipse of the moon for about two hours and it became very dark.

CCLXXXIII This year too occurred the battle of Walad Kaltabū, which is a place near Ráshid, where the Abyssinians and the Muhammadan troops met and fought. In this battle was killed Sheikh Míri, the Sheikh of el Ḳallábát, and Sheikh Aḥmad walad 'Abūd of the SHÁÍḲÍA SOWÁRÁB cavalry and many men; and the major of the battalion, and 'Ali Agha el Ṣahbi, the *Sanjak* of the MOGHÁRBA, and the *Malik* Sa'ad of the SHÁÍḲÍA cavalry were all taken prisoners and ransomed.

CCLXXXIV And towards the end of the year the Ḥakimdár led a large expedition against the MEKÁDA, and left Sulaymán Káshif Abu Dáūd to act for him at el Khartoum.

CCLXXXV In *el Ḳa'ida* of the same year Mírmírán Aḥmad Pasha with Firhád Bey, *Míralái* of the *Gehadía*, arrived with troops from el Maḥrūsa to assist the Ḥakimdár, and overtook him on the road as he was returning without having met the Abyssinians. Then they went back together to el Khartoum and stayed there until the beginning of 1254[2].

CCLXXXVI In *Rabí'a el Awal* 1254 dispatches came for Khūrshid Pasha, permitting him to go back to el Maḥrūsa and appointing Aḥmad Pasha to succeed him as Ḥakimdár of the Sudan.

CCLXXXVII So Khūrshid Pasha made all preparations for his family and belongings and set forth by boat; and this was a great sorrow to all the people, and when he bid them farewell they began to weep, and of Sheikh 'Abd el Ḳádir it is even said that he abstained from eating or drinking for two days from grief at the parting.

CCLXXXVIII And when Aḥmad Pasha heard of the affliction of this Sheikh he sent for him and promised him all prosperity and happiness, until his grief was assuaged; for Khūrshid Pasha had recommended him strongly to his successor. And indeed Aḥmad Pasha fulfilled his promises, because he entrusted him with the whole direction of the Government and never issued a single order except by his advice, so that Sheikh 'Abd el Ḳádir had more influence than a Governor...

CCLXXXIX (The author describes how Aḥmad Pasha devoted himself to reorganization and efficiency and put a stop to unauthorized looting by the soldiery, so that the prosperity and security of the country increased greatly "and prices fell until the *ardeb* of *dhurra* could be bought for five

[1] 1838 A.D. [2] 1838 A.D.

piastres." It is remarked that Khūrshid Pasha had collected the scattered natives, relieved the effects of past famines and stamped out sedition; but Aḥmad Pasha even surpassed him in the success of his measures and attained to great popularity, for he was fairspoken, no lover of bloodshed, firm of will, sparing of words, and insisted on his orders being carried out without procrastination.)...

CCXC And he remained at el Khartoum for a time and set the affairs of the provinces in order; and then he went to the neighbourhood of Walad Medani, leaving behind him 'Abd el Ḳádir Agha to act for him at el Khartoum. And while he was away in those parts, in *Ramaḍán* of the same year, His Highness...Effendína Muḥammad 'Ali Pasha honoured the country with a visit and entered el Khartoum...(The author speaks of the Ḥakimdár returning, and the reception of him and the chief functionaries by the Pasha, and their joy thereat. Muḥammad 'Ali Pasha then went south with the Ḥakimdár "as far as the mountains of Fázoghli," and held a reception for all the chief Sheikhs of the country, such as Sheikh Aḥmad Abu Sin, and presented them with robes.)...

CCXCI Then His Highness turned his attention to searching for mines and remained for some time in those parts. Afterwards he returned to el Khartoum, in the month of *el Ḥigga* in the same year, and after a short stay there returned to el Maḥrūsa.

CCXCII The Ḥakimdár, however, remained awhile in the [southern] mountains and came back to el Khartoum early in 1255[1]. Thence he proceeded to Dongola and stayed a few days there. He then turned back and reached Shendi, where he heard news of the flight of Aḥmad walad el Mek. So he pursued him accompanied by some troops and the *Malik* Kanbál; but the latter was killed the same year.

His Highness then returned to el Khartoum.

CCXCIII On the 4th of *Showál* in the same year died the learned Sídi Muḥammad el Bulaydi, the *Mufti*.

CCXCIV In 1256[2] the Ḥakimdár went to the neighbourhood of el Táka with the *Gehadía* and cavalry composed of *Delatía*, MOGHÁRBA and SHÁÍḲÍA, and remained there till the district had submitted. Then he made it a *mudíría* and appointed as governor Kūrkatli 'Omar Káshif.

CCXCV The same year there was a very high Nile; and Aḥmad Háshim, the vice-governor [*wakíl el mudíría*] died; and His Excellence Muṣṭafa Bey, the Governor of el Khartoum, returned from Kordofán to el Khartoum sick and there died.

CCXCVI After the return of the Ḥakimdár from el Táka he appointed Ḥamdi Mūsa Bey *Mírálái* to succeed Muṣṭafa Bey as Governor of

[1] 1839 A.D. [2] 1841 A.D.

el Khartoum and the whole of the Gezíra of Sennár proper, and Ḥamdi Bey held this post during the lifetime of the late Aḥmad Pasha.

CCXCVII Now H. E. the Ḥakimdár gave himself no rest, but was always visiting again and again the districts of his *ḥakimdária*, one time going to the [FUNG] mountains, and another to Kordofán and Teḳali; and finally he returned to el Khartoum in 1257[1], and in *Ramaḍán* died there.

CCXCVIII After his death the affairs of the *ḥakimdária* fell into disorder, and confusion reigned owing to the division of the country into seven provinces, each one with its own *Amír Lewa* as Governor.

CCXCIX Then, the same year, came Menekli Aḥmad Pasha as a reformer, but no reforms resulted and nothing was settled, for each governor concerned himself only with the work of his own province and failed to render full obedience to the reformer.

CCC For a time the latter stayed at el Khartoum: then he went to el Táka with the army, taking with him el Arbáb Muḥammad Dafa-'alla and Sheikh 'Abd el Ḳádir and Sheikh Aḥmad Abu Sin.

At el Táka he took captive a number of the rebels and brought them back to el Khartoum when they were all executed.

CCCI And Menekli Aḥmad Pasha stayed at el Khartoum until '61[2] and then proceeded to el Maḥrūsa in company with el Arbáb Muḥammad Dafa'alla and Sheikh Abd el Ḳádir walad el Sheikh el Zayn...

(The author says the two Sheikhs were received in audience by Muḥammad 'Ali Pasha, and Sheikh 'Abd el Ḳádir made a speech of which the eloquence amazed the Pasha, who conferred upon him the decorations of a *Mirálái* set in jewels. The two Sheikhs were also shown round Cairo and Alexandria and other places.)...

CCCII Finally the Pasha appointed Khálid Pasha as their Ḥakimdár and recommended them to his care; and in *Muḥarram* 1262[3] Khálid Pasha entered el Khartoum in company with those we have mentioned. There also accompanied him Sheikh Ibráhím el Hínami as *Ḳáḍi* over the whole Sudan. For awhile His Excellency stayed at el Khartoum: then he undertook a tour of inspection which took him into every quarter of his *ḥakimdária*. At one time he visited el Táka, at another the mountains of Fázoghli and the mines of Ḳassán, at another Kordofán and the mines of Shaybūn. And he remained in power as Ḥakimdár until the latter part of 1266[4].

CCCIII Then 'Abd el Laṭíf Pasha came as Ḥakimdár in the place of Khálid Pasha, in *Rabí'a el Ákhir* of the same year, and the latter returned to el Maḥrūsa after 'Abd el Laṭíf Pasha had importuned

[1] 1842 A.D. [2] 1845 A.D. [3] 1845 A.D. [4] 1850 A.D.

him [to do so] and repeated complaints had been made on the subject. In fact had not Sheikh 'Abd el Ḳádir been charged to reply for the people on his behalf he would have been ruined.

CCCIV 'Abd el Laṭíf Pasha stayed at el Khartoum busying himself with hearing cases and petitions innumerable[1], and he did no other work unless it were what he did in the matter of renewing and beautifying the buildings of the present *ḥakimdáría*.

CCCV In his time Rufá'a Bey, the Director of Schools, came, and with him *Ḳáimaḳám* Bayūmi Effendi and many Effendis and gentlemen; and the Ḥakimdár continued at el Khartoum and never left it; and nothing happened in the *ḥakimdáría* except the dismissal of Sheikh Idrís 'Adlán from the position of Sheikh of the [FUNG] mountains and the appointment of his brother's son 'Adlán in his stead, and the matter of Ḥasan Mismár, the Superintendent of Customs, who was beaten and imprisoned, and what followed, and the dismissal of Ḥasan Khalífa el 'Abádi, who had been in charge of the road across the Abu Ḥammad desert, from the sheikhship, and his imprisonment, and what followed, and the appointment of his brother Ḥusayn Khalífa as Sheikh, and the granting to Sheikh 'Abd el Ḳádir of the rank of *mu'áwin* of the *ḥakimdáría* in addition to his being *Sheikh el Masháikh* of the whole of the Gezíra, and the extreme deference paid to him, and also to Sheikh Aḥmad Abu Sin.

CCCVI Early in 1268[2] Rustum Pasha arrived as Ḥakimdár of the Sudan and 'Abd el Laṭíf Pasha retired to el Maḥrūsa. In his days the Members of the Council, Mahr Bey and the others, visited the country; but his period of rule was short: in fact he stayed a few days in el Khartoum, visited Walad Medani district, returned thence sick and died at el Khartoum.

CCCVII In *Ramaḍán* of the same year Ismá'íl Pasha Abu Gebel was appointed to succeed Rustum Pasha. He came to el Khartoum and stayed there awhile, and then went to the district of Khashm el Baḥr. Thence he proceeded to the eastern districts, toured them awhile, and finally returned to el Khartoum until he was recalled in *Sha-'abán* '69[3].

CCCVIII He was succeeded as Ḥakimdár by Selím Pasha, who lay sick at el Khartoum until his recall at the end of *Gemád el Awal* '70[4].

CCCIX Selím Pasha was succeeded by Sirri 'Ali Pasha Arnáóṭ: he never left el Khartoum except to visit Sennár, and his rule was brief for he was recalled in *Gamád el Akhír* '71[5].

[1] reading لاحصرلها for لاحضرلها.
[2] 1851 A.D.
[3] 1853 A.D.
[4] 1854 A.D.
[5] 1855 A.D.

CCCX The next Ḥakimdár was Garkas 'Ali Pasha. He stayed at el Khartoum for some time. And in his days Effendína 'Abd el Ḥalím Pasha honoured the country with a visit, but he did not remain for long, for cholera, known as *el ríḥ el aṣfar*, broke out; and when the epidemic was at its height, namely in *Ragab* '73[1], the doctors advised a change of air for him, so he went by boat up the White Nile, and thence returned to Berber without leaving his boat once until he reached el Khartoum. From Berber he returned to el Maḥrūsa.

CCCXI Now this epidemic killed great numbers of the people and penetrated to every part of the Sudan; and among the notables who died from it was Sheikh Abd el Ḳádir el Sheikh el Zayn, *Sheikh el Mashάikh* of the Gezíra of Sennár and el Khartoum, a noble and good man, and one of the greatest in the land. He died at el Khartoum and was buried there, and every community was represented at his burial, as well as the Ḥakimdár and the vice-Ḥakimdár.

CCCXII There also died Sheikh Yásín, *Sheikh el Mashάikh* in Kordofán Province, one of the greatest in the land; and Sheikh el Ṭerayfi ibn el Sheikh Aḥmad el Rayyaḥ el 'Araki; and the *feki* 'Omar Baḳádi, the famous man of learning (God bless him!); and many of the nobles.

CCCXIII And 'Ali Pasha Garkas, after the departure of H. E. 'Abd el Ḥalím Pasha, remained as Ḥakimdár until the coming of Effendína Muḥammad Sa'íd Pasha.

CCCXIV The last-named [returned] to Egypt in '73[2] after a short stay at el Khartoum, and [before] his return he dismissed the Ḥakimdár and appointed Arákíl Bey el Armani Governor of the whole of the Gezíra of Sennár and el Khartoum on the 16th of *Rabí'a Thάni* 1273[3].

CCCXV Arákíl Bey remained Governor until his death in '75...

(The author says he was a skilful and well-endowed statesman of kind disposition, and all went well during the first part of his rule because he took the advice of Sheikh el Zubayr, who had succeeded his father Sheikh 'Abd el Ḳádir; but mischief-makers caused a breach between them and el Zubayr fled to Cairo "and remained there as a *mu'άwin* in the Interior." Arákíl Bey then ceased taking the advice of any of the native notables of influence and increased his severity, so that he completely alienated most of the Sheikhs, and some of them even revolted and took to the hills.)...

CCCXVI In *Ragab* 1275[4] Ḥasan[5] Bey Saláma el Garkasi was appointed in his stead as Governor. This Bey was a man of bad natural attributes, coarse and rough, ignorant of statesmanship and unfitted for rule, but withal regular in his prayers, a keeper of faith and temperate.

[1] 1857 A.D. [2] 1857 A.D. [3] 1857 A.D.
[4] 1859 A.D. [5] reading حسن for حسين.

CCCXVII In *Muḥarram* 1278[1] he was recalled, and Muḥammad Rásikh Bey, the Governor of Kordofán, was appointed in his place.

He reached el Khartoum in *Ṣafar* of the same year.

CCCXVIII Rásikh Bey was fond of ease and enjoyment, and did no work except to begin building the fort which stands on the east bank of the Nile, opposite the fort of the *ḥakimdária*.

CCCXIX He was the last of the Governors (*Mudíriyyūn*) who were restricted to the control of the province of el Khartoum and the Gezíra.

CCCXX Only a short account has been given of these and of the Ḥakimdárs who were appointed after the late Aḥmad Pasha, for they made no great mark, and no important events happened [in their days]. We have therefore contented ourselves with merely enumerating them and recording their names. The real power of the *ḥakimdária* and its proper organization had ceased with Aḥmad Pasha; and in the same way the *régime* of the *Ḳáḍis* who were held in awe by the people and could speak authoritatively ceased with the late *Ḳáḍi* el Saláwi, and after him things fell into decay, and the *Ḳáḍis*, as has been seen, were mere names with no authority.

CCCXXI Rásikh Bey continued to hold the position of Governor until the good news was received of the appointment of His Excellence Mūsa Pasha as Ḥakimdár of the Sudan. And the people rejoiced at this news and were sure that it meant relief and security.

CCCXXII Mūsa Pasha arrived on the 4th of *Ṣafar* '79[2] to the joy and relief of all men, and after its time of trial the *ḥakimdária* regained its splendour.

CCCXXIII After the *firmán* had been read, Mūsa Pasha sent for all the Governors and the Sheikhs of the provinces and the notables, and on their arrival at el Khartoum he thoroughly reorganized the system of Government and fixed the taxation...(The author explains how, in his care for the interests of the people, Mūsa Pasha made the yearly taxes payable in three instalments and caused each taxpayer to be provided with a *sirki* on which was entered the amount he had to pay and a note of each payment made to the *ṣerráf*.)...

CCCXXIV He also created district *náẓirs* (*nuẓár akṣám*) and officials over the people, and as *náẓir* over all he appointed el Zubayr 'Abd el Ḳádir, who had been *Sheikh el Masháíkh*. All this he did that the people might tread the paths of civilization and progress. He also ordered them to wear Turkish clothes.

CCCXXV (The author speaks of the improvement in the state of affairs occasioned by these reforms, and then mentions an expedition made by

[1] 1862 A.D. [2] 1863 A.D.

Mūsa Pasha to the Abyssinian border, where, failing to meet the Abyssinians, he turned his attention to the AWLĀD NIMR—who had retired there from Shendi after the murder of Ismá'íl Pasha—and broke their power. He went on to el Táka, and finally returned to Khartoum the same year. There he received news of his promotion to be *Ferik*, and the event was duly celebrated by the populace.)...

CCCXXVI On the 3rd of *Muḥarram* 1280[1] Mūsa Pasha set out for el Maḥrūsa to meet His Excellency the Khedive and was greatly honoured and returned, after a short stay, to his *ḥakimdária*, and el Khartoum was honoured by his arrival on the forenoon of a Friday in *Gemád el Ákhir* 1280...

CCCXXVII (The author now suddenly breaks off his history to say that he will give a short *résumé* of the events that happened during the *régimes* of Mūsa Pasha's successors.

CCCXXVIII He then recounts in fulsome language how in 1282[2] Ga'afir Muẓhar Pasha came to Khartoum with Ga'afir Ṣádiḳ Pasha, the new Governor-General, as the latter's *wakíl*, and at once proceeded to el Táka and repressed a rebellion there. On the 17th of *Showál* 1282[3] he returned to Khartoum and by virtue of a *firmán* received from Egypt took the place of Ga'afir Ṣádiḳ Pasha as Governor-General. On the 18th of *Showál* the *firmán* was publicly read and a formal reception held, and the new Governor-General appointed 'Ali Bey Faḍli to be his *wakíl*.

CCCXXIX In 1283[4] the Governor-General was summoned to Cairo and sent up the Red Sea to Maṣṣáwa on a mission of enquiry. After his return to Cairo he was sent back again to Khartoum in 1284[5]. His departure, journey and return were celebrated in a poem addressed to him by Sheikh el Amín Muḥammad, the Chief of the *'Ulema*. He then remained at Khartoum and carried on the Government with great success. Eulogies of his modesty, generosity and other virtues are poured forth in a stream of nauseous adulation.

CCCXXX In 1288[6] the catastrophe of his recall befel the Sudan, and universal grief was shown.)...

CCCXXXI And while they were distracted with uncertainty and conjecture and were relieving the tension by clinging to the ropes of hope, lo! they were overwhelmed with a great disaster and stricken by a terrible blow, by comparison with which their previous affliction was of no account, for in the month of *Ragab* el Khartoum and its neighbourhood suffered a calamity such as had never been known, namely the appointment of one who was in every respect the opposite of his predecessor, and whose name [viz. Mumtáz, *i.e.* "Distinguished"] was completely distinguished [Ar. "*mumtáz*"] from his character; for his character was that of those men of whom God in His precious

---

[1] 1863 A.D.　　　　[2] 1866 A.D.
[3] 1866 A.D.　　　　[4] 1867 A.D.
[5] 1868 A.D.　　　　[6] 1871 A.D.

Book spoke the words "Be ye separated[1] this day [from the righteous], O ye evildoers!"

CCCXXXII This substitute, whose works were perversion and substitution, arrived on the 2nd of *Ramaḍan* in this year, and from the day of his arrival he terrorized the people by such wholesale injustice as had never been experienced by them individually or collectively at the hands of any of the rulers who preceded him, and as would, if mentioned, blacken the pages of the records and cause the heart of the historian to bleed for pity. Therefore we have drawn a veil over the details and recognized that to shroud the foulness of his deeds in a short summary is preferable to expounding them at length.

[1] reading امتزو for امترو.

D 7 (NOTES)

I The first page of *Mek* 'Adlán's MS. is missing and the second page begins with "...'*el Kaṣṣábi.*' *Their religion....*" The first paragraph, as far as that point, is translated from Muḥammad 'Abd el Mágid's MS., which is to all intents and purposes the replica of that of *Mek* 'Adlán.

The description of Sóba bears a strong resemblance to that given in the tenth century by Ibn Selím and quoted in Vol. I, p. 171 above.

For the date of the foundation of Sennár see note to para. VIII.

Sóba lies a few miles upstream of Khartoum on the Blue Nile and is the ancient 'Aloa. It is described as follows by Abu Ṣáliḥ the Armenian, writing at the beginning of the thirteenth century A.D. "Town of 'Alwah. Here there are troops and a large kingdom with wide districts, in which there are 400 churches. The town lies to the east of the large island between the two rivers, the White Nile and the Green Nile. All its inhabitants are Jacobite Christians. Around it there are monasteries, some at a distance from the stream and some upon its banks. In the town there is a very large and spacious church, skilfully planned and constructed, and larger than all the other churches in the country; it is called the church of Manbalî. The crops of this country depend upon the rise of the Nile, and upon the rain. When they are about to sow their seed, they trace out furrows in the field and bring the seed and lay it at the side of the field, and beside it they lay a supply of the drink called '*mizr*,' and go away; and afterwards they find that the seed has been sown in the ground and the *mizr* has been drunk. So again at the time of harvest they reap some of the corn, and leave beside the rest of it a supply of *mizr*; and in the morning they find the harvest completed; and they say that this is done by beings of a different order from ours." (Trans. Butler and Evetts, pp. 262 *et seq.*)

The churches were under the jurisdiction of the see of S. Mark at Alexandria.

Ruins to be seen at Kutráng, Kasemba and other places (see Vol. I, p. 48) probably represent the remains of some of the 400 churches: they are in red brick and of a meagre description, almost level with the ground.

Alvarez, some four hundred years later, also records the existence of ancient Christian churches hereabouts. Yáḳūt, el Mas'ūdi and Eutychius all mention that the particular form of Christianity in vogue was the Jacobite or monophysite (see Abu Ṣáliḥ, p. 264, note).

The most flourishing period of the Christian kingdom of 'Aloa may have been between 1100 and 1300. Budge (Vol. II, pp. 303–306) gives a good *résumé* of the subject. A description of the ruins at Sóba may be found in Budge, Vol. I, 324, and a photograph of them in Peacock's *Report*, p. 6. A very full discussion of the whole question of Christianity in the

Sudan will be found in Letronne (*Matériaux*...), and reference should be made to Part I, Chap. 3 and Part II, Chap. 2 above for further information *re* Sóba and 'Aloa.

"*A hostel occupied by the Muhammadans*" is in the Arabic رباط معمورة بالمسلمين. See note to D 7, para. II, and see explanatory note in Vol. I, p. 171 *re* Ibn Selím's use of the same word.

The spelling "*Ṣóbá*" for "Sóba" is unusual and incorrect.

The *mizr* spoken of is the older form of the modern *merissa* (native beer). El Tūnisi (*Voy. au Dârfour*, p. 224) speaks of "le *mizr*, le *oum-bulbul*, sorte de vin rouge." He explains it in a note (p. 426) as "une boisson fermentée et enivrante, tout à fait analogue au *bouza* qu'on prépare en Egypte." "*Bouza*" and "booze" are no doubt the same word and so both appear to be of the same derivation as the word "*merissa*."

"*Ḳassábi*" is the fine white variety of millet which is still grown in large quantities in the Gezíra.

II This paragraph closely resembles D 3, V and D 3, 157 (*q.v.*).

The word translated "*hostel*" is again رباط. In D 3 the word used is قصر. In Muḥammad 'Abd el Mágid's MS., in place of بنى له رباط we have بنى لهم رباطا.

"*El Ís*" is definitely written أَلِيسْ in at least one copy. See D 3, 153 (note).

III By the AWLÁD ḌAYFULLA are probably meant the ḌAYFULLÁB, *i.e.* the family of the author of D 3.

For Idrís el Arbáb see D 3, 141 and note thereto.

Muḥammad 'Abd el Mágid's MS. gives 912 for 913.

V Cp. Jackson, *Tooth of Fire*..., p. 17.

VII Cp. Jackson, p. 22.

"*Because he was the more powerful*" is كونه هو الكبير.

VIII There is no warrant for deriving "*Sennár*" (سنار) from "*sin*" (سن, a tooth) and "*nár*" (نار, fire). Schoff (*Periplus*..., p. 61) identifies Sennár with the ancient Cyeneum. The author of the *Periplus* says that it is three days' journey inland from Adulis to Coloe (modern Kohaito), and from Coloe to the city of the Auxumites (*i.e.* Axum) "there is five days' journey more; to that place all the ivory is brought from the country beyond the Nile through the district called Cyeneum and thence to Adulis." Cyeneum may correspond geographically with Sennár but it certainly does not philologically as the former is spelt Κυηνεῖον.

910 A.H. is the generally accepted date of the foundation of the FUNG kingdom: cp. Bruce. The original MS. may, however, have given 915 (٩١٥) in mistake for 910 (٩١٠), or the last of the three figures may have been indeterminate, for one other MS. I have seen gives 915, and another gives 910, and in the MS. here translated there is a marginal note to "910" implying that the text read "915" and that the copyist made the emendation: the note is الموافق لما تقره ٩١٠.

X Gerayf Ḳumr, or Gerayf East, is on the east bank of the Blue Nile a few miles outside Khartoum. Jackson (p. 19) wrongly translate "Gereif *Gimri*."

XI Cp. *A.-E. Sudan* (which reproduces Stewart's *Report...*), p. 229, where "Khamir" (خمير) is a mistake for Ḥimyar (حمير), "Beni Abbas" (بني عباس) for 'Abs (عبس), "Ziban" (زيبان) for Dhubian (ذبيان), "Ferára" (فرارة) for Fezára (فزارة), and "Shaker" (شكر) for Yashkur (يشكر).

The tribes mentioned are well-known Arabian tribes, frequently mentioned in the Sudan *nisbas*.

The Beni Yashkur are a branch of Ḳays 'Aylán (see Wüstenfeld, D and ABC, XXVIII (note)). From the remarks of the author of ABC one gathers that the Shukría are intended here to represent the descendants of the Beni Yashkur.

Of the 'Abs Burton says "Those ancient clans the Abs and Adnan have almost died out....The Abs, I am informed, are to be found near Kusayr (Corseir) on the African coast, but not in Al-Hijaz" (*Pilgrimage...*, II, 119).

XIII See note to BA, CCXVI for this and following paragraphs.

For the following chronology of the kings cp. Appendix 1, BA, CCXVI, D 2, II, *Anglo-Eg. Sudan*, p. 328, Bruce, Cailliaud, Tremaux, Na'ūm Bey and Jackson, in all of which similar lists are given though the dates vary to some extent.

XVII Of Ṭabl Cailliaud says (Vol. II, p. 256): "fut tué à Chendy par les gens du roi de cette ville."

XX See remarks *re* the battle of Kalkól in the note to BA, CCXVI, and also D 3, 241 and 141.

XXI Sheikh Idrís el Arbáb's biography is given in D 3 (No. 141): see also Jackson, pp. 27, 28.

XXII Ḥasan wad Ḥasūna's biography is given in D 3 (No. 132).

XXIII For Ibráhím el Būlád and "Khalíl" see AB, 89–101; D 3, 6, etc.

XXIV The biography of Muḥammad el Miṣri is No. 195 in D 3.

XXV Tág el Dín's biography is No. 67 in D 3.

XXVI Cp. D 3, VIII. The same words قدم على ("*inspired*") are used in both cases: see note to D 3, V. "*Obtained direction in the right way*" is اخذ طريق القوم.

XXVIII El Rubáṭ was son of Bádi Síd el Ḳūm (see Cailliaud, II, 256). In his reign the Abyssinians repeatedly invaded Sennár, but no mention is here made of the fact. An account of the circumstances will be found in the note to para. L and Appendix 2.

XXIX In the text, as in that used by Jackson (*q.v.* p. 35), the people attacked by Bádi are called "Shakká" (شكا) and there is a marginal note saying "perhaps Shilluk" (شلك). "Shilluk" is certainly the right reading: cp. Stewart (*Report...*) or *Anglo-Eg. Sudan*, p. 229.

XXXII Bruce noted this fact concerning the nomenclature of the villages round Sennár.

XXXIII The word "*el Maḥrūsa*" is used throughout D 7 instead of the usual "Miṣr" (Cairo): it means literally "the well-guarded," and is an epithet applied to any large town.

XXXVI Cp. Jackson, pp. 34 and 82.

Cailliaud (II, 258) in 1821 describes Sennár and says: "Au centre domine l'ancienne résidence des aïeux de Bâdy. C'est une construction en briques cuites, élevée de quatre étages; abandonnée, ainsi que toutes ses dépendances, elle est déjà à demi délabrée."

Poncet in 1699 says (p. 19): "the King's Palace is surrounded with high Walls of Brick bak'd in the Sun, but has nothing regular in it. You see nothing but a confus'd Heap of Buildings, without Symmetry or Beauty."

XXXVIII Cp. Poncet (p. 19): "When we had almost past over the Court, they oblig'd us to stop short before a Stone, which is near to an open Hall, where the King usually gives Audience to Embassadors." Burton (*Pilgrimage*..., II, p. 31) uses the word "*dakka*" for a stone bench at Medína.

XLI "*Um Laḥm*" is several times mentioned in D 3 (see Nos. 84, 88, 157, 165), and is similarly identified with 1095 A.H. (1684 A.D.).

XLII Bádi el Aḥmar would appear to be the king whom Poncet found reigning in 1699. Bruce gives his dates as 1701 to 1726, but I agree with Jackson (*q.v.* p. 98, note) in thinking those dates must be less accurate than the dates given by Cailliaud (1687–1714) or D 7. Poncet describes him thus: "That Prince is Nineteen Years of Age, black, but well shap'd and of a Majestick Presence, not having thick lips, nor flat Nose like the Rest of his Subjects." In other words, he was more of an Arab than a negro type and therefore likely to have been paler in complexion (*i.e.* "Aḥmar").

The rebellion referred to here and Bádi's exploit are also mentioned in D 3, 153 (*q.v.*). Cp. Jackson, pp. 35–36. El Amín Arádib *walad 'Agib* was presumably one of the 'ABDULLÁB of Ḳerri. Cailliaud (II, 256) notes that Bádi's vizier was Náṣir el Tamáni.

XLIII The biography of this saint is given in D 3 (No. 125). From D 3 and the statements of his descendants it seems that his real name was Ḥammad and not Aḥmad.

The reading ٢٧ is given, and not ٢٢, in other copies.

XLIV "*The news of his doings reached the* FUNG *in the south*...," etc., is as follows in the Arabic:

بلغت اخباره الي الفنج بالصعيد وهم جنود لولو فصمموا علي عزله لانهم
همِ الذين يعزلون ويولون من يريدوا في الملوك بدون قتل

Lūlū is not mentioned elsewhere: Jackson (p. 36) assumes it to be the commander's name.

The "*slaying*" referred to may be the ceremonial slaying of the king as practised at Sennár (*vide* Bruce, and cp. Vol. I, p. 50 and note to D 5 (*a*), VI), or the sense may be no more than the obvious one, that the military were all-powerful and that no one could oppose them.

XLV Cailliaud (II, 256) mentions that Ounsa died at Sennár of small-pox.

XLVII We have seen from the preceding paragraphs that the succession to the throne had been purely patrilinear. For the OUNSÁB see BA, 214 and D 2, I: they were the royal family.

XLVIII "Abu Shelūkh" (ابو شلوخ) has been quite incorrectly called "Abu Shilluk" (ابو شلك) by several writers. Westermann is thus led into using the name as evidence of what may perhaps be taken as true on different grounds, namely that the FUNG were racially an offshoot of the SHILLUK. "Shelūkh" are the cuts on the face used by most Sudanese Arabs: "*mushellakh*" is the usual adjective to describe one so marked.

The Sheikhs of the HAMAG, it will be seen, only usurped the royal functions in fact, but were very careful not to attempt to do so in name. They acted as "kingmakers," but in deference to public opinion never failed to insist upon the existence of a king of the royal house. Their position in some respects resembled that of the hereditary viziers under the fifth dynasty in ancient Egypt (*q.v.* Breasted, *Hist.*, pp. 113, 114).

XLIX Contrast D 1, CLXXX, and compare D 2, VIII and XXX.

"*ANWÁB*" is a curious plural formed from "NŪBA."

L For this war with Abyssinia see Jackson, Chap. III, and Budge (Vol. II, p. 203). The latter says: "'Îyâsû I, 'Adyâm Sagad I, king of Abyssinia, invaded Sennaar because Bâdî had stopped certain presents which 'Îyâsû had sent to the king of France. A battle was fought on the Dinder river, and the Abyssinian army was defeated with great slaughter." As Budge says later that 'Îyâsû I was murdered in October 1706, and that Bádi Abu Shelūkh reigned from 1724 to 1762, "'Îyâsû I" must be an error for "'Îyâsû II."

Jackson (p. 48) gives a variant translation of paras. L–LVI—not differing to any extent from D 7. We note, however, that the "el Amín" of para. L was el Amín Mismár, the 'Abdullábi, of Ḳerri. The only MSS. I have seen give simply "el Amín."

The Abyssinian account of the war, as gathered from the Portuguese records, admits the defeat but shows that Sennár was actually abandoned by Bádi and that but for a brilliant manoeuvre carried out by Khamís, the Fūr, the Abyssinians would probably have been completely victorious.

It may be as well to give here a brief historical *résumé* of the previous relations between Sennár and Abyssinia. The first detailed record of these relations will be found in the *Historia Aethiopiae* of P. Petri Paez, who was a Jesuit father, born about 1564. (See Beccari, *Rerum Aethiop....*, Vol. III, pp. 327–354, 370 ff.; and cp. Bruce, *loc. cit.*) 'Abd el Ḳádir II had been on good terms with the great Abyssinian conqueror Susneôs ("Socinios") but had been deposed by his brother 'Adlán I. He fled to Tchelga, a frontier district of Abyssinia leased to Wad 'Agíb by a special arrangement (see Bruce, Vol. III, p. 300) and under the joint protection of the two, but was subsequently killed in a local rebellion. About 1613 we have Bádi Síd el Ḳūm, who had succeeded 'Adlán I and was son of 'Abd el Ḳádir, sending a present of two indifferent horses to Susneôs: he appears not to have been satisfied with the treatment meted out to his father. About a year later, el Rubáṭ having succeeded his father Bádi, Susneôs, irritated by a number of incidents that had occurred, entered into a league with "Naêl filho de Agub" (Náil wad 'Agíb, an 'Abdullábi ?) and sent his generals to make a series of raids into the provinces of Sennár (including Sūákin), and considerable loot was captured yearly. In 1619, as the marginal summary puts it, "Melcâ Christôs, Ionaêl et Oald Haureât regnum Funye invadunt, pluribus praeliis hostes profligant, regem capiunt et, universa regione depopulata, a Suaquêm usque ad Fazcolô (*i.e.* Fázoghli), ingenti praedi onusti ad Imperatorem redeunt." [Extracts from the Portuguese of Paez will be found in Appendix 2. See also Bruce, Vol. III, pp. 311–319.]

After the expedition just described, to quote Bruce (*loc. cit.*), "Still the vengeance of Socinios was not satisfied. The Baharnagash, Guebra Mariam," was commanded to march "against Fatima, queen of the Shepherds[1], called at that time Negusta Errum[2], queen of the Greeks. This was a princess who governed the remnant of that antient race of people, once the sovereigns of the whole country, who, for several dynasties, were masters of Egypt, and who still, among their ancient customs, preserved that known one, of always placing a woman upon the throne. Her residence was at Mendera, on the north-east of Atbara, one of the largest and most popular towns in it." Mendera, that is Mundera, was on the great east-to-west trade and pilgrim route, and its queen, the modern representative of Candace, derived her income from the fact. She surrendered to Guebra Mariam and was taken to Abyssinia but was released and sent back home with presents.

The Abyssinians no doubt considered Sennár, or at least that portion of the kingdom which was bounded by Abyssinia, as theoretically a subject state. For instance, Ludolfus, basing his history chiefly on the works of Tellez and the Jesuit memoirs, says in Bk. I, Chap. XVI (published 1681 and translated by Gent in 1684) that to the south Abyssinia is bounded by "the Kingdom of Sennar or Fund, governed by its peculiar king, formerly a tributary to the Abessines, but now absolute"; and in Bk. II, Chap. XVIII, we find "as for the king of Sennar, he has often revolted and made warr upon the Abessines."

Menelik II was of the same opinion so late as 1891: see note to D I, CLXXXIII.

Between the reigns of el Rubáṭ (died 1642) and Bádi "Abu Shelūkh" (*acc.* 1723) there seems to have been a period of comparative peace.

The el Amín walad Mismár mentioned here is not to be confused with the Muḥammad el Amín walad Mismár of paras. LXXVII *et seq.*: see Na'ūm Bey, *Hist. Sudan*, II, 99.

LI Khamís is mentioned by Bruce (Vol. II, p. 635): "Hamis, prince of Dar Fowr had been banished from his country in a late revolution occasioned by an unsuccessful war against Selé and Bagirma, and had fled to Sennaar, where he had been kindly received by Baady, and it was by his assistance the Funge had subdued Kordofan."

Muḥammad Abu el Kaylak was probably the greatest man that the Sudan produced in the seventeenth and eighteenth centuries. His sons and grandsons were virtually supreme in the Gezíra after his death until the Turkish conquest, and he himself not only conquered and administered Kordofán but also raised himself to the position of a dictator at Sennár.

I do not think that there can be much doubt but that he was one of the HAMAG by race, though Jackson (p. 51) says (rashly, I think) that the "general consensus of native opinion" is in favour of his being a Ga'ali, and quotes an account of him given by the *Mek* of the GAMŪ'ÍA from which it would appear that Abu el Kaylak's mother was HAMAG and his father a Gamū'i

[1] The BEGA tribes, that is. [2] *I.e. el Rūm.*

(*i.e.* of Ga'ali extraction). The term "HAMAG" is often used as almost the equivalent of barbarians, and, on the other hand, in so far as the HAMAG have Arab blood in them, it is supposed to be derived from BENI 'ABBÁS (*i.e.* Ga'ali) ancestors. In fact, where some people would say that the GAMŪ'ÍA were partly HAMAG, the GAMŪ'ÍA put it differently and speak of the HAMAG (*e.g.* Abu el Kaylak) as being partly Ga'ali. There is, however, the possibility that Abu el Kaylak was called a Hamagi because of his mother belonging to that race. Such an example of the survival of a matrilineal system would be by no means anomalous.

From Bruce (Appendix 28, p. 226) one would suppose that Abu el Kaylak was the son of Sheikh Ṣubáḥi. The vizier 'Adlán is repeatedly referred to as his brother and in 1176 (1762 A.D.) wrote a letter of recommendation for Bruce signed "el Sheikh 'Adlán son of el Sheikh Ṣubáḥi." But Ṣubáḥi was the Sheikh of Khashm el Baḥr (see para. LXXII) and one of the KAMÁTÍR (RUFÁ'A), which Abu el Kaylak certainly was not, so it is evident that Bruce was simply misled by the use of the term "*akhu*." From para. LXXII it is clear that 'Adlán and Abu el Kaylak were bosom friends.

As regards Abu el Kaylak's career: in Appendix 46 (pp. 416–7) Bruce says (1772): "From these two provinces [viz. the Gezíra and southern Kordofán] are all the riches of the kingdom; and they are both in the hands of the two brothers, Adelan, and 'Abd el Calec, who have killed two kings, and keep the third [*i.e.* Ismá'íl] without forces or revenue."

Again, on p. 425, Bruce says: "News brought (Aug. 1st) that the people of Darfoor have marched with an army to take Kordofan, which, it is apprehended, they soon will do, being about 12,000 horse, and an infinite number of foot. There are at Kordofan about 1500 horse, with Mahomet Abou Calec; who, it is thought, will fall back on Sennaar, if not surrounded...."

Browne, writing in 1793 from Dárfūr, says (p. 307): "A king of the name of Abli Calik is the idol of the people of Kordofân where he reigned about fourteen years ago and is renowned for probity and justice."

The following Tree, compiled from D 7, will be found useful in following the career of Abu el Kaylak's descendants:

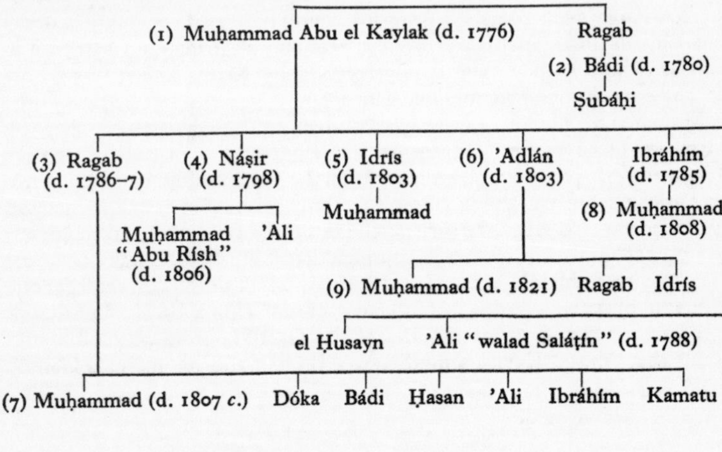

The name "Abu el Kaylak" is alleged (by *feki* Muḥammad 'Abd el Mágid of the 'OMARÁB, for whom see D 3, 113 note) to be more correctly "Abu Lakaylak." He explains "*Lakaylak*" as a diminutive of "*lak*," meaning 100,000, and says the nickname was given because Sheikh Muḥammad commanded 100,000 men. This, however, is not very convincing.

LVII 'Abd el Laṭíf el Khaṭíb's biography is No. 9 in D 3.

The text is corrupt here, reading thus:

وتجاري علي........

علي فعل امور ذميمة من النهب والقتل حتى انه تجارا على

الخطيب عبد اللطيف العالم المشهور وقتله..........

The MS. of Muḥammad 'Abd el Mágid omits the middle line.

"*The FUNG nobility*" is كبراء الدولة من الفنج. Cp. paras. LXI and LXII.

LVIII Cp. MacMichael (*Tribes*..., pp. 9–11), and Jackson (p. 50) who adds el Amín Mismár (for whom see para. L) among the commanders. The FUNG army was probably composed largely of 'ABDULLÁB from Ḳerri if we may judge from the names "'Abdulla walad 'Agíb," "Shammám walad 'Agíb," "el Amín Mismár" and "'Agayl." Khamís the Fūr was probably assisting the FUNG in Kordofán during the war: see the first passage from Bruce quoted in the note to LI.

LXI "*FUNG nobles*" here is اكابر دولة الفنج: cp. paras. LVII and LXII.

LXII "*Great men of the FUNG*, that is slaves of the king," is كبراء الفنج وهم عبيد الملك: cp. paras. LVII and LXI.

It would appear that slaves had attained in Sennár to a position analogous to that of the *Mamlūks* in Egypt.

LXIV Cailliaud says (II, 256) that Bádi died at Sūákin.

LXVII Cailliaud speaks of Náṣir (II, 256) as "tué à el-Bouqra par Bády Ouâled Regeb."

LXVIII "*FŪÁRI*" may be a plural formed from FŪR: cp. "ANWÁB" in para. XLIX. Jackson (p. 59) says: "Ahmed wad Mahmud, Sheikh of the Furs." Muḥammad 'Abd el Mágid's MS., however, gives "Ḳawáría."

"*Prayer-mat*" is موطا. Jackson (p. 59) translates "pen."

LXIX It was in Ismá'íl's reign that Bruce visited Sennár. In the text Bruce speaks of him as "white in colour as an Arab," with short black hair; but in the MS. notes (Vol. VI, p. 417) he speaks of him ("the *mek*") as having "woolly hair and black flat features."

LXXI The reading '89 instead of '83 is adopted from another MS.

LXXII The reading "1198" as the date of Abu el Kaylak's death is obviously an error, as his successor died in 1194 A.H. (see para. LXXXVI). Two other MSS. to which I had access, and which agree with that here translated as regards other dates, give 1190.

As regards the relationship between Abu el Kaylak and 'Adlán see note to para. LI. Cp. also para. CC.

Feki Muḥammad 'Abd el Mágid writes to me of 'Adlán walad Ṣubáḥi: "He was one of the KAMÁTÍR, a learned and pious man. His tomb is at

Sennár and is still visited. In times of distress people call upon him saying 'Yá 'Adlán, Wali and Sulṭán.' He has performed many miracles, and has a marvellous power of curing club-footedness (*el nabt*). If one has a club-foot and visits him on seven Saturdays, by God's leave one will be healed of it."

"*Khashm el Baḥr*" was the name given to the district bordering on either side of the river from Sennár southwards. Muḥammad 'Abd el Mágid writes to me again on this subject: "It was the custom of the kings to grant to the man they put in charge of these villages the rank of 'Sheikh of Khashm el Baḥr,' and to the man they put in charge of the cultivable lands the rank of 'Sheikh of the lands of the villages of Khashm el Baḥr.' The inland villages, which water from wells, were called 'the rainland villages' (*ḥillál el ḳuṭr*) and also had two Sheikhs, one for the villages and one for the lands: the former was called 'Sheikh of the rainland villages,' and the latter 'Sheikh of the lands of the rainland villages.'"

LXXIII Of Ismá'íl Cailliaud (II, 256) notes "mort du côté de Saouákin."

LXXV Abu 'Ali's full name was Abu 'Ali wad Muḥammad wad 'Adlán wad Náíl, Náíl being the ancestor of the AWLÁD NÁÍL section.

LXXVII Muḥammad el Amín (walad Mismár) was Sheikh of Ḳerri, an 'Abdullábi. He had apparently succeeded the Sheikh 'Agíb of para. LXXVI. Bádi his brother seems to have succeeded him, but when Bádi died, or was deposed, he again became Sheikh and did not die till 1790 (see para. CXII).

The reading "*Aḥmad walad 'Ali*" for "Muḥammad" is correct and occurs in other MSS.: cp. paras. LXXIX, CCI and CCIII and note to CCI.

Jackson gives (p. 61) "Mohammed wad Ali."

LXXXI El Amín walad 'Agíb is the Muḥammad el Amín of para. LXXIX, etc. (cp. note to para. L). "Wad 'Agíb" was practically the hereditary title of the 'ABDULLÁB.

LXXXIV "*His uncle*" is Abu el Kaylak. Jackson (p. 63) is in error in making el Amín give Bádi the *coup de grâce*. Such MSS. as I have seen all agree with the text as translated.

LXXXVI Ragab was son of Abu el Kaylak.

LXXXVIII Jackson (p. 63) makes Náṣir the victor. No MSS. that I have seen do so.

XC Cp. D 3, IV (note) and Jackson (p. 63).

XCI In para. CIV it is Ibráhím's brother 'Ali who is called "Walad Saláṭín."

XCII The AWLÁD NIMR are the Ga'ali *Meks* of Shendi.

XCIII For "*fásher*" cp. el Tūnisi (*Voy. au Ouadây*, p. 98): "Le mot de Ouârah, chez les Ouadayens, est analogue au mot de Fâcher chez les Fôriens...Au Dârfour, la dénomination de Fâcher s'applique également à la grande place qui est devant la demeure du sultan...et à cette demeure elle-même. Ou donne encore ce nom, hors de Tendelty, à la ville, ou au bourg, ou au village où le sultan s'établit. Mais au Ouadây, le nom de Fâcher ne s'applique qu'à la grande place qui est devant le *palais*...."

XCV Sa'ad ibn el Mek Idrís was the Ga'ali *Mek* of Shendi. According to Cailliaud's list (III, 106) he ruled for 40 years.

XCVI The Arabic of the three phrases given is

(a) يا سنار جاتك نار.

(b) النار طفاها السيل.

(c) انا وانت.

C 'Abūd lies south-west of Wad Medani, in the Gezíra.

CI Ḥegázi's biography is given in D 3 (No. 133).

"*Said he would inspire them*" is اوعدهم بقدومه عليهم—a technical phrase for which cp. para. XXVI above.

CIV Inṭaraḥná is west of Rufá'a.

For 'Ali "walad Saláṭín" cp. note to para. XCI.

CVI From Cailliaud (II, 256) it seems that after 'Adlán's death his son Rubáṭ reigned for a month and was then put to death by Náṣir at Sennár. See para. CX.

CVII The Arabic of the quotation is

اليس من العجايب ان مثلي يري ما قل ممتنعا عليه وتوكل باسمه الدنيا جميعا وما من ذاك شئ في يديه

CVIII Awkal is said by Cailliaud to have reigned 18 months and to have been killed by Náṣir at el Dámer (Vol. II, p. 256).

CIX Cailliaud (II, 256) says Ṭabl reigned a year and 5 months and "fut tué à Chendy par Ouâlad-Agyb."

CX This Bádi is Bádi V. For Rubáṭ see note to CVI. Cailliaud omits Ḥasab Rabbihi.

CXII Cp. notes to paras. LXXVII and LXXXI.

CXIV This is Bádi VI.

CXVII See Na'ūm Bey (*Hist. Sud.* II, 87) for such tales.

The Sultan 'Abd el Raḥman el Rashíd reigned from 1785 to 1799. Murád Bey, the *Mamlūk*, was defeated by Napoleon's army in July 1798, made Governor of Upper Egypt in 1800, and died in 1801.

Aḥmad Pasha el Gazár was Governor of Acre at the time the French besieged it. He is said to have been "a monster of rapacity and cruelty" (Paton, I, 259).

CXVIII "*Came to him*" is the technical قدم عليه (see note to para. XXVI).

CXX The author appears to fluctuate in his estimate of Náṣir's character; or else remarks from another hand have been inserted in the text. The MS. of Muḥammad 'Abd el Mágid agrees with that translated. Cp. para. CCCXVI.

CXXI Cp. D 3, 133. For "*Ḥusayn*" Jackson (p. 68) gives "Hassan." Such other MSS. as I have seen give "Ḥusayn."

CXXIII This Sírū is north of Omdurmán, so "advanced into the Gezíra" (دخلوا الجزيرة) is probably an error: the southern Sírū (*q.v.* para. CXXVII) can hardly be meant here. It is too far from the FEZÁRA and BENI GERÁR country.

Háshim, the Musaba'áwi Sultan, had lately been expelled from Kordofán by the KUNGÁRA and had fled to Shendi. He was eventually put to death there by the *Mek* Nimr (see Burckhardt, and MacMichael, *Tribes*..., p. 63).

CXXIV See note to CLXXVII.

CXXVII Idrís and 'Adlán were Náṣir's own brothers. This Sírū is on the west bank just south-west of Karkóg. Deberki is nearly due east of Karkóg.

CXXVIII This 'Abdulla walad 'Agíb is the one first mentioned in para. CXII. See also CXXXVIII.

CXXIX "*Gave him protection*" is اعطاه الزمام.

CXXXII Bádi walad Ragab had been actually killed by Aḥmad walad 'Ali, but (see LXXXIV) the latter was merely the ally of Náṣir and the other sons of Abu el Kaylak. Aḥmad's grievance had been his deposition from the sheikhship, but a more mortal quarrel existed between Bádi and Náṣir on account of the former's having flogged the latter (see LXXVII). In the result Bádi was deposed and killed, and here we have 'Adlán handing over Náṣir, his own brother, to Bádi's son for vengeance to be taken. Jackson (p. 69) gives "Sahi" (صاحي) or "Hyas" (حياص) for "Ṣubáḥi" (صباحي) which is obviously the correct reading.

Sheikh Dafa'alla el 'Araki is repeatedly alluded to in D 3.

CXL See para. CCIX. The reference (المرحوم جنتمكان) is to Ismá'íl Pasha.

CXLI Jackson (pp. 70, 71) wrongly attaches the following description of 'Abdulla walad 'Agíb to "Agib."

CXLIV The *Mek* Sa'ad was mentioned in para. XCV. According to Cailliaud's list (III, 106) Musá'ad (*q.v.* para. CXLIX) succeeded Sa'ad.

This is, according to tribal accounts, quite correct. The ruling family at Shendi were the SA'ADÁB, and Musá'ad inherited in due course. Then Muḥammad walad Nimr, also a Sa'adábi, rebelled and tried to enlist the aid of the HAMAG towards the realizations of his pretensions. The HAMAG (*i.e.* 'Adlán) played Muḥammad false as related in D 7; but his son Nimr (see para. CXLVI) escaped and took refuge with the SHUKRÍA nomads for a time, and then returned in 1801 (see para. CL) and relegated Musá'ad to an inferior position. Jackson (p. 71) has confused Muḥammad walad Nimr and his son Nimr walad Muḥammad. Cailliaud (copied by Budge, Vol. II, p. 206) made the error of allotting Musá'ad and Muḥammad each 13 years and not noting that they overlapped; and Jackson makes things worse by putting in definite dates (which Cailliaud did not), viz. Musá'ad 1778–1791 and Muḥammad 1791–1804. See Part III, Chap. 1 (*k*) on the subject.

CXLV See paras. XCII–XCIV. It had been on the advice of the GA'ALIÍN of Shendi (AWLÁD NIMR) and others that the king had enslaved Abu el Kaylak's daughters.

CXLIX "*MAGÁDHÍB*" = AWLÁD EL MAGDHŪB. Cp. D 1, CXXV; D 3, 123; and D 7, CCLXIV.

CL This *Mek* 'Ísáwi was a Gamū'i, the eponymous ancestor of the ÍSÁWÍA section and nephew of Bábikr Sulaymán (*q.v.* note to para. CCXII).

CLI 'Awaḍ el Kerím Abu Sin was the grandson of the Abu 'Ali of para. LXXV. His father was 'Ali, and his son was the well-known Aḥmad Bey Abu Sin (see para. CCXC and Part III, Chap. 2 (*d*)).

CLII Yūsef's biography is No. 256 in D 3.

CLIII "*The historian states...*" is قال المورخ (*sic* in each MS. seen).

CLV Muḥammad walad Ragab walad Muḥammad [*sc.* Abu el Kaylak] was 'Adlán's nephew.

"*Kamtūr*" is Muḥammad Kamtūr (see para. CCIV) of Khashm el Baḥr (*q.v.* note to para. LI).

Bádi VI had been deposed by Idrís walad Muḥammad (see para. CLXI) and Ránfi set up in his place.

Muḥammad walad Náṣir [*sc.* walad Abu el Kaylak] "Abu Rísh" was 'Adlán's nephew.

CLVII The quotation runs تحسبهم جميعا وقلوبهم شتي.

CLXI So, too, Cailliaud (II, 257): "Rânfa régna 5 ans. Fut tué à Sennâr par Mohammed Regeb. Le trône fut vacant pendant un an et demi, ensuite revint à Bâdy, fils de Tabl."

CLXII 'Ali Baḳádi is the *feki* whose biography is numbered 68 in D 3.

CLXIV The Gedíd referred to is the village on the Blue Nile a little above Khartoum.

CLXV The text gives ... فتبارزوا ١٢١٢ الي كسله الي اوايل سنة....

Another MS. gives ... تبارزو ١٢٢١ الى كسلا وأقام بها فى أوائل سنه....

CLXVI For "*Harába*" (هرابة) Jackson (p. 73) gives Meheria (مهرية ?). Muḥammad 'Abd el Mágid's MS. gives "Hawáwa."

CLXVII Sulaymán is presumably the Ḥág Sulaymán Aḥmad of paras CXVIII and CLXVIII.

CLXXV The 'ARAKIÍN had great religious influence owing to their alleged nobility of descent and the number of their *fekis*. See D 3 *passim*.

The emendation in the final sentence is adopted from another MS.

CLXXVII An "el Arbáb Dafa'alla" is mentioned in paras CXXIV, CXXXI and CXXXVI (*i.e.* about 1797). In this paragraph (CLXXVII), *i.e.* about 1808, we have "el Arbáb Dafa'alla walad Aḥmad" or "el Arbáb Dafa'alla." In para. CXCVI, *i.e.* in 1821, we have "el Arbáb Dafa'alla walad Aḥmad Ḥasan"; and in paras CXCVII, CCX, CCXIV and CCXVIII "el Arbáb Dafa'alla walad Aḥmad" or "el Arbáb Dafa'alla." Probably the same man is meant in each case. See note to para. CCXVIII.

"*Arbáb*" is properly a title: see Jackson, p. 94, and cp. Poncet, p. 8: "The Erbab or Governour of this province...lives at Argo."

CLXXIX To cast earth upon a person's head is to show contempt for him. The Arabic is ... حثوا التراب علي.

CLXXXIV It is noteworthy that all the five sons of Muḥammad Abu el Kaylak whose children are mentioned at all named their (eldest?) sons Muḥammad after Abu el Kaylak.

CLXXXV "*Yellow fever*" is حمي صفراوية.

Ḥámid walad Abu 'Aṣá is No. 113 in D 3.

"*Muḥammad Nūrayn*" is either another form of, or a mistake for, Muḥammad Nūr, for whom see the introduction to D 3 and ABC, XI.

Ibráhím 'Abd el Dáfa'i is mentioned again as a poet in para. CCXXXV. He was possibly the son of that 'Abd el Dáfa'i el Ḳandíl whose biography is in D 3 (No. 4). The question of his authorship of D 7 is discussed in the Introduction.

The Arabic of his verses is:

دع العين تبكي دهرها بتوجد علي غضيض بحر كان بالعلم مزبدا

هو الحبر ابن الحبر ضيف الاهنا لقد حاز فخرا في الانام وسوددا

In Muḥammad 'Abd el Mágid's copy, in the first line, غيض occurs for غضيض, and in the second line we have نجل for ابن and الهنا for الاهنا. The sense is unaffected.

CLXXXVIII El Labayḥ was the Rufá'i Sheikh. His headquarters were at Káwa.

CLXXXIX "*Gibiṣ*" (جبص) is a purely Sudanese word, and is variously explained. The idea of stickiness seems to be primarily involved.

CXC Cp. para. CCXXXII. Sheikh Ḥasan was the son of the 'Abd el Raḥman ibn Ṣáliḥ ibn Bán el Nuḳá whose biography is in D 3 (No. 25). See Introduction to D 3.

CXCI Náṣir "walad 'Agíb" is the Náṣir walad el Amín of paras CXL and CLXXXVI: see para. CCIX. "Walad 'Agíb" was practically a hereditary title. Na'ūm Bey (II, 99)—followed by Budge (II, 204) and Jackson (p. 105)—gives three separate persons in succession (Náṣir wad el Amín, Amín ibn Náṣir and Náṣir wad 'Agíb) by error for one.

CXCII El Sayyid Muḥammad 'Othmán el Mírghani was the great-grandfather of Sir Sayyid 'Ali el Mírghani, K.C.M.G. He entered the Sudan by way of Maṣṣáwa from Mekka in 1817 and visited Kordofán as well as Sennár. In Kordofán he married a Dongoláwía, and his son el Sayyid el Ḥasan was born at Bára. The shrine erected over the latter's afterbirth at Bára is described by Seligman in the volume of *Essays and Studies presented to William Ridgeway*. El Sayyid el Ḥasan visited Mekka and finally returned and settled at Kassala. His son el Sayyid Muḥammad 'Othmán II resided at Maṣṣáwa and died in Egypt in the Khalífa's time, leaving two sons, el Sayyid Aḥmad, who lives at Kassala, and el Sayyid 'Ali, who lives at Khartoum and Omdurmán. The Mírghanía *ṭariḳa* is a branch of the Khatmía.

CXCIII "*Aḥmad*" is given in the Arabic by error for "Ḥammad." 'Awaḍ el Kerím Abu Sin had a number of sons, and the best known of them, Aḥmad Bey (see paras CCXC, etc.), lived on into Turkish days. One of Aḥmad Bey's brothers was named Ḥammad; and other copies I have seen give "Ḥammad" and say both he and his father "were killed by the BAṬÁḤÍN." The text of D 7 gives "BAḤṬÁGIYYŪN" but no such people exist.

"*Religious Sheikhs*" is مشايخ السجاجيد.

CXCV See para. CLV.

CXCVIII Ḥasan was Abu el Kaylak's grandson. Of him and Wad 'Adlán Cailliaud, who accompanied Ismá'íl Pasha in 1821, speaks as follows: "Ces deux usurpateurs, ennemis l'un de l'autre...n'accordaient au roi légitime que la faible part qu'il leur avait plu de lui assigner. A'dlân [*i.e. Walad 'Adlán*] tenait sa cour au village de Moûna, où il tentait de se former une petite province: il avait le don de se faire aimer, et son parti était plus fort que celui de Regeb [*i.e. Ḥasan Ragab*]. Au mois d'avril, le bruit des brillans succès d'Ismâyl sur les Chaykyés et de l'approche de son armée, vint jeter l'alarme dans le Sennâr. A'dlân et Regeb sentirent alors que leur intérêt commun exigeait qu'ils réunissent leurs forces pour repousser un ennemi également redoutable pour tous deux. Ils formèrent donc une alliance momentanée, et prirent l'engagement réciproque d'agir de concert contre le pacha, tant que le danger subsisterait....Sur ces entrefaites, Regeb, abusant de la confiance d'A'dlân, conçut le projet de se débarrasser de son compétiteur par une lâche trahison...vers la fin de mai, A'dlân, livré au sommeil, fut assailli par une foule d'assassins qui enfoncèrent ses portes: il se lève, saisit ses armes, et se défend avec fureur; mais couvert de blessures, il succombe sous le fer d'Abdallah-Niknitt el d'Idris-Ouâd-A'quindi, écuyers de Regeb, payés par lui pour commetre cet attentat. Regeb croyait alors avoir vaincu tous les obstacles; mais les troupes d'A'dlân...firent éclater l'horreur que leur inspirait une action aussi atroce....A Gondâl, le 1er juin, ces mêmes troupes, commandées par le ministre d'A'dlân, en vinrent aux mains avec celles de Regeb....Regeb remporta l'avantage; mais cette victoire fut loin d'augmenter la force de son parti. Quelques jours après, ayant appris que l'armée d'Ismâyl avait passé le fleuve Blanc et qu'elle s'avançait sur Sennár, Regeb ne songea qu'à fuir...et alla se réfugier dans les montagnes sur les confins de l'Abyssinie. Alors Bâdy...réunit à lui l'ancien parti d'A'dlân, et se porta au-devant du pacha jusqu'à Ouâd-Modyen [*i.e. Wad Medani*]." (Cailliaud, pp. 233–5.)

CC See note to para. LXXII.

CCI–CCII See note to para. LXXVII where Aḥmad is called "walad 'Ali."

CCVI See Part III, Chap. 1 (*k*) and Chap. 2 (*a*).

CCVII "*Foretold by shaking...*" is ترمز بحروف مقطعة—a method of divination.

CCIX Cailliaud's narrative (Vol. II, 192 *et seq.*) may be compared. Náṣir walad el Amín is Cailliaud's "Lod-A'guyb" (*i.e.* Wad 'Agíb): the two narratives agree remarkably closely as to Ismá'íl's movements.

CCX The *Ḳáḍi* Aḥmad el Saláwi was known to Werne as he accompanied Aḥmad Pasha's Kassala expedition. Werne (p. 253) says: "This great Kadi is a hypocritical but intelligent Mograbin, drinks stoutly his wine in private...and...during Ramazan, when even the poor half-starved soldiers fasted, openly set them the fine example of eating and drinking before his tent."

CCXI See note to para. CXCVIII. Cailliaud mentions this expedition against Ḥasan walad Ragab (Vol. II, 238 *et seq*): it was under the command of Díwán Effendi (*q.v.* para. CCXIV) and consisted of 400 irregular horse.

The murderers of Walad 'Adlán were put to death by impalement.

The *Mek* Bádi is thus described by Cailliaud: "Il était vêtu d'une large chemise de toile blanche, les jambes nues, de longues sandales aux pieds, la tête couverte du bonnet particulier aux méliks [*i.e. the* '*taḳia*,' *for a description of which see* Vol. I, pp. 248 and 249]...Bâdy est un homme de quarante ans environ, d'une taille moyenne, robuste, d'une figure pleine et agréable, ayant les cheveux crêpus et le teint de couleur cuivrée, qui est celui de la race des Foungis." (II, 298–9.)

CCXII This is evidently the expedition referred to by Cailliaud (II, 307–8). It started on August 22nd and only took eighteen days. Cailliaud's

"Djamélyehs" refers to the GAMŪ'ÍA. "Leur chef fut tué...on leur prit trois cents chameaux, beaucoup de boeufs, et de moutons."

Idrís el Miḥayna was related as follows to the present *mek* of the GAMŪ'ÍA, Náṣir:

Sulaymán
- Miḥayna
  - Idrís
    - 'Abd el Ḳádir
    - Maḳbūl
- Bábikr
  - Ibráhím
    - Náṣir el Mek

The Muḥammad Sa'íd Effendi mentioned is the same as the "Díwán Effendi Sa'íd" of paras CCXIV, CCXV, for Cailliaud mentions that "Divan Effendy" commanded this expedition.

CCXIII The reading منازل occurs in other MSS.

Cailliaud accompanied the expedition to Fázoghli (Cailliaud, Vol. II, Chaps. XXXVI–XLIII).

There is no other record, so far as I am aware, of the taxation fixed by Ismá'íl Pasha: Cailliaud gives no information on the subject. There was no regular budget until 1881 (see Dehérain, p. 181), and nothing is known of the details of taxation previous to the time of Khūrshid Pasha (for which see Dehérain, p. 182).

A *riál* at present is worth, in the Gezíra, 10 piastres (2*s*.), and in most other parts (*e.g.* Kordofán) 20 piastres. An exhaustive note on the subject of the currency in use in Egypt in 1845 is added to his edition of el Tūnisi's *Voyage au Ouaday* by Dr Perron (see pp. 675–682). Among the silver coins there were (1) the "*riál abu madfa'a*" (the Spanish dollar of Charles IV, value 20 pt. 28 paras), (2) the "*riál 'agūz*" (a worn and defaced coin), (3) the "*riál abu arba'a*" (the same as No. 1, except that IIII occurs instead of IV. Date 1798. "Très recherché au Soudan"), (4) the "*riál abu shubbák*," or "*riál abu ibra*," or "*riál abu nukṭa*" (Austrian), (5) the "*riál abu ṭayra*" (Russian), the "*riál chinco*" or "*abu shagera*" (5-franc piece). Nos. 4 (the Austrian thaler, or talari) and 5 were also known as "*riál ḳushli*" (value 20 pt.).

Cailliaud writing of Berber in 1821 similarly says "Les piastres d'argent d'Espagne, sur-tout celles de Charles IV, y sont préférées: mais celles où le nom du prince est écrit Charles IIII, par quatre I, et qu'ils nomment 'réal France abou-arba...' obtiennent sur les autres un surcroît de valeur qui va à 2 francs et plus" (Vol. II, 118); and again (Vol. II, 296), writing of Sennár, "l'argent qui a cours dans le pays sont les piastres d'Espagne: mais ici, comme au Barbar, celles qui portent l'empreinte de Charles IIII, par quatre I, obtiennent une préférence marquée."

If the *riál* be reckoned at its very lowest possible value, viz. 10 pt., the taxation specified in para. CCXIV still appears almost unbelievably onerous, and to amount to something approaching confiscation.

As no mention is made of camels, which presumably were not taxed per head because there was no means of counting them, we may assume that a tribute was, in the case of the nomads, demanded from the whole tribe. It may also be taken for granted that it was not paid and that the herds of the nomads were, practically speaking, spoils of war for any official who could catch them (see note to CCLXXXIX).

CCXIV The spread of the false rumours mentioned was described by Díwán Effendi to Cailliaud (*q.v.* Vol. III, 75–76).

An insurrection actually occurred at el Ḥalfáya (*op. cit.* Vol. II, 93; cp. also Dehérain, pp. 94–96).

CCXV Sa'ad 'Abd el Fattáḥ (*q.v.* para. CCLXXVII) was one of the 'ABÁBDA.

A "*mu'allim*" was a clerk and a "*mubáshir*" a kind of superintendent.

For the move to Wad Medani in March 1822 cp. Cailliaud, III, 89.

CCXVI Several accounts of the murder of Ismá'íl Pasha by *Mek* Nimr are extant. Cailliaud had parted from the Pasha, luckily for himself, and only heard of the murder when he arrived at Marseilles on 11th December 1822. He gives the following description, based presumably on the first account received in Cairo: "Arrivé à Chendy, il commit l'imprudence grave de s'éloigner de son camp, et d'aller dans un village voisin célébrer par un banquet nocturne, avec un petit nombre des siens, le bonheur d'être bientôt rendus à leurs foyers. Nimir où Nêmr, ancien roi de la province ...avait voué à Ismâyl une haine éternelle. A la faveur des ténèbres, il accourut à la tête de sa troupe chargée de matières combustibles, et en un clin d'oeil un vaste incendie enveloppa la maison où le jeune prince et ses amis dormaient dans une sécurité perfide. Il leur fut impossible de se frayer une issue à travers les flammes, et ils périrent suffoqués....Nimr prit la fuite avec ses complices, et se retira dans le Darfour." (Vol. III, 336, etc.)

The last detail is certainly wrong: Nimr fled towards Abyssinia not Dárfūr.

Rüppell was at Shendi in 1824 and gives a rather different account (see *Reisen*..., p. 111). Ismá'íl Pasha gave Nimr two days in which to produce 1000 slaves as tribute. Nimr protested that this was impossible. Ismá'íl struck him and threatened him with impalement, and Nimr pretended to give way. He then persuaded the Pasha to leave his boat and stay in the village, and, under pretext of furnishing fodder for the horses, piled masses of *dura* stalks outside the house where the Pasha was. When night came and Ismá'íl and his companions were half drunk, Nimr set fire to the *dura* stalks, and Ismá'íl and his friends were burnt to death.

Werne (1840) also gives the story with slight variations and additions: *e.g.* Nimr was given *three* days to pay the impost, and Ismá'íl struck him on the face with his pipe-stem as he knelt asking for a longer period of grace (see Werne, p. 77).

Zaydán (II, 164) speaks of a time limit of five days and a demand for a boat-load of gold and 2000 men—modified finally to 20,000 *riáls* of silver and 2000 men. Ismá'íl was then persuaded to attend a dancing entertainment to which all the inhabitants also assembled, and at a given signal the straw was lit and the Pasha and his suite driven within its circle and killed.

The account given in D 7 is practically the same as that given by Rüppell.

Of Nimr himself Cailliaud (II, 300) says: "On m'avait prévenu de son caractère hautain, de sa fierté: je le trouvai assis sur un *engareb* lisant le Coran....Nimir est un homme de six pieds; il a le regard dur, l'humeur sombre; il est réfléchi, plein d'orgueil et d'audace, studieux et dévot." See also note to CCCXXV.

CCXVII "*Kadakhdár*" is said to have been a title denoting "Master of the Household."

CCXVIII El Arbáb Dafa'alla (previously called "el Arbáb Muḥammad walad Aḥmad") is mentioned by Werne (p. 77). Speaking of Ismá'il Pasha's murder he says: "At the same time, the father of our Defalla [*q.v.* paras CCC, CCCI], Mohammed Adlan Defalla, Great Sheik of the Fungh, on the Gesira, murdered all the Turkish soldiers to be found in his countries." Our author omits this! Werne adds (p. 78) that this same el Arbáb Dafa'alla "fled from the Gesira, and, according to report, died in Habesch." See note to CLXXVII.

The family of el Arbáb Dafa'alla are said to have been SURŪRÁB, *i.e.* GAMŪ'ÍA, but they intermarried with the FUNG royal house (see note to para. CCC). Their headquarters were at el Surayba. Abu Shóka is a few miles south of Sennár (see Marno's map).

The people of 'Abūd were nearly all KAWÁHLA.

"*Delatía*" were irregular troops such as were later called Bashi Bazūks.

CCXIX Cp. Cailliaud, III, 337–8; Rüppell, 111–2; Dehérain, 98; Werne, 77; and Budge, II, 212.

The Arabic of the last sentence is:

ودخل على الفقيه احمد الريح في خلوته فامر بحرقهم جميعا

CCXX This "*Walad 'Agíb*" is the Náṣir walad el Amín of para. CCIX. For Sheikh Khógali see D 3, 154.

CCXXII Kutráng is on the east bank of the Blue Nile below el Kámlín.

By "*el Ḳubba*" is meant, as usual, the site of Sheikh Khógali's tomb at Khartoum North. Werne's translator (p. 17) calls it "Chobba."

CCXXIV El 'Ádayk is a colloquial name for the Blue Nile.

CCXXV The 'AḲÁḲÍR are a section of GA'ALIÍN.

CCXXVIII El Naṣūb is a hill in the Buṭána between the Blue Nile and Kassala Province.

CCXXIX Bashír walad 'Aḳíd (*q.v.* para. CCLXVI) was one of the MÍRAFÁB of Berber.

Um 'Arūḳ ("mother of roots") was properly a large *ḥaráz* tree and gave its name to a site on the west bank of the White Nile close to the site of the present *Commandanía* of Omdurmán.

CCXXXII See para. CXC.

CCXXXIII Sabderát is just east of Kassala. Werne (pp. 217–8) refers to this expedition. Sabderát was destroyed and the population put to the sword.

CCXXXV Cp. para. CLXXXV for Ibráhím 'Abd el Dáfa'i.

Sheikh Aḥmad el Ṭaib ibn el Bashír's tomb, built in 1906, is at the village, called after him "Sheikh el Ṭaib," on the west bank some twenty-five miles below Omdurmán. He introduced the Sammánía *ṭaríḳa* into the Sudan. He himself adopted it, when at el Medína, from its founder "el Sammáni." Sheikh el Ṭaib's descendants speak of themselves as

GAMŪ'ÍA, but it is said that as a matter of fact the Sheikh's father, el Bashír, was a Baza'i from Kordofán who married one of the GAMŪ'ÍA of the SURŪRÁB section and settled permanently on the Nile.

Sheikh el Ṭaib's full name was Aḥmad el Ṭaib ibn Bashír ibn Málik ibn el feki Muḥammad ibn el feki Surūr.

"*El Sammáni's*" full name was Muḥammad ibn 'Abd el Kerím, and he is alleged to have been a Ḳurashi. He was born in 1130 A.H. (1718 A.D.) at el Medína and was taught by Sheikh Muḥammad ibn Sulaymán el Kurdi. He was then instructed in the tenets of the Khalwatía *ṭariḳa* by el Sayyid Muṣṭafa ibn Kamál el Dín el Bekri and adopted it. Later he founded the Sammánía *ṭariḳa* himself. It was so called because he was by trade a seller of *samn* (fat). He died in 1189 A.H. (1775 A.D.). Cp. also Burton, *Pilgrimage...*, I, 162.

CCXXXVII Cp. Budge (II, 213), who says 'Othmán Bey succeeded in 1825. *Muḥarram* is the first month of the year and *Ṣafar* the second.

The *Gehadia* were trained troops drawn by the Turks from subject races. They were not irregulars as were the "*Delatia*": see para. CCLXVII. For "*Mubáshir*" see note to CCXIV.

CCXXXVIII Budge (*loc. cit.*) has mistranslated and misunderstood the Arabic.

Sheikh Shanbūl walad Medani, or an ancestor of the same name, was eponymous ancestor of the "SHENÁBLA" of the Gezíra. These are not to be confused with the quite distinct SHENÁBLA nomads of Kordofán, but are connected with the KAWÁHLA. Their ancestor is said to have come from Ṣubía in Yemen. Arbagi was their headquarters. Medani the son of Shanbūl was killed in 1883 with Hicks Pasha.

CCXLIII Ḳubbat Khógali was the usual military camping place. It was healthy, and troops could easily be marched thence to Berber Province (cp. Werne, p. 17).

CCXLIV This Sheikh el Zayn was great-grandson of the el Nūr walad Mūsa Abu Ḳussa whose biography is in D 3 (No. 217). He was a Ya'aḳū-bábi and his full name was el Zayn walad el Sheikh Sálim (see Jackson, *Yacubabi Tribe...*).

El Kū'a (or el Kí'án)—meaning literally "a bend" or "elbow" (*sc.* of the river)—is a district on the Blue Nile south of Sennár.

CCXLV For "*Bayraḳia*" some copies give "*Barayḳia*". The literal meaning is probably "standard-bearers" (*i.e. Baraḳdária*).

CCXLIX Sheikh 'Abd el Ḳádir was the son of the Sheikh el Zayn of para. CCXLIV (cp. Jackson, *Yacubabi Tribe...*, p. 3).

Idrís walad 'Adlán was met by Werne, who calls him (1840) "After Aburow [*i.e. Abu Róf*] the most powerful ruler in the peninsula" (p. 161).

Idrís walad 'Adlán was a brother of the Muḥammad walad 'Adlán who was murdered by Ḥasan Ragab (see Cailliaud, II, 238).

CCL The Arabs meant are the ḤAMMADA, Sheikh Abu Gin's people.

The Sírū mentioned is the one near Sennár.

CCLII "*He fixed...*," etc., is ربط الاموال على الفدان. A *feddán* = 1·038 acres (5024 square yards).

CCLIII The date 1243 (for 1247) is given in the other MSS.

CCLIV Khalífa was Sheikh of the 'ABÁBDA.

CCLV El 'Aṭísh lay between Roṣayreṣ and Lake Tsana in what is now Abyssinia. It was the headquarters of a *Káshif* (see Werne, p. 197).

CCLVI A *ḳada'a* is about 5⅓ *feddáns*.

When Muḥammad 'Ali reproached Khūrshid Pasha for not sending more money to him the latter replied "When my Sennárians cultivate ten times as much as they do they will still only have corn and beasts and no money to give you." Khūrshid Pasha had pleaded their poverty, to which the Pasha's reply had been "They have two Niles and I only one: make the lazy work as I do in Egypt and they will become rich" (Brun Rollet, *Bull. Soc. Geog.* 1855, IX, p. 367, quoted by Dehérain, p. 168).

Between 1830 and 1838 the taxation rose to 3,125,000 francs, and between 1838 and 1842 to 5,000,000 (Dehérain, pp. 182, 183).

CCLIX Ḥammadnulla is presumably the Ḥammadnulla walad Malák of D 3, 128.

"*Budanáb*" for "*Budatáb*" is adopted from Muḥammad 'Abd el Mágid's MS. They are a section of MAḤASS and their present representatives live at Burri on the outskirts of Khartoum: cp. ABC, VI.

The making of Khartoum into the official capital of the Sudan dates from this time (1830). In 1822 a permanent military camp only had been made there (Dehérain, p. 117, quoting Werne, *Expedition zur Entdeckung der Quellen des Weissen Nil*, pp. 44–5). Cp. also Holroyd, p. 167. He visited Khartoum in 1837. It had then 15,000 inhabitants and many houses "built of sunburnt bricks."

CCLXII 'Abd el Ḳádir walad Ḍayfulla was a Gamū'i (FITÍḤÁB section, ḤAMAYDÁNÍA subsection). He is buried at el Debba in Gayli district.

CCLXIII This expedition was a failure and Khūrshid Pasha suffered defeat. Aḥmad Pasha in 1840 said to Werne (*q.v.* p. 8): "First Darfur, and now Taka, will pay no tribute, nor have they done so since Churschid Pascha was in the Chaaba (the forests where he was defeated)." The enemy had been the HADENDOA under Sheikh Muḥammad Dín "the defeater of the Turks under Churschid Pasha" (Werne, p. 55)..."It seemed to us most wonderful that the Haddenda, a tribe that numbers over 80,000 fighting men, did not set on us, and give us a lesson such as Churschid Pascha had received from them" (p. 176)..."The fatal defeat of Churschid Pascha, in which he also lost two guns, to recover which a whole battalion, save one or two men, were sacrificed" (p. 177). Khūrshid Pasha managed however to get 3000 head of cattle and some cash as tribute (see Werne, p. 109).

CCLXIV Ḥammad walad el Magdhūb is No. 123 in D 3.

"*The ruler of...Nile*" is حاكم اقليم الخلفاية والبحر الابيض.

CCLXXI "*Makáda*" is a synonym for Abyssinians or Abyssinia. Werne uses the word *passim* in this sense. See, too, his remarks (p. 247).

CCLXXV The cholera evidently spread westwards. El Tūnisi speaks of it ("*el haoua el-asfar*") in Wadái in 1838 (*Voy. Darfour*, p. 283).

CCLXXVI Ragab walad Bashír is said to have been one of the 'ABDULLÁB.

CCLXXVII El Senūssi was no doubt the son of the Baḳádi who is mentioned (No. 68) in D 3 and in para. CLXII above.

Muḥammad ibn el Ḥág and Muḥammad 'Ali were MAḤASS, el Ṭerayfi was an 'Araki and Sheikh Muṣṭafa the same.

Sa'ad 'Abd el Fattáḥ's son, Sheikh Ḥasan, was a *Ḳáḍi* in Dongola a few years ago, and died on the pilgrimage.

CCLXXX The village of 'Awag el Darb opposite el 'Aylafūn is called after the man here mentioned. "*Sheikh Idrís*" is Idrís wad el Arbáb of el 'Aylafūn.

CCLXXXI The Gezíra of Sennár comprised all that "the Gezíra" does now. The term is so used (*e.g.*) in Marno's map (1870). Muṣṭafa Bey was of course subject to the Governor-General (*Ḥakimdár*): his title as given here is "*Mudír 'alá 'umūm gezíra Sennár.*" See note to paras CCXCV, CCXCVII, CCCXIV and CCCXVII.

CCLXXXIII Sheikh Míri is mentioned by Werne (p. 75): he says (in 1840) "Under their lately deceased Sheikh Myri, who possessed more than ninety suits of chain armour...the Tokruri [*i.e.* the TAKÁRÍR] enjoyed a pretty considerable power, highly dangerous for their frontier neighbours, as they had also for warfare about a hundred muskets, a large number for these lands; but since Sheikh Myri's death they have sadly declined in power and force." Mansfield Parkyns also mentions him (II, 357).

'Ali Agha is also mentioned (Werne, p. 144): "Ali Aga, whose family name is Sobi, leader of 300 Magrabins...." He was "wofully slashed in an attack by the Turks on Makada. Never have we seen on any skull such severe scars...." He was "descended from one of the principal families of Fez."

Of the *Malik* Sa'ad Werne (p. 160) says "The Schaigies every morning wait on the old Sheik Melek Saat, and kiss his hand. They never steal or make a prize of anything, without preserving the best of it for him, and in all ways provide for and attend to him, as if he was still in possession of his old rank and dignities." And again (p. 137) "The Schaigie Melek Saat, whose father yet [*sc.* 1840] rules the old Dongola, had received, a month before the present chasua [*i.e. the expedition by Aḥmad Bey to Kassala*], some hundred blows of the stick at the order of the Pascha."

CCLXXXIV Sulaymán Káshif was a Circassian. He led Aḥmad Pasha's White Nile exploration expedition. He lived at Kerreri (see Werne, pp. 14, 62, 63, 186, etc.).

CCLXXXVI Aḥmad Pasha was a Circassian, "stolen from his native land when only six years old" (Werne, p. 156).

CCLXXXIX From the nomads in the east Aḥmad Pasha used to demand 20 pt. poll-tax on adult males and a tenth of all produce and animals (see Werne, p. 61).

CCXC 'Abd el Ḳádir Agha is probably Werne's "Abd el Kader, the jovial Topschi Baschi," the commandant of artillery (Werne, pp. 28, 139).

Aḥmad Abu Sin was the greatest of the SHUKRÍA Sheikhs: he attained to the rank of Bey and was given practically complete control over the Arab tribes in and east of the Gezíra. Werne describes him (p. 54) as "a handsome large man, with noble countenance, and his character is described by all as vigourous, able, and generous."

Baker's description of him is also worth quoting: "He was the most magnificent specimen of an Arab that I have ever seen. Although upwards of eighty years of age, he was as erect as a lance, and did not appear more than between fifty and sixty; he was of Herculean stature, about six feet three inches high, with immensely broad shoulders and chest; a remarkably arched nose; eyes like an eagle, beneath large, shaggy, but perfectly white eyebrows; a snow-white beard of great thickness descended below the middle of his breast...As a desert patriarch he was superb, the very perfection of all that the imagination could paint, if we would personify Abraham at the head of his people" (*Nile Tributaries...*, p. 111).

CCXCII Kanbál was a Sháíḳi. Werne says of him (1840): "Even now, though dead, Kamball still lives in the people's mouths: they have a great number of songs about him, in which he is described, on account of his cruelty and savage deeds, constantly wandering round, without grave, rest, or peace, as the punishment of his crimes. He was shot in the back, most likely by the soldiers of Achmed Pascha, in a fight between them and the Schaigies of Melek Hammet" (Werne, p. 177).

Werne himself, however, speaks of Kanbál as "a distinguished soldier, an honest man, and general favourite, and from his generosity to the poor, ever in debt." He was extraordinarily brave and much valued by Aḥmad Pasha. "After his death the Pascha himself took charge of his infant son, had him educated, and allows him 500 piastres a month" (p. 179). This son was the lately deceased Bashír Bey Kanbál who was "*mudáwin* of Arabs" in Kordofán.

"*Hammet*" is the same as Aḥmad walad el Mek. He did not submit to the Turkish government but fled for the Abyssinian border. The Pasha took Kanbál's SHÁÍḲÍA in pursuit and rode himself with them from Berber to Abu Ḥaráz, where "Hammet" was captured: he was not however put to death.

CCXCIV It was this expedition which Werne accompanied. Its object was primarily to collect tribute from the HADENDOA. "I need money, much money—want it most badly," said Aḥmad Pasha to Werne. He also hoped to open up the Abyssinian trade routes and conquer that country (Werne, p. 8). He took with him about 10,000 regulars, and about the same number of irregulars and camp-followers (Werne, p. 197). The expedition was conducted in a perfectly haphazard manner but the ḤALANḲA and HADENDOA submitted eventually and the town of Kassala was founded (see Dehérain, pp. 108–110; Lepsius, *Letters*, p. 200; Werne *passim*; and Budge, Vol. II, pp. 214–217).

CCXCV This Musṭafa Bey is the man mentioned as Governor of the Gezíra of Sennár in para. CCLXXXI. As we see from the next paragraph and para. CCCXIV the control of the two (Khartoum and the Gezíra) was generally vested in one man.

CCXCVIII The seven provinces, according to Budge (II, 217), were Fázoghli, Sennár, Khartoum, Kassala, Berber, Dongola and Kordofán.

CCXCIX "*Reformer*" is "*munaẓam*" (منظم). It is not certain from the text and the context whether the author intends to say that Menekli Pasha was made Governor-General (*Ḥakimdár*) as were his predecessors and successors, or that an experiment was being made in decentralization, which was abandoned as a failure and tried again in 1856 (see para. CCCXIV).

According to Lepsius, who writes in 1844 (January), Aḥmad Pasha Menekli was "the new Governor of the Southern Provinces." Lepsius also says "On the sudden death, by poison, of Ahmed Pasha, the governor of the whole Sudan, at Chartûm...the south is divided into five provinces, and placed under five pashas, who are to be installed by Ahmed Pasha Menekle" (*Discoveries in Egypt...*, pp. 133–135).

CCC This el Arbáb Muḥammad Dafa'alla is the son of the el Arbáb Dafa'alla mentioned previously, and is the man mentioned by Werne as accompanying Aḥmad Pasha's Kassala expedition in 1840. Werne calls him (p. 37) "Mohammed Defalla, a great Sheikh of the neighbourhood of Wollet-Medina...his relations of the old royal family have whole heaps of such" (*sc.* armour as that he wore). Again Werne says (p. 76) "Defalla has already given many causes for suspecting his fidelity and both his own and father's names are too often connected with that of Nimr."

He is referred to as "our herculanean neighbour" and "our fat friend." His command consisted of 150 men (p. 78). He married Naṣra, the sister of Idrís walad 'Adlán (see Werne, p. 160).

CCCII The "*mines of Shaybūn*" were once famous. Russegger in 1838 (p. 200) says "The bed of every stream in the vicinity of Jebel Sheibun and Tira...exhibits a gold-bearing alluvium." As a matter of fact Mr S. C. Dunn tells me that at Shaybūn itself there was never any gold; but the people of Shaybūn, the SHAWÁBNA, used to get it from the north side of Gebel Kinderma, a day's journey away. The Arabs thought the gold was from Shaybūn itself.

Khálid Pasha was Governor-General when Petherick visited Khartoum. He was "a veteran soldier of the Syrian and Arabian wars...by birth a Greek" (Petherick, *Egypt...*, p. 127).

CCCV Rufá'a Bey and Bayūmi Effendi were both members of the first educational congress held in Egypt in 1836 under the presidency of Mukhṭár Bey. A portrait of Rufá'a Bey is extant (see Zaydán, II, 192–193).

Ḥasan Khalífa and Ḥusayn Khalífa were sons of the Khalífa mentioned in para. CCLIV.

"*Mu'áwin of the Ḥakimdária*" = *Náib Ḥakimdár* = Assistant Governor-General.

"*Sheikh el Mashdíkh*" or "Sheikh of Sheikhs" was a rank invented by the Turks (see MacMichael, *Tribes...*, p. 33). 'Abd el Ḳádir's authority would be confined to the Gezíra and north of Khartoum and would not extend, *e.g.*, to Kordofán (cp. paras CCCXI and CCCXII).

CCCX "*Garkas*" or "*Sharkas*" = "Circassian."

By "'*Abd el Ḥalím Pasha*" is meant Prince Ḥalím Pasha, who visited the Sudan during Sa'íd Pasha's viceroyalty of Egypt. Zaydán (II, 202) says "In his [Sa'íd Pasha's] days certain privileges (امتيازات) were conferred on the Sudan, and Prince Ḥalím Pásha *was appointed as its Governor-General* ('*Ḥakimdár*')." This is no doubt inaccurate.

CCCXII For Yásín (*i.e.* Yásín Muḥammad Dólíb) see MacMichael (*Tribes*.... p. 33). He was a Dólábi of Khorsi, the grandfather of the *feki* Dardíri of D 1.

'Omar Bakádi was presumably a relative of the men mentioned in paras CLXII and CCLXXVII.

CCCXIV The author of D 7 is quite precise and consistent as to this administrative change. It seems from D 7 that after the conquest of the country a Governor-General (*Ḥakimdár*) was appointed with practically absolute powers. Subject to him were the Governors of Provinces. This system remained in force until the death of Aḥmad Pasha in 1842, Khartoum and the Gezíra forming a single province.

Then (para. CCXCVIII) the Sudan was divided into seven provinces, without (it is implied) any Governor-General.

Later in the year, according to D 7, came Menekli Pasha and attempted some reforms without much success. What these reforms were remains vague, and Lepsius (see note to para. CCXCVIII) throws little light on the matter. But in any case decentralization seems to have failed, and with the succession of Khálid Pasha in 1845 the Governor-Generalship was certainly revived. On this point there is no contradiction and Petherick, *e.g.*, speaks of Khálid Pasha (1845–1850) as "Governor-General." There can also be little doubt that D 7 is correct in saying that Khálid Pasha's six successors were all Governor-Generals.

But in 1857 (says D 7) came Sa'íd Pasha and appointed Arákíl Bey, not Governor-General, but only "Governor of the whole of the Gezíra of Sennár and el Khartoum" (مدير عموم جزيرة سنار والخرطوم); *i.e.* the other governors of provinces were independent of him. Arákíl Bey's successors, Ḥasan Bey and Rásikh Bey, we are told, held the same position; but apparently it was a failure, as Mūsa Pasha was in 1863 made Governor-General (see paras CCCXIX and CCCXXI). If these facts are true they have generally been overlooked as Arákíl Bey and his two successors always appear in lists of "Governor-Generals of the Sudan." The fact that they alone were Beys (the usual rank of a provincial governor) while all the rest were Pashas lends strong support to the account given by D 7.

Petherick, in spite of his having called Khálid Pasha (1845–1850) "Governor-General," writes in 1859 as follows (see *Upper Egypt...*, p. 128): "The town of Khartoum contained two different administrations, one the Governor-Generalship, and the other the Local Authority of the province, with a population of about sixty thousand inhabitants. Since the visit of the present Viceroy to Khartoum in the year 1847, the Governor-Generalship has been abolished, the governor of each province now communicating directly with the Minister of the Interior at Cairo."

The state of affairs described was no doubt true of 1859 (though it was altered in 1863 when Mūsa Pasha was given the Governor-Generalship); but it seems that the provincial governors had not been independent since 1847 but only since 1857.

Arákíl Bey was a brother of Nubar Pasha and a Christian Armenian. In 1862 his body was disinterred and sent to Egypt (see Petherick, *Travels...*, p. 77).

For el Zubayr see note to CCCXXIV.

CCCXVI Other MSS. correctly give "*Ḥasan*" for "*Ḥusayn*."

CCCXIX The Arabic is as follows:

هو اخر المديريون الذين انفردوا بولاية مديرية الخرطوم والجزيرة

See preceding note.

CCCXX For el Salâwi see para. CCXXXVI.

CCCXXI Baker's description of Mūsa Pasha Ḥamdi is as follows: "This man was a rather exaggerated specimen of Turkish authorities in general, combining the worst of oriental failings with the brutality of a wild animal" (*Albert Nyanza*, p. 8). He was originally a Circassian slave bought by a Turk in Cairo market. He entered the army, was caught by the Arabs in the Syrian war, and escaped. He was then sent to the Sudan and rose in turn to be a colonel of infantry, Governor of Khartoum, *aide-de-camp* to the Governor-General, a commander of irregular cavalry, Governor of Dongola, of Berber, and of Kordofán. He was dismissed the service for inhuman treatment of prisoners, but was later appointed Governor of Kena in Egypt, Chief of Police in Cairo, President of the Council, and finally Governor-General of the Sudan and a general of division for operations against Abyssinia and the White Nile. Murder and torture were no more to him than pastimes. (See Petherick, *Central Africa*..., Vol. I, pp. 51, 52, 147.) To judge from Baker's and Petherick's descriptions of the Sudan in this man's time, the reforms described by D 7 are purely chimerical.

CCCXXIV A *náẓir* is properly an overseer.

Of el Zubayr 'Abd el Ḳádir (*q.v.* CCCXV above) Jackson (*Yacubabi Tribe*..., p. 4) says that after his return from Egypt "he was made President of the Court of Appeal by Jaafer Pasha but later served for about four years as Sub-Governor of Sennâr with the rank of Bimbashi. He quarrelled with his Governor Yusef Pasha (some time between 1879 and 1882) and both were recalled to Khartoum; but on the outbreak of the Mahdiist movement he offered to raise a battalion in Sennâr. He accordingly went to Sennâr but was so unpopular with the people that the Government decided to remove him quietly: he was put on board a sailing-boat by night but in midstream the sailors threw him overboard and he was drowned at the age of 59 in the year 1885."

CCCXXV Cp. Baker (*Nile Tributaries*..., pp. 140, 278–280): "Mek Nimmur" (the son that is of the man who killed Ismá'íl Pasha) "was a most unpleasant neighbour to the Egyptian Government, and accordingly he was a great friend of the King Theodorus; he was, in fact, a shield that protected the heart of Abyssinia...Upon several occasions expeditions on a large scale had been organized against Mek Nimmur by the Governor-General of the Sudan; but they had invariably failed; as he retreated to the inaccessible mountains...." In March 1862 Baker visited Nimr: "Since our departure from the Egyptian territory, his country had been invaded by a large force, according to orders sent from the Governor-General of the Soudan. Mek Nimmur as usual retreated to the mountains, but Mai Gubba and a number of his villages were utterly destroyed by the Egyptians" (p. 444).... "Mek Nimmur's territory was an asylum for all the blackguards of the adjoining countries..." (p. 451, and cp. Werne, p. 78). Baker found him "a man of about fifty, and exceedingly dirty in appearance" (p. 458). Baker interceded, on his return, with Mūsa Pasha for Nimr, but Mūsa Pasha "declared his intention (1862) of attacking him after he should have given the Abyssinians a lesson, for whom he was preparing an expedition in reply to an insolent letter that he had received from King Theodore...upon a question of frontier....Mūsa Pasha subsequently started with several thousand men to drive the Abyssinians from Gallabat...but upon the approach of the Egyptians, they fell back rapidly. ...The Egyptians would not follow them, as they feared the intervention of the European powers" (pp. 559–561).

CCCXXVII Other MSS. correspond.

CCCXXVIII *Feki* Muḥammad 'Abd el Mágid's MS. breaks off with the mention of the repression of the rebellion in Kassala (Táka).

CCCXXXI The quotation is from the 36th chapter of the Ḳurán (Sale, p. 333).

APPENDIX I

The Chronology of the Fung Kings

A

N.B. *Br.* = Bruce; *Ca.* = Cailliaud; and MS. refers to D 7 in the following.

	Name of King (MS.)	Date of accession (MS.)			
1.	'Omára Dūnḳas ("*'Amru ibn 'Adlán*," *Br.*)	1504	Bruce 1504	Cailliaud 1484	42 years
2.	[1]'Abd el Ḳádir I ibn 'Omára Dūnḳas	1533	„ 1551	Cailliaud	10 „
3.	[1]Náíl ibn 'Omára Dūnḳas	1543	„ 1534	„	12 „
4.	'Omára Abu Sakaykín ("*ibn 'Omára Dūnḳas*," *Ca.*; "*'Amru ibn Náíl*," *Br.*)	1554	„ 1559	„	8 „
5.	[2]Dekín walad Náíl ("*Ṣáḥib el 'Áda*," *Ca.*)	1562	„ 1570	„	17 „
		[Cailliaud inserts Dôrah			8 „]
6.	[2]Ṭabl I ("*ibn 'Abd el Ḳádir*," *Br.*, *Ca.*)	1577	Bruce 1590	Cailliaud	4 „
7.	Ounsa I ("*ibn Ṭabl*," *Ca.*)	1589	„ 1593	„	12 „
8.	'Abd el Ḳádir II ("*ibn Ounsa*," *Br.*)	1598	„ 1606	„	3 „
9.	'Adlán I "walad Áya" ("*ibn Ounsa*," *Br.*)	1604	„ 1610	„	4 „
10.	Bádi I, "Síd el Ḳūm" ("*Abu el Rubáṭ*," *Ca.*; "*ibn 'Abd el Ḳádir*," *Br.*)	1611	„ 1615	„	7 „
11.	el Rubáṭ ("*ibn Bádi I*," *Ca.*, *Br.*)	1614	„ 1621	„	27 „
12.	Bádi II ibn el Rubáṭ, "Abu Duḳn"	1642	„ 1651	„	37 „
13.	Ounsa II walad Náṣir (nephew of "Abu Duḳn")	1677	„ 1689	„	12 „
14.	Bádi III ibn Ounsa II, "el Aḥmar"	1688–9	„ 1701	„	27 „
15.	Ounsa III ibn Bádi III	1715	„ 1726	„	3 „
16.	Nūl ("*ibn Bádi*," *Br.*)	1718	„ 1729	„	4 „
17.	Bádi IV ibn Nūl, "Abu Shelūkh"	1723	„ 1733	„	40 „
18.	Náṣir ibn Bádi IV	1761	„ 1766	„	8 „
19.	Ismá'íl ibn Bádi IV	1768	„ 1769	„	7 „

(Bruce's chronology ends with 1772)

[1] Bruce and Cailliaud give these two in inverted order.

[2] Between these two Bruce and Cailliaud insert "Douro" or "Dôrah" or "Dâour" (see note).

	Name of King (MS.)	Date of accession (MS.)			
20.	'Adlán II	1776–8	—	Cailliaud	12 years
	[1]Rubáṭ ("*ibn 'Adlán II*," *Ca.*)	1788	—	,,	30 days
21.	[1]Awkal ("*ibn Ounsa*," *Ca.*)	1788	—	,,	1 yr, 6 mths
22.	[1]Ṭabl II	1788–9	—	,,	1 yr, 5 mths
23.	[1]Bádi V ("*ibn Dekin*," *Ca.*)	1789	—	,,	1 year
24.	[2]Ḥasab Rabbihi	1789	—	,,	—
25.	Nowwár	1790	—	,,	1 year
26.	Bádi VI walad Ṭabl II (first reign)	1790	—	,,	6 years
27.	[3]Ránfi	(date not given)	—	,,	5 ,,
28.	[3]Badi V walad Ṭabl II (second reign)	1803, deposed in 1821	—	,,	16 ,,
					"335 années de règne" (*Ca.*)

[1] Rubáṭ was a pretender appointed in antagonism to Awkal, Ṭabl II and Bádi V, or to Bádi V alone (see paras CVIII to CX).

[2] Omitted by Cailliaud.

[3] Between 27 and 28 Cailliaud inserts an interregnum of $1\frac{1}{2}$ years.

B

The dates as given by Na'ūm Bey correspond with those of the MSS., with the immaterial proviso that, in converting the Muhammadan date to the corresponding Christian date, a difference of one year frequently appears (*e.g.* Na'ūm Bey "1505," MS. "1504," etc.). This is owing to the fact that the first or last day of the Muhammadan year does not coincide with that of the Christian year, or, in other words, any given Muhammadan year falls partly in one Christian year and partly in another.

Professor Budge accepts Na'ūm Bey's dates (Vol. II, pp. 201–204).

C

Between Dekín and Ṭabl I (Nos. 5 and 6) Bruce and Cailliaud insert a third king. Bruce speaks of him as "Douro," son of Dekín, with a reign of three years (1587–1590). Cailliaud gives "Dôrah ou Dâour, fils de Dakyn...8 ans." Mr Jackson, in his appendix (*Tooth of Fire*, p. 98), gives "Dudu" and adds a note "also given as Duda, Darru, Dor, and Dora." The Arabic transliteration of these names in the order given is as follows:

دورو دوره داور دودو دوده درو دور دوره

It would therefore appear not unlikely that the king's name was Dáūd, *i.e.* داود

He was probably omitted by an oversight of the author. As he was the son of the preceding king, and not a mere usurper, it is unlikely that he was left out from any ulterior motive.

D

Adding together the information to be gathered from Bruce, Cailliaud and the MS., as to the relationships between the first fifteen or sixteen kings, we obtain the following genealogical tree of the OUNSÁB.

- (1). 'Omára Dūnḳas
  - 2 (or 3). 'Abd el Ḳádir I
    - 6. Ṭabl I
      - 7. Ounsa I
        - 8. 'Abd el Ḳádir II
          - 10. Bádi I, "Síd el Ḳūm" (or "Abu el Rubáṭ" Ca.)
            - 11. el Rubáṭ
              - 12. Bádi II, "Abu Duḳn"
              - Náṣir
                - 13. Ounsa II
                  - 14. Bádi III, "el Aḥmar"
                    - 15. Ounsa III
        - 9. 'Adlán I, "Walad Áya"
  - 3 (or 2). Náíl
    - 5. Dekín, "Ṣáḥib el 'Áda" or "Síd el 'Áda"
      - 6. (Douro, or Dôrah, etc.) Br. and Ca.
    - 4. ("'Amru" *i.e.* 'Omára Abu Sakaykín) Br.
  - 4. ('Omára Abu Sakaykín) Ca.

The 16th (or 17th) king, Nūl, was only connected with the above on his mother's side (see para. XLVII, MS.).

E

In place of the date 1504 (the date of the foundation of the FUNG kingdom) Cailliaud gives 1484, and he is alone in doing so. He then states the numbers of years that each king (including "Dôrah") reigned: the total down to 1821 A.D. he gives as 335 years; but in adding up this total he omits 6 months + 5 months + 30 days, so 336 years would be more correct. To this must be added the interregnum of $1\frac{1}{2}$ years in the time of Ránfi, which Cailliaud mentions but does not include in the total; and the result is 337 to 338 years.

The dates of accession are not given except in the case of 'Omára Dūnḳas.

Now it is very suspicious that if 337 be subtracted from 1821 the result is 1484. I say suspicious advisedly, because, in the first place, one notes that the period from 910 A.H. (1504 A.D.) to 1236 A.H. (1821 A.D.) covers 327 lunar years, namely the period given in the MS., and that, if eight years be added on account of the inclusion of "Dôrah" ("Douro," etc.) as given by Cailliaud, we arrive at 335 lunar years, namely the number quoted by Cailliaud. The period from 1504 A.D. to 1821 A.D. covers only

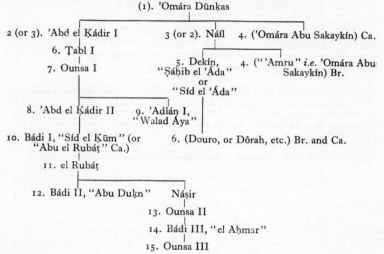

318 solar years. Secondly, the length of each reign must have been given in lunar years in the Arabic MS. consulted by Cailliaud, and if Cailliaud had wished to give in each case the exact equivalent in solar years he must have used fractions (which he did not do), or the total would have necessarily been wrong.

Thus, apparently, we have Cailliaud obtaining the figure 1484 A.D. by subtracting 337 lunar years from the solar date 1821 A.D., and not noticing that 337 lunar years only equal 327 solar years.

He also adds 12 years to 'Omára Dūnḳas's reign. Bruce and the MS. only give 30 years, but Cailliaud gives 42. The above, I think, accounts for the difference between the date 1504, which I take to be correct, and Cailliaud's "1484"; and it vitiates Cailliaud's chronology[1].

[1] Of the chronological list he accepted Cailliaud says (Vol. II, p. 255): "Je m'étais procuré, chez les érudits de la ville [Sennár], plusieurs listes chronologiques des rois Foungis du Sennâr":...(etc., as quoted in the introduction). "Enfin... j'en obtins une du roi Bâdy lui-même..."; and to this Cailliaud adds in a note "Elle était écrite en arabe: j'en dois la traduction à l'obligeance de M. Agoub, professeur d'arabe au collège royal de Louis-le-Grand." So if there is blame to be apportioned perhaps M. Agoub rather than Cailliaud should be the scapegoat.

APPENDIX II

Extracts from the Portuguese of C. Beccari's "Rerum Aethiopicarum Scriptores Occidentales Inediti a saeculo XVI ad XIX." (12 Vols.)

Extract I

From Paez, *Historia Aethiopiae*, Vol. III, pp. 353, 354. Susneôs lays waste Sarquî (Çarquî[1]) and enters into a league with Náíl: this in the reign of el Rubáṭ ibn Bádi at Sennár.

Depois foi caminhando devagar e entrou em sua corte de Gorgorrâ; e nam esteve alli mais que duas semanas, porque logo tornou a sair e foi pollo caminho de Tacuça e Tancâl a terra que chamam Gunquê, e dalli mandou chamar a Naêl filho de Agub, com que primeiro tinha concerto, e como veio, beixou o pe ao Emperador e prometeo do servir dalli por diante e nam tornar mais a seu senhor Urbât rey de Senaar, e o Emperador lhe deo ricos vestidos e pecas de ouro e *depois (*sic*) guiou Naêl ao Emperador ate chegar a terra del Rey de Fûnye e deo na terra Çarquî e matou muytos e cativou suas molheres e filhos e queimou suas casas. Fez isto o Emperador por cinco causas. A primeira porque, mandando elle muyto ricas peças de presente ao Rey de Badê, elle nam respondeo como debia, e mandou dous cavallos muyto ruins. A 2ª, porque deo Naêl nas terras que pertecem a Dambiâ e fez muyto dano e, mandandolhe dicer o Emperador se fora aquello com seu consentimento ou nam?, ouvindo este recado, calou e nam respondeo. A 3ª, porque Alêb criado do Emperador fugio pera elle come muytos cavallos e lebou os atabales de Maçagâ, e o Emperador lhe escreveo que nam detivese la seu criado, que elle lhe perdoava, e que, se nam quisesse vir, que lhe mandase os atabales, e elle nam quis facer huma cousa nem outra. A 4ª, porque, indose a gente Chucên a Çarquî, os agassalhou e depois os seus lhe ficeram muyto maltratamento e nam lhes deixaram enterra seus mortos sem que pagasem, pollo que elles quiseram facer amizade com seu senhor o Emperador e, quando vinham, deram nelles os de Çarquî e mataram muytos e tomaram suas molheres e filhos. A 5ª, porque, vindo pera o Emperador a may de Joseph filho de Gibarâ, a tomou a gente de Çarquî e nam a deixaram passar. Por tod estas cousas se enfadou o Emperador e fez amizade com Naêl e destruio as terras del Rey de Badê sugeto a el Rei de Senaar.

Translation[2]

Afterwards he went away slowly and entered his district of Gorgorrâ, but he did not remain there more than two weeks, for he then left and went by Tacuça and Tancâl to the country called Gunquê, and thence summoned

[1] In the index "Çarquî" is described as "regio in regno Funye."
[2] With this passage compare Bruce, Vol. III, Bk. III, pp. 311–319.

Náíl walad 'Agíb, with whom he previously had an agreement. When Náíl came he kissed the foot of the Emperor and promised to serve him from thenceforward and never more to return to his liege lord Rubáṭ the king of Sennár. The Emperor gave him rich garments and ornaments (?) of gold, and Náíl afterwards accompanied (?) the Emperor until he reached the land of the king of Fung and descended on the Çarquî[1] country and killed many and captured their women and children and burnt their homes. This the Emperor did for five reasons. The first because, when he sent the king of Bádi [King Bádi?] many costly presents, the latter had not replied as was due but had sent two very poor horses. The second because, Náíl having raided lands belonging to Dambia and done much damage, and the Emperor having sent to him [the king?] to ask whether this was with his consent or not, [the king?] on receipt of the message kept silence and made no reply. The third because, when Alêb[2], the Emperor's servant, absconded to him with many horses and took with him the kettledrums of Maçagâ, and when the Emperor wrote to him not to detain the servant, and said that he would pardon him, and that if he was unwilling to come back he should send him the kettledrums, [the king] was unwilling to do the one thing or the other. The fourth because, [when some Chucên people came?] to Çarquî, he gave them lodging but subsequently illtreated [them?] grossly and would not allow them to bury their dead unless they paid, because they wished to make friendship with his lord the Emperor; and when they arrived the Çarquî people fell upon them and killed many of them and took captive their women and children. The fifth because, when the mother of Joseph son of Gibarâ was on her way to the Emperor, the people of Çarquî took her and would not let her pass. For all of these reasons the Emperor was exasperated and made friendship with Náíl and laid waste the lands of the king of Bádi [King Bádi?] subject to the king of Sennár.

EXTRACT II

Paez, Vol. III, p. 370.

The Abyssinian generals make war on the Fung and take much booty: this in 1618.

Estando ainda o Emperador em Çalabaçâ, lhe chegou carta do Cantiva Za Guiorguís, em que decia que tinha dado em as terras Bertâ, Caebâ, Batêl e outras que senhorea el Rey de Funye Erobât e que cativara muytas molheres e meninos, queimara suas casas e tomara muyto fato. Depois soube o Emperador como Erobât mandara muyta gente de pe e de cavallo pera que guardasem a terra de Çarquî. Tambem lhe disseram como o Abuna Isaac, a quem tinha mandado pera Ethiopia o patriarche de Alexandria abba Marcos, morrera da terra de Senaar muyto tempo depois que o tomou Erobât; o que Emperador sintio muyto e alevantou logo de Çalabaçâ e foi caminhando ate Dabolâ, e dalli mandou a Jonaêl com muyta gente a as terras Gemâ e Çabên e dando nellas tomou muytas vacas e fato e tornou, e o Emperador alevantou logo de Dabolâ, passou por Bêd e foi a terra Tançal e mandou a Jonaêl, ao Cantîba Za Guiorguís e a Caba

---

[1] Bruce, *loc. cit.*, "Serke."   [2] Bruce, *loc. cit.*, "Alico."

Christos com muyta gente de guerra pera da na terra de Çarquî, e chegando la em sete dias, o siguinte muyto cedo se puseram em ordem e os del Rey de Funye estavam ja aparelhados com muytos cavallos e gente de pe; mas, dando batalha *foram desbaratados os Balôus e morreram muytos e a Jonaêl lhe trouxeran 326 cabeças e tomaram muytos cavallos, malhas, capacetes, espinguardas, atabales e camelos e tornaram com grande alegria onde estava o Emperador que os recebeo com muyta festa, mas dalli a 8 dias morreo de fevre o Cantîba Za Guiorguîs, e o Emperador o chorou muyto, porque o amava e era seu parente; e assi pus em seu lugar por Cantîba de Dambiâ a seu filho mais velho.

Translation

While the Emperor was still at Çalabaçâ there reached him a letter from the Cantîba Za Guiorguîs in which the latter stated he had attacked the lands of Bertâ, Caebâ Batêl and others which were under the rule of Rubáṭ the King of the FUNG and had captured many women and children, burnt their houses and taken much booty. The Emperor learnt later how Rubáṭ had sent many footmen and horsemen to defend the district of Çarquî. He was also told how the Abuna Isaac, to whom the Patriarch of Alexandria had sent Abba Marcos to Ethiopia [? *Whom Abba Marcos the Patriarch of Alexandria had sent to Ethiopia*?] had died in [*lit.* "*from*"] the land of Sennár a long time after Rubáṭ had seized him. The Emperor felt this greatly, and at once started from Çalabaçâ and journeyed as far as Dabolâ, and thence sent Jonaêl with a large force to the districts of Gemâ and Çabên; and he fell upon them and took many cows and goods and returned. Then the Emperor at once set forth from Dabolâ and, passing by Bêd, went to Tançal district and despatched to Jonaêl the Cantîba Za Guiorguîs and Caba Christos with a large body of troops to attack the land of Çarquî. And he [Jonaêl] reached [Çarquî] in seven days and on the following day very early set forth his array. And the troops of the king of Sennár were already standing ready with many cavalry and footmen. But when battle was joined the Balôus were routed and many were killed and 326 heads were brought to Jonaêl, and many horses and suits of mail and helmets and muskets and camels and drums were taken, so that they returned with great elation to the place where the Emperor was, and he received them with lavish entertainment. But eight days later the Cantîba Za Guiorguîs died of fever; and the Emperor sorrowed greatly for he loved him like a father, and so appointed in his place as Cantîba of Dambiâ his eldest son.

EXTRACT III

Paez, Vol. III, p. 372. The Emperor, after wintering at Gorgorra moves to Debaroâ. In 1619 Melcâ Christôs and others invade the Sennár territories in force.

Partindo Abeitahûn Melcâ Christôs e Jonaêl, foram como o Emperador lhes mandou e, chegando destruiram todas as terras de Funye, matando e cativando muyta gente e tomaram muytos cavallos e armas e atabales, e chegando a Abromelâ (com ser serra tam forte que, revelandose huma vez a gente daquella terra contra el Rey de Dequin, veio elle com todo seu poder e nam a pode entrar e assi se tornou). Elles a subiram por força de armas e mataram muytos e tomaram alli seu Rey e o trouxeram presso e chegando ao Emperador com grande festa e alegria lhe presentaram aquelle Rey com os escravos, armas e cavallos que tomoram em suas terras. Tambem Dêye Azmâch Oald Haureât foi como lhe mandou seu senhor e, caminhando 19 dias, chegou a Ateberâ terra de Fûnye e logo domingo antes de meio dia deo nella e venceo ao capitam que alli estava, e fugindo elle, mataram muytos dos seus e cativaram suas molheres e filhos de maneira que tudo ficou despovoado e tomaram muyta prata e ouro, peças e vestidos ricos, muytos camellos, espingardas, malhas e capacetes, e tres pares de atabales, com o que todos os do exercito ficaram cheos, e assi lhe sucedeo ao Emperador Seltân Çaguêd o que o nem hum de seus antecessores, porque em huma mesma semana destruio desde Çuaquên ate Fazcolô, de onde tiram o ouro, cumprindolhe nosso Senhor o que desejava. Como Dêye Azmâch Oald Haureât teve esta victoria, tornou logo dando graças a Deos.....Por estas victorias, que Deos N. Senhor deo ao Emperador de Çuaquên ate Fazcolô, fez grandes festas e deo muytos louvores ao Senhor, de quem lhe vieram tantas merces. E nisto se occupou ate o mes de mayo de 1619.

Translation

Abeitahûn Melcâ Christôs and Jonaêl set forth as the Emperor had ordered them and on arrival laid waste all the lands of the FUNG, killing and capturing many people and taking many horses and arms and drums; and reaching Abromelâ (which was so strong that on one occasion, when the people of that country had fared against the king of Dekín [King Dekín?], he came with all his power but was unable to effect an entry and so returned), they subdued it by force by arms and killed many and there captured its king and brought him prisoner to the Emperor with great celebration and joyfulness and handed him over together with the slaves and arms and horses taken in his country. Also Dêye Azmâch Oald Haureât, as commanded by his lord, journeyed 19 days and reached Atbara [in?] the FUNG territory and at once, on a Sunday, before noon, fell upon it and defeated its local chieftain and put him to flight and killed many of his people and captured his women and children in such manner that the whole district was depopulated, and took much silver and gold, pieces of cloth and rich garments, many camels, muskets, suits of mail and helmets and three pairs of drums, so that all the troops were sated. Thus the Emperor Sultan Çaguêd [*i.e.* SUSNEÔS] was successful beyond all his predecessors, for in a single week he wrought destruction from Sūákin to Fázoghli, whence they bring gold, understanding what Our Lord desired.

When Dêye Azmâch Oald Haureât had won this victory he returned forthwith giving thanks to God...(*descriptions of festivities, etc., follow*)... For these victories which Our God granted to the Emperor from Sūákin to Fázoghli he made great festivity and offered many thanksgivings to the Lord from whom had come to him so great favours. In this he occupied himself until the month of May 1619.

INDEX

N.B. 1. *Where figures are in italics the reference is to notes.*

2. *The references are generally in groups of three. The first (Roman figures) denotes the Part, the second (ordinary figures) denotes the chapter, the third (Roman) denotes the section.*

3. *T. = a tribe, S.T. = a sub-tribe, Ar.T. = an Arabian (non-Sudan) tribe, G. = a "gebel," V. = a village, W. = wells, R. = river.*